Menu Celebrations!

Especially for my friend Bobbie:
enjoy;

My Best to You
Lee Cannon
6/29/95-

Menu Celebrations!

Meal planning for the family
every day of the year

Lee Cannon

OWL BAY
Publishers

Published by Owl Bay Publishers, Inc.
Post Office Box 6461
Montgomery, Alabama 36106

ISBN 0-9638568-9-8

Manufactured in the United States of America

Table of Contents

❧ ❧ ❧

Special Menu Plans
(for every season of the year)

🍒 🍒 🍒

Introduction

THE ONE QUESTION A MEAL MANAGER asks every day is "What shall we have for dinner?" Included in this text is a dinner or lunch menu for every day of the year, along with recipes and general information concerning family meal planning. The purpose of this general information is to strengthen the foods and nutrition skills and knowledge of today's meal manager.

Every home has a meal manager, and it makes no difference who it is. It can be a wife, husband, sibling, roommate or a domestic. Meal management is a serious responsibility that requires knowledge of basic nutrition, planning, purchasing, storing, preparing and serving food. There are three basic requirements that the food should meet: it should 1) look good, 2) taste good and 3) be good for you. In this order of importance, these are necessary requirements to guarantee that the people will eat and enjoy the food and ultimately develop and maintain the state of good nutrition.

One of the greatest changes in meal planning today is the amount of time people are willing to spend on the total sequence of eating. Even though time is limited, the demand for good eating is of the utmost importance. In addition to planning for adequate nutrition, there are other goals the meal manager must consider. For example, the food purchased cannot use more than its fair share of the income and the food must be of the kind that the people will expect and accept. The cultural background and physical condition of family members will determine what is acceptable. It is hoped that increased knowledge and practice will lead to better and more efficient eating habits for the family.

While this book is presented as a cookbook for the public, it will be equally useful for classes in basic meal planning. The study of meal planning will prepare one for home and family life which includes, within a broad spectrum, feeding the family and fulfilling social responsibilities with a feeling of pride, security and ease.

Following are certain concepts around which the content of this book was built.

1. Nutrition is the study of the foods we eat and the use of these foods to our bodies. It is also a study of the process by which food is selected, prepared, consumed and becomes part of the human body.
2. Food contains nutrients that work together to serve the needs of the body.
3. No one food contains all the essential nutrients in the appropriate amounts. Combinations are needed for best growth and health, therefore, a variety of foods must be eaten every day.
4. Dietary fiber is needed for healthy functioning of the body.
5. The way food is processed, stored and prepared for eating can influence the nutrient content of the food, as well as its safety, appearance and taste.
6. Each nutrient, carbohydrate, protein, fat, vitamin, mineral and water, has a specific function in the body.
7. The human body can synthesize some nutrients. Others must be obtained from the food eaten. All nutrients are supplied if the USDA food guide is followed

The meals in this book have been developed with several important points in mind.

1. Meal planning and preparation must not require too much time.
2. Most meals are economical, though some have a touch of "elegance" which is not inexpensive.
3. The use of commercially pre-prepared and convenience foods are minimized due to economy and quality.
4. Less fat has been included in the recipes because present surveys indicate that most Americans eat too much fat.
5. Less salt is used in preparation. However, the final salt content is the responsibility of the individual.

6. Less sugar is used wherever possible. Again, it is not necessary to deprive people of all pleasurable desserts, because by exercising portion control, sugar in the diet can be decreased. Instead of cutting six servings from an eight-inch pie, make it eight or ten.

7. Food is naturally beautiful. It has a variety of bright colors, textures and shapes. All these attributes are considered in the meals presented in this book.

8. Simplicity in planning, preparing and presenting food helps to preserve the natural endowments of foods.

9. The final meal, when presented, should look good, taste good and be good for you.

After studying a recipe, even a cook with limited experience will challenge something about it. A simple example would be a tomato sauce recipe that specifies that seeds should be removed by straining. This is a time-consuming task, and unless for health reasons, is unnecessary. This is a step that can be eliminated without altering the palatability of the sauce. The wise, creative cook will not be a slave to a recipe. Challenge and change a recipe to your own use. This is called "personalizing" a recipe. In buying food for these menus, staple foods, more frequently used in the preparations of all meals, can be purchased in larger quantities than are required merely for a seven-day plan. Examples of such foods are flour, sugar, cocoa, vinegar, oil and shortening. It is much more expensive to make frequent trips to the market and purchase in small lots than to stock in quantity. Stock up at sale time.

At the beginning of each week there is an essay preceding the week's meals. The essays contain basic information which will assist the meal manager in making decisions concerning the planning, preparation and serving of easy but elegant meals to family and friends.

Many cookbooks are read by people who do not cook. Therefore, the factual information, as well as the menus with at least one new recipe for every day of the year, should be of benefit to the "readers" as well as the "doers." One meal each week will have complete recipes along with a plan of work. Meal managers should plan their meals by the week. However, this planning is successful only if it is done with flexibility in mind. The wise planner considers the constantly changing physical and social needs of the family. The results can be good, nutritious meals achieved through an informal, relaxed approach to what can be a very pleasurable task.

Good living and good eating go together when you can prepare interesting, delicious and nourishing meals using a minimum amount of our most precious commodities: time, energy and money.

January

January - First Week

Many people can successfully combine meal management at home with activities away from home. By planning, meals at home can please the family and properly budget time, energy and money. The benefits of planning ahead include:
1. Energy and time in shopping and cooking are saved.
2. Money is saved because less expensive foods can be put into menus and prevent costly, unplanned meals.
3. A major goal in planning is to serve foods that are nourishing.
4. More variety in foods can be obtained.
5. Good meal-planning habits can be formed.

No aspect of home life has undergone more dramatic change than preparing and eating food; yet, in spite of change, families today can retain a high degree of individuality and still have well-planned meals. A happy note about family eating habits is that even though more meals are eaten away from home, most families still spend more time together eating than in any other activity.

Fortunately, families no longer believe there is only one "right" way to plan meals. This freedom of planning gives a fresh, challenging, exciting approach to meal planning. There is no magic formula to achieve a successful family meal. Each meal planner is free to create or innovate to meet the family's needs and health. Good nutrition is the basic key to good health. Nutritious family meals can happen every day without creating emotional upheavals or economic crises if the United States Department of Agriculture's "Daily Food Guide" is followed.

USDA Daily Food Guide

Use from these basic food groups every day:

Milk Group: 3 or more glasses for children (smaller glasses for some children under 8). 4 or more glasses for teenagers. 2-3 or more glasses for adults. Cheese, ice cream and other milk products can supply part of the milk.

Meat Group: 2 or more servings (meats, fish, poultry, eggs, or cheese, dry beans, peas, nuts as alternates).

Vegetable and Fruit Group: 4 or more servings (include dark green or yellow vegetables; citrus fruit or tomatoes).

Bread and Cereal Group: 4 or more servings (enriched or whole grain; added milk improves nutritional values).

Fat, Sweets and Alcohol Group: limit intake.

Here are three pointers issued by the U.S. Departmentof Agriculture on how to use the food guide:
1. Choose at least the minimum number of servings from each of the first four food groups.
2. Select additional foods to round out the meals. These additional foods should add enough calories to complete your food energy needs for the day.
3. Try to include some meat, poultry, fish, eggs or milk at each meal to assure adequate protien.

Since more than half of today's homemakers are employed outside the home, time is especially precious. Time can mean money to a person as well as a business. A person who spends unnecessary hours in meal preparation is wasting valuable time.

The criterion for a lovely, gracious and tasty meal is not the length of time spent in cooking, but what the food looks like and tastes like. The answer is planning ahead. A few minutes used in planning will pay dividends on time and energy spent in meal preparation. (See meal preparation schedules included with the complete meals.)

Whenever possible prepare twice as much food as needed and freeze half of it. Many cooked foods can be held three or four days in the refrigerator to be served again with a little change in appearance. Also, a good vegetable soup made from the week's leftovers can be a real crowd-pleaser. Just remember: If the food looks good, tastes good and is good for you, the meal is a success.

We need to become increasingly aware of getting the most from our food dollar. That means pre-planning activities such as:

1. Rotate pantry and freezer supplies.
2. Follow newspaper food ads and clip coupons for special values.
3. Shop wisely and eliminate food waste.
4. If there is a choice of brands or types, check the cost-per-unit to get the best buy.
5. Keep handy a planning notebook for making shopping lists, planning menus, and for writing notes to yourself.
6. Make a pocket in your notebook to stash coupons, so that they are close at hand and you won't forget them.
7. Have a number of air-tight containers handy at all times for storing. They should be translucent or have see-through lids, so you will know what is stored inside.
8. Store foods in the same spot so your family will know where to find them. For instance, cheeses can be wrapped separately, then stored together in one place.
9. To get the most nutritive value, it is essential to serve some foods at the peak of their freshness.

How often have you wondered "how much is enough" in a recipe? A good recipe will always tell you how many *servings* it will supply, but this does not mean number of people. The size, age, gender and activity of the family members will determine how much food should be prepared. A family of four with two preschoolers will need fewer servings than the family with two teenage boys. Number of servings in a recipe does not allow for seconds or leftovers.

What size is a serving? For meat, a serving is 2 to 3 ounces of lean, cooked meat without bone. This is equivalent to 3 to 4 ounces of raw, lean meat, 5 ounces if bone or fat is present. Two eggs equals one serving. As a meat substitute 1 cup cooked dried beans or peas, or $1/4$ cup peanut butter is a serving. The following portions are considered a serving: 1 slice (1 ounce) of bread, 1 ounce of ready-to-eat cereal, $1/2$ to $3/4$ cup of cooked cereal, grits or pasta, $1/2$ cup of a fruit or vegetable, or a portion as ordinarily served, such as 1 medium apple, 1 banana, 1 potato, or $1/2$ grapefruit.

Some people plan carefully to eliminate leftovers, others plan carefully to have leftovers. In this latter case, we call them "planned-overs." These foods are cooked to be used later. The excess cooked foods should be carefully wrapped to exclude air and stored in the freezer or refrigerator. The frozen product can be stored for many weeks, but products stored in the refrigerator have a storage life of approximately one week. Potatoes are an excellent example of "planned-overs." They can be simmered in their skins. Some of the freshly-cooked potatoes can be seasoned and served. The refrigerated ones are then ready for frying or creaming, hashbrowns, potato salad, casseroles, soups, stews, croquettes, and many other preparations. Other prime "planned-overs" candidates include rice, various other vegetables, spaghetti sauce, dressings, ham, roasts, bread and casseroles.

Because wasted food means wasted money, make sure that you never throw away good food. Save both large and small amounts of leftovers and make wise use of them. This means that you have to think up a use for the leftovers, especially when there's only a small amount. Here are some ways to put small amounts of various foods to good use:

Egg yolks (note: 2 yolks = 1 whole egg) can be used in cream puddings and fillings, custards, sauces, salad dressings and scrambled eggs. Egg whites can be used in angel food cakes, cookies, fluffy frostings, fruit whips and meringues. Hard-cooked eggs can be put to use in casseroles, salads, sandwiches, pizzas and stuffed vegetables. Meat drippings can go in gravies, casseroles, soups, stews and sauces or French dip sandwiches. Fruits can be used in salads, fruit cups, sauces, shortcakes, upside-down cakes, cobblers and parfaits. Cooked pastas can be included in casseroles, meat loaf and salads. Dry bread can make French toast, croutons, stuffings, crumb toppings and coatings. Soft bread can be used in bread puddings, meat loaf and stuffings. Leftover cakes or cookies can be used in brown betty, cottage pudding, crumb crusts, and crumb toppings. Dilute evaporated milk with equal parts of water and use as whole milk in cooking. Vegetables can be used in salads, relishes, casseroles, soups and stews. Leftover raw vegetables can be converted to a great stew, soup or congealed salad.

To preserve the quality of leftover food, cool cooked food quickly, cover and refrigerate. Cover egg yolks with cold water and refrigerate in a tightly-covered container for up to two days. Refrigerate egg whites in a tightly-covered container up to ten days. Using leftovers wisely represents a saving in money and time. Finding interesting, attractive ways to serve them is always a challenge. Leftovers are often as good the second time around.

As we start the new year, we are confronted with several points that will influence our meal planning:

1. Economy following the festive season.
2. Use of leftovers from holiday eating.
3. Changes from the traditional holiday food.
4. More time to cook during January.
5. Good time to try new recipes for the coming year.
6. Always keep in mind that good nutrition can be obtained by following the USDA "Daily Food Guide."

SUNDAY
Do Ahead Sunday Dinner
Pork chops and rice in wine sauce
Green beans with parsley butter
Mayonnaise drop biscuits
Fresh fruit salad with honey mustard dressing
Sweet potato pie

Plan of Work
Day before:
1. Wash green beans, break off tips and strings, cut into 2-inch pieces. Store in refrigerator.
2. Prepare honey mustard dressing.
3. Section oranges and grapefruit.
4. Prepare sweet potato pie.
Before being gone for a two hour period (like going to church):
5. Set the table.
6. Prepare the pork chops and wine sauce and place in oven 2 hours before serving time (before going to church).
About 30 minutes before the meal is to be served, and the pork chops are still cooking:
7. Prepare the biscuits and place on baking sheet and bake just before serving.
8. Cook green beans.
9. Assemble the salad. This meal can be served 30 minutes after arriving home.
ENJOY!!

PORK CHOPS AND RICE IN WINE

4 large pork chops
Salt and pepper
1/2 teaspoon poultry seasoning
4 thick slices of onion

4 green pepper rings
1/2 cup uncooked rice
1 (15 ounce) can tomato sauce
3/4 cup dry white wine

Place pork chops in a casserole. Sprinkle salt, pepper and poultry seasoning over meat. Place one onion slice and one green pepper ring on each chop. Sprinkle rice between chops. Combine the tomato sauce and wine and pour over the chops. Cover tightly and bake at 350° for 1-$^1/_2$ hours or until tender. 4 servings.

GREEN BEANS WITH PARSLEY BUTTER

1/2 pound fresh green beans
1/2 cup water
1/2 teaspoon salt (optional)
Black pepper

3 tablespoon butter or margarine, melted
2 tablespoons chopped fresh parsley
2 tablespoons lemon juice

Break or cut off and discard tips of green beans. Break beans into 2-inch lengths. Place in small sauce pan. Add ¼ cup water and ½ teaspoon salt. Cover with a close-fitted lid. Cook until steam flows around base of lid. Turn down heat to lowest point, do not remove lid. Cook about 10 minutes or until crisp and tender. Drain off water. Add butter, parsley and lemon juice. Add salt and pepper to taste. Toss well and serve hot. 4 servings.

FRESH FRUIT SALAD WITH HONEY MUSTARD DRESSING

1 large yellow or pink grapefruit
2 oranges
1 large ripe banana

1 cup chilled sliced fresh strawberries
1 kiwi, peeled and sliced
Honey mustard dressing

Peel and section grapefruit and oranges. Reserve juice. Peel and slice banana, dip slices in reserved juice. Combine grapefruit, oranges and banana. Place in lettuce-lined bowl. Top with kiwi slices. Serve dressing separately. 4-6 servings.

To section grapefruit or orange:

With a sharp knife, cut a flat piece off both ends of the fruit, barely cutting into the flesh. Pare the fruit as you would an apple with an up and down motion, cutting into the fruit and cutting away all of the outer white membrane. With a small sharp knife, cut down one side and up on the other side of each section. This will extract the section free from membrane. Do this over a bowl to catch the juice for dipping bananas.

HONEY MUSTARD DRESSING FOR FRUIT OR VEGETABLE SALAD

3 tablespoons cider vinegar
3 tablespoons honey
6 tablespoons mayonnaise
1 tablespoon Dijon mustard

1-2 tablespoons finely chopped onion
1 ½ tablespoons chopped fresh parsley
1/8 teaspoon salt
1/2 cup vegetable oil

Heat vinegar and honey in a small saucepan over low heat stirring until honey dissolves. Pour into a bowl and cool. Whisk in mayonnaise, mustard, onions, parsley and salt. Gradually whisk in oil. Refrigerate. Bring to room temperature before using. Makes about 1 ½ cups. Store in refrigerator.

MAYONNAISE DROP BISCUIT

2 cups self-rising flour
1 teaspoon sugar
1/2 teaspoon salt

1/4 cup mayonnaise
3/4 cup milk

Combine all ingredients in a large mixing bowl. Drop mixture by heaping tablespoon about 1-inch apart on greased cookie sheet. Bake in 400° oven for 15 minutes or until brown. Yield - 12 biscuits.

SWEET POTATO PIE

5 medium sweet potatoes, cooked, peeled and
    mashed, or 1 (24-ounce) can of yams, drained
1/2 cup butter or margarine, softened
1 cup brown sugar, firmly packed
3 eggs, slightly beaten
1/2 teaspoon nutmeg
1/2 teaspoon ginger

2 teaspoons cinnamon
1 teaspoon vanilla extract
1/2 teaspoon salt
1 cup evaporated milk
Whipped cream or topping
1 commercial deep (9-inch) pie crust or 2 shallow
    (9-inch) pie crusts

Cream butter with brown sugar. Add eggs and mix thoroughly with electric mixer. Add remaining ingredients (except whipped cream). Beat well. Pour into one deep pie crust or two shallow 9-inch pie crusts. Bake in a 350° oven for 60 minutes or until center is firm. Top each slice with whipped cream or topping before serving. 6-8 servings.

MONDAY
Lima bean and tuna casserole*
Fresh green salad, Italian dressing
Onion cheese bread
Left over Christmas dessert

LIMA BEAN AND TUNA CASSEROLE

2 (10-ounce) packages frozen baby lima beans
1/2 tablespoon butter
2 tablespoons flour
1 cup dairy sour cream, at room temperature
1/4 cup chopped fresh parsley

1/2 teaspoon salt (optional)
1/8 teaspoon pepper
1 (6 1/2-ounce) can chunk light tuna in water,
    drained and flaked *
1 1/2 cups shredded Cheddar cheese

Preheat oven to 350°. Cook lima beans according to package directions. Drain and reserve liquid (2/3 cup). Melt butter in small saucepan. Stir in flour until smooth. Remove from heat and gradually stir in reserved liquid. Bring to a boil, stirring constantly. Boil and stir one minute. Stir in sour cream, pimiento and parsley. Add salt and pepper to taste. Place half of the beans in a 1 1/2 quart baking dish, then one half of the tuna. Spread one half of the sour cream sauce over the top. Sprinkle with one half of the cheese. Repeat layers. Bake 25 to 30 minutes or until heated throughout. Allow to stand for 5 minutes before serving. 6 servings. * 1 cup diced ham may be used.

TUESDAY
Chopped beef steak
Sauteed potatoes and green peppers
Apple and nut salad
Blueberry muffin*
Lemon Sherbert Cookies

BLUEBERRY MUFFINS

1 ½ cups all-purpose flour
¾ cup sugar
1 ½ teaspoons baking powder
¼ teaspoon salt
½ teaspoon cinnamon
1 egg, beaten

¼ cup plus 2 tablespoons butter or margarine, melted
½ cup milk
1 ½ cups blueberries, fresh or dry frozen
2 tablespoons all-purpose flour

Preheat oven to 400°. Combine flour, sugar, baking powder, salt and cinnamon. Sift twice. Combine egg with melted butter and milk. Add to flour mixture and stir until smooth. Combine blueberries with flour. Fold in blueberries. Fill greased muffin tins one-half full and bake in hot oven about 25 minutes or until muffins are well browned. Serve warm or at room temperature. Yield, 1 dozen.

WEDNESDAY
Braised chicken and rice
Buttered spinach
Tossed grapefruit salad*
Whole wheat bread slices, jam
Left over Christmas dessert

TOSSED GRAPEFRUIT SALAD

1 quart torn romaine lettuce
2 cups torn bibb lettuce
2 cups grapefruit sections (see page 7)

1 cup red onion rings
4 bacon slices, cooked crisp and crumbled
Celery seed dressing

Combine the romaine and bibb lettuce, grapefruit segments, onion and bacon. Toss lightly. Serve with dressing. 6 servings.

Celery Seed Dressing

½ cup sugar
1 teaspoon salt
1 teaspoon dry mustard
½ teaspoon paprika

1 small onion, grated
⅓ cup cider vinegar
1 cup vegetable oil
1 teaspoon celery seed

Place sugar, salt, mustard, paprika, onion and vinegar in blender container. Blend. While motor is still running, remove lid and slowly add oil; a clear thick emulsion will form. Pour in jar and stir in celery seed. Cover and store in refrigerator.

THURSDAY
Hot turkey salad*
Cheese grits
Whole wheat toast and jam
Baked apple with almond topping
Iced tea

HOT TURKEY SALAD

2 cups cooked, cubed turkey (use leftover if available)	1 teaspoon salt
2 cups chopped celery	2 tablespoons lemon juice
1/2 cup blanched almonds	1/2 cup mayonnaise
1/3 cup chopped green pepper	4 slices Swiss cheese
2 tablespoons chopped pimiento	2 tablespoons (1/4 stick) butter or margarine, melted
2 tablespoons finely chopped onion	1 cup cracker crumbs

Combine turkey, celery, almonds, green pepper, pimiento, onion, salt, lemon juice and mayonnaise. Put into 4 buttered individual baking dishes or a buttered 1-quart baking dish. Top with slices of cheese. Combine butter and cracker crumbs and sprinkle on top. Bake in a moderate oven (350°) about 20 minutes. 4 servings.

FRIDAY
Penne with Marinara tomato sauce*
Green salad / Garlic bread
Ice milk with frozen peach slices

PENNE IN MARINARA TOMATO SAUCE

2 large onions, chopped (2 cups)	2 (16 ounce) cans diced tomatoes, undrained
4 cloves garlic, crushed	2 teaspoons oregano
1/2 pound mushrooms, chopped or 1 (8-ounce) can mushroom stems and pieces	1 teaspoon sweet basil
	1/2 teaspoon crushed red pepper
1/4 cup water	1 1/2 teaspoons dried parsley flakes or 1 tblsp fresh
4 cups (32 ounces) tomato sauce	12 ounces penne (small tubular macaroni)

Cook onions, garlic and mushrooms in 1/4 cup water until slightly tender, about 10 minutes. Stir in tomato sauce, tomatoes and spices. Simmer over low heat about one hour, stirring occasionally. Do not cover. If the mixture gets too thick, add tomato juice. Cook penne according to package directions. Drain and top with sauce. 6 servings.

SATURDAY
Baked fish fillet with savory sauce
Rice pilaf
Buttered fresh spinach
Cole slaw
Bread sticks
Cherry pie with Whipped cheese topping*

CHERRY PIE WITH WHIPPED CHEESE TOPPING

1 (16 ounce) can pie cherries
$^1/_4$ teaspoon salt
3 tablespoons corn starch
$^3/_4$ cup honey

1 tablespoon butter or margarine
$^1/_4$ teaspoon almond extract
Pastry for 8 or 9-inch double crust pie
Whipped cheese topping (recipe follows)

Drain cherries and set aside. Combine juice with salt and corn starch. Add honey and cook over medium heat, stirring constantly, until thickened and clear. Add butter and stir until melted. Remove from heat and gently stir in cherries and almond extract. Set aside to cool. Line 8-inch pie plate with your favorite pastry recipe or commercial pastry. Spoon in cooled filling. Top with lattice strips of pastry, sealing and fluting edges. Bake at 425° for 30 to 35 minutes, or until bubbly and crust is lightly browned. Top with cheese topping. 6 to 8 servings.

Whipped Cheese Topping

2 cups (8 ounces) shredded Cheddar cheese $^1/_4$ cup light cream or half & half

Allow cheese to come to room temperature. In a mixing bowl, beat cheese until fairly smooth. Gradually add cream and continue to beat until mixture is smooth and fluffy.

January - Second Week

If a meal is well planned it will look good, taste good and be good nutritionally. But planning does not end here; the meal must also be satisfying. This gives us three more things to think about.

First, the meal should contain foods that will prevent hunger. This means the meal should contain some fat and protein, because these nutrients remain in the stomach longer and are more slowly digested. A mixture of carbohydrates with fat or protein is ideal.

Second, a satisfying meal should be so composed that it does not produce feelings of discomfort. Meals too high in fat can cause discomfort. For this reason, the meal planner should be careful and not plan rich meals for people who prefer simple foods. This can be done by eliminating unnecessary sauces, whipped cream, rich desserts and other high-calorie foods.

The third point is to plan meals, hearty or light, in relation to the activity of the diners. People who are physically active can tolerate heavier meals than those who sit at work all day or are otherwise inactive.

The temperature of foods when served contribute to the satisfying qualities or enjoyment of meals. For a meal to taste good there must be a contrast in the temperatures of the foods served. Most connoisseurs demand that food be served at the proper temperature. This means that hot foods should be served hot and cold foods should be served cold.

Few people find a meal consisting of foods at one temperature, either all hot or all cold, pleasing, regardless of the season or weather. The temperature does not necessarily affect the nutritive value, but it does affect the fun of eating. Basically, hot foods are enjoyed more during cold weather and cold foods in hot weather, but regardless of the weather, some temperature contrast makes the meal more acceptable. Hot soup with hot bread and cold salad is a terrific light lunch in the winter time.

A good meal planner must also understand the importance of texture and plan for it deliberately. Texture in food means its crispness, crunchiness, hardness, softness, or smoothness. A meal with several textures is more enjoyable. A well-planned meal should contain one crisp food, one chewy food and others that are soft or smooth or crunchy. Foods that provide crispness are raw or slightly-cooked vegetables, toasted bread, crusty rolls or crackers. Chewy foods are mainly meats. Well-cooked vegetables, fruits, bread, boiled fish, cooked cereal and some casseroles are the soft foods. Smooth foods are puddings, sauces and gravies.

A lunch meal of omelet, mashed potatoes, buttered peas, plain gelatin salad, sliced white bread and apple sauce, for example, is all of the same texture. It would be more interesting if it were an omelet, sliced tomatos, buttered peas, fresh fruit salad, whole wheat toast and jam. A dull meal becomes exciting by altering the texture. Even children seem to get more fun out of eating when raw carrots or apple slices are added for crispness.

Every cook wants to hear the phrase, "I love the flavor of this dish." Good flavor will entice us to eat even when we are not hungry. Flavor is experienced through tongue taste, sense of smell and the sense of touch. The ability to experience flavor differs among individuals and even in the same individual from time to time. People are better tasters when they are rested, free from emotional stress, calm and collected. Also, cooks have said that it is difficult to prepare a good-tasting meal when they are tired, worried or depressed. A happy cook is a good cook.

The main factor in flavor is the aroma of food, as is demonstrated when you walk into the kitchen, take a breath and say, "Mom, what's for dinner?" When the posterior nasal passage is closed by swelling, as when you have a cold, the sense of smell is lost and all food tastes alike. It is the aroma that makes us enjoy hot roast beef, fresh baked bread and spice cake.

Smell is also subject to fatigue. This means that you lose your sensitivity to odor after a while. Hence, after being in a fish market for a while, the fish odor seems less powerful. For this reason, some people eat faster so they do not lose the sense of smell. So, if we like a certain food, we eat it faster; if we don't like it, we eat slower. Likewise, by waiting between courses at the table, we increase our enjoyment of each course. So stay rested, happy and free from colds to enjoy foods.

With the beginning of a new year everyone is watching the food budget. It is a known fact that the highest percentage of our food dollar is spent on meat and meat products so this will naturally be the place to cut down on the food bill. One very economical idea is to use canned meat products. This week we will use tuna. It is economical as well as versatile. It is ready to eat or use in other recipes and is invaluable for a quick main dish for any meal. It is so easy to figure the cost of tuna because there is absolutely no waste such as bone or fat. For dieters, tuna is also packed in water instead of oil.

SUNDAY
Sunday Brunch
Egg and sausage casserole
Cheese grits / Hot biscuits and jam
Icy crisp fruit bowl*
Sugar cookies

ICY CRISP FRUIT BOWL

1 cup sugar	1 cup sliced pear chunks (do not peel)
1 cup water	2 cups fresh sliced (or frozen and thawed) peaches
1/4 cup lemon juice	1 cup fresh strawberry halves
1 cup sliced fresh plums or halved canned plums	Whipped cream or sour cream
1 cup seedless grapes	Chopped nuts or toasted coconut
1 cup sliced fresh nectarines (if available)	

Combine sugar and water in a saucepan. Bring to a boil, stirring to dissolve the sugar. Simmer for 5 minutes. Cool completely and add lemon juice. Cut fruit directly into lemon syrup. Cover and refrigerate. Serve cold, topped with whipped cream or sour cream and garnished with chopped nuts or toasted coconut. Makes about 2 quarts. Store extra in refrigerator.

MONDAY
Old fashioned chicken and dumplings*
Turnip greens
Raw vegetable tray
Brownies

OLD FASHIONED CHICKEN AND DUMPLINGS

2 ½ pound chicken, cut up	1 rib of celery, cut in ½ inch pieces
3 quarts water	1 teaspoon salt
1 bay leaf	¼ teaspoon pepper
1 onion, quartered	¼ cup flour

Place chicken in a large stew pot, cover with water, add remaining ingredients except flour. Bring water to a boil, turn heat down and simmer until chicken is tender and easily penetrated with a fork (about 45 minutes). Take chicken from the broth and remove meat from the bones. Set aside meat and discard skin and bones. Strain the broth (about 2 quarts) and return it to the pot. Remove 1 cup of broth and set aside for the dumplings. Blend 1 cup of broth with the flour. Add this to remaining broth while stirring. Cook with continued stirring until broth is slightly thickened. Add cut-up chicken meat to broth, and add dumpling strips slowly, one at a time. Cover, turn heat down, and let dumplings simmer for 15 minutes. Add cut up chicken meat to the broth. Serve in a bowl. Serves 6.

Dumplings

2 cups all-purpose flour	1 teaspoon baking powder
1 teaspoon salt	1 cup chicken broth

Sift together flour, salt and baking powder. Add broth to dry mixture, blending and kneading to make a stiff dough. Roll mixture on a well-floured surface. to a thickness of $^1/_8$-inch. Cut into 1x3-inch strips. Spread the strips on waxed paper to dry for about one hour.

TUESDAY
Beef roast
Buttered steamed corn and mushrooms*
Marinated sliced tomato and onion ring
Garlic bread sticks
Baked apples

BUTTERED STEAMED CORN WITH MUSHROOMS

3 tablespoons butter or margarine	1 (10-ounce) package frozen whole kernel corn or 1
1 cup (3-4 ounces) sliced fresh mushrooms, or 1	(16-ounce) can whole kernel corn, drained
(4-ounce) can mushrooms, stems and pieces	¼ teaspoon salt
3 green onions, sliced ⅛ inch, use tops	⅛ teaspoon pepper

In a 2-quart saucepan, melt butter. Add mushrooms. cook, uncovered, over medium heat, stirring occasionally, until tender (4-6 minutes). If using canned mushrooms, cook until heated (2-3 minutes). Stir in onions, corn, salt and pepper. Cover and continue cooking, stirring occasionally, until vegetables are crisply tender, about 5 minutes. 4 servings.

WEDNESDAY
Linguini with parsley and basil*
Tossed green salad with Italian dressing
Bread Sticks
Ice milk with fruit topping

LINGUINI WITH PARSLEY AND BASIL

1 cup firmly packed fresh parsley
1 ½ teaspoons dried whole basil
1 teaspoon garlic salt
½ teaspoon black pepper
2 cloves garlic, crushed

½ cup olive oil
½ cup grated Parmesan cheese
1 (7-ounce) package thin linguini
⅓ cup pine nuts (optional)
Additional Parmesan cheese

Combine parsley, basil, garlic salt, black pepper, garlic and oil in container of an electric blender. Process until pureed. Remove from blender and stir in ½ cup of Parmesan cheese. Prepare linguini according to package directions. Drain. Combine linguini and sauce, tossing well. Pour into serving dish and sprinkle with nuts. Top each serving with additional Parmesan cheese. Serve hot. 6 servings.

THURSDAY
Surprise burgers*
Green bean casserole
Potato salad
Crustless Pumpkin pie*

SURPRISE 'BURGERS

1 beef boullion cube
½ cup boiling water
2 slices bread, cubed
1 pound ground beef
⅔ cup instant nonfat dry milk
½ cup coarsely grated carrot
2 tablespoons grated onion

1 egg
½ teaspoon salt
¼ teaspoon pepper
¼ teaspoon savory
8 sandwich buns, buttered
1 cup chopped olives (optional)*
1 cup shredded sharp Cheddar cheese

Dissolve boullion cube in boiling water, pour over bread. Combine beef, milk, carrot, onion, egg, salt, pepper and savory. Add bread mixture, mixing just enough to blend. Spread meat mixture on both halves of bun. Place under broiler a few minutes, until lightly brown. Top each 'burger with 1 tablespoon olives and 1 tablespoon Cheddar cheese. Return to broiler just until cheese begins to melt. Sandwich bun halves together and serve immediately. 8 servings. Note: Try other "surprises" in place of olives, such as pickle relish, chopped peanuts, mustard, ketchup, tomato slices, etc.

CRUSTLESS PUMPKIN PIE

3 eggs
³/₄ cup honey
¹/₂ teaspoon ginger
¹/₂ teaspoon nutmeg
1 teaspoon cinnamon

¹/₂ teaspoon salt
1 ³/₄ cup pumpkin
1 cup undiluted evaporated milk
Sweetened whipped cream (optional)

Beat eggs slightly. Add honey, ginger, nutmeg, cinnamon, salt and pumpkin. Mix well. Add milk. Pour into buttered 9-inch pie pan. Bake at 325° one hour, or until knife blade comes out clean. Cool thoroughly before cutting. Serve in pie shaped wedges, topped with sweetened whipped cream, if desired. 6 servings.

FRIDAY
Beef stroganoff (Use left over cooked beef)
Mashed potatoes
Buttered peas
Honey Waldorf salad*
Whole wheat toast with strawberry preserves

HONEY WALDORF SALAD

3 large red apples, unpeeled
1 tablespoon lemon juice
1 cup chopped celery
¹/₂ cup coarsely chopped pecans or walnuts

¹/₂ cup calorie reduced mayonnaise
1 tablespoon honey
Lettuce cups

Core and quarter apples. Do not peel. Dice apples and place in a bowl. Add lemon juice, stir to cover all apple pieces. Add celery and nuts. Combine mayonnaise and honey. Stir until smooth then toss with apple mixture. Serve in lettuce cups. 4 servings.

SATURDAY
Shrimp Pie Supper
Shrimp pie
Buttered steamed asparagus
Caesar salad
Buttermilk corn sticks
Applesauce cake with topping

Plan of Work
Day before:
1. Steam and peel shrimp. Store immediately in refrigerator.
2. Prepare applesauce cake.
3. Prepare salad dressing and refrigerate.
Early on the day of serving:
4. Prepare seasoned mashed potatoes and refrigerate (not necessary to do this at the last minute).
5. Prepare asparagus for cooking (wash and cut). Refrigerate.

6. Wash and tear salad greens. Place in zip lock plastic bags, ready to be tossed.

7. Combine and sift dry ingredients for corn sticks.

30 minutes before serving: (Congratulations, you have already completed most of the preparation. This will be a relaxed final preparation.)

8. Remove cake from refrigerator. Should be served at room temperature.

9. Preheat oven to 400°.

10. Final preparation of shrimp. Assemble the pie. Place in preheated oven.

11. Cook asparagus.

12. While asparagus is cooking, combine cornstick ingredients and place in oven 15 minutes before shrimp is finished cooking.

Serve and Enjoy!

SHRIMP PIE

1 pound fresh or frozen, cooked, peeled shrimp,	*1 teaspoon Worcestershire sauce*
or three 4 1/2-ounce cans shrimp	*1/8 teaspoon pepper*
2 tablespoons margarine or cooking oil	*2 cups seasoned mashed potatoes*
1 large onion, sliced	*1 tablespoon chopped parsley*
1 (10 1/2-oz) can condensed cream of celery soup	*Melted butter or margarine*
1 (4 oz can mushroom stems and pieces, drained	*Paprika*

Thaw frozen shrimp or drain and rinse canned shrimp in cold water. Melt margarine or heat oil in heavy skillet; add onions and cook over moderate heat, stirring often, until tender but not brown. Remove from heat and add soup, mushrooms, Worcestershire sauce, pepper and shrimp. Mix well. Combine mashed potatoes and parsley. Spoon or flute a high standing border of potato mixture around inside edge of a well-greased 10x1-inch pie plate. Brush potatoes with melted butter and sprinkle with paprika. Pour shrimp mixture into center. Set pie plate on a sheet of foil (to catch drippings). Bake in 400° oven for 30 minutes or until potatoes are hot and lightly browned. 4-6 servings. May be made and served in individual au gratin dishes.

BUTTERED STEAMED ASPARAGUS

24 fresh asparagus spears	*2 tablespoons melted butter or margarine*
1/2 teaspoon salt (optional)	*(optional)*

Wash asparagus. Remove scales and cut off tough bottoms. Place asparagus in sauce pan and barely cover with boiling water. Add salt if desired. Cover with well fitted lid and cook over medium heat. When steam begins to escape around the rim of cover, turn heat down to lowest setting. Do not remove cover. Cook for 15 minutes before removing cover. If still not tender crisp, cook 3-5 minutes longer. Drain. Add butter if desired, and serve hot. 4-6 servings.

CAESAR SALAD

8 cups washed and torn romaine lettuce	*1 cup croutons*
or fresh spinach	*1/4-1/2 cup (1-2 ounces) Parmesan cheese*

Place lettuce or spinach in a large bowl. Toss with dressing. Add croutons and cheese. Toss lightly and put into a salad serving bowl.

Dressing

½ cup olive oil

1-2 cloves garlic, crushed

1 tablespoon plus 1 teaspoon lemon juice

1 teaspoon Worcestershire sauce

¼-½ teaspoon freshly ground pepper

1 tablespoon chopped anchovy fillets (optional)

Combine all ingredients in small bowl. Mix thoroughly and toss with salad.

BUTTERMILK CORNSTICKS

1 ⅓ cups cornmeal

⅓ cup flour

1 teaspoon double acting baking powder

½ teaspoon baking soda

1 tablespoon sugar

½ teaspoon salt

1 cup buttermilk

1 egg, beaten

2 tablespoons melted shortening or oil

Combine cornmeal, flour, baking powder, soda, sugar and salt. Sift twice. Combine buttermilk, egg and shortening, and add to dry ingredients. Stir until smooth. Bake in well greased hot* cornstick pan at 400° for 25 minutes or until brown. 12 cornsticks.

*Grease cornstick pan and heat before adding batter.

APPLESAUCE CAKE WITH TOPPING

2 ½ cups sifted flour

1 teaspoon ground cinnamon

½ teaspoon salt

½ teaspoon ground cloves

½ teaspoon ground nutmeg

⅔ cup butter or margarine, softened

1 cup sugar

1 ⅓ cups warm applesauce

1 ¼ teaspoons baking soda

⅓ cup raisins

⅓ cup chopped nuts (optional)

Whipped cream or whipped topping

Grease a 9x9x2-inch baking pan, line bottom with waxed paper and grease again. Combine flour, cinnamon, salt, cloves and nutmeg, and sift. Mix butter and sugar until well blended. Stir in 2 tablespoons of the applesauce. Add baking soda to the remaining applesauce in small bowl, stirring until mixture foams and looks bubbly. Stir into butter mixture alternately with dry ingredients, mixing until smooth after each addition. Stir in raisins and nuts. Pour into prepared pan. Bake in 350° oven for 45 to 50 minutes or until cake springs back when touched. Cool in pan. Cut into 9 squares. Top with whipped cream or whipped topping. 9 servings.

January - Third Week

Change. It's often easier said than done. Life-long eating and exercise habits develop gradually over many years and are hard to change. However, there is growing evidence that the American public is changing as people become increasingly aware of the benefits of more healthful behavior and habits.

Adopting a more healthful approach to eating and exercise are two significant changes that people can make to preserve fitness and promote general good health. A better diet and more exercise can affect many of the key risk factors associated with some diseases. Excess weight, for example, is not a direct disease risk factor, but it increases the risk of heart attack by increasing the chance of developing high blood pressure, diabetes and high blood cholesterol. Changing your diet can reduce the risk of these health dangers.

Exercise not only serves an important function in weight control by using calories, but, far more important, it improves health by increasing physical fitness. Exercise improves circulation, allows the body to use oxygen more effectively, improves muscle and skin tone and, in general, helps to keep the body in top form. Like any other behavior change, changing your eating and exercise habits may not be too easy. To do so, it is important to remember that all behavior change involves three basic steps:

1. Become aware of current patterns and the need for a change.
2. Master the necessary information to make the change possible.
3. Make the change a permanent part of everyday life.

Most people eat what they are used to eating. Favorite foods are developed for reasons of comfort. Familiar recipes are prepared out of habit. It takes time, thought and effort, as well as a full understanding of the need, to change your food habits. A healthy body is the objective and is well worth the effort.

As you begin to develop your Healthy Diet Plan, some long standing eating habits may go, but many favorite recipes will remain. As old patterns are replaced by new more healthful ones, it gets easier. A new confidence also emerges as your new food variety leaves the spices of life and eating enjoyment intact.

The fresh approach to a Healthy Diet Plan:

1. Meet your daily requirements for protein, vitamins, minerals and other nutrients by following the USDA food guide (see Introduction).
2. Control calorie intake and maintain desirable weight.
3. Avoid eating excessive amounts of foods high in fat and cholesterol.

Fresh fruits fit easily into these guidelines. They are low in calories, virtually fat free and a rich source of vitamins and minerals. Fresh fruits are the ideal companion for a healthy diet that emphasizes weight control and the reduction of excess fat, sugar and cholesterol. Offering the best of nature's goodness, these foods can play a vital role in changing your eating habits easily, conveniently and deliciously. A healthy diet must contain adequate protein, vitamins and minerals.

The world of fresh fruits is an adventure in nutritious eating. Spanning a bountiful spectrum of natural goodness, fresh fruits offer today's consumer a wide variety of flavors, colors and textures. Ranging from apples to watermelons, few foods offer such an abundant source of essential nutrients. Fruits contribute nearly all of the vitamin C (92%), about half of the vitamin A and about one-fourth of some B vitamins obtained from food.

Various trace minerals in very small amounts are essential for health maintenance and are found in fruits. Raw fruits are especially valuable for several other reasons. There is minimal vitamin and mineral loss, whereas certain nutrients, such as vitamin C and minerals, are partially lost in some cooking procedures.

Raw fruits are also an excellent source of fiber that is inadequate in many American diets. Fiber adds bulk to the diet which many nutrition experts believe helps to reduce intestinal disorders. Attention must be given to calorie control and maintaining ideal weight by planning a nutritious, well balanced eating pattern suitable for your lifestyle and retraining your tastes in favor of low calorie foods and moderate sized portions. A balanced diet is the basic foundation of any effective nutrition plan and is essential to a low calorie program.

Moderation and variety are the cornerstones of a balanced diet. Everyone needs proteins, carbohydrate, fat, vitamins and minerals. Without them your body cannot function. All essential nutrients must be supplied by the food you eat.

On a low-calorie diet, your choice of foods is as important as the amount you eat. A balanced diet includes a little of everything and eliminates the extremes. Increase fruit consumption and reduce total fat consumption, because fat contains more than twice as many calories as protein or carbohydrates. Therefore, excessive amounts of fat in the diet should be avoided to preserve ideal weight. Happy New Year and eat healthy.

SUNDAY
Sunday Night Supper
Zippy glazed baked ham
Baked sweet potatoes
Mandarin Brussels sprouts
Layered spinach salad
Rye bread slices
Quick mini sundaes with honey chocolate sauce

Plan Of Work

Day before:
1. Prepare mini sundaes
2. Prepare Layered salad
3. Trim ham of as much fat as possible.
Three hours before serving:
4. Put ham in oven and bake for 2 hours for a six pound ham
5. One hour before serving put sweet potatoes in oven with ham
6. 45 minutes before serving, remove ham from oven, brush with glaze and cook 30 minutes longer.
7. Allow ham to cool 15 minutes before serving
8. During the cooling time, prepare the Brussels sprouts.
Enjoy!

ZIPPY GLAZED HAM

1 (6-pound) boneless or butt end of ham   *¼ cup light flavored honey*
1 cup catsup   *¼ cup prepared mustard*

Preheat oven to 325°. Trim as much fat as possible from ham. Insert meat thermometer if desired. Bake for 2 hours. Combine catsup, honey and mustard. Baste ham with mixture during last 30 minutes of baking. Cool ham for 15 minutes before slicing and serving. 10-12 servings.

BAKED SWEET POTATOES

8 medium sized sweet potatoes   *¼ cup vegetable oil*

Scrub sweet potatoes with brush to remove any defects in skin. Cover each potato with oil. Place on baking sheet. Bake at 400° for ³/₄ to 1 hour or until soft to touch. May be served immediately or cut X in top and press down on four cut corners to expose the interior.

MANDARIN BRUSSELS SPROUTS

3 (10-ounce) packages frozen Brussels sprouts   *3 tablespoons honey*
1/4 cup (1/2 stick) butter or margarine   *1 (11-ounce) can mandarin oranges, drained*
1/2 teaspoon salt   *3 tablespoons slivered almonds, toasted*
1/4 teaspoon ginger

In 3-quart saucepan, cook Brussels sprouts according to package directions. Drain well; set aside. In same saucepan, melt butter. Stir in Brussels sprouts, salt, ginger and honey. Cover; cook over medium heat, stirring occasionally, until heated through (5 to 7 minutes.) Stir in oranges and almonds. Cover; let stand one minute. 6 - 8 servings.

LAYERED SPINACH SALAD

1 quart torn fresh spinach   *1 cup mayonnaise*
2 cups fresh mushroom slices   *1/2 teaspoon sugar*
1 1/2 cups fresh onion rings (red onions if available)   *1/2 teaspoon curry powder*
2 (10 oz) packages frozen peas, thawed, drained   *2 bacon slices, crisply cooked and crumbled*

In a 2 1/2 quart salad bowl, layer spinach, mushrooms, onions and peas. Combine mayonnaise, sugar and curry powder. Spread over salad to seal. Cover; refrigerate overnight. Top with bacon before serving. 8 servings.

QUICK MINI SUNDAES WITH HONEY CHOCOLATE SAUCE

1 quart vanilla ice cream   *softened Honey chocolate sauce*

Spoon 2 tablespoons of honey chocolate sauce into bottom of 12 custard cups. Fill remainder of cup with ice cream. Top with Honey chocolate sauce. Freeze immediately. To serve: Turn ice cream filled cups upside down onto dessert plate. Serve one or more per person, as desired. 12 custard cup sized sundaes.

Honey Chocolate Sauce

1 tablespoon corn starch   *1/2 cup water*
3 tablespoons cocoa   *3/4 cup marshmallow creme*
1/2 cup (1 stick) butter or margarine   *1 teaspoon vanilla*
1/2 cup honey

Combine cornstarch, cocoa, butter, honey and water in a heavy saucepan. Bring to a boil, stirring constantly. Remove from heat, add marshmallow creme and vanilla. Stir until smooth and well blended. Makes 2 cups.

MONDAY
Chicken baked in mushroom sauce*
Buttered noodles
Steamed spinach
Fresh fruit salad, no dressing
Carrot muffins

CHICKEN BAKED IN MUSHROOM SAUCE

1 broiler-fryer chicken, cut into serving pieces
¼ cup (½ stick) butter or margarine
1 teaspoon salt
½ teaspoon pepper

1 large onion, sliced
1 (4 ounce) can sliced mushrooms
1 (10 ½-ounce) can cream of mushroom soup
⅓ cup sherry wine

In large shallow baking pan, place butter. Put in heated oven until butter is melted. Place chicken pieces in melted butter and turn until completely coated. Sprinkle salt and pepper on chicken. Bake in 400° oven for 15 minutes skin side down. Remove from oven; turn skin side up and place onion slices over chicken; add mushrooms. In bowl, combine mushroom soup and wine; pour over chicken. Reduce temperature of oven to 350° and bake about 1 hour or until fork can be inserted in chicken with ease. 4 - 6 servings.

TUESDAY
Ham and corn casserole (use left over ham)*
Carrot and cabbage salad
Whole wheat rolls
Raspberry yogurt with frozen raspberries

HAM AND CORN CASSEROLE

3 tablespoons flour
1 ½ cups milk
½ teaspoon dry mustard
1 tablespoon Worcestershire sauce
1 teaspoon salt
¼ teaspoon pepper

1 (15 ¼ ounce) can whole kernel corn, drained
1 medium onion, chopped
¼ cup chopped green pepper
2 cups cubed cooked ham
1 ¼ cup shredded Cheddar cheese, divided
3 tablespoons buttered bread crumbs

Combine flour and ½ cup milk, blending until smooth. Heat remaining milk. Stir in flour mixture, stirring constantly until smooth and thick. Add mustard, Worcestershire sauce, salt and pepper. Mix thoroughly. Add corn, onion, green pepper, ham and ¾ cup cheese. Mix and pour in 2-quart baking dish. Top with remaining cheese and bread crumbs. Bake at 375° for 55 minutes. Makes 6 servings.

WEDNESDAY
Spaghetti and meat sauce
Garden salad, oil and vinegar dressing
Hot buttered Italian bread
Hot cranapple crisp*

HOT CRANAPPLE CRISP

3 cups unpeeled sliced "delicious" apples (4 apples)
*1 (16 ounce) can whole cranberry sauce**

Whipping cream, whipped

Combine apples and cranberry sauce in mixing bowl and mix thoroughly. Pour into a greased 2-quart casserole. Distribute evenly in pan. Sprinkle topping (below) over cranberry apple mixture. Bake, uncovered, in 350° oven for 45 to 55 minutes. This can be served hot or cold. Top each serving with a tablespoon of whipped cream. Makes 6 - 8 servings.

Topping

1 1/2 cups minute oatmeal, uncooked
1/2 cup brown sugar, packed
1/2 cup flour

1/4 teaspoon salt
1/3 cup chopped pecans (optional)
1/2 cup melted butter or margarine

Combine oatmeal, sugar, flour and salt. Add pecans if desired. pour over melted butter and mix well. Note: In lieu of canned cranberry sauce, use 2 cups crushed whole cranberries and 1 1/4 cups sugar and mix well.

THURSDAY
Parmesan fish fillets*
Broiled vegetable kabobs
Scalloped potatoes
Corn muffins
Fresh fruit

PARMESAN FISH FILLET AND KABOBS

8 large cherry tomatoes
8 slices (1/4-inch thick) zucchini
8 medium sized mushrooms
8 large pitted olives

8 (1-inch) pieces green pepper
4 frozen flounder fillets
1/2 cup commercial Italian dressing
Grated Parmesan cheese

Alternate vegetables on each of 4 9-inch metal skewers. Place frozen fillets on greased rack of broiler pan; brush with dressing. Broil 4 to 5 inches from heat 4 minutes. Brush with dressing; carefully turn over. Place kabobs on rack. Brush fillets and kabobs with dressing. Broil 3 minutes; turn kabobs and brush both kabobs and fillets with dressing. Broil until fillets flake easily with fork, 2 to 3 minutes longer. To serve, brush fillets with dressing and sprinkle with cheese. 4 servings. **Note:** Any combination of vegetables can be substituted; cut into sizes recommended above.

FRIDAY
Sloppy chicks on sesame seed bun*
Potato salad
Marinated sliced tomatoes, onions and cucumbers
Ice cream with blueberry topping

SLOPPY CHICKS

2 cups cooked, chopped chicken
1 (8 ounce) can tomato sauce
1/3 cup brown sugar, firmly packed
1/4 cup vinegar

1 1/2 teaspoons chili powder
1 tablespoon prepared mustard
4 sandwich buns

In a large skillet combine chicken, tomato sauce, sugar, vinegar, chili powder and mustard. Simmer 15 to 20 minutes, or until heated through. To serve, spoon filling into buns. 4 servings.

SATURDAY
Curried shrimp with hot marmalade soy dip*
Buttered broccoli
Jellied vegetable juice
Finger rolls
Triple strawberry trifle*

CURRIED SHRIMP WITH HOT MARMALADE SOY DIP

2 (10 ounce) packages frozen breaded shrimp
1/2 cup (1 stick) butter or margarine

1 teaspoon curry powder
Hot marmalade soy dip

Cream together butter and curry powder. Spread curry butter over both sides of frozen shrimp. Arrange in shallow baking pan. Broil about 3 inches from heat for 8 to 10 minutes or until hot and browned, turning once. Serve with hot marmalade soy dip. 6 servings.

Hot Marmalade Soy Dip

2/3 cup orange marmalade
1/2 cup lemon juice
1/2 cup soy sauce

2 cloves garlic, minced
Dash ginger
2 teaspoons corn starch

Combine ingredients; mix well. Cook, stirring constantly, until clear and thickened. Serve hot with shrimp.

TRIPLE STRAWBERRY TRIFLE

1 (3 5/8-ounce) package vanilla-flavored pudding
   and pie filling
1 1/2 cups milk
1 (4 oz) container frozen whipped topping, thawed

1 baked (8-inch) sponge cake layer, home made
   or commercial
1/3 cup orange juice
2 cups sliced sweetened strawberries, halved, divided

Prepare pudding mix as directed on package using milk as the liquid. Cover with waxed paper and cool to room temperature. Fold in 1 cup of whipped topping. Cut cake into 1 1/2-inch cubes; place in 1 1/2-quart serving bowl or individual dishes and sprinkle with orange juice. Spoon 1/2 cups strawberries evenly over cake cubes; spoon on pudding, covering cake completely. Chill at least 2 hours. Top with remaining whipped topping and strawberry halves, if desired. 6 servings.

January - Fourth Week

In planning meals at the beginning of this new year, remember to include a variety of vegetables. Vegetables give both nutritive value and appetite appeal to our diets. In order to plan the needed amount of nutrients, vegetables are usually placed in a group with fruits. From this group, you need to choose four or more one-half cup servings each day.

As stated before, be sure to include one serving of a food high in vitamin C each day. Foods in this category include citrus fruits such as oranges, lemons, grapefruit, limes and tomatoes. Also include one serving of a food high in vitamin A at least every other day. Brightly pigmented yellow and dark green vegetables and fruits contain generous amounts of carotenoids, an outstanding source of provitamin which is converted to vitamin A in the body. Vitamin A is stored in the body, so a good source every other day is adequate. The remaining servings may be of any vegetable or fruit, including those valued for vitamins A or C.

In deciding which of the many vegetables to serve at a meal, remember to vary their color, texture, flavor, size, shape and method of preparation. Mashed sweet potatoes served at the same meal with mashed pumpkin would seem too similar for most people, while mashed sweet potatoes served with green beans or broccoli would add variety.

Think how drab our diets would be without the color and crispness of fresh tossed salads, the tang and texture of relishes, or the distinctive flavors of other vegetable dishes.

Vegetables are not only an excellent source of vitamins and minerals, but they are also low in calories. One-half cup of most vegetables contain less than 50 calories, while starchy vegetables such as corn, boiled potatoes, lima beans and peas supply from 50 to 100 calories per half cup.

Some vegetables are known for the protein they contribute to our diet. These are mature dry legumes such as dry peas and members of the bean family, including kidney, Lima, garbanzo, navy, pinto and soybeans. These also provide B vitamins including folic acid along with iron and other trace minerals and fiber in addition to the vegetable protein. These foods are low in fat and contain no cholestrol.

SUNDAY
Penne with creamy vegetable sauce*
Fresh garden salad with seasoned rice vinegar
Italian bread
Lemon sherbert with pound cake

PENNE WITH CREAMY VEGETABLE SAUCE

1 (12 ounce) package of penne or other pasta	*12 ounces cream cheese, softened*
1 (4 ounce) can of mushrooms, stems and pieces, drained	*1 cup half & half*
	1/2 cup grated Parmesan cheese
1 (10 ounce) package of frozen chopped broccoli, thawed	*3/4 teaspoon salt*
	1/2 teaspoon pepper

Cook pasta according to package directions. Remove from heat, drain and keep hot. Combine mushrooms and broccoli; set aside. Place cream cheese in a quart size saucepan. Place over medium heat, stir until cheese is melted. Add half and half, stir until smooth. Stir in Parmesan cheese until well blended. Add salt, pepper and broccoli mixture. Correct seasoning. If mixture is too thick, add a little half and half. Place pasta on individual serving plate and top with vegetable sauce. 6-8 servings.

MONDAY
Roast shoulder of lamb with mustard sauce coating*
Oven baked potato slices
Relish tray
Hot buttered English muffins with raspberry jam

> *"Tell me what you eat and I will tell you what you are."*
> *Brillat-Savarin, French gastronomist*

ROAST SHOULDER OF LAMB WITH MUSTARD SAUCE COATING

3 pounds boneless lamb shoulder, rolled and tied
2 cloves garlic, cut in slivers
Salt to taste
Pepper to taste
½ cup Dijon mustard

½ teaspoon ground rosemary
½ teaspoon thyme
1 clove garlic, crushed
1 teaspoon soy sauce
Fresh parsley

Wipe the lamb shoulder with a damp cloth. Cut shallow slits all over the meat and insert the garlic slivers in them. Sprinkle the lamb with salt and pepper and place on a rack in a roasting pan, fat side up. Roast in the center of a 400° oven for 30 minutes. Combine the mustard, rosemary, thyme, crushed garlic and soy sauce. Remove the lamb from the oven and coat it completely with the mustard sauce (a basting brush can be used). Roast for an additional hour for a total cooking time of 90 minutes or to an internal temperature of 140° for a medium-rare roast. When the lamb is done, let it rest at room temperature for about 10-15 minutes before carving. Carve in ½-inch thick slices and garnish with fresh parsley. 6-8 servings.

TUESDAY
Chopped beef steak with mushroom gravy
Mashed Potatoes
Baked tomato halves
Cauliflour salad
4 o'clock scones *

4 O'Clock Scones

2 cups sifted all-purpose flour
½ teaspoon salt
1 tablespoon sugar
1 tablespoon plus 1 teaspoon baking powder
1 tablespoon plus 1 teaspoon solid shortening

1 egg, well-beaten
½ to ⅔ cup milk
Melted butter
Sugar

Sift together flour, salt, sugar and baking powder. Cut in shortening. Stir ½ cup milk into the egg; gradually add to flour mixture. If necessary, add remaining milk. Knead lightly on floured board; roll to ½-inch thickness in form of a circle. Cut in wedges. Place on baking sheet, brush with melted butter and sprinkle with sugar. Bake in hot over (400°) for 15 minutes. 15 scones.

WEDNESDAY
Tahitian Chicken*
Buttered green beans
Green salad
Hot rolls, butter
Iced chocolate pound cake

TAHITIAN CHICKEN

1 (2 ½ pound) frying chicken, cut up	⅛ teaspoon ground allspice
1 teaspoon salt, divided	⅛ teaspoon ground cloves
½ cup flour	2 chicken bouillon cubes
¼ teaspoon black pepper	1¼ cups water
½ teaspoon monosodium glutamate (optional)	3 tablespoons lime juice
2 tablespoons margarine or cooking oil	3 tablespoons cornstarch
1 cup sliced onion	1 can (20 ounces) pineapple chunks, undrained
¼ cup firmly-packed dark brown sugar	2 bananas, peeled and halved lengthwise and crosswise

Combine ½ teaspoon salt, flour, pepper and monosodium glutamate in plastic or paper bag. Shake each piece of chicken in the bag separately to coat well. Brown in cooking oil. Pour off all excess fat. Remove chicken. Add onion and cook over medium heat, stirring frequently, until transparent. Stir in brown sugar, remaining ½ teaspoon salt, allspice, cloves, bouillon cubes, 1 cup water and lime juice. Heat. Return chicken to skillet and bring to a boil. Reduce heat, cover and simmer about 40 minutes or until tender. Turn chicken pieces after 20 minutes. Remove chicken to a warm platter; keep warm. Blend together cornstarch and remaining ¼ cup water. Stir into liquid in skillet. Cook over medium heat, stirring, until thickened and boiling. Add pineapple and bananas; heat through. Serve over chicken. 4 servings.

THURSDAY
Broiled ham slices with raisin sauce
Buttered Brussels sprouts
Carrot and raisin salad
Corn bread
Pineapple delight*

PINEAPPLE DELIGHT

1 (8 ¼ ounce) can crushed pineapple, undrained	½ cup (1 stick) butter or margarine, sliced in pats
1 (9 ounce) yellow cake mix	Vanilla ice cream, whipped cream or whipped topping (optional)
1 cup chopped pecans	

Preheat oven to 375°. Spread pineapple in 8-inch pie plate. Cover evenly with dry cake mix. Sprinkle pecans over top of cake mix. Place pats of butter on top of pecans. Bake for 20 minutes or until top is brown and crusty. Serve warm. Cut into pie shaped wedges, topped with vanilla ice cream or whipped cream. Makes 6 to 8 servings. Store left overs covered in refrigerator.

FRIDAY
Soy barbecued shrimp*
Oven browned potatoes
Stir fried zuchinni and onions
Cabbage and pineapple salad
Hot buttered French bread
Iced chiffon cake

SOY BARBECUED SHRIMP

2 pounds fresh shrimp
2 cloves garlic, crushed
½ teaspoon salt
½ cup soy sauce

½ cup lemon or lime juice
3 tablespoons finely chopped parsley
2 teaspoons dehydrated onion flakes
½ teaspoon pepper

Shell and de-vein shrimp, leaving tails on. Arrange shrimp in shallow dish. In small bowl mash garlic with salt. Stir in remaining ingredients. Pour marinade over shrimp, marinate for 2 hours, and thread shrimp on skewers. Grill 3 minutes, basting with marinade. Turn. Grill 5 minutes more, basting several times. Use any remaining marinade as dip for the French bread. 4 servings. (May be broiled in oven.)

SATURDAY
(Informal Saturday Night Supper)
Ranch style chicken breasts
Baked potatoes
Sauteed and steamed mixed vegetables
Hot rolls (commercial)
Sherried crunch pie

Plan of Work
Day before:
1. Prepare pie 90 minutes before meal is served
2. Prepare potatoes and place in oven
3. Prepare chicken and place in oven
4. Prepare vegetables for steaming
5. 15 minutes before potatoes are cooked, steam vegetables
A simple meal if pie is prepared ahead of time.

RANCH STYLE CHICKEN BREASTS

4 whole chicken breasts, skinned and boned   *½ cup (1 stick) butter or margarine, melted*
2 (1 ounce) packages dried Ranch Style dressing mix

Cut whole breast in half. Dip in melted butter. Dredge in dry salad dressing mixture. Bake skin side up at 375° for 45 minutes. 8 servings.

BAKED POTATOES

8 large baking potatoes
Oil
Butter (optional)

Sour cream (optional)
Salt
Pepper

Scrub potatoes, pierce skin with fork several times to allow steam to escape. Rub with oil. Bake at 375° for one hour or until soft to the touch. Protect the hands with towel or mitts and slightly roll potato to soften the center. To serve, cut an X on top of the skin of the potato. Gently press open. Sprinkle lightly with salt and pepper. Pass the butter and/or sour cream if desired. 8 servings.

SAUTEED AND STEAMED MIXED VEGETABLES

5 green peppers, cut into wide strips
3 large onions, sliced
3 ribs celery, sliced
3 tablespoons vegetable oil

3 tablespoons water
1 (8 oz) can mushrooms, stems and pieces, drained
Salt
Pepper

Saute peppers, onions and celery in oil until tender, not brown, stirring constantly. Add water. Cover and simmer for 5 minutes. Add mushrooms and seasonings. Heat through. Serve hot. 6 - 8 servings.

HONEY SHERRIED CRUNCH PIE

1 envelope (1 tablespoon) plain gelatin
1/2 cup sweet sherry wine
1 (3 1/4 ounce) package vanilla pudding and
 pie filling mix (not instant)
1 1/2 cups milk

1/4 cup honey
1/2 cup heavy cream, whipped
1 (9 inch) baked pie shell
1 cup coarsely crushed peanut brittle

Soften gelatin in wine. Prepare pudding mix according to directions on package, using 1 1/2 cups milk as the liquid. Remove from heat; add softened gelatin and stir until dissolved. Add honey. Cool completely, about 1 hour. When pudding mixture is partially thickened, fold in whipped cream. Pour into pie shell. Cover with peanut brittle; pat down gently. Chill until served. 6 - 8 servings.

February

February - First Week

VISITING THE SUPERMARKET is a very important trip for the food shopper today. It is almost a game. The market is handsome in design, air conditioned or heated, and often has music in the background. Baby sitting is sometimes supplied. Samples and gimmicks abound. Here are a few tips on how to win at the supermarket game.

Plan your menu for a week in advance. Decide which meats, fish, fruits and vegetables you and your family enjoy eating. What good buys are available that can be included? Make these menus fun - your family deserves it! Also include snacks: fresh vegetables, dried fruits, cheese, nuts and baked crackers are nourishing choices.

Before shopping, examine the contents of your refrigerator and your cupboard for leftovers or partly-filled boxes. These leftovers mean money because you may not have to buy these items on the next shopping trip.

Read the food section of your newspaper for store specials, coupons and flyers. You can often save a great deal of money with coupons and specials. But use coupons only when you need them - don't buy things unnecessarily. Overbuying is a waste of money.

Think about your store layout. Jot down aisle numbers and what's in them. Then make up a shopping list in the same order as the items are located in the store, saving you time once you are there. Stick to your list unless you spot a real bargain.

Contact a friend and shop together. You can chip in for large quantities and divide them at home. This will save money and gas. It is best not to shop with children and spouses.

The best time to shop is when you're not tired or hungry. Being tired means you may get confused and miss the week's best buys; hunger tempts you to buy more than you really need.

Follow your aisle strategy and shop according to your shopping list. Select meats, poultry, dairy products and frozen foods last to keep them fresh and as cold as possible.

Most stores have unit pricing, which means that price per ounce or pound is listed under each item on the shelf. Compare which container gives you the most food for the money. While other foods are inviting, you can save money if you follow your list and buy only what you need.

Store brands offer a good blend of quality and economy. Generic foods can also be money savers. They are generally packaged with a plain black and white label and no brand name. They are usually equal nutritionally to branded products, but they may be lacking in flavor and appearance.

Growing conditions or the weather can determine price and quality of fruits and vegetables, so look for the freshest produce possible. Handle fresh fruits and vegetables carefully to prevent bruising. Refrigerate as soon after purchase as possible. Don't buy too much at a time, and don't keep it around too long. Usually a week is the maximum storage time, except for apples, citrus fruits and root vegetables. While fresh, luscious tomatoes are perfect for salads; less expensive canned tomatoes are better for cooked dishes.

Label reading has become a very popular part of the shopping trip. Knowing how to read labels can pay big dividends in savings, flavor and nutrition, so always allow time for label reading in the store. If your vision is poor, invest in a pocket magnifying glass and take it with you to the store. Other shoppers noticing your care will probably admire you, and just might ask for your advice on shopping tips.

Examine the ingredients listed on the container. They are listed by weight in descending order. Nutrition information is also provided on labels and should be read. If the label carries the title "Nutrition Facts" it is the new label recently approved by the Food and Drug Administration. It will include:

1. Standardized serving size (1 cup, 1 tablespoon, etc.) that is considered an average serving.
2. Percent of daily value for certain nutrients. The labels are based on a 2000 calorie daily diet. Decide whether you need more or less calories per day, then use these percentages to determine how a food fits into your daily diet. Nutrients included are total fat, saturated fat, cholesterol, sodium, carbohydrates, sugar, proteins, vitamins A and C, calcium and iron.
3. Protein: It is difficult to state the percentage of protein required per person because it depends on the individual need. Most people need no more than 50 grams per day (4 calories per gram).

SUNDAY
Winter Sunday Supper
Creamy and chunky potato soup
Beef roll-ups
Neopolitan green beans
Freezer dinner rolls
Cantelope and melon salad with ginger cream dressing
Nut bars

Plan Of Work
Day before:
1. Prepare nut bars
Early in the day:
2. Wash and prepare green beans
3. Prepare salad dressing
1 ¹/₂ hours before dinner:
4. Remove rolls from freezer
5. Prepare soup and keep warm
6. Prepare beef roll-ups
7. While roll-ups are baking, steam beans and add remaining ingredients

CREAMY AND CHUNKY POTATO SOUP

¹/₂ pound (8 or 9 slices) bacon, chopped
1 large onion, finely chopped
4 - 5 medium potatoes, peeled and cubed
1 cup water
1 (10 ¹/₂ ounce) can cream of chicken soup

1 cup sour cream
1 teaspoon salt (optional)
¹/₂ teaspoon pepper
2 tablespoons chopped fresh parsley
  (or 1 tablespoon dried)

In a 2- or 3-quart saucepan, cook bacon until limp. Add onion and cook on medium heat until onion is cooked, not brown. Add potatoes and water. Cook for about 10 minutes or until potatoes are tender. Add remaining ingredients. Mix well and simmer for 5 minutes. 4 to 6 servings.

BEEF ROLL-UPS

2 ¹/₂ cups biscuit mix
1 cup milk
1 ¹/₂ pounds ground beef
2 eggs, beaten
1 teaspoon salt
1 teaspoon pepper

¹/₂ teaspoon garlic salt
¹/₂ teaspoon celery salt
1 tablespoon Worcestershire sauce
1 (10 ¹/₂ ounce) can cream of mushroom soup
1 (3 ounce) package cream cheese, softened
Fresh parsley

Add milk to biscuit mix and mix. Roll out biscuit dough on floured surface into 1/2 inch thick rectangle approximately 8x10 inches. Mix beef with eggs, salt, pepper, garlic salt, celery salt and Worcestershire sauce. Spread beef mixture over biscuit dough. Roll as for jelly roll. Cut into ½-inch slices. Place slices, cut side down, in greased pan. Bake in preheated 350° oven for 30 minutes or until browned.

Combine undiluted soup and cream cheese. Heat until smooth. Top each serving with soup mixture and garnish with fresh parsley. 6 servings.

NEAPOLITAN GREEN BEANS

1 pound fresh green beans or 1 (16 ounce)	*½ cup chopped celery*
packages frozen green beans	*¼ cup chopped green peppers*
¼ cup water	*1 tablespoon dried chopped onion or ¼*
1 (14 ½ or 16 ounce) can diced tomatoes	*cup fresh, chopped*

Cook beans the nutritional way. Wash green beans. Place beans and water in a 1-quart saucepan with a well-fitted lid. Place on high heat. When steam begins to flow around the edge of the lid and the lid can swirl, reduce heat to lowest level and cook 15 minutes. Do not raise the lid until beans have finished cooking. Drain the water from the beans. Add tomatoes, celery, peppers and onions. Cook over medium heat about 15 minutes or until heated through. 6 servings. Approximately 30 calories per serving.

FREEZER DINNER ROLLS

5 ½ to 6 ½ cups unsifted flour	*1 ¼ cups water*
½ cup sugar	*½ cup milk*
1 ½ teaspoons salt	*⅓ cup butter or margarine*
2 packages active dry yeast	*2 eggs at room temperature*

In a large bowl, thoroughly mix 2 cups flour, sugar, salt and undissolved active dry yeast. Combine water, milk and butter in a saucepan. Heat over low heat until liquids are very warm (120°‑130°). Butter does not need to melt. Gradually add to dry ingredients and beat 2 minutes at medium speed of an electric mixer, scraping bowl occasionally. Stir in enough additional flour to make a soft dough. Turn out onto lightly floured board; knead until smooth and elastic, about 8 to 10 minutes. Cover with plastic wrap, then a towel. Let rest for 20 minutes. Punch dough down. Shape into desired shapes for dinner rolls. Place on greased baking sheets. Cover with plastic wrap and foil, sealing well. Freeze until firm. Transfer to plastic bags. Freeze up to four weeks. Remove desired number of rolls from freezer and place on greased baking sheet. Cover; let rise in warm place, free from draft, until doubled in volume, about 1 ½ hours. Bake at 350° 15 minutes or until golden brown and done. Remove from baking sheet and cool on wire racks. (4 dozen rolls, total)

GINGER CREAM DRESSING
(for Fruit Salad)

½ cup mayonnaise	*½ teaspoon ginger*
2 tablespoons sugar	*dash of salt*
1 tablespoon lemon juice	*½ cup heavy cream, whipped*
½ teaspoon grated lemon peel	

Blend mayonnaise, sugar, lemon juice, lemon peel, ginger and salt until smooth. Fold in whipped cream and chill. Makes about 1 ½ cups dressing.

NUT BARS

2 cups unsifted flour, divided
²/₃ cup firmly-packed dark brown sugar
1 teaspoon baking powder
½ cup butter or margarine
4 eggs, well beaten

½ cup firmly packed dark brown sugar
1 ½ cups dark corn syrup
2 teaspoons vanilla extract
1 teaspoon salt
1 cup chopped walnuts or pecans

Grease 13x9x2-inch baking pan. Combine 1 ½ cups of the flour, ⅓ cup brown sugar and baking powder. Cut in butter with pastry blender or 2 knives until very fine crumbs form. Pat firmly and evenly into bottom of prepared pan. Bake in oven at 350° for 15 minutes. Combine eggs, ⅓ cup brown sugar, remaining ½ cup flour, corn syrup, vanilla and salt until well mixed. Pour over partially baked layer. Sprinkle with nuts. Bake in oven at 350° for 35 to 40 minutes or until set. Cut into bars while still warm. (32 bars)

MONDAY
Barbeque Sandwich
Quick and easy Brunswick stew *
Cole Slaw
Sesame seed buns
Chocolate cake

QUICK AND EASY BRUNSWICK STEW

2 large onions, chopped
2 tablespoons butter or margarine, melted
1 (10 ounce) can barbeque beef
2 (10 ounce) cans barbeque pork
1 (10 ounce) can barbeque chicken
1 (16 ounce) can tomatoes

1 (16 ounce) can creamed corn
1 (16 ounce) can whole kernel corn, drained
2 potatoes, peeled and diced or 2 cans potatoes,
* drained and diced*
¼ cup soy sauce
2 tablespoons Worcestershire sauce

In a large pan, saute onions in melted butter until tender, not brown. Add remaining ingredients and cook at medium heat for 20 minutes. 10 servings, freeze leftovers.

TUESDAY
Jan's poppy seed chicken*
Buttered rice
Steamed asparagus
Lettuce wedge, commercial dressing
Pound cake with chocolate sauce

JAN'S POPPY SEED CHICKEN

2 cups sour cream
1 (10 ³/₄ ounce) can cream of celery soup
½ cup plus 2 tablespoons milk
3 tablespoons poppy seed

4 cups chicken meat, cooked and chopped
1 cup buttered cracker crumbs
1 tablespoon sesame seeds (optional)

Combine sour cream, soup, milk and poppy seed. Stir until smooth. Add to chicken. Place mixture in a 2-quart baking dish. Cover with crumbs and top with sesame seed. Bake at 350° for 40 minutes. 6 servings.

WEDNESDAY
Baby beef roast
Roasted herb potatoes*
Fresh spinach in cream cheese
Sliced tomatoes and onions
Vanilla ice cream

ROASTED HERB POTATOES

3 tablespoons cooking oil	1/4 cup grated Parmesan cheese
3 cloves garlic, crushed	1/4 teaspoon salt
1 tablespoon dried rosemary, crushed	1/4 teaspoon pepper
4 medium potatoes, unpeeled, sliced 1/3 to 1/2 inch thick	

Spray a 10x15-inch cookie sheet with cooking spray. In a small bowl, combine oil, garlic and rosemary. Arrange potato slices on cookie sheet. Brush with oil mixture. Sprinkle with Parmesan cheese. Bake in a 400° oven for 30 minutes or until lightly brown and crisp. 4-6 servings.

THURSDAY
Liver and onions supreme*
Scalloped potatoes
Baked tomato halves
Toasted English muffin
Orange sherbet

LIVER AND ONIONS SUPREME

1 pound beef liver slices	1/2 cup dry bread crumbs
1 egg, slightly beaten	1/2 teaspoon salt
1 tablespoon milk	1 medium onion, sliced
1/2 cup grated Parmesan cheese	3 tablespoons butter or margarine

Combine egg and milk. In another dish combine cheese, bread crumbs and salt. Dip liver in egg mixture, then in crumb mixture. Saute onion in 1 tablespoon butter until tender; remove from skillet. Brown liver in 2 tablespoons butter, 2 to 3 minutes on each side or to desired doneness, adding more butter as required. Return onion to skillet; heat. Serve hot. 4-6 servings.

FRIDAY
Flounder amandine *
Rice pilaf
Buttered wholed kernel corn
Marinated beets and onion salad
Egg bread (cornbread)
Peach yogurt with peach topping

FLOUNDER AMANDINE

2 pounds flounder fillets or other fish fillets,
  fresh or frozen
¼ cup flour
1 teaspoon seasoned salt
1 teaspoon paprika

¼ cup (½ stick) melted butter or margarine
½ cup sliced almonds
2 tablespoon lemon juice
4 to 5 drops liquid hot pepper sauce or to taste
1 tablespoon chopped parsley

Thaw frozen fillets. Cut fillets into serving size portions. Combine flour, seasoned salt and paprika; mix well. Roll fish in flour mixture. Place fish in a single layer, skin side down, in a well greased baking pan, 15x10x1-inch. Drizzle 2 tablespoons melted butter over fish. Broil about 4 inches from source of heat 10 to 12 minutes or until fish flakes easily when tested with a fork. Saute almonds in remaining 2 tablespoons melted butter, stirring constantly. Remove from heat. Add lemon juice, hot pepper sauce and parsley; mix. Pour over fish. Serve at once. 6 servings.

SATURDAY
Linguini primavera *
Crisp vegetable salad, Italian dressing
Hot garlic bread
Apple pizza

LINGUINI PRIMAVERA

1 bunch broccoli (about 1 pound)
2 small zucchini
½ pound fresh asparagus
1 1 pound package linguini
2 large cloves garlic, crushed
2 cups cherry tomatoes, halved
¼ cup olive oil
1 teaspoon dried leaf basil, crumbled
½ pound mushrooms, thinly sliced

½ cup frozen green peas, thawed
¼ cup chopped fresh parsley
1 ½ teaspoons salt
½ teaspoon black pepper
½ teaspoon crushed red pepper
½ cup (½ stick) butter or margarine
1 cup heavy cream
½ cup freshly grated Parmesan cheese

Wash and trim broccoli, zucchini and asparagus. Cut broccoli into bite size pieces; cut zucchini into thin slices; cut asparagus into 1-inch pieces. Cook in boiling water until crisp-tender; drain; put in a large bowl. Cook linguini according to package instructions; cook only 9 minutes in boiling water; drain. Saute garlic and tomatoes in oil in a large skillet. Stir in basil and mushrooms; cook 3 minutes. Stir in peas, parsley, salt, black and red peppers; cook 1 minute more. Add mixture to vegetables in bowl. Melt butter in same skillet; stir in cream and cheese. Cook over medium heat, stirring constantly, until smooth. Add linguini, toss to coat. Stir in vegetables; heat gently just until hot. 6-8 servings.

February — Second Week

Many shoppers feel that they have conquered the "Supermarket game." Before they are convinced of this, they should take a good look at the contents of their grocery cart. Often the shopper wonders, "Why did I buy that when I really don't need it?" Such questions can be answered by looking at the factors that influence why we choose the products we do.

    There are many sales techniques to encourage you to buy at the supermarket. They are part of good merchandizing and efficient store operation. To be aware of the psychology that is used to influence purchases is an aid to the shopper.

Social influences can be a big factor in grocery shopping. A shopper might select an expensive frozen cake, or a frozen entree convenience item even though it costs more money simply because friends have talked about the item. Unconsciously we may follow the advice of famous celebrities in TV commercials when we are making shopping decisions. Often, advertising will indicate how the buyer can be somebody special by purchasing the product.

Understanding your own family's needs and wants will help to give you a better grasp on food buying. All families are different and, therefore, the amount of money that they will spend for food varies. Size of family and stage in family life cycle influence food buying (infant, teen age or adult). Choices are also related to whether the meal planner is employed outside the home.

Before starting a shopping trip, spend time gathering information that will minimize the amount of time you have to spend at the supermarket. It will save total food dollars.

Organize the shopping list. After planning the meals, you may want to organize it by food type. For example, list meats or proteins and include fruits, vegetables, and breads that would work into these meals. Keep the list flexible. You might list green vegetables and then make comparisons as to the cost after you reach the store. Be sure to check supplies on hand and then list ingredients that you need to buy. Keep an on-going list in the kitchen and jot down items or thoughts as the week goes by.

Review recipes so that you know what you will actually need (to avoid extra trips to the market) and the form you need to purchase. Be prepared to make some substitutions because canned or frozen may be less expensive than fresh. If it's seasonal, fresh may be the best buy.

Be sure to read and save the newspaper ads and clip coupons you will be able to use. Don't be tempted by ads for products you don't need. Saving seven cents on an 89 cent item is no bargain if it wasn't on the grocery list.

Select your grocery store carefully. Generally all stores run specials throughout a given week. If you want to shop around, determine if stores are close enough to make the energy cost worth the price of shopping in several stores. If the stores are not located very near each other, you might shop one store one week and buy enough of their bargain items to last two weeks, then shop the second store the next week for their bargain items.

You may find that shopping the same old store is not necessarily the most economical method. It may be necessary to change your habits and switch to another store. As you try to economize, you may need to make other choices in your shopping habits. Some shoppers are now finding that warehouse markets or cooperatives where the customer does most of the work offer lower prices.

Do not shop hungry. Shop after eating. Consumers who are not hungry are not as likely to make impulse purchases. If you must fit grocery shopping into the end of a busy day, eat an apple before going to the store. Don't shop hungry.

Whenever possible try to shop without children or spouse because they are likely to exert pressure to buy items that may not be on your grocery shopping list. The person who regularly does the shopping is accustomed to the grocery store and is not as likely to be influenced by new items or impulses.

Most grocery stores are designed in a similar pattern for shopping. As you enter, you will pick up a cart almost immediately and follow a right-handed pattern of traveling through the store. The right-handed traffic pattern is designed for the majority of customers who find it easier to reach to the right to pick up items instead of across the body.

Produce is located at the front of most grocery stores and is considered an impulse item by the merchandiser. In beautiful condition and well displayed, it will tempt the shopper. Because it is so highly perishable it must be sold as rapidly as possible. Do not be tempted if it is not on the list.

Grocers know that almost all people entering the store will move along this aisle.

As you continue around the edge of the grocery store, you will find the meat department, the dairy department, baked goods and the deli. Some shoppers go directly to the meat, fish and poultry counters and make these purchases first. This helps in planning meals around the meat specials, because meat does take the biggest chunk, roughly one-third, of the food dollar. "Price per serving" provides the true cost for a meal. Boneless meat yields four servings per pound, Bone-in meat yields two to three servings per pound and meat with substantial bone and fat yield one or two servings per pound. Therefore boneless, although more expensive, may prove to be a better buy.

Throughout the store, specials are often used as "loss leaders." Loss leaders are advertised specials that are moderately priced and have wide appeal. They are designed to bring customers into the store with the expectation that they will buy other merchandise that is not on sale. Shoppers need to be aware of regular prices so that they can recognize true bargains.

Fresh items and high demand items tend to be one and the same. The dairy section is as far from the entrance as possible so that you will need to pass by various items of merchandise on your way to pick up needed dairy foods. The dairy department offers an array of nutritious foods for the consumer. It also provides a pull date on the food package that assures the consumer of the freshness of the item.

The pull date means the item must not be sold beyond that date to guarantee good quality. It is located on the top of the milk container, on the bottom of cottage cheese and sour cream cartons and is usually stamped on the plastic wrap of cheese products. Egg cartons are stamped with the pull date on the rim that you open. Refrigerated dough products are stamped with a freshness date on the bottom of the can which means that the item is best if used by that date.

Colors, shapes, textures, smells and tastes will arouse the senses and attract you as a customer to buy some items that are available in the grocery store and are not on your list. It is pleasant to visit a grocery store and see how your own senses are aroused as you travel down the aisles.

Remember, supermarkets are generally arranged so people will have to walk over most of the store to reach the necessary basic food items on the grocery list, such as meat, milk, frozen juice and bread. Walking every aisle once a week for essential items may be good for business, but it may not be good for your pocketbook unless you stick to the grocery list.

Many shelves are layered so that the most popular or the least expensive items are on the lower shelves. People who come into the store to buy these basic items will have to reach down to get them. On the other hand, impulse items or new products will be located at eye level. Impulse items will often be scattered among the staples. Again, sticking to the shopping list can help you avoid impulse buying. Studies indicate that about three-fourths of all purchases come from spontaneous decisions that were made in the supermarket.

Many products are displayed as units: cookies and sauces may be near the ice cream, or crackers and dips put with the cheese. Spaghetti is a low-profit staple, and the sauce is a high-profit impulse item. They are often located near each other so that the shopper will not forget to pick them up.

Advertisers use a variety of merchandizing methods to help promote sales of products. These can range from colorful banners or beautiful displays to the aroma of freshly-brewed coffee or baked goods. Even harder to resist are the free bite-sized samples that may turn into items in the shopping cart.

One must also be aware that shoppers seem to associate mass displays with bargains. These mass displays or end-aisle displays may actually be bargains or they may be regularly priced articles displayed in a basket.

Multiple pricing has a remarkable power of suggestion. If cans are marked 4 for $1.00, sales soar. Sometimes there is a small saving from buying these multiple priced items. However, surveys show that people buy them thinking they are getting a bargain, when actually they are paying the regular price.

When comparing prices, be sure to look at the unit pricing that is available on each of the grocery shelves. Unit pricing gives the cost per unit, pound, ounce, pint, serving, or other measure for the product. Unit pricing helps the shopper make comparisons among sizes, forms or brands of a given product. Next week, a review of shopping tips.

SUNDAY
Easy Swiss steak *
Buttered rice
Minted peas and carrots
Bread sticks
Green salad with oil and vinegar dressing
Gingerbread topped with lemon sauce

EASY SWISS STEAK

2 pound round beef steak (cut ½ to 1 inch thick)
Salt and pepper to taste
½ cup flour
2 tablespoons shortening
1 onion, sliced thin

½ green pepper, chopped finely
1 (8 ounce) can tomato sauce
1 (4 ounce) can mushrooms or stems and pieces,
  drained
²/₃ cup hot water

Cut meat into serving sized pieces. Add salt and pepper to meat to taste. Pound flour into meat with meat mallet. In a skillet, brown meat in shortening; add onions, green pepper, tomato sauce, mushrooms and hot water. Cover tightly and simmer for 1 hour or until meat is tender; serve with rice. 8 servings. If it gets too dry, add 4 ounces (½ cup) tomato sauce plus ⅓ cup hot water.

MONDAY
Meat loaf with mushroom sauce topping
Mashed potatoes
Broccoli Parmesan
Fruited cabbage salad *
Whole wheat bread
Vanilla ice cream topped with creme de Menthe

FRUITED CABBAGE SALAD

6 cups shredded cabbage
1 orange, peeled and cut in segments or 1 can
  Mandarin orange, drained
¼ cup sliced celery
1 tablespoon minced fresh parsley
3 tablespoons sugar
1 tablespoon corn starch

¼ teaspoon salt
¼ teaspoon dry mustard
⅛ teaspoon pepper
1 cup apple juice
⅓ cup white vinegar
1 egg, beaten
1 red apple, cored and cut in wedges

Combine cabbage, oranges, celery and parsley in a large bowl. Cover and chill in refrigerator for several hours. Combine sugar, corn starch, salt, mustard and pepper in saucepan. Stir in apple juice and vinegar. Beat in egg with a rotary beater. Cook over medium heat, stirring constantly, until mixture coats a spoon. Remove from heat. Cool. Pour dressing in a jar. Cover and chill in refrigerator. Immediately before serving, add apples and dressing to cabbage mixture; toss gently to mix. 6 servings.

TUESDAY
Portuguese soup *
Grilled cheese sandwich
Spinach salad
Crumb cake

PORTUGUESE SOUP

6 cups chicken stock or canned chicken broth
1 pound smoked sausage, sliced, 1/4 inch thick
4 medium potatoes, peeled and diced
1 (15 1/2 ounce) can kidney beans, drained
1 (16 ounce) can tomatoes

1/2 medium head of green cabbage, coarsely chopped
1 medium onion, chopped
2 large carrots, chopped
1 green bell pepper, diced
6 garlic cloves, crushed

Combine all ingredients in large pot. Bring to a boil. Reduce heat; simmer until thick, stirring occasionally, about 2 hours. Season with pepper. (Can be prepared 2 days ahead; refrigerate. Rewarm before serving.) 6 servings.

WEDNESDAY
Salmon cheese pie*
Buttered green beans
Orange and grapefruit with French fruit dressing
Vanilla ice cream on a brownie

SALMON CHEESE PIE WITH WHITE SAUCE TOPPING

1 (1 pound) can salmon
1/4 small onion, finely chopped
1 cup shredded Cheddar cheese
4 sprigs parsley, chopped
1 can refrigerator biscuits (10 biscuits)
2 slices white bread, cut in small pieces

1 cup milk, hot but not boiling
1 teaspoon dry mustard
1/2 teaspoon salt
White pepper to taste
1 cup frozen peas, thawed

Heat oven to 375°. Drain salmon and remove bony section and skin. Flake into a bowl. Combine onion, cheese and parsley. Add to salmon. Mix lightly with a fork a put into a greased 9-inch pie pan. Place biscuits on top and bake for 20 minutes. While salmon is baking, prepare white sauce. Put bread, milk, mustard, salt and pepper into blender container, cover and process until smooth. Pour into saucepan and add peas (stirring constantly). Correct seasoning. Keep sauce hot until pie is baked. To serve, cut pie into wedges and spoon hot sauce over biscuits. 4 - 6 servings.

THURSDAY
Turkey medallions with caviar spaghetti
Mixed vegetable salad with ranch dressing
French rolls
Frozen lemon yogurt laced with citrus sauce

TURKEY MEDALLIONS AND CAVIAR SPAGHETTI

1 pound turkey steaks or sliced turkey breast	*2 tablespoons cooking oil*
1 egg, beaten	*1 pound spaghetti or perciatelli**
1 tablespoon milk	*1 ½ cups heavy cream*
1 ½ cups dry bread crumbs	*Juice of ½ lemon*
Salt to taste	*1 small jar caviar*
Pepper to taste	*Lemon wedges*
2 tablespoons butter or margarine	

With mallet, flatten turkey steaks or slices between sheets of waxed paper to expand to about double. Cut into bite sized medallions. Combine egg and milk. Set aside. Season bread crumbs lightly with salt and pepper. Dip medallions into egg and milk mixture, then into seasoned bread crumbs. Saute medallions, a few at a time, in butter and oil over medium heat and transfer to heated plate to keep warm. Cook spaghetti in 6 quarts boiling, salted (optional) water until al dente. Warm cream over very low heat and just before pasta is done, stir in lemon juice and caviar and heat through. Drain pasta and turn onto heated deep serving platter. Toss pasta with half of the cream sauce. Pour the remaining cream sauce over the spaghetti and top with turkey medallions. Serve with lemon wedges. 6 - 8 servings.

* Long tubular pasta; more hollow and slightly larger in diameter than spaghetti.

FRIDAY
Sweetheart Supper (Valentines Day)
Baked ham with cherry sauce
Buttered spinach with egg topping
Candied sweet potatoes
Fruit and oatmeal muffins
Ruby red salad with horseradish dressing
Chocolate tort with raspberry sauce

Plan Of Work

Day before:
1. Cook sweet potatoes, finish next day, 1 hour before meal.
2. Prepare chocolate torte and raspberry sauce.
3-4 hours before serving:
3. Cook ham.
4. Make cherry sauce. Set aside to reheat before serving on hot ham.
1 hour before serving:
5. Wash spinach and place in pan. Do not cook until last minute.
6. Finish preparing sweet potatoes and place in oven.
30 minutes before serving:
7. Mix muffins and cook.
15 minutes before serving:
8. Cook spinach.

BAKED HAM WITH CHERRY SAUCE

Purchase a smoked ham. Bake according to package directions or bake at 325° for 15 minutes per pound for a large ham, 20 to 25 minutes per pound for a small ham or 25 to 30 minutes for a half ham. During last 30 minutes, remove skin and excess cover fat. Continue to cook until thermometer placed in center of thickest section of meat (if one is used) registers 170° or until brown. Do not cover ham or use water in pan.

Cherry sauce for ham

1/4 cup sugar	*1 tablespoon lemon juice*
1 1/2 tablespoons corn starch	*1/2 teaspoon cinnamon*
1 (16 1/2 ounce) can tart red cherries, undrained	*1/8 teaspoon ground cloves*

Combine sugar and cornstarch in sauce pan. Stir in cherries with syrup or liquid. Cook, stirring constantly until mixture boils and thickens. Add lemon juice, cinnamon and cloves. Serve hot over ham. Yield 2 cups.

BUTTERED SPINACH

2 pounds fresh spinach or 2-3 (10 ounce)	*1/2 teaspoon salt (optional)*
* packages frozen spinach*	*2 - 4 tablespoons butter or margarine*
1/4 cup water	*1 hard cooked egg, grated*

Remove tough stems from fresh spinach. Wash thoroughly, leaving as much water as possible on the leaves. Place in a 2 quart sauce pan with a well fitted lid. Add water, and salt, if desired. Cover tightly and place on high heat. Cook until steam is expelled at the base of the lid and the lid swirls when turned. Turn heat to the lowest point, do not remove lid. Cook for about 10 minutes. Drain. Add butter and toss to mix. Place in a serving dish and top with grated egg. 8 servings.

CANDIED SWEET POTATOES

2 pounds sweet potatoes	*1 teaspoon pumpkin pie spice*
1/2 cup brown sugar, packed	*1/3 cup sherry*
1 cup orange juice	*2 tablespoons butter or margarine*

Cook potatoes in boiling salted water for 30 minutes or until almost tender. Drain. Peel and cut into serving pieces. Place potatoes in shallow 1 1/2-quart baking dish. In a sauce pan, combine remaining ingredients and bring to a boil. Boil 3 minutes. Pour over potatoes. Bake at 350° for 1 hour or less, basting often to glaze well. 8 servings.

FRUIT AND OATMEAL MUFFINS

1 egg	*1/2 cup sugar*
3/4 cup milk	*1 tablespoon baking powder*
1 apple, grated, not peeled	*1 teaspoon salt*
1/2 cup vegetable oil	*1 teaspoon nutmeg or pinch of ground cloves*
1 cup all purpose flour	*2 teaspoons cinnamon*
1 cup quick oats	

Beat egg. Add milk, apple and oil. Combine remaining ingredients. Pour egg mixture into dry ingredients. Stir only until dry ingredients are moistened. Fill 12 greased muffin pans ³/₄ full. Bake in 400° oven for 15 to 20 minutes. Yield 12 muffins.

RUBY RED SALAD

1 tablespoon plain gelatin	*3 cans stewed tomatoes with onions and peppers,*
2 tablespoons water	*undrained*
3 (3 ounce) boxes rasberry flavored gelatin	*Hot sauce to taste*
1 ¹/₂ cups boiling water	

Add 2 tablespoons water to gelatin to soften. Disolve plain gelatin and raspberry gelatin in boiling water. Add remaining ingredients. Mix and pour in appropriate mold. Chill until firm. 8 servings.

Dressing

1 cup sour cream	*1-2 tablespoons horseradish*

Combine sour cream and horseradish. Stir until well mixed.

CHOCOLATE TORTE

1 cup sugar	*16 (1 ounce) squares semi sweet chocolate*
2 cups (1 pound) softened butter or margarine	*8 eggs, slightly beaten*
2 tablespoons Amaretto	

In a 2-quart saucepan, combine sugar, butter, Amaretto and chocolate. Cook, stirring constantly, until chocolate is melted and mixture is smooth. Add a little of the chocolate mixture to eggs beating constantly, then add eggs to the chocolate mixture. Mix well. Pour into a greased 9-inch spring form pan. Bake in 350° oven for 45-50 minutes. Cover and chill 4 hours. Cover with topping or use one of the glazes. Garnish with raspberry sauce.

Topping

¹/₂ cup whipping cream	*¹/₂ cups chopped almonds*
2 tablespoons confectioners sugar	

Whip cream adding sugar slowly. Add almonds. Mix well. Spread on cake

Glaze 1

1 (6 ounce) package chocolate chips	*¹/₂ cup whipping cream*

Combine ingredients in a small sauce pan and cook over low heat stirring constantly until chocolate is melted. Spread on cake.

Glaze 2

1 (6 ounce) package semi-sweet chocolate	*Pinch of salt*
¹/₂ cup sour cream	

In a small sauce pan, melt chocolate over low heat, stir in sour cream and salt. Spread on cake.

Raspberry Sauce

2 (10 ounce) packages frozen raspberries
1 tablespoon corn starch

½ cup cold water
1 tablespoon lemon juice

Thaw raspberries. Strain. Discard seeds. In a small saucepan mix cornstarch and water until smooth, stir in puree. Stir constantly over medium heat until thickened and boiling: boil 1 minute. Remove from heat; stir in lemon juice. Serve warm. To serve with torte: spoon sauce on plate, top with torte that has been covered with whipped cream topping or glaze.

SATURDAY
Glazed pork loin *
Seasoned turnip greens
Oven steamed carrots
Marinated sliced tomatoes
Whole wheat bread
Apple sauce and tea cakes

GLAZED PORK LOIN

2 tablespoons cooking oil
1 large onion, finely chopped (1 cup)
2 cloves garlic, crushed
1 cup bottled chili sauce
½ cup lemon juice

⅓ cup molasses
3 tablespoons Dijon-style mustard
1 tablespoon Worcestershire sauce
¼ cup dark rum
1 (4 to 5) pound pork loin

Heat oil in medium sauce pan; add onion and garlic. Saute 5 minutes until onion is tender but not brown. Stir in chili sauce, lemon juice, molasses, mustard and Worcestershire sauce; bring to boiling; lower heat, cover and simmer 20 minutes. Stir in rum. Place meat on rack in large shallow baking dish. Do not add water or cover. Roast in a slow oven at 325° for 2 ½ hours. Brush meat with glaze. Continue roasting for 1 hour or until meat thermometer registers 170°, basting frequently with additional glaze. 6 - 8 servings.

February - Third Week

Here are some more tips to review to help you beat the supermarket game. The shopper who can relate the catch jingle or the song that advertises a famous name brand is most likely to purchase that item in the grocery store. Advertisers know that consumers need to be aware of the product offered for sale, what the product does and where it can be bought. Advertising provides a service for the consumer as well as for the merchant.

Shoppers should make some real cost comparisons between highly-advertised name brand goods and house brands or generic brands sold in the grocery store. Often 3 or 4 cents or more per item will make a sizable difference in the total grocery bill.

Be aware of the non-food items that will tempt you in the grocery store. Non-food items such as towels, clothing, housewares, beauty aids, motor oils, auto accessories and pet foods are but a few of the variety of high-profit items that are now being stocked by most modern supermarkets. Do some shopping and comparing of prices to determine whether buying at a discount store will provide a better bargain than buying these non-food items at your grocery store. Convenience will surely enter into your final decision, and sometimes is more important than saving a few cents.

Take time to look over the day-old bread reduced for quick sale. Try to keep the grocery list flexible enough to include unplanned bargains from the slightly-damaged rack. Don't rush as you shop. Take time to read the labels and give yourself enough time to think over the best buys and try to find the best bargains.

Fortunately, frozen foods come late in the grocery shopping trip so they won't defrost before checkout. The frozen section now includes a number of tempting convenience items that may or may not be on your grocery shopping list. Convenient foods are not always more costly than their home-made counterparts. Many frozen main dishes do cost more and contain smaller amounts of desirable high protein ingredients such as meat and cheeses than the meals you would prepare yourself. When you buy these, check them while they're cooking to determine if it contains more sauces than the main ingredient.

As convenience becomes more important in our busy lives, shoppers will find a wider range of ready-to-eat foods provided by the grocer. Delis, catering and small cafes within the grocery store will be tempters unless you can stick to the basic grocery list.

The shopper will find one last tempter when reaching the checkout counter - high profit items such as candy, gum and toys. This is the place where children may pressure parents for unplanned items that sometimes go into the basket while waiting in line at the checkout stand. This is another reason for shopping without children. Parents will buy rather than create a scene. If you feel that you are tempted, take the time for the pre-shopping steps before taking a grocery trip. Plan a grocery list, check supplies on hand, review recipes, read newspaper ads, collect coupons and select a store that offers the most bargains on your list.

In review, don't shop when you are hungry. Shop without children or spouses. For those especially subject to temptation, try to cut the number of shopping trips down to a minimum. Stick to the shopping list. You will find that you have purchased all of the necessary food for the week and you won't need to go to a more costly convenience store during the week.

Develop your own plan for shopping in the supermarket of your choice. Use your understanding of the psychology of food buying to feel more in control as you buy groceries each week.

It is helpful to know the sales techniques designed to influence our buying. They are usually the most efficient ways of doing business. No one is forcing us to buy, but we do need to be aware of the psychology used in the supermarket so that we can make more rational choices and win at the supermarket game.

SUNDAY
Baked turkey breast
Oven baked potatoes
Steamed and buttered cabbage wedge
Fresh tomatoes and onion in oil and vinegar dressing
Warm bagels with reduced calorie cream cheese
Coffee ice cream topped with burnt sugar sauce *

BURNT SUGAR SAUCE

1 ½ cups sugar
½ cup water

⅓ cup bourbon

In a dry heavy skillet, add sugar. Stir constantly with a fork over moderately high heat until melted and a deep caramel color occurs. Slowly pour in water a little at a time while continuing stirring until all sugar is dissolved. Add bourbon and simmer for 2 minutes. Cool and refrigerate. To reheat, set in a pan of barely simmering water and stir until sauce reaches desired consistency. Serve over ice cream.

MONDAY
Puttanesca pasta *
Tossed green salad, Italian dressing
Hot garlic bread
Peach crisp

PUTTANESCA PASTA

1 pound of spaghetti or rotini
2 tablespoons olive oil, divided
1 large onion, sliced
6-8 cloves garlic, crushed
3 (14 ½ ounce) cans diced tomatoes
⅓ cup pitted ripe olives
⅓ cup capers, rinsed

5-6 canned anchovies, drained, chopped
2 teaspoons dried oregano
1 tablespoon fresh rosemary or ½ tablespoon dried
Garlic salt to taste
Pepper to taste
¼ cup finely chopped Italian parsley

Cook pasta according to package directions, add 1 tablespoon oil to water to prevent sticking. Drain. Meanwhile, heat 1 tablespoon olive oil in large non-stick skillet. Add onions and garlic and saute. Stir in tomatoes, olives, capers, anchovies, oregano, rosemary, salt and pepper. Stir well and adjust seasoning. Cook 15 minutes over moderate heat. Toss ¾ of sauce with pasta. Pour pasta in large flat serving dish and pour remaining sauce over it. Sprinkle with parsley. 6-8 servings.

TUESDAY
Grilled hamburgers on sesame seed buns
Quick and easy corn casserole *
Hot kidney bean salad
Sliced tomatoes, onions, pickles, lettuce
Saucepan brownies *

QUICK AND EASY CORN CASSEROLE

1 (16 ounce) can cream style corn
1 (16 ounce) can whole kernel corn, undrained
1 cup sour cream

1 (8 ½ ounce) box cornbread or corn muffin mix
½ cup (1 stick) butter or margarine, melted

Combine all ingredients in large bowl. pour into lightly greased 9x13-inch dish and bake at 350° for 45 minutes or until center is firm. Refrigerate or freeze leftovers for another meal. Makes 10-12 servings.

SAUCEPAN BROWNIES

½ cup butter or margarine
2 squares (1 ounce each) unsweetened chocolate
1 cup sugar
2 eggs, beaten

³/₄ cup self-rising flour
1 teaspoon vanilla
³/₄ cup chopped nuts

Preheat oven to 350°. Grease bottom of a 9-inch square baking pan. Melt butter and chocolate in a saucepan over low heat. Remove from heat. Stir in remaining ingredients in order listed. Mix well. Spread in prepared pan. Bake 30 minutes. Cool in pan. Cut into 14 or 16 squares.

WEDNESDAY
Turkey tetrazzini *
Carrot and cabbage salad
Bread sticks
Fresh fruit cup with Kirsch *

TURKEY TETRAZZINI

10 ounces fresh mushrooms, sliced thin
  (about 4 cups)
¼ cup plus 1 tablespoons butter or margarine,
  divided
¼ cup flour
1 ³/₄ cups milk
2 cups chicken broth (canned or homemade)
¼ cup dry white wine

10 ounces spaghettini or linguini
3 cups coarsely chopped cooked turkey
1 cup frozen peas, thawed
²/₃ cup grated Parmesan cheese, divided
Salt to taste
Pepper to taste
¹/₃ cup fine bread crumbs

In a saucepan cook mushrooms in ¼ cup butter over moderate heat, stirring, until most of the liquid is evaporated. Stir in flour and cook over low heat for 3 minutes. Add milk, broth and wine, stirring. Bring to a boil, continue stirring and simmer for 5 minutes. Cook spaghettini "al dente" and drain well. Combine spaghettini, mushroom sauce, turkey, peas, salt and pepper to taste and stir in 1/3 cup Parmesan cheese. Transfer to 3-quart casserole. Combine ⅓ cup Parmesan cheese with bread crumbs and sprinkle over top. Dot with remaining butter. Bake at 375° for 30 to 40 minutes. 4 servings.

FRESH FRUIT CUP WITH KIRSCH

2 oranges
1 grapefruit
¼ pound seedless grapes
1 apple, unpeeled

2 tablespoons lemon juice
¼ cup sugar
2 tablespoons Kirsch or orange juice
4 cherries or strawberries

Peel orange and grapefruit and remove sections (**SEE PAGE 7**). Cut orange sections in half and grapefruit sections in quarters. Cut grapes in half if large. Core apples and cut into ½-inch cubes and combine with lemon juice. Combine all fruits and blend in sugar. Add Kirsch or orange juice. Keep chilled. Serve in compote topped with cherry or strawberry. 4 servings

THURSDAY
Vegetable Plate
Lima beans in sour cream *
Buttered broccoli
Baked sweet potato
Rye bread and butter
Apple cobbler

LIMA BEANS IN SOUR CREAM

1 (10 ounce) package frozen Lima beans
1/2 cup finely chopped onion
2 tablespoons butter or margarine
1 (2 ounce) jar chopped pimiento

1/2 cup sour cream
Salt to taste
Cayenne pepper to taste

Cook Lima beans according to package directions. Drain. Saute onions in butter until tender, not brown. Combine Limas, onions, pimiento, sour cream, salt and cayenne. 4 servings.

FRIDAY
Pork chops supreme
Quick glazed carrots
Green rice pilaf
Ever green salad with yogurt cumin dressin
Egg bread
Rum cream cake *

RUM CREAM CAKE

4 eggs
2/3 cup sugar
1/2 teaspoon salt
2/3 cup sifted flour
1/2 cup cornstarch

1/2 cup dark rum
1 recipe custard filling (follows)
1 cup heavy cream, whipped
2 tablespoons chopped nuts

Grease two 9-inch diameter x 1 ½-inch deep layer cake pans. Beat eggs in large mixing bowl on medium speed of electric mixer until fluffy. Gradually add sugar and salt, beating about 12 minutes or until mixture is doubled in bulk and mounds slightly when dropped from a spoon. Sift flour and corn starch over egg mixture. Fold in gently until well mixed. Pour into prepared pans. Bake in 350° oven about 25 minutes or until cake springs back when touched. Cool 10 minutes. Remove from pans; cool completely on wire rack. Split each layer in half. Sprinkle cake layers with rum. Put bottom layer on serving plate. Spread with ⅓ of the custard filling. Repeat with remaining cake and custard filling, ending with cake layer. Frost with whipped cream. Garnish with nuts.

Custard Filling

1/2 cup sugar
1/4 cup cornstarch
1/8 teaspoon salt

2 cups milk
3 egg yolks, slightly beaten
1 1/2 teaspoons vanilla

Combine sugar, cornstarch and salt in top of a double boiler. Gradually stir in milk. Cook over boiling water, stirring constantly, until mixture thickens enough to mound when dropped from a spoon. Cover and cook 10 minutes, stirring occasionally. Stir about ½ cup hot mixture into egg yolks, then stir all into hot mixture. Cook 2 minutes, stirring constantly. Remove from boiling water and stir in vanilla. Chill. 10-12 servings.

SATURDAY
Romantic Dinner for Two
Cream cheese with Jezebel sauce and crackers
Fancy fish fillets
French green beans with water chestnuts and almonds
Buttered Franconia potatoes
Spinach salad for two
Cream biscuits
Fresh strawberries with Kirsch

Plan Of Work
Early in the day:
1. Prepare Jezebel sauce.
2. Wash, peel and prepare potatoes.
3. Wash and hull strawberries. Dry thoroughly between paper towels. Place in zip lock bag and store in refrigerator.
1 ½ hours before serving:
4. Prepare biscuits and place in refrigerator until time to cook.
1 hour before serving:
5. Prepare fish. Put in oven 20 minutes before serving.
6. Complete preparation of potatoes and put in oven.
7. Prepare green beans. Cook at last minute so they will be hot. Be sure to keep items hot until served.

CREAM CHEESE WITH JEZEBEL SAUCE

8 ounce jar pineapple preserves
8 ounce jar apple jelly
¼ cup horseradish
¼ cup dry mustard

1 teaspoon black pepper
1 (3 ounce) package reduced calorie cream cheese
Crackers

In a small saucepan, thoroughly mix first 5 ingredients. Heat slowly until thoroughly mixed. Cool. Spread a small amount of cream cheese on a cracker. Top with sauce mixture. Or place a block of cream cheese on a tray with Jezebel sauce in a small bowl on the same tray. Put crackers in a separate container. Allow guests to serve themselves.

FANCY FISH FILLETS

½ pound fillet of sole (dry well with paper towels)
1 tablespoon butter or margarine
3 large mushrooms, sliced or 4-ounce can sliced
  mushrooms, drained

1 cup white seedless grapes
¼ cup sour cream
¼ cup mayonnaise
1 teaspoon lemon juice

Place fillets in individual greased au gratin dishes or small baking dishes. Melt butter in small pan over low heat. Saute mushrooms 3-5 minutes. Add grapes, stir gently. Add remaining ingredients, stirring until blended. Spoon sauce over fillets. Cover with foil and bake at 325° for 20 minutes. (2 servings)

FRENCH GREEN BEANS WITH WATER CHESTNUTS & ALMONDS

1 (10 ounce) package frozen green beans,
* French style*
1 can sliced water chestnuts, drained

2 tablespoons butter or margarine (optional)
Coarse ground black pepper
¼ cup toasted, slivered almonds

Cook beans according to package directions. Add water chestnuts and heat thoroughly. Season to taste with butter and black pepper. Top with almonds.
To toast almonds: Place slivered almonds in a shallow pan. Heat in oven only until lightly browned (5 - 10 minutes). Watch carefully. (2 servings)

FRANCONIA POTATOES

2 medium sized baking potatoes
2 tablespoons vegetable oil

salt and pepper to taste

Wash and peel potatoes. Place in small saucepan. Cover with water. Bring water to a boil and boil for 10 minutes. Remove from water and rub with vegetable oil. Sprinkle with salt and pepper. Bake in a 400° oven until brown, about 15- 20 minutes. 2 servings.

SPINACH SALAD FOR TWO

1 pound raw spinach, stem ends removed

1 hard cooked egg, sieved or grated

Dressing

⅓ cup red wine vinegar
1 clove garlic, crushed
1 teaspoon salt

¼ teaspoon hot pepper sauce
Pinch dry mustard
1 cup olive oil

Combine all dressing ingredients and shake well. Wash spinach, dry between paper towels and coarsely chop. Coat (don't drown) the spinach leaves with dressing; toss and garnish with the egg. Keep extra dressing in the refrigerator for any tossed green salad. Just be sure to take it out in time for the oil to come to room temperature and then shake it well.

WHIPPED CREAM BISCUITS

1 (8 ounce) carton whipping cream
2 cups self -rising flour

1 teaspoon sugar

Combine all ingredients. Mix just until dough follows fork around bowl. Turn out onto a lightly floured surface; knead gently for 30 seconds. Roll or pat to ½ inch thick and cut with biscuit cutter. Bake on ungreased cookie sheet in 450° oven for 12-15 minutes. 16 medium sized biscuits. Freezes well.

FRESH STRAWBERRIES WITH KIRSCH

1 pint strawberries, washed and hulled   Kirsch
Powdered sugar

Sprinkle strawberries with powdered sugar and drizzle with Kirsch a few hours before dinner.

February - Fourth Week

The food shopping habits of the American people are changing. The American male is becoming more involved in shopping, meal planning and food preparation. Surveys show that approximately 42 percent of the men do the regular family food shopping and 47 percent do the regular family cooking, while 75 percent cook part time.

When men do the shopping, they purchase foods that are easy to prepare, versatile and recognizable. Men usually do not like mixtures in which the food items cannot be identified. When women shop they tend to visit each aisle, while men do not. Women tend to read food labels more often, are more cost-conscious, use coupons more, stick more closely to prepared shopping lists, are more daring in trying new products and appear to pay more attention to nutrition and health.

It is interesting to watch a man buy a piece of beef. He buys for flavor, so he selects one that is well marbled (that is, with white streaks of fat embedded within the muscle tissue). A woman selects one with practically no cover fat and no marbling. She buys for economy (who wants to pay for fat?) and for fewer calories.

Although grocery shopping patterns vary widely between the husband and wife in the upper income ranges of two-wage-earner families, they tend to complement each other and are apt to shop together at least one a month. On joint trips, couples generally buy more than on individual trips, but the differences between them in individual shopping trips balance out on the joint ventures, except that the nutrition concerns of the men don't change. Half of these families eat dinner out at least once a week. The husbands prepare dinner in 32 percent of the families, and 10 percent prepare more than three dinners per week. More than one-third of the men shop alone for the ingredients that will go into the meals they prepare.

According to surveys, meal preparation activities — except for "special" meals — were considered chores by 62 percent of the wives and 75 percent of the husbands. Yet, one-third of the couples enjoyed one "special" meal per week at home, and 25 percent had two or three. Because of changing roles of men and women, all members of the family should learn as much as possible concerning planning, purchasing, preparing and serving good quality, nourishing meals to the family.

Visit the stores in your shopping area. Walk around to determine the layout. Check prices of frequently-used items. Take notes on your observations of the store operations. Then sit down and rate the stores. Try your first and second choices to see how they do under actual shopping conditions before you decide. Here are some of the things to observe as you look around the unfamiliar markets. They are not listed in order of importance — only you can know if a particular practice is of importance to you.

General Appearance: Is the store cluttered with advertising posters, banners and other gimmicks? Is there a directory to help you find things? Are the front and aisle displays filled with junk foods and impulse items?

Pricing: Are most items singly priced or are they, for example, 3 for 67 cents? Do the shelf tags carry unit prices (price per pint, pound or count)? Are the items individually price marked even if the cash registers use a scanning device for ringing up the sale?

Frozen foods: Are the foods solidly frozen? Is the temperature of the box near zero degrees? Are frozen foods piled near the front of the freezer where temperatures may not be low enough for long storage? Are stacks of products left in the aisle thawing while the clerk is checking out customers or is out to lunch?

Dairy, Meat and Egg Boxes: Are the eggs refrigerated? Is the temperature in these boxes 42° or lower? Are they clean? Do the meat labels give the species, primal cut and retail name (like "Beef Chuck Steak")?

Produce: Is it wilted, poorly-trimmed, dirty or untidily thrown into the case? Is there adequate variety for your needs? Are there too many impulse items such as salad dressings, croutons, salad seasonings, etc.?

Grocery: Are there too many "out of stock" signs on the shelves? Are marked down items in such bad condition (dented on seams, swollen or badly rusted) that they should not be sold?

Check stand area: Is the service good? Are checkers friendly and efficient? Are the checkstands cluttered with impulse items? Do you leave with a feeling that you would like to return because the store really cares about pleasing you?

SUNDAY
Family Supper
Pot roast with vegetable medley
Tossed salad with creamy herb dressing
Freezer white bread
Grape streusel

Plan Of Work
7 hours before dinner is served:
1. Remove bread dough from freezer. When thawed, shape into loaves, place in loaf pans and let it rise.
2. Make creamy herb dressing.
3. Peel and cut vegetables.
4. Prepare topping for streusel
5. Set the table (if no one is coming for lunch.)
2 hours before dinner:
6. Prepare the pot roast and vegetables and start cooking.
7. Finish preparation of the streusel and place in oven 1 hour before dinner is served.
8. Put bread in oven 35 minutes before dinner is served. Reduce heat in oven to 350°.

POT ROAST WITH VEGETABLE MEDLEY

1 (2-3 pound) beef rump or chuck roast	*1 bay leaf*
2 tablespoons flour	*1 rib celery, cut in 8 pieces*
¼ teaspoon salt	*2 cups beef bouillon*
½ teaspoon thyme	*½ cup red wine or beef bouillon*
Dash pepper	*1 teaspoon Worcestershire sauce*
½ teaspoon dry mustard	*6 large carrots, peeled, cut into chunks*
2 tablespoons butter or margarine	*6 potatoes, peeled, cut into large cubes*
2 cloves garlic, crushed	*6 large onions, peeled, quartered*

Rub meat with flour, salt, thyme, pepper and dry mustard. Melt butter in Dutch oven; add meat, brown on both sides. Reduce heat; add garlic, bay leaf, celery, bouillon, wine and Worcestershire sauce. Cover; simmer ½ hour turning meat every 15 minutes. Add carrots, potatoes and onions; continue cooking for 45 minutes or until tender. 8 servings.

CREAMY HERB DRESSING

½ cup milk
½ cup sour cream
1 tablespoon lemon juice
1 teaspoon dried parsley flakes

½ teaspoon dried oregano
½ teaspoon dried basil
¼ teaspoon salt
pepper to taste

Combine in jar with well-fitted lid. Shake vigorously before serving. Average serving is 1 tablespoon dressing for 1 cup greens. Refrigerate left overs.

FREEZER WHITE BREAD

12 ½ to 13 ½ cups unsifted flour
½ cup sugar
2 tablespoons salt
²/3 cup instant nonfat dry milk solids

4 packages active dry yeast
¼ cup (½ stick) softened butter or margarine
4 cups very warm tap water

In a large bowl, thoroughly mix 4 cups flour, sugar, salt, dry milk solids and undissolved active dry yeast. Add butter. Gradually add tap water to dry ingredients and beat 2 minutes at medium speed of electric mixer, scraping bowl occasionally. Stir in enough additional flour to make a soft dough. Turn out onto lightly floured board; knead until smooth and elastic, about 15 minutes. Cover with a towel. Let rest for 15 minutes.
 Divide dough into 4 equal pieces. Form each piece into a smooth round ball. Flatten each ball into a mound 6 inches in diameter. Place on greased baking sheets. Cover with plastic wrap. Freeze until firm. Transfer to plastic bags. Freeze up to four weeks. Remove from freezer; place on ungreased baking sheets. Cover; let stand at room temperature until fully thawed, about 4 hours. Roll each ball to 12x18 inches. Shape into loaves. Place in greased 8 ½ x 4 ½ x 2 ½-inch loaf pans. Let rise in warm place, free from draft, until doubled in bulk, about 1 ½ hours. Bake at 350° about 35 minutes or until done. Remove from pans and cool on wire racks.

GRAPE STREUSEL
Filling

2 tablespoons cornstarch
½ cup sugar
1 teaspoon cinnamon
 Dash salt

4 cups sliced, unpeeled apples
3 tablespoons lemon juice
1 ½ pounds grapes (red, green and/or blue-black)
 halved and seeded, if necessary (about 4 cups)-
 Do not halve green seedless grapes

Streusel topping

½ cup butter or margarine
²/3 cup sugar
1 cup flour

1 teaspoon cinnamon
½ cup chopped nuts

In a large bowl, blend cornstarch with ½ cup sugar, cinnamon and salt. Add grapes, apples and lime juice. Toss to coat. Turn into greased 1 ½-quart baking dish. In a small bowl, blend butter, ⅔ cup sugar, flour and cinnamon until it resembles coarse cornmeal. Add nuts. Top filling with streusel topping. Bake in 375° oven for 40-50 minutes, or until streusel is golden and fruit is tender. Serve warm. 6-8 servings.

MONDAY
Sausage quiche *
Buttered peas
Marinated beet and onion salad
Peach yogurt with peach topping

SAUSAGE QUICHE

½ pound lean bulk hot sausage	*2 eggs, beaten*
1 small onion, finely chopped	*⅔ cup evaporated milk*
1 cup shredded sharp Cheddar cheese	*2 teaspoons parsley flakes*
2 tablespoons flour	
1 unbaked pie crust (8 or 9 inch, commercial	
or home made)	

Fully cook sausage and drain well. Combine sausage, onions, cheese and flour. Spread on pie crust. Beat together eggs milk and parsley flakes. Slowly pour over sausage mixture. Bake on baking sheet 35-40 minutes at 375° or until filling is set. 4 servings.

TUESDAY
Hawaiian pork *
Chow mein noodles
Buttered green beans
Walking fruit salad *
Chocolate chip cookies

HAWAIIAN PORK

1 pound pork shoulder	*2 tablespoons soy sauce*
1 tablespoon cooking oil	*1 tablespoon vinegar*
1 (8 ounce) can pineapple chunks	*1 tablespoon corn starch*
1 green pepper, cut into strips	*Chow mein noodles*
½ cup apricot or peach preserves	

Remove as much visible fat as desired from the meat. Cut meat into strips. In a non-stick skillet, brown meat in oil; drain. Drain pineapple, reserving liquid. Add water to reserved liquid to measure 1 cup; pour over meat. Cover; simmer 20 minutes, stirring occasionally. Add green pepper and pineapple. Cover; continue simmering 10 minutes. Stir in combined preserves, soy sauce, vinegar and cornstarch. Cook, stirring occasionally, until thickened. Serve over noodles. 4 servings.

WALKING FRUIT SALAD

³/₄ pound seedless grapes, pulled from stems
1 red apple, cored and cubed
¹/₂ cup raisins

¹/₄ cup toasted slivered almonds
1 head iceberg lettuce, cored, rinsed, drained
and chilled

In bowl, mix grapes, apple, raisins and almonds. Carefully remove lettuce leaves from head, one at a time. Put ½ cup of fruit-nut mixture in each lettuce cup. (Can be served as a snack; omit lettuce.) 6-8 salads. Note: A walking salad has no dressing. Therefore, one can eliminate the lettuce and carry the salad anywhere.

WEDNESDAY
Baked polenta casserole *
Buttered zucchini and tomatoes
Tossed green salad with Greek olives and Italian dressing
Hot garlic bread
Frozen raspberry yogurt with raspberry sauce

BAKED POLENTA CASSEROLE

1 pound bulk sausage
1 cup chopped onion
1 (16 ounce) can tomatoes
1 (8 ounce) can tomato sauce
1 (4 ounce) can sliced mushrooms, drained
1 teaspoon salt
¹/₂ teaspoon pepper
¹/₂ teaspoon oregano
¹/₄ teaspoon garlic powder
³/₄ cup flour

³/₄ cup corn meal
³/₄ cup Parmesan cheese
1 tablespoon sugar
1 tablespoon baking powder
³/₄ teaspoon salt
³/₄ cup milk
1 egg, beaten
3 tablespoons cooking oil
1 ¹/₂ cups shredded sharp Cheddar cheese

Brown sausage and onion. Stir in undrained tomatoes, tomato sauce, mushrooms, salt, pepper, oregano and garlic powder. Simmer, covered, for 5 minutes. Sift together flour, corn meal, Parmesan cheese, sugar, baking powder and ³/₄ teaspoon salt. Make a well in dry ingredients and add milk, egg and oil; stir until combined. Spread in bottom of 13x9x2-inch baking dish. Pour meat mixture over batter. Bake at 400° for 30 minutes. Top with Cheddar cheese and bake 5 minutes longer. (6 servings)

THURSDAY
Vegetable soup
Broiled cheese and onion sandwich *
Stacked spinach salad
Broiled and sweetened grapefruit halves

BROILED CHEESE AND ONION SANDWICHES

2 tablespoons butter
1/4 teaspoon salt
2 medium onions, thinly sliced
6 slices white bread, toasted
Butter, softened

6 tablespoons chili sauce
6 thick slices Cheddar cheese (about 12 ounces)
3 slices bacon, cooked crisp
6 thinly sliced green pepper rings

In a skillet, melt butter, add salt, onions and saute. Butter toast; place on broiler pan. Spread each slice of toast with 1 tablespoon chili sauce. Divide onions over toast. Top each with a slice of cheese. Broil until cheese melts. Garnish each with crumbled bacon and green pepper ring. 6 open faced sandwiches.

FRIDAY
Mayflower fish fillet *
Rice pilaf
Buttered corn on the cob
Corn muffins
Bananas Mexicana

MAYFLOWER FISH FILLET

2 pounds fish fillets, fresh or frozen (any kind)
1/4 cup butter or margarine, melted
2 tablespoons lemon juice
1 teaspoon grated onion
1 teaspoon salt

1/8 teaspoon liquid hot pepper sauce
Dash pepper
Chopped parsley
1 (one-pound) can whole cranberry sauce

Thaw frozen fillets. Cut into serving-sized portions and place in a well greased baking dish, 12x7 1/2x2 inches. Combine butter, lemon juice, onion and seasonings; pour over fish. Bake in a moderate oven, 350°, for 25 to 30 minutes or until fish flakes easily when tested with a fork. Sprinkle with parsley and serve with cranberry sauce. 6 servings.

SATURDAY
Marinated chicken Veronique *
Seasoned buttered asparagus
Steamed rice
Orange and avocado salad
Hot rolls
Custard pie

MARINATED CHICKEN VERONIQUE

4 half chicken breasts, skinned and boned
Marinade (recipe follows)
3/4 pound fresh grapes (blue-black, red or green),
*   pulled from stems*
1 tablespoon butter

1 tablespoon cooking oil
1/4 cup water
1 1/4 cups heavy or light cream
Parsley sprigs
Steamed rice

Cut each chicken breast diagonally into 4 or 5 strips. Put in bowl with marinade. Let stand 5 minutes. Meanwhile, halve grapes; seed if necessary. Set aside. Heat butter and oil in skillet. Remove chicken pieces from marinade (reserve marinade) and saute quickly, 2 minutes per side. Remove chicken from pan and keep warm. Deglaze pan with water.* Stir cream into remaining marinade in bowl; then pour mixture into pan. Cook and stir over medium heat to thicken slightly. Put chicken and grapes into sauce. Heat through. Adjust seasonings. Pour into heated bowl. Garnish with parsley sprigs. Serve with steamed rice. 4 servings.

Note: To deglaze, remove excess fat, add a little broth, wine or water, and stir with sediment left in pan. Heat and stir so that a gravy or sauce is formed.

Marinade

2 tablespoons cornstarch
3 tablespoons dry sherry
1 tablespoon soy sauce

½ teaspoon powdered ginger, or ½ teaspoon
grated ginger root
1 small clove garlic, crushed

Combine all ingredients.

March

March - First Week

NOW THAT THE FOOD IS BOUGHT and brought home, what happens to it? It must be stored properly. The proper storage of food immediately after it has been brought home is an important factor in the prevention of loss or waste from deterioration. When food is left in the car or on the kitchen table it is exposed to extremes in temperature which will jeopardize its safekeeping and quality. Food storage areas should always be kept clean and orderly.

All food while being stored, prepared and served should be protected against contamination. All perishable food must be stored at a temperature that will protect it against spoilage. The length of time that foods may be held satisfactorily and without appreciable deterioration depends on the product and its quality when stored as well as the condition of the storage areas.

After food has been purchased, head home as soon as possible. Don't do errands while the food is in the warm car, because bacteria and molds love those cozy temperatures and will start to multiply at a rapid rate. If you must do errands, do them before you shop or keep an ice chest in the car for perishables.

As soon as you return home, put the cold items into the refrigerator or freezer right away. Meat for the freezer is wrapped in freezer paper, labeled and dated, so you will have a record of what it is and how old it is. Store vegetables in plastic bags in a crisper. Do not wash until ready to use.

Do not put canned goods, boxes or bags of food under the sink. This is a favorite spot for insects and rodents. Also there are pipes that might leak causing rusty cans and deterioration of boxes and bags.

Cupboards for storing food should be far from the stove or other sources of heat. Heat dries up mixes, flour and bread and encourages insect infestation. Use these cupboards near the stove for dishes or cooking utensils, and use the coolest spots for foods. Following these rules might require rearranging the kitchen.

Children often have accidents because household items such as cleaning fluids, furniture polish and window cleaners are stored next to salad dressings, ketchup, oils and vinegar. Children cannot distinguish the difference.

If all meal planners would mark the date of purchase on cans and jars at the time they are first put on the shelf, it would be a reminder to use the product before it reaches one year of age.

If you are suspicious of a food's safety because of some physical appearance such as badly rusted or swollen cans or signs of leakage, DO NOT TASTE IT. Throw it away. The life you save may be your own. Tasting does not always tell you if a food is safe. Any doubts, throw it out!

SUNDAY
Oven baked chicken breasts
Buttered English peas
Grated carrot salad *
Cornbread casserole
Pineapple upside down cake

GRATED CARROT SALAD

4 cups coarsely grated carrots	2 tablespoons sugar
1 cup chopped celery	1 teaspoon lemon juice
1/2 cup dark raisins	1/4 teaspoon celery seed
1/3 cup mayonnaise	1/4 teaspoon salt
1/4 cup vegetable oil	1/4 teaspoon dry mustard
Small onion, cut into chunks	

Toss carrots, celery and raisins in a large bowl. Puree remaining ingredients in a blender or food processor to make about 1 cup dressin g. Toss half the dressing with the vegetables. Refrigerate remaining dressing and use another time. It keeps at least a week. 4 cups salad.

MONDAY
Meat balls in fresh tomato sauce *
Garliced spaghetti squares
Garden salad with blue cheese dressing
Italian bread sticks
Mixed fruit cup in rosé wine

MEATBALLS IN FRESH TOMATO SAUCE

1 1/2 pounds ground beef	1 garlic clove, crushed
1/2 cup dried bread crumbs	2 tablespoons red wine vinegar
2 tablespoons grated onion	1 tablespoon sugar
1 egg white	1/2 teaspoon celery seeds
1/4 teaspoon pepper	1/2 teaspoon paprika
1/4 cup water	1/4 teaspoon thyme
2 tablespoons oil	1/2 teaspoon oregano
4 large tomatoes (about 1 1/2 pounds) each	1/2 teaspoon fennel seed
cut into wedges	2 teaspoons cornstarch
1 medium onion, sliced	1 tablespoon water

In a large bowl, combine beef, bread crumbs, onion, egg white, pepper and water. Shape mixture into 1-inch meatballs. Bake in 325° oven for 20 minutes. Place meatballs in skillet; add tomatoes, onion, garlic, vinegar, sugar, celery seeds, paprika, thyme, oregano and fennel seed. Heat to boiling. Reduce heat to low; cover and simmer 15 minutes, stirring occasionally. With slotted spoon, remove meatballs and vegetables to large platter. In a cup, combine cornstarch and 1 tablespoon water. Over low heat, gradually stir cornstarch mixture into simmering liquid in skillet and cook, stirring constantly, until slightly thickened and smooth. Pour over meatballs and vegetables. 6 servings.

TUESDAY
Baked potato soup *
Ham sandwiches on whole wheat bread
Pineapple and cottage cheese salad
Apple pie

BAKED POTATO SOUP
(use leftover baked potatoes)

1 quart water	*1 quart milk*
6 chicken bouillon cubes	*4 medium-sized prebaked potatoes, peeled & cubed*
2 tablespoons butter or margarine	*2 teaspoons chopped parsley (optional)*
2 ribs celery, chopped	*4 slices toasted bread, each cut into four triangles*
2 carrots, peeled and shredded	*4 slices cheese*

Bring water to a boil in saucepan; dissolve bouillon cubes in water. In frying pan, over medium heat, melt butter. Stir in celery and carrots; cook until tender; stir into broth. Add milk, potatoes and parsley to broth. Simmer 30 minutes, stirring occasionally. Just before serving, top toast slices with cheese; broil until cheese melts. Float cheese triangles on bowls of steaming soup. 8 servings.

WEDNESDAY
Broccoli cassserole
Turnip greens with ham cubes
Macaroni salad
Corn sticks
Apple upside down cake *

APPLE UPSIDE DOWN CAKE

¹/₄ cup (¹/₂ stick) butter or margarine	*¹/₄ teaspoon nutmeg*
¹/₂ cup firmly packed brown sugar	*1 large spice cake mix*
2 large red cooking apples, sliced (not peeled)	*¹/₄ cup apricot or peach preserves*
2 teaspoons lemon juice	*1 tablespoon orange juice or liqueur*
¹/₂ teaspoon cinnamon	

Melt butter in saucepan. Add sugar, apple slices, lemon juice, cinnamon and nutmeg. Cook for 3 to 5 minutes or until apples are slightly tender. Pour into a greased 9x9x1 ¹/₂-inch cake pan. Prepare cake mix according to package directions; pour over apple mixture and bake. Allow cake to cool for 5 minutes after baking and then invert onto serving plate. Combine preserves and orange juice or liqueur and heat until hot and well mixed. Pour over top of inverted cake. Yield: 1 9-inch cake.

THURSDAY
Early Spring Barbecue (served indoors)
Sliced beef barbecue
Scalloped corn
Mixed bean casserole
Old fashioned cauliflower slaw
Large sesame seed buns
Butterscotch shortbread cookies
Homemade peach buttermilk ice cream

Plan of Work

Day before:

1. Prepare shortbread cookies.

9:00 a.m.:

2. Prepare the beef for barbecuing.
3. At 10:00 o'clock, start cooking meat.
4. After meat is started, prepare beans, place in baking dish already to bake.

Two hours before dinner is served:

5. Put the beans in oven to cook.
6. Prepare the slaw and refrigerate until ready to serve.
7. Ice cream can be prepared after the slaw. Be sure the freezer keeps it frozen until served.
8. Prepare corn casserole. Do not cook until one hour before serving.

SLICED BEEF BARBECUE

8 pounds boneless rolled chuck roast	*2 bay leaves*
2 (14 ounce) bottles catsup	*4 medium onions, chopped*
1 teaspoon chili powder	*1 large green pepper, chopped*
10 whole cloves	*2 tablespoons Worcestershire sauce*
1 teaspoon dry mustard	*1 cup cider vinegar*
1 teaspoon cinnamon	*1 teaspoon ginger*
1 teaspoon allspice	*1 teaspoon black pepper*
2 cloves garlic, crushed	*2 teaspoons salt*

Place meat in roaster. Mix remaining ingredients and pour over the meat. Cook in slow oven, 250°, for 6 hours. Remove meat, slice and cover with sauce. Makes great sandwich on large buns. Serves 25 for sandwiches; serves 12 for dinner.

SCALLOPED CORN

2 (16 ounce) cans whole kernel corn	*2 cups fresh bread crumbs*
2 (16 ounce) cans cream style corn	*2 tablespoons butter or margarine, melted*
2 medium-sized onions, chopped	*1 1/2 cups milk*
1/2 cup chopped green pepper	*Salt and pepper to taste*

Combine all above ingredients in a large mixing bowl. Correct seasoning. Pour into a 2-quart baking dish. Bake, uncovered, in 350° oven for 50 minutes. 8-10 servings.

MIXED BEAN CASSEROLE

1 (16 oz) can baked beans (without tomato sauce)	*1/4 cup water*
1 (16 ounce) can red kidney beans, drained	*1/2 cup honey*
1 (16 ounce) can green lima beans, drained	*1-1/2 teaspoon dry mustard*
1 medium onion, chopped	*1 teaspoon salt*
4 slices bacon, chopped	*1/2 teaspoon pepper*
1/4 cup wine vinegar	*1/2 cup chili sauce or catsup*

In large mixing bowl, combine all ingredients. Pour into a greased 9x13 baking pan. Bake at 300° for 2 hours, stirring after the first hour to mix well. Cook longer if too soupy. 8 servings.

OLD FASHIONED CAULIFLOWER SLAW

1 cup mayonnaise	*1 cup thinly-sliced radish*
1 cup sour cream	*1/4 cup sliced green onion*
1 package cheese-garlic dressing mix	*1/2 cup snipped watercress*
1 tablespoon plus 1 teaspoon caraway seed	*2 tomatoes, cut into wedges*
1 large head cauliflower	

Combine mayonnaise, sour cream, dressing mix and caraway seeds. Chill while preparing remaining ingredients. Cut cauliflower in half and discard core. Cut into thin slices and combine with radishes, onions and watercress. Add mayonnaise mixture and toss. Chill 1-2 hours. Garnish with tomato wedges. Serves 10-12.

BUTTERSCOTCH SHORTBREAD COOKIES

1 cup butter or margarine	*2 1/4 cups all-purpose flour*
1/2 cup brown sugar, firmly packed	*1 teaspoon salt*
1/4 cup granulated sugar	

Cream butter and sugar. Stir in flour and salt. Mix well (use hands). Roll or pat on floured surface, 1/2 inch thick. Cut in any desired shape. Place on ungreased cookie sheet. Bake in 300° oven 25-30 minutes. Store in airtight container. Yield: 7 dozen.

PEACH BUTTERMILK ICE CREAM

1 tablespoon (1 envelope) unflavored gelatin	*4 cups whipping cream*
1 cup sugar	*1 tablespoon vanilla extract*
2 cups buttermilk	*2 cups mashed fresh peaches*
1 egg, beaten	*1/4 cup sugar*
1/4 teaspoon salt	

In a 1-quart saucepan, combine gelatin, sugar and buttermilk. Dissolve sugar and gelatin over low heat, stir occasionally. Gradually add hot mixture to egg, stirring constantly. Stir in salt , cream and vanilla. Combine mashed peaches with sugar; add to mixture. Chill; churn-freeze. Yield: approximately 3 quarts.

FRIDAY
Poached fish in cream sauce
Steamed rice in chicken broth
Buttered fresh green beans
Ceasar Salad
Pineapple bran muffins *

PINEAPPLE BRAN MUFFINS

1 cup all purpose flour	*1 cup wheat bran cereal*
1 tablespoon baking powder	*1/3 cup skim milk*
1/2 teaspoon salt	*1/4 cup vegetable oil*
3 tablespoons firmly packed brown sugar	*1 (8 ounce) can crushed pineapple in juice,*
1 egg, slightly beaten	*not drained*

Combine flour, baking powder, salt and brown sugar. Set aside. Combine egg, cereal, milk and oil. Stir to combine. Let stand about 2 minutes or until cereal is softened. Stir in pineapple including juice. Add flour mixture, stirring only until combined. Pour into 12 greased 2 ½-inch muffin-pan cups. Bake in 400° oven about 25 minutes or until muffins are golden brown. Serve warm. 12 muffins.

SATURDAY
Ham and chicken Eugenie *
Mashed potatoes
Steamed, buttered broccoli
Grapefruit and apple salad with poppy seed dressing
Buttered hot French bread
Baked custard

HAM AND CHICKEN EUGENIE

2 center slices ready to eat ham (¼ inch thick)	*2 ribs celery, finely chopped*
¼ cup (½ stick) butter or margarine	*1 teaspoon minced onion*
*3 chicken breasts, split in half **	*½ cup half & half or milk*
Salt	*1 (10 ¾-ounce) can cream of chicken soup*
Pepper	

Cut ham in 6 serving portions. Saute in 1 tablespoon of the butter until lightly brown on both sides. Place each portion in a shallow baking pan. In the same skillet, lightly saute the chicken breasts in remaining butter. Place one on each ham portion. Sprinkle very lightly with salt and pepper. Combine celery, onion, cream and soup. Pour ½ cup over each portion of ham and chicken. Cover tightly. Bake in 350° oven for one hour. 6 servings. * May remove skin and bone, if desired.

March - Second Week

SOME OF THE MOST PERISHABLE of all foods are the dairy products. If a few rules are followed in their handling, then all is well.
• **Concentrated milk:** This is milk from which approximately ⅔ of the water has been removed by evaporation. To increase the keeping quality of fresh concentrated milk, it may be quickly frozen and held frozen until ready to use. For better quality it should be used soon after defrosting. It should be kept frozen or refrigerated at all times. It can be refrigerated for as long as two weeks and frozen for as long as six weeks and retain its sweetness and flavor. This type of milk is not available in all markets.
• **Cottage cheese and other uncured cheeses:** Cottage cheese is perishable. It needs to always be kept covered and in the refrigerator. It should keep for at least five days after the "pull date" on the carton. It deteriorates rapidly if left out of the refrigerator. When serving the uncured products such as cottage, ricotta, farmers or bakers cheeses, always use a clean spoon or knife to avoid contamination. Creamed cottage cheese keeps longer than the low fat product.
• **Yogurt:** One of the most popular of dairy products, yogurt should be stored in the refrigerator at all times. Because of the acid produced during fermentation, which inhibits bacterial growth, the product has improved keeping qualities. However, with longer storage, the whey tends to separate from the milk curd causing a "weeping" of the product. If an unpleasant taste or odor should develop during storage, discard the product.
• **Non-fat dry milk solids:** If properly handled, this product should keep for a relatively long time. After opening the package, it should be tightly closed and stored in a cool, dark, dry place. For best

quality, it should not be kept beyond 2 or 3 months after the package is opened. If the package is not tightly closed and is kept in a damp atmosphere, it will soon become lumpy and develop off flavors. When this happens it should be discarded.

• **Fresh fluid milk products:** Whole milk, low fat milk and skim milk are all very perishable. Get them home from the store and into the refrigerator as quickly as possible for best quality and longer storage life. If properly stored and handled, these products should keep for at least one week beyond the pull date.

Minimum shelf life of dairy products is the time between the processing date and the pull date. If properly handled, most products will keep at least a week beyond the pull date.

PULL DATES

Product	(Days after processing)
All fluid milks	10 days
Cottage cheese	13 days
Sour cream	21 days
Yogurt	30-35 days

• **Eggs:** Eggs also need to be refrigerated as soon as possible after shopping. Under proper refrigeration, eggs will keep for about 3 weeks after the pull date and still retain their quality. The pull date on most brands of eggs is 21 days after packing.

Eggs provide a nearly perfect medium for the growth of bacteria. Dishes such as quiches, souffles and custards or any food that contains a large amount of eggs in a moist product should be refrigerated if there are any leftovers. Do not leave custard pie, deviled eggs or similar products out of the refrigerator longer than two hours. Commercial mayonnaise, while containing eggs, also contains vinegar or lemon juice, the acid of which inhibit growth of bacteria. Therefore, it can be safely stored in a cool place if refrigeration is not available. Never eat cracked eggs; cook thoroughly or discard them. They could be contaminated and cause illness. In storing eggs, remember one day left at room temperature is the same as storing in the refrigerator for one week.

SUNDAY
Don't beware of this Ides of March Sunday
Oriental rib chops en brochette
Herbed rice
Barbecued vegetable aspic salad
Commercial hard rolls
Gingerbread with lemon sauce

Plan Of Work
(A real no-fuss dinner for company)
The day before:
1. Marinate rib chops
2. Prepare aspic
3. Prepare gingerbread
About one hour before dinner:
4. Prepare herbed rice.
5. Final preparation of rib chops for grilling.
To be grilled just before dinner.

ORIENTAL LAMB RIB CHOPS EN BROCHETTE

4 (1-inch thick) lamb rib chops	*2-3 cloves garlic, crushed*
²/₃ cup soy sauce	*2 teaspoons sugar*
²/₃ cup oil	*2 green peppers, cut in pieces*
Juice of 2 lemons	*1 can water chestnuts, drained*
1 teaspoon ground ginger	*Pineapple chunks*

Place lamb chops on shallow glass baking dish. Combine soy sauce, oil, lemon juice, ginger, pepper, garlic and sugar in measuring cup. Pour over lamb chops. Cover and refrigerate several hours or overnight. Pour off marinade and set aside. Thread lamb chops on skewers (optional). Broil or grill 6-7 inches from source of heat 15 minutes or to desired doneness, brushing frequently with marinade. Alternately thread green pepper pieces, water chestnuts and pineapple chunks on skewers. Broil or grill for 10 minutes, brushing with marinade. 4 servings.

HERBED RICE

2 cups chicken broth (or 2 cups water and 2	*2 tablespoons dried chopped chives*
* chicken bouillon cubes)*	*¹/₄ teaspoon basil leaves*
1 cup uncooked regular rice, medium or long grain	*¹/₄ teaspoon savory leaves*
3 tablespoons butter or margarine	*¹/₄ teaspoon garlic salt*

Bring chicken stock to boil quickly in 2 ½-quart covered saucepan. Stir in rice with a fork, cover and simmer for 12 to 14 minutes or until all stock is absorbed. Remove from heated area. Meanwhile, melt butter in saucemaker over low heat. Add herbs and garlic salt; heat herb butter for 3 minutes. Pour herb butter over cooked rice, tossing lightly with a fork to mix. Serve immediately. 4-6 servings. All herbs may be doubled in volume.

BARBECUED VEGETABLE ASPIC SALAD

2 envelopes unflavored gelatin	*2 teaspoons sugar*
¹/₄ cup water	*1 ¹/₂ teaspoons salt*
2 (8 ounce) cans tomato sauce	*¹/₈ teaspoon pepper or Tabasco sauce*
1 ¹/₂ teaspoons prepared mustard	*1 ¹/₂ cups cooked vegetables (i.e., peas, carrots, corn,*
2 teaspoons Worcestershire sauce	* beans, chopped cabbage, or combination of these)*
2 tablespoons minced onion	*Grated Parmesan cheese*
1 ¹/₂ tablespoons vinegar	

Sprinkle gelatin in cold water to soften. Combine tomato sauce, mustard, Worcestershire sauce, onion, vinegar, sugar, salt and pepper. Simmer for 3 minutes. Remove from heat, add softened gelatin and stir until thoroughly dissolved. Chill to unbeaten egg white consistency. Fold in vegetables. Lightly sprinkle the bottom of a mold with Parmesan cheese. Turn in gelatin mixture and chill until firm. Unmold on salad greens. 6 servings.

GINGERBREAD WITH LEMON SAUCE

1 ¹/₂ cups flour	*¹/₂ cup shortening, butter or margarine*
1 teaspoon baking soda	*¹/₂ cup sugar*
¹/₂ teaspoon baking powder	*1 egg, beaten*
¹/₂ teaspoon salt	*¹/₂ cup boiling water*
1 teaspoon cinnamon	*¹/₂ cup molasses*
1 teaspoon ginger	

Combine flour, soda, baking powder, salt, cinnamon and ginger. Sift twice. In mixing bowl, blend shortening and sugar; add egg, boiling water and molasses; stir. Add flour mixture and stir. Pour into 8-inch baking pan. Bake at 350° for 30-40 minutes or until done. Serve warm, topped with lemon sauce. 6-9 servings.

Lemon Sauce

1/3 cup butter or margarine
1 cup sugar
1/2 cup light syrup
1 cup evaporated milk (skim or regular)

1/4 cup lemon juice
1 teaspoon grated lemon rind
1/4 teaspoon salt

Combine butter, sugar and syrup. Cook over low heat for 3-4 minutes. Add remaining ingredients and blend well. Serve hot over gingerbread.

MONDAY
Chicken a la king supreme *
Buttered peas and carrots
Cottage cheese and pear salad
Ice cream with butterscotch topping

CHICKEN A LA KING SUPREME

3 tablespoons chicken fat or butter
1 cup chopped celery
3 tablespoons chopped green pepper
1/4 cup flour
1 cup chicken broth (without fat)
1 cup half & half or milk
1 egg yolk
1 (2 ounce) jar chopped pimiento, drained

2 tablespoons capers (drained)
3 cups cooked, chopped chicken
1 1/2 teaspoons salt
1 tablespoon Worcestershire sauce
Tabasco sauce to taste
Almonds
Rice or chow mein noodles

Melt fat, add celery and green pepper; cook slowly for 5 minutes. Add flour; stirring constantly. Gradually add broth and milk. Cook until thick. Beat egg yolk and add a little of the sauce; then slowly add this mixture to the remaining sauce. Add remaining ingredients and seasonings except almonds. Add almonds just before serving. Serve hot in pastry shells, toast shells, on mounds of fluffy rice or chow mein noodles. 6-8 servings.

TUESDAY
Baked chicken breast
Buttered peas / Tabouli salad *
Rye bread and butter
Cream cheese pound cake topped with chocolate swirl

TABOULI SALAD

1 cup bulgar (cracked wheat)
4 cups boiling water
2 tablespoons olive oil
1/4 cup fresh lemon juice
3 green onions with tops, finely chopped

2 medium tomatoes, finely chopped
1/4 cup finely-chopped fresh mint or 1 teaspoon dried mint
1/4 cup finely-chopped fresh parsley
Freshly ground black pepper to taste

In a large heat-proof bowl, combine bulgar and boiling water. Cover and allow to stand for 1 hour, or until most of the water is absorbed. Drain bulgar, using cheesecloth to help extract most of the moisture. Combine oil and lemon juice. Add to bulgar along with onions, tomatoes, mint, parsley and pepper. Gently toss mixture with a fork and refrigerate at least 1 hour to allow flavors to blend. Serve chilled or at room temperature. 6 servings.

WEDNESDAY
St. Patrick's Day Dinner
Endive and pasta soup *
Shepherd's pie *
Spinach souffle
Irish soda bread
Irish delight parfait

ENDIVE AND PASTA SOUP

1 quart chicken stock or canned broth with all fat removed
2 chicken bouillon cubes or 2 teaspoons instant chicken bouillon
½ pound fresh endive, washed and coarsely chopped
1 teaspoon dried basil
1 medium-sized onion, chopped

2-3 cloves garlic, chopped
5 scallions (green onions) sliced thinly (use tops)
¼ cup pastina (a tiny pasta)
Black pepper
Parmesan cheese, grated

In a large saucepan, heat broth to boiling. Add endive and basil. Reduce heat to a simmer. In a small microwave-safe dish, cook onions, garlic and scallions for about 3 minutes, or until the onion is tender and translucent. Add the onion mixture and pastina to the liquid. Simmer uncovered for 30 minutes. Cool slightly. Serve warm with a sprinkle of Parmesan cheese. 4 - 6 servings.

SHEPHERD'S PIE

2 cups well-seasoned mashed potatoes (can use leftovers)
2 egg yolks
2 egg whites
⅛ teaspoon salt
2 cups finely-chopped lamb or any cooked meat
2 tablespoons parsley

⅓ cup chopped celery
½ cup cream or leftover gravy
¼ teaspoon salt
¼ teaspoon paprika
1 tablespoon butter (optional)
½ cup (2 ounces) shredded Cheddar cheese

Add egg yolks to the mashed potatoes. Beat in until very light. Whip the 2 egg whites until foamy, add salt, continue beating until stiff. Fold them lightly into the potatoes. Spread the bottom of a greased 1 ½ quart baking dish with ½ of the potatoes. Combine meat, parsley, celery, cream or gravy, salt and paprika. Spread the meat mixture over potatoes. Cover the meat mixture with the remaining potatoes. Dot with butter and sprinkle with the shredded cheese. Bake in hot oven, 400°, about 20 minutes or until the top is brown. 6 servings.

THURSDAY
Pork fajitas *
Cottage fried potatoes
Hot Italian bread
Pineapple cream fluff *

PORK FAJITAS

1 pound lean boneless pork
2 cloves garlic, minced or crushed
1 teaspoon oregano, crumbled
1/2 teaspoon cumin
1 teaspoon seasoned salt
2 tablespoons orange juice
2 tablespoons vinegar
Dash of hot pepper sauce
1 tablespoon cooking oil

1 medium onion, peeled and sliced
1 green pepper, seeded and sliced
4 flour tortillas
Green onion tops, sliced (optional)
Shredded lettuce (optional)
Sour cream (optional)
Shredded Cheddar cheese (optional)
Bottled salsa (optional)

Slice pork across grain into 1/8-inch strips (partial freezing makes slicing easier). Marinate pork strips in garlic, oregano, cumin, salt, orange juice, vinegar and hot pepper sauce for 10 minutes. Heat heavy skillet, griddle or wok until hot (if using electric griddle or wok, use 400°). Add the tablespoon of oil, onion, green pepper and pork strips; stir fry until the pork is no longer pink, about 3-5 minutes. Serve in flour tortillas and accompany with sliced green onion, shredded lettuce, sour cream, shredded Cheddar cheese and salsa, if desired. 4 servings.

PINEAPPLE CREAM FLUFF

4 slices canned pineapple, drained
12 large marshmallows, quartered or 48 miniatures
1 cup heavy cream, whipped

1/2 cup freshly grated or shredded coconut
(canned or frozen may be used)

Dice pineapple, add marshmallows. Chill thoroughly. Drain; and, just before serving, fold into whipped cream. Spoon into 4 compotes and sprinkle with coconut. 4 servings.

FRIDAY
Sauteed scallops in pastry shells
Buttered broccoli
Baked tomato halves
Fruit and mushroom salad *
Pecan pie

FRUIT AND MUSHROOM SALAD

1/2 cup calorie reduced mayonnaise
1 (20 ounce) can chunk pineapple unsweetened
  juice, drained (reserve juice)
2 medium bananas, sliced 1/4 inch thick

1 orange, peeled, sectioned and cut up
1/2 pound fresh mushrooms, sliced
Lettuce cups
Ground nutmeg

Combine mayonnaise and 1 tablespoon pineapple juice. One hour before serving, toss with pineapple chunks, bananas, orange and mushrooms. Chill. Spoon into lettuce cups. Sprinkle with nutmeg. 4-6 servings.

SATURDAY
Cubed steak Parmigiana *
Buttered linguini
Sauted peppers and mushrooms
Greek salad
Garlic bread
Iced carrot cake

CUBED STEAK PARMIGIANA

6 beef cubed steaks
3 tablespoons flour
½ teaspoon salt
⅛ teaspoon pepper
1 egg
2 tablespoons water
⅓ cup fine, dry bread crumbs
⅓ cup grated Parmesan cheese
3 tablespoons cooking oil

1 (15 ounce) can tomato sauce
1 tablespoon sugar
1 clove garlic, crushed
½ teaspoon leaf oregano
½ cup grated Parmesan cheese
3 slices (4 ounces) mozzarella cheese, halved
½ teaspoon basil leaves
Leaf oregano

Combine flour, salt and pepper; dredge steaks. Combine eggs and water. Combine bread crumbs, ⅓ cup Parmesan cheese and basil leaves. Dip each steak in egg mixture and dredge in crumb mixture, coating evenly. Measure oil into a 13x9-inch roasting pan; place in oven and preheat oven to 375° (5-10 minutes). Place breaded steaks in the pan and bake, uncovered, at 375° for 25 to 30 minutes or until golden brown. Pour off drippings. Combine tomato sauce, sugar, garlic and leaf oregano and pour over meat. Sprinkle with ½ cup Parmesan cheese. Bake 20 minutes. Place a slice of Mozzarella cheese on each steak and sprinkle oregano over cheese. Bake 3-5 minutes, until cheese is melted. 6 servings.

March - Third Week

MEAT, FISH AND POULTRY SHOULD BE stored immediately in the refrigerator. Prepackaged meats can be kept in the original wrappers, but loosen wrapper on one end to allow good circulation of air. Rewrap fresh meat with wax paper, which remains loose to allow air circulation. Plastic wrap has a tendency to cling and not allow air circulation. Follow the "Storage Time Chart" to keep food at its maximum quality.

STORAGE TIME CHART

Type of meat, Poultry or fish	Refrigerator 38° to 40°	Freezer 0° or below
Roasts		
Beef	4-6 days	6-9 months
Veal and lamb	3-5 days	6-9 months
Pork	4-6 days	3-6 months
Steaks and chops		
Beef	3-4 days	6-8 months
Pork veal and lamb	2-3 days	3-4 months

STORAGE TIME CHART (cont'd)

Ground meat

Beef, veal and lamb	1-2 days	3-4 months
Pork	1-2 days	1-3 months
Variety meats (liver, kidney)	1-2 days	3-4 months
Luncheon meats	1 week	2 months

Sausage

Fresh pork	1 week	2 months
Smoked	3-7 days	2 months
Dry and semi-dry, unsliced	2-3 weeks	2 months
Frankfurters	5-7 days	2 months
Bacon	5-7 days	2 months

Smoked ham

Whole or half	1 week	2 months
Slices	3-4 days	2 months
Corned beef	1 week	2 weeks
Leftover cooked meat	2-4 days	2-3 months

Poultry

Raw	2 days	6 months
Cooked	2-4 days	2-3 months

Fish

Raw	1 day	2-4 months
Cooked	2-4 days	2-3 months

Frozen cooked combination foods

Meat pies	3 months
Swiss steak	3 months
Stews	3-4 months
Meat dinners	3-4 months

Frankfurters, bacon, sliced smoked ham, smoked sausage and luncheon meats could lose some quality if frozen. Therefore, it is not recomended that they be frozen.

SUNDAY
Sunday Night Supper
Glazed cornish hen *
Buttered new potatoes
Broccoli Parmesan
Green salad with French dressing
Hot rolls
Lemon merangue pie

GLAZED CORNISH HEN

4 (16 - 20 ounce) Cornish hens
2 cups seasoned dry stuffing mix
1 (8 ounce) can pineapple tidbits
1/4 cup chopped celery
1/4 cup sliced green onions
Melted butter or margarine

2 tablespoons honey
2 tablespoons soy sauce
2 tablespoons toasted sesame seeds
1 tablespoon cornstarch
1/2 teaspoon ground ginger
Dash garlic powder

Thaw hens; wash and pat dry. Prepare stuffing according to package directions. Drain pineapple, reserving juice; add water to make ½ cup. Set aside. Add pineapple, celery and green onion to stuffing. Cool completely. Stuff each hen with stuffing mixture. Close cavity with wooden picks; truss with string. Arrange hens in roasting pan without rack. Brush hens with butter. Roast at 350° for 1 hour. In saucepan, combine reserved juice, honey, soy sauce, sesame seeds, cornstarch, ginger and garlic powder. Cook, stirring constantly, until thickened and translucent. Baste hens with soy mixture; continue roasting for 30 minutes, basting again after 15 minutes. Place hens on platter; pour remaining sauce over hens. 4 servings.

MONDAY
French style vegetable stew *
Tuna sandwich on rye
Relish tray
Blueberry dessert

FRENCH STYLE VEGETABLE STEW

1 large onion, chopped
2 cloves garlic, crushed
2 small zucchini, thinly sliced
1 medium-sized green pepper, cut into thin strips
½ cup olive oil or salad oil
1 medium eggplant, pared, cut into strips
3 tablespoons flour

4 medium tomatoes, peeled, cut into eighths
¼ cup catsup
1 tablespoon salt
1 teaspoon cider vinegar
½ teaspoon crushed oregano leaves
¼ teaspoon pepper

In Dutch oven, saute onion, garlic, zucchini and green pepper in oil until onion is transparent. Coat eggplant with flour; add eggplant and tomatoes to sauteed vegetables. Combine catsup, salt, vinegar, oregano and pepper; pour over vegetables. Cover; simmer 30-35 minutes; stir occasionally, or until vegetables are tender. 8-10 servings.

TUESDAY
Ham with pineapple mustard sauce *
Baked sweet potato slices
Buttered peas / Fruit salad
Cornbread
Chilled applesauce

HAM WITH PINEAPPLE MUSTARD SAUCE

1 precooked buffet ham
1 (8 ounce) can pineapple tidbits
1 tablespoon butter or margarine
1 egg

1 tablespoon honey
2 tablespoons Dijon mustard
1 teaspoon prepared horseradish

Bake the precooked ham at 325° for 15 minutes per pound. Drain pineapple, reserving juice. Place juice in saucepan. Add butter, egg, honey, mustard and horseradish. Cook, stirring constantly, over medium heat until thickened. Do not boil. Fold in pineapple. Serve with ham.

WEDNESDAY
Sauteed cube steaks
Mashed potatoes
Squash casserole
Orange and onion salad
Carrot muffins
Marble cheesecake *

MARBLE CHEESECAKE

1 cup Graham cracker crumbs
3 tablespoons butter or margarine, melted
3 tablespoon sugar
3 (8 ounce) packages cream cheese, softened
³/₄ cup sugar

3 tablespoons flour
1 teaspoon vanilla
3 eggs
1 (1 ounce) square unsweetened chocolate, melted

Combine crumbs, butter and 3 tablespoons sugar. Press onto bottom of 9-inch springform or deep dish pie pan. Bake at 350° for 10 minutes. Combine cream cheese, ³/₄ cup sugar, flour and vanilla, mixing at medium speed on electric mixer until well blended. Add eggs, one at a time, mixing well after each addition. Add chocolate to 1 cup of batter; mix until well blended. Spoon plain and chocolate batters alternately over crust; cut through batter with knife several times for marble effect. Bake at 450° for 10 minutes. Reduce oven temperature to 250°. Continue baking for 30 minutes. Loosen cake from rim of pan; cool before removing rim of pan. Chill. 1 9-inch cheesecake. (8-10 servings)

THURSDAY
Too Busy To Cook For Company
Chicken breasts with fresh lemon sauce
Wild rice
Florentine vegetables
Black raspberry molded salad
Finger rolls (commercial)
Fudgy oatmeal drops

Plan Of Work

Most of this meal can be prepared the day before. A good meal for the busy hostess.
Day before:
1. Prepare the gelatin salad.
2. Prepare the oatmeal drops.
3. Prepare the Florentine vegetables.
About 1 hour before dinner is served:
4. Prepare chicken dish.
5. While chicken is cooking, prepare the rice.

CHICKEN BREASTS WITH FRESH LEMON SAUCE

16 small skinless, boneless chicken breast halves
   (about 4 ounces each)
¹/₂ teaspoon salt

2-3 tablespoons butter or margarine
1 quart chicken stock or broth
Fresh lemon sauce (recipe below)

Trim and discard any fat from the chicken breasts; pat dry and sprinkle with the salt. In a large skillet, melt 2 tablespoons butter over moderately high heat. When the foam subsides, add as many breasts as fit in a single layer and saute for 2 minutes on each side, until very lightly browned. Repeat with remaining chicken, adding more butter as necessary. As they are sauteed, transfer the chicken breasts to a Dutch oven. Pour 1 cup of stock into the skillet and bring to a boil, scraping up the brown bits that cling to the bottom of the pan. Pour mixture into Dutch oven and add remaining 3 cups of stock. Bring to a boil over high heat, reduce heat to low and simmer covered for 8-10 minutes, until meat is springy to the touch. To serve arrange chicken breasts on a warmed platter and spoon some of the fresh lemon sauce over the center of each breast. Pass remaining sauce separately. If you want to serve the dish cold, refrigerate the chicken in the stock until chilled. Arrange on a platter and coat with chilled or slightly warmed sauce. 8 servings.

Fresh Lemon Sauce

6 egg yolks at room temperature
1 tablespoon plus 1 teaspoon all-purpose flour
2 cups chicken stock or broth
1/4 cup fresh lemon juice
Salt to taste
White pepper to taste

In a double boiler, stir the yolks until blended. Stir in the flour and then the stock. Cook over simmering water, stirring constantly, until the sauce thickens, 10-12 minutes. Continue to cook, stirring for 2-3 minutes longer. Add lemon juice and season to taste with salt and pepper. 2 1/2 cups.

WILD RICE

1 cup wild rice
1 teaspoon salt
4 cups water
1/4 cup butter or margarine

Rinse wild rice under running water using a strainer or in a bowl of water. Drain. Place rice in a heavy saucepan with salt and water. Bring to a boil; reduce heat and simmer, covered, until the kernels are open and tender, but not mushy, about 45 to 55 minutes. Drain excess liquid. Melt butter and stir into the cooked wild rice. (If wild rice is not available, purchase the combination of regular and wild.)

FLORENTINE VEGETABLES

1/2 cup lemon juice
1/3 cup olive oil
2 cups chicken broth
4 chicken bouillon cubes
3 cloves garlic, crushed
Pinch of red pepper flakes
1/2 teaspoon salt
2 teaspoons coriander seed or 1 teaspoon powder
1/2 teaspoon dried thyme, crumbled or 2 fresh sprigs
1/2 teaspoon dried oregano
1 teaspoon sugar
2 leeks (white part only) cut crossways into 1/2-inch pieces
3 carrots, scraped and cut into 1/2-inch pieces
4 ribs celery, cut into 1-inch pieces
2 red bell peppers cut into 1 inch pieces
1/4 pound green beans cut into 1-inch pieces
1/2 pound mushrooms, cut in half

In a saucepan, combine the first 11 ingredients. Bring to a boil and simmer 5 minutes. Add leeks and carrots and simmer 5 minutes. Add celery, bell peppers and green beans and simmer 3 minutes. Add mushrooms and simmer 3 minutes. Transfer vegetables to a shallow baking dish (11 1/2 x 8 1/2) with a slotted spoon. Boil cooking liquid until reduced to 1/2 cup (about 2 minutes). Pour over vegetables in baking dish. Chill overnight or 3 hours. Serve at room temperature. 6 to 8 servings.

BLACK RASPBERRY MOLDED SALAD

1 (3 ounce) package black raspberry flavored gelatin
1 ¼ cups hot water
³⁄₄ cup Burgundy wine
⅓ cup canned pineapple tidbits, drained

½ cup finely-diced celery
⅓ cup slivered almonds
Lettuce or curly endive
Calorie reduced mayonnaise

Add hot water to gelatin and stir until dissolved. Cool. Add Burgundy. When slightly thickened, add pineapple, celery and almonds. Pour into 6 individual salad molds or 1 quart ring mold. Chill until set. Unmold on lettuce or curly endive. Serve with mayonnaise. 6 servings.

FUDGY OATMEAL DROPS

3 cups quick oats
½ cup cocoa
½ cup undiluted evaporated milk
2 cups sugar

½ cup (1 stick) butter or margarine
1 cup miniature marshmallows
¼ teaspoon vanilla extract

Place oats in large bowl. Mix cocoa, milk, sugar and butter in a saucepan. Cook over medium heat; stir constantly until a full boil. Boil 1 minute. Remove from heat. Add marshmallows and vanilla; stir until melted. Pour over oats; stir with fork until well-mixed. Drop from teaspoon onto waxed paper; work rapidly. Let stand until firm. 3½ dozen drops.

FRIDAY
Baked cheese pudding
Stewed tomatoes
Oriental sprout salad *
Angel food cake with fresh peach sauce

ORIENTAL SPROUT SALAD

1 cup slivered ham
2 cups homegrown sprouts or 1 can (16 ounces)
  bean sprouts, drained
1 cup sliced fresh mushrooms
1 (8 ounce) can sliced water chestnuts, drained
1 (6 ounce) package frozen Chinese pea
  pods, thawed
2 green onions with tops, chopped
5 cups (about 12 ounces) Chinese cabbage or
  celery , thinly sliced

2 tablespoons sesame seeds, toasted
½ cup soy sauce
¼ cup vinegar
2 tablespoons oil
2 teaspoons sugar
¼ teaspoon Tabasco sauce or to taste
⅛ teaspoon dry mustard

In medium bowl, combine meat, sprouts, mushroom, water chestnuts, pea pods and onions; toss. Place Chinese cabbage into large salad bowl; top with meat mixture. Sprinkle with sesame seeds. In a small bowl, combine soy sauce, vinegar, oil, sugar, Tabasco sauce and mustard; blend well. Pour over salad. 4-6 servings.

SATURDAY
Double thick lamb chops grilled with herb butter*
Barley pilaf
Minted carrots and peas
Cabbage and pineapple salad
Frozen lemon dessert

DOUBLE-THICK LAMB CHOPS GRILLED WITH HERB BUTTER

6 loin lamb chops, cut double thick
½ cup butter or margarine
1 teaspoon chopped fresh tarragon or
　½ teaspoon dried
½ teaspoon dried dill or 1 teaspoon fresh

½ teaspoon dried rosemary or 1 teaspoon fresh
1 tablespoon fresh parsley, chopped
2 tablespoons dry red wine vinegar or lemon juice
Salt
Pepper

Remove excess fat from lamb chops and secure ends with toothpicks. Place them over a medium fire and grill, turning several times until they are nicely browned. Centers should be pink; 2-inch chops will take about 7 minutes on each side. Combine butter, tarragon, dill, rosemary, parsley and wine in a small pan; simmer for a few minutes at one side of grill. Sprinkle chops well with salt and pepper and pour a spoonful or two of herb butter over each chop as it cooks. 6 servings.

March - Fourth Week

There are a few foods normally stored in the refrigerator that can be left in a cool place for one or two days: eggs in the shell (for one night only), hard cheeses, such as Cheddar, Provolone and Parmesan, and raw vegetables stored in plastic bags and secured by a rubber band or twister. Margarine, butter, pickles, olives and fruit are a few more. A few items that should not be kept at room temperature for even one night are fresh or cooked meat, fish, cooked vegetables, canned goods after they have been opened, milk and cottage cheese.

Each year, pick out one month to go through your pantry to check for food products over one year old. Even if safe, some foods lose quality if stored too long. Check for leaking or swollen cans, and old open packages of flour, rice, dry milk and similar products that are not used very often. These should be discarded to give you more room in the storage area.

A good rule to follow when storing meat, fish, poultry, dairy products and other perishable products is to keep them CLEAN, COLD AND COVERED.

SUNDAY
Meat cakes with mushroom sauce
Rice and bran pilaf *
Green beans and onions
Carrot and raisin cookies *
Orange yogurt

RICE AND BRAN PILAF

½ cup uncooked long-grain brown or white rice	*¼ cup sliced water chestnuts*
2 chicken bouillon cubes	*1 cup wheat bran cereal*
½ cup butter or margarine	*¼ teaspoon ground sage*
½ cup chopped onion	*½ teaspoon basil leaves*
½ cup chopped celery	*¼ teaspoon pepper*
1 (2 ½ ounce) jar (½ cup) sliced mushrooms,	*½ cup water*
* drained*	

Cook rice according to package directions, but do not use salt called for in package directions; use bouillon cubes. Melt butter in large skillet. Stir in onion, celery, mushrooms and water chestnuts. Cook over medium heat, stirring occasionally, until celery is almost tender. Gently stir in cooked rice, cereal, sage, basil, pepper and water. Cover and cook over very low heat for about 15 minutes. Serve immediately. 6 servings.

CARROT-RAISIN COOKIES

¼ cup butter or margarine, softened	*2 cups biscuit mix*
⅓ cup sugar	*½ teaspoon cinnamon*
1 egg	*½ cup raisins, chopped*
1 teaspoon vanilla	*½ cup finely-shredded carrots*

Beat butter and sugar with electric mixer at medium speed until well blended, about 2 minutes. Add egg and vanilla; beat well. Add biscuit mix and cinnamon; mix until blended. Add raisins and carrots; mix well. Drop by teaspoonfuls onto greased baking sheet, about 2 inches apart. Flatten slightly with spoon. Bake at 350° until set but not dry, about 10 minutes. Remove from baking sheet while still warm. Cool on rack. 48 cookies.

MONDAY
Beef bourguignon *
Mashed potatoes
Stir-fry zucchini
Tomato and cottage cheese salad
Whole wheat rolls
Chocolate pudding

BEEF BOURGUIGNON

1 ½ pounds boneless chuck, cut into 1-inch cubes	*1 (6 ounce) can tomato paste*
2 tablespoons butter or margarine	*1 cup red wine and ³/₄ cup sherry or 1 ³/₄*
2 large onions, quartered	* cups beef bouillon*
1 (4 ounce) can button mushrooms, drained or	*1 cup beef bouillon*
* ½ pound fresh, quartered*	*1 bay leaf*
2 tablespoons cornstarch	*Dash of pepper*

In Dutch oven, brown meat in butter. Remove beef. Add onions and mushrooms, cook 10 minutes. Remove vegetables from pan. Add cornstarch and tomato paste, stir until blended; stir in wine and sherry or beef bouillon. Bring to boil. Add beef, vegetables and remaining ingredients. Cover, simmer 1 ½ hours or until done, stirring occasionally. 6 servings.

TUESDAY
Turkey burgers *
Cottage fried potatoes
Cabbage and apple salad
Lemon sherbert / tea cakes

TURKEY BURGERS

1 pound cooked turkey, ground
8 single saltine crackers, crushed
2 tablespoons catsup
1 tablespoon lemon juice
1 tablespoon dried onion flakes

1 teaspoon Worcestershire sauce
1/2 teaspoon paprika
1 teaspoon horseradish (optional)
1/2 teaspoon pepper sauce (optional)
4 bacon slices

Combine ground turkey with remaining ingredients except bacon slices. Shape into 4 patties. Wrap each pattie with bacon slice around outer edge, securing with wooden picks. Broil over preheated charcoal 3 inches from source of heat for 5-6 minutes on each side, or until done. (Can be broiled in oven.) 4 servings.

WEDNESDAY
Welcome Spring Dinner
Black bean soup
Carrot ring with bacon broccoli sauce
Baked tomato halves
Relish tray with vegetables
Hot buttered English muffins
Applesauce crisp

Plan Of Work
Early in the day:
1. Prepare tomatoes and refrigerate.
2. Prepare topping for apple crisp.
3. Cook rice, prepare all vegetables and bacon for the carrot ring.
4. Prepare black bean soup.
About one hour before dinner:
5. Complete preparation of carrot ring.
6. Place dessert, tomatoes and carrot ring in the oven at the same time.
7. While cooking, prepare bacon broccoli sauce.
8. Reheat bean soup before serving.

BLACK BEAN SOUP

1 (16 ounce) package (2 cups) dry black beans
1 large onion, chopped
1 large green pepper, chopped
1 large garlic clove, crushed

1 (15 ounce) can tomato sauce
2 teaspoons salt (optional)
1/2 teaspoon pepper
1-2 ham hocks or ham bone (optional)

Rinse beans with running cold water and discard any stones or shrivelled beans. In 5-quart saucepot over high heat, heat beans and 8 cups water to boiling; boil 3 minutes. Remove saucepot from heat; cover and let stand one hour. In a microwave-safe pan, cook onion, green pepper and garlic at high setting until tender (about 3 minutes). Stir onion mixture into undrained beans; add tomato sauce, salt and pepper. Heat to boiling. Reduce heat to low; add ham hocks; cover and simmer mixture about 2 hours or until beans are tender, stirring occasionally. Remove ham bones. Remove meat from bones, chop finely and add ham pieces back to bean mixture. 9 servings.

CARROT RING WITH BACON BROCCOLI SAUCE

3 cups cooked rice	*1 tablespoon flour*
2 cups shredded carrots	*⅛ teaspoon leaf marjoram, crushed*
1 tablespoon butter or margarine	*1 cup milk*
⅓ cup finely chopped green pepper	*1 egg, slightly beaten*

Stir rice and carrots together in a large bowl. Melt butter in saucepan. add green pepper and cook over low heat until pepper is tender-crisp. Mix in flour and marjoram. Gradually blend in milk; cook and stir to make a smooth sauce. Mix a small amount of hot sauce with egg; blend into hot sauce. Cook and stir until sauce is thick. Combine thoroughly with rice and carrots. Spoon into a greased 4-cup ring mold; press firmly into mold. Bake in 400° oven for 30 minutes. Invert onto serving plate.

Sauce

6 bacon slices	*White pepper*
½ cup (1 stick) butter or margarine	*4 cups (1 quart) milk*
½ cup chopped onion	*2 tablespoons dry sherry*
½ cup flour	*1 (4 ounce) jar sliced mushrooms, drained*
1 teaspoon salt	*3 cups broccoli flowerets, cooked tender-crisp*
½ teaspoon dry mustard	*5 hard-cooked eggs, each cut into eighths*

In microwave, oven or skillet, cook bacon slices until done but not too crisp. Drain on paper towel. Snip into pieces ³/₈-inch wide. Melt butter in large saucepan, add onion and cook until tender. Stir in flour, salt, mustard and pepper. Gradually blend in milk. Cook and stir over medium heat until hot and thickened. Stir in sherry, bacon and mushrooms. Fold in broccoli and eggs. If necessary, return to low heat until sauce is hot. Correct seasonings. Place in serving bowl or chafing dish. Spoon over individual servings of rice ring. 6 servings.

BAKED TOMATO HALVES

3 large tomatoes	*1 ½ tablespoons chopped parsley*
⅓ teaspoon salt	*2 tablespoons finely-chopped celery*
³/₄ teaspoon prepared mustard	*1 teaspoon oregano (optional)*
1 teaspoon chopped onion	*1 teaspoon butter or margarine*

Wash tomatoes, remove stem end, and cut crossways in half. Sprinkle tomatoes with salt, and spread the cut side with mustard. Mix onion, parsley, celery and oregano. Place over mustard on tomatoes. Dot each half with butter. Bake in moderate oven at 350° for 30 minutes or until tender. 6 servings.

APPLE SAUCE CRISP

1 one-pint jar (2 cups) applesauce
¹/₂ cup firmly packed brown sugar
¹/₂ cup flour
³/₄ teaspoon cinnamon

³/₄ teaspoon nutmeg
¹/₂ cup oats
¹/₂ stick (¹/₄ cup) butter or margarine, melted

Spread applesauce evenly in lightly greased 9-inch casserole dish. In a bowl, combine brown sugar, flour, spices and oats. Stir in melted butter, mix well. Sprinkle oat mixture over apple sauce. Bake at 350° for 25-30 minutes, or until brown. Serve warm. (Recipe can be easily doubled or tripled and baked in a 9x13-inch dish.) Can be served with a topping of whipped cream, whipped topping or vanilla ice milk. 6 servings.

THURSDAY
Oven fried chicken *
Potatoes au gratin
Cauliflower/ broccoli
Cranberry salad
Oatmeal bread
Coffee ice cream pie

OVEN FRIED CHICKEN

1 (2 ¹/₂ pound) frying chicken, cut into
  serving pieces
1 cup flour
2 teaspoons salt
¹/₄ teaspoon pepper
2 teaspoons paprika

2 eggs, slightly beaten
3 tablespoons milk
²/₃ cup grated Parmesan cheese
¹/₃ cup fine dry bread crumbs
2 tablespoons butter or margarine
2 tablespoons fat

Preheat oven to 400°. If desired, remove chicken skin. Combine flour, salt, pepper and paprika, set aside. Combine egg and milk, set aside. Combine cheese and crumbs, set aside. Dip chicken pieces in flour mixture, then in egg mixture and then in the Parmesan cheese mixture. Set the chicken aside for 5 minutes. Melt butter and fat in baking dish. Place chicken in dish skin side down. Bake in 400° oven for 30 minutes, turn and bake 30 minutes more. 4 servings.

FRIDAY
Broiled salmon with cucumber sauce *
Confetti rice
Peas with bacon chips
Orange and grapefruit salad
Corn muffins
Chocolate velvet pudding with bananas

BROILED SALMON WITH CUCUMBER SAUCE

¹/₄ cup (¹/₂ stick) butter or margarine, melted
2 tablespoons lemon juice
4 salmon steaks
1 medium cucumber, pared and diced
¹/₂ teaspoon salt

¹/₄ teaspoon pepper
1 tablespoon chopped chives
¹/₂ cup sour cream
2 teaspoons lemon juice

Combine butter and lemon juice; brush on both sides of steaks. Broil steaks about 6 inches from source of heat, about 8 minutes on each side until fish flakes easily, brushing occasionally with butter and lemon juice mixture. Keep warm. Combine cucumber with remaining ingredients, mix well. Serve over hot steaks. 4 servings.

SATURDAY
Garlic soup *
Grilled ham and cheese sandwiches
Citrus salad
Chocolate chip cookies

ZUPPA di AGLIO
(Garlic Soup)

1 tablespoon butter or margarine
Vegetable cooking spray
2 slices bread, cut into cubes
8 large cloves garlic, crushed
8 sprigs fresh parsley (leaves only), chopped fine

$3/4$ cup dry red wine (Burgundy)
4 cups chicken broth
$1/4$ teaspoon black pepper
2 tablespoons grated Parmesan cheese

Over medium heat in heavy saucepan coated with cooking spray, add butter and heat. Add bread and garlic. Cook until golden brown, stirring constantly. (Do not burn.) Add parsley, wine, broth and pepper. Cover and cook 2 minutes. Sprinkle each serving with Parmesan cheese. Serve immediately. 4 servings.

April

April - First Week

SEAFOOD! FRESH FROM COAST TO COAST. Seafood is plentiful. Seasonal variations do occur. But as with vegetables, which are picked at the peak of flavor, fish can be caught when they are available, frozen and canned, and held in reserve until the demand exceeds the immediate supply. Thus the market supply is kept fairly regular despite seasonal variation.

Fish is economical. There is very little waste in most forms. If fish is boned or filletted at the market, it is almost 100 percent edible - and with only a little shrinkage in cooking.

Seafood is easy to prepare. Unless the dish is a complicated casserole, almost any fish can be prepared in less than half an hour. Boiled shrimp can be ready to serve in 5 minutes, counting the time it takes the water to boil... even if the shrimp is frozen.

Weight-conscious Americans delight in low-calorie fish. Fish is high in poly-unsaturated fats. Fish can be used in a multitude of ways to vary the diet for almost anyone. Also, it is probably the most nutritious of all meats. High in taste-tempting flavor appeal, low in calories and saturated fats, high in nutritional value, seafood is the best protein buy on the market.

The qualities that make fish popular are also those which make it nutritious. For example, the natural tenderness and flavor, ease of preparation and short cooking time are a result of the kind of protein and the small amount of connective tissue found in fish. The elements needed for good health - protein, minerals, vitamins, fats and carbohydrates - are all found in fish. Seafood cannot contain everything needed for good health, but it comes close.

There are several things to remember in preparing fish. Avoid overcooking fish. Fish is cooked when it loses its transparent look, and the flesh flakes easily when tested with a fork. Sprinkle fish with salt and pepper and a generous amount of lemon or lime juice; let stand several hours in refrigerator before cooking. This improves the flavor.

When purchasing a whole fish, allow ½ pound per person. With steaks and fillets, allow ⅓ pound per person. One pound of fish yields 2 cups of cooked, flaked fish. One and a half pounds of raw shrimp yields ¾ pound when cooked and shelled, enough for four people. One pint of oysters for frying, boiling or raw serves four.

Use all left-over cooked fish. Flake the meat from the bones and skin to use in salads, casserole dishes, chowders or any recipe calling for canned or flaked fish. Also flaked fish may be frozen for future use. Discard the skin.

Always tightly cover fish stored in the refrigerator. Remove fish from its paper wrappings, wipe off with a damp cloth, and place in a covered dish or roll in waxed paper. Store in the coldest part of the refrigerator.

Line the baking pan or broiler pan with aluminum foil when cooking fish in the oven. It is easier to remove the fish when cooked and helps with the dish washing, too.

Dry fish thoroughly before frying to prevent the fat from spattering. Place fish in frying pan flesh side down to prevent curling. Have fat hot but not smoking. Turn to brown on both sides. When broiling, baking or planking lean fish, baste frequently with melted butter or other fat to avoid dryness.

Keep frozen fish frozen until ready to use. It may be cooked before or after thawing, but requires a longer time to cook if cooked frozen.

Slice a lime or lemon and add to water when cooking fish. This improves the flavor and keeps it from falling apart.

Oysters and clams should be cooked only until tender (they curl around edges). Note that crab and processed lobster are already cooked when purchased.

Do not overcook shrimp. Drop cleaned shrimp in boiling salted water (spices may be added) and when it comes to a boil again, remove from heat, cover and let stand for 5 minutes, then drain.

SUNDAY
Stuffed pork chops *
Caramelized tomatoes
Southern turnip greens
Waldorf salad
Coffee ice cream with crunch topping *

STUFFED PORK CHOPS

2 tablespoons butter or margarine
2 cloves garlic, crushed
½ cup onions, chopped
½ cup mushrooms, chopped
¼ cup parsley

1 teaspoon oregano
1 teaspoon basil
2 tablespoons Dijon mustard
¼ cup bread crumbs
4 pork chops (1 ½-inch thick) with pocket

Melt butter in skillet; add garlic, onion and mushrooms. Saute until onion is tender. Add parsley, oregano, basil, mustard and bread crumbs. Mix well. Stuff mixture into pocket of pork chops. Bake in 375° oven for 1 hour. 4 servings. **Note:** Ask butcher to cut the pockets.

CRUNCHY TOPPING FOR ICE CREAM

¼ cup plus 1 tablespoon butter or margarine, melted
³/₄ cup wheat bran cereal
⅓ cup firmly packed brown sugar

½ cup shredded coconut
2 tablespoons all-purpose flour
½ teaspoon cinnamon
¼ teaspoon nutmeg

Combine all ingredients in medium-sized mixing bowl. Mix well. Spread mixture evenly in a shallow baking pan. Bake in 350° oven about 8 minutes; stir once or twice while mixture bakes. Topping will not be crisp while hot, but will become crisp on cooling. Use for topping for molded gelatin and fruit salads, fruit, ice cream or pudding. Yield: approximately 1 ½ cups.

MONDAY
Chopped steak in Oriental mushroom sauce
Noodles
Buttered asparagus
Avocado, grapefruit salad with French dressing *
Finger rolls
Chocolate yogurt with chocolate sauce

FRENCH DRESSING

½ cup lemon juice or vinegar
½ teaspoon salt
⅛ teaspoon pepper
⅛ teaspoon cayenne

1 teaspoon paprika
1 teaspoon sugar (optional)
1 cup olive oil or vegetable oil

Place lemon juice, salt, pepper, cayenne, paprika and sugar in blender. With the motor running slowly, add the oil. A temporary emulsion will form. Shake or beat vigorously before using. Yield: 1 ½ cups.

TUESDAY
Last Fling Mardi Gras Dinner
Commercial salsa and dippers
Artichoke balls
Spinach stuffed sole (or any white fish fillet)
Parsley buttered potatoes
Baked tomatoes
Lettuce wedge with Chiffonade dressing
Commercial sourdough rolls
Orange chiffon pie

Plan Of Work
Early in the day:
1. Prepare dressing.
2. Prepare orange chiffon pie.
About 1 ½ hours before dinner:
3. Prepare the spinach stuffed sole. Keep in refrigerator until baking time.
4. Prepare baked tomatoes. Place in oven about 15 minutes before the sole.
5. Prepare potatoes and start cooking about 15 minutes before the sole.
6. Put sole in oven about 30-40 minutes before dinner is served.
7. Prepare salad last minute.

ARTICHOKE BALLS

1 (14 ounce) can artichoke hearts
2 eggs, beaten
2 cups Italian seasoned bread crumbs, divided
¼ cup Parmesan cheese, divided
6 cloves garlic, crushed
3 tablespoons salad oil

Drain and finely-chop artichoke hearts. Add eggs, 1 cup crumbs and 2 tablespoons cheese; mix well. Saute garlic in salad oil; add to artichoke mixture and mix well. Refrigerate for 30 minutes. Combine 2 tablespoons Parmesan cheese and 1 cup bread crumbs. Roll artichoke mixture into balls, the size of a walnut; roll balls in crumb and cheese mixture. Refrigerate until served. Yield: about 25 balls.

SPINACH STUFFED SOLE

½ pounds fresh mushrooms, thickly sliced
2 tablespoons butter or margarine
½ pound fresh spinach, shredded
¼ teaspoon oregano, crushed
¼ teaspoon garlic powder
4 fillets of sole (about 1 pound) or any fish fillet
Juice from ½ lemon (about 1 tablespoon plus 1 teaspoon)
4 ounces sliced Mozzarella cheese

In medium-sized skillet, saute mushrooms in butter about 5 minutes or until tender. Add spinach. Continue cooking about 1 minute or until spinach is barely wilted. Remove from heat. Drain. Add oregano and garlic powder and mix. Place ¼ mixture in center of each fillet. Roll fillet around mixture and place, seam side down, in greased 1 ½ quart shallow baking dish. Sprinkle with lemon juice. Cover each roll with 1 slice of cheese. Bake in 425° oven for 20-25 minutes or until fish is done. Sprinkle with paprika, if desired. 4 servings. NOTE: Substitute 1 package (10 ounce) thawed frozen chopped spinach (well drained) for fresh spinach. After sauteeing mushrooms, remove from heat and drain. Stir in spinach, oregano and garlic powder. Continue as in recipe above.

PARSLEY BUTTERED POTATOES

6-9 medium potatoes, pared and quartered
½ cup (1 stick) butter or margarine, melted

¼ cup finely minced fresh parsley

Place potatoes in boiling water, just to cover. Cook until just tender. Place in serving dish. Pour on butter and sprinkle with parsley. 6-9 servings.

BAKED TOMATOES DELUXE

3 (14 ½ ounce) cans diced tomatoes
³/₄ cup sugar
1 ½ cups coarse bread crumbs (left over biscuit)

1 teaspoon salt
¼ teaspoon pepper
3 tablespoons butter or margarine

Combine tomatoes, sugar, crumbs, salt and pepper. Pour into greased 1 ½ quart baking dish. Dot with butter. Bake in 350° oven about 35-40 minutes until brown and bubbly. 6-9 servings.

CHIFFONADE DRESSING

1 cup French dressing
2 teaspoons finely chopped parsley
2 teaspoons finely chopped pimiento
1 teaspoon chopped capers

2 hard cooked eggs, yolks and whites
chopped separately
¼ teaspoon salt
⅛ teaspoon cayenne pepper

Just before serving, combine French dressing with remaining ingredients. Mix well. Yield: 1 ½ cups.

ORANGE CHIFFON PIE

4 eggs, separated
1 envelope unflavored gelatin
³/₄ cup sugar, divided
½ cup orange juice
¼ teaspoon salt
2 tablespoons lemon juice

2 teaspoons grated orange peel
¼ teaspoon cream of tartar
1 cup whipping cream, whipped
1 9-inch Graham cracker crust
Orange slices, optional

In small mixing bowl, beat egg yolks at high speed until thick and lemon colored, about 5 minutes. In medium saucepan, combine gelatin, ¼ cup sugar, orange juice and salt. Let stand 1 minute. Gradually stir in beaten yolks. Cook, stirring constantly, over medium heat until mixture thickens slightly, about 5 minutes. Remove from heat and stir in lemon juice and orange peel. Chill, stirring occasionally, until mixture mounds when dropped from a spoon, 30-45 minutes. Wash and dry beaters. In large mixing bowl, beat egg whites and cream of tartar at high speed until foamy. Add remaining ½ cup sugar, 1 tablespoon at a time, beating constantly, until sugar is dissolved* and whites are glossy and stand at soft peaks. Fold chilled yolk mixture and whipped cream into egg whites. Pile mixture into crust. Chill until firm, at least 3 hours. Garnish with orange slices, if desired.
*Rub a bit of meringue between thumb and forefinger to feel if sugar has dissolved.

WEDNESDAY
Dean's Zucchini Parmesan *
Cottage fried and steamed potatoes
Green beans with ham chips
Carrot and celery sticks / Cornsticks
Pound cake with fresh peach sauce

DEAN'S ZUCCHINI PARMESAN

1 pound ground beef	1 teaspoon salt
2 medium sized onions, chopped	1/4 teaspoon garlic salt
1 large green onion, chopped	1 cup (4 ounces) shredded Cheddar cheese
2 tablespoons olive oil	1 teaspoon oregano
1 (10 ounce) can tomatoes and green chilies	1/4 teaspoon black pepper
1 (8 ounce) can tomato sauce	4 medium zucchini, sliced 1/4 inch thick
1 (6 ounce) can tomato paste	1/2 cup grated Parmesan cheese
1 large green pepper, chopped	

Saute beef and onions in oil until beef is cooked and onion is tender, stirring constantly. Add tomatoes and green chilies, tomato sauce, tomato paste and green pepper; simmer for 10 minutes. Add salt, garlic salt, Cheddar cheese, oregano and pepper. Add zucchini and simmer 10 minutes while stirring. Place in greased 2 quart baking dish and sprinkle Parmesan cheese on top. Bake in preheated 350° oven for 15 minutes. 6-8 servings.

THURSDAY
Split pea soup *
Egg salad sandwiches
Crunchy celery slaw *
Cherry cobbler

SPLIT PEA SOUP

2 cups dry split peas (not necessary to pre-cook)	1/2 cup finely-chopped carrots
2 quarts water	1/2 cup finely-chopped onion
1 or 2 ham hocks	1 tablespoon lemon juice
1/2 cup finely-chopped celery	Salt and pepper to taste

Place first 6 ingredients into a large kettle. Boil gently about 2 hours or until the consistency desired for soup. Remove ham hock. If desired, press peas through a coarse sieve or processor to get puree. Remove meat from bone and chop. Return to soup. Add lemon juice, add salt and pepper to taste. Add water, if needed, while cooking. 8 servings.

CRUNCHY CELERY SLAW

4 cups thinly sliced celery	2 tablespoons cider vinegar
1/3 cup coarsely-chopped carrots	2 teaspoons salt
1/2 cup raisins	1/2 teaspoon ground white paper
1/2 cup coarsely-chopped walnuts	2/3 cup plain yogurt
1/3 cup salad oil	

In a large bowl, combine celery with carrots, raisins and walnuts; set aside. Blend together oil, vinegar, salt and pepper; stir in yogurt. Pour over celery mixture; toss lightly. Serve on lettuce leaves, if desired. 8 servings.

FRIDAY
Cajun shrimp *
Buttered rice
Peas with sauteed onions
Congealed spring salad
French bread
Frosted fudge cake *

CAJUN SHRIMP

1 pound shrimp, raw, peeled
2 tablespoons butter or margarine
3 cloves garlic, crushed
¹/₄ cup lemon juice
3 tablespoons Worcestershire sauce
2 tablespoons Pickapeppa sauce

¹/₄ teaspoon cayenne pepper
³/₄ teaspoon salt
4 drops hot pepper sauce
1 teaspoon sugar
¹/₄ cup white wine (optional)

In medium-sized skillet, melt butter; add garlic, cook until golden color, not brown. In a small bowl, combine the remaining ingredients. Add to garlic butter. Bring to a boil; turn heat down, simmer for 5 minutes. Add shrimp; bring to a boil and cook for 5 minutes or until the shrimp has turned pink. Serve shrimp in an au gratin dish with lots of the liquor or on rice. If rice is not used, serve hard bread for dunking in the juice. 2-4 servings.

FROSTED FUDGE CAKE

2 cups sugar
2 cups flour
1 cup butter or margarine (2 sticks)
¹/₄ cup cocoa
1 cup water

¹/₂ cup buttermilk
2 eggs, slightly beaten
1 teaspoon soda
1 teaspoon vanilla

In a large mixing bowl, combine sugar and flour. In a saucepan, combine butter or margarine, cocoa and water. Bring to a boil; pour over sugar mixture; stir well by hand. Add buttermilk, eggs, soda and vanilla. Mix well and pour into a greased 9x13-inch pan. Bake at 375° for 45-50 minutes, or until cake leaves sides of pan. Five minutes before cake is done, prepare frosting; pour over hot cake.

Frosting

¹/₂ cup butter or margarine (1 stick)
¹/₄ cup cocoa
¹/₄ cup plus 2 tablespoons milk

1 cup chopped pecans
1 teaspoon vanilla
1 (16 ounce) box confectioner's sugar

In a saucepan, combine butter, cocoa and milk. Heat until butter melts and mixture boils rapidly while stirring constantly. Remove from heat, add vanilla and sugar and beat until smooth. Add nuts, mix well. Pour on hot cake. Cool in refrigerator about 1 hour before serving.

SATURDAY
Best-ever chicken casserole *
Broccoli with lemon butter
Fresh vegetable relish tray
Whole wheat bread
Lemon bisque

BEST-EVER CHICKEN CASSEROLE

2 cups cooked, coarsely-chopped chicken	*3 ounces slivered almonds*
4 hard-cooked eggs	*1 teaspoon salt*
2 cups cooked rice	*2 tablespoons lemon juice*
1 ½ cups celery, chopped	*1 cup bread crumbs*
1 medium onion, chopped	*2 tablespoons butter or margarine, melted*
1 cup mayonnaise	*Grated Parmesan or Romano cheese (optional)*
2 (10 ½ ounce) cans cream of mushroom soup	

Preheat oven to 350°. Combine all ingredients except bread crumbs, butter and cheese. Pour into a 9x13-inch baking dish. Combine bread crumbs with melted butter or margarine. Spread over chicken mixture. Top with cheese. Bake in oven for 50 minutes. Serve hot. 6-8 servings.

April - Second Week

HEADING THE LIST OF ESSENTIALS for good health is protein, necessary for building and repairing body tissues. It is known that fish — along with meat, milk, egg and cheese — contains abundant amounts of excellent proteins. Seafood has more of this protein per ounce than either meat or dairy products and is higher in amino acids than meat, dairy products or any vegetable or cereal grain. The protein composition of fish is similar to that of human tissue and is, therefore, more easily used by the body.

Just four ounces of fish will supply about half of the total protein required each day. The rest can easily be supplied by cereal, vegetables and dairy products. Although different kinds of fish differ in fat content, all fish are lower in fat than other red meats. The fats found in fish are of polyunsaturated, which is of great importance in planning today's diet.

Fish that live on or near the ocean bottom are considered "lean fish" and the fat content is not more than 5 percent. These lean fish, often called ground fish, are sea trout, sheepshead, grouper, black and red drum, flounder, snapper and bluefish. In lean fish, the fat is concentrated in the liver.

Fish that swim near the surface of the sea are generally called "fat fish." In these fish the oil is distributed all through the tissues. These fish include Spanish mackerel, pompano and mullet. The fat content is over 5 percent. All shellfish, oysters, clams, scallops, shrimp, lobster and crabs, are considered lean fish. Shellfish have some carbohydrate in the form of glycogen in their makeup. From this comes the sweet taste.

Carbohydrate content of fish is low and not of real consequence, since the average diet gets enough from other foods. Minerals are not required by the body in large amounts, but the small amount needed can be supplied by fish and shellfish. Minerals supplied by seafoods are iodine, calcium, magnesium, chlorine, potassium, phosphorus and sulfur. The iron content of fish is a little less than that of red meat. An average serving of 6 oysters provides more iron than the daily adult requirements.

Fish and shellfish contain adequate amounts of vitamins which are extremely important to good health. Fish liver oil supplies vitamins A and D which are fat soluble. Fish also supply adequate amounts of water-soluble B vitamins, such as thiamine, riboflavin, niacin, pyridoxine, biotin and B12.

Fish, combined with fruits and vegetables, can furnish all vitamins that are necessary for good nutrition. With the plus of easy fixing and eating, seafood just makes good sense in today's world.

SUNDAY
Easter Dinner with All the Frills
Rolled roast leg of lamb with apricot filling *
Oven steamed and baked potatoes *
Baked spinach and artichokes *
Tomato aspic with avocado and celery *
Cheese biscuits *
Coconut cream pie *

Plan Of Work

Day before:
1. Prepare aspic.
2. Prepare coconut cream pie
3. Prepare spinach and refrigerate.
4 Hours before dinner is served:
4. Prepare lamb roast and put in oven.
1 ¹/₂ hours before dinner is served:
5. Prepare potatoes and place in oven. Remove from oven before raising heat on lamb. Return to warm.
6. Put spinach in oven. Remove before raising heat on lamb. Return to warm.
7. Prepare biscuits, hold in refrigerator until lamb is removed from oven. Raise temperature and cook.

ROLLED ROAST OF LAMB WITH APRICOT FILLING

1 (8 ounce) package of dried apricot halves	*4 tablespoons butter or margarine at room*
2 tablespoons lemon juice	*temperature*
1 teaspoon salt	*¹/₂ teaspoon garlic powder*
1 cup water	*¹/₂ (8 ounce) package herbed bread stuffing*
1 (5 ounce) can sliced water chestnuts,	*7 pound leg of lamb, boned, trimmed of fat*
drained and diced	*(reserve bones)*

Put apricots into a saucepan and bring to a boil with lemon juice, salt and 1 cup of water. Simmer, covered, 5 minutes, then drain, reserving the liquid. When cool enough to handle, cut each apricot half into 3 or 4 pieces. Mix apricots with the rest of the ingredients, except lamb. Add enough of the reserved apricot liquid to bring to the consistency of a spread. Open out the leg of lamb and spread the apricot stuffing evenly over the inside. Then roll up the lamb and tie well with kitchen twine. Wrap rolled lamb with its bones around it in a tight package of heavy-duty foil. Refrigerate over night. Two hours before cooking time remove from refrigerator. Do not unwrap. Put lamb package in a shallow baking pan in a preheated 375° oven and roast, allowing 35 minutes per pound of lamb (weighed without bones). Remove from oven 30 minutes before end of cooking time. Raise the temperature to 400°. Unwrap lamb, discard bones, and return lamb to pan. Put back in oven 30 minutes to brown. Let stand 20 minutes before carving. 8 servings.

OVEN STEAMED AND BAKED POTATOES

6 large potatoes
3 tablespoons vegetable oil

Salt to taste
Pepper to taste

Peel potatoes. Rub with oil and put in baking dish. Sprinkle with salt and pepper. Cover with aluminum foil. Bake in 350° oven for 30 minutes. Remove foil, turn potatoes and continue to bake 30 minutes until potatoes are cooked and slightly brown. 6 servings.

BAKED SPINACH AND ARTICHOKES

3 (10 ounce) packages frozen chopped spinach
1 tablespoon butter or margarine
Salt to taste (optional)
2 (6.5 ounce) jars marinated artichokes,
drained, reserve juice

3 (3 ounce) packages cream cheese
¼ cup (½ stick) butter or margarine
¼ cup plus 2 tablespoons milk
¼ teaspoon pepper
⅓ cup grated Parmesan cheese

Cook spinach according to package directions. Drain very thoroughly. Season with butter, salt and liquid from 1 jar of artichokes. Cut artichokes in small pieces and spread over bottom of 1 ½ quart baking dish. Spread spinach over artichokes. Place cheese, butter, milk and pepper in blender. Blend until smooth. Pour cheese mixture over spinach. Sprinkle with Parmesan cheese. Refrigerate about 24 hours before cooking in a 375° oven for 35-40 minutes. 6-8 servings.

TOMATO ASPIC WITH AVOCADO AND CELERY

2 envelopes unflavored gelatin
½ cup cold water
2 cups tomato juice or vegetable juice
1 medium onion, sliced
3 sprigs parsley, chopped
2 tablespoons cider vinegar

1 tablespoon lemon juice
2 teaspoons sugar
½ teaspoon salt
1 cup diced avocado
½ cup finely-chopped celery
Calorie reduced mayonnaise

Soften gelatin in cold water. Combine remaining ingredients except avocado and celery. Simmer about 15 minutes and then strain, if desired. Add gelatin to hot juice and stir. Chill until partially set; add avocado and celery. Pour into individual molds or one large ring mold and chill until set. Unmold on curly lettuce and serve with mayonnaise on the side. 4-6 servings.

CHEESY BUTTER BISCUITS

3 cups biscuit mix
1 cup milk
³/₄ cup (3 ounces) shredded Cheddar cheese, divided

½ teaspoon garlic powder
¼ cup (½ stick) butter or margarine

Combine biscuit mix, milk, ½ cup cheese and garlic powder. Form ball. If dough is too sticky, gradually mix in enough biscuit mix to make dough easy to handle. Be careful not to add too much biscuit mix. Turn onto surface dusted with biscuit mix. Shape into balls. Roll in melted butter and place on ungreased cookie sheet. With a fork, flatten to within ½ inch and brush top surface with melted butter and remaining cheese. Bake in 450° oven for 8-10 minutes. 16- 18 biscuits.

COCONUT CREAM PIE

1 cup sugar, divided	*1 cup flaked coconut, divided*
3 tablespoons cornstarch	*2 tablespoons butter*
¼ teaspoon salt	*1 ½ teaspoons vanilla, divided*
3 eggs, separated	*½ teaspoon cream of tartar*
2 cups milk	*1 (9 inch) deep dish pie shell, baked*

In medium saucepan, combine ⅔ cup sugar, cornstarch and salt. In bowl beat together egg yolks and milk until blended. Gradually stir milk mixture into sugar mixture. Cook over medium heat, stirring constantly, until mixture thickens and bubbles. Boil, stirring constantly, for 1 minute. Remove from heat. Stir in ¾ cup coconut, butter and 1 tablespoon vanilla. Pour into baked pie shell. Set aside. In large mixing bowl, beat egg whites and cream of tartar at high speed until foamy. Add remaining ⅓ cup sugar, 1 tablespoon at a time, beating constantly, until sugar is dissolved and whites are glossy and stand in soft peaks. Beat in remaining ½ teaspoon vanilla. Spread meringue over filling, starting with small amounts at edges and sealing to crust all around. Cover pie with remaining meringue, spreading evenly in attractive swirls. Sprinkle with remaining ¼ cup coconut. Bake in 350° oven until peaks are lightly browned, 12-15 minutes. Cool at room temperature.

Banana cream pie:

Prepare cream filling as above, omitting coconut. Peel and slice 3 medium bananas. Arrange half of banana slices over bottom of pie shell. Cover with half of filling. Top with remaining banana slices and filling. Prepare meringue, spread over filling and bake as above. 1 9-inch deep dish pie.

MONDAY
A Neighborly Lunch
Mulligatawny soup *
Cantaloupe and melon chunks, no dressing
Cream cheese and olive sandwich on whole wheat bread
Orange yogurt

MULLIGATAWNY SOUP

1 large green apple (Granny Smith),	*¼ cup flour*
coarsely chopped	*2 cups water or chicken broth*
2 large carrots, scraped and sliced ½ inch thick	*1 (8 ounce) can tomato sauce*
¼ cup chopped celery	*2 teaspoons instant chicken bouillon or 8 cubes*
1 small green pepper, cut in small pieces	*1 teaspoon curry powder*
1 cup chopped onion	*Salt and pepper to taste*
2 tablespoons butter	*2 cups cubed cooked chicken*

Cook apples, carrots, celery, green peppers and onions in butter, stirring constantly, until tender. Stir in flour and mix thoroughly. Add remaining ingredients and simmer 1 hour. Freeze leftovers. 6-8 servings. Celery, green peppers, onion, curry powder and chicken may be increased as desired.

TUESDAY
Baked chicken slices
Cauliflower and nut casserole *
Mashed potatoes
Popovers
Greek salad

CAULIFLOWER AND NUT CASSEROLE

1 medium head cauliflower (about 2 pounds),   *1 teaspoon dry mustard*
  broken into flowerets   *¹/₃ cup coarsely chopped pecans or walnuts*
1 cup sour cream   *¹/₃ cup coarsely chopped pecans or walnuts*
1 cup (4 ounces) shredded Cheddar cheese   *¹/₄ cup fine dry bread crumbs*
1 tablespoon flour   *1 tablespoon butter or margarine, melted*
2 teaspoons seasoned chicken stock base   *1 teaspoon dried marjoram leaves, crumbled*
  (or instant chicken bouillon)   *¹/₂ teaspoon onion salt*

Heat one inch of salted water (¹/₂ teaspoon salt to 1 cup water) in Dutch oven to boiling. Add cauliflower. Heat to boiling, reduce heat to low and cover. Simmer until tender, about 15 minutes; drain. Mix sour cream, cheese, flour, stock base, and mustard. Place cauliflower in baking dish, 10x6x2 inches. Spoon cheese mixture over cauliflower. Sprinkle nuts over the cheese layer. Combine bread crumbs, butter, marjoram and onion salt. Sprinkle over cheese and cauliflower. Bake in 400° oven until hot and bubbly, 15-20 minutes. 4-6 servings.

WEDNESDAY
Onion soup
Shrimp salad with mustard mayonnaise *
Ripe tomato slices
Hot French bread
Fresh peach compote, Cream cheese pound cake

SHRIMP SALAD WITH MUSTARD MAYONNAISE

4 pounds shrimp, cooked and peeled   *2 tablespoons finely-chopped onion*
2 ribs celery, chopped   *2 tablespoons Dijon mustard*
1 green bell pepper, chopped   *1 teaspoon dry mustard*
¹/₂ Vidalia or Bermuda onion, chopped   *1 tablespoon Worcestershire sauce*
1 teaspoon salt   *Salt to taste*
1 pint (2 cups) mayonnaise,   *Ground white pepper to taste*
  (homemade may be used)   *Lettuce*

Combine shrimp, celery, bell pepper, onion and 1 teaspoon salt in large mixing bowl. In medium bowl combine remaining ingredients except lettuce and mix well. Cover and chill. Toss with shrimp mixture. Line individual salad plates or large salad bowl with lettuce leaves. Turn shrimp mixture on the lettuce. 6 servings.

THURSDAY
Grilled ham slices
Steamed potatoes and green peppers
Squash pudding *
Apple and nut salad
Oatmeal cookies

SQUASH PUDDING

1 pound summer squash
2 tablespoons butter or margarine
1 egg, well beaten
1/2 cup half & half or milk

2 tablespoons brown sugar
1/4 teaspoon nutmeg
3/4 teaspoon salt
Pepper to taste

Slice squash in 1/2-inch slices. Cook in lightly salted water until tender; drain. Add butter, egg, half and half, brown sugar, nutmeg, salt and pepper; mix well. Place in 1-quart baking dish. Bake in 400° oven for 20 minutes. 4-6 servings.

FRIDAY
Good Friday and Lent Dinner
Baked Red Snapper with sour cream stuffing *
Sauteed whole kernel corn
Green beans with mushrooms
Pineapple and cucumber salad
French rolls
White Charlotte Russe with strawberry topping *

BAKED RED SNAPPER WITH SOUR CREAM STUFFING

3-4 pounds dressed Red Snapper or other
  dressed fish, fresh or frozen
1 1/2 teaspoons salt

Sour cream stuffing
2 tablespoons olive oil

Thaw frozen fish. Clean, wash and dry fish. Sprinkle inside and out with salt. Stuff fish loosely. Close opening with small skewers or wooden picks. Place fish in well-greased baking pan. Brush with fat. Bake in moderate oven, 350°, for 40-60 minutes or until fish flakes easily when tested with a fork. Baste occasionally with oil. Remove skewers. 6 servings.

Sour Cream Stuffing

3/4 cup chopped celery
1/2 cup chopped onion
1/4 cup (1/2 stick) melted butter or margarine, melted
1 quart dry bread crumbs
2 tablespoons grated lemon rind

1/4 cup lemon, peeled and diced
1/2 cup sour cream
1 teaspoon paprika
1 teaspoon salt

Cook celery and onion in butter until tender. Combine all ingredients and mix thoroughly. Makes approximately 1 quart stuffing.

WHITE CHARLOTTE RUSSE WITH STRAWBERRY TOPPING

³/₄ cup evaporated skimmed milk
1 envelope unflavored gelatin
¹/₄ cup water
2 egg whites, room temperature
¹/₄ cup sugar, divided

¹/₂ teaspoon lemon juice
2 tablespoons brandy
18 fresh strawberries, washed, stem ends
  removed, sliced

Pour milk in medium-sized bowl. Place in freezer until milk is partially frozen. Chill beaters. In a medium bowl, beat egg whites until frothy. Gradually add 2 tablespoons sugar. Whip until very stiff. In a very small saucepan, soften gelatin in water. Place over moderate heat and stir until dissolved. Cool. Whip partially-frozen milk until foamy. Gradually add remaining 2 tablespoons sugar and dissolved, cooled gelatin . Whip until very stiff. Fold beaten egg whites into whipped milk. Combine lemon juice and brandy. Fold brandy mixture into the whipped milk mixture. Pour into one-quart serving dish or individual serving dishes. Chill at least 2 hours before serving. Top each serving with sliced strawberries. 6 servings.

SATURDAY
Lunch
Italian minestrone *
Fresh garden salad with creamy Italian dressing
Sour dough rolls / Pineapple cake

ITALIAN MINESTRONE

2 tablespoons olive oil
2 medium onions, chopped
1 medium carrot, chopped
1 large or 2 medium ribs celery, sliced
2 cloves garlic, crushed
2 (14 ¹/₂ ounce) cans chicken or beef broth
1 (14 ¹/₂ ounce) can stewed tomatos, undrained
1 cup shredded cabbage
³/₄ cup vegetable juice
1 ¹/₂ teaspoons dried basil, crushed

1 (15 oz) can cannelloni or Great Northern
  beans, rinsed and drained
1 medium zucchini, sliced ¹/₄-inch thick
¹/₂ of a 9-oz pkg frozen Italian style greens
  beans or 5 ounces fresh broccoli
2 oz packaged spaghetti or linguine, broken
2 oz prosciutto or fully-cooked ham, diced
salt and pepper to taste
¹/₄ cup finely shredded Parmesan cheese

In a large Dutch oven or kettle, heat oil. Add onions, carrots, celery and garlic in hot oil. Cook until onion is tender but not brown. Stir in the chicken or beef broth, undrained tomatoes, cabbage, vegetable juice and basil. Bring to boiling; reduce heat. Cover and simmer for 20 minutes. Stir in the beans, zucchini, green beans or broccoli, spaghetti or linguine and prosciutto or ham. Return to boiling; reduce heat. Cover and simmer for 10 to 15 minutes more or until vegetables and pasta are tender. To serve, ladle soup into bowl; top with Parmesan cheese. 6-8 servings.

April - Third Week

Most varieties of fresh fish are more abundant during certain seasons of the year. It is important to be able to recognize the desirable characteristics of fresh fish.

Fresh fish in the whole or drawn form should have the following characteristics:

Flesh: Firm, elastic flesh not separating from the bones indicates that fish are fresh and have been carefully handled.

Odor: Fresh and mild. A fish just taken from the water has practically no "fishy" odor. The fishy odor becomes more pronounced with the passage of time, but it should not be disagreeably strong when the fish are purchased.

Eyes: Bright, clear and full. The eyes of the fresh fish are clear and transparent; as the fish becomes stale, the eyes become cloudy and often turn pink. When fish are fresh, the eyes often protrude, but with increasing staleness they tend to become sunken.

Gills: Red and free from slime. The color gradually fades with age to a light pink, then gray and finally brownish or greenish.

Skin: Shiny, with color unfaded. When first taken from the water, most fish have an iridescent appearance. Each species has its characteristic markings and colors that fade and become less pronounced as the fish loses freshness.

Fresh fillets and steaks are the most commonly-bought forms of fresh fish, and should be judged by the following standards:

Flesh: Fresh-cut in appearance; the color should resemble that of freshly-dressed fish. It should be firm in texture, without traces of browning around the edges and without the dried-out appearance which give evidence of moisture loss.

Odor: Fresh and mild, if any odor at all.

Wrapping: If the fillets or steaks are wrapped, the wrapping should be of moisture-proof, vapor-proof material. There should be little or no air space between the fish and the wrapping.

The many kinds of shellfish available today reveal the modernization of the processing, packaging and shipping of seafood. The common varieties of shellfish, shrimp, clams, oysters, crabs and lobsters, have distinct appearances and flavors. The most popular of the shellfish is shrimp. They are usually sold headless since the tail is the edible portion of the shrimp. These may be purchased fresh or frozen; in the shell or peeled. "Peeled" shrimp, with the shell removed, are also usually deveined (have had the sand vein removed).

Shrimp should have a mild odor with firm meat. The color of fresh shrimp varies with the species — Browns, Whites, Pinks, Royal Reds. The colorful names of the species describe the shrimp perfectly. Poorly-handled shrimp often have black spots on the meat and have a strong iodine flavor and smell. Shrimp are sold according to size or grade. Count refers to the number of headless shrimp per pound and may be described by such general terms as: Jumbo - 15 or less per pound; Large - 15-30 per pound; Medium - 30-42 per pound; and Small - 42 or more per pound.

Most people purchase clams and oysters in the fresh form, already shucked. However, if purchased in the shell, the clam or oyster should be alive, and the shell should close tightly when tapped gently. Freshly-shucked clams are pale orange to deep orange in color and are packed with little or no free liquor. Freshly-shucked oysters should be plump and have a natural creamy color and clear liquid. There should be no more than 10 percent liquid by weight when oysters are purchased in a container. An excess of liquid indicates poor quality and careless handling. Oysters are packed in three grades: Selects - large; Standard - medium; and Stewing - very small. Freshly-shucked clams and oysters, when packed on ice in the refrigerator and handled properly, will remain fresh from a week to 10 days.

Crabs and lobsters should show movement of the legs when they are to be purchased alive. Lobsters can be purchased cooked or uncooked, frozen in the shell. Cooked crabs and lobsters should have bright red shells and be free of any disagreeable odor. Cooked crabmeat can be purchased in 1-

pound cans as (1) lump meat - whole lumps of white meat from the large body muscles that operate the swimming legs, (2) flake meat - small pieces of white meat from the body, (3) flake and lump meat - a combination of the first two kinds, or (4) claw meat - brownish-tinted meat from the claws.

Pasteurized crab meat is also marketed in 1-pound cans. Pasteurization is a simple process which prolongs by months the shelf life of crabs under refrigeration. After crab meat is steam-cooked in the shell, the meat is picked from the shell and packed in 1-pound cans. The cans are hermetically sealed and placed in retorts which heat the crab meat to a specific temperature for a designated time capable of retarding bacterial growth.

Frozen lobster tails are mottled. The color of the shell varies with the species, but are usually described as olive green with white spots and tinges of reddish yellow to orange. The meat is white and clear, and should be hard frozen when purchased. They should have no odor.

While scallops grow to be quite large, a very small amount of meat is taken from each one in the United States because only the adductor muscle (the muscle which opens and closes the shell) is eaten. The scallop should have a sweetish odor before it is cooked. The meat of the large sea scallops is white, orange or pink, while the meat of the smaller calico or bay scallop is either creamy white, light tan or pinkish. The large sea scallop shell is saucer-shaped and grows as large as 8 inches in diameter. The abductor muscle in these sea scallops may be as large as 2 inches in diameter. Sea scallops are taken from deep water in the middle and north Atlantic states. Bay scallops are found in shallow waters from New England to the Gulf of Mexico. Calico scallops are strictly southern and produced mostly in North Carolina and Florida. They are found in deep water and resemble the bay scallop in flavor. The meat of the bay and calico scallop is much sweeter than that of the sea scallop.

SUNDAY
Casual Sunday Night Buffet
Tuna, nut pate with crackers
Cheesey lasagna
Squash wheels and mushrooms
Radicchio, orange and onion salad
Hot garlic Italian or French bread
Fresh strawberry compote
Cookie of choice

Plan Of Work
Day before:
1. Prepare tuna pate
2. Prepare meat mixture and cheese sauce for lasagna. (The whole dish may be prepared the day before; refrigerate and cook just before serving.)
3. Wash and remove stems of strawberries. Make puree. Dry remaining strawberries and store in air-tight plastic bags. Refrigerate until next day.
Early in the day:
4. Prepare bread and wrap in foil. Heat just before serving.
1 ½ hours before dinner:
5. Prepare vegetables; cover and refrigerate until cooked. Timing of cooking vegetables depends on method of cooking, microwave or convection oven.
1 hour before dinner:
6. Prepare salad. Assemble just before serving.
7. Cook lasagna.

TUNA, NUT PATE

2 (7½ ounce) cans tuna fish (water packed) drained and flaked	½ to 1 cup sour cream
1 cup coarsely chopped pecans or walnuts	Tabasco sauce to taste
2 (1¼ ounce) packages Italian salad dressing mix	2 tablespoons chopped pimiento, drained
	Parsley sprigs or coarse ground pepper

Combine tuna, nuts and dressing mix. Mix thoroughly. Add sour cream to the desired consistency and Tabasco; mix thoroughly. Put into a 1-quart mold. Chill until ready to serve. Unmold on plate and smooth with spoon. Garnish with pimiento and parsley sprigs and sprinkle top with coarse ground black pepper. Serve with a spatula on assorted crackers.

CHEESY LASAGNA

10 ounces lasagna noodles, barely cooked (al dente)	Sauce
Meat mixture	½-pound (2 cups) sharp Cheddar cheese, shredded

Place half the noodles in a greased 13x9-inch baking pan. Add a thick layer of the meat mixture, then a layer of sauce. Repeat layers. Top with shredded Cheddar cheese. Bake at 325° for 20 minutes. Can be made the day before and refrigerated, then baked as needed. 6 servings.

Meat Mixture

1 pound hamburger or bulk sausage	2 (6 ounce) cans tomato paste
1 tablespoon oil (optional)	1 cup water
1 large onion, chopped	1 bay leaf, crushed
6 sprigs fresh parsley, chopped	Salt to taste
3 cloves garlic, crushed	Pepper to taste
3 ½ cups whole peeled tomatoes, diced (28-ounce can or use fresh)	

Heat oil in skillet. Add meat, onion, parsley and garlic. Cook until meat is lightly browned. Add tomatoes, tomato paste, water, bay leaf, salt and pepper. Simmer, uncovered, for 45 minutes.

Sauce

¼ cup (½ stick) butter or margarine	3 egg yolks, slightly beaten
1 onion, chopped fine	1 cup grated Parmesan cheese
3 tablespoons flour	1 cup shredded Cheddar cheese
2 cups milk	

Melt butter in medium-sized skillet; cook onions until tender, not browned. Stir in flour. Slowly stir in milk and cook over low heat until smooth and thickened. Stir a small amount of sauce into egg yolks. Return all egg mixture to the sauce, add both cheeses and cook, stirring, over low heat until cheese is melted.

SQUASH WHEELS AND MUSHROOMS

2 cups (½ pound) yellow squash, cut in ¼-inch slices	1 teaspoon basil leaves
2 cups (½ pound) zucchini, cut in ¼-inch slices	¼ teaspoon salt
1 ½ cups (¼ pound) whole mushrooms	⅛ teaspoon pepper
2 tablespoons butter, margarine or olive oil, melted	⅛ teaspoon garlic powder
	¼ cup grated Parmesan cheese

Arrange squash in four sections in a ring in a 10-inch pie plate, alternating yellow and zucchini squash for color. Place mushrooms in center of pie plate. Drizzle melted butter or oil over all. Sprinkle with basil, salt, pepper, garlic powder and cheese. Cover with plastic wrap, turning back one edge to vent. Cook in microwave on high power setting for 5-6 minutes or until vegetables are tender-crisp, turning dish once. Let stand 2 minutes before serving. 4-6 servings. NOTE: If conventional oven is used, cover with foil and bake 35-45 minutes.

RADICCHIO, ORANGE AND ONION SALAD

6 large navel oranges
1 teaspoon red wine vinegar
1/2 teaspoon salt
Pepper to taste
3 tablespoons olive oil, divided

1 large head of radicchio (about 1/2 pound) shredded into 1/2-inch strips
1 large red or Vidalia onion, sliced crossways, about 1/8- 1/4-inch thick, keep slices intact

Remove orange peel and membrane with sawing motion. Over a bowl, release segments from orange. Squeeze the membrane to extract all the juice. Whisk vinegar into orange juice, add salt and pepper to taste; whisk 2 tablespoons olive oil into juice until incorporated. In medium bowl, toss radicchio with half the dressing. Toss orange segments with remaining dressing, add pepper to taste. Arrange radicchio and orange on large serving platter.*
Saute onion slices in 1 tablespoon oil until tender and slightly browned. Keep slices whole. Arrange onions on top of salad and serve. 6 servings.
* Individual salads may be served.

HOT GARLIC ITALIAN BREAD

1 (8 ounce) loaf Italian bread
1/2 cup butter or margarine, softened

1-2 teaspoons garlic salt

Slice bread into 1/2-inch slices, do not cut all the way through. Butter one side of each slice. Sprinkle over butter with garlic salt. Wrap in aluminum foil and heat. 6 servings.

FRESH STRAWBERRY COMPOTE

1/3 cup sugar
1 cup orange-flavored liqueur *
2 pints whole fresh strawberries, washed and stemmed

1 cup whipping cream, whipped stiff and sweetened to taste, or 2 cups whipped topping

Combine sugar and liqueur. Reserve 4-6 attractive berries for garnish. Add remaining berries to sugar mixture, tossing gently to coat. Marinate in refrigerator for 2-3 hours. Puree enough marinated berries to make one cup; fold into whipped cream. Spoon remaining berries and juice into 4-6 stemmed glasses. Top with whipped cream and garnish with the reserved berries. 4-6 servings. * Orange juice may be used for children.

MONDAY
Broiled fish fillet with lemon butter
Brussels sprouts with cheese sauce *
Steamed cauliflower
Apple and nut salad
Whole wheat toast triangles
Cherry cheesecake

BRUSSELS SPROUTS WITH CHEESE SAUCE

2-3 (10 ounce) packages frozen Brussels sprouts	1/8 teaspoon black pepper
2 tablespoons butter or margarine	1/4 teaspoon dry mustard
2 tablespoons flour	1 cup milk
1/4 teaspoon onion powder	1 cup shredded processed or sharp Cheddar cheese

Cook Brussels sprouts according to package directions; drain. In one-quart saucepan, melt butter, blend in flour, onion powder, pepper and mustard. Add milk, stirring to make a smooth mixture. Cook over low heat, stirring constantly, until mixture thickens. Add cheese, continue to cook and stir until cheese is melted. Correct seasoning. Serve over Brussels sprouts. 6 servings

TUESDAY
Chicken, dressing and broccoli *
Cole slaw and orange slices
Fruit cocktail pudding and sauce

CHICKEN, DRESSING AND BROCCOLI

4 cups herb seasoned stuffing cubes	3 green onions with tops, thinly sliced
1 (10 ounce) package frozen chopped broccoli	6 eggs, beaten
1 cup cooked, cubed chicken	1 1/2 cups milk
1/2 cup shredded Cheddar cheese	2 tablespoons blanched almonds, sliced

Place 2 cups of the stuffing cubes in a greased 8x8x2-inch baking dish. Layer broccoli, chicken, cheese and onions over stuffing. Sprinkle with remaining stuffing cubes. Combine eggs and milk. Pour over casserole mixture. Top with sliced almonds. Cover and refrigerate several hours or overnight. Bake in a 350° oven until golden brown, about 50-60 minutes. 4-6 servings.

WEDNESDAY
Popover Pizza Bake *
Chef's salad with French dressing
Cappucino Creme *

POPOVER PIZZA BAKE
Base

1 pound ground beef	1 (10 1/2 ounce) can pizza sauce with cheese
1 pound fresh mushrooms, sliced	1 teaspoon oregano, crushed
1/2 cup chopped green pepper	1 teaspoon garlic salt
1/2 cup chopped onion	1 1/2 cups (6 ounces) shredded Mozzarella cheese

Popover Top

2 eggs	1/2 teaspoon salt
1 cup milk	1/2 cup grated Parmesan cheese
1 tablespoon vegetable oil	1/2 cup thinly-sliced ripe pitted olives (optional)
1 cup all-purpose flour	

In large skillet or Dutch oven, cook and stir ground beef, mushrooms, green pepper and onion until meat is browned. Thoroughly drain off fat. Stir in pizza sauce, oregano and garlic salt. Simmer 10 minutes. Meanwhile, prepare Popover Top. In small bowl of electric mixer, blend together eggs, milk and oil. Add flour and salt. Beat at medium speed about 1 ½ minutes or until smooth. Do not over-beat. Spoon hot beef mixture into shallow 2-quart baking dish. Sprinkle with Mozzarella cheese. Pour top evenly over base. Sprinkle with Parmesan cheese and olives. Bake in 400° oven for 30 minutes or until puffy and golden brown. Serve immediately. 6-8 servings. **Note**: If prepared spaghetti sauce is available or frozen, use 3 or 4 cups and eliminate the base, and add cooked ground beef.

CAPPUCINO CREME

1 (7 ounce) jar marshmallow creme   *³/₄ cup finely-chopped almonds*
1 cup coffee-flavored yogurt or ice cream

Mix all ingredients with electric mixer until well-blended. Pour into 4 dessert or parfait dishes; freeze. 4 servings. (Walnuts may be substituted for almonds.)

THURSDAY
Chopped steak with Oriental mushroom sauce *
Buttered noodles
Sauteed green and red peppers
Beet and onion salad
Fruit and oatmeal cookies

CHOPPED STEAK WITH ORIENTAL MUSHROOM SAUCE

2 pounds ground round steak   *¹/₄ teaspoon pepper*
¹/₂ cup beef bouillon   *¹/₄ cup cracker crumbs*
¹/₂ teaspoon onion salt

Combine meat, bouillon, onion salt, pepper and cracker crumbs. Mix thoroughly. Shape into 6 patties. Pan broil or oven broil to desired doneness. Serve topped with Oriental mushroom sauce. 6 servings

ORIENTAL MUSHROOM SAUCE

2 tablespoons bottled oyster sauce   *¹/₄ cup (¹/₂ stick) butter or margarine*
2 tablespoons dry sherry   *1 pound small fresh mushrooms*
2 teaspoons soy sauce   *¹/₄ cup finely-chopped onion*
¹/₂ teaspoon sugar

Combine oyster sauce, sherry, soy sauce and sugar. Set aside. In large skillet, heat butter over medium heat until sizzling. Add mushrooms and onion. Cook about 10 minutes or until liquid has evaporated and mushrooms and onion begin to turn golden brown around edges. Reduce heat to medium. Add oyster sauce mixture. Cook and stir 1-2 minutes or until mushrooms are glossy and sauce thickens. Serve over chopped steaks. 2 cups.

> *"Friends are like good melons. Shall I tell you why? To find one good, you must a hundred try."*
>
> *Claude Mermet*
> *French Poet*

Crab cakes *
Baked potatoes
Buttered carrots
Cabbage and apple salad
Corn muffins
Ice cream with toffee nut sauce

CRAB CAKES

1 ½ slices fresh white sandwich bread	*½ teaspoon ground mustard*
3 egg whites or 2 whole eggs	*¼ teaspoon ground allspice*
1 tablespoon mayonnaise	*¼ teaspoon cayenne pepper*
1 ½ tablespoons lemon juice	*3 tablespoons fresh parsley or 1 tablespoon dried*
2 teaspoons Worcestershire Sauce	*1 pound fresh lump crabmeat or 2 (7 ½ ounce)*
1 ¼ teaspoon paprika	*cans white crabmeat*
½ teaspoon curry powder	*2 teaspoons olive oil*

Place bread in a food processor and process to soft crumbs. Set aside. In medium bowl, combine egg whites or eggs, mayonnaise, lemon juice, Worcestershire sauce, paprika, curry powder, mustard, allspice, cayenne and parsley. Add crabmeat and bread crumbs and toss gently, taking care not to break up crabmeat lumps. Shape mixture into a dozen ⅔-inch thick patties and place on a baking sheet lined with wax paper. Refrigerate for 20 minutes to dry out patties slightly. (Can be made a day ahead; cover with plastic wrap and refrigerate.) In a 10-inch non-stick skillet, heat 1 teaspoon olive oil (more if desired) over moderate heat. Add half of the patties and fry until golden brown, about 3 minutes on each side. Repeat with other half of patties. Keep warm. Serve immediately. 12 patties.

Baked pork loin
Almond pilaf *
Fresh green beans with Savory
Tomato and cottage cheese salad
One-hour hot rolls
Saucy baked apple

ALMOND PILAF

2 tablespoons butter or margarine	*½ cup currants*
1 small onion, chopped	*3 cups chicken broth or stock*
2 cups long grain rice	*¼ cup (1 ounce) toasted, slivered almonds*

In a medium flame-proof baking dish, melt butter over moderate heat. Add the onion and saute until softened, about 2 minutes. Add the rice and stir until the grains are well-coated; stir in the currants. Add the stock and bring to a boil. Cover baking dish, reduce heat to low, and simmer about 15 minutes or until the liquid is absorbed. Remove from heat and stir in almonds. Serve hot. 6-8 servings.

April - Fourth Week

FISH AND SHELLFISH MUST BE KEPT under refrigeration or packed in ice to preserve freshness and flavor. The three primary causes of breakdown in the quality of fish are bacterial action, oxidation of the oil or flesh, and enzymic action in the flesh. When frozen or stored at very low temperatures, fish will remain fresh and tasty several months since the bacterial and enzymic action will be retarded. Using moisture- and vapor-proof material for wrapping will prevent excessive oxidation.

Fresh fish should be stored in the refrigerator at 35° or 40° in their original wrappers immediately after they are received, and are at their best in quality if used the day of purchase. However, they can be kept in the meat keeper or coldest part of the refrigerator or packed in ice for two days.

Fresh shellfish are best if used the day of purchase, but they may be kept in the refrigerator on ice for two days with the exception of oysters and clams which may be held for a week to ten days if packed in ice in the refrigerator. If the shellfish is not to be used the day it is purchased, however, it is best to freeze it as soon as possible, always wrapping it in moisture- and vapor-proof material.

The most highly recommended method for freezing fish to prevent drying out and moisture loss is glazing. This method coats the fish with ice, causing a seal which prevents drying. It is as efficient as the better known method of freezing the fish in a block of ice, and takes less freezer space for storage. To glaze the fish, clean it, place in a single layer on a tray loosely wrapped. As soon as the fish is frozen, dip it quickly in ice cold water. If the fish is completely frozen, a glaze will form immediately. If the glaze does not form, return the fish to the freezer until it is completely frozen. Repeat the glazing process three or four times. A thin coat of ice will result from each dipping. Handle the fish carefully to keep from breaking the glaze. Wrap the fish in air-tight wrapping such as aluminum foil, polyethylene or laminated papers.

Thawing of fish should be scheduled so that fish is used as soon as possible after it is thawed. Fishery products should never be re-frozen and they should be used the same day they are thawed. Thaw fish by placing it in the refrigerator in its wrapping. Allow 18 to 24 hours for a 1-pound package. If it must be thawed more quickly, place the package under cold running water to thaw. Allow 1 to 2 hours for a 1-pound package. Never thaw fish in warm water or at room temperature because flavor, moisture and freshness are lost. The bacteria in fish grow rapidly at room temperature and cause a marked decrease in the quality of the fish.

SUNDAY
Fish fillets Parmigiana *
Buttered broccoli spears
Crisp spinach salad with orange segments and almond slivers
Bran Muffins
Peach shortcake

FISH FILLET PARMIGIANA

1 (8 ounce) can tomato sauce
1 teaspoon oregano leaves
2 teaspoons Worcestershire sauce
1 pound fish fillets, cut into 8 equal portions
Salt to taste

Pepper to taste
½ cup chopped onion
4 slices American cheese, folded in half
¼ cup crushed potato chips
2 tablespoons grated Parmesan cheese

In a small bowl, combine tomato sauce, oregano and Worcestershire sauce. Spoon half of sauce into 10x8x2- inch baking dish. Add 4 fillets; sprinkle with salt, pepper and onion. Top each with cheese and a second fillet. Spoon remaining sauce over fish. Cook in 350° oven for 20 to 25 minutes. To serve, combine potato chips and Parmesan cheese; sprinkle on fish while hot. Let stand several minutes before serving. 4 servings.

MONDAY
Beef Julienne with asparagus *
Buttered rice
Fresh vegetable medley with French dressing
French bread and butter
Sugar cookies *

BEEF JULIENNE WITH ASPARAGUS

1 ½ pounds boneless round steak	*⅛ teaspoon pepper*
2 tablespoons butter or margarine	*1 ½ cups beef broth*
1 clove garlic, crushed	*¼ cup cornstarch*
¼ cup finely chopped onion	*⅓ cup water*
1 (12 ounce) package frozen cut asparagus	*1 (4 ounce) can mushrooms, unsliced*
2 teaspoons salt	*3 cups hot cooked rice*

Cut meat into strips about 3 inches long and ⅛ inch thick. Saute meat, garlic and onions in butter over medium heat, stirring constantly, until meat loses its red color. Add asparagus, salt, pepper and beef broth to skillet and bring to a boil. Lower heat, cover and simmer 8 - 10 minutes, or until asparagus is just tender. It should not be overcooked. Blend cornstarch with water. Add to beef-asparagus mixture, add mushrooms. Cook until thickened and clear. Serve over hot rice. 6 servings.

SUGAR COOKIES

1 cup butter or margarine, softened	*1 cup all-purpose flour*
1 cup granulated sugar	*1 teaspoon soda*
1 cup powdered sugar	*½ teaspoon salt*
1 cup vegetable oil, minus 1 tablespoon	*1 teaspoon cream of tartar*
2 eggs, well beaten	*Granulated sugar*
1 teaspoon vanilla	

Cream butter; gradually add granulated sugar and powdered sugar while beating. Add oil, eggs and vanilla and beat until well mixed. Combine flour, soda, salt and cream of tartar. Stir dry ingredients into sugar mixture. Chill at least 2 hours or longer. Shape into 1-inch balls. Place on ungreased cookie sheet. Dip glass in sugar and press on cookie ball to flatten. Bake in 350° oven for 12 -15 minutes, or until lightly browned. Remove from cookie sheet immediately. Keep in air tight container. Approximately 10 dozen cookies.

TUESDAY
Rigatoni with Italian sausage and tomatoes *
Tossed salad with oil and vinegar dressing
Hot garlic bread
Vanilla yogurt with a berry topping

RIGATONI WITH ITALIAN SAUSAGE AND TOMATOES

6 Italian sausages, about 1 ¹/₂ pounds	*2 teaspoons Italian seasoning*
1 tablespoon olive oil or 3 tablespoons water	*1 teaspoon fennel seed*
1 medium onion, finely chopped	*1 teaspoon garlic salt*
3 cloves garlic, crushed	*Salt to taste*
1 (16 ounce) can tomatoes	*¹/₂ teaspoon pepper*
1 (8 ounce) can tomato sauce	*¹/₂ pound rigatoni, uncooked (5 cups cooked)*
3 tablespoons minced parsley	*Parmesan cheese*

Cut sausages into 2-inch pieces. In a fry pan, heat oil over medium-high heat. Cook sausages until done and golden brown. Drain off excess fat; add onion and garlic. Cook until onions are tender. Add tomatoes, tomato sauce, parsley, Italian seasoning, fennel seed and garlic salt. Cook over medium heat 10 minutes. Season with salt and pepper. Remove sausage and set aside. Meanwhile, cook rigatoni according to package directions, al dente; drain well. Put pasta back into pan it was cooked in, add ¹/₂ the sauce (not sausage), toss, and put on a large platter, making a well in the center. Put sausages in well and pour remaining sauce over pasta and sausages. Serve with freshly grated Parmesan cheese. 4 servings.

WEDNESDAY
Barbecued rump roast *
Baked stuffed potatoes
Buttered spinach
Gourmet onions on cucumber and tomato slices *
Custard pie

BARBECUED RUMP ROAST

2 pounds beef rump roast	*3 whole allspice berries*
1 ¹/₂ tablespoons Worcestershire sauce	*Salt to taste*
3 tablespoons lemon juice	*Pepper to taste*
1 tablespoon vinegar	*¹/₄ cup olive oil or salad oil*
1 teaspoon mustard seeds	

Place roast in a bowl. Combine Worcestershire sauce, lemon juice, vinegar, mustard seeds, allspice berries, salt and pepper; heat thoroughly. Pour this sauce over meat and let stand several hours, turning several times to have the meat well covered with sauce. Drain, saving sauce. Heat oil and brown meat in deep skillet, then pour sauce over meat and cover closely. Cook slowly until tender, about 3 hours, adding water if necessary. Serve sauce with meat. 6 servings.

GOURMET ONIONS WITH CUCUMBER AND TOMATO SLICES

2 large onions, white skin or Vidalia, finely chopped	*Garlic salt to taste*
¹/₂ cup sugar	*Tabasco sauce to taste*
1 cup vinegar	*¹/₂ to 1 teaspoon monosodium glutamate (optional)*
2 cups water	*1 large cucumber, sliced*
¹/₂ cup mayonnaise	*3 tomatoes, sliced*
1 teaspoon dill seed	*6 lettuce cups*

Chop onions. Combine sugar, vinegar and water. Add onions. Marinate 6 hours or overnight. Drain thoroughly. Add mayonnaise, dill seed. garlic salt, Tabasco and monosodium glutamate. Place sliced cucumber and tomatoes in lettuce cups; top with onions. 6 servings. Onions make a great hors d'oeuvre. Serve with crackers.

THURSDAY
Ladies Luncheon
Molded ham and potato salad
Pineapple casserole
Rolled asparagus sandwiches
Black bottom ice cream dessert

Plan of Work
Great luncheon for a busy hostess. Almost all of the preparation can be done ahead of time.
Day before:
1. Prepare salad. Chill.
2. Prepare pineapple casserole. Cook at the last minute.
3. Prepare asparagus sandwiches and keep refrigerated, covered, to bake at the last minute.
4. Ice cream dessert can be prepared and kept in the freezer, covered.
The morning of the luncheon:
5. Unmold salads to be ready to serve
6. Set the table; fix the flowers; relax
7. In the last 30 minutes, bake the casserole and the sandwiches.

MOLDED HAM AND POTATO SALAD

1 envelope plain gelatin	*1 teaspoon prepared mustard*
¼ cup cold water	*2 cups ground cooked ham*
1 (10 ³/4) ounce can of condensed cream	*½ cup finely chopped celery*
of potato soup	*2 tablespoons chopped pimiento*
½ cup milk	*2 tablespoons sliced green onions*
½ cup sour cream	*¼ teaspoon dried dillweed*
1 teaspoon lemon juice	

Soften gelatin in cold water. In medium saucepan, combine soup and milk; bring to a boil, add gelatin to dissolve. Remove from heat, stir in sour cream, lemon juice and mustard. Cool. Add remaining ingredients, mix and pour into individual molds. Chill until firm. Unmold and serve with mustard sauce. 6-8 servings.

Mustard Sauce

1 cup sour cream	*¼ teaspoon dillweed*
3 tablespoons prepared mustard	

Combine all ingredients; correct seasoning by adding more mustard, if desired.

PINEAPPLE CASSEROLE

2 (20 ounce) cans pineapple chunks
1 cup sugar
1/4 cup plus 3 tablespoons flour

2 cups shredded sharp Cheddar cheese
1/2 cup butter or margarine
1 1/2 cups fine cracker crumbs

Drain pineapple; reserve 3 tablespoons of the juice. Combine sugar and flour and stir in juice. Add cheese and pineapple and mix well. Spoon into a buttered 1 1/2-quart casserole. Combine butter and cracker crumbs and sprinkle over pineapple. Bake, uncovered, at 350° for 20-30 minutes or until crumbs are lightly browned. 6-8 servings.

ROLLED ASPARAGUS SANDWICHES

1 (8 ounce) package cream cheese, softened
3 (4 ounce) packages blue cheese, crumbled
1 tablespoon chives, chopped fine
2 teaspoons Worcestershire sauce

1 loaf white bread, crust removed
2 (15 oz) cans asparagus spears, well drained & diced
1/2 cup butter or margarine, melted

Combine cheeses, chives and Worcestershire sauce. Beat with an electric mixer for 1 minute. Roll bread flat with rolling pin. Spread cheese mixture on each slice of bread. Place an asparagus spear on edge of bread and roll in each slice of bread. Arrange on cookie sheet, seam side down. Brush with melted butter. Bake in 350° oven for 15 minutes. May be made ahead of time and frozen. Bake at time of serving. 20 sandwich rolls.

BLACK BOTTOM ICE CREAM DESSERT

36 vanilla wafers, crushed
2 (1 ounce) squares chocolate, melted
2 cups sifted powdered sugar
1/2 cup (1 stick) butter or margarine
2 eggs, separated

1 teaspoon vanilla
Pinch salt
1/2 cup chopped nuts
1 quart vanilla ice cream, slightly softened

Place half of crumbs on bottom of greased 8-inch square pan or pie pan. Combine chocolate, sugar, butter, egg yolks, vanilla and salt. Beat well. Beat egg whites until stiff. Fold into chocolate mixture. Spread over crumbs. Cover crumbs with nuts. Spread on ice cream; sprinkle with remaining crumbs. Freeze. 6-8 servings.

FRIDAY
Crab bisque *
Ham slices (left over)
Sweet potato souffle with nut topping
Stir fry zucchini
Apple muffins
Fruit cup

CRAB BISQUE

2 tablespoons butter or margarine
2 green onions, minced, use tops
2 (10 1/2 ounce) cans cream of celery soup
3 cups milk
1 cup whipping cream
1/2 teaspoon Old Bay seasoning
1 teaspoon Worcestershire sauce

1/2 teaspoon garlic salt
1/4 teaspoon white pepper
Hot sauce to taste
8 ounces crab meat or 2 (6 1/2 ounce) cans crab meat
2 hard cooked eggs, finely-chopped
1/2 cup dry sherry
Chopped parsley

In a 2-quart saucepan, saute onions in butter until cooked but not brown. Add soup, milk, cream, seasoning, Worcestershire sauce, garlic salt, pepper, hot sauce and crab meat. Simmer until hot. Add eggs and sherry. Heat and serve. Garnish with chopped fresh parsley. **Note:** Crab meat can be fresh or frozen.

SATURDAY
Oven crispy chicken
Potato casserole
Steamed carrots and onions
Molded fruit salad
One-hour dinner rolls *
Millionaire pie

ONE HOUR DINNER ROLLS

2 cups all-purpose flour
1 tablespoon sugar
1 teaspoon baking powder
1 teaspoon salt

1/4 cup shortening
1 1/4 ounce package dried yeast
1/4 cup warm water
3/4 cup buttermilk

Sift flour, sugar, baking powder and salt into a large mixing bowl; blend in shortening. Dissolve yeast in warm water, add buttermilk and mix well. Add yeast mixture to the dry ingredients, all at one time. Mix until mixture forms a ball. Sprinkle flour lightly on a board and knead the mixture until it is smooth. If sticky, add more flour to board and hands. Pat dough 1/4 to 1/2-inch thick and cut with 2-inch cutter. Place rolls on greased baking sheet. Spread with melted butter; cover lightly with a clean towel. Allow to rise in a warm place until almost double, about 1 hour. Bake in 400° oven for 15 minutes. 12 rolls.

May

May - First Week

"SUMMERTIME AND THE LIVING IS EASY," are the words from a well-known song. The idea is truly wonderful. However, if we take it too seriously and make summertime *too* easy and relaxed, especially in preparing, transporting and serving food at outings, it could cause a holiday catastrophe such as food poisoning.

Whether the outing is a long haul, a short trip or just in your own backyard, the occasion will be a glorious one if you prepare and serve foods in a safe manner. When you are waiting outside during hot weather, a little attention will prevent food spoilage and illness.

Everyone has heard the statement, "keep hot foods hot and cold foods cold." It's really necessary and not difficult if you understand the principle of food sanitation. To transmit disease, the food must contain a disease-forming agent such as bacteria, mold or virus, or be handled in a way that permits contamination from the person preparing it or from the surroundings.

Once the food is contaminated, the proper environment must be provided for the contamination to grow and spread: a warm climate, moisture and nutrients. Follow these precautions during the summer to prevent food poisoning.

1. When cooking hamburgers outside, don't allow the meat to stay unrefrigerated for more than one hour at the most. Cook in small batches that will be used quickly, so they don't sit around to allow bacteria to grow. Ground meat has millions of little surfaces exposed, so it is easily contaminated. Keep unused meat in a refrigerated container.

2. Always wash your hands thoroughly with soap and water before and after handling raw meat, especially ground meat.

3. Never handle meat if you have cuts, sores or infections of any kind on your hands.

4. If raw meat is carried to the grill on a tray, wash the tray before putting cooked meat on it. Cooking would destroy contamination on the outside of raw meat; putting the cooked meat back on the same unwashed tray could cause recontamination. Don't even use the same knife; wash it before reusing.

5. Know which foods cause problems: all raw meat, fish, poultry, anything containing eggs and dairy products. It is best to keep foods, cooked or uncooked, at 40° or below until it is time to prepare or serve them. If the food will be eaten hot, be sure it is heated thoroughly. The only way to know if the interior of an ice chest is 40° is to pack a small thermometer with the food.

6. If the outing involves fishing, supply an ice chest with crushed ice for chilling the fish. Some people prefer to use dry ice or to use regular crushed ice with a few handfuls of ordinary table salt sprinkled over it. This can reduce the temperature in the chest to below freezing, but this technique can be used only in a plastic lined ice chest or cooler.

7. A favorite outdoor dessert is strawberry shortcake with good old-fashioned whipped cream on top. Don't let whipped cream stand at a warm temperature. Keep it refrigerated until it's served, because whipped cream can be contaminated easily. Avoid custard or cream pies on outings for the same reasons. Don't carry homemade mayonnaise; it's made with raw eggs and is easily contaminated. Take only commercially processed mayonnaise and sandwich spreads on outings.

8. Never allow perishable foods (anything that comes from an animal) to stand at room temperature for more than two hours. In warm weather, make that one hour or less.

9. Don't use or drink water from a spring or well you are not familiar with. It could be contaminated. Don't even wash fruit in anything but safe drinking water. If in doubt, carry your own water.

10. On an outing, the tendency is to relax and expose food that people will pick up and eat as they roam around, especially fried chicken and stuffed eggs. Often the bugs will take over. They carry disease-forming organisms on their feet or spread them by regurgitation, so keep food covered.

11. Wash hands thoroughly before handling perishable foods to be eaten cold, such as stuffed eggs or cold cuts for sandwiches. Fingers spread germs.

There are several signs of food spoilage that everyone should be aware of, such as off color, off odor, off taste, a sour taste in a normally bland food, an alcoholic taste in fruit juices, sliminess on the surface of meat and, of course, mold on the surface where mold is not supposed to be. A food can have some of these signs and still be good, but it's better to be safe than sorry. When in doubt, throw it out.

Watch young children, because they like to pop berries from bushes into their mouths and they could get a poisonous one. Don't diaper your baby in places which might come in contact with food, and wash your hands before handling food.

Foodborne illness can cause symptoms similar to and often mistaken for a virus infection, such as diarrhea, vomiting and stomach cramps. They can occur anytime from 2 hours to 24 hours after eating contaminated food, depending on the organisms responsible. With young children or the elderly, the results can be severe. Only about one out of 100 people die from food poisoning, but that's too many.

So, always remember to keep cold foods cold and hot foods hot. Keep all surfaces clean, including the hands that prepare and serve. Have wonderful, happy, safe and sanitary holiday outings all summer.

SUNDAY
May Day Dinner
Pork roast with apple sauce
Baked acorn squash
Savory green beans
Layered tomato and cheese salad
Cheese and onion muffins
Chocolate delights
Pineapple Sherbert (commercial)

Plan Of Work
Day before:
1. Prepare chocolate delights.
2. Corn sticks can be prepared. Reheat before serving.
3 hours before serving:
3. Prepare roast for baking and place in oven.
1 hour before serving:
4. Place acorn squash in oven to cook.
5. Prepare salads and place in refrigerator
6. Prepare green beans.
Roast, squash, beans and corn sticks must be served hot.

ROAST PORK WITH APPLE SAUCE

5 pound bone-in fresh pork shoulder or fresh ham	*¹/₄ teaspoon pepper*
1 large onion, peeled	*¹/₂ teaspoon dried basil leaves*
1 teaspoon salt	*1 quart apple sauce*

Wipe pork with dry towel. Place meat in roasting pan. Cut onion into 8 slices and place on roast. Sprinkle meat with salt, pepper and basil. Cover tightly with lid or aluminum foil. Bake at 375° for one hour. Reduce heat to 350° and bake for 1 hour and 45 minutes or until meat thermometer registers 170°. Pass the apple sauce. 6-8 servings. **Note**: If thermometer is used, it must be inserted in the thickest muscle, not touching bone or embedded in fat.

BAKED ACORN SQUASH

3 large acorn squash   *3 tablespoons brown sugar or honey*

Cut squash in half lengthwise. Scoop out seeds; add $^1/_4$-inch of water. Bake in 400° oven for 20 minutes. Place 1 tablespoon brown sugar or honey in each half while still hot. Serve immediately. 6 servings.

SAVORY GREEN BEANS

2 pounds fresh green beans   *2 cloves garlic, crushed*
2 tablespoons olive oil   *$^1/_2$ teaspoon savory*

Wash and remove ends of green beans. Place in pan, add 1 cup water and cover with well-fitted lid. Place on high heat; when steam begins to flow freely around the rim of the lid, turn heat down to the lowest point, do not remove lid, and cook about 10 to 15 minutes or until crisp tender. Drain. Heat oil in skillet; add garlic and cook until garlic is light brown. Add beans and stir fry. When heated through, add savory. Remove from heat and serve hot. 6 servings.

LAYERED TOMATO AND CHEESE SALAD

3 large, ripe tomatoes   *$^1/_4$ teaspoon pepper*
*2 cups cottage cheese ***   *Curly endive or other salad greens*
1 tablespoon finely minced onion   *Salad dressing (optional)*
1 teaspoon salt

Peel chilled tomatoes and cut each into 4 slices. Season cheese with onion, salt and pepper; pile generously on half the tomato slices. Spread mixture to edge of slices and top with second slice of tomato. Season with salt and pepper. Arrange on beds of curly endive and serve with any desired dressing. 6 servings.
*Can save a small amount of cheese to put on top of the second tomato slice, with a bit of green lettuce under it for garnish.

CHEESE AND ONION MUFFINS

$^3/_4$ cup canned French fried onions   *$^1/_3$ cup shredded Cheddar cheese*
1 $^1/_2$ cup biscuit baking mix   *$^1/_2$ cup milk*
$^1/_4$ teaspoon onion powder

Crush onions, reserving ¼ cup. Combine ½ cup onions with remaining ingredients; beat well for ½ minute. Grease 12 muffin cups. Divide half of the batter among the muffin cups; sprinkle with half of the reserved onions. Repeat with remaining batter and crushed onions. Bake at 375° for 20-30 minutes or until firm. Serve warm. Yield: 12 muffins.

CHOCOLATE DELIGHTS

1 ³/4 cup all-purpose flour
1/3 cup cocoa
1/4 cup sugar
Pinch of salt
³/4 cup (1 1/2 sticks) butter or margarine
1/3 to 1/2 cup strong coffee. chilled
12 ounces semisweet chocolate chips, melted

²/3 cup sugar
2 tablespoons (1/4 stick) butter or margarine, melted
2 tablespoons milk
2 teaspoons coffee liqueur
2 eggs, slightly beaten
1/2 cup finely-chopped, toasted walnuts or pecans

Sift flour, cocoa, sugar and salt; pour into large bowl. Add butter and blend until consistency of coarse meal. Gradually mix in coffee. Knead dough briefly on floured board, then form into log. Wrap in plastic or aluminum foil and refrigerate several hours or overnight.

Lightly grease tiny muffin cups (diameter of top of each cup should about 1 ³/4 inches). Cut the dough into 4 pieces. Working with 1/4 of dough at a time (keep remainder in refrigerator), pinch off enough dough to line muffin cups by pressing lightly with fingers. Repeat with remaining dough. Chill.

Combine chocolate, sugar, butter, milk and coffee liqueur in medium bowl and blend well. Add eggs and beat until smooth. Stir in chopped nuts. Fill muffin cups ²/3 full. Bake at 350° until filling is set, about 20-25 minutes. Let cool in pans 15 minutes, then remove. Transfer to wire racks and let cool completely. Chocolate delights can be prepared ahead of time and frozen. Makes 4 dozen.

MONDAY
Hot spinach soup
California turkey salad *
Hot rolls
Honey nut dessert squares *

CALIFORNIA TURKEY SALAD

1 (8 ounce) bottle French dressing
1/2 cup (2 ounces) crumbled Blue cheese
4 bacon slices, cooked crisp and crumbled
1 1/2 quarts shredded lettuce
2 tomatoes, chopped

1 small green pepper, cut in chunks
2 cups cooked, chopped turkey
2 hard cooked eggs, chopped
1 avocado, peeled and chopped

Combine dressing, cheese and bacon; mix well. Chill. Put lettuce on platter, top with tomato, green pepper, turkey, eggs and avocado. Garnish with additional bacon, if desired. Serve with dressing. 6 servings.

HONEY NUT DESSERT SQUARES

3 cups crushed shredded wheat cereal
   (9 large biscuits)
1 1/4 cups finely chopped nuts
3 tablespoons sugar
1/2 teaspoon ground cinnamon
1/4 teaspoon ground cloves
1/8 teaspoon salt

³/4 cup butter or margarine, melted
1 cup sugar
1/2 cup water
1/2 cup honey
2 tablespoons lemon juice
Vanilla ice cream or sweetened whipped cream,
   if desired

Combine shredded wheat, nuts, 3 tablespoons sugar, cinnamon, cloves and salt. Spread evenly in well-greased 9x9x2-inch baking pan. Pour melted butter evenly over shredded wheat mixture. Bake until lightly brown, 25 minutes, in 400° oven. While shredded wheat mixture is baking, mix 1 cup sugar and water in heavy saucepan. Heat to boiling; reduce heat. Simmer 5 minutes, stirring constantly. Stir in honey and lemon juice. Simmer 5 minutes. Remove shredded wheat mixture from oven. Pour syrup evenly over mixture immediately; press down with back of spoon. Let stand at room temperature 4 to 6 hours. Cut into squares. Serve with vanilla ice cream or sweetened whipped cream. 16 squares.

TUESDAY
Enchilada casserole *
Buttered broccoli
Tossed fresh vegetable salad *
Super moist coconut cake *

ENCHILADA CASSEROLE

1 cup chopped onion	1 (6 ounce) can tomato paste
1 clove garlic , crushed	1 (3 ounce) can chopped green chiles, drained
2 tablespoons butter or margarine	1 teaspoon salt
2 pounds ground beef	1 (8 ounce) package tortilla chips
1 (10 ½ ounce) can cream of mushroom soup	3 cups (12 ounces) shredded sharp Cheddar cheese
1 (8 ounce) can tomato sauce	Sour cream (optional)

Saute onion and garlic in butter. Add meat; brown. Stir in soup, tomato sauce, tomato paste, chiles and salt; cook until mixture begins to boil. Place half of tortilla chips in bottom of 13x9-inch baking dish. Pour meat mixture over tortilla chips. Top with remaining tortilla chips and cheese. Bake at 375° for 20 to 25 minutes. Serve with sour cream, if desired. 6-8 servings.

TOSSED FRESH VEGETABLE SALAD

1 head lettuce	¼ cup salad oil
¼ head Chinese cabbage	1 tablespoon lemon juice
¼ head curly endive	1 tablespoon wine vinegar
1 large cucumber, sliced	½ teaspoon salt
2 medium-sized fresh tomatoes, cut in wedges	¼ teaspoon pepper
½ cup thawed frozen peas, uncooked	¼ teaspoon monosodium glutamate (optional)

Tear or cut salad greens into small pieces; arrange in salad bowl. Make a design of cucumber, tomato wedges and peas in clusters. Just before serving, sprinkle salad with oil, lemon juice, vinegar, salt, pepper and monosodium glutamate then toss salad and serve. 6 servings.

SUPER MOIST COCONUT CAKE

1 (18 ½ ounce) white cake mix	1 (9 ounce) container whipped topping
1 cup evaporated milk	½ to 1 cup flaked coconut
1 cup sugar	

Prepare cake according to package instructions. Pour into greased 9x13x2-inch pan. Bake according to directions. When done, punch holes in top. Combine milk and sugar in a small saucepan; bring slowly to a boil. Pour milk and sugar mixture over top of hot cake as soon as it comes from the oven. Cool. Spread cake with whipped topping and top with coconut. 12 servings.

WEDNESDAY
Oyster stew *
Caesar bean salad *
Toasted tear-offs *
Fresh fruit

OYSTER STEW

2 (12 ounce) cans oysters, fresh or frozen	*4 cups oyster liquor and half & half, combined*
2 slices bacon, chopped	*1 ½ teaspoons salt*
½ cup chopped onion	*¼ teaspoon white pepper (black may be used)*
1 (10 ¼ ounce) can cream of potato soup	*2-3 tablespoons chopped parsley*

Thaw frozen oysters. Drain oysters; reserve liquor. Fry bacon until crisp. Remove bacon from fat, cook onion in bacon drippings until tender. Add soup, oyster liquor mixture, salt and pepper. Heat, stirring occasionally. Add bacon and oysters. Heat 3-5 minutes longer or until edges of the oysters begin to curl. Correct seasoning. Sprinkle parsley on each serving. 6 servings.

CAESAR BEAN SALAD

½ cup vegetable oil	*2 (16 ounce) cans kidney beans, heated, then drained*
¼ cup lemon juice	*1 medium head romaine lettuce*
½ cup grated Parmesan cheese	*1 cup seasoned croutons (commercial or home made)*
½ teaspoon garlic salt	*2 tablespoons chopped fresh parsley*
¼ teaspoon black pepper	*3 eggs, hard-cooked, cut in wedges*

In medium bowl, combine oil, lemon juice, cheese, garlic salt and pepper; mix well. Add warm beans; toss gently. Cover and chill. Line salad bowl with romaine leaves. Pour beans on top and sprinkle with croutons and parsley. Garnish with egg wedges. 6 servings.

TOASTED TEAR-OFFS

³⁄₄ cup (1 ½ sticks) butter or margarine	*1 loaf French bread*
1 ¼ cups (5 ounces) shredded sharp Cheddar cheese	*Chopped parsley*

Cream butter with 1 cup cheese. Slice bread into 1-inch slices, slicing only ³⁄₄ way to bottom. Cut loaf through the center lengthwise just ³⁄₄ way to the bottom. Spread inside cut surfaces with the cheese mixture. Sprinkle the remaining ¼ cup cheese and parsley over the top. Wrap loaf in heavy duty foil; seal securely. Heat on grill or in oven for 15 to 20 minutes or until cheese melts. Turn once, if heated on grill. 1 loaf toasted bread.

THURSDAY
Hot turkey pot pie *
Buttered asparagus
Molded cabbage and celery salad *
Skillet coffee cake with topping *

HOT TURKEY POT PIE

4 cups cooked, cubed turkey
¹/₂ cup butter or margarine
1 ¹/₂ cups chopped onion
4 green peppers, finely chopped
1 (4 ounce) can chopped green chiles
¹/₂ cup plus 2 tablespoons flour
5 cups turkey broth (chicken bouillon may be substituted)

2 cups (8 ounces) shredded Cheddar cheese
Salt
Freshly ground black pepper
2 (10 ounce) packages frozen patty shells, thawed,
*   or your favorite pie crust, rolled thick*
1 egg, beaten

Place turkey in a 2-quart baking dish. Melt butter in a saucepan. Add the chopped onion, peppers and chiles. Cook over low heat, stirring frequently, for about 10 minutes, or until vegetables are tender. Stir flour into vegetables and cook for 1 minute. Remove from the heat and stir in the broth. Cook, stirring constantly, until the mixture comes to a boil and is thickened. Remove from heat, add cheese and stir until melted. Adjust the seasoning. Spoon over cubed turkey. Place thawed patty shells very close together on a lightly-floured board and pinch edges together to make a sheet of dough. Roll out into shape to fit the top of the casserole. If using your own favorite pastry crust, roll out thick to fit casserole. Place crust on casserole. Seal the edges and brush with beaten egg. Make 3 gashes in center to allow the steam to escape. Place baking dish on a cookie sheet and cook in a very hot oven (450°) for 30 minutes. Reduce temperature to 325° and cook 30 minutes longer. 6 servings.

MOLDED CABBAGE AND CELERY SALAD

1 envelope plain gelatin
¹/₄ cup cold water
1 cup hot water
¹/₄ cup mild vinegar
1 tablespoon lemon juice

2 tablespoons sugar
¹/₂ teaspoon salt
¹/₂ cup finely-shredded cabbage
1 cup sliced celery
2 tablespoons chopped pimiento

Soften gelatin in cold water. Add sugar, salt and hot water and stir until dissolved. Add vinegar and lemon juice. Cool. When mixture begins to thicken, add remaining ingredients. Pour into 1 quart mold that has been rinsed in cold water and chill. When firm, unmold on bed of lettuce or endive. Garnish with mayonnaise. 6 servings.

SKILLET COFFEE CAKE

1 (18 ¹/₂ ounce) package yellow cake mix   *1 tablespoon grated orange rind*

Prepare cake mix according to instructions, adding 1 tablespoon grated orange rind. Pour into well-oiled electric fry-pan and bake 35 minutes at 280° with cover vent open for the last five minutes. Uncover; quickly sprinkle topping evenly over cake. Cover, turn off. Let stand 10 minutes longer before cutting. This sets the topping. Uncover, cut into squares and serve right from fry-pan. 16 servings.

Topping

½ cup brown sugar, packed	½ cup coarsely chopped nuts
¼ cup graham cracker crumbs	2 tablespoons butter or margarine, melted
1 tablespoon grated orange rind	1 ½ teaspoons cinnamon

Combine sugar, crumbs, orange rind, nuts, butter and cinnamon. Beat until blended. Additional nuts may be sprinkled on top. (optional).

FRIDAY
Foil baked fish *
Skillet vegetables *
Lettuce slice with creamy blue cheese dressing *
Corn bread
Cocoa pudding *

FOIL BAKED FISH

4 fresh whole white fish, cleaned (2 pounds in all)	¼ cup chopped chives
2 tablespoons butter or margarine	¼ cup chopped onion
½ cup chopped parsley	2 tablespoons lemon juice
½ cup chopped dill sprigs	

Rinse fish; allow to drain. Sprinkle lightly with salt. Make stuffing by combining butter, parsley, dill sprigs, chives, onion and lemon juice. Stuff and wrap each fish separately in aluminum foil, sealing the edges carefully. Bake in 400° oven for 20 minutes. Unwrap, remove to a hot platter, garnish with parsley and lemon slices. 4 servings.

SKILLET VEGETABLES

¼ cup (½ stick) butter or margarine	Salt to taste
3 cups thinly-sliced celery	Pepper to taste
1 (10 ounce) package frozen corn	Dash of nutmeg
1 (16 ounce) can tomatoes	

Melt butter in saucepan or large skillet. Add celery, cover and cook 5 minutes. Add corn and tomatoes and cook 10 minutes, until corn is tender. Season to taste. 6 servings.

LETTUCE WITH CREAMY BLUE CHEESE DRESSING

Head lettuce, 1-inch thick slice per serving	2 tablespoons finely-chopped onion
2 ounces blue cheese, crumbled	1 ½ teaspoons lemon juice
1 clove garlic, crushed	⅛ teaspoon sugar
½ cup dairy sour cream	¼ teaspoon monosodium glutamate (optional)
½ cup mayonnaise	1 carrot, scraped and shredded
1 teaspoon garlic salt	

Arrange lettuce slices on individual salad plates. Combine remaining ingredients, except carrots, and stir until smooth. Spoon on lettuce, sprinkle with shredded carrots. 4-6 servings. (Increase blue cheese to 4 ounces and use dressing as a dip for raw vegetables.)

COCOA PUDDING

2 tablespoons butter or margarine
1/2 cup sugar
1 egg
1 cup milk
2 1/2 cups all-purpose flour

2 1/2 teaspoons baking powder
1/2 cup cocoa
1/4 teaspoon salt
1/4 teaspoon baking soda

Cream butter and sugar until light and fluffy. Add egg and beat well. Mix and sift dry ingredients. Add dry ingredients alternately with milk to sugar mixture. When well mixed, pour into boiling syrup.

Syrup

3 cups water
2 cups sugar

1/4 cup (1/2 stick) butter or margarine
1 cup chopped nuts

Combine in a deep skillet (2-quart size) all ingredients. Bring to boiling point. When boiling well, add pudding mixture to syrup. Cover; when steaming well, turn to simmer position for 30 minutes. Do not remove lid until done. 6-8 servings.

SATURDAY
Italian style meat patties *
Buttered rice
Layered vegetable casserole *
Pineapple and cottage cheese salad
Vanilla yogurt with fruit topping

ITALIAN STYLE MEAT PATTIES

1 1/2 pounds ground raw meat (combine beef,
   veal and pork)
3 eggs
1/3 cup grated Parmesan cheese
2 tablespoons all-purpose flour
1 teaspoon salt
1/4 teaspoon black pepper

6 thin slices cooked ham
3/4 cups shredded Swiss cheese
2 eggs
2 tablespoons water
Flour
1/4 cup butter, margarine or shortening

Combine meat, 3 eggs, Parmesan cheese, 2 tablespoons flour, salt and pepper. Divide into 12 equal portions; shape each portion into a thin patty about 4 inches in diameter. Half of these will be used as bottom patties to be covered with filling; the remainder will be tops. On each of the bottom patties, place a slice of ham (cutting ham if necessary) and one heaping tablespoon of cheese. Cover with remaining patties, pinching edges to seal. Refrigerate until one hour before serving time. Then beat 2 eggs with 2 tablespoons water and dip each patty into eggs, then into flour, coating both sides. Brown well in heavy pan in melted butter or shortening; cover and cook on top of range or bake in oven at 350° for 45 minutes. A little water may be added to pan if needed. 6 servings.

LAYERED VEGETABLE CASSEROLE

1 medium eggplant, peeled and sliced	*2 tomatoes, sliced*
4 summer squash, sliced	*Pepper to taste*
1 medium-sized green pepper, cut into	*Salt to taste*
bite-sized pieces	*⅓ cup salad oil*
10 whole okra pods, cut in half	*Parmesan cheese (optional)*

Layer vegetables in 1-quart baking dish. Sprinkle salt and pepper over each layer. Pour oil over all vegetables. Cover. Bake at 350° for 1 ½ hours. Remove from oven, uncover, sprinkle with Parmesan cheese. Return to oven and heat for 5 minutes. 6 servings.

May - Second Week

NOTHING RUINS A HOLIDAY LIKE a case of food poisoning. Food poisoning is the great master of disaster. You could be up half the night with an upset stomach, headache and nausea and think you've caught a "flu bug" or virus that's going around. But that may not be the case.

A lot of people who think they have the flu are really suffering from a mild case of food poisoning caused by tiny organisms called bacteria. There is probably not much you can do to prevent the flu. But you can prevent food poisoning; the job starts when you shop for food at the market. You then have to keep working to prevent food poisoning as you store, prepare, cook and serve food at home. Food poisoning prevention can be broken down into three simple steps: Keep hot food hot, keep cold food cold, and keep all food clean.

Germs that cause food poisoning are usually killed when you boil, broil or roast foods. However when food stays at room temperature for longer than 2 hours, some bacteria may start to multiply. Some organisms even produce poisons that are destroyed by heating and cause food poisoning. Once food is cooked, keep it hot until served. Refrigerate leftovers at once. Remember, often germs do not change the taste, odor or appearance of foods.

Here are some tips to prevent food poisoning while cooking meat or poultry:
1. Allow frozen products more time to cook. You generally need to cook an unthawed product one and one half times longer than a thawed product.
2. Cover leftovers to retain moisture. Reheat all the way through. Bring gravies to a rolling boil.
3. Germs do not multiply very fast if the temperature is 40° or below. So, store meat, poultry, eggs, milk, cheese and other perishables in the refrigerator.
Here are some tips on how to safely store meat and poultry:
1. Meat and poultry may be stored as purchased in plastic wrap for a day or two. For longer storage time, remove from store wrapping and wrap very loosely in wax paper or plastic wrap. The refrigerator temperature should be set to 40°. Use a thermometer to check your setting.
2. Cover meat and poultry leftovers and store in the refrigerator. Use in two days. Use covered container or wrap tightly to store in freezer. Keep in mind that warm leftovers will raise the interior temperature of the refrigerator somewhat.
3. In preparing meat and poultry salads, make sure that all ingredients are thoroughly chilled. After mixing, place in shallow containers that will allow the heat gained during mixing to be removed quickly. Place in the refrigerator.

The best way to thaw meat and poultry is in the refrigerator. Or, place on a tray in a double brown grocery bag and leave at room temperature. Double bags provide insulation and allow even thawing to occur (one hour per pound, and no longer).

At the market, always pick up meat, poultry and dairy products last, and get them home and into the refrigerator or freezer quickly. Don't leave them in the car trunk on a warm day while you do other errands.

Keep germs off meat, poultry and dairy products by washing utensils, platters and counter tops with soap and water before and after touching raw meat and poultry. Wash utensils and platters after they have come in contact with raw meat and poultry and before they touch any cooked product. The same goes for your hands, or rubber gloves.

Germs are a natural part of our environment, so you need to be careful to keep things clean, especially your hands. Be sure to bandage cuts and sores before you handle food. Keep pets out of areas where food is prepared in the kitchen. Teach children to wash their hands before handling food. Ground meat must be handled carefully and cooked until it is brownish-pink in the center. Never serve it raw. (Sorry, tartare lovers!) Ground meat requires special care. When it is ground, germs on the surface can spread quickly throughout the meat.

Know what kind of ham you've bought. Some need to be cooked; others are fully cooked and can be eaten as they come from the package. Check the label, and if you have any doubts, cook the ham, 15 minutes per pound.

Cook poultry products completely. If you prepare the turkey, chicken or duck the day before you plan to cook it, store it in the refrigerator. Store giblets separately. This rule also applies to stuffings. Always stuff the bird right before roasting. If the bird is stuffed, stuff loosely to allow heat penetration. Refrigerate leftover poultry and stuffing in separate dishes, within two hours.

Use only clean, unbroken, odor-free eggs any time eggs are not going to be thoroughly cooked, such as in soft-cooked eggs, poached eggs, scrambled eggs, omelets, uncooked salad dressings, ice cream or soft custard. Cracked or soiled eggs can contain harmful bacteria, and should be used only in recipes that call for thorough cooking. If you doubt the safety of the egg, discard it.

SUNDAY
Brunch
Scalloped bacon and eggs *
Sauteed mushrooms
Lettuce wedges with Green Goddess dressing
Toasted English muffins with orange marmalade

SCALLOPED BACON AND EGGS

¼ cup chopped onion	*1 cup (4 ounces) shredded sharp Cheddar cheese*
2 tablespoons butter or margarine	*6 eggs, hard-cooked, sliced*
2 tablespoons all-purpose flour	*1 ½ cups crushed potato chips*
1 ½ cups milk	*10 to 12 slices bacon, crisp-cooked and crumbled*

Saute onions in butter until tender; blend in flour. Add milk. Cook, stirring constantly, until mixture is thickened and bubbly. Add cheese; stir until melted. Place a layer of egg slices in 1 ½ quart baking dish. Cover with half the cheese sauce, half the bacon and half the potato chips. Repeat layers; end with potato chips. Bake at 350° for 15 minutes or until heated through. 4-6 servings.

MONDAY
Sesame broiled steaks with pineapple slices *
White rice in consomme / Eggplant supreme
Salad greens with dressing royale *
Iced carrot cake

SESAME BROILED STEAKS WITH PINEAPPLE SLICES

2 pounds beef chuck steak, cut ³/₄ inch thick
Instant unseasoned meat tenderizer
  (unless steak is already tender)
¹/₃ cup soy sauce
2 tablespoons cooking oil
2 tablespoons lemon juice

2 tablespoons water
¹/₄ teaspoon hot sauce
1 tablespoon honey
1 (8 ³/₄-ounce) can pineapple slices, drained
2 tablespoons sesame seed, oven-toasted for 8 minutes

Sprinkle all sides of meat with tenderizer (optional), using 1 teaspoon total. To ensure penetration, pierce deeply at ¹/₂-inch intervals with a long-tined fork. Combine soy sauce, cooking oil, lemon juice, water and hot sauce. Place meat in shallow pan. Pour soy mixture over meat. Cover and refrigerate for 1 to 2 hours. Drain meat, reserving marinade. Place meat on unheated rack of broiler pan. Broil 3 to 4 inches from heat for 7 minutes; brush with marinade. Turn meat; broil 4 minutes more. Meanwhile, combine remaining marinade and honey. Arrange pineapple slices around meat, brush meat and pineapple with marinade mixture. Continue broiling 2 to 3 minutes for medium rare, longer for extra doneness. Sprinkle with sesame seed. 4-6 servings.

DRESSING ROYALE

¹/₂ cup sour cream
²/₃ cup mayonnaise
2 tablespoons brown sugar
2 teaspoons salt

2 tablespoons white wine vinegar
2 tablespoons coarse ground black pepper
¹/₂ pound bacon, diced and cooked (optional)

Combine sour cream and mayonnaise. Add sugar, salt, vinegar and pepper. Chill. Spoon dressing over salad greens. Sprinkle with bacon bits just before serving. 4 servings.

TUESDAY
Southern catfish or mullet with herb butter *
Wild rice
Buttered Brussels sprouts
Fresh tomato and onion slices with basil dressing
Corn sticks
Pecan tarts

SOUTHERN CATFISH OR MULLET WITH HERB BUTTER

2 pounds pan-dressed catfish or mullet, fresh
  or frozen
1 cup fine corn flake crumbs

1 teaspoon salt
Oil for frying
Herb butter

Thaw fish, if frozen; wash and dry. Combine crumbs and salt. Roll fish in crumb mixture (or shake a few at a time in crumb mixture in a paper bag) until well coated. Heat oil (approximately ⅛-inch deep) in skillet. Place fish in single layer in hot oil; fry 2 or 3 minutes, or until brown. Turn carefully and fry 2 to 3 minutes on second side or until fish flakes easily when tested with a fork (drain on paper towel). Serve herb butter over hot fish. 4-6 servings.

Herb Butter

½ cup (1 stick) softened butter or margarine
1 tablespoon finely-chopped parsley
1 tablespoon finely-chopped chives or green onions
1 tablespoon lime or lemon juice

½ teaspoon salt
Liquid hot pepper sauce to taste
Freshly ground black pepper to taste

Cream butter until smooth and fluffy. Beat in parsley, chives, juice, salt, pepper sauce and black pepper. Yield is a little over ½ cup.

WEDNESDAY
Middle of the Week Lamb Dinner
Cheddar cheese wafers and white Zinfandel wine
Gourmet shoulder lamb chops
Sauteed potatoes, Serbian style
Asparagus Dijon
Pineapple and cheese salad
Commercial sour dough rolls
Cherry turnovers

Plan Of Work
Day before:
1. Make cheese wafers and cherry turnovers.
2. Lamb chops can be prepared the day before and cooked at the last minute, just before serving.
Several hours before serving:
3. Prepare asparagus. Cook at the last minute.
One hour before serving:
4. Prepare the potatoes.
5. While potatoes are cooking, prepare salad; place in refrigerator until serving time. (If unable to determine the time of cooking or preparation, the whole meal can be prepared starting two hours before serving.)

CHEDDAR CHEESE WAFERS

½ cup (1 stick) butter or margarine, softened
2 cups (8 ounces) shredded, sharp Cheddar cheese,
   room temperature
¼ cup grated Parmesan cheese

1 cup all-purpose flour
¼ cup finely-chopped nuts
¼ teaspoon cayenne pepper

Combine all ingredients thoroughly by hand or processor. If blended by hand, take about 4-5 minutes. Shape into a roll 1 ½ inches in diameter. Wrap in waxed paper or plastic wrap; chill. Slice and place on an ungreased cookie sheet. Bake in 350° oven for 10-15 minutes or until nicely browned. About 4 dozen wafers.

GOURMET SHOULDER LAMB CHOPS

1 large onion, finely chopped
10 cloves garlic, crushed

18 strips bacon
6 thick shoulder lamb chops

Combine onions and garlic. Place evenly on top of each lamb chop, Wrap each chop with 3 strips of bacon and secure with wooden pick. Broil chops 4 minutes on each side, 3 inches from source of heat. 6 servings.

SAUTEED POTATOES, SERBIAN STYLE

5-6 large potatoes
1 medium onion, sliced
¼ cup olive oil

¼ teaspoon salt
Pepper to taste
¼ cup chopped fresh parsley

Peel and quarter potatoes and place in a saucepan. Add onion, oil, salt and pepper. Barely cover with water; simmer until potatoes are tender and most of the water is gone. Drain and top with parsley. 5-6 servings.

ASPARAGUS DIJON

3 tablespoons butter or margarine
3 tablespoons flour
1 ½ cups milk
1 teaspoon salt
⅛ teaspoon pepper

2 tablespoons lemon juice
2 tablespoons Dijon mustard
½ cup sour cream
2 (15 ounce) cans asparagus spears, drained
⅓ cup grated Parmesan cheese

Melt butter, add flour; blend well. Slowly add milk and cook until thickened, stirring constantly. Add salt, pepper, lemon juice, mustard and sour cream. Arrange asparagus spears in greased 1 ½ quart baking pan. Spoon sauce over asparagus. Sprinkle with Parmesan cheese. Cook at 350° until mixture is hot and cheese browns. 6 servings. If there is too much sauce, store in refrigerator for future use.

PINEAPPLE AND CHEESE SALAD

2 (20 ounce) cans pineapple chunks, drained
2 (3 ounce) packages cream cheese, chilled
French dressing (commercial)

6 Lettuce cups
Paprika

Drain pineapple. Cut cream cheese into small cubes. Combine pineapple and cheese cubes. Toss lightly with dressing. Serve in lettuce cups and top with paprika. 6 servings.

CHERRY TURNOVERS

3 cups sifted all-purpose flour
3 tablespoons granulated sugar
1 ½ teaspoons salt
½ teaspoon cinnamon

1 cup shortening
5-6 tablespoons water
1 (20 ounce) can prepared cherry pie filling
Powdered sugar

Combine flour, granulated sugar, salt and cinnamon. Cut in shortening with pastry blender until mixture is uniform. Sprinkle dough with water, a tablespoon at a time, stirring it with a fork until just enough has been added so dough can be patted into a ball. Divide pastry in half. On a lightly-floured surface, roll one half into a 10x15-inch rectangle. Cut into six 5-inch squares. Repeat with other half of dough. Place about 2 measuring tablespoons of fruit filling in center of each square. Moisten pastry edges with water. Fold over one half of pastry to form a triangle. Seal edges firmly with a fork. Prick top with fork for steam to escape. Place on ungreased baking sheets. Bake at 425° for 12 to 15 minutes or until lightly browned. Cool slightly; sprinkle with powdered sugar. 12 turnovers. Freeze leftovers.

THURSDAY
Hot and chunky cucumber soup *
Ham sandwich on whole wheat bread
Pineapple and cottage cheese salad
Banana cake and topping *

HOT AND CHUNKY CUCUMBER SOUP

4 cups milk	2 chicken bouillon cubes
1/4 cup butter or margarine	3 tablespoons minced parsley
1/2 cup finely-chopped celery	1 teaspoon Worcestershire sauce
1 cup finely-chopped onion	2 teaspoons salt
1/4 cup flour	1/8 teaspoon pepper
2 cups finely-diced, pared cucumber	1/4 cup sour cream (optional)

Scald milk in double boiler over simmering water. Melt butter in heavy saucepan. Add celery and onion; mix well. Cover. Cook over moderate heat 15 to 20 minutes, stirring occasionally; do not brown. Add flour; mix well. Add hot milk. Cook until thickened, stirring constantly. Add cucumber and bouillon cubes and continue to cook until tender, about 20-30 minutes. Stir frequently. Add parsley and Worcestershire sauce. Season with salt and pepper to taste. Mix well. Garnish each portion with a dab of sour cream or paprika or a cucumber slice, as desired. 6 servings

BANANA CAKE AND TOPPING

2 cups flour	1 1/2 cups sugar
1 teaspoon soda	2 eggs
1 teaspoon baking powder	1 cup mashed bananas
1 teaspoon salt	3/4 cup buttermilk
1/2 cup shortening	1 teaspoon vanilla

Sift together flour, soda, baking powder and salt. In separate bowl, cream shortening and slowly add sugar; gradually add eggs and beat well. In another bowl, combine bananas, buttermilk and vanilla. Alternately add flour mixture and wet ingredients to shortening mixture, beginning and ending with flour mixture. Pour into a greased 13x9-inch pan and bake in 350° oven for 35 to 40 minutes. Add topping and broil in oven for 2 minutes

Topping

2/3 cup brown sugar, firmly packed	1 teaspoon vanilla
1/4 cup light cream or evaporated milk	1 cup chopped nuts
6 tablespoons butter or margarine	1 cup coconut

Combine brown sugar, cream, butter, vanilla, nuts and coconut. Cook over medium heat until butter and sugar are melted. Pour on baked banana cake. Broil a few minutes in oven with door open. Watch carefully so topping doesn't burn.

FRIDAY
Chinese beef with green peppers *
Buttered noodles
Buttered cabbage / Green salad
Raisin bread

CHINESE BEEF WITH GREEN PEPPERS

2 teaspoons cornstarch
3 tablespoons soy sauce
2 tablespoons vegetable oil
1 clove garlic, cut in half

1 pound beef round or tenderloin, sliced thin
    and cut in strips
1 large green pepper, sliced in ¹/₄-inch strips

Dissolve corn starch in soy sauce. Set aside. Preheat oil and garlic in Wok or electric skillet at 375°. Remove garlic. Stir-fry beef and peppers about 3 minutes, until beef loses its redness and peppers are crisp-tender. Add soy sauce mixture. Cook and stir until thickened, about 1 minute. 4 servings.

SATURDAY
Baked turkey breast
Jalpeno stuffed potatoes *
Buttered beets with egg slices
Green salad
Cheese and onion loaf *
Chocolate yogurt or ice milk

JALAPENO STUFFED POTATOES

4 hot baked potatoes
1 tablespoon butter or margarine
1 tablespoon milk

¹/₄ teaspoon salt
1 cup (¹/₄ pound) Jalapeno pepper pasteurized
    processed cheese spread

Slice tops from baked potatoes; scoop out centers to form a shell. Mash potatoes; combine with butter, milk and salt. Beat until fluffy. Stir in process cheese spread; fill shells. Bake at 375° for 20 minutes. 4-8 servings.

CHEESE AND ONION LOAF

1 loaf (16 ounces) Vienna bread, unsliced
¹/₂ cup (1 stick) butter or margarine

2 cups thinly-sliced onion
1 cup (4 ounces) shredded Cheddar cheese

Slice bread about ³/₄ of the way through into ¹/₂-inch slices. Melt butter in a large skillet. Saute onions until tender and butter is absorbed, about 6 minutes. Reserve ¹/₃-cup of the cooked onion mixture. Distribute the onion mixture between bread slices. Reserve ¹/₂-cup of the cheese. Sprinkle small amount of cheese between each slice of bread. Spread reserved onions and cheese over top of bread. Bake at 350° until cheese melts and bread is warm, about 8 minutes. Serve immediately. 6-8 servings.

May - Third Week

FAMILY REUNIONS TRADITIONALLY BRING together families and friends. One favorite entree is roast beef. It can be a disaster, so be careful. It is usually no food safety problem if cooked thoroughly, served hot, and refrigerated after the meal. But rare roast beef, served with pan drippings, is another matter since it provides the perfect spot for bacteria to grow and develop.If you must serve rare beef at buffets, cook it at least to an internal temperature of 140°. Heat the pan drippings to the boiling point before serving. And don't let the meat stand more than 2 hours at room temperature. Refrigerate leftovers promptly. If gravy or drippings are kept for a second meal, boil them a few minutes before serving.

Creamed vegetables are a buffet favorite, but are perishable, too. Serve them hot, and don't let them stand more than 2 hours at room temperature. Refrigerate quickly after the meal.

Your family may enjoy meals every day without problems, but on holidays when large groups get together, the types and larger quantities of food present different problems. You may not have enough refrigerator space. Holiday meals are fun but need careful planning. Don't try to feed more people than you can handle. Consider the size and quantity of the cooking equipment you have, your supply of eating utensils and dishes. Figure out how much refrigerator space you'll need to store foods, and keep them all clean, cold and covered for happy holiday eating.

SUNDAY
Old-fashioned chicken pie *
Eggplant almondine *
Buttered green beans
Tossed salad
Hot rolls with butter
Apple chip cake *

OLD-FASHIONED CHICKEN PIE

1 (4-5 pound) stewing chicken, cut up	*¼ teaspoon pepper*
2 sprigs parsley	*¼ cup plus 2 tablespoons flour*
4 ribs celery, sliced	*¼ cup (½ stick) butter or margarine or water*
1 carrot, sliced	*Salt and pepper to taste*
1 onion, sliced	*Dash of tabasco (optional)*
2 teaspoons salt	*12 refrigerator biscuits*

Place chicken in a deep skillet and barely cover with water. Add parsley, celery, carrot, onion, 2 teaspoons salt and ¼ teaspoon pepper. Bring water to a boil and then reduce heat to a simmer and cook, covered, until tender, about 30 minutes. Let chicken cool in broth for 1 to 2 hours. Cut meat from the bone in bite-sized pieces. discard vegetables and reserve broth. In a saucepan, reduce broth to 3 cups over high heat. Combine flour and butter and add to reduced broth. Whisk until smooth. Season to taste with salt, pepper and tabasco. Place chicken in a 1 ½ quart shallow casserole, cover with gravy and top with 12 uncooked biscuits. Overlap the biscuits so they cover the pie completely. Bake in a 450° oven for 15 to 20 minutes. 6 servings. Note: If butter is not used, mix flour with a little water to make a smooth, thin paste before adding to broth.

EGGPLANT ALMONDINE

1 ½ pounds eggplant
1 teaspoon salt
½ cup (1 stick) butter or margarine
½ cup chopped almonds
⅔ cup finely-chopped onion

¼ cup chopped parsley
¾ cup cracker crumbs
2 eggs, beaten
2 tablespoons milk
1 cup shredded, sharp Cheddar cheese

Peel eggplant and cut into cubes. Place in saucepan, add small amount of water and salt. Bring to a boil; cover, and simmer 15 minutes or until tender. Drain and beat until fluffy with electric mixer. In medium-sized sauce pan, melt butter; add almonds. Saute until golden in color. Remove almonds and set aside. Add onions to butter in skillet; cook over low heat until transparent. Add parsley and crumbs; stir in eggplant. Add eggs, milk and almonds. Turn mixture into a greased 1-quart casserole and bake in a 400° oven for 15 minutes or until hot. Top with Cheddar cheese and bake until cheese has melted. 6 servings

APPLE CHIP CAKE

1 ½ cups oil
2 cups sugar
3 eggs, well-beaten
3 cups flour
1 teaspoon salt

1 teaspoon soda
3 cups chopped apples
1 cup chopped pecans
2 teaspoons vanilla

Combine oil, sugar and eggs. Sift together flour, salt and soda. Add to egg mixture. Add apples, pecans and vanilla. Pour into well greased and floured tube pan. Bake in 325° oven for 1 hour.

Glaze

½ cup (1 stick) butter or margarine
1 cup dark brown sugar, firmly packed

¼ cup milk

In a sauce pan, melt butter and sugar; bring to a boil and boil for 2 ½ minutes. Add milk and mix well. Pour mixture over hot cake. Let set in pan for 2 hours before removing cake.

MONDAY
Corn and beef stuffed peppers *
Cottage fried potatoes *
Carrot sticks, celery, stuffed olives
Bagels and cream cheese
Fresh fruit

CORN AND BEEF STUFFED PEPPERS

4 large green peppers
1 tablespoon oil
1 pound ground beef
¾ cup chopped onion
1 (8 ounce) can whole kernel corn, drained
1 teaspoon salt

⅛ teaspoon pepper
¼ teaspoon basil
¾ cup (3 ounces) shredded, sharp Cheddar cheese
1 (10 ½ ounce) can tomato soup,
   diluted with ⅓ cup water
¼ cup water

Wash peppers thoroughly; remove top, seeds and membranes. Chop tops. Heat oil in large skillet; saute beef, onion and pepper tops over medium heat until meat is browned. Stir in corn, salt, pepper and basil. Turn into large bowl; clean skillet. Fill peppers with meat mixture and arrange in skillet. Sprinkle peppers with cheese; pour soup over peppers; add remaining ¼ cup water to bottom of frypan. Cover; simmer for 60 minutes or until tender. 4 servings.

COTTAGE FRIED POTATOES

3 bacon slices	*1 teaspoon salt*
3 cups thinly-sliced potatoes, peeled or unpeeled	*¼ teaspoon pepper*

Cook bacon slices in a frypan until crisp. Remove from pan and crumble. Fry potatoes in the bacon fat until well browned; sprinkle with salt and pepper. Cover the pan and cook over low heat until potatoes are tender. Sprinkle with bacon pieces before serving. 4-6 servings.

TUESDAY
Shrimp and noodle verdi *
Buttered broccoli with bacon *
Orange pecan salad
Hot buttered English muffins with Jam

SHRIMP AND NOODLE VERDI

8-9 ounce package green noodles, cooked, drained	*1 (10 ³/₄ ounce) can cream of mushroom*
5 green onions, sliced, use tops	*or cream of chicken soup*
2 to 3 pounds shrimp, cooked and shelled	*1 teaspoon prepared mustard*
1 cup sour cream	*2 eggs, slightly beaten*
1 cup mayonnaise	*1 ½ cup (6 ounces) shredded sharp Cheddar cheese*

Combine noodles and onions. Place in a greased 9x13-inch baking dish. Top with shrimp. In large mixing bowl, combine sour cream, mayonnaise, soup, mustard, eggs and 1 cup Cheddar cheese. Pour over noodles and shrimp. Bake in 350° oven for 30 minutes or until bubbly.
Final cooking can be done in microwave oven. Cook on medium-high for 10 to 12 minutes. After 5 minutes, rotate dish ¼-turn. After next 5 minutes, top with Cheddar cheese, rotate ¼-turn and cook 2 minutes longer. Let stand 5 minutes outside of oven before serving. 6 servings.

BUTTERED BROCCOLI WITH BACON

1 ½-pounds broccoli, trimmed and cut into	*½ teaspoon salt*
* desired pieces*	*1-2 tablespoons Parmesan cheese*
1-2 tablespoons butter or margarine	*6 slices bacon, cooked and crumbled*

Cover broccoli with water, add salt and bring to a boil. Simmer 4-5 minutes or until broccoli stalks are barely tender when pierced with a sharp pointed knife. Drain. Arrange broccoli on serving platter. Dot with butter; sprinkle with Parmesan cheese and crumbled bacon. 6 servings.

ORANGE PECAN SALAD

1 (8 ounce) bottle oil and vinegar dressing
2 tablespoons orange juice
1 teaspoon orange rind
2 quarts coarsly-chopped assorted greens

1 cup orange slices
1/2 cup chopped dates
1/2 cup chopped pecans

Combine dressing, orange juice and orange rind; mix well. Combine greens, orange slices, dates and pecans; toss lightly. Toss with dressing before serving. 6 servings.

WEDNESDAY
Elegant crab dish *
Baked sweet potatoes
German-style cabbage and apples *
Bunker Hill brown bread *
Pineapple chunks in white creme de menthe

ELEGANT CRAB DISH

6 slices Holland rusk or toast
2 large tomatoes (6 slices)
1 1/2 pounds crab meat, flaked, or 2 (6 1/2 ounce)
  cans, drained and flaked

Dressing
8 slices bacon, cooked and crumbled
2 eggs, hard-cooked and grated

Place one slice Holland rusk or toast on individual serving plate. Top with one slice of tomato, then crab meat. Pour dressing over crab; sprinkle with bacon crumbles and top with grated egg. 6 servings.

Dressing

1/2 cup mayonnaise
1/4 cup chili sauce

1 tablespoon lemon juice
1 tablespoon horseradish sauce

Combine all ingredients; stir until well-mixed.

GERMAN-STYLE CABBAGE AND APPLES

2 tablespoons butter
1/3 cup finely-chopped onion
2 tablespoons sugar
1/3 cup red wine vinegar
1 teaspoon salt
4 cups shredded red cabbage

1 cup diced cooking apple (approximately
  1 large apple)
2 tablespoons sugar
1 cup sour cream at room temperature
Apple slices (optional)

In skillet, melt butter; saute onion with 2 tablespoons sugar for 5 minutes. Stir in vinegar, salt and cabbage; cover and simmer for 10 minutes. Add apple and 2 tablespoons sugar; cover and cook about 5 minutes. Transfer to heated platter; spoon sour cream over center of cabbage. Garnish with apple slices, if desired. 6 servings.

BUNKER HILL BROWN BREAD

1 ½ cups flour	½ cup currants
⅓ cup sugar	2 eggs, slightly beaten
2 teaspoons soda	1 ½ cups buttermilk
1 ½ teaspoons salt	¾ cup light molasses
1 cup wheat germ	¼ cup cooking oil
1 cup fine graham cracker crumbs	

Combine flour, sugar, soda and salt in a large bowl. Stir well to blend. Add wheat germ, crumbs and currants. Mix well. In separate bowl, combine eggs, buttermilk, molasses and oil. Mix well. Add egg mixture to dry ingredients; stir until all ingredients are moistened. Pour batter into 2 well-greased and lightly-floured 1-pound coffee cans (do not cover). Bake in 350° oven for 55-60 minutes or until a wooden pick inserted in the center comes out clean. Cool 10 minutes in cans. Loosen bread with sharp knife or spatula and remove from cans. Cool completely. 2 round loaves.

THURSDAY
Cheeseburger pie *
Fresh spinach in garlic butter *
Marinated tomatoes and onion rings
Easy strawberry Bavarian *

CHEESEBURGER PIE

1 pound ground beef	1 (9-inch) pastry shell, unbaked
1 (8 ounce) can tomato sauce, divided	2 cups (8 ounces) shredded, sharp Cheddar cheese
½ teaspoon oregano	1 egg, beaten
1 teaspoon salt	¼ cup milk
¼ teaspoon pepper	½ teaspoon dry mustard
¼ cup chopped onion	½ teaspoon Worcestershire sauce
½ cup very fine bread crumbs	¼ cup chili sauce
¼ cup chopped green pepper	

Crumble and brown beef in skillet. Drain off excess fat, if necessary. Add ½ cup tomato sauce, oregano, salt, pepper, crumbs and green pepper. Spread in pastry-lined pie pan. Combine cheese, egg, milk, mustard and Worcestershire sauce. Spread over filling. Bake for 30 minutes in 425° oven. Combine remaining tomato sauce with chili sauce (not necessary to heat). Serve pie in wedges with tomato/ chili sauce topping. 6-8 servings.

GARLIC BUTTER

½ cup (1 stick) butter, at room temperature	3 tablespoons finely-chopped garlic
1 tablespoon lemon juice	Salt and freshly-ground black pepper to taste

Cream the butter and beat in the lemon juice, a little at a time. Beat in the garlic and season with salt and pepper. Serve over hot spinach. Yield: about ¾ cup.

EASY STRAWBERRY BAVARIAN

1 (16 ounce) package frozen strawberries,
  defrosted and drained (save juice)
1/4 cup cold milk
2 envelopes unflavored gelatin
1/2 cup juice drained from strawberries,
  heated to boiling

1/4 cup sugar
2 egg yolks
Red food coloring (optional)
1 cup heavy cream
1 cup crushed ice, drained

Pour cold milk into blender container, add gelatin and hot juice. Cover and process at STIR for about 1 minute. When gelatin is dissolved. Remove cover; add strawberries, sugar, egg yolks and food coloring, if desired, and continue processing (on LIQUIFY) until strawberries are liquefied. Add cream and crushed ice and continue processing until ice is liquefied. Pour at once into serving dishes. Let set 5 to 10 minutes before serving. 6-8 servings.

FRIDAY
Mother's Day Out Dinner
World's Fair chicken
Buttered noodles
Fresh asparagus with hot wine and mayonnaise sauce
Fresh fruit salad with cherry cream dressing
Hot buttered French bread
Chocolate Rounds
Commercial strawberry ice milk (optional)

Plan Of Work
Day before:
1. Prepare chocolate rounds
2 hours before dinner:
2. Prepare chicken and place in oven.
3. While chicken is cooking, prepare fruit and dressing for salad. Refrigerate until ready to serve.
4. Prepare bread. Do not heat until chicken is out of oven.
25 minutes before chicken is done:
5. Boil water and cook noodles.
6. Prepare asparagus.
7. Remove chicken from oven; raise temperature, place bread in oven.
8. Assemble salad.
9. Complete meal and serve. Bread will be ready in time.

WORLD'S FAIR CHICKEN

3 whole broiler-fryer chicken breasts, halved
2 tablespoons butter or margarine
1 teaspoon salt
1/4 teaspoon pepper
1/2 cup blanched, slivered almonds
1/2 cup raisins

1/4 cup chopped chutney
1 1/2 cups orange juice
1/2 teaspoon cinnamon
1/2 teaspoon curry powder
1/16 teaspoon or a pinch of thyme

In greased large shallow baking pan place chicken in single layer, skin side up. Dot with butter. Sprinkle salt and pepper on chicken. Bake in 425° oven for 15 minutes. In saucepan, combine almonds, raisins, chutney, orange juice, cinnamon, curry and thyme; simmer about 10 minutes or until flavors blend. Pour sauce over chicken. Reduce heat to 350° and bake about 1 hour longer or until fork can be inserted in chicken with ease. 6 servings.

BUTTERED NOODLES

1 (8 ounce) package noodles
3 quarts boiling water

1 teaspoon salt
$1/4$ cup butter or margarine

Add up to 1 teaspoon salt to boiling water. Add noodles and stir to separate. Return to boiling. Boil, uncovered, stirring occasionally, 5-7 minutes or until al dente. Drain. Serve immediately. If noodles are to be held a short time, drain and return to pot. Toss with a little vegetable oil or butter; cover. 6 servings.

STEAMED FRESH ASPARAGUS WITH HOT WINE AND MAYONNAISE SAUCE

1 tablespoon instant minced onions
$1/_4$ cup sauterne
2 tablespoons chopped parsley

1 tablespoon lemon juice
$3/_4$ cup mayonnaise
1 pound fresh asparagus, steamed

Add onion to wine, let stand 10 minutes. Add remaining ingredients. Heat over hot but not boiling water; stir until blended. Serve over steamed asparagus. 4-6 servings.

CHERRY CREAM DRESSING

1 cup sour cream
$1/2$ cup Maraschino cherry juice

1 tablespoon lemon juice

Combine sour cream, cherry juice and lemon juice. Chill. Serve over mixed fresh fruit.

HOT BUTTERED FRENCH BREAD SLICES

1 loaf French bread

$1/4$ cup ($1/2$ stick) butter or margarine, softened

Slice bread, do not cut completely through the bottom. With soft butter, spread on one side of each slice. Wrap bread in foil. Heat before serving.

CHOCOLATE ROUNDS

$1/2$ cup shortening
1 cup sugar
2 eggs
1 teaspoon vanilla
2 tablespoons water

2 squares (1 oz. each) unsweetened chocolate, melted
2 cups biscuit mix
1 cup chopped nuts
Quick chocolate frosting

Combine shortening, sugar, eggs, vanilla, water and chocolate. Stir in biscuit mix and nuts. Drop dough by teaspoonfuls onto ungreased baking sheet. Bake at 350° for 15 minutes. Cool and frost with Quick Chocolate Frosting. About 4 dozen cookies.

Quick Chocolate Frosting

1 cup powdered sugar   *2-3 tablespoons water or milk*
1/4 cup cocoa

Combine all ingredients; blend.

SATURDAY
Broiled ham with pineapple slices *
Buttered Brussels sprouts
Cabbage and carrot salad
Onion rolls
Caramel banana pudding *

BROILED HAM WITH PINEAPPLE SLICES

Center-cut ham slices, 1/2-inch thick   *6 pineapple slices*

Trim excess fat from ham slices. Clip edge of ham slightly. Place on broiler rack. Broil one side. Turn ham; place pineapple slices on ham. Broil until brown. 6 servings.

CARAMEL BANANA PUDDING

1/4 cup butter or margarine   *3 eggs, separated*
1 1/2 cups firmly-packed brown sugar   *1 teaspoon vanillia extract*
3 tablespoons all-purpose flour   *Vanilla wafers*
Dash of salt   *3 or 4 bananas*
1 (13 ounce) can evaporated milk   *2 tablespoons sugar*
3/4 cup water

Melt butter in top of a double boiler; stir in brown sugar, flour, salt. Gradually stir in evaporated milk and water; cook until thickened, stirring constantly (about 15 or 20 minutes). Beat egg yolks until thick and lemon colored. Stir some of hot mixture into yolks; add to remaining hot mixture, stirring constantly. Cook 2 minutes longer or until thickened. Remove from heat and stir in vanilla. Cool. Line bottom and sides of a lightly-greased 1 3/4-quart casserole with vanilla wafers. Slice enough bananas to cover bottom layer; top with half of pudding. Layer with vanilla wafers, remaining banana slices and remaining pudding. Beat egg whites (at room temperature) until soft peaks form; gradually add 2 tablespoons sugar and continue beating until stiff peaks form. Spread over pudding. Bake at 350° for 10 minutes or until top is brown. Serve warm or chilled. Left overs good the second day. 8 servings.

May - Fourth Week

WITH MAY COMES THE GATHERING OF FRIENDS for reunions and other outdoor festivities. One popular food that is often served at picnics is fried chicken. Foods such as this are usually cooked inside in deep fat. When frying, the cook should be aware of the dangers involved. Here are some safety points for deep frying in the kitchen.

One cause of kitchen fires is overheated fats used in deep fat frying. Avoid splattering fat onto a hot element or onto an open flame. Do not heat fats above 400° and work carefully around hot fats.. If fat should happen to ignite in the kitchen, smother the flames. If possible put a lid on the pan. Turn off the gas or electricity. Aluminum foil is effective in smothering a flame by keeping air away from the fire. Baking soda can be sprinkled on the flames. Do not pour water on a fat fire! A grease fire will spread if water is poured on it because the water causes the hot fat to spatter. If you receive a burn while cooking, immediately apply ice to the burned area. Keep ice in direct contact with the burned area until medical help comes or for at least 20 minutes. Immediate application of ice is important to reduce the damage inflicted by the burn.

Certain precautions can be taken to minimize the possibility of fires and burns while deep-fat frying. Pans should always have the handles positioned over the counter rather than protruding out from the range. Never leave a pan of hot fat unattended. Remember that the fat will bubble up when moist foods are added to it; avoid putting so much fat in the container that the fat overflows when moist foods are added. Carefully add foods to hot fat to reduce the likelihood of splashing and splattering. Have the lid of the deep-fat fryer or a roll of aluminum foil within reach in case they should be needed.

Deep-fat frying, broiling and other cookery procedures, are only dangerous when you forget to consider kitchen safety. There is no good reason for fires of any kind in the kitchen. Think safety.

Rules for frying chicken

1. Cut up a whole chicken into serving pieces. Pre-cut chicken loses moistness and flavor.
2. Small chickens have more flavor, but large chickens have more meat. Make a choice.
3. Remove skin before frying. Skinned chicken can be crispier, and it contains less fat.
4. Place dark meat in center of the skillet, because these pieces take longer to cook.
5. Never season with salt and pepper before frying, but generously season immediately after removing from the skillet.
6. Drain chicken for at least one minute on a paper towel to drain off excess fat.
7. Oil must be very hot to cook faster and give less time to absorb fat.

SUNDAY
Chicken quiche *
Stewed tomatoes
Buttered baby Limas
Mushrooms in the greens salad *
Pineapple sherbert

CHICKEN QUICHE

5-6 broiler-fryer chicken thighs (1 ½ cups cubed)
4 slices bacon
¼ cup chopped onion
¼ cup chopped green pepper
2 (9 inch) frozen pie shells
½ teaspoon salt
¼ teaspoon pepper

⅛ teaspoon nutmeg
1 cup (4 ounces) shredded Swiss cheese
½ cup (2 ounces) shredded Cheddar cheese
3 eggs slightly beaten
¾ cup milk
¾ cup sour cream

Remove bones from thighs and chop chicken into bite-sized cubes. In a large fry pan, fry bacon until crisp. Remove bacon and crumble. Pour off all but ¼-cup bacon drippings. Over medium heat, saute cubes of thighs, onion and green peppers for about 15 minutes. Drain and spread sauteed ingredients over bottom of two frozen pie shells; sprinkle with salt, pepper and nutmeg. Add crumbled bacon. Sprinkle with Swiss and Cheddar cheese. Combine eggs, milk and sour cream; pour over ingredients in both pie shells. Bake in 400° oven for 20 minutes. Reduce heat to 350° and continue baking for 30-40 minutes more, until puffy and a knife when inserted near the center comes out clean. Slice each pie into 6 pieces. (Leftovers can be reheated and served next day or eat one quiche and freeze the other.) 12 servings.

MUSHROOMS IN THE GREENS SALAD

½ pound fresh mushrooms, sliced
1 medium avocado, peeled and sliced
1 medium zucchini, thinly sliced
1 pint cherry tomatoes, halved
¼ cup sliced green onions (use tops)
1 teaspoon sugar

1 teaspoon salt
½ teaspoon coarse-ground black pepper
*3 tablespoons vegetable oil ***
*2 tablespoons cider vinegar ***
Lettuce leaves or salad greens

In medium-sized bowl, combine mushrooms, avocado, zucchini, tomatoes and onions. Sprinkle with sugar, salt and pepper. Combine oil and vinegar. Pour over mushroom mixture. Toss until well coated. Serve on lettuce leaves. 6 servings.
*5 tablespoons seasoned rice vinegar may be substituted for oil and vinegar.

MONDAY
Beef cube goulash *
Mashed potatoes
Green beans in garlic sauce *
Cole slaw
Apple muffins with fruit preserves

BEEF CUBE GOULASH

2 pounds beef round, cut in 1-inch cubes
2 cups chopped onion
¼ cup (½ stick) butter or margarine
2 tablespoons commercial steak sauce
2 teaspoons salt

2 teaspoons paprika
2 (8 ounce) cans tomato sauce
2 tablespoons flour
½ cup chopped parsley

Trim excess fat from meat. Pre-heat broiler. Place meat and onions in broiler pan. Brush them with butter and steak sauce; brown lightly under the broiler, tossing so that second side also browns. Reset oven to 350° and remove pan. Combine salt, pepper, tomato sauce and flour, stirring to make a smooth mixture. Cover meat with sauce; cover tightly with foil. Place in the oven; bake for 2 hours. Serve sprinkled with parsley. 6 servings.

GREEN BEANS IN GARLIC SAUCE

1 ½ pounds green beans   Salt to taste
3 tablespoons olive oil   Pepper to taste
4 cloves garlic, crushed

Wash and trim green beans. Cook in boiling water for 5 minutes. Drain well; dry thoroughly with paper towel. In a large skillet, heat olive oil; add garlic and heat, do not brown. Add beans; saute until heated through and slightly browned.

TUESDAY
Pollo Alla Cacciatore *
Stir fry zucchini and yellow squash
Tomato cheese aspic *
French bread rolls
Pass the chocolate mints

POLLO ALLA CACCIATORE

2 ½ to 3 pounds cut-up chicken, or 3-4   2 teaspoons fennell seed
   boned chicken breasts, split   ½ teaspoon caraway seeds
2 garlic cloves, crushed   ¼ teaspoon cinnamon
1 medium onion, chopped fine   2 teaspoons oregano
2 cans (15 to 16 ounces) tomatoes or canned   2 bay leaves
   diced tomatoes   1 ½ teaspoons salt
1 (6 ounce) can tomato paste   1 teaspoon crushed red pepper (optional)
½ cup dry white wine   1 (8 ounce) package spaghettini
1 teaspoon sugar

Remove skin from chicken. Place in a shallow pan with pieces barely touching. Combine garlic, onion, canned tomatoes, tomato paste, white wine, sugar, fennel seeds, caraway seeds, cinnamon, bay leaves, salt and pepper. Pour over chicken pieces; cover and bake at 350° until the chicken is tender, about 1 hour. Remove cover and continue cooking for 30 minutes, basting occasionally. Cook spaghettini according to package directions (al dente). Place on individual serving plates. Remove the bay leaves from the chicken mixture and place the chicken pieces on the spaghettini with the sauce liberally spooned over them. 6 servings.

TOMATO CHEESE ASPIC

1 envelope unflavored gelatin   1 teaspoon Worcestershire sauce
¼ cup cold water   Dash of Tabasco
½ teaspoon celery salt   2 tablespoons vinegar
½ teaspoon salt   2 tablespoons finely-chopped chives
½ teaspoon sugar   1 cup cottage cheese
2 cups tomato juice or vegetable cocktail juice

Sprinkle gelatin over water. Let stand a few minutes until softened. Combine celery salt, salt, sugar and tomato juice; heat until almost boiling. Add gelatin and stir until dissolved. Add Worcestershire sauce, Tabasco, vinegar and chives; mix well. Pour into 6 individual molds or 1 quart-sized mold. Chill. When mixture begins to congeal, press a spoonful of cottage cheese in the center of each mold or interspersed throughout the large mold. Chill until firm. Unmold. 6 servings.

WEDNESDAY
Baked ham with applesauce glaze *
Baked sweet potatoes
Buttered broccoli
Spinach salad
Hot biscuits
Apple cobbler

BAKED HAM WITH APPLESAUCE GLAZE

Canned smoked ham   *Applesauce*

Place ham on rack in open roasting pan. Do not add water. Do not cover. Roast in a slow oven, 325°. Allow 18-20 minutes per pound for roasting. During the last 20-30 minutes of roasting time, spread applesauce over meat and return to oven to finish roasting.

THURSDAY
Swedish meatballs
Toasted onion rice *
Stir fry snow peas
Pineapple and grapefruit mold *
Hard rolls
Chocolate pound cake slices

TOASTED ONION RICE

1 cup uncooked rice
1 (4 ounce) can sliced mushrooms, drained
1 (1 ³/₈ ounce) package dehydrated onion soup mix

1 tablespoon butter
2 cups boiling water (chicken or beef broth
  may be used)

Place rice in 1 ½ quart baking pan. Toast, in oven, at 400°, stirring occasionally, until golden. Add remaining ingredients. Cover; reduce temperature to 350° and bake 25-30 minutes longer. 6 servings.

PINEAPPLE AND GRAPEFRUIT MOLD

1 (20 ounce) can pineapple tidbits with juice
1 (3 ounce) package lemon-flavored gelatin
1 (3 ounce) package cherry-flavored gelatin
²/₃ cup Maraschino cherry juice or grenadine syrup
³/₄ cup orange juice

⅓ cup lemon juice
2 cups grapefruit sections (either fresh or
  well-drained canned)
Curly lettuce
Sour cream or mayonnaise

In small saucepan, heat pineapple juice only; bring to a boil. Stir in lemon and cherry-flavored gelatins. Stir in cherry juice or grenadine syrup, orange juice and lemon juice. Chill until gelatin begins to set up. Add pineapple tidbits and grapefruit sections. Pour into a 6-cup mold. Chill. Unmold on curly lettuce or endive. Top with a dollop of sour cream or mayonnaise. 6 servings.

FRIDAY
Spring Catfish Supper
Fillet of catfish in wine sauce *
Green bean and corn bake *
Lyonnaise carrots *
Iceberg lettuce with Monticello dressing *
Bread sticks (commercial)
Baked caramel pudding *

Plan Of Work

Early in the day:

1. Prepare green bean and corn casserole, ready to bake.
2. Prepare the salad dressing. It must be allowed to set for 2 hours before using.
3. If time is limited, carrots can be prepared at this time also. Carrots do not change color when reheated
4. Baked custard may be prepared early and reheated if you want to serve it warm.

About 1 hour before serving:

5. Assemble all ingredients for the catfish dish. Start cooking about 20 minutes before serving and serve immediately.

35 minutes before serving:

6. Place green bean casserole in oven.
7. Prepare salad and add dressing just before serving.
8. Heat custard pudding while eating dinner.

FILLET OF CATFISH IN WINE SAUCE

1/3 cup white seedless raisins
1 1/2 pounds catfish fillets (or any white fish fillet)
1/4 cup flour
1/2 teaspoon sage
3/4 teaspoon pepper
1 tablespoon butter or margarine

Vegetable coating spray
3 tablespoons lemon juice
1/4 cup plus 2 tablespoons dry white wine
1/4 cup plus 2 tablespoons dry sherry
1/2 tablespoon soy sauce

Soak raisins in water to cover until softened (about 10 minutes) and drain. Cut fish into 6 servings. Combine flour, sage and pepper. Dip fish lightly into the seasoned flour. Heat butter in a 10-inch skillet coated with cooking spray. Add coated fish; top with lemon juice and drained raisins. Reduce heat to low. Cover pan and cook slowly about 10 minutes. Remove cover; turn fillets carefully and brown on the other side. Combine wine, sherry and soy sauce. Add to skillet. Bring to a boil, reduce heat and simmer until sauce has reached desired thickness (but not too dry), about 5 to 8 minutes. Fillets will be very tender. Remove from pan carefully. 6 servings.

GREEN BEAN AND CORN BAKE

1/4 cup (1/2 stick) butter or margarine
1/2 cup chopped onion
1/2 cup chopped celery
1/2 cup chopped green pepper
1 (16 ounce) can French style green beans, drained
1 (16 ounce) can whole kernel corn, drained

1/2 cup (2 ounces) shredded sharp Cheddar cheese
1 (8 ounce) carton sour cream
1 (10 1/2 ounce) can cream of celery soup
1 cup crushed cheese crackers
1 cup slivered almonds
1/4 cup (1/2 stick) melted butter or margarine

Saute the onion, celery and green pepper in ¼ cup butter. Combine beans, corn, sour cream, celery soup and sauteed vegetables and mix well. Pour into buttered 2-quart casserole. Top with crushed crackers and almonds. Drizzle with melted butter. Bake at 350° for 30 minutes. 6 servings. Good leftover or to freeze.

LYONNAISE CARROTS

12-18 carrots
¼ cup water

¼ cup (½ stick) butter or margarine

Scrape carrots; cut into halves or thirds. Wash, do not shake off any water from the surface of the carrots. Place carrots in a pan that will be almost full when carrots are added. Add water and butter. Pan must have a well-fitted lid. Cover. Place on high heat. When steam is expelled around the rim and the lid twirls when turned, turn heat down to lowest point immediately. Do not lift lid. Simmer about 15 to 20 minutes. Drain and serve. 6 servings.

MONTICELLO DRESSING

⅔ cup salad oil
1 tablespoon sesame (benne) seed
1 small clove garlic, crushed

1 teaspoon salt
½ teaspoon white pepper
⅓ cup tarragon or wine vinegar

Pour salad oil into small saucepan. Add sesame seed; heat over low heat 5-7 minutes. Remove from heat. Add garlic, salt, pepper and vinegar. Place in covered jar; cool, then chill 2 hours or longer. Shake well before serving. Will dress a quart of chopped western iceberg lettuce. 1 cup dressing.

BAKED CARAMEL PUDDING

1 ½ cups biscuit mix (do not pack)
½ cup brown sugar, Packed
½ cup milk

1 teaspoon vanilla
½ cup coarsely chopped nuts

Topping

¾ cup brown sugar, packed
3 tablespoons butter or margarine
1 teaspoon vanilla

1 cup boiling water
Whipped cream or whipped topping (optional)

Combine biscuit mix and ½ cup sugar. Add milk and vanilla. Stir to blend. Spread batter into a greased 11x7x1-inch pan. Sprinkle nuts over the batter. Combine topping ingredients except whipped cream. Pour over batter and nuts. Bake in a 350° oven for 30-35 minutes. Spoon into dessert dishes. Serve warm with whipped cream or topping. 6-8 servings.

SATURDAY
Vichyssoise (French potato soup) *
Ham and egg salad in pita bread
Asparagus in aspic *
Grapes, canteloup, melon in creme d'menthe

VICHYSSOISE

1 can (10 ½ ounce) condensed chicken broth
1 can (10 ³/4 ounce) cream of potato soup
1 soup can of milk

1 (8 ounce) package cream cheese, softened
4-5 green onions, chopped (use tops)
2 tablespoons finely chopped chives

Add broth, soup, milk, cheese and onions into a blender jar. Blend until smooth. Pour into a two quart saucepan. Heat and stir, do not boil. Chill 6 hours. Serve cold, topped with chives. 4-6 servings.

ASPARAGUS IN ASPIC

1 envelope unflavored gelatin
2 tablespoons cold water
1 (6 ounce) package lime flavored gelatin
1 ½ cups boiling water
2 (15 ounce) cans cut-up asparagus
1 cup mayonnaise

1 cup milk
2 tablespoons tarragon vinegar
½ teaspoon salt
1 cup (4 ounces) shredded sharp Cheddar cheese
3 tablespoons grated onion
Tabasco sauce, to taste

Soften unflavored gelatin in water. Combine lime flavored gelatin and unflavored gelatin and dissolve in boiling water. Chill until slightly thick. Drain asparagus; reserve ¼ of the liquid. Combine liquid with mayonnaise, milk, vinegar, salt, and gelatin mixture, and stir until smooth. Add asparagus, cheese, onion and hot sauce. Pour into 6-cup mold and chill. 6-8 servings.

June

June - First Week

JUNE IS DAIRY MONTH and a good time to write about our most celebrated food: milk. A country is as strong as its people; and one reason the American people are healthy and strong is because we have had plenty of milk. In addition to its other attributes, milk builds strong bones and teeth due to its excellent supply of calcium and phosphorous. Milk has always been an important source of other nutrients that are necessary for proper development. Maximum retention of these valuable nutrients is assured as milk is stored, processed, transported and distributed in its many different forms.

Even though there are many different forms of milk on today's market, the most prevalent are pasteurized and homogenized milks. Pasteurization is a process by which milk is heated to a high temperature and held there long enough to destroy all pathogenic organisms and most of the nonpathogenic bacteria so that it can be safely consumed. All nutrients are retained with the exception of slight losses in some of the vitamins. All pasteurized milk is homogenized, which is part of the pasteurization process. The heated milk is channeled to the homogenizer where it is forced under high pressure through tiny openings. Nothing is added or removed. It is simply treated mechanically to break up the fat into smaller globules which are dispersed uniformly throughout the milk. This simply means that the milk remains uniform throughout and has a slightly richer taste. Also, a softer curd is formed during digestion and perhaps the milk is easier to digest.

In addition to these two treatments, today's milk appears on the market in many forms to appeal to the varied tastes of consumers. The secret is to read the label to be certain that the milk you are buying is the one to suit your needs, such as whole milk, low fat milk, skim milk, low fat chocolate milk, or ultra high-temperature milk, among others. It is easy to maintain good nutrition with the nutrients found in milk. For the non-milk-drinkers, there is a vast array of great dairy products to suit the taste and need, such as yogurt, ice cream, ice milk and a multitude of cheese varieties.

Since milk is so perishable, always follow the "Three C's" to retain high quality: always keep it Clean, Cold and Covered. Do not allow milks of any kind to remain at room temperature any longer than is absolutely necessary. If left at room temperature with the cap off, organisms may enter and grow and multiply and could cause illness.

The fat content of the product is important for the meal planner. The rich flavor of milk is influenced by the fat content. If family members are restricted to a low fat diet, the adjustments can be helped by selecting a milk product with the desired fat level. Regardless of the fat content, all other nutrients remain the same.

Following are the most used milk products that are found in all markets.

1. Whole milk has a fat content of 3.25 percent.

2. Extra rich milk has a fat content of 4 percent.

3. Low fat milk will be labeled with the fat content and will usually be one of the following, 2 percent, 1 percent, $^1/_2$ percent, or skim milk, usually 0.01 percent.

4. Yogurt will vary in fat content from non-fat up to whole milk yogurt. Read the label to determine the fat content.

5. Cultured buttermilk may be made from whole milk (3.25 percent fat) or skim milk (0.5 percent fat). It is produced by fermentation of milk with lactic acid producing bacteria to give it the characteristic flavor and aroma.

6. Non-fat dry milk solids are produced by spray-drying skim milk. For best quality, the package should be kept tightly closed in a cool, dark, dry place. Quality will remain good for 2 to 3 months after opening the package if properly stored. As the product is used, put the remainder in a smaller container with a tight-fitting lid. To reconstitute, follow package directions, Refrigerate 2 to 3 hours before using to improve flavor. Keep the reconstituted product in the refrigerator.

SUNDAY
Minute steaks
Cottage fried potatoes
Elegant green bean casserole *
Fruit with poppy seed dressing
Hot whole wheat rolls
Fresh strawberry pie *

ELEGANT GREEN BEAN CASSEROLE

2 (16 ounce) cans cut green beans, drained
3/4 cup sour cream
3/4 cup cream of mushroom soup
5 cloves garlic, crushed or 1/2 plus 1/8
   teaspoon garlic powder

1 cup (4 ounces) shredded sharp Cheddar cheese
1 cup crushed saltine crackers
1/4 cup (1 stick) butter or margarine, melted
1 (2.8 ounce) can French fried onion rings

Combine green beans, sour cream, soup and garlic. Put in a greased 1 1/2 quart baking dish. Combine saltines, cheese and butter. Spread on top of vegetable mixture. Bake, uncovered, at 350° for 50 minutes. Remove from oven, top with onion rings. Bake 10 minutes longer. 6 servings.

CHOCOLATE CHIFFON CAKE WITH CREME FILLING

2 eggs, separated
1 1/2 cups granulated sugar
1 3/4 cups sifted cake flour
1 teaspoon salt
1/2 cup buttermilk powder
3/4 teaspoon soda

1/3 cup oil
1 cup water
2 ounces unsweetened chocolate, melted (cool)
1/4 to 1/2 cup grated unsweetened chocolate
Creme filling

In small mixer bowl, beat egg whites until foamy. Beat in 1/2 cup of the sugar, 1 tablespoon at a time; continue beating until stiff and glossy. Set meringue aside. Sift remaining sugar, flour, salt, soda and buttermilk powder into a large mixer bowl. Add oil and 1/2 cup water; beat one minute on high speed, scraping bowl constantly. Add remaining water, egg yolks and chocolate. Beat one minute, scraping bowl occasionally. Fold in meringue. Grease and flour baking pan, 13x9x2-inches or 2 round layer pans, 8 or 9x1/2-inches. Pour batter into pan(s). In a 350° oven bake oblong pan 40 to 50 minutes, layer pans 30 to 35 minutes, or until wooden pick inserted in the center comes out clean. Cool and split to make 4 layers. Fill layers and frost with creme filling, sprinkling each layer with 1 or 2 tablespoons grated unsweetened chocolate. Refrigerate at least 8 hours.
If cake flour is not available, substitute 1 1/2 cups sifted all-purpose flour. Powdered buttermilk is available in supermarkets.

Creme filling

1 1/2 cups chilled whipping cream
1 (8 ounce) package cream cheese, softened
2/3 cup brown sugar, packed

1 teaspoon vanilla
1/4 teaspoon salt

In a chilled bowl, beat cream until stiff. Set aside. In a separate bowl, blend cream cheese, sugar, vanilla and salt. Fold into whipped cream.

MONDAY
Baked chicken quarters
Oven steamed sweet potatoes with whole onions
Marinated vegetable nut salad *
Whole wheat bagel with cream cheese
Pineapple sherbert

MARINATED VEGETABLE-NUT SALAD

³/₄ cup cider vinegar
³/₄ cup sugar
1 tablespoon water
1 teaspoon salt
¹/₂ teaspoon pepper
1 (16 ounce) can small English peas, drained

1 (12 ounce) can whole kernel corn, drained
1 (2 ounce) jar chopped pimiento, drained
1 cup finely-chopped celery
1 cup finely-chopped onion
¹/₂ cup roasted peanuts

In small saucepan, combine vinegar, sugar, water, salt and pepper. Bring to a boil and boil one minute. Cool completely. Combine peas, corn, pimiento, celery and onion. Pour cooled marinade over vegetables. Refrigerate overnight. Drain and just before serving add toasted peanuts. 6 servings.

TUESDAY
Tuna loaf with egg and olive sauce *
Steamed and stir-fry potatoes
Buttered peas
Molded lettuce salad with cottage cheese dressing *
Lemon pudding

TUNA LOAF WITH EGG AND OLIVE SAUCE

2 (6 ¹/₂ ounce) cans tuna (packed in water)
³/₄ cup milk
1 ¹/₂ cups bread crumbs, soft
2 tablespoons sweet pickle, chopped

1 tablespoon lemon juice
1 egg, slightly beaten
1 teaspoon salt

Drain water from tuna and flake. Into a large mixing bowl, add tuna, milk, crumbs, pickle, lemon juice, egg and salt, Blend well. Pack the mixture into a loaf pan. Bake in 350° oven for 30 minutes or until golden brown. Invert on a platter and serve with egg and olive sauce. 6 servings.

Egg and Olive Sauce

2 tablespoons butter or margarine
2 tablespoons flour
1 cup milk

2 eggs, hard cooked and chopped coarsely
6 pimiento stuffed olives, chopped

Melt butter, stir in flour to make a smooth paste; gradually add milk. Cook, stirring constantly, until thick and smooth. Combine eggs and olives with the medium white sauce. Pour over loaf. 6-8 servings.

MOLDED LETTUCE SALAD WITH COTTAGE CHEESE DRESSING

1 (3 ounce) package of lime-flavored gelatin
2 cups lukewarm water
2 cups shredded lettuce

½ cup radishes, sliced
1 teaspoon salt
½ teaspoon white pepper

Dissolve gelatin in water. Cool until partially set. Place lettuce, radishes, salt and pepper into a 1 ½ quart mold. Pour chilled gelatin over vegetables. Chill until firm. Serve with cottage cheese dressing. 6 servings.

Cottage Cheese Dressing

½ cup cottage cheese
⅛ teaspoon salt
1 ½ teaspoons lemon juice

2 tablespoons mayonnaise
Few drops Tabasco sauce

Cream cheese; add remaining ingredients; mix well. Serve on vegetable salad.

WEDNESDAY
June Graduation Dinner for Four (or 8)
Gourmet pork chops in wine
Baked and buttered sweet potato slices
Succotash
Asparagus salad
Sourdough wheat rolls
Fruit melange

Plan Of Work
Day before:
1. Prepare asparagus salad, refrigerate.
Early in the day:
2. Prepare pork chops and marinade. Marinate chops, place in refrigerator.
3. Shell Lima beans.
4. Prepare mixed fruit and refrigerate.
1 ½ hours before serving:
5. Put pork chops in oven.
6. Prepare sweet potatoes, put in oven 30 minutes before serving.
30 minutes before serving:
7. Prepare the succotash.

GOURMET PORK CHOPS IN WINE

4 ¾-inch pork chops
½ cup white dinner wine
¼ cup honey
Salt and pepper to taste

½ cup chopped green onions
½ green pepper, sliced
2 teaspoons corn starch

Trim fat from chops. Arrange in baking pan. Combine wine, honey, salt and pepper. Pour over chops and marinate for 1 hour or more. Bake, uncovered, at 300° (slow) 1 hour, basting with sauce to glaze. Add onions and green pepper. Continue baking until tender, about 30 minutes longer. Remove to a hot platter. Moisten corn starch with a little of the sauce to make a smooth paste. Add to sauce in pan. Stir until smooth and thick. Serve over chops. 4 servings.

BAKED SWEET POTATO SLICES

1 medium sweet potato per person
2 tablespoons vegetable oil

½ cup (1 stick) butter or margarine, melted
Salt and pepper

Wash and rub oil on the outside of each potato. Slice into ¼-inch slices. Place potato slices on a cookie sheet; brush with butter and sprinkle with salt and pepper. Cover. Bake in 400° oven for 15 minutes. Remove cover. Turn slices and brush with butter , sprinkle with salt and pepper. Bake another 15 minutes or until tender.

SUCCOTASH

2 cups Lima beans, fresh, shelled
1 (1 ½ ounce) package frozen whole kernel corn

2 tablespoons butter or margarine
½ green pepper, chopped coarsely

In a 1-quart saucepan, place Lima beans, cover with boiling water and simmer until tender-crisp. Drain. Cook corn according to package directions. Drain. In a 2-quart saucepan, melt butter; add green pepper and cook over low heat until tender-crisp. Add beans and corn to green pepper and heat. Do not overcook. Keep crisp but tender. Correct seasoning. 4-6 servings.

ASPARAGUS SALAD

2 (10 ounce) packages frozen asparagus spears or
  2 pounds fresh asparagus, cooked
²/₃ cup finely chopped nuts
3 tablespoons soy sauce

2 tablespoons vegetable oil
2 tablespoons sugar
1 clove garlic, finely chopped
¼ teaspoon ground ginger

Cook asparagus according to package directions or fresh asparagus until crisp-tender; drain and cool. Combine nuts, soy sauce, oil, sugar, garlic and ginger in small bowl; stir until sugar dissolves. Pour over asparagus; toss. Cover and refrigerate until chilled. Toss just before serving. 4-5 servings.

FRUIT MELANGE

1 (12 ounce) package frozen mixed fruit, thawed
2 tablespoons chopped Maraschino cherries
2 tablespoons chopped nuts

½ cup whipped cream
2 tablespoons toasted coconut

Divide fruit among 4 compotes. Top each with ½ tablespoon cherries and ½ tablespoon nuts; top with whipped cream, then ½ tablespoon toasted coconut. 4 servings.

THURSDAY
Baked fish fillets
Stir fry zucchini
Sunshine Lima beans *
Raw vegetable relish tray
Raisin bread and butter / Fruit cocktail pudding

SUNSHINE LIMA BEANS

2 (10 ounce) packages frozen Lima beans
1 small onion chopped
1/2 cup butter or margarine, melted
3 tablespoons flour
1 teaspoon curry powder

1 cup milk
1 (16 ounce) can sliced peaches, drained
3 tablespoons butter or margarine, melted
Curry powder

Cook beans according to package directions; drain. Place in 9x11-inch baking dish. Saute onion in 1/4 cup butter until translucent. Add flour and curry powder, stirring until smooth. Gradually add milk, stirring until thickened. Pour sauce over beans and gently toss. Arrange peach slices on top of bean mixture. Brush with 3 tablespoons butter. Sprinkle with curry powder. Serve immediately. 6-8 servings.

FRIDAY
Spaghetti in clam sauce
Green salad with Italian dressing
Italian bread slices / Glazed sand cake *

GLAZED SAND CAKE

1 (18.5 ounce) package yellow cake mix
1/2 cup corn starch
1/2 cup sugar
1 cup water
4 eggs
1/2 cup oil

1 teaspoon vanilla
1 cup light corn syrup
1/4 cup sugar
1/4 cup butter or margarine
1/2 cup bourbon (optional)
Whipped cream (optional)

Combine cake mix. corn starch and 1/2 cup sugar; add water, eggs, oil and vanilla. Beat at medium speed for 3 minutes. Pour into greased bundt pan or 12-inch tube pan. Bake in 350° oven 50-60 minutes. Cool 15 minutes in pan. In small saucepan, combine corn syrup, 1/4 cup sugar and butter. Stir over medium heat until smooth. Remove from heat and add bourbon. Remove cake from pan and pierce thoroughly with fork. Brush while warm with half the sauce. Let stand 1 hour. Repeat, using remaining sauce. Store, tightly-covered, for up to one week. Can be served plain or topped with whipped cream.

SATURDAY
Shrimp with cashew nuts *
Buttered brown rice
Cabbage and carrot slaw
Popovers *
Ice cream and fruit sauce

SHRIMP WITH CASHEW NUTS

2 tablespoons cooking oil
2 pounds raw shrimp, shelled and deveined
1/4 cup finely-sliced green onions, use tops
1 (10 ounce) package frozen peas
1 cup chicken bouillon
1/2 cup sliced water chestnuts

1 teaspoon salt
1/2 teaspoon ground ginger
1/4 cup soy sauce
1 tablespoon plus 1 teaspoon corn starch
1/2 cup dry roasted cashew nuts

Heat oil in skillet. Add shrimp and sliced green onions. Cook, stirring constantly, until shrimp turn pink and onions are tender. Add peas, chicken bouillon, water chestnuts, salt and ginger. Cover; bring to a boil and simmer for 5 minutes or until peas and shrimp are tender. Blend soy sauce and corn starch. Stir in shrimp mixture and cook until sauce is clear and slightly thickened. Stir in cashew nuts. Serve immediately with hot rice or fried noodles. 4 servings.

POPOVERS

1 cup flour   *2 eggs*
½ teaspoon salt   *1 cup milk*

Sift flour and salt into mixing bowl. Add unbeaten eggs and ½ cup of milk. Beat until smooth, using rotary beater, whisk or spoon. Add remainder of milk and mix well. Fill well-oiled deep muffin pans or glass custard cups ⅓ to ½ full. Avoid excess fat in pans, as it reduces volume and gives misshapen products. Bake at 400° about 40 minutes, until they are well-risen and brown, then quickly slash the tops with a paring knife. Turn off heat, and allow popovers to dry in oven, approximately 10 minutes. Popovers should be firm to the touch when removed from the oven, otherwise they will collapse. Serve immediately. 10 large popovers.

June - Second Week

CHEESE HAS BEEN A USEFUL and versatile food for thousands of years. It is made in many countries around the world. Its use in the United States is almost unlimited: it is used in casseroles, combined with other foods, sandwiches, snacks and even desserts.

Cheese is the principle ingredient in many cooked dishes, and is considered a meat substitute because cheese, which is made from milk, contains complete protein. It contains the essential amino acids which are needed to build and maintain a healthy body. Cheese contains in concentrated form almost all the protein and usually most of the fat, essential minerals, vitamins and other nutrients found in milk. A one-inch cube or one-ounce slice of Cheddar type cheese is the equivalent of two-thirds of a glass of milk in calcium and protein. Most of the cheese in this country is made from cow's milk.

The proper storage of cheese in the home is very important. To prevent loss of flavor and moisture, natural cheese should be stored in the refrigerator in a tightly-covered container. To prevent mold contamination, cheese should be stored in its original wrapping. After opening, the cut surface may be covered with wax paper, plastic wrap or aluminum foil to protect it from drying. The proper refrigerator temperature for cheese is 40° to 45°.

Soft, unripened cheese, such as cottage cheese and cream cheese, should be stored, tightly covered, in the coldest part of the refrigerator. Like milk, cheese should be kept in the refrigerator at all times except when being used. Cheddar is the cheese most commonly used for cooking in this country. It is available in natural and processed forms, and varies in flavor from mild to very sharp. Cheddar and other hard cheeses are best for cooking because they melt into a smooth, tender consistency instead of becoming gummy as softer cheeses do. But they do require cooking care. To avoid separation and toughening, cheese should be cooked at a low temperature and not over-cooked. For top-of-the-range dishes, it should be heated in the top of a double boiler, over simmering water. For baked dishes, the oven temperature should be moderate, 350°. For grilled dishes, such as grilled cheese sandwiches, the cheese should be placed 5 inches from the heat, broiled at a moderate rate, and broiled only until the cheese melts.

Technically, natural cheese is classified by the method of producing curd, the animal source of the milk, the fat content of the milk and the type of microorganism responsible for ripening (mold or bacteria). During the ripening process or aging, the flavor, texture and appearance of the cheese are developed. For convenience, natural cheeses are classified according to moisture content as:
1. Hard - Cheddar, Edam, Gruyere, Provolone, Swiss, Romano, and others.
2. Semi-hard - Brick, Bel Paese, Fontina, Gouda, Jack, Munster, and others.
3. Soft - Limburger, Brie, Camembert, Mozzarella, Cottage, Ricotta, Cream, Neufchatel, Roquefort, and others.

The term "natural" in regard to cheese merely distinguishes it from blended or modified cheese. It does not mean that it does not contain added color, salt, or other additives.

The versatility of cheese is amazing. It can be used in every course of any kind of meal.

SUNDAY
Welcome Summer Brunch
Gazpacho cup
Florentine egg turnovers with mustard sauce
Baby Brussels sprouts
Relish tray
Croissants and strawberry preserves
Melon cooler parfait

Plan Of Work

Day before:
1. Prepare Gazpacho.
2. Wash Brussels sprouts.
3. Prepare mustard sauce.
4. Prepare cream cheese sauce for the dessert.
One hour before serving:
5. Prepare the turnovers. Bake 25 minutes before serving.
6. While turnovers are baking, prepare melon balls and refrigerate. Assemble at time of serving.
15 minutes before serving:
7. Cook Brussels sprouts.
8. Warm mustard sauce.
A very easy, but delightful meal.

GAZPACHO CUP

2 large tomatoes, peeled, coarsely chopped	*1 cup tomato or vegetable juice*
1 small cucumber, peeled, coarsely chopped	*1 tablespoon wine vinegar*
1/2 medium onion, finely chopped	*1/2 teaspoon salt*
1/2 green pepper, chopped	*1/8 teaspoon pepper*

Combine all of the ingredients in a large bowl. Cover and refrigerate at least two hours, before serving to blend flavors. Leftovers will keep several days in refrigerator. Serve very cold. 6 servings. Note: If you want to serve as a beverage before the meal, puree in a blender. If not, serve in a cup with a spoon.

FLORENTINE EGG TURNOVERS WITH MUSTARD SAUCE

2 eggs
1 tablespoon lemon juice
6 hard-cooked eggs, chopped
1 (10 ounce) package frozen chopped spinach,
   thawed and drained

½ cup (2 ounces) shredded Cheddar cheese
3 tablespoons instant minced onion
1 (8 ounce) package refrigerated crescent rolls
Mustard sauce

In medium bowl, beat 1 egg with lemon juice. Stir in chopped eggs, spinach, cheese and onion. Set aside. Separate roll dough into triangles. Spread about ⅓ cup reserved egg- spinach mixture in center of each of 8 triangles. Top with remaining triangles. Pinch edges to seal. Place on greased baking sheet. Beat remaining egg and brush on top of each turnover. Bake in 350° oven until golden brown, about 15 to 20 minutes. Serve warm with mustard sauce. 4 servings.

Mustard Sauce

1 egg
¼ cup water
¼ cup vinegar
2 tablespoons sugar

1 ½ tablespoons dry mustard
1 tablespoon butter or margarine
¼ teaspoon salt
Dash of nutmeg

Place all ingredients in blender container or small mixing bowl. Cover and blend or beat with electric or rotary beater at medium speed until well blended. Pour into small saucepan. Cook over medium heat, stirring constantly, just until sauce begins to boil. Remove from heat. Refrigerate extra sauce.

BABY BRUSSELS SPROUTS

2 (10 ½ ounce) packages of frozen Brussels
   sprouts or 1 pound fresh
¼ cup vegetable or peanut oil

¼ cup water
Salt to taste
Pepper to taste

If using fresh, pick tiny sprouts because they are more tender; wash and drain. Heat oil in a covered skillet over medium heat. Add sprouts, then water. Cover and simmer for 8-10 minutes, or until the sprouts are barely tender, yet still green. Do not over-cook. Season with salt and pepper. 4 servings.

MELON COOLER PARFAIT

1 (8 ounce) package Neufchatel cheese
½ cup frozen lemonade or limeade concentrate, thawed

4 cups assorted melon balls

Place Neufchatel cheese and lemonade concentrate in food processor or blender container; process until well blended. Spoon melon balls into parfait glasses or individual bowls; top with cheese mixture.

MONDAY
Pot roast with vegetables
Peas and cheese salad
Yorkshire pudding
Brown sugar cake with coconut crunch topping *

BROWN SUGAR CAKE WITH COCONUT CRUNCH TOPPING

½ cup (1 stick) butter or margarine
2 cups brown sugar, packed
2 eggs
½ cup hot water
½ cup sour milk (or ½ cup sweet milk with 1 ½ teaspoons vinegar)

2 ½ cups sifted cake flour
½ teaspoon soda
2 teaspoons baking powder
1 teaspoon vanilla

Cream butter. Add 1 cup brown sugar. Cream well. Beat together 1 cup brown sugar and eggs. Beat into creamed mixture. Combine water and milk and add alternately with flour, soda and baking powder which have been sifted together. Mix thoroughly. Stir in vanilla. Pour batter into 13x9x2-inch greased pan. Bake in moderate oven (375°) about 35 minutes. While still warm, top with coconut crunch topping.

Broiled Coconut Crunch Topping

¾ cup brown sugar
⅓ cup flour
1 teaspoon cinnamon
¼ cup butter or margarine, melted

½ cup chopped nuts
½ cup shredded coconut
¼ cup milk

Combine brown sugar, flour and cinnamon. Stir in butter, nuts, coconut and milk. When brown sugar cake is removed from oven, spread lightly with topping. Place under broiler, about 3 inches from source of heat. Allow to cook (mixture bubbles) about 3 minutes. Watch carefully to avoid scorching.

TUESDAY
American stir-fry *
Buttered brown rice
Molded broccoli salad *
Carrot muffins
Angel food cake wedge with lemon curd topping *

AMERICAN STIR-FRY

2 tablespoons plus 2 teaspoons cornstarch
2 tablespoons Worcestershire sauce
1 ½ cups beef broth
½ cup soy sauce
2 tablespoons ketchup
2 pounds ground beef

1 tablespoon vegetable oil
2 medium onions, chopped
3 ribs celery, diagonally sliced
4 carrots, sliced thin
1 (8 ounce) can mushroom stems and pieces, drained

Dissolve cornstarch in Worcestershire sauce. Combine beef broth, soy sauce, ketchup and Worcestershire sauce mixture. Set aside. Preheat electric skillet or wok at 375°. Stir-fry beef until browned. Remove from wok. Heat oil in wok. Stir-fry onion, celery and carrots until crisp-tender, about 4 minutes. Add mushrooms, beef and beef broth mixture. Cook and stir until thickened. Serve hot with rice. 6-8 servings.

MOLDED BROCCOLI SALAD

4 eggs, hard cooked　　　　　　　　　　*3 tablespoons lemon juice*
2 (10 ounce) packages frozen chopped broccoli　*1 cup mayonnaise*
1 ½ envelopes unflavored gelatin　　　　*Tabasco sauce to taste*
1 (10 ½ ounce) can consomme　　　　　*½ teaspoon garlic salt*
2 tablespoons Worcestershire sauce　　　*½ teaspoon monosodium glutamate (optional)*

Slice eggs. Cook broccoli according to package directions, drain and cool. Place gelatin in small bowl and cover with ½ can of consomme. Heat remaining consomme; add softened gelatin and heat until gelatin is dissolved. Combine eggs, broccoli, gelatin mixture, Worcestershire sauce, lemon juice, mayonnaise, Tabasco sauce, garlic salt and MSG. Pour into a greased 1 ½ quart mold. Chill, unmold and serve. 6-8 servings.

LEMON CURD

Grated rind of 2 lemons　　　　　　　*1 cup butter or margarine*
½ cup lemon juice　　　　　　　　　　*4 eggs well beaten*
2 cups sugar

Combine lemon rind, juice and sugar in top of double boiler. Add butter. Heat, stirring constantly, until butter is melted. Stir a little of the hot mixture into the beaten eggs; then add eggs to the mixture in the double boiler. Continue cooking until the mixture thickens, about 15 minutes. Place in jar. Refrigerate until needed. Use as filling for tarts or topping for cake or ice cream.

WEDNESDAY
Speedy macaroni and cheese *
Spinach stuffed tomatoes *
Congealed fruit salad
Butter cookies

SPEEDY MACARONI AND CHEESE

1 (7 ounce) package elbow macaroni　　　*⅓ cup chopped onions*
8 ounces fresh mushrooms, sliced　　　　*2 tablespoons chopped pimiento*
2 tablespoons butter or margarine　　　　*4 eggs, hard cooked and chopped*
2 (10 ³/₄ oz) cans condensed cream of chicken soup　*2 cups (8 ounces) shredded Cheddar cheese*

Cook macaroni according to package directions; drain. Meanwhile, saute mushrooms in butter. Combine soup, onion, pimiento, eggs, cheese, mushrooms and macaroni. Turn into 2-quart rectangular baking dish. Bake at 350° for 25 to 30 minutes. 6 servings.

SPINACH STUFFED TOMATOES

6 large or 8 medium tomatoes　　　　　*2 (9 ounce) packages frozen, chopped,*
Garlic salt　　　　　　　　　　　　　*creamed spinach, thawed.*
Freshly ground pepper　　　　　　　　*²/₃ cup crushed bread stuffing mix*
3 tablespoons melted butter or margarine　*2 tablespoons grated Parmesan cheese*
½ cup finely chopped onion

Using a sharp paring knife, cut the tops from the tomatoes in a zig-zag fashion. Scoop tomato pulp from the inside (reserve for salads, casseroles or sauces). Sprinkle the insides of the tomato cups lightly with garlic salt and ground pepper. Melt butter in a skillet. Saute onion until transparent, about 5 minutes. Remove from heat. Add creamed spinach and crushed bread crumbs. Blend well. Spoon spinach mixture into tomatoes. Place in a buttered casserole. Sprinkle each with cheese Bake, uncovered, in 350° oven for about 20 minutes or until heated through. 6-8 servings.

THURSDAY
Salmon casserole *
Savory green beans
Butterscotch muffins
Apple sauce
Cookies

SALMON CASSEROLE

2 cups cooked rice	1/2 teaspoon celery salt
2 tablespoons chopped parsley	1/4 teaspoon pepper
1/4 cup (1/2 stick) butter or margarine	1/4 teaspoon nutmeg
1/4 cup flour	2 tablespoons lemon juice
2 cups milk	1 cup (4 ounces) shredded Cheddar cheese
1 teaspoon salt	1 (16 ounce) can salmon, flaked

Combine rice and parsley. Spread mixture in a greased 2-quart baking dish. In a saucepan, melt butter; add flour and stir to make a smooth paste. Add milk gradually, stirring constantly. Cook over medium heat until thick and smooth. Add salt, celery salt, pepper, nutmeg, lemon juice and cheese. Stir until cheese is melted. Add salmon. Pour mixture over rice. Bake 30 minutes at 375°. 6 servings.

FRIDAY
Parmesan liver saute *
Buttered linguini
Baked honey buttered acorn squash
Congealed perfection salad
French rolls
Cake

PARMESAN LIVER SAUTE

1 1/2 pounds beef liver, 1/2-inch thick	1/2 cup (1 stick) butter or margarine
1/3 cup grated Parmesan cheese	1/4 pound Mozzarella cheese, cut into 6 slices
1/3 cup fine cracker crumbs	Tomato sauce, catsup or chili sauce (optional)
1/2 teaspoon paprika	

Cut liver into 6 serving pieces. Combine Parmesan cheese, crumbs and paprika. In skillet, melt 1/2 cup butter; dip liver slices in butter, then coat both sides with crumb mixture. About 10 minutes before ready to serve, saute liver on both sides in remaining 1/2 stick butter until golden. Place on oven-proof platter and top with Mozzarella cheese slices. Place under broiler just long enough to melt cheese slightly. Top each serving with a spoonful of tomato sauce, if desired. 6 servings.

June   **153**   *Menu Celebrations!*

SATURDAY
Sausage-eggplant jambalaya *
Broccoli in butter almond sauce
Beet and onion salad Bread sticks
Fresh lemon pie *

SAUSAGE-EGGPLANT JAMBALAYA

1 tablespoon cooking oil
1 medium onion, chopped
1/2 cup chopped green pepper
1/2 cup chopped celery
2 cloves garlic, crushed
1 medium sized eggplant, peeled and
  cut into 1-inch pieces

1/2 pound bulk sausage, lightly cooked
1/2 pound smoked sausage, cut in 1 inch pieces
1 cup uncooked rice
1 cup water
1 teaspoon garlic salt
1/4 teaspoon pepper

In a 2-quart saucepan, add oil, onion, pepper, celery and garlic. Saute until vegetables are soft, not brown. Add eggplant cubes, browned bulk sausage and smoked sausage. Heat. Add rice, water, salt and pepper. Bring to a boil. Cover, turn heat down to low. Cook until rice is tender, 15 to 20 minutes. 6 servings.

FRESH LEMON PIE

1 cup sifted flour
1/2 teaspoon salt
1/3 cup shortening
3 to 3 1/2 tablespoons cold water
1 1/4 cups sugar

3 tablespoons flour
1/8 teaspoon salt
3 eggs, well beaten
1 large lemon
1/2 cup water

Sift flour and salt, cut in shortening until mixture resembles coarse cornmeal. Sprinkle cold water over mixture. Mix with fork. Form into a ball. Refrigerate dough for 10 minutes. Roll out pastry 1 inch in diameter larger than a 9-inch pie pan. Place the pastry in the pie pan and crimp crust edges. Set aside. Combine sugar, 1 tablespoon flour and salt. Add eggs. Blend until smooth. Grate lemon peel from lemon. Peel lemon and cut into paper thin slices. Remove seeds. Add lemon slices, peel and water to sugar mixture. Blend well. Pour into pastry-lined pie pan. Bake at 400° for 35 minutes. Let pie set 15 minutes before serving. 6-8 servings. Deep dish 9-inch commercially-prepared crust may be used.

June - Third Week

EGGS MAKE ONE OF THE BEST inflation-fighting main dishes. Eggs contain a complete protein. That is, like milk, meats, fish and poultry, egg protein contains all of the essential amino acids that are needed to build and maintain body tissue. Two eggs will provide the same amount of protein as a serving of meat. In addition to good quality protein, eggs are a good source of iron, vitamin A, B vitamins and fats. Because of the nutritive value, the basic four guidelines suggest that 3 or 4 eggs be included in the diet each week.

Care must be taken in buying eggs. Buy only refrigerated eggs, for eggs should be refrigerated from the time they are laid until they are used. Fresh eggs have a rough, dull surface. If possible, buy eggs that are government graded for size and quality. Government quality grades appear on the carton. The most common grade found in the market is grade A, although grade AA and grade B may also be available. When broken into a dish or frying pan, a fresh egg will have a white that is thick and stands up well around a firm, high yolk. As the egg ages, the white will become thin and runny.

Most recipes call for large eggs. However, the smaller ones can be used if they are a good buy. The standards for size grades of eggs and minimum weight per dozen eggs are as follows:

1. Extra Large   27 ounces
2. Large   24 ounces
3. Medium   21 ounces
4. Small   18 ounces

The size of the egg has nothing to do with quality. To get the best buy, calculate the cost per ounce for the various sizes and buy the cheapest.

One popular method of preparation of eggs is to hard-cook them. This, by the way, is a misnomer, because you should never really hard-cook eggs. The perfect hard-cooked egg has a tender white, a yolk properly set, and not the faintest darkening of the yolk where the white encircles it. The dark line around the yolk of a hard-cooked egg comes from a chemical reaction caused by too much heat. Another prime consideration about hard-cooked eggs is that you have to be able to peel them cleanly.

Here's how to hard-cook an egg to eliminate the dark line and to peel easily. First prick the shell at the large end of each egg with a drafting pin to let out air, because there is always a bubble of air in there which will expand when the egg is heated and can crack the shell. Next, lay the eggs in a sauce pan and cover them with cold water. Put the pan on high heat and bring the water to a boil; remove it from the heat, cover the pan and let it stand for about 17 minutes. Then transfer the eggs to a bowl of ice water to cool. To peel, crack the egg all over by gently tapping it against the sink. Start peeling at the large end and hold the egg under a thin stream of cold water. Hard cooked eggs will keep in the refrigerator for 2 to three days.

At Easter time, eggs are left at room temperature for decorating or picked from the yard during egg hunts. Do not eat these eggs. They have open pores due to cooking, which serve as a great entrance for bacteria from soil or handling. Discard them after the Easter holidays.

SUNDAY
Dad's Day Dinner
Indonesian spareribs
Beefy rice and mushrooms
Frosted tomatoes
Lettuce wedge with thick Roquefort dressing
Cream biscuits
Chocolate lover's cheese cake

Plan of Work
Day before
1. Prepare salad dressing
2. Prepare biscuits

Early in the day
3. Make sauce for ribs.
4. Prepare the tomatoes. Refrigerate until ready to broil.
5. Wash head of lettuce. Do not cut until ready to serve.
6. Prepare cheese cake.

One hour and forty-five minutes before serving
7. Start cooking the ribs. Brush with sauce every 20 minutes.

Thirty minutes before serving
8. Prepare rice and start cooking.
9. Cut biscuits, and bake 15 minutes before serving.
10. Broil tomatoes 7-8 minutes before serving.

INDONESIAN SPARERIBS

4 pounds spareribs
1 tablespoon hickory smoked salt
1/4 teaspoon black pepper
1 tblsp plus 1 teaspoon coriander seed, crushed
1 tablespoon plus 1 teaspoon cumin seed, crushed
1/3 cup soy sauce

1 teaspoon monosodium glutamate (optional)
2 tablespoons instant minced onion
1/2 teaspoon grated ginger
1/4 cup salad oil
1 1/2 tablespoons brown sugar
1/3 cup lime or lemon juice

Cut spareribs into serving pieces. Place on rack in a shallow pan. Combine remaining ingredients; mix well. Brush sauce over ribs to coat all sides. Bake in 325° oven for 1 1/2 hours or until ribs are tender and brown. Baste with sauce every 20 minutes. 6 servings.

BEEFY RICE AND MUSHROOMS

6 green onions, sliced (use tops)
2 tablespoons butter or margarine
2 (10 1/2 ounce) cans consomme

1 cup water
1 cup rice
2 (4 oz) cans mushrooms stems and pieces, drained

In a 2-quart saucepan, cook onions in butter until tender. Add remaining ingredients. Heat to boiling. Reduce heat. Cover; simmer 20 to 25 minutes or until all liquid has been absorbed. 6-8 servings.

FROSTED TOMATOES

6 tomatoes
Salt to taste
Pepper to taste
1 tablespoon finely-minced green onion
1 tablespoon finely-minced green pepper

1 tablespoon finely-minced parsley
1 egg white, room temperature
1/3 cup mayonnaise
Parmesan cheese, grated

Cut top off of tomatoes. Hollow out a small well in the center. Season with salt and pepper. Combine onion, green pepper and parsley. Place in well and over top of each tomato. (Make sure that tomato can stand firmly.) Broil 2 minutes. Beat egg white until stiff. Fold the mayonnaise into the egg white. Frost each tomato top. Sprinkle cheese on top. Broil until egg white is lightly browned. 6 servings.

THICK ROQUEFORT DRESSING

1 small onion, chopped
1/4 cup chopped fresh parsley
1 cup mayonnaise
1/2 cup sour cream
1/4 cup wine vinegar

1/4 teaspoon pepper
1 teaspoon garlic salt
4 ounces Roquefort (or blue) cheese, crumbled
1 tablespoon lemon juice

Combine all ingredients and blend with beater or blender. Chill. Yield: 2 cups.

CREAM BISCUITS

1 (3 ounce) package cream cheese, softened
1/2 cup butter or margarine, softened

1 cup self rising flour

Blend cheese and butter thoroughly. Stir in flour. Mix with hands. Form a roll two inches in diameter and 6 inches long. Wrap in plastic or foil and store in refrigerator 6-8 hours or overnight. When ready to serve, slice into 1/2- to 3/4-inch circles. Bake at 350° for 15 minutes or until lightly brown. Yield: 12 biscuits. Note: Low fat cream cheese may be used.

CHOCOLATE LOVER'S CHEESE CAKE

2 (8 ounce) packages cream cheese, softened
1/2 cup sugar
1/2 teaspoon vanilla

2 eggs
4 squares semisweet chocolate, melted, slightly cooled
1 chocolate-flavored pie crust, 9 inch (commercial)

Combine cream cheese, sugar and vanilla at medium speed with electric mixer until well blended. Add eggs; mix until blended. Blend in melted chocolate when mixture is smooth. Pour into crust. Bake at 350° for 40 minutes or until center is almost set. Refrigerate overnight. Top with assorted fresh fruit if desired. 8 servings.

MONDAY
Luncheon
Baked mushroom omelet with wine sauce
Buttered Lima beans
Congealed ambrosia salad *
Rye toast with butter and blackberry jam
Pound cake with ice cream and topping

CONGEALED AMBROSIA SALAD

1 (3 ounce) package orange gelatin
1/2 cup sugar
1 cup boiling water
3 oranges, peeled and cut into 1-inch pieces

1 (8 1/2 ounce) can crushed pineapple, undrained
1 cup flaked coconut
1 cup chopped pecans
1 (8 ounce) carton commercial sour cream

Dissolve gelatin and sugar in boiling water; chill until mixture starts to thicken. Fold in oranges, pineapple, coconut, pecans and sour cream and blend well. Pour into a 13x9x2-inch pan or mold. Chill until firm. 10-12 servings.

TUESDAY
Pork roast
Rice pilaf
Celery au gratin *
Carrot and green pepper sticks
Whole wheat muffins
Shortbread cookies

CELERY AU GRATIN

1 large stalk celery
1 (10 ½ ounce) can chicken broth or
  1 ¼ cups chicken stock
¼ cup butter or margarine

¼ teaspoon ground nutmeg
⅛ teaspoon ground black pepper
2 cups soft bread crumbs
1 cup shredded Swiss cheese

Trim end of celery. Remove celery stalk base and cut off tops. (Save tops for soups, stews, etc.) Cut stalks crosswise into 6 or 12 slices. Place in a large skillet. Add chicken broth; bring to boiling point. Reduce heat. Cover and simmer for 8 minutes or until celery is crisp tender. Remove celery to a buttered 12x6x2-inch baking dish; cover to keep warm. In a medium saucepan, melt butter; remove from heat; stir in nutmeg and black pepper. Add bread crumbs; stir until butter and crumbs are mixed. Blend in cheese. Spoon over celery wedges. Bake, uncovered, in a moderate oven, 375°, for 12 minutes or until cheese melts and crumbs brown. 6 servings.

WEDNESDAY
Oven fried fish *
Duchess potatoes
Creamed peas *
Sliced tomatoes and cucumber
Corn muffins
Angel food cake with fruit topping

OVEN FRIED FISH

1 ½ pounds fish fillets or steaks
¾ teaspoon salt
¼ teaspoon pepper
¾ cup milk
¾ cup fine bread or cracker crumbs

3 tablespoons melted butter, margarine or
  bacon drippings
Paprika
Lemon wedges
Parsley

Cut fillets or steaks into 4 serving size portions. Combine salt, pepper and milk. Dip each piece of fish into milk mixture, and then into bread or cracker crumbs. Place in a 2-quart baking dish. Pour the melted butter over the fish. Bake at 350° until firm and golden, about 25-30 minutes. (Test for doneness by using a fork to see if the fish will flake easily.) Serve garnished with paprika, lemon wedges and parsley. 4 servings.

CREAMED PEAS

1 (16-17 ounce) can green peas
1 (5 ⅓ ounce) can (⅔ cup) evaporated milk or
  evaporated skim milk

3 tablespoons butter or margarine
3 tablespoons flour
½ teaspoon onion salt

Pour off liquid from peas and add to the evaporated milk. In small saucepan, melt butter; stir in flour and salt. Add the cold liquid all at one time and cook, stirring constantly, until sauce is smooth and thick. Add peas. Heat only until hot. Do no overcook. Correct seasoning. 4 servings.

THURSDAY
Swiss chicken *
Old-fashioned fruit conserve *
Buttered spinach
Orange and onion slices with French fruit dressing
Hot rolls / Brownie squares

SWISS CHICKEN

4 chicken breast halves, boned	1 ½ tablespoons flour
½ teaspoon salt	½ teaspoon salt
1 egg, beaten	½ teaspoon pepper
1 cup dry bread crumbs	1 ½ cups milk
¼ cup vegetable oil	⅓ cup white wine
1 ½ tablespoons butter or margarine	1 cup (4 ounces) shredded Swiss cheese, or 4 slices

Sprinkle each breast half with salt and pound flat. Dip in egg and then in bread crumbs. Heat oil in large skillet; add chicken and brown lightly on each side. Place in 2-quart shallow baking dish and set aside. In small saucepan, melt butter; stir in flour, salt and pepper to make a smooth paste. Slowly add milk, stirring constantly. Cook until smooth and thick. Remove from heat, stir in wine; pour sauce over chicken. Bake at 350° for 45 minutes. Remove from oven; top with cheese and bake for 5 more minutes. 4 servings.

OLD-FASHIONED FRUIT CONSERVE

1 (16 ounce) can peach halves, undrained	⅓ cup dark seedless raisins
1 (16 ounce) can jellied cranberry sauce	¼ teaspoon ground cloves

Drain peaches, reserving juice. In small saucepan, combine juice, cranberry sauce, raisins and cloves; bring to a boil. Reduce heat and simmer for 5 minutes or until cranberry sauce melts. Add peach halves and warm through. Serve warm with turkey or chicken. Yields about 1 ½ cups of sauce.

FRIDAY
Chicken-spaghetti casserole *
Green salad
Garlic bread
Spumoni ice cream

CHICKEN-SPAGHETTI CASSEROLE

¼ pound spaghetti	⅓ cup milk
2 cups peas, canned or frozen	¼ cup sherry
1 ½ cups cold, diced chicken	1 ½ cups chicken broth
1 small onion, chopped	3 slices white bread, in pieces
1 (8 ounce) can mushrooms, stems and pieces	1 (2 ounce) jar pimiento, drained
2 tablespoons butter or margarine	¼ cup grated Parmesan cheese

Cook spaghetti according to package directions, al dente; drain well and put into a greased 2-quart casserole. Add peas and chicken. Saute mushrooms and onions in butter; add to spaghetti in baking dish. Put the milk, sherry, broth and bread into blender container; cover and process until smooth. Remove feeder cap and add pimiento; immediately turn blender off. Pour into saucepan and cook until thickened, stirring constantly. Pour over ingredients in casserole, mix well with a fork. Sprinkle with cheese. Bake about 30 minutes at 350°. 6-8 servings.

SATURDAY
Cook inside, but eat Al Fresco style.
Getchi shrimp *
Spinach salad *
Hot garlic bread
Almond orange sponge cake *

GETCHI SHRIMP

2 gallons water
1 tablespoon salt
5 pounds hot smoked link sausage,
  cut in 2-inch pieces

1 stalk celery, cleaned and cut into 2-inch pieces
4-6 large onions, each cut into wedges
12 ears corn
6 pounds shrimp, unpeeled

In an 18-quart pan, bring water to a boil, add salt and sausage and cook for 20 minutes. Add celery and onions, cook until onions are translucent. Add corn, bring to a boil and cook for 5 minutes. Add shrimp, bring to a boil and cook 5 to 10 minutes, until shrimp are pink and done. Turn heat to low. Each guest serve him or her self, using a slotted spoon; one ear of corn per person. Serve cocktail sauce. 12 servings.

Cocktail Sauce

3 cups catsup or chili sauce
¹/₄ cup prepared horseradish

¹/₄ cup lemon juice (add 2 tblsp extra for tart flavor)
Hot sauce to taste

Combine all ingredients. Stir until thoroughly mixed. Refrigerate until needed.
Cover table with paper. Use all disposable dinner ware. No clean up.

SPINACH SALAD
Salad

1 pound (5-6 cups) spinach
1 (5 ounce) can sliced water chestnuts, drained
¹/₄ pound fresh mushrooms, washed and sliced or
  1 (5-ounce) can bean sprouts, well drained

¹/₄ head lettuce, chopped
¹/₄ pound bacon, fried crisp and crumbled
6 fresh strawberries

Combine all ingredients in a large salad bowl. Just before serving, toss with dressing. 6 servings.

Dressing

1 medium-sized onion, thinly sliced and
  separated into rings
1 cup salad or olive oil
¹/₄ cup vinegar

1 teaspoon Worcestershire sauce
1 teaspoon salt
¹/₂ cup catsup
¹/₂ cup sugar

Place onion rings in a bowl. Mix remaining ingredients and pour over onion rings. Store in refrigerator. Best if made the day before.

ALMOND ORANGE SPONGE CAKE

1 cup sliced almonds, divided
1 ¼ cup granulated sugar, divided
2 eggs, separated
1 teaspoon vanilla
2 tablespoons finely-ground orange peel

⅓ cup plus 2 tablespoons orange juice
1 cup cake flour
Pinch of salt
1 (3 ounce) package cream cheese, softened
½ cup confectioners sugar

Preheat oven to 350°. Butter and flour a 12-cup Bundt pan and set aside. Spread the almonds on a baking sheet and toast in oven until golden brown (do not burn). Let cool. Reserve ⅓ cup; set aside. In a food processor or blender, process the remaining nuts and 2 tablespoons of the granulated sugar until finely ground. In a large bowl or mixer, beat the egg yolks on medium speed until they turn pale yellow, about 1 minute. Gradually beat in 1 cup of the granulated sugar until thick and light, about 5 minutes. Beat in the vanilla, orange peel and ⅓ cup of orange juice. In two batches, sift the cake flour over the batter and fold in. Fold in the finely-ground almonds. In a large bowl, beat the egg whites on medium speed until frothy. Add the salt and continue beating until a soft peak forms, about 2 minutes. Beat in the remaining 2 tablespoons of granulated sugar; beat until a stiff peak forms. Fold ¼ of the egg whites into the batter, then fold in the remaining egg whites. Pour the batter into the prepared Bundt pan and bake for 45 minutes or until a wooden pick inserted into the center comes out clean. Let cool on a rack for 10 minutes. Invert the cake onto the serving plate. In a small bowl, beat the cream cheese until smooth. Add the confectioners sugar and beat until blended. Stir in the remaining 3 tablespoons of orange juice. Dribble the orange glaze over the top of the warm cake, allowing it to cascade down the sides. Sprinkle the reserved nuts over the top. Serve at room temperature. (This cake can be made up to 2 days in advance. Wrap well and refrigerate. Warm to room temperature before serving.)

June - Fourth Week

FOLLOWING ARE SUGGESTIONS OR WAYS to cut down on the amount of fat in cooking and eating. Remember that 1 gram of fat contributes 9 calories while 1 gram of protein or carbohydrate only contributes 4 calories to the diet. So, cutting down on unnecessary fat means cutting calories drastically.
1. Trim as much fat as possible from meat before and after cooking. Cook meat or poultry on a rack so the fat will drain off.
2. Roast, bake, broil or simmer meat without the addition of fat.
3. Cut down on fried, batter-fried or breaded and fried foods, because they do absorb fat during cooking.
4. Remove skin from chicken and turkey.
5. Chill meat or poultry broth until the fat becomes solid, Spoon off the fat and use the broth.
6. Dry peas and beans contain minimal amounts of fat unless fat is added in cooking. Use cooked dry peas or beans occasionally as a main dish or as a side vegetable dish, but use smallest amount of fat for flavor in cooking.
7. Cut down on or eliminate dressing on salad or use low-calorie dressings.
8. Use low-fat or skim milk.

9. Use sour cream in salads in place of mayonnaise, because sour cream contains 25 calories per tablespoon; mayonnaise contains 100 calories per tablespoon.
10. Cook without fat whenever possible.
11. Update old recipes by cutting down as much as possible in the amount of fat used.
12. Season vegetables with spices, herbs and lemon juice or bouillon, and use little or no fat.
13. Cut out high-fat desserts; use as much fresh fruit as possible.
   Remember, good food does not have to be fattening.

SUNDAY
Pork chops in pineapple sauce *
Steamed rice
Buttered asparagus
Cabbage and apple salad
Butterscotch cheesecake bars *

PORK CHOPS IN PINEAPPLE SAUCE

2 tablespoons butter or margarine	*2 tablespoons water*
8 pork chops	*3 cups hot cooked buttered rice*
1 teaspoon salt	*Pineapple sauce*

In a large skillet, melt the butter. Add pork chops. Brown on both sides, sprinkle with 1 teaspoon salt. Add water and cover. Cook slowly until meat is fork tender, about 45 minutes. Spoon pineapple sauce over pork chops. Cook slowly to glaze well, about 10 minutes. Serve pork and sauce over cooked rice. 6-8 servings.

Pineapple sauce

1 (8 ounce) can pineapple chunks (unsweetened)	*2 teaspoons soy sauce*
1/3 cup brown sugar, packed firmly	*1/4 teaspoon salt*
2 tablespoons corn starch	*3/4 cups seedless raisins*
1/3 cup vinegar	

Drain pineapple chunks; reserve juice. Add enough water to juice to make 1 cup liquid. Combine liquid, brown sugar, corn starch, vinegar, soy sauce and salt in a saucepan. Mix well; cook, stirring constantly, over medium heat until clear and thickened. Stir in raisins and pineapple chunks.

BUTTERSCOTCH CHEESECAKE BAR

1 (12 ounce) package butterscotch flavored morsels	*1 (8 ounce) package cream cheese, softened*
1/3 cup butter or margarine	*1 (14 ounce) can sweetened condensed milk*
2 cups graham cracker crumbs	*1 teaspoon vanilla extract*
1 cup chopped nuts	*1 egg*

In medium saucepan, melt morsels and butter; stir in crumbs and nuts. Press half of the mixture firmly onto bottom of greased 13x9-inch pan. In large mixer bowl, beat cheese until fluffy; beat in milk, vanilla and egg. Mix well. Pour into prepared pan; top with remaining crumb mixture. Bake 25 to 30 minutes at 350° or until wooden pick inserted near center comes out clean. Cool to room temperature; chill before cutting into bars. Refrigerate leftovers. 24 bars.

MONDAY
Teriyaki lamburgers on sesame buns *
Cottage potatoes
Vegetable salad mold *
Angle food cake with strawberry fluff *

TERIYAKI LAMBURGERS ON SESAME BUNS

1 ½ pounds lean ground lamb	2 tablespoons vinegar
½ cup soy sauce	2 cloves garlic, crushed
½ cup brown sugar	½ teaspoon ground ginger
2 tablespoons cooking oil	½ teaspoon salt

Divide lamb into 6 equal parts and shape into patties. Combine soy sauce, sugar, oil, vinegar, garlic, ginger and salt. Place patties in shallow pan. Pour marinade over lamb patties. Refrigerate for 2-3 hours. Turn occasionally. Drain. Grill 1-3 inches from charcoal or source of heat, or in skillet for about 5 minutes on each side, or to desired degree of doneness. 6 servings. Serve on sesame seed buns.

VEGETABLE SALAD MOLD

1 (3 ounce) package lemon gelatin	1 cup cottage cheese
1 cup boiling water	½ cup mayonnaise
1 (8 ounce) can (or 1 cup) mixed vegetables,	¼ cup sweet pickle relish
drained	½ teaspoon garlic salt

Empty gelatin into a bowl, add water and stir until gelatin is dissolved. Set aside to cool. Combine vegetables, cottage cheese, mayonnaise, relish and garlic salt. Mix lightly. Stir in gelatin mixture, Pour into 1-quart mold. Chill until firm. 6 servings.

STRAWBERRY FLUFF

1 (10 ounce) package frozen strawberries,	1 egg white
partially thawed	

Combine partially-thawed strawberries and egg white in 4-quart mixing bowl. Beat with electric mixer at highest speed until mixture is very thick and will form stiff peaks, about 6-8 minutes. Serve over angel food cake.

TUESDAY
Tuna frittata*
Buttered beets
Fresh garden salad with creamy Italian dressing
Cheese bread sticks
Quick mayonnaise cake *

TUNA FRITTATA

1 (6 ½ ounce) can tuna fish, drained, flaked
1 (15 ounce) can mixed vegetables, drained
1 (4 oz) can mushrooms, stems and pieces, drained
2 tablespoons instant minced onions
½ teaspoon dehydrated parsley flakes

5 eggs slightly beaten
¼ teaspoon seasoning salt
1 teaspoon salt
¼ teaspoon pepper
2 tablespoons butter or margarine

In a large mixing bowl, combine all ingredients except the butter. Stir until well blended. Melt butter in a heavy 9- inch skillet. Pour in the fish mixture. Cover; cook over moderately low heat for 30 minutes or until firm. Cut into wedges and serve hot. 4-6 servings.

QUICK MAYONNAISE CAKE

1 (18 ½ ounce) package chocolate cake mix
   (with pudding in the mix)
1 cup mayonnaise

1 cup water
3 eggs

In large mixing bowl, combine all ingredients. Beat at medium speed for 2 minutes, or 300 strokes by hand, or in a food processor for 30-45 seconds. Pour into greased 9x13x2-inch pan, or two 9-inch layer pans. Bake at 350° for 35 minutes or until center springs back when lightly touched. Cool in pan for 10 minutes. Remove. Cool on wire rack. Fill or frost as desired.

WEDNESDAY
Barbecued country ribs
Baked beans
Low calorie potato salad *
French bread
Fruit and cookies

LOW CALORIE POTATO SALAD

5 cups cooked, peeled potatoes, cubed
1 cup chopped celery
½ cup chopped green pepper
⅓ cup chopped sweet pickle
1 ½ cups sour cream
2 tablespoons white wine vinegar

4 green onions chopped
1 teaspoon salt
¼ teaspoon pepper
4 eggs, hard-cooked, chopped
Curly endive (optional)

Combine potatoes, celery, green pepper and sweet pickle. Combine sour cream, vinegar, onion, salt and pepper. Stir sour cream mixture into potato mixture; add eggs. Mix until evenly coated. Cover and chill. Garnish with endive, if desired. 6-8 servings.

THURSDAY
Apple cider chicken *
Buttered noodles
Roasted green and red peppers
Strawberry pretzel salad *

APPLE CIDER CHICKEN

1 broiler-fryer (about 3 lbs) cut into serving pieces
1 small onion, chopped
2 cloves garlic, crushed
1 ¹/₂ cups apple cider

¹/₂ teaspoon pepper
1 ¹/₂ teaspoons ground ginger
2 cups cooked rice or noodles

Place chicken in baking dish. Combine onions, garlic, cider, pepper and ginger. Add to chicken and marinate for at least 4 hours, longer if possible. Turn chicken pieces occasionally. Place in oven at 350° for 1 hour or until chicken is tender and well browned. Serve with rice or noodles. 4 servings.

STRAWBERRY PRETZEL SALAD

2 cups crushed pretzels
2 tablespoons sugar
³/₄ cup (1 ¹/₂ sticks) butter or margarine, melted
1 (8 ounce) package cream cheese
1 cup powdered sugar
1 (9 ounce) package frozen whipped topping

1 (3 ounce) package strawberry-flavored gelatin
1 (3 ounce) package lemon-flavored gelatin
2 cups boiling water
1 (20 ounce) crushed pineapple, undrained
1 (10 ounce) package frozen strawberries, thawed

Combine pretzels, sugar and melted butter. Put in bottom of 9x13-inch baking dish. Bake 7 minutes at 400°. Cool. Combine cheese, powdered sugar and whipped topping. Spread evenly over first layer. Add gelatin to boiling water, stir until dissolved; add pineapple and strawberries. Cool slightly and pour over second layer. Refrigerate until set. 14-16 servings. Refrigerate leftovers and serve again, or share with a friend.

FRIDAY
Roast beef
Piquant rutabagas *
Buttered peas and onions
Fresh spinach salad

PIQUANT RUTABAGAS

3 cups peeled and diced rutabagas
1 cup boiling water
2 tablespoons butter or margarine, melted
1 tablespoon light brown sugar

2 tablespoons soy sauce
1 tablespoon lemon juice
1 teaspoon Worcestershire sauce

Cook rutabagas in boiling water until tender, about 20 minutes. Drain. Combine remaining ingredients in a small saucepan. Heat thoroughly, do not boil. Pour sauce over rutabagas and mix gently. Serve hot. 4-6 servings.

SATURDAY
Roma Dinner
Antipasto
Veal parmigiana / Linguini
Marinated tomatoes and cucumber slices
Hot garlic Vienna bread
Strawberries with peach sauce

Plan Of Work

Day before:

1. Prepare the marinated tomatoes and cucumber slices.
2. Prepare peach sauce and refrigerate.
3. Prepare sauce for veal Parmigiana.

Early in the day:

4. Prepare items for the antipasto. Cover dish with plastic wrap and refrigerate.
5. Prepare the bread. Wrap and refrigerate until about 10 minutes before dinner is served.
6. Clean strawberries, dry in a paper towel, seal in airtight plastic bag and refrigerate.

About 1 hour before serving:

7. Do final preparation and bake the veal dish.

About 20 minutes before serving:

8. Prepare the linguini.
9. Heat the bread.

This is an easy Italian dinner.

Buona Saluta!

ANTIPASTO

Antipasto (before the pasta) is an individual plate consisting of a variety of salad foods and hors d'oeuvres. Combine as you wish. Be creative, but not overpowering, Here are some that may be arranged against a border of chopped lettuce or Italian celery. Choose what you want from the following:

Prosciutto (Italian ham, Cut paper thin if possible)
Italian salami
Pepperoni
Capocollo (Smoked pork)
Mozzarella cheese
Swiss cheese
Provolone (smoked cheese)
Hard cooked egg quarters
Pickled artichoke hearts
Ripe olives, plain or in olive oil

Peperoncini (small green pepper, pickled in vinegar)
Canned whole mushrooms
Radishes
Pimiento
Anchovy fillets
Celery hearts
Carrot sticks, green beans, zucchini slices
  marinated in Italian dressing
Peeled, cooked shrimp marinated in Italian dressing

• • •

VEAL PARMIGIANA

1 (6 ounce) can tomato paste
1 can water
1/2 teaspoon basil
1/4 teaspoon oregano leaves
1/8 teaspoon garlic powder
1 teaspoon thyme
1 tablespoon brown sugar
1 teaspoon Worcestershire sauce
1 tablespoon butter or margarine

2 teaspoons season salt
1/4 teaspoon black pepper
2 eggs, beaten slightly
2 pounds veal cutlets, cut 1/2-inch thick
1 cup fine dry bread crumbs
1/2 cup olive oil
1/4 cup grated Parmesan cheese
1/2 pound Mozzarella cheese slices

Combine tomato sauce, water, basil, oregano, garlic powder, thyme, brown sugar, Worcestershire sauce and butter. Cook until thickened, stirring constantly. Set aside. Combine season salt, pepper and eggs. Dip cutlets into egg mixture then into bread crumbs. Brown on both sides in hot oil. Place cutlets in 9x13x2-inch baking dish. Pour sauce over meat and sprinkle with Parmesan cheese. Cover, using aluminum foil, if necessary, and bake in 350° oven for 30 minutes. Remove cover and top cutlets with slices of Mozzarella cheese. Continue baking until cheese melts. 4-6 servings.

MARINATED TOMATOES AND CUCUMBER SLICES

1 cup salad oil (part olive oil is best)
⅓ cup wine vinegar
1 tablespoon plus 1 teaspoon Worcestershire sauce
1 ½ teaspoons salt
¼ teaspoon pepper
2 tablespoons sugar

2 teaspoons sweet basil
¼ teaspoon thyme
3-4 green onions, chopped (use tops)
2 medium tomatoes, cut into wedges
1 large cucumber, peeled and sliced

In mixing bowl, combine oil, vinegar, Worcestershire sauce, salt, pepper, sugar, basil, thyme and onion. Mix well. Add tomatoes and cucumbers. Marinate overnight (if possible). 6 servings.

HOT GARLIC VIENNA BREAD

1 loaf Vienna bread
½ cup butter or margarine

1 teaspoon garlic salt

Slice bread into ½-inch slices. Butter one side of each slice. Sprinkle with garlic salt. Assemble loaf. Wrap in aluminum foil. Heat. 6 servings.

STRAWBERRIES WITH PEACH SAUCE

6 large, fresh peaches (about 2 ½ pounds)
1 cup unsweetened white grape juice
1 cup water
3 tablespoons fresh lemon juice
1 teaspoon grated orange peel

¼ cup orange flavored liqueur, such as
    Grand Marnier or Cointreau
½ cup powdered sugar
1 quart strawberries, cleaned and sliced

Drop peaches briefly into boiling water to remove skins. Quarter peaches, discarding the stone, and place in medium saucepan. Pour in grape juice and 1 cup water; cover and poach over moderately low heat until tender, about 10 minutes. Drain, reserving ½ cup of liquid, In a food processor or blender, combine peaches with reserved liquid, lemon juice, peel, orange liqueur and sugar; puree until smooth. Pour mixture into serving bowl. Cover and refrigerate until chilled. Serve over fresh, sliced strawberries. 6 servings.

July

July - First Week

The charm of eating in summer or early fall is the availability of luscious, good-looking, highly-nourishing fruits and vegetables which are the main source of several essential vitamins and minerals and are also important for dietary fiber. Dark green leafy vegetables are the most concentrated source of nutrients. Fruits and vegetables are especially health-promoting because they are low in fat, sodium, and sugar, and have no cholesterol factors. Cholesterol has been linked to high blood pressure and heart disease.

Eating plenty of fresh fruits and vegetables, at least 5 to 9 servings per day, can help everyone in following the *Dietary Guidelines for Americans*, published by the U.S. Department of Agriculture. Here's how:

The *Dietary Guidelines* say:
• Eat a wide variety of foods;
• Maintain ideal weight;
• Avoid too much fat, saturated fat and cholesterol;
• Eat foods with adequate starch and fiber;
• Avoid too much sugar and sodium.

Most fruits and vegetables best retain their nutrients and peak quality when stored unwashed and refrigerated in air-tight containers or plastic bags. Citrus fruits and apples do best in ventilated bags. Items safely stored outside the refrigerator, preferably in a cool, dry place, include onions, potatoes, sweet potatoes (short time only), winter squash, rutabaga, pumpkin, and bananas. Most fruits and tomatoes may be held at room temperature up to 3 days or until ripe. All berries and cut or fully ripe fruit should be refrigerated.

Nutrients can be conserved when preparing fruits and vegetables by:
• Storing as short a time as possible;
• Cooking only until tender-crisp, not soft;
• Reducing the surface area; that is, limiting the amount of chopping (cut large pieces and slices);
• Saving the cooking liquid for soups, stews, and beverages;
• Cooking with the smallest amount of water;
• Serving as soon as cooked (not holding);
• Cooking in their skins and eating the skins or peeling later;
• Never use baking soda in cooking fruits or vegetables, as this will destroy some nutrients.

Cooking Techniques

Boiling/Steaming: Add washed vegetables to small amount of boiling unsalted water; simmer covered until tender-crisp. When steaming, vegetables do not come into contact with the water, so nutrients are not leached out.

Stir-Fry: Add coarsely-chopped vegetables to small amount (2 to 4 tablespoons) of hot vegetable oil in shallow wide pan or wok, and cook, stirring often, until just tender-crisp, glossy and bright.

Baking: Many vegetables can be baked in their skins, with most nutrients retained. Pierce skins to allow steam to escape.

Pressure Cooking and Microwave: Vegetables are quickly cooked with a minimum amount of water. Nutrients are retained if overcooking is avoided. Pressure cooking is a good way to cook root vegetables or winter squash.

Words like "rich" and "moderate" have little meaning in reference to nutrients. Mere presence of a nutrient does not necessarily make that food an important source of the nutrient. To be mentioned as a source, an item should contain at least the following amount or percentage of the U.S.D.A. requirements per serving: vitamin A, 25%; vitamin C, 25%; folic acid, 15%; iron, 10%; calcium, 10%; riboflavin or thiamine, 10%; protein, 10%; crude fiber, 0.5 g.; potassium, 400 mg.

SUNDAY
Chicken Florentine *
Fruit and vegetable slaw
Italian bread
Peach cake

CHICKEN FLORENTINE

6 chicken breast halves
1 cup Italian seasoned bread crumbs
2 tablespoons olive oil
2 tablespoons (¼ stick) butter or margarine
2 cups Sauce Marinara
½ cup dry red wine
1 ½ cups boiling chicken stock
1 cup uncooked long grain rice
¼ cup sliced black olives

2 (10 ounce) packages frozen chopped spinach, thawed and pressed dry
1 cup ricotta or cottage cheese
2 eggs, beaten
½ teaspoon crushed marjoram
½ teaspoon salt
¼ teaspoon nutmeg
¼ cup grated Parmesan cheese

Coat chicken with bread crumbs. Heat oil and butter in large skillet. Add chicken breasts and saute until brown. Remove from pan and set aside. Combine Sauce Marinara and wine. Place 1 cup sauce-wine mixture in skillet. Add chicken stock, rice and olives; stir thoroughly, scraping bottom of skillet. Place in a lightly-oiled 3-quart casserole. Arrange chicken skin-side down atop rice. Cover tightly with foil and bake at 350° for 20 minutes. Turn chicken, re-cover with foil and bake another 25 minutes. (Dish may be cooked ahead to this point.) While chicken is baking, combine spinach, ricotta, eggs, marjoram, salt and nutmeg. Spoon spinach mixture around edge of baking dish. Pour remaining sauce-wine mixture over chicken. Sprinkle with Parmesan cheese. Bake uncovered, until spinach mixture is heated, 10 to 15 minutes more. (6 servings) Note: This dish can also be prepared with cooked chicken or turkey, which would be added after rice is baked.

Sauce Marinara

2 tablespoons olive oil
2 cloves garlic, crushed
1 (28 ounce) can tomato puree or equivalent of diced tomatoes
1 tablespoon sugar

1 tablespoon fresh minced parsley
1 teaspoon oregano
1 teaspoon basil
1 teaspoon salt
¼ teaspoon pepper

In a 3-quart saucepan, heat olive oil and saute garlic until golden brown. Add remaining ingredients and simmer for 15 minutes with the lid only partially covering pan to prevent spattering. (May be refrigerated for 2 weeks or frozen up to 6 months.)

FRUIT AND VEGETABLE SLAW

1 medium head lettuce
1 unpeeled red apple, cut into thin strips
1 cup coarsely-grated carrots
1 cup finely chopped cucumber
2/3 cup orange juice
2 tablespoons lemon juice

1 tablespoon brown sugar
1 egg, beaten
1/2 teaspoon salt
1/2 teaspoon dried basil, crumbled
1/2 teaspoon dried mint, crumbled

Core, rinse and thoroughly drain lettuce. Finely shred lettuce, place in bottom of 1 1/2-quart salad bowl. Arrange apple, carrot and cucumber on top. In top of double boiler, combine orange juice, lemon juice, brown sugar, egg, salt, basil and mint. Set over hot water and cook, stirring constantly, until slightly thickened. Remove from heat and cool before adding to salad. Right before serving, add dressing to salad and toss slightly. (6 servings.) Note: Low heat setting can be used instead of double boiler, stir constantly.

PEACH CAKE

1 1/3 cup cooking oil
1 (18 1/2-ounce) box yellow cake mix
1 (3 ounce) box instant vanilla pudding
2 eggs
1 1/3 cups water
1 (16 ounce) can peach pie filling*

3/4 cup chopped nuts
1 teaspoon cinnamon
1/3 cup sugar
1/2 teaspoon nutmeg
1/4 cup powdered sugar
Hot water

Spread oil in jelly roll pan (10 1/2x15 1/2x1-inch). Add to the same pan cake mix, pudding, eggs and water; stir in pan until all dry ingredients are moistened but still lumpy. Spread batter evenly in pan. Cover with pie filling. Sprinkle nuts over filling. Combine cinnamon, sugar and nutmeg. Sprinkle cinnamon sugar over all. Bake at 350° for 25 minutes. Remove from oven. Combine powdered sugar with enough hot water to make a thin glaze. Drizzle glaze over top of cake in a lacy fashion. Refrigerate leftovers. To use as snacks, cut 2x2 1/2x1-inch pieces. Yield: 50. Note: Any fruit pie filling can be used.

MONDAY
Al Fresco Supper on the Fourth
Herbed Boursin and crackers *
Tangy barbecued chicken quarters *
Mushroom potato salad *
Foil-grilled zucchini and tomatoes *
Hot barbecued bread *
Pecan crumb cake *
Chocolate ice cream *
Soft drinks, other drinks as desired

Plan Of Work

The day before:

1. Prepare barbecue sauce (save enough or double amount to pass when eating).
2. Marinate chicken.
3. Prepare boursin and refrigerate until ready to use.

Early in the day:

4. Prepare zucchini and tomato packets, ready to cook.
5. Prepare potato salad and refrigerate until ready to use.
6. Prepare bread wrapped in foil and refrigerate until ready to heat.
7. Prepare cake.

Two hours before serving:

8. Put chicken in smoker or on grill 30 minutes before serving.
9. Place zucchini packets on grill.

Ten minutes before serving:

10. Put bread in oven or grill to heat.

HERBED BOURSIN

8 ounces calorie-reduced cream cheese, softened	½ teaspoon thyme
¼ cup butter or margarine	½ teaspoon basil
1-2 cloves garlic, crushed	½ teaspoon garlic salt
1 teaspoon dried parsley	½ teaspoon monosodium glutamate, optional
1 teaspoon wine vinegar	¼ teaspoon Tabasco sauce
1 teaspoon Worcestershire sauce	Coarsely-ground black pepper

Combine all ingredients except the coarsely-ground pepper. Cover with wax paper or plastic wrap and refrigerate until ready to use. Shape into a flat mold ½ inch thick. Cover with the coarsely ground pepper. Surround with fresh parsley. Serve with assorted crackers.

TANGY BARBECUED CHICKEN QUARTERS

2 broiler-fryers, quartered	2 cups evaporated milk
2 cups commercial mayonnaise-type salad dressing	1 tablespoon salt
2 cups cider vinegar	1 tablespoon black pepper (more if desired)

Combine salad dressing, vinegar, milk, salt and pepper. Pour over chicken. Chicken must be completely covered. Marinate 6-8 hours or overnight. Drain. Cook chicken in smoker 1 ½ hours or on grill about 1 ½ to 2 hours, basting every 15 minutes. Serve hot with additional marinade. Make fresh marinade; do not use sauce in which chicken was marinated. (6 servings.)

MUSHROOM POTATO SALAD

1 ¼ pounds potatoes (5 medium)	1 teaspoon dried dill or 1 tablespoon fresh dill
½ pound fresh mushrooms, thickly-sliced	½ teaspoon pepper
½ cup sour cream	1 medium size red onion, thinly sliced
½ cup mayonnaise or salad dressing	¼ cup chopped dill pickle
1 teaspoon salt	4 eggs, hard cooked, sliced

Wash potatoes. In medium-size saucepan, heat 2 inches water to boiling. Add potatoes. Cover. Boil gently for 25 to 30 minutes or until potatoes are tender. Remove. Add mushrooms to same water. Simmer, uncovered, 5 minutes. Drain thoroughly. Meanwhile, in a large bowl combine sour cream, mayonnaise, salt, dill and pepper. Peel and dice potatoes. Combine potatoes, mushrooms, onion, pickle, egg slices. Add dressing. Toss gently to coat. Serve immediately or cover and chill. (6-8 servings.)

FOIL-GRILLED ZUCCHINI AND TOMATOES

5-6 medium zucchini (about 7-8 cups), sliced 1/4-inch thick
1/2 cup olive oil or salad oil
5 medium tomatoes
1 large onion
3 cloves garlic, crushed (garlic salt may be used, omit additional salt)

2 teaspoons dried thyme, crushed
Salt to taste
Pepper to taste
Juice of 2 lemons

Lightly brush oil on 6 sheets of heavy-duty foil and arrange equal amounts of zucchini on each. Slice tomatoes. Divide tomato slices among pieces of foil. Slice onion very thin and place on top of zucchini and tomatoes. Sprinkle each serving with olive oil, garlic, thyme, salt, pepper and lemon juice. Wrap packages securely and grill over medium hot coals, turning once or twice, for 20-25 minutes or until vegetables are tender. (6 servings).

HOT BARBECUED BREAD

1/2 cup (1 stick) soft butter or margarine
1 tablespoon prepared mustard
1/2 cup grated Parmesan cheese

1/2 teaspoon garlic salt
1/4 cup parsley, snipped
1 long loaf French bread (about 18 inches long)

Combine first five ingredients. Cut bread in one-inch slices, cutting to, but not through, bottom crust. Spread butter mixture generously on one side of each slice. Wrap loaf in foil. Heat 350° about 25-30 minutes.

PECAN CRUMB CAKE

1 (18.5 ounce) box yellow or lemon cake mix (reserve 2/3 cup for topping)
1/2 cup (1 stick) butter or margarine, melted
4 eggs, well beaten, divided
1/2 cup dark brown sugar, packed

2/3 cup reserved cake mix
1 1/2 cups white syrup
1 teaspoon vanilla
1 1/2 cups pecans, coarsely chopped

Combine cake mix less 2/3 cup, butter and one egg. Pat mixture into a 9x13-inch baking dish and bake for 15 minutes at 350°. Meanwhile, combine sugar, reserved cake mix, syrup, vanilla, remaining 3 eggs, and pecans. Mix well. Pour over partially cooked cake. Increase oven temperature to 375°. Return cake to oven. Cook until surface is fairly firm, about 30-35 minutes. Cool, cut into squares of desired size.

CHOCOLATE ICE CREAM

1 quart milk
1 cup cocoa
1 cup light corn syrup
5 eggs

2 cups sugar
1 quart whipping cream
1 tablespoon vanilla extract

In a 2-quart saucepan, combine 2 cups milk, cocoa and corn syrup. Bring to a boil over medium heat, stirring constantly. Cool. In large mixing bowl, beat eggs until foamy; gradually beat in sugar. Add cocoa mixture. Stir in 2 cups milk, cream and vanilla. Chill. Churn-freeze. (Yield: 1 gallon)

TUESDAY
Broiled Sirloin Steak and Tomato Halves *
Buttered Limas and pimiento
Fresh vegetable salad
Crusty popovers *
Caramel cake and frosting

BROILED SIRLOIN STEAK AND TOMATO HALVES

1 beef sirloin steak, cut 1-2 inches thick	*Salt and pepper*

Set regulator for broiling. Place steak on rack in broiler pan, so the top of 1-inch steak is 2-3 inches from the heat and 2-inch steak is 3-5 inches from the heat. Broil. When one side is browned, season, turn and finish cooking on the second side. Season. Steaks cut 1 inch thick require 18-20 minutes for rare and 20-25 minutes for medium. Steaks cut 2 inches thick require 30-40 minutes for rare and 35-45 minutes for medium. (4 servings)

Tomato Halves

2 large tomatoes	*$1/4$ teaspoon salt*
2 tablespoons cracker crumbs	*$1/4$ teaspoon paprika*
2 tablespoons prepared horseradish	*2 teaspoons chopped parsley*
1 tablespoon lemon juice	

Cut tomatoes in half crosswise. Carefully remove stem end. Combine cracker crumbs, horseradish, lemon juice, salt and paprika. Spread cracker mixture evenly over tomato halves; sprinkle with parsley. Place on rack in broiler pan 2-3 inches from heat. Broil 3-5 minutes or just until heated.

CRUSTY POPOVERS

1 whole egg	*2 tablespoons melted calorie-reduced margarine*
2 egg whites	*$1/4$ teaspoon salt*
$1/2$ cup instant non-fat dry milk	*1 cup whole wheat flour*
1 cup water	*Vegetable cooking spray*

In large mixing bowl, combine whole egg and egg whites. Beat until light, add dry milk, water, margarine and salt. Blend well. Gradually beat in flour. Coat 2-inch muffin tins with cooking spray. Fill each cup $2/3$ full of batter. Bake in 400° oven for 35-40 minutes or until popovers are high, crusty and well-browned. Remove from cups at once. Cut a small slit on the side of each popover to allow steam to escape. Serve hot. Store leftovers in refrigerator. (Yield: 18)

WEDNESDAY
Cheese and mushroom pie *
Buttered green vegetable
Orange pecan tossed salad *
Iced chocolate angel food cake

CHEESE AND MUSHROOM PIE

½ pound mushrooms, sliced	3 tablespoons butter or margarine
½ cup chopped celery	3 tablespoons flour
¼ cup chopped onion	1 ½ cups milk
1 clove garlic, crushed	4-6 Swiss cheese slices
2 tablespoons butter or margarine	Double crust for 9-inch pie
⅓ cup cashew nut pieces (coarsely chopped)	

Saute mushrooms, celery, onion and garlic in butter until tender. Add cashews and cook one minute. Line pie pan with bottom crust. Place vegetables in crust carefully. In small saucepan, melt butter. Add flour, stirring to make a smooth paste; add milk gradually, stirring constantly. Cook until sauce is smooth and thick. Pour over vegetables. Top with slices of Swiss cheese. Adjust top crust. Make slits to release steam. Bake at 350° for 40 minutes or until brown. Cool for about 4-5 minutes before serving. (6 servings)

CONGEALED JEWEL SALAD

2 (3 ounce) packages pineapple flavored gelatin	1 cup chopped raw cranberries
1 cup hot water	½ cup canned crushed pineapple
½ teaspoon salt	½ cup diced celery
1 cup cold liquid (drained pineapple syrup plus water)	½ cup chopped walnuts or pecans

Dissolve gelatin in hot water. Add salt and pineapple juice-water mixture. Chill until slightly thickened. Fold in remaining ingredients. Turn into one-quart mold or into 6 individual molds. Chill until firm. Unmold onto bed of crisp lettuce, decorate with additional nut halves or pieces and serve with dressing of your choice. 6 servings.

THURSDAY
Tuna casserole with cheese swirls *
Buttered broccoli
Jellied vegetable salad / Bread
No-crust cheese cake *

TUNA CASSEROLE WITH CHEESE SWIRLS

3 tablespoons butter or margarine	1 (6 ½ ounce) can water-packed tuna, drained
⅓ cup chopped green pepper	1 cup cooked peas, drained
⅓ cup chopped onion	1 tablespoon lemon juice
¼ cup biscuit mix	2 cups biscuit mix
1 (10 ½ ounce) can condensed cream of mushroom or celery soup	½ cup cold water
1 ½ cups milk	¾ cup shredded processed American cheese

In saucepan, melt butter; add pepper and onion. Cook until tender. Gradually stir in biscuit mix, soup and milk. Heat to boiling over medium heat, stirring constantly for 1 minute. Stir in tuna, peas and lemon juice. Pour mixture into ungreased baking dish, 11 ½x7 ½x1 ½ inches (2-quart oblong). Combine 2 cups biscuit mix and water to make a soft dough. Gently shape dough into a ball on floured surface. Knead 5 times. Roll dough into a rectangle, 15x19 inches; sprinkle with cheese. Roll up, beginning at wide side. Seal well by pinching edges into dough. Cut into twelve 1 ¼-inch slices. Place slices, cut side down, on hot tuna mixture. Bake 20-25 minutes at 425°. Cutting slices is easier when rolled dough is frozen. (4-6 servings)

NO CRUST CHEESE CAKE

2 (8 ounce) packages cream cheese, softened	1 cup sour cream
2/3 cup sugar	3 tablespoons sugar
1/8 teaspoon salt	1 teaspoon vanilla flavoring
3 eggs	Salt, dash
1/2 teaspoon almond extract	Toasted slivered almonds (optional)

Beat cheese until fluffy. Gradually beat in 2/3 cup sugar and salt. Add eggs, one at a time, beating well after each addition. Add almond extract. Pour into buttered 9-inch pie pan. Bake at 350° for 30 minutes. Combine sour cream, 3 tablespoons sugar, vanilla and salt. Spread over top of cake. Return to oven and bake 10 minutes longer. Sprinkle with almonds. Cool before serving. (6-8 servings)

FRIDAY
Short cut lasagna *
Mixed vegetables with oil and vinegar dressing
Garlic bread
Fresh peach ambrosia *

SHORT CUT LASAGNA (Use uncooked noodles)

1 1/2 pounds ground beef	1 (12 ounce) package Swiss cheese slices
1/2 pound lasagna noodles, uncooked	1 (8 ounce) can tomato sauce
3 1/2 cups spaghetti sauce	1/4 cup Parmesan cheese
1 pound (2 cups) cottage cheese	

Cook beef until pink color disappears. Stir to break meat apart. Dip noodles in boiling water. Grease a 9x13x2-inch pan. Cover bottom with uncooked lasagna noodles (approximately 3 1/2 noodles); cover with 1³/4 cups spaghetti sauce, then with 1/2 of the cooked beef. Sprinkle with 1 cup cottage cheese. Cover all with half the slices of Swiss cheese. Repeat layers. Cover last layer of Swiss cheese with tomato sauce, and sprinkle on the Parmesan cheese. Cover with heavy duty foil squeezed tightly around the edges. Bake in pre-heated oven at 350° for 1 1/2 hours. (6-8 servings)

FRESH PEACH AMBROSIA

2 pounds (about 8 medium) fresh peaches, sliced	2 tablespoons lemon juice
1 cup sliced bananas	1/3 cup shredded coconut
2 tablespoons sugar	

Combine peaches, bananas, sugar and lemon juice. Chill. Spoon into serving dish. Top with shredded coconut. 6-8 servings. (For extra festivity, add champagne, Chablis, or any favorite semi-sweet wine instead of lemon juice.)

SATURDAY
Sweet and sour frankfurter crepes *
Buttered green beans
Jellied vegetable salad *
Oatmeal cookies

SWEET AND SOUR FRANKFURTER CREPES

1 (8 ounce) can pineapple chunks
2 tablespoons butter or margarine
1 medium onion, chopped
1 green pepper, chopped
2 tablespoons cornstarch
1/4 cup brown sugar, packed
1 teaspoon instant chicken bouillon granules

Dash salt
3/4 cup water
1/4 cup vinegar
1 tablespoon soy sauce
6 franks, cut diagonally in 1/4-inch slices
9 (8 inch) crepes

Sweet and Sour Filling

Drain pineapple, reserve syrup. In a skillet, melt butter; cook onion and green pepper until tender but not brown. Combine corn starch, brown sugar, bouillon granules and salt. Combine reserved pineapple juice, water, vinegar and soy sauce and add to cornstarch mixture. Blend into vegetables, cooking and stirring until mixture is thick. Add franks and pineapple.

Crepes

3/4 cup flour
1 teaspoon sugar
1/4 teaspoon salt
1 cup buttermilk

1/2 cup milk
2 eggs, slightly beaten
1 tablespoon cooking oil

In a bowl combine flour, sugar and salt. Add buttermilk, milk, eggs and oil; beat with rotary beater (or electric mixer) until well blended. Heat a lightly-greased 8-inch skillet or crepe pan. Using a 1/4-cup measure, pour 1/4 cup batter into pan. Lift and tilt skillet to spread batter. Brown on one side only. Invert pan over paper toweling; remove crepe to cool. Repeat to make 9-10 crepes, greasing skillet occasionally.

To assemble: Using the above or a favorite crepe recipe, cook crepes and spoon about 4 tablespoons filling along center of unbrowned side of each crepe. Fold the 2 opposite edges of crepe so they overlap on top of filling. Roll loosely and place seam side down in 9x13x2-inch baking dish. Spoon remaining filling over crepes. Cover and bake at 375° until heated through, about 20-25 minutes. (6-9 servings)

JELLIED VEGETABLE SALAD

1 (3 ounce) package lemon flavored gelatin
1 teaspoon unflavored gelatin
1 cup boiling water
1 cup cold water
1 tablespoon finely chopped onion
1/2 teaspoon salt

1/4 cup chopped green pepper
1/4 cup shredded carrots
1/4 cup diced celery
1/4 cup thinly-sliced radishes
Lettuce leaves

Combine flavored and unflavored gelatin. Dissolve in boiling water. Add cold water, onion and salt. Chill in refrigerator until mixture begins to thicken. Gently stir in green pepper, carrots, celery and radishes. Pour into a quart mold or 6 individual molds. Chill until set. Unmold and serve on lettuce. (6 servings)

July - Second Week

How do Americans feel about fruits and vegetables on the dinner table? According to recent surveys, the demand for French fries, fresh fruit and vegetable salads, fresh vegetables and frozen greens is rising. Consumption is up in frozen corn, carrots, cauliflower and broccoli, as well as French fries. This is also shown in the increased number of "salad bars" and salad meals in restaurants. America's eating habits are improving, but modern produce counters present a few problems that should be cleared up for meal managers.

People often say they like locally-grown fresh fruits and vegetables because they are not covered with wax. If you select a bright, shiny piece of fruit or a vegetable for your family, you are automatically buying a waxed product.

Nature protects most plants, flowers and fruits with a shield of wax which keeps in moisture and prevents sun damage. Most home-grown fruits and vegetables retain their nutrients and peak quality unwashed and refrigerated in airtight plastic bags, but this cannot be done commercially. So, after the fruits and vegetables have been picked, a thorough "bath" is given in the packing house. The washing process includes soaking and scrubbing in a detergent and rinsing in hot water. This removes the natural protective wax from the fruit or vegetable, so man-made wax is applied to replace nature's coating. Without this wax, the fruit would quickly become soft, perhaps decay, and lose a great deal of its juice content and nutrients. While there is admittedly a cosmetic effect, the principal function of the wax is to retard shriveling and dehydration of the product. Waxing cannot improve the quality of inferior products. All waxes on fruits and vegetables have been approved by the U.S. Food and Drug Administration as completely safe and edible materials. So, if home-grown fruits and vegetables are not available, use eye-appealing waxed ones for quality, flavor and nutrition.

SUNDAY
24-Hour sauerbraten *
Mashed potatoes
Buttered Brussels sprouts
Carrot and cabbage salad / Corn muffins
New Orleans bread pudding with tipsy sauce *

24-HOUR SAUERBRATEN

4 pounds rump or bottom round of beef	*½ teaspoon ground sage*
2 teaspoons dry mustard	*6 whole cloves*
1 tablespoon water	*3 beef bouillon cubes*
2 tablespoons dried parsley flakes	*2 cups boiling water*
2 tablespoons grated lemon peel	*½ cup dried onion flakes*
1 teaspoon salt	*½ cup cider vinegar*
1 teaspoon thyme	*2 or 3 tablespoons shortening*
1 teaspoon whole black peppercorns	*Flour*

Place beef in close-fitting pan. Combine mustard and 1 tablespoon water; let stand 10 minutes for flavor to develop. Combine mustard with parsley flakes, lemon peel, salt, thyme, black pepper, sage, cloves, bouillon cubes, boiling water, onion flakes and vinegar; pour over meat. Cool. Place in refrigerator to marinate 24 hours, turning several times. Remove meat from marinade. Brown on all sides in shortening. Add marinade. Cover and simmer until tender, about 2 ½ to 3 hours. Remove meat and make gravy, using 1 ½ tablespoons flour to each cup liquid left in pan. (8-10 servings)

NEW ORLEANS BREAD PUDDING WITH TIPSY SAUCE

½ loaf French bread or ½ pound day-old bread
1 quart milk
2 eggs
1 cup sugar

1 tablespoon vanilla extract
¼ cup (½ stick) butter, melted
¾ cup dark raisins
Tipsy or Bourbon Sauce

Soak bread in milk; crush until well-mixed and crumbled. In separate bowl beat eggs, gradually stir in sugar, vanilla and raisins, Add to milk mixture. Pour butter in bottom of 2-quart shallow baking pan. Pour milk mixture over butter in baking pan. Butter will float on top. Bake at 325° for one hour or until set. Cool. Cut in squares and serve topped with sauce. Serve pudding and sauce warm. (6 servings)

Tipsy or Bourbon Sauce

¼ pound (1 stick) butter or margarine, softened
1 cup sugar
¼ cup boiling water

1 egg, beaten
¼ cup Bourbon (optional)

In top of double boiler, melt butter. Stir in sugar and boiling water. Cook, stirring constantly over hot water until sugar is dissolved. Pour egg into hot mixture slowly, stirring continually to prevent egg from curdling. Stir for three minutes. Cool. Add Bourbon. Sauce must be served warm. (6 servings)

MONDAY
Beef cubes on buttered pasta *
Tossed salad with Italian dressing
Garlic bread / Creme de menthe parfait *

BEEF CUBES ON BUTTERED PASTA

⅓ cup flour
1 pound boneless top of the round, cut into
   1-inch cubes
2 tablespoons butter or margarine
1 teaspoon dried thyme
1 tablespoon wine vinegar
1 (10 ½ ounce) can consomme or 1 ¼ cups beer
½ teaspoon salt

¼ teaspoon pepper
½ teaspoon sugar
1 bay leaf
3 onions, sliced
8 ounces spaghettini
¼ cup butter or margarine
Parmesan cheese

Place flour in paper sack, shake beef cubes, a few at a time, in the bag to coat. Brown meat in butter. Combine thyme, vinegar, consomme or beer, salt, pepper, sugar, bay leaf and onions. Pour over beef in skillet. Bring to a boil. Reduce heat; cover and simmer 1 hour or until meat is tender. Cook spaghettini according to package directions. Drain, toss with butter. serve meat and sauce over the pasta, topped with Parmesan cheese. (4 servings)

CREME DE MENTHE OR CREME DE COCOA PARFAIT

Creme de menthe or creme de cocoa
Vanilla or chocolate ice cream, or both

Whipped topping or whipped cream

In parfait glasses, arrange alternating layers of creme de menthe or creme de cocoa and vanilla or chocolate ice cream, or some of both flavors. Top the parfait with whipped topping or whipped cream.

TUESDAY
Savory tuna loaf with parsley sauce*
Buttered Lima beans
Green salad
Bread sticks
Fresh strawberry pie *

SAVORY TUNA LOAF WITH PARSLEY SAUCE

2 eggs, beaten
1/2 cup milk
2 cups soft bread crumbs
1/4 cup minced onion
1 tablespoon dehydrated parsley flakes

1/4 teaspoon thyme
1 teaspoon salt
1/4 teaspoon pepper
3 cans (6 1/2 or 7 ounces each) tuna in vegetable oil

Combine eggs, milk, bread crumbs and seasonings in mixing bowl; blend together. Add tuna; mix thoroughly. Turn into foil-lined loaf pan, 8 1/2x4 1/2x2 3/4-inches. Bake in 375° oven for 1 hour. Turn loaf onto platter; remove foil. (Turn right side up onto another platter.) Garnish with lemon slices. Serve with parsley sauce. 6 servings.

Parsley Sauce

1 can condensed cream of celery soup
1/2 cup milk

2 tablespoons chopped parsley

Combine undiluted soup and milk; stir over low heat until hot. Add parsley.

FRESH STRAWBERRY PIE

1 pound (16 ounces) fresh strawberries
1 cup sugar
2 tablespoons corn starch

1/3 cup strawberry flavored gelatin
1 frozen 9-inch deep dish pie crust, baked

Wash strawberries, remove the stems and cut in half. Crush enough strawberries to equal one cup. Place remaining berries in the pie crust. Combine crushed berries, sugar and corn starch. Cook over medium heat until thick and clear. Stir in gelatin; mix well. Pour strawberry mixture over the berries in the crust. Refrigerate until firm. Serve topped with whipped cream or whipped topping. 8 servings.

WEDNESDAY
Bacon-wrapped beef patties
Asparagus supper casserole *
Marinated raw vegetables
Sesame seed buns / Soft molasses cookies

ASPARAGUS SUPPER CASSEROLE

1 pound fresh asparagus or 1 (10 ounce)
   package frozen asparagus
4 or 5 eggs, hard-cooked
1/4 cup butter or margarine
1/4 cup sifted flour
1 1/2 cups milk
1/2 cup Sauterne or any white dinner wine

3/4 teaspoon seasoned salt
3 tablespoons frozen chopped chives or
   chopped green onion
1/2 cup shredded Cheddar cheese
1 large tomato
1/4 cup fine dry bread crumbs
1 tablespoon butter, melted

Cook asparagus; drain and cut into bite-size pieces. Arrange in a 1 ½-quart baking dish. Slice eggs and arrange over asparagus. Melt ¼ cup butter, blend in flour; stir in milk. Cook, stirring, until thickened. Blend in wine, salt, chives or green onion, and cheese. Pour over asparagus. Cut tomato into thin slices and arrange over sauce; sprinkle with bread crumbs mixed with the butter. Bake in moderate oven, 375°, about 25 minutes. (4 servings)

THURSDAY
Sausage stroganoff
Hot rice
Grapefruit and avocado with French dressing
Frosted cream puff bars *

FROSTED CREAM PUFF BARS

1 cup boiling water
½ cup butter or margarine
1 cup flour
4 eggs

1 teaspoon almond flavoring
Frosting
½ cup blanched almonds

Pour water into saucepan, add butter, and cook until butter is melted and water is boiling. Add flour quickly while boiling; stir vigorously until dough forms a ball. Remove from heat. Add eggs one at a time, beating well after each addition. Add almond flavoring. Spread on 10x15-inch greased cookie sheet. Bake at 350° for 45 minutes. Make frosting. Spread over cooled bar base. Top with blanched almonds. (15-18 bars)

Frosting

⅓ cup butter or margarine, softened
2 tablespoons grated orange rind
1 teaspoon almond extract
¼ teaspoon salt

2 unbeaten egg whites
1 pound powdered sugar
1 tablespoon milk

Cream butter, orange rind, almond extract and salt until fluffy. Add egg whites and sugar alternately, a little at a time, beating well after each addition. Add milk and beat. If necessary, add more milk to make desired spreading consistency. (Yield: about 2 cups)

FRIDAY
Sweet-sour pork chops *
Buttered snow peas
Broccoli and cauliflower salad
Hard rolls
Ice cream with strawberry topping

SWEET-SOUR PORK CHOPS

6 rib pork chops, ½-inch thick
1 tablespoon shortening
Salt
Pepper
1 cup catsup
1 cup pineapple juice

2 tablespoons brown sugar
2 tablespoons lemon juice
¼ cup minced onion
2 teaspoons Worcestershire sauce
1 teaspoon salt
¼ teaspoon ground cloves

Brown chops in shortening; drain excess fat. Sprinkle lightly with salt and pepper. Combine catsup, pineapple juice, brown sugar, lemon juice, onion, Worcestershire sauce, salt and cloves. Pour over chops. Cover, simmer for 45 minutes, basting occasionally, or until meat is tender. Skim excess fat from sauce. 6 servings. (About 2 cups sauce.)

SATURDAY
Granny's Birthday Luncheon (Granny does no work)
Bloody Bloody Marys *
Pita crackers *
Shrimp salad with mustard dressing *
Stuffed zucchini boats * / Relish tray:
Carrot and pepper sticks / Deviled eggs *
Refrigerator cloverleaf rolls * / Pecan cherry cake *

Plan Of Work
The day before:
1. Prepare the Pecan cherry cake
2. Prepare Pita crackers
Early in the day:
3. Have ingredients ready for Bloody Bloody Marys
4. Prepare Zucchini boats, ready to bake
5. Eggs can be prepared
6. Vegetables can also be scraped and cut; store covered in the refrigerator.
7. Shrimp can be purchased freshly steamed at most meat markets. Peel, de-vein and chill until ready to complete final preparation.
Three hours before serving:
8. Start preparation for rolls.
Two hours before serving:
9. Prepare rolls for last rising.
Minutes before serving:
10. Place rolls in oven
11. Make final preparations for serving
Allow time for a happy hour before serving to enjoy the Bloody Marys and Pita crackers.

BLOODY BLOODY MARY

3 ounces vegetable juice or tomato juice
1 1/2 ounces Vodka
1 teaspoon lemon or lime juice
1/8 teaspoon Worcestershire sauce (a good dash)

1/8 teaspoon Tabasco sauce (adjust to taste)
Pepper, optional (adjust to taste)
8-inch celery stalk or wedge of lemon or lime

Combine all in shaker. Mix thoroughly. Add ice to individual glass and fill with mixture. Add one celery stalk to each glass. Lime or lemon wedge can be used as garnish, attached to rim of glass. (1 serving)

PITA CRACKERS

1 package pita bread (white)
1/2 cup (1 stick) butter or margarine, softened

2 tablespoons Bouquet Garni (crushed)
3/4 teaspoon garlic powder

Cut pita bread in serving size pieces, and split open. Mix butter with Bouquet Garni and garlic powder. Spread small amount of butter mixture on crackers. Bake in 325° oven for 6 minutes. Cool and serve. Can be used as a snack or with a dip.

SHRIMP SALAD WITH MUSTARD DRESSING

1/4 cup plus 2 tablespoons wine vinegar
1/4 cup plus 2 tablespoons Dijon mustard
3/4 cup salad oil (preferably olive oil)
Salt to taste

3/4 teaspoon freshly ground black pepper, or to taste
3 cups shrimp, cooked, peeled, de-veined, chilled
6 lettuce cups

In small bowl, combine vinegar and mustard. With a whisk add oil a few drops at a time, while whisking vigorously. When mixture thickens, add salt and pepper. Serve immediately. (If left over, shake well before using again.) Toss with shrimp and serve in lettuce cups. (6 servings)

STUFFED ZUCCHINI BOATS

6 medium-sized zucchini
1 can (12 ounce) whole kernel corn, drained
2 teaspoons seasoned salt

2 eggs, beaten
1/4 cup chopped green onions (use tops)
1/2 cup (2 ounces) shredded sharp Cheddar cheese

Wash zucchini and cut off ends. Do not pare. Cook whole in boiling water about 5 to 7 minutes. Cut squash in half lengthwise. With tip of spoon carefully remove squash from shells. Chop into small pieces; combine with corn, seasoned salt, eggs, and onions. Pile mixture lightly into zucchini shells. Place in 2-quart oblong baking dish. Sprinkle with shredded cheese. Bake, uncovered, in moderate oven (350°) for 30 minutes or until tender and lightly browned. (6 servings)

DEVILED EGGS

8-10 hard-cooked eggs
2 tablespoons lemon juice or wine vinegar
3 tablespoons prepared mustard
1/2 teaspoon thyme
1 teaspoon salt

1/2 teaspoon cayenne pepper
1 teaspoon curry powder
1/2 cup pickle relish and juice
Mayonnaise
Caviar, pickle relish, olive slices as garnish

Slice eggs in half lengthwise. Remove yolks, place in mixer bowl and mash well. Add lemon juice, mustard, thyme, salt, pepper and curry. Mix with electric mixer until smooth. Stir in pickle relish and as much mayonnaise as it takes to make a smooth spreadable mixture. Adjust seasoning. Fill eggs. Garnish with a bit of caviar, pickle relish or sliced olives. Do not add too much liquid. The mixture will be runny. Plan for at least two halves per person. Refrigerate leftovers. They will keep a couple of days. (6-10 servings)

REFRIGERATOR CLOVERLEAF ROLLS

1 package active dry yeast
1/4 cup warm water
1/2 cup boiling water
1/2 cup shortening

1/4 cup sugar
1 teaspoon salt
1 egg
3 1/2 cups sifted flour

Sprinkle yeast over warm water; dissolve. Pour boiling water over shortening in blender container; cover and process until blended. Remove cover. Add sugar, salt and egg; process until thoroughly blended. Add yeast mixture and process until thoroughly mixed. Measure flour into mixing bowl. Add liquid ingredients from blender container; stir thoroughly. Cover and refrigerate until about 2 hours before baking. Grease muffin cups. Punch down dough and roll into small balls, ³/₄ inch to 1 inch in size. Put three balls into each muffin cup and let rise until double in bulk. Bake 10 to 15 minutes in 400° oven. Brush with melted butter after removing from oven. (2 dozen)

PECAN CHERRY CAKE

1 ¹/₂ cups granulated sugar	³/₄ cup drained, chopped Maraschino cherries
1 (8 ounce) package cream cheese, softened	¹/₂ cup chopped pecans
1 cup (2 sticks) butter or margarine	¹/₂ cup finely-chopped pecans
1 ¹/₂ teaspoons vanilla	1 ¹/₂ cups sifted powdered sugar
4 eggs	2 tablespoons milk
2 ¹/₄ cups sifted all-purpose flour	Cherries - optional
1 ¹/₂ teaspoons baking powder	Nuts - optional

Combine sugar, cheese, butter and vanilla; mix well. Add eggs, one at a time; mix well. Combine 2 cups flour and baking powder; gradually add to sugar mixture. Toss remaining flour with cherries and chopped nuts; fold into batter. Sprinkle greased tube pan with ¹/₂ cup finely-chopped nuts; pour batter into pan. Bake at 325° for 1 hour and 20 minutes. Cool 5 minutes. Remove from pan; cool thoroughly. Combine sugar and milk; drizzle over cake. Garnish with cherries and nuts, if desired.

July - Third Week

The potato is among nature's most versatile products. It is eaten in all seasons and is very good for you. As for the number of calories, it has no more than an apple, but has more nutrients. The toppings and sauces added to the potato add the calories. Learn to enjoy the bare baked potato without toppings.

A medium-sized baked potato provides as much vitamin C as an orange; it furnishes B vitamins including thiamin, niacin and hard-to-find vitamin B6 (pyrodoxine), plus important trace minerals such as copper, magnesium and small amounts of iron and vegetable protein. The potato's potassium level is as great as the banana's — but it contains fewer calories. It also adds to the daily fiber intake.

There are four basic types of potatoes sold in food stores and all are delicious. You can find the oval, reddish-brown-skinned russet; the red-skinned round; the beige-skinned long white; and the beige-skinned round white. A medium-sized potato makes one 6- to 8-ounce portion, or one cup.

New potatoes are not a variety, but simply potatoes that go directly from the field to the market without being put in storage.

Supermarket potatoes are usually graded by federal or state officials. Sizes will vary, but it is best to purchase those of medium size. This facilitates even cooking. Select potatoes free from wrinkles or wilted skins. Avoid buying potatoes that are sprouting or with dark spots, cut surfaces or greenish tints.

To store them, gently wipe newly purchased potatoes with a dry cloth. Put them in a cool dark place that's well-ventilated. A temperature between 45-50° is ideal. At this temperature, potatoes should keep well for several weeks.

Greening of potatoes comes from allowing them to have a prolonged exposure to light. Should they have green spots after you've stored them a while, cut spots off or the potato will taste bitter.

Do not refrigerate potatoes. Below 40°, they will develop a starchy-sweet taste as the result of accumulated sugars. This increased sugar will cause the potato to darken when cooked.

Cook potatoes with their skins on if possible to conserve nutrients. Potatoes retain nutrients better if cooked whole. They may be halved, sliced or diced if shorter cooking time is required. To keep cut potatoes from turning dark, dip them in cold water to which a little lemon juice or ascorbic acid has been added. Don't soak them; soaking potatoes too long can result in loss of water-soluble vitamins.

To save energy, bake a bunch of potatoes and save! Yes, you can bake all the potatoes you need for a week or two at the same time, which will save many oven hours on your electric or gas bill. Cool and store them, covered, in the refrigerator, then use them as you need them.

To prepare standard oven-baked potatoes, scrub potatoes under cold running water; cut off blemishes, pat dry and prick in several places with skewer or fork. Potatoes wrapped in foil or rubbed with salad oil before baking have softer skins than those baked with skins exposed and/or dry. This is a matter of preference.

All medium-sized potatoes require 45 to 60 minutes in a 400° oven to become soft when pinched with mitted hands, or tested with a fork.

To prepare microwave oven-baked potatoes, scrub, pat dry and prick uniformly-sized potatoes with skewer or fork. Place in a spoke pattern with the smaller ends toward the center, in microwave oven. Follow oven manual for cooking time. Most ovens require four to five minutes to bake a medium-sized potato, plus two minutes for each additional one cooked at the same time. It is important to turn potatoes over halfway through microwave baking time.

SUNDAY
Parmesan chicken *
Broccoli with sour cream sauce *
Sliced tomatoes, cucumber and onion slices
Whole wheat rolls, commercial
Butterscotch brownies

PARMESAN CHICKEN

¹/₄ pound (1 stick) butter or margarine	*³/₄ cup Parmesan cheese*
¹/₄ cup cracker meal	*1 (2 ¹/₂- to 3-pound) fryer, cut in serving pieces*

Melt butter. In small bowl, combine cracker meal and Parmesan cheese. Dip chicken first in melted butter, then in cracker meal mixture. Place, skin side up, in baking dish. Bake uncovered at 350° for 1 ½ hours. (4-6 servings)

BROCCOLI WITH SOUR CREAM SAUCE

2 (10 ounce) packages frozen broccoli spears	*1 teaspoon vinegar*
2 tablespoons butter or margarine	*¹/₈ teaspoon pepper*
2 tablespoons finely-chopped onion	*1 cup sour cream*
2 teaspoons sugar	*¹/₄ cup chopped nuts (optional)*

Cook broccoli according to package directions. In top of double boiler melt butter; saute onion until tender. Stir in sugar, vinegar and pepper. Gently blend in sour cream. Place top of double boiler over warm, not boiling, water. Heat until sauce is warm. Serve over broccoli. Top with nuts. (6 servings)
Note: Can be prepared in sauce pan over low heat, if watched carefully.

MONDAY
Spinach fettuccine Alfredo *
Baked tomato halves
Coleslaw with vinaigrette dressing *
Peach yogurt

SPINACH FETTUCCINE ALFREDO

1 (12 ounce) package spinach fettuccine
1 egg yolk (optional)
²/₃ cup light cream (sour cream or half & half
   may be substituted)

¹/₂ cup (1 stick) butter or margarine
2 cloves garlic, crushed
¹/₂ cup grated Parmesan cheese
Additional cheese for topping, if desired

Cook noodles according to package directions. While noodles are cooking, beat egg yolk lightly with a fork and add to cream. Combine butter and garlic and melt. Drain noodles; place in warm serving bowl or platter. Over the noodles pour egg and cream mixture, melted butter mixture and grated cheese. Toss noodles with fork and spoon until well blended. Top with additional grated cheese, if desired, and serve immediately. (4 servings as main dish, 8 servings as side dish)

COLE SLAW WITH VINAIGRETTE DRESSING

1 small head cabbage (about 1 pound)
¹/₄ cup sliced pimiento-stuffed green olives
¹/₃ cup olive oil
3 tablespoons red wine vinegar
1 tablespoon drained and chopped capers

¹/₂ teaspoon salt
¹/₈ teaspoon pepper
¹/₄ teaspoon red pepper flakes
1 cup cherry tomatoes, cut in half
¹/₄ cup chopped parsley

Trim outer leaves from cabbage; quarter and core. Chop coarsely (about 6 cups). In a large bowl combine cabbage with olives. Combine oil, vinegar, capers, salt, pepper and red pepper flakes in a large screw-top jar. Cover; shake well. Pour dressing over cabbage and toss with cherry tomatoes; sprinkle with parsley. Toss again before serving. (4-6 servings)

TUESDAY
Roast pork loin
Baked potatoes (with salt and pepper topping only)
Corn and green bean casserole *
Apple nut salad
Skillet cornbread
Low calorie rice pudding *

CORN AND GREEN BEAN CASSEROLE

1 (16 ounce) can French-style green beans, drained
1 (16 ounce) can whole kernel corn, drained
¹/₂ cup chopped celery
¹/₂ cup chopped onions
¹/₄ cup chopped green pepper
¹/₂ cup (2 ounces) shredded sharp Cheddar cheese

¹/₂ cup sour cream
1 (10 ¹/₂-ounce) can cream of celery soup
Salt and pepper to taste
¹/₄ cup (¹/₂ stick) butter or margarine
2 cups crushed cheese crackers
¹/₂ cup slivered almonds*

Combine beans, corn, celery, onions, pepper, cheese, sour cream, soup, salt and pepper. Pour into greased 1 $1/_2$-quart baking dish. Combine butter and crushed crackers well. Spread over casserole. Sprinkle almonds over top. Bake 45 minutes at 350°. Can be topped with almond sauce. (6 servings)

LOW-CALORIE RICE PUDDING

2 cups water
$1/_2$ cup uncooked rice
$1/_2$ teaspoon salt
$1/_2$ cup raisins
2 cups instant non-fat dry milk

$1/_2$ cup sugar
1 cup warm water
1 teaspoon vanilla
Almond sauce (optional)

Combine 2 cups water, rice, salt, raisins, non-fat dry milk, sugar, 1 cup warm water, and vanilla. Pour into a greased 1-quart baking dish. Cover. Bake in 375° oven for one hour. (6 servings)

Almond Sauce

1 cup evaporated skim milk
$1^1/_2$ cups sugar

$2/_3$ cup butter or margarine
$1/_2$ teaspoon almond flavoring or extract

Combine first three ingredients in a saucepan; boil one minute. Add flavoring if desired. Yields about 2½ cups.

WEDNESDAY
Baked chicken
Steamed new potatoes
Sauteed green peppers
Fresh vegetable with sweet and sour dressing *
Sliced rye bread
Cheese crumble apple pie *

SWEET AND SOUR DRESSING

1 teaspoon dry mustard
2 tablespoons cornstarch
$1/_4$ teaspoon salt
1 tablespoon sugar

$1/_2$ cup vinegar
3 tablespoons finely-chopped onions
1 $1/_3$ cups water

Combine mustard, cornstarch, salt, sugar, vinegar, onions and water in a sauce pan. Bring to a boil; boil for two minutes, stirring constantly. Pour into a jar, cover and refrigerate. Serve on vegetable salads. (2 cups)

CHEESE CRUMBLE APPLE PIE

1 unbaked pie shell, 9 inch (make a high rim on pie crust)

Topping

$1/_2$ cup all-purpose flour
$1/_3$ cup sugar
$1/_3$ cup firmly-packed brown sugar

$1/_3$ teaspoon cinnamon
5 tablespoons butter or margarine

Combine flour with sugars and cinnamon; cut in butter. Set aside.

Filling

5-6 cups peeled, thinly-sliced cooking apples
  (approx. 1 ½ pounds)
1 tablespoon fresh lemon juice

1 ½ cups (6 ounces) shredded Cheddar cheese
1 tablespoon plus 1 teaspoon all-purpose flour
¼ teaspoon nutmeg

Toss together apples and lemon juice. Combine cheese, flour and nutmeg; toss with apples. Arrange apples in pie crust. Sprinkle on topping. Bake 40-50 minutes in 375° oven.

THURSDAY
Sesame steaks *
Baked potato
Buttered green beans with almonds
Lettuce wedges - light Ranch dressing
Bits of Brickle ice cream pie *

SESAME STEAKS

1 pound sirloin steak, cut ½-inch thick
1 tablespoon lemon juice
2 tablespoons salad oil
½ cup soy sauce
1 tablespoon brown sugar
1 teaspoon onion salt

½ teaspoon black pepper
½ teaspoon garlic powder
½ teaspoon ginger
1 tablespoon sesame seed
½ teaspoon monosodium glutamate

Cut steak into 3 or 4 serving-size pieces; place in flat baking dish. Combine remaining ingredients; pour over steak, being sure to coat all sides. Let stand 1 hour or longer, (for a strong Oriental flavor, overnight) turning once or twice. Broil 3 inches from heat a few minutes on each side to desired degree of doneness. Serve with rice or baked potato. (4 servings)

BITS OF BRICKLE ICE CREAM PIE

Vanilla ice cream, softened
2 (3 ounce) Bits of Brickle or Heath candy bars,
  crushed
1 (9 inch) graham cracker pie shell, baked or
  commercial
1 ½ cups sugar

1 cup evaporated milk
3 ounces Bits of Brickle or Heath candy bars,
  crushed (optional)
¼ cup butter or margarine
Dash of salt
3 tablespoons maple syrup

Spoon enough ice cream to fill crust ¾ full; spread evenly. Sprinkle crushed candy over ice cream. (Save some for topping.) Add more ice cream until crust is heaping full. Sprinkle remaining candy on top. Cover with plastic wrap and freeze. Leave at room temperature for several minutes before slicing and serving. Top with sauce and serve. Sauce served best warm or at room temperature. (Makes one large deep pie or two small shallow ones.) Sauce may be passed separately.

Sauce

Combine sugar and milk in medium sauce pan and remaining ingredients. Heat until sugar is dissolved and mixture is smooth. (Could have some crunchiness due to candy pieces.)

FRIDAY
Late Friday Night Supper
Health spa soup *
Boiled shrimp and red sauce
Pear and cottage cheese salad
Caramel cake with easy caramel frosting *

HEALTH SPA SOUP

1 (10 ounce) package frozen chopped broccoli
1 large carrot, peeled and thinly sliced
1 medium potato, peeled and thinly sliced
$^1/_2$ chopped onion
1 (14 $^1/_2$-ounce) can chicken broth, plus 2
  chicken bouillon cubes

$^1/_2$ bay leaf
1 teaspoon curry powder
$^1/_2$ teaspoon salt
1 $^1/_2$ cups buttermilk
Lemon slices

In Dutch oven, combine broccoli, carrot, potato, onion, broth, bay leaf, curry powder and salt. Cover and bring to a boil. Turn down heat; simmer 10 minutes or until tender. Blend until smooth in blender or food processor. In same Dutch oven, combine broccoli mixture and buttermilk. Heat 5 minutes over medium heat, stirring ccasionally. Garnish with lemon slices. May be served cold or hot. Makes 4 (1 cup) servings.
Note: Home made chicken stock may be used, approximately 1 ½ cups.

CARAMEL CAKE WITH EASY CARAMEL FROSTING

2 cups flour
2 $^1/_4$ teaspoons baking powder
$^3/_4$ teaspoon salt
1 cup plus 2 tablespoons sugar
$^1/_2$ cup butter or margarine

$^2/_3$ cup minus 1 tablespoon milk
1 teaspoon vanilla
2 eggs, unbeaten
$^1/_2$ cup finely-chopped nuts

Combine and sift flour, baking powder, salt and sugar. Cream butter, add dry ingredients and milk alternately. Add eggs and nuts. Beat for 1 minute. Pour batter into a greased and floured 9-inch cake pan. Bake in 350° oven for 40 minutes. Cool in pan on rack for 5 minutes. Remove from pan. Cool thoroughly on rack before frosting. Cake may be baked in 2 (8 inch) layer pans for 25 minutes.

Easy Caramel Frosting

$^1/_2$ cup (1 stick) butter or margarine
1 cup brown sugar, firmly packed

$^1/_4$ cup milk
1 $^3/_4$ to 2 cups sifted powdered sugar

In a 1-quart saucepan, melt butter; add brown sugar and cook, over low heat, stirring constantly, for 2 minutes. Add milk and continue to cook and stir until mixture comes to a boil. Remove from heat, cool. Add powdered sugar gradually until of right consistency to spread.

SATURDAY
Festive Summer Brunch Buffet
Screwdrivers * or orange juice
Baked ham slices (served cold) *
Gratin chicken and mushrooms *
Fresh asparagus with citrus butter *
Fresh fruit with poppy seed dressing *
Pronto pumpernickel bread * or commercial sweet rolls
Quick and Easy chocolate ice cream and raspberry sauce *

Plan Of Work

Day before:

1. Cook ham, cool.

2. Cook chicken breasts for the Gratin. Continue final preparation the next day.

3. Prepare poppy seed dressing and grapefruit sections. Refrigerate.

Early in the day:

4. Prepare screwdrivers and refrigerate.

5. Prepare ice cream and place in freezer.

6. Prepare raspberry sauce.

7. Complete food preparation of chicken dish. Refrigerate until 30 minutes before dinner is served, and place in oven.

8. Wash and prepare asparagus for last minute cooking

9. Prepare only dry ingredients for biscuits. Finalize preparations 30 minutes before serving, to serve biscuits hot.

20 minutes before serving:

10. Cook asparagus

11. Slice ham, place on serving dish with all garnishes. Place on buffet table.

12. Complete all cooking.

SCREWDRIVER

Ice   *Orange juice*

1 ¹/₂ ounces of vodka

Put ice and vodka in a highball glass. Fill with orange juice. Stir. Make on individual demand.

BAKED HAM SLICES

3-pound fully-cooked boneless ham

Remove all wrappings. Place in a 350° oven for about 45 minutes. Chill.

GRATIN CHICKEN AND MUSHROOMS

4 chicken breast halves, skinned and boned	*1 small onion, finely-chopped*
1-2 tablespoons butter or margarine	*2 tablespoons all-purpose flour*
1 small carrot, pared, coarsely-chopped	*³/₄ cup milk, hot*
1 rib celery, coarsely-chopped	*¹/₄ cup dry white wine*
2 sprigs parsley	*¹/₂ teaspoon fresh lemon juice*
¹/₄ teaspoon salt	*¹/₄ teaspoon dried tarragon, crumbled*
¹/₂ pound fresh mushrooms	*Salt*
¹/₄ cup (¹/₂ stick) butter or margarine, divided	*Pepper*
Freshly-ground pepper	*¹/₂ cup (2 oz) shredded Gruyere or Swiss cheese*

Butter chicken breasts; cut them in half. Place in large skillet with 2 inches of cold water; add carrot, celery, parsley and salt. Cook covered, over medium heat, to a boil, then adjust heat to maintain a simmer for 12 minutes. Allow breasts to cool to tepid in liquid, drain. Reserve broth for other use. Wipe dirt and grit from mushrooms with damp paper toweling. Trim and discard stem ends. Cut mushrooms into ¼-inch slices. Heat 2 tablespoons of butter in large skillet over medium heat. When foam subsides, add the mushrooms. Saute, tossing, until mushrooms begin to exude liquid, about 3 minutes. Increase heat to high; saute, tossing until liquid has evaporated and mushrooms are golden brown, about 5 minutes. Cut chicken breasts into bite-size pieces; combine with mushrooms. Melt 2 tablespoons butter in medium sauce pan over medium heat. When foam subsides, add onion; saute until softened, about 5 minutes. Sprinkle flour into pan; stir until blended. Reduce heat to low; cook, stirring constantly, 4 minutes. Remove from heat. Slowly stir in milk and wine until smooth. Return sauce to heat; simmer, stirring, until smooth and thickened, about 5 minutes. Add lemon juice, tarragon, salt and pepper to taste. Combine sauce with mushrooms and chicken. Transfer to a greased, 1-quart baking dish; sprinkle with cheese. Bake in 350° oven until sauce is bubbly and cheese is deep golden brown, about 25 minutes. Serve hot. (4 servings)

FRESH ASPARAGUS WITH CITRUS BUTTER

2 to 2 ½ pounds or 1 large bunch asparagus
½ cup water
¼ pound (½ stick) butter or margarine
¼ cup orange juice
1 tablespoons lemon juice

Break off asparagus stalks as far down as they snap easily. Wash asparagus and place in medium-size sauce pan. Pan should be almost full. Add ½ cup water. Cover with a well-fitted lid. Cook over high heat until steam flows out around rim of the lid. (Do not lift lid.) Turn heat down to lowest heat point. Cook until crisp-tender. Test after five minutes. Melt butter, add orange juice and lemon juice. Stir until well mixed. Drain cooked asparagus. Stir in butter mixture. Serve hot. (6 servings)

FRESH FRUIT WITH POPPY SEED DRESSING
Fresh Fruit Mixture

1 cup grapefruit sections
1 cup unpeeled apple chunks
1 cup banana slices
½ cup grapes
Lettuce cups

Combine grapefruit, apple and bananas. Immediately pour any excess grapefruit juice on apples and bananas to prevent darkening. Chill mixture. Arrange on individual lettuce cups. Serve with poppy seed dressing. (4-6 servings.)

Poppy Seed Dressing

1 egg
¼ cup sugar
1 teaspoon poppy seed
1 teaspoon dry mustard
1 teaspoon chopped onion
½ teaspoon paprika
½ teaspoon salt
¼ cup honey
1 ¼ cups salad oil

In blender container add egg, sugar, poppy seed, mustard, onion, paprika, salt and honey. Blend for 5 seconds. Remove center cover insert and add salad oil, slowly. Blend until mixture is thick and smooth. (Yield: 2 cups)

PRONTO PUMPERNICKEL BREAD

1 (13 ³/₄-ounce) package hot roll mix   *¹/₄ cup molasses*
³/₄ cup unsifted rye flour   *1 ¹/₂ teaspoon caraway seeds*
1 egg, separated

Prepare hot roll mix according to package directions. Add rye flour, egg yolk, molasses and caraway seeds. Let bread rise according to package directions, about 45 minutes. When double in size, punch down and shape into round loaf. Place on greased baking sheet. Let rise again for 45 minutes, or until double in size. Lightly beat egg white and brush on bread. Bake at 375° for 40 minutes or until brown. 1 loaf.

QUICK AND EASY CREAMY CHOCOLATE ICE CREAM

1 (13 ounce) can evaporated milk   *1 teaspoon vanilla*
³/₄ cup chocolate syrup   *¹/₂ cup whipping cream*
1 tablespoon sugar

Pour milk into large bowl. Chill beater. Freeze bowl of milk, only until crystals form around edge. Whip until fluffy. Fold in syrup, vanilla, sugar and whipping cream. Pour into 2-quart container. Freeze 4-6 hours. (Makes 8, 1-cup servings or 2 quarts) Place ¼ cup of raspberry sauce on serving plate and top with ice cream.

Raspberry Sauce

1 (10 ounce) package frozen raspberries, thawed   *1 tablespoon raspberry or orange flavored liqueur*
2 tablespoons sugar

Combine all ingredients in electric blender container; process until smooth. Strain through double layer of cheese cloth, if desired.

July - Fourth Week

A meal takes on a touch of elegance when mushrooms are included. Using mushrooms as food dates back to ancient Greece, when they were looked upon as the "food of the gods." Gourmet chefs recognize mushrooms as one of the most versatile of foods — delicate in flavor, low in calories, delicious raw, sauteed, and cooked with vegetables, meats and eggs. Yet there are those who have never discovered how mushrooms can make ordinary dishes *out* of the ordinary. However, mushrooms do require some special care after purchase.

To store fresh mushrooms, place unopened package in refrigerator. Once film wrap has been removed, cover remaining mushrooms with a damp paper towel and refrigerate. They'll stay fresh for several days.

Basic preparation: never soak or peel fresh mushrooms, because flavor and nutritive value is in the skin. If bottom of stem looks dry and brown, trim away a thin slice and discard. Other than that, you should find a good use for every bit of the mushrooms you buy. Just before using, wipe with a damp cloth or rinse quickly and gently with cold water and drain. Then, slice, chop, mince or use whole.

Equivalents for fresh mushrooms:
1 pound: about 12 large, 18 to 20 medium, or 30 to 40 small mushrooms
1 pound whole: about 5 cups sliced, 6 cups chopped
1 pound sliced and cooked: about 1 $^3/_4$ cups
1 pound diced and cooked: about 2 cups

Mushrooms are domestically cultivated all year long. Washed mushrooms may be eaten raw; cap and stalk are edible, the caps considered to be a delicacy. Highest quality mushrooms are free from blemishes, firm, with short stems and unopened veil at the base of the cap. Mushrooms with spots or slight darkening or exposed gills may still be fresh and safe, but will not keep well. Mushrooms are a moderate source of riboflavin, fiber, and a fair amount of phosphorus, but a surprise nutrient is that 1 cup contains more potassium than $^1/_2$ cup of orange juice and half as much as a medium banana. The nutritive value is really an extra bonus, since mushrooms are probably eaten more for their innate flavor and taste appeal. They are low in sodium and recommended for special diets: only 90 calories per pound and 17 calories per 3 $^1/_2$-ounce serving.

SUNDAY
Beef roast
Milanese rice *
Buttered mixed vegetables
Tossed salad with lemon Blue cheese dressing *
Hard rolls
Lemon cake

MILANESE RICE

$^1/_2$ cup (1 stick) butter or margarine	Salt to taste
1 large onion, chopped	Pepper to taste
1 $^1/_2$ cups long grain rice, uncooked	$^1/_2$ cup mushrooms, fresh or canned
4 $^1/_4$cups chicken broth	1 cup grated Parmesan or shredded Swiss cheese
$^1/_3$ cup Chablis or other white dinner wine	

In a heavy skillet, melt the butter and saute the onion until soft but not brown. Add the rice and cook until it begins to brown, stirring constantly. Bring chicken broth to a boil and add to rice. Add the wine. Bring back to a rapid boil and stir in salt, pepper and mushrooms. Reduce heat and continue to cook, stirring frequently. When all liquid is absorbed, rice should be cooked. This takes about 25 minutes. Stir in the cheese; serve. (6 servings)

LEMON BLUE CHEESE DRESSING

2 ounces Blue cheese, crumbled	Black pepper
$^1/_4$ cup lemon juice	$^3/_4$cup salad oil or olive oil

Mash Blue cheese with fork. Add remaining ingredients and mix well. Serve over tossed green salad. (little over 1 cup)

MONDAY
Meat loaf
Oven roasted potatoes
Seasoned turnip greens
Creamy apple slaw *
Double orange bread *
Fresh strawberries topped with sour cream and brown sugar

CREAMY APPLE SLAW

1 tablespoon white vinegar
2 teaspoons lemon juice
1 teaspoon sugar
1/4 teaspoon prepared mustard
1/8 teaspoon salt

3/4 cup sour cream
3 cups shredded cabbage
2 cups unpeeled, cubed apples (dipped in lemon juice)
1/4 cup grated carrots
3 tablespoons finely-chopped celery

To make dressing: Combine and mix well, vinegar, lemon juice, sugar, mustard and salt. Stir in sour cream, cover and chill. When ready to serve, combine cabbage, apples, carrots and celery. Add dressing and toss to combine. (Yield: 5 cups, 4 servings)

DOUBLE ORANGE BREAD

2 1/2 cups all-purpose flour
3/4 cup sugar
1/2 cup wheat germ
1 tablespoon baking powder
1 teaspoon salt
1/2 teaspoon soda

1 cup orange juice
1/3 cup oil
1 egg, slightly beaten
1/2 cup chopped pecans
2 tablespoons grated orange rind

Combine flour, sugar, wheat germ, baking powder, salt and soda. Stir well to blend. Add remaining ingredients. Stir just to moisten dry ingredients. Pour into a well-greased 9x5x3-inch loaf pan. Bake at 350° for 50-55 minutes or until a wooden pick inserted in the center comes out clean. Remove from pan immediately. Cool. Wrap in a foil or plastic wrap and refrigerate for several hours or overnight for easier slicing. 1 loaf.

TUESDAY
Quick Supper Before the Theater
Chicken and Dumplings (in haste) *
Mashed potatoes (optional)
Peas and carrots in lemon butter *
Green salad with creamy herb dressing *
Strawberry Bavarian parfait *

Plan Of Work

Day before:
Cook chicken and remove meat from bones. Have 2 cups measured and ready to complete the Chicken and Dumplings the next day.

1 ½ hour before serving time:
1. Prepare peas and carrots
2. Assemble the salad
3. Complete the Chicken and Dumplings
4. Prepare Bavarian Parfait before being seated

CHICKEN AND DUMPLINGS (IN HASTE)

¼ cup flour
¼ teaspoon salt
Dash pepper
⅛ teaspoon poultry seasoning
¼ cup water

2 cups chicken stock
2 cups cooked, cubed chicken
½ cup water
1 ½ cups biscuit mix

Combine flour, salt, pepper, and poultry seasoning with ¼ cup water until smooth. Stir into chicken stock. Cook, stirring constantly, until thickened, about 2 minutes. Add chicken. Cover and simmer while making dumplings. Add ½ cup water to biscuit mix; stir 18 times. Drop by a tablespoon onto hot chicken mixture to make 12 dumplings. Cover pan tightly and simmer 15 minutes. Do not lift lid during cooking. (4 servings)

PEAS AND CARROTS IN LEMON BUTTER

4-6 carrots, scraped, cut into ½-inch slices
½ cup water
1 (10 ounce) package frozen peas
1 tablespoon butter, margarine

1 tablespoon lemon juice
Salt to taste
¼ teaspoon pepper (optional)

Add carrots to water in a quart-size sauce pan with a well-fitted lid. Cover, place on high heat. Cook until steam is expelled around the rim of the lid. Turn heat to lowest point. Do not raise lid. Cook for about five minutes. When carrots are tender, add peas. Heat until peas are thawed and hot. Drain. Add butter and lemon juice for seasoning. Correct seasoning before serving. (4-6 servings)

CREAMY HERB DRESSING

¼ cup milk
¼ cup sour cream
1 ½ teaspoons lemon juice
½ teaspoon dried parsley flakes

¼ teaspoon dried oregano
¼ teaspoon dried basil
⅛ teaspoon salt
¼ teaspoon pepper

Combine all ingredients. Mix well. Chill 1 hour before serving. Yield: ½ cup. Double if more dressing is desired.

STRAWBERRY BAVARIAN PARFAIT

*1 (16 ounce) package frozen strawberries,
defrosted and drained (save juice)*
¼ cup cold milk
2 envelopes unflavored gelatin
*½ cup juice drained from defrosted berries,
heated to boiling*

¼ cup sugar
2 egg yolks
Red food coloring (optional)
1 cup heavy cream
1 cup crushed ice, drained

Pour cold milk into blender container, add gelatin and hot juice. Cover and process at STIR for about 1 minute. When gelatin is dissolved, push LIQUEFY button and remove cover; add sugar, strawberries, egg yolks and food coloring if desired, and continue processing until strawberries are liquefied. Add cream and crushed ice and continue processing until ice is liquefied. Pour at once into serving dishes. Let set 5 to 10 minutes before serving. (6-8 servings)

WEDNESDAY
Clam chowder *
Ham and tomato sandwiches on rye
Fresh vegetable salad with Italian dressing
Peach cobbler *

CLAM CHOWDER
(Quick but Elegant)

1 large onion, chopped
1 tablespoon butter or margarine
*1 (6 ½-ounce) can minced or chopped clams,
undrained*
1 (10 ³/₄-ounce) can cream of potato soup

1 small (5 ⅓-ounce) can of evaporated milk
1 small (5 ⅓-ounce) can filled with whole milk
Salt to taste
Pepper to taste

Saute onions in butter over medium heat; do not brown. Add clams, soup, evaporated milk and whole milk. Stir and heat. Season to taste. Serve hot. (4 servings)

PEACH COBBLER

1 cup flour
1 cup sugar
1 cup milk

1 (1 pound) can sliced peaches
½ cup (1 stick) butter or margarine
Dash of cinnamon

Combine flour, sugar and milk; beat until smooth and consistency of pancake batter. Pour into greased square baking dish. In a sauce pan, bring undrained peaches to a boil. Pour over batter; do not stir. Slice butter over fruit; sprinkle with cinnamon. Bake at 350° for 30 minutes, or until crust rises to the top and browns. If fresh or frozen peaches are used in place of the canned peaches, add ¼ cup water and an additional 1 cup sugar and bring to a boil. (4-6 servings)

THURSDAY
Braised pork chops
Orzo and parsley gratin *
Asparagus spears with vinaigrette sauce *
Bagels with calorie-reduced cream cheese
Chilled fruit medley

ORZO AND PARSLEY GRATIN

2 teaspoons salt
1 pound orzo
6 garlic cloves, unpeeled
1 cup heavy cream
1 cup chicken broth (or canned broth)

1 cup grated Parmesan cheese (divided)
1 1/4 cup minced fresh parsley leaves (divided)
1/4 cup dry bread crumbs
3 tablespoons cold butter or margarine

In a 4-quart sauce pan, place about 3 quarts of water with two teaspoons salt. Bring to a boil. Stir in orzo and garlic cloves. Boil for about 10 minutes or until orzo is al dente. Drain in colander. Rinse orzo under running cold water and drain thoroughly. Remove garlic cloves and peel them. Place garlic in a large bowl and mash. Whisk the garlic with the cream. Add broth, 3/4 cup Parmesan cheese, 1 cup of parsley, and salt and pepper to taste. Mix well. Pour mixture into a buttered 2-quart baking dish. Smooth top. In small bowl combine bread crumbs, remaining cheese and parsley. Sprinkle the mixture over the orzo, and dot with butter cut into small pieces. Bake in a 325° oven for 1 hour and 15 minutes or until it is bubbly and golden on top. Refrigerate leftovers. (10 servings)

ASPARAGUS SPEARS WITH VINAIGRETTE SAUCE

1/4 cup salad oil
1/4 cup vinegar
2 tablespoons chopped parsley
2 tablespoons chopped pimiento
2 tablespoons sweet pickle relish

1/2 teaspoon salt
1/2 teaspoon sugar
2 hard-cooked eggs, chopped
2 (15 ounce) cans asparagus spears

To make vinaigrette sauce, combine all ingredients except the asparagus, and chill. Heat asparagus; drain. Serve vinaigrette sauce over asparagus. (6 servings)

FRIDAY
Broiled fish fillet in lemon butter
Parsley buttered new potatoes
Spinach with egg topping
Peas and cheese cubes with creamy Italian dressing *
Cheese puffs *
Lemon sherbet

CREAMY ITALIAN DRESSING

2 tablespoons tarragon vinegar
1 cup mayonnaise
1/2 small onion, finely-chopped (or 1 tablespoon
   instant minced onion)
1 tablespoon sugar

³/4 teaspoon Italian herbs
1/4 teaspoon salt
1/4 teaspoon garlic powder
Dash pepper (more if desired)

Put into blender container vinegar, mayonnaise, onion, sugar, Italian herbs, salt, garlic powder, and pepper. Cover and process at BLEND. Chill until ready to serve. (1 1/4 cups)
Note: If instant onion is used, mix by hand instead of blender.

CHEESE PUFFS

1 cup water
1/2 cup (1 stick) minus 1 tablespoon
   butter or margarine
³/4 teaspoon salt

Pinch nutmeg
1 cup all-purpose flour
4 eggs, room temperature
2 1/4 cups (9 ounces) shredded Gruyere cheese

Combine water, butter, salt and nutmeg in a large sauce pan. Bring to boil. Remove from heat. Immediately stir in flour. Place over low heat and beat vigorously until dough forms a ball. Remove from heat. Cool 3 or 4 minutes. Beat in eggs one at a time; beat until completely absorbed before adding another. Mixture should be glossy, smooth and firm. Blend in cheese. Drop by heaping teaspoons onto a greased cookie sheet. Space evenly. Bake in 425° oven for 25 to 30 minutes or until puffed and brown. Cool. Slit side of each puff. Serve warm or at room temperature. May be frozen. Can be used as hors d'oeuvre or bread. (2-3 dozen puffs)

SATURDAY
Noon Meal for Children
Tuna and chip salad *
Grilled cheese sandwiches
Raw carrot and pepper sticks with Ranch dressing
Apple pie with ice milk

TUNA AND CHIP SALAD

1 (6 1/2 ounce) can chunk tuna (water packed), drained
1 cup cooked rice
1/4 cup finely-chopped onion
1 tablespoon vegetable oil
1/4 teaspoon pepper
1 teaspoon vinegar

1 teaspoon salt
1/2 teaspoon Tabasco sauce
2 tomatoes, finely diced
1 small head lettuce, finely shredded
2 cups corn chips, coarsely crushed (optional)

Break tuna into bite-sized pieces. Stir in rice, onion, oil, vinegar, salt, Tabasco, tomatoes and lettuce. Chill. At serving time add corn chips and toss lightly. (6 servings)

August

August - First Week

Fruits with their wide variety of colors, texture, shapes, flavors and aromas make an enjoyable contribution to the daily diet. The food guide recommends one serving of a good source of vitamin A at least every other day, and one serving or two servings of vitamin C every day. These servings can be either a vegetable or a fruit. For example, vitamin A can be supplied by ½ cup of spinach or ½ of a medium sized cantaloupe. You may get your allowance of vitamin C from ½ cup of broccoli or one medium orange. For one counting calories, you would choose cantaloupe, not avocado, for Vitamin A, or grapefruit over blueberries for vitamin C. If choosing canned fruit, choose one canned with no sugar added or in light syrup rather than one canned in heavy syrup.

Other examples of fruits high in vitamin A are apricots, papaya, peaches, prunes and watermelon. A few examples of fruits high in vitamin C are blueberries, grapefruit, lemons, limes, oranges, pineapple, strawberries and tangerines. Cantaloupe and watermelon are good sources of both vitamin A and C. Remember, three to five servings a day of fruits and vegetables are great for a healthy diet, but more is even better.

Following are a few suggestions to follow when shopping for fruit:
1. Don't buy just because the price is low. Some bargains may be undesirable.
2. Buy only what you need because fresh fruits are perishable.
3. Shop carefully and don't buy damaged or deteriorated fruits. The waste in preparation may offset the price reduction.
4. Don't buy on size only. Large fruits are not always the best quality nor are they always economical.
5. Appearance is not everything. A fruit with a poor color and a superficial blemish may have excellent eating quality.
6. Buy in season. Quality is usually higher and price more economical.
7. Shop for fruits in greatest supply. Usually they are good choices and reasonably priced.
8, Don't pinch fruit when selecting. Rough handling causes spoilage and waste. Also, the grocer's loss is passed on to the customer.
9. Buy fruits that are mature, ripe, well colored and free of bruises, skin punctures and decay.
10. Remember, at the produce counter you are your own best judge of quality.

Most fruits should be stored clean and dry in the refrigerator. If necessary, most of them can be stored at room temperature if not above 70°.

Here are some general statements concerning nutrition from fruits and vegetables.
1. Half of the vitamin A in the food supply (51%) is from fruits and vegetables.
2. Fruits and vegetables supply 94% of the vitamin C in this country.
3. Unless fruits and vegetables are consumed, it is almost impossible to get enough vitamin C from food.
4. Vitamin C is not stored in the body to any large extent. Therefore, it is desirable to consume fruits and vegetables daily to get the vitamin.
5. 20% of the iron in the food supply comes from fruits and vegetables.
6. 43% of the folic acid and other B vitamins come from fruits and vegetables.
7. Fruits and vegetables are relatively low in calories.
8. Fruits and vegetables are an important source of fiber in the diet.
9. A major part of the vitamin K comes from fruit and vegetables.
10. Excess water and heat will destroy much of the water soluble vitamins, vitamins B and C particularly. Use water sparingly in preparation of fruits and vegetables.

SUNDAY
Braised pork steaks
Sweet potatoes
Parmesan mushroom bake *
Waldorf salad
English muffins with butter and preserves
Old-fashioned grasshopper pie *

PARMESAN MUSHROOM BAKE

2 pounds mushrooms
1/4 cup (1/2 stick) butter or margarine
1 cup Italian style bread crumbs
1/3 cup Parmesan cheese

1 teaspoon garlic salt
1/4 teaspoon black pepper
2 tablespoons dried parsley flakes

Wash and dry mushrooms. Remove stems to be used for other dishes. Toss mushroom caps with 2 tablespoons melted butter. Place in 1 1/2 quart baking dish. Combine crumbs, cheese, salt, pepper and parsley flakes. Sprinkle over mushrooms. Dribble remaining melted butter over cheese mixture. Bake in 350° oven for 25 minutes. 4-6 servings.

OLD-FASHIONED GRASSHOPPPER PIE

32 large marshmallows or 3 cups of miniatures
1/2 cup milk
1/4 cup creme de menthe
3 tablespoons white creme de cocao
1 cup heavy cream

Green food coloring
1 (9 inch) baked chocolate cookie
(or commercial) crust *
Shaved chocolate or maraschino cherries

Heat marshmallows and milk over moderate heat, stirring constantly, until melted. Chill until thickened; blend in liqueurs. Whip cream until stiff. Remove 1/2 cup and set aside for garnish. Fold marshmallow mixture into remaining whipped cream. Fold in a few drops of green food coloring. Pour into pie crust. Chill at least 3 hours. Garnish with whipped cream and shaved chocolate or chopped maraschino cherries. 1 pie.

Chocolate Cookie Crust

1/2 cup butter or margarine, melted
1 1/2 cup chocolate cookie crumbs

Combine melted butter and crumbs. Press mixture firmly and evenly into bottom of a 9-inch pie plate. Bake at 350° for 10 minutes.

MONDAY
Quick pasta cheese casserole *
Buttered spinach
Green salad with honey mustard dressing
Garlic toast
Rice pudding with Bourbon or orange sauce

QUICK PASTA CHEESE CASSEROLE

1 (12 ounce) package elbow macaroni
1 large onion, chopped
2 teaspoons butter, margarine or bacon fat
$^1/_2$ cup milk
1 (10 $^1/_2$-ounce) can of cream of chicken soup
1 (10 $^1/_2$-ounce) can of cream of tomato soup

1 teaspoon leaf oregano
$^1/_2$ teaspoon sweet basil
2 teaspoons garlic salt
6 thin slices American cheese
2 tomatoes, sliced thin
$^1/_2$ cup dry bread crumbs, buttered, or
    crushed wheat germ

Cook macaroni according to package directions; drain. Brown onions in butter; add both soups, oregano, basil, garlic salt and heat. Mix with macaroni. Pour into 2 greased (1 ½ quart) casseroles. Arrange 6 cheese slices on top of one casserole. Put a row of overlapping tomato slices down the center. Cover with crumbs or wheat germ. Bake at 350° for 25 minutes. 4-6 servings. Cover and freeze second casserole to be used when desired. Before serving, thaw, cover with 6 additional cheese slices, tomatoes and crumbs and bake.

RICE PUDDING WITH BOURBON OR ORANGE SAUCE

1 (3 ½-ounce) package vanilla flavored
  pudding and pie filling mix
2 ½ cups milk

1 cup cooked rice
½ cup raisins
Bourbon or orange sauce

Combine pudding mix, milk, rice and raisins in a saucepan. Cook, stirring, until thick. Pour into individual serving dishes. Just before serving, spoon sauce over rice pudding. 4 servings.

Bourbon or Orange Sauce

¼ cup (½ stick) butter or margarine
½ cup sugar

1 egg yolk, beaten
¼ cup Bourbon or orange juice

Melt butter; stir in sugar. Stir until sugar dissolves. Whip in egg yolk gradually; cool to room temperature, and add Bourbon or orange juice. Yield: approximately 1 cup.

TUESDAY
Oriental beef with vegetables *
Buttered rice
Fresh fruit salad with citrus dressing *
Bread sticks
Brownies

ORIENTAL BEEF WITH VEGETABLES

1 pound round steak
½ teaspoon cornstarch
1 tablespoon soy sauce
2 tablespoons cooking oil
1 large onion, sliced
1 green pepper, cut in thin strips

3-4 tomatoes cut in wedges
2 teaspoons cornstarch
1 tablespoon vinegar
⅓ cup water
1 tablespoon soy sauce.

Cut steak into thin strips, ½ inch by 2 inches. Combine ½ teaspoon cornstarch with 1 tablespoon soy sauce. Mix with beef. Saute beef with hot oil until barely cooked. Remove steak from skillet. Brown onions and peppers, add tomatoes and cook for about 2 minutes. Add meat. Combine remaining ingredients. Add to meat mixture. Cook over medium heat until sauce is thick and clear, stirring constantly. Serve over rice or Chinese noodles. 4-6 servings.

CITRUS DRESSING FOR FRUIT SALAD

½ cup orange juice   *2 eggs, beaten*
½ cup lemon juice   *1 cup sugar*

Combine all ingredients in a 1-quart saucepan. Bring to a boil, stirring constantly. Simmer three minutes. Chill and serve on fruit salad or as a dip for fruit tray.

WEDNESDAY
Baked fish fillet with savory sauce *
Baked tomatoes
Sauteed green peppers
Cole slaw
Biscuits
Orange refrigerator torte

BAKED FISH WITH SAVORY SAUCE

1 pound fish fillets   *½ teaspoon powdered mustard*
Salt to taste   *2 teaspoons water*
1 tablespoon chopped onion   *1 teaspoon fresh lemon juice*
¼ teaspoon tarragon leaves   *½ cup mayonnaise*
⅛ teaspoon ground black pepper   *Paprika*

Wipe fish with damp cloth and place in a baking dish. Sprinkle with salt. Combine onion, tarragon, black pepper, mustard and water, let stand 10 minutes for flavors to blend. Add lemon juice and mayonnaise. Spread on fish. Bake in preheated very hot oven (425°) for 25-30 minutes or until brown. Garnish with paprika. 4 servings. Note: This sauce is also excellent served on cooked broccoli.

ORANGE REFRIGERATOR TORTE

This four-layer refrigerator cake is almost delicate enough to be classed as a pudding — each bite melts in your mouth. Be sure the sauce is hot when you fill the cake so the layers will soak it up.

2 (8 inch) sponge cake layers, or 1 orange   *1 cup orange juice*
   chiffon tube cake   *5 tablespoons lemon juice*
3 eggs separated   *1½ cups whipping cream*
½ cup sugar   *Sugar*
2 tablespoons cornstarch   *Preserved orange slices or fresh orange*
Dash of salt   *sections for garnish*

Slice each cake layer in half horizontally, making four layers in all. Beat egg whites until stiff, but not dry. In the top part of a double boiler, add the sugar, cornstarch and salt; stir in orange juice, lemon juice and slightly beaten egg yolks. Cook over hot water, stirring constantly, until thickened; remove from heat. Fold beaten egg whites into the orange sauce *while it is still hot*. Spread filling between the cake layers, use a spatula to spread excess filling onto sides of cake until all has been absorbed into the cake. Refrigerate overnight. Several hours before serving time, whip cream and sweeten to taste. Frost top and sides of cake. Refrigerate until time to serve, then garnish top of cake with preserved orange slices or orange segments. 8-10 servings.

THURSDAY
A Friendship Day Gathering (Supper)
Wine of choice
Artichoke and onion spread
Crackers, carrots and celery sticks
Crispy oven fried chicken
Russian style potatoes
Dilly creamed peas and carrots
Orange and grapefruit salad with celery seed dressing (see index)
Light corn bread loaf
Pineapple sherbet (commercial)
Mint chocolate chip cookies

Plan Of Work

Day before
1. Prepare mint chocolate chip cookies.
1 ½ hours before serving
2. Section grapefruit and orange and prepare salad dressing.
3. Prepare artichoke spread. Bake, refrigerate, and reheat before serving.
4. Prepare chicken and place in oven.
5. Prepare potatoes and place in oven with chicken.
6. Scrape and cut carrots, thaw frozen peas and chop onions for the carrots and peas dish.
7. Prepare corn bread. Place in oven during the last 30 minutes of baking the chicken. As soon as the chicken comes out, turn oven down to 350°. Put in artichoke spread to heat.
8. Cook carrots and peas as cornbread is cooking.

ARTICHOKE AND ONION SPREAD

1 (14 ounce) can artichoke hearts, drained and finely chopped	*³/₄ teaspoon garlic salt*
	1 teaspoon hot sauce
½ medium onion, finely chopped	*Parmesan cheese*
1 cup mayonnaise	*Curry powder*
1 cup grated Parmesan cheese	

Combine artichoke hearts, onion, mayonnaise, 1 cup Parmesan cheese, garlic salt and hot sauce in a 1-quart baking dish. Sprinkle top with Parmesan cheese and top with curry powder. Bake in 350° oven for 60 minutes. Serve warm with crackers. Yield: about 3 cups. Will serve 25 for hors d'oeuvres. Recipe may be doubled.

CRISPY OVEN FRIED CHICKEN

1 broiler-fryer (2 ½ to 3 pounds) cut into serving pieces	*1 teaspoon marjoram, crushed*
½ teaspoon salt	*2 teaspoons grated lemon peel*
1 teaspoon onion salt	*½ cup fresh lemon juice*
½ teaspoon thyme, crushed	*½ cup water*

Sprinkle chicken pieces with salt, rubbing well into flesh. Place chicken in shallow baking pan, skin side down. Combine seasonings, lemon peel, juice and water; pour over chicken. Bake, uncovered, at 400° for about 40 minutes. Turn chicken and continue baking, basting with pan drippings once or twice, until chicken is done and skin is crispy, about 35 minutes.

RUSSIAN STYLE POTATOES

4 medium potatoes	*Pepper to taste*
1 small onion finely-chopped	*2 tablespoons butter or margarine*
Salt to taste	*3 tablespoons sour cream*

Peel potatoes and cut into cubes. Place potatoes and onions in a saucepan. Cover with water and simmer until tender. Drain. Combine butter and sour cream. Add to potatoes. Add salt and pepper. Stir to coat potato with the sauce. Let stand a few minutes before serving. 4 servings.

DILLY CREAMED PEAS AND CARROTS

¾ cup water	*1 (10 ounce) package frozen peas, thawed, drained*
2 medium carrots, scraped and sliced	*2 green onions, sliced, use tops*
⅓ cup butter or margarine	*½ teaspoon salt*
1 tablespoon cornstarch	*⅛ teaspoon pepper*
1 cup half & half or milk	*½ teaspoon dried dill weed*

In 2-quart saucepan, bring water to a boil. Add carrots. Cover; cook over medium heat until carrots are crisply tender (8-10 minutes). Drain; set aside. In same saucepan, melt butter. Stir in cornstarch until smooth. Stir in carrots, half-and-half, peas, green onions, salt, pepper and dill weed. Cook over medium heat stirring constantly, until mixture comes to a boil and is thickened (5-7 minutes). Boil, stirring constantly, 1 minute. 4-6 servings.

LIGHT CORN BREAD LOAF

½ teaspoon soda	*2 cups self-rising cornmeal*
2 cups buttermilk	*¾ cup sugar*
1 cup self-rising flour	

Add soda to buttermilk. Combine flour, cornmeal and sugar; add to buttermilk mixture. Pour into two well-greased loaf pans. Bake in 350° oven for 30-40 minutes.

MINT CHOCOLATE CHIP COOKIES

⅓ cup dark brown sugar, packed
⅓ cup sugar
⅔ cup butter or margarine
1 egg, slightly beaten
1 teaspoon vanilla

1 ¼ cups flour
½ teaspoon salt
½ teaspoon baking soda
½ cup chopped nuts, pecans or walnuts
1 (6 ounce) package mint chocolate chips

Cream together sugars and butter. Add egg and vanilla to the creamed mixture. Sift flour, salt and baking soda together. Add to the creamed mixture. Add nuts and chocolate chips. Drop a heaping teaspoonful of batter on an ungreased cookie sheet about 2 inches apart. About 4 dozen cookies.

FRIDAY
Broccoli and mushroom quiche *
Glazed carrots
Red apples and raisin salad
Hot buttered French bread
Marble ice cream pie * or Quick chocolate sauce over vanilla ice cream

BROCCOLI AND MUSHROOM QUICHE

1 (10 ounce) frozen chopped broccoli
1 (4 ounce) can mushrooms, drained
1 (9 inch) pie crust, unbaked
1 cup Swiss or Cheddar cheese, shredded

3 eggs, beaten
1 cup heavy cream or evaporated milk
¼ teaspoon salt
1 tablespoon butter or margarine

Cook broccoli according to package directions, drain. Place in bottom of pie crust, add mushrooms, cover with cheese. Combine eggs, cream and salt, carefully pour over vegetables; dot with butter. Place pan on cookie sheet. Bake at 350° for 40 minutes or until quiche puffs up and browns slightly. Cool 30 minutes at room temperature before serving. 4-6 servings.

MARBLE ICE CREAM PIE

1 baked (9 inch) pie shell, pastry or crumb crust
1 quart vanilla ice cream

½ cup chocolate sauce
⅓ cup heavy cream, whipped

Soften ice cream until it can be scooped into baked pie shell. Pour chocolate in an irregular design over the ice cream. Decorate edge with whipped cream. Put into freezer and freeze until firm and ready to use.

Quick Chocolate Sauce

2 cups sugar
¼ cup cocoa
¼ cup butter or margarine

1 large can evaporated milk
2 teaspoons vanilla

Mix sugar and cocoa and stir over low heat for 2 minutes. Add butter and evaporated milk. Turn up heat, and bring to a boil. Boil for 1 minute. Remove from heat and add vanilla. Can use over plain ice cream, also. Keeps several weeks in refrigerator. 3 cups.

SATURDAY
Lunch
Cheese strata *
Raw green peppers and celery sticks
Potato salad
Hot dog buns
Lemon and Sherry surprise *

CHEESE STRATA (Baked cheese sandwich)

12 slices bread, crust removed   *3¹/₂ cups milk*
Butter   *¹/₂ teaspoon salt*
¹/₂ pound sliced sharp American cheese   *¹/₄ teaspoon pepper*
4 eggs, beaten

Butter bread slices on both sides. In a long 2-quart buttered baking casserole, layer 6 slices bread; top with cheese slices and with 6 slices bread. Combine eggs, milk, salt and pepper; pour over sandwiches. Refrigerate 6 hours or overnight. Bake 50-60 minutes in a 325° oven or until a knife inserted in the center comes out clean. 6 servings.

LEMON AND SHERRY SURPRISE

1 (3 ounce) package lemon flavored gelatin   *1 cup Sherry*
1 ¹/₂ cups boiling water   *Whipped cream or topping*

Dissolve gelatin in boiling water. Cool. Add Sherry. Pour into individual parfait glasses. Refrigerate until set. Garnish with whipped cream or whipped topping and lemon slices. 4-6 servings.

August - Second Week

To get the best flavor from store-bought tomatoes, a lot depends on how you handle them once you get them home. First and foremost, they should never be refrigerated. Refrigeration kills flavor in tomatoes. Secondly, they'll probably need some kitchen ripening. This is natural. They're sent to the market mature, but under ripe, because if they were fully ripe they would mush upon arrival. Consequently, most of the tomatoes in the stores range from pale pink to rosy red in color, and are too firm for full appreciation. As with bananas, pears, melons and avocados, a little tender loving care will make all the difference.

To ripen store-bought tomatoes, simply place them stem-side-up on your kitchen counter or in a fruit bowl (remember that tomatoes are listed botanically as a fruit). Leave them at room temperature until they reach a bright tomato-red color and yield gently to the touch. To hasten the ripening process they may be kept in a special fruit ripening bowl which is available in department stores and supermarkets. The covered bowl traps the ethylene gas which the tomatoes (and all fruit) give off during the ripening process. The more concentrated the gas becomes, the faster the ripening. The bowl is properly ventilated to prevent the build-up of carbon dioxide. The ripening bowl also helps keep the fruit from drying out. Another way of ripening tomatoes is to place them for a few days in a paper bag with several air holes punched in it; the principle is the same as with the ripening bowl. And if you place a lime in with the tomatoes, it will speed the ripening even more, because limes give off more ethylene gas than any other fruit.

Tomatoes are a great nutrition-boost to the diet. There are only about 30 calories in a medium tomato. And they are high in vitamin C, and contain vitamin A, plus other vitamins and minerals, They've become our third most popular vegetable and are used in all sorts of dishes, from soups to salads to sauces and countless others.

SUNDAY
Sunday Night Company Dinner
Glazed pork and beef balls
Sweet potatoes 'n peaches
Garlic butter spaghetti squash
Green salad with tomato French dressing
Toasted English muffin halves
Cocoa Bundt cake (no egg yolks, no fat)

Plan Of Work

Day before
1. Prepare glaze for pork and beef balls. Reheat before serving.
2. Prepare pork and beef balls, refrigerate and cook 45 minutes before serving.
3. Prepare cocoa Bundt cake, Keep well covered to keep moist.

Early in the day
4. Prepare tomato French dressing.
5. Prepare spaghetti squash and reheat before serving.
6. Prepare salad greens and refrigerate.

45 minutes before serving
7. Prepare sweet potatoes and bake.
8. Bake pork and beef balls.

GLAZED PORK AND BEEF BALLS

1 egg, beaten	*1 tablespoon Worcestershire sauce*
¹/₂ teaspoon salt	*1 tablespoon instant minced onion*
¹/₈ teaspoon pepper	*¹/₂ cup corn flake crumbs*
1 teaspoon dry mustard	*³/₄ pound ground ham or bulk pork sausage*
³/₄ cup milk	*³/₄ pound ground beef*

Combine all ingredients. Shape into 12 balls. Place in shallow baking pan. Spoon honey orange or pineapple glaze over balls. Bake at 350° for 40 minutes. To serve, place balls on warm plate, spoon hot glazed mixture of your choice on each serving. 6-8 servings.

Honey Orange Glaze

1 cup firmly-packed brown sugar	*¹/₂ cup orange juice*
¹/₂ cup liquid honey	

Combine ingredients and spoon over pork and beef balls.

Pineapple Glaze

1 (8 ¼ ounce) can crushed pineapple, drained,
  reserving 2 tablespoons pineapple syrup
1 cup firmly-packed brown sugar

2 tablespoons lemon juice
2 tablespoons prepared mustard

Place pineapple and reserved juice in small bowl. Add remaining ingredients; stir. Spoon over pork and beef balls.

SWEET POTATOES 'N PEACHES

2 (1-pound 3-ounce) cans yams or sweet
  potato halves, drained
1 (1 pound) can sliced peaches, drained, reserving
  ³/₄ cup peach syrup

³/₄ cup brown sugar, packed
1 teaspoon mace
¼ cup (½ stick) butter or margarine, melted

Layer sweet potatoes and peach slices in a buttered 13x9x2-inch baking dish. Combine reserved peach syrup, brown sugar, mace and butter. Pour over sweet potatoes and peaches. Bake in 325° oven for 30 minutes. 6-8 servings.

GARLIC BUTTERED SPAGHETTI SQUASH

1 medium-sized spaghetti squash
¹/₃ cup butter or margarine

2 cloves garlic, crushed
Parmesan cheese - optional

Cut squash in half, lengthwise, and clean out the seeds. Place squash, cut side down, in a saucepan. Add 2 inches of water; bring to a boil and cook, covered, for 25-30 minutes or until the squash is tender. Drain squash and cool. Using a fork, remove spaghetti like strands from inside the squash. Melt butter, add garlic and cook slowly over low heat about 1 minute. Do not allow garlic to burn. Stir garlic butter into the squash strands. Serve hot, topped with Parmesan cheese, if desired. 6 servings.

TOMATO FRENCH DRESSING

1 (10 ³/₄-ounce) can condensed tomato soup
¹/₃ cup salad oil

¼ cup vinegar
½ teaspoon dry mustard

Combine ingredients in a jar; shake well before using. (Or mix in an electric blender.) Serve with salad greens. Makes about 1½ cups.
Variations: To 1 recipe of tomato French dressing add any one of the following: 4 slices bacon, cooked and crumbled; ¼ cup crumbled blue cheese; 1 medium clove garlic, minced; ¼ cup sweet pickle relish.

COCOA BUNDT CAKE
(No Fat, No Cholesterol)

Butter-flavor no-stick cooking spray
1 ¹/₃ cups unsifted cake flour (or all-purpose flour)
2 tablespoons corn starch
2 teaspoons baking powder
½ teaspoon baking soda
¼ teaspoon salt
¹/₈ teaspoon cinnamon

½ cup plus 2 tablespoons unsweetened cocoa
½ cup plus 2 tablespoons granulated sugar, divided
½ cup dark or light corn syrup
½ cup plus 2 tablespoons warm water
2 teaspoons vanilla extract
4 large egg whites
Pinch of cream of tartar

Position a rack in the center of the oven and preheat it to 350°. Coat the Bundt pan with cooking spray. Dust the pan with 2 tablespoons sifted cocoa, and tap out excess cocoa. Sift the flour, corn starch, baking powder, baking soda, salt, cinnamon and ½ cup cocoa into a large bowl. Make a well in the center of the dry ingredients and add ½ cup of sugar, corn syrup, water and vanilla, but do not blend together at this time. Set aside. In another large bowl, with an electric mixer, whip the egg whites with the cream of tartar until foamy. Add the remaining 2 tablespoons of sugar and whip the whites until stiff but not dry. Remove the bowl of whites from the stand. With the mixer on low speed (it's not necessary to wash the beaters), beat the cocoa and corn syrup mixture until well blended. Stir about 1 cup of the egg whites into the chocolate batter to lighten it. then gently fold in the remaining whites, Turn the batter into the prepared Bundt pan. Bake for about 45 minutes, or until the top is springy to the touch and a wooden pick inserted in the center comes out clean. Cool the cake in the pan on a rack for about 5 minutes, then top with another rack or plate and invert. Lift off the pan. Cool. Frost if desired.

No Fat Frosting

1 cup confectioners sugar	1 tablespoon hot coffee
2 tablespoons cocoa	

Sift together the sugar and cocoa. Add milk or coffee and mix. Spread frosting over the top of warm cake allowing it to run down the sides. Add more confectioners sugar for a stiffer frosting.

MONDAY
Baked chicken spaghetti *
Tomato aspic
Hot cheese biscuits
Melon and cantaloupe balls on lemon sherbet

BAKED CHICKEN SPAGHETTI

¼ pound spaghetti, cooked	⅓ cup milk
1 (16 ounce) can peas, drained	¼ cup sherry
1 ½ cups cooked, chopped chicken	1 ½ cups chicken broth
1 medium onion, chopped	3 slices white bread, in small pieces
1 (8 oz) can mushroom, stems and pieces, drained	1 (2 ounce) jar chopped pimiento
2 tablespoons butter or margarine	Salt and pepper to taste
1 teaspoon dried basil	¼ cup grated Parmesan cheese

Put spaghetti in greased 2-quart baking dish. Add peas and chicken. Saute onion, mushrooms and basil in butter. Add to spaghetti in baking dish. In saucepan, combine milk, wine, broth and bread. Cook over low heat until thickened, stirring constantly. Add pimiento. Season sauce with salt and pepper. Pour sauce over ingredients in baking dish. Mix well with a fork. Sprinkle with cheese. Bake at 350° for 30 minutes. 6 servings.

TUESDAY
Swiss seafood bake *
Hot rice / Buttered broccoli
Carrot slaw Bread sticks
Crunchy apple cobbler *

SWISS SEAFOOD BAKE

3 tablespoons butter or margarine
¼ cup chopped green onions (use tops)
3 tablespoons flour
⅛ teaspoon cayenne pepper
1 cup milk
1 ½ cups (6 ounces) shredded Swiss cheese

½ cup chopped Spanish green olives
1 (10 oz) package frozen scallops, thawed
1 pound shrimp, cooked, shelled and deveined
1 (8 oz) can mushroom stems & pieces, drained
Hot cooked rice

Melt butter. Add onions and saute 3 minutes. Blend in flour and cayenne pepper. Gradually add milk and cook over low heat, stirring constantly, until thickened. Add cheese and continue cooking, stirring occasionally, until cheese is melted. Add olives, scallops, shrimp and mushrooms. Mix well. Pour into greased 1½-quart baking dish. Bake at 325° for 35-45 minutes. Serve over rice. 6 servings.

CRUNCHY APPLE COBBLER

6 cups thinly-sliced apples, unpeeled
½ cup uncooked rolled oats
½ cup frozen apple juice concentrate,
  thawed but undiluted

1 teaspoon cinnamon
¼ teaspoon cloves
2 tablespoons raisins
⅓ cup crunchy cereal (such as Grape Nuts)

Layer the oats on the bottom of an 8-inch square non-stick pan or pan sprayed with non-stick vegetable spray. Add the apple slices. Combine the apple juice concentrate, cinnamon and cloves; pour over the apples and oats. Sprinkle the raisins on top. Cover with foil and bake in a 350° oven for 1 hour. Remove the foil. Cover the top of the apples with crunchy cereal and bake an additional 10 minutes. 6 servings.

WEDNESDAY
Meat loaf
Oven steamed potatoes, carrots and onions
Gazpacho ring *
Plain muffins with orange marmalade
Fresh fruit

GAZPACHO RING

2 envelopes unflavored gelatin
1 (12 ounce) can (1 ½ cups) vegetable juice
1 cup canned whole tomatoes, drained and
  chopped, juices reserved
¼ teaspoon garlic powder
1 teaspoon Worcestershire sauce
Dash hot sauce

2 green onions, finely-chopped
½ carrot, grated
1 stalk celery, finely-chopped (use tops)
½ green pepper, finely-chopped
½ small cucumber, peeled and finely-chopped
1 small avocado, diced (optional)
Salad greens

In a 2-quart saucepan, combine gelatin with 1 cup vegetable juice; let stand 1 minute. Stir over medium heat until dissolved, about 1-2 minutes. Measure remaining vegetable juice and add reserved tomato liquid from whole tomatoes to equal 2 ½ cups; combine with gelatin mixture. Stir in reserved tomatoes, lemon juice, garlic powder, Worcestershire sauce and hot sauce. Chill until the mixture is the consistency of egg whites. Fold in onions, carrot, celery, green pepper, cucumber and avocado; turn into 6-cup ring mold. Chill until firm. To serve, unmold onto a serving plate; garnish with salad greens, if desired. 6 servings.

THURSDAY
Quick and easy tuna chow mien on crisp noodles *
Carrot, cheese sticks, pickle tray
Whole wheat bread
Cup custard with whipped topping

QUICK AND EASY TUNA CHOW MIEN ON CRISP NOODLES

1 tablespoon butter or margarine	Milk
1/4 cup chopped onion	Salt and pepper (optional)
1 (10 1/2-ounce) can cream of chicken soup	1 (5 ounce can) chow mien noodles
1 (8 1/2 ounce) buffet can of peas	2-3 green onions, chopped (use tops)
1 (6 1/2 or 7 ounce) can of tuna fish in water	2 tablespoons chopped pimiento
1 cup thinly-sliced celery	

In quart-sized saucepan, melt butter, add onion; stir and cook until tender, about 2 minutes. Add soup. Heat to boiling, stirring. Add peas (include liquid), tuna and celery. Heat gently just until bubbling hot (celery should still be crisp when served). If mixture appears too thick, add a small amount of milk and heat again. Adjust flavor. Serve over crisp canned chow mien noodles. Top each serving with green onions and pimiento. 4 servings.

FRIDAY
Parmesan veal chops *
Scalloped tomatoes
Corn saute
Fresh vegetable relish tray
Apple sauce bread *
Coffee ice cream with butterscotch sauce

PARMESAN VEAL CHOPS

4 veal chops	1/2 cup grated Parmesan cheese
Salt	2 tablespoons butter or margarine
Pepper	3/4 cup Sauterne or other white dinner wine
Flour	3 green onions, chopped
1 egg, slightly beaten	2 tblsp green onion tops, chopped (optional)

Score fat on edges of chops; sprinkle with salt and pepper and dredge with flour. Dip chops in egg, then in cheese; brown slightly in butter. Add wine and green onions; cover and simmer until meat is tender and wine is almost evaporated. Sprinkle with additional chopped green onion tops when served. 4 servings.

APPLE SAUCE BREAD

1/2 cup butter, margarine or shortening	1 teaspoon baking soda
3/4 cup sugar	1 teaspoon salt
2 eggs	1 teaspoon cinnamon
1 teaspoon vanilla	1/2 teaspoon nutmeg
2 cups sifted flour	1 cup applesauce
1 teaspoon baking powder	1/2 cup chopped walnuts or pecans

Cream butter until soft, add sugar gradually, continuing to cream together until fluffy. Add eggs and vanilla and beat well. Combine and sift together the next six ingredients; add to first mixture and mix thoroughly. Add applesauce and nuts and mix only until blended. Pour into loaf pan, and let stand 20 minutes before baking in a moderate oven (350°) for 1 hour. Cool before slicing.

SATURDAY
Vegetable dip with carrots, celery and crackers *
Minute steak in garlic butter
Creamed potatoes
Lettuce wedge with sour cream paprika dressing *
Sour dough rolls / Iced lemon cake

VEGETABLE DIP

1 (10 oz) package frozen chopped spinach, thawed
1 (8 ounce) can sliced water chestnuts, drained, chopped finely
1 bunch green onions (about 5) chopped finely (use tops)
1 cup mayonnaise

1 cup sour cream
1 (5 ⅛ oz) package dried vegetable soup
1 teaspoon lemon juice
½ teaspoon monosodium glutamate (optional)
Tabasco to taste

Squeeze water thoroughly from the spinach. Chop a little more. Add water chestnuts, onions, mayonnaise, sour cream, dried soup, lemon juice, MSG, and Tabasco. Mix well. Refrigerate 4 hours or overnight. Serve with carrot sticks, celery and crackers. If thick, serve with a spreader. Yield: approximately 1 quart.

SOUR CREAM PAPRIKA DRESSING

¼ cup cider vinegar
¾ teaspoon salt
⅛ teaspoon ground black pepper
1 teaspoon paprika
½ teaspoon instant minced onion

¼ teaspoon instant minced garlic
½ to ¾ cup salad or olive oil
1 cup sour cream
⅓ cup catsup

Combine vinegar, salt, pepper, paprika, onion and garlic. Gradually beat in oil with electric beater or blender. Gradually stir in sour cream and catsup. Beat until smooth. (Flavors blend better if allowed to stand in refrigerator 24 hours.) Serve over lettuce, or raw fresh vegetables. Yield: 2 ⅓ cups.

August - Third Week

It only takes a few mistakes to lose valuable vitamins, and Vitamin C is the most perishable of all. Overcooking foods and pouring the water down the drain is a real waste: overcooking destroys valuable nutrients and discarding the cooking water wastes water-soluble nutrients. Too much light will also destroy some B vitamins as well as C. At least half the vitamin C in orange juice is lost when it is reconstituted in a blender and left to set a few hours in a well-lighted place. Also, air is destructive to vitamin C, and air is beaten into the juice by the whirling blender blades. To avoid Vitamin C loss in orange juice, reconstitute quickly and store covered in the refrigerator. It is best to thaw frozen juice in its own container, then shake it with cold water in a covered container. Choose containers that match the volume of the juice, since extra-large containers mean more air is present.

SUNDAY
Beef continental *
Couscous with parsley *
Peas with onions
Orange and onion slices with French dressing
Apple pie with French pastry *

BEEF CONTINENTAL

2 pounds sirloin tip roast, cubed	1/3 cup cooking oil
1/2 cup flour	1 cup dry red wine
1/2 teaspoon salt	1 clove garlic, crushed
1/4 teaspoon pepper	1 large onion, sliced thin

Combine flour, salt and pepper. Place in plastic bag. Add beef cubes; toss until beef is well-coated. Place beef in 1 1/2-quart baking dish. Combine remaining ingredients, pour over meat. Cover, bake at 350° for two hours or until beef is tender. Can be refrigerated overnight and heat at 350° for 30 minutes before serving. 4-6 servings.

COUSCOUS WITH PARSLEY

2 tablespoons olive oil	Pepper to taste (freshly-ground preferred)
1 small onion, chopped	1 cup couscous
1 1/3 cups water	2 tablespoons lemon juice
1/4 teaspoon Tabasco sauce	1/4 cup chopped fresh parsley
Salt to taste	

Heat olive oil in saucepan; add onions and cook until tender, not brown. Add water, Tabasco sauce, salt and pepper and bring to a boil. Add couscous, stir and cover. Remove from heat and let stand for 5 minutes. Stir in lemon juice and parsley and serve. 4 servings.

APPLE PIE WITH FRENCH PASTRY

Pastry for 2-crust pie	1 teaspoon cinnamon
5 1/2 cups cooking apples	1/4 teaspoon nutmeg
3/4 cups sugar	1 tablespoon butter or margarine
2 tablespoons flour	

Line 9-inch pie plate with pastry. Pare, core and slice apples. Place in pastry-lined pie plate. Combine sugar, flour, cinnamon and nutmeg. Sprinkle over apples. Dot with butter. Wet edge of lower crust. Place top crust over apples and press edges together. Cut several slits in upper crust. Bake at 400° for 30-40 minutes, or until apples are tender and crust is golden brown. 1 pie.

French Pastry

2 cups flour	1 small egg, beaten
1/2 teaspoon salt	1/4 cup water
1/2 teaspoon baking powder	1 1/2 teaspoons vinegar
3/4 cup shortening	

Combine flour , salt, baking powder and shortening; blend until mixture takes on the texture of small peas. Combine and mix egg, water and vinegar; add to dry ingredients and toss until the dough forms a ball. Turn onto floured board. Divide into 2 pieces; roll half for lower crust and other half for upper crust. Pastry for one 2-crust pie.

MONDAY
New Orleans Monday Night Supper
(Clothes washing day, no time to cook)
Red beans and rice
Vegetable salad with creamy tart dressing
Hot buttered French bread (commercial)
Pound cake topped with ice cream and fruit

Plan Of Work
Day before:
1. Place beans in water to soak overnight
2. Prepare pound cake
Six hours before serving:
3. Prepare and cook beans
Last hour before serving:
4. Prepare bread. Put in oven about 20 minutes before serving.
5. Prepare rice and salad

RED BEANS AND RICE

1 pound dried kidney beans	*1 tablespoon salt*
1 ham hock	*1 teaspoon black pepper*
1 ³/₄ quarts water	*1 dash Tabasco sauce*
¹/₂ teaspoon cayenne pepper	*1 ¹/₄ teaspoon thyme leaves*
¹/₂ teaspoon sugar	*1 (4 ounce) can tomato sauce*
1 tablespoon plus ¹/₂ teaspoon oregano	*1 cup chopped parsley*
4-5 green onions, chopped (use tops)	*¹/₂ pound Polish sausage, sliced*
1 tablespoon Worcestershire sauce	*¹/₂ pound smoked sausage, sliced*
1 large or 2 small cloves garlic, crushed	*6 cups steamed rice*

Sort and wash beans. Place in a large Dutch oven and cover with water about 2 inches above beans. Allow to set overnight. Add water to equal 1 ³/₄ quarts water. Add ham hock and bring to a boil; reduce heat, cover and simmer for 3 hours. Add pepper, sugar, oregano, onions, Worcestershire sauce, garlic, salt, pepper, Tabasco sauce, thyme, tomato sauce and parsley; cover and cook for 1 ¹/₂ hours. Correct seasoning. Add water if mixture gets to thick. Add Polish sausage and smoked sausage and cook 30 minutes more. Serve over steamed rice. 6 servings.

STEAMED RICE

3 cups water	*1 ¹/₂ teaspoons salt*
1 ¹/₂ tablespoons butter or margarine	*1 ¹/₂ cups brown rice*

Measure water into a heavy 2-quart saucepan and bring to a boil; add butter and salt. Stir in rice. Cover saucepan, lower the heat and simmer 20 minutes or until the rice is tender and all the water is absorbed. 4 ½ cups rice.

VEGETABLE SALAD WITH CREAMY TART DRESSING

1 large cucumber (or 2 small)	*3 green onions, chopped*
1 cup cherry tomatoes cut in half	*1 tablespoon lemon juice*
½ cup bean sprouts	*Salt to taste*
³/₄ cup sour cream or yogurt	*Seasoned pepper to taste*
¼ cup plus 2 tablespoons buttermilk	

Peel and slice cucumber. Add tomatoes and bean sprouts. Combine sour cream, buttermilk, onions, lemon juice, salt and pepper. Add to vegetables and toss just before serving. 6 servings.

CREAM CHEESE POUND CAKE

¼ pound (1 stick) butter	*6 eggs*
½ pound (2 sticks) margarine	*3 cups all-purpose flour*
1 (8 ounce) package cream cheese, softened	*2 tablespoons baking powder*
2 ½ cups sugar	*2 teaspoons vanilla*

Cream butter, margarine and cheese. Beat in sugar. Add eggs, one at a time. Combine flour and baking powder. Add to butter mixture, blend thoroughly. Add vanilla. Pour into greased tube or bundt pan. Bake at 325° for 1 ½ hours.

TUESDAY
Tuna loaf
Broccoli Parmesan *
Steamed carrots
Caesar salad
Two-hour loaf bread *
Butterscotch pudding

BROCCOLI PARMESAN

3 (10 ounce) packages frozen broccoli spears	*⅛ teaspoon marjoram*
3 tablespoons butter or margarine	*½ teaspoon dry mustard*
2 tablespoons minced onion	*1 chicken bouillon cube*
3 tablespoons flour	*2 ½ cups milk*
³/₄ teaspoon salt	*³/₄ cup grated Parmesan cheese*
Pepper to taste	*Paprika*

Cook broccoli according to package directions and put into 2- quart bake and serve dish. Melt butter and saute onions. Blend in flour, salt, pepper, marjoram and mustard. Add bouillon cube and milk. Cook until thick, stirring constantly. Continue cooking and add ½ cup cheese, stirring until melted. Pour over broccoli; garnish with paprika and ¼ cup cheese. Bake at 375° for 20-25 minutes. Can be put together and baked at last minute. 6-8 servings.

TWO-HOUR LOAF BREAD

2 ²/₃ cups luke-warm water
2 envelopes active dry yeast
2 teaspoons honey or sugar

6 ½ to 7 ½ cups all-purpose flour
2 teaspoons salt

In a large bowl, combine water, yeast and honey. Stir briefly and let stand until the yeast dissolves and begins to foam, 5 to 10 minutes. Stir 3 cups of the flour and the salt into the yeast mixture and beat well until smooth and bubbly. Gradually add enough of the remaining flour, 1 cup at a time, to make a fairly soft dough; do not add more flour than the dough can absorb. Turn out onto a lightly-floured surface and knead lightly until dough is just barely nonsticky, about 2 minutes. Place in oiled bowl and turn to coat with a light film of oil. Cover and let rise in warm draft-free place until doubled in bulk, about 30 minutes. Punch down dough and divide in half; place each half in well-greased 9x5x3-inch loaf pan. Cover and let rise in warm, draft-free place until doubled in bulk, about 30 minutes. Bake loaves in 400° oven for 30 minutes, or until tops are browned and bottoms sound hollow when tapped. Turn out onto racks and let cool before storing. 2 loaves.

WEDNESDAY
Meat cakes with mushroom sauce
Oven baked new potatoes
Country style zucchini *
Vegetable juice aspic
Biscuit
Fresh fruit

COUNTRY-STYLE ZUCCHINI

3 medium zucchini
Salt
2 tablespoons butter or margarine

¼ teaspoon pepper
¼ teaspoon dried basil leaves
3 tablespoons grated Parmesan cheese

Cut zucchini into ½ inch slices. Place slices on paper towels. Sprinkle lightly with salt; let stand two minutes. Pat dry. Place butter in skillet. Melt over medium heat. Saute zucchini, turning occasionally, until edges are golden brown, about 5 minutes. Season with pepper and basil; stir in grated cheese. Serve warm. 4-6 servings.

THURSDAY
No Meat Today
Scalloped eggplant *
Stewed tomatoes
Broccoli with Hollandaise sauce
Three bean salad
Apple walnut bread slices *

SCALLOPED EGGPLANT

1 medium-sized eggplant
1 medium onion, finely-chopped
1 medium-sized green pepper, finely-chopped
1 egg, slightly beaten

1 cup milk
Dash of black pepper
1 cup crushed cracker crumbs
¼ cup (½ stick) butter or margarine

Peel eggplant; cut into chunks. Cook in boiling salted water until tender. Drain. Mash eggplant, add chopped onion and green pepper. Combine egg and milk, add black pepper and cracker crumbs; add eggplant mixture. Pour mixture into greased 1 ½ quart casserole. Dot with butter and bake at 350° for 30-40 minutes. 4-6 servings.

APPLE WALNUT BREAD

6 cups all-purpose flour
1 ³/₄ cups sugar
2 tablespoons baking powder
2 ½ teaspoons salt
3 cups milk

2 eggs, beaten slightly
1 ½ cups raisins
1 ½ cups walnuts, coarsely-chopped
2 cups finely-chopped apples

Mix flour, sugar, baking powder and salt. Combine milk and eggs, and stir into dry ingredients, blending well. Stir in raisins, nuts and apples. Turn into two greased and floured loaf pans, 9x5x3 inches. Bake in preheated oven, 350°, for 1 hour and 15 minutes.
Variation: For more concentrated apple flavor, use 3 cups apple juice instead of 3 cups milk. Because juice is sweeter than milk, reduce sugar to 1 ½ cups.

FRIDAY
Pork chops supreme *
Linguine misto *
Steamed yellow squash and onions
Tropical fruit salad with pineapple dressing *
Bread sticks
Coffee ice cream with chopped nut topping

PORK CHOPS SUPREME

8 thin pork chops
¼ cup cooking oil
1 cup flour
½ teaspoon salt

¼ teaspoon black pepper
1 (10 ½ oz) can condensed cream of mushroom soup
½ cup dry white wine
1 (4 ounce) can mushrooms, drained

Trim chops of excess cover fat. Heat oil in heavy skillet. Put flour, salt and pepper in plastic bag. Shake chops, one at a time, in bag until well-coated with flour. Shake off excess flour. Brown chops in hot oil. Place chops in shallow baking pan, do not overlap. Combine soup, wine and mushrooms. Pour over chops. Cover, bake at 350° for 1 hour. Remove cover last 15 minutes of cooking. 4 servings. Note: Browning can be omitted. If so, then eliminate the 1/4 cup of oil.

LINGUINE MISTO

4 medium carrots, scraped
1 (4 ounce) package linguine
1 tablespoon oil (preferably olive oil)
2 cloves garlic, crushed
½ pound fresh mushrooms, sliced
1 medium onion, thinly-sliced

1 celery rib, thinly-sliced
2 tablespoons lemon juice
1 ½ teaspoons oregano leaves
½ teaspoon salt
⅛ teaspoon pepper
¼ cup water

Cut each carrot lengthwise into thin slices; then cut slices into thin strips. Prepare linguine as package directs; drain and keep warm. In 12-inch skillet over medium heat, heat oil; add carrots, garlic, mushrooms, onion, celery, lemon juice, oregano, salt and pepper. Cook 3 minutes, stirring often. Add water; reduce heat to low, cover and cook about 10 minutes longer or until carrots are tender-crisp. Add linguine to carrot mixture; toss. 4 servings.

TROPICAL FRUIT SALAD WITH PINEAPPLE DRESSING

1 cup pineapple chunks
1 orange, sectioned or 1 can Mandarin
  oranges, drained

1 banana, sliced
1 avocado, peeled, sectioned (optional)
Lettuce

Combine all fruits, serve in a lettuce-lined bowl. Top with pineapple dressing.

Pineapple Dressing

½ cup sugar
1 tablespoon flour
1 egg, slightly beaten

³/₄ cup pineapple juice
¼ cup lemon juice

Combine all ingredients, cook over low heat, stirring constantly, until thick. Cool before mixing with fruit. 4 servings.

SATURDAY
Barbecued chicken on the grill
Cabbage casserole *
Corn on the cob
Seasoned sliced tomatoes, onions and cucumber
Barbecue bread (commercial)
Pineapple float *

CABBAGE CASSEROLE

1 medium head cabbage
1 tablespoon sugar
2 tablespoons butter or margarine
1 onion, sliced

1 green pepper, sliced
2 cups (one 16-oz can) canned tomatoes, drained
³/₄ cup shredded Cheddar cheese

Cut cabbage into 6 slices and cook in boiling salted water for about 10 minutes or until tender-crisp. Place in greased 2-quart casserole. Saute sugar, butter, onion and pepper until tender. Add tomatoes. Pour mixture over cabbage and sprinkle with shredded cheese. Bake at 350° until heated through. 6 servings.

PINEAPPLE FLOAT

1 quart pineapple sherbet
1 liter ginger ale

1 20-ounce can pineapple rings, drained

In each serving dish, place 2 scoops of pineapple sherbet. Fill with ginger ale. Garnish with pineapple placed around straw for sipping. 1 serving.

August - Fourth Week

Colorful salads really brighten the dinner table, adding sunny flavor and worlds of good nutrition to a meal. Salads are versatile: they can be tossed, arranged, molded, frozen, refrigerated or heated. Salads can be used to any advantage: they can be heavy if the entree is light, they can be light when the entree is heavy. If an essential nutrient is missing in the entree, it can be added in a salad. They can serve as a main dish, , a vegetable, a dessert and even as a soup, like gazpacho.

Ingredients in salads can supply essential nutrients to the diet. For example, protein is supplied through meat, cheese and legumes. Vitamin A, B, C and essential minerals are supplied through carrots, broccoli, cabbage, cauliflower, peas, Brussels sprouts, cucumber, lettuce, tomatoes and fresh fruits. They can supply a good source of carbohydrates through rice and pastas.

It is so easy for a cook to be creative and prepare a salad that is different, delicious, nutritious and inexpensive. Take advantage of roadside stands for lower cost, ripe, flavorful fruits and vegetables. A good salad depends in large part on the quality of the materials used, so remember:
• Buy only top quality produce that is in season. They are also more economical. Poor quality produce has lost its flavor and much of the nutrients.
• Buy only the quantity to be used, and use them while they are fresh.
• Buy pre-packaged greens carefully. Make sure you can see what you're getting.

After buying crisp, fresh salad greens at the market, be sure to keep them that way. Wash greens thoroughly in cold water and pat them dry with a cloth towel or paper towels. Wrap clean, dry greens in a towel and store them in the refrigerator crisper to chill or put the wrapped greens in a plastic bag and store in the refrigerator.

SUNDAY
Chicken and spinach divan *
Buttered vermicelli (thin pasta)
Fruit salad with poppy seed dressing
Cornbread / Creamy coconut pie *

CHICKEN AND SPINACH DIVAN
(Using microwave or oven cooking)

1 pound boneless, skinless chicken breasts	*½ teaspoon dry mustard*
2 tablespoons dry white wine or chicken broth	*Pepper to taste*
10 oz fresh spinach (5 cups), washed and trimmed	*1 ¼ cups milk (low fat preferred)*
* or 1 (10 oz) package frozen chopped spinach*	*½ cup grated Parmesan cheese*
2 tablespoons butter or margarine	*Paprika*
3 tablespoons flour	

Split chicken breast into 4 equal portions; place in a 2-quart microwave-safe baking dish, cover with wine or broth. Cover with plastic wrap, vent one corner, or with a lid. Cook in microwave until juices from the chicken are no longer pink, about 5-7 minutes. Set aside. Thaw frozen spinach (does not need to be cooked). If fresh spinach is used, place it in a 2-quart casserole, cover with lid or plastic wrap, vented. Cook in microwave for 3 minutes; set aside. Melt butter in skillet, stir in flour, mustard and pepper. Blend in milk and juices from chicken using a wire whip, if available. Cook until smooth and thickened. Stir in ¼ cup of cheese, continue stirring until well blended. Place spinach around chicken in the 2-quart baking dish. Pour sauce over all and sprinkle with remaining cheese. Lightly dust with paprika. Microwave on high until hot, about 2 minutes, or bake in 350° oven about 15 minutes or until hot throughout. 4 servings.

CREAMY COCONUT PIE

1 (6 ounce) package instant vanilla pudding
   and pie filling
2 cups milk
1 cup sour cream

1 teaspoon vanilla extract
1 teaspoon almond extract
1 cup moist, flaky coconut, divided
1 (9 inch) deep-dish pie crust (commercial), baked

Combine pudding, milk, sour cream, vanilla extract, almond extract and 1 cup less 2 tablespoons coconut. Blend thoroughly. Pour into baked pie crust. Place in refrigerator; allow to set at least 2 hours. To serve, top with whipped cream or whipped topping; sprinkle with remaining 2 tablespoons coconut.

MONDAY
Pork chops on fruited pilaf
Randy's squash casserole *
Bibb lettuce with oil and vinegar dressing
Bacon bread *
Frozen chocolate yogurt with chocolate sauce

RANDY'S SQUASH CASSEROLE

1 ½ to 2 pounds yellow summer squash
1 large onion, chopped
Salt to taste
Pepper to taste
1 cup shredded sharp Cheddar cheese

½ cup milk
2 eggs, beaten
6 saltine crackers
1 tablespoon Parmesan cheese

Wash and slice squash. Combine with onion in medium-sized saucepan. Add ½ cup water, cover and cook over high heat until steam expels around edge of lid. Turn heat down to lowest point immediately. Cook about 7-10 minutes or until tender. Drain. Combine squash mixture with salt, pepper, Cheddar cheese, milk, eggs and crackers, mix and correct seasoning. Pour into a 2-quart casserole. Top with Parmesan cheese. Bake in 350° oven for 1 hour. 6 servings.

BACON BREAD

7 ¼ cups all-purpose flour
3 tablespoons sugar
2 teaspoons salt
1 teaspoon coarsely-ground black pepper
2 packages active dry yeast

1 ½ cups milk
¾ cup water
½ pound bacon, crisp-cooked and crumbled
⅓ cup reserved bacon fat
1 egg (at room temperature)

Combine 2 ½ cups flour, sugar, salt, pepper and undissolved yeast. Combine in saucepan milk, water and reserved bacon fat; heat to warm (120-130°). Gradually add to dry ingredients; beat 2 minutes at medium speed of mixer. Add egg and 1 cup flour. Beat at high speed 2 minutes. Stir in crumbled bacon and enough additional flour to make soft dough. On floured board, knead 4-5 minutes. Divide dough in half. Shape into 2 loaves. Place in 2 greased 8 ½x4 ½x2 ½-inch loaf pans. Cover; let rise in warm draft-free place until doubled, about 45 minutes. Bake at 375° for 30 minutes or until done. Remove from pans; cool on racks. 2 loaves.

TUESDAY
Roast beef
Potatoes Delmonico *
Buttered green beans
Pineapple-orange spinach salad *
Biscuits / Caramel cake

POTATOES DELMONICO

¼ cup butter or margarine
3 tablespoons flour
½ teaspoon salt
¼ teaspoon pepper
½ teaspoon garlic salt

1 ½ cups hot milk
1 cup (4 ounces) shredded Cheddar cheese
4 hard-cooked eggs, sliced
4 cups sliced (¼-inch slices) cooked potatoes
Paprika

Melt butter, Add flour and seasonings; stir until well blended. Slowly add milk, stirring constantly. Continue cooking until smooth and thick. Remove from heat; blend in ½ cup cheese. Pour entire mixture over sliced potatoes and hard-cooked eggs. Mix well, put into a well-greased casserole. Sprinkle with ½ cup cheese and paprika. Bake 1 hour at 350°. 6 servings.

PINEAPPLE-ORANGE SPINACH SALAD

1 (15 ½ ounce) can pineapple tidbits
5 cups spinach leaves
4 strips bacon, cooked and crumbled
1 cup sliced mushrooms
1 orange, peeled and sliced crosswise
3 tablespoons sliced almonds, toasted
½ cup cooking oil
3 tablespoons orange juice

2 tablespoons vinegar
1 tablespoon Dijon mustard
1 teaspoon dill weed
½ teaspoon grated orange rind
¼ teaspoon garlic powder
¼ teaspoon salt
Dash pepper

Drain pineapple, reserving ¼ cup juice. Set aside. Thoroughly clean spinach; drain and tear into bite-sized pieces. In salad bowl, combine spinach, bacon, mushrooms, orange, pineapple and almonds. Thoroughly blend reserved juice, oil, orange juice, vinegar, mustard, dill, orange rind, garlic powder, salt and pepper. Toss ½ cup dressing with salad. Serve remaining dressing with salads. 4 servings.

WEDNESDAY
Layered Italian casserole *
Buttered broccoli
Tossed vegetable salad
Garlic bread
Angel food cake with fresh fruit topping

LAYERED ITALIAN CASSEROLE
Cream Sauce

¼ cup (½ stick) butter or margarine
¼ cup flour
3 cups light cream or milk
1 cup chicken broth

½ cup grated Parmesan cheese
1 teaspoon salt
¼ teaspoon pepper

Melt butter in saucepan. Stir in flour, cook 1 minute. Lower heat, stir in cream and broth until smooth; cook, stirring constantly, until thick and smooth. Stir in cheese, salt and pepper; cook until cheese melts. Cover, keep warm.

Meat Layer

1 large onion, chopped
2 tablespoons butter or margarine
1 pound ground beef
1 pound bulk sausage
1/4 teaspoon cinnamon
1/4 teaspoon allspice

1/4 teaspoon nutmeg
2 teaspoons salt
1/2 teaspoon pepper
1 (6 ounce) can tomato paste
1/4 cup dry white wine

Saute onions in butter, add meat, cook until done, drain off fat. Add spices, tomato paste and wine. Bring to a boil, simmer for 15 minutes.

Pasta

1 pound noodles
3 eggs

2 tablespoons butter, soften
3/4 cup Parmesan cheese

Cook noodles according to package directions. Beat eggs, add 1/2 cup Parmesan cheese and butter. Stir into pasta. Spoon 1/2 pasta into 2-quart baking dish. Pour 1 cup cream sauce over pasta. Add all meat mixture. Pour 1 cup cream sauce over meat. Top with remaining pasta and cover with remaining cream sauce. Sprinkle with remaining Parmesan. Bake at 350° for 35 minutes. Cool 15 minutes. Cut into squares for serving. 6 servings.

THURSDAY
Meat loaf
Rice casserole
Brussels sprouts with creamy egg sauce *
Grapefruit and avocado salad
Sweet potato biscuit with orange marmalade *

BRUSSELS SPROUTS WITH CREAMY EGG SAUCE

1 quart fresh Brussels sprouts
1/4 cup butter
1/4 cup chopped onion
1/4 cup flour
1 teaspoon salt

1/8 teaspoon pepper
2 cups milk
3 hard-cooked eggs
3 tablespoons minced parsley

Remove outer wilted leaves from sprouts. Cut off stem ends. Wash and soak in salted water (2 tablespoons salt to 1 quart of water) for 30 minutes. Drain. Cook in boiling salted water about 15 minutes or until tender. Drain, keep hot. Melt butter. Cook onion in butter until tender; add flour and seasonings; blend. Add milk, stirring constantly, and cook until thickened. Cut eggs into halves, lengthwise. Remove yolks. Cut whites into quarters or eighths and add to sauce. Arrange sprouts in serving dish. Top with egg sauce and sprinkle with yolk of egg which has been pressed through a sieve. Garnish with minced parsley. 6 servings.

SWEET POTATO BISCUITS

1 cup mashed sweet potatoes
²/₃ cup milk
¼ cup (½ stick) butter or margarine, melted
1 ¼ cups all-purpose flour

1 tablespoon plus ½ teaspoon baking powder
2 tablespoons sugar
½ teaspoon salt

Combine potato, milk and butter. Combine and sift flour, baking powder, sugar and salt. Add to potato mixture. Stir slightly to form a soft dough; turn onto floured board and knead about 20 seconds. Pat to ½-inch thick, and cut with a biscuit cutter dipped in flour. Bake at 475° for 12 minutes. 10-12 medium biscuits.

FRIDAY
Teens Hobo Party
(Back-to-School Celebration)
Jerky strips
Spinach dip in a salad puff bowl with king size dip chips
Oven barbecued ribs
Baked bean medley
Sliced baked potatoes
Corn on the cob with garlic dressing
Apple sour cream slaw
Hobo bread
Ice cream sandwiches (commercial)
Crisp chocolate chip cookies

Plan Of Work

Jerky can be prepared several days ahead. Store in air-tight container. May refrigerate, but not necessary.
Day before:
1. Prepare salad puff bowl. Wrap carefully and chill.
2. Prepare cookies.
3. Prepare hobo bread.
4. Prepare sauce for ribs.
Early in the day:
5. Cook beans and reheat before serving.
6. Prepare spinach dip, cover and refrigerate.
7. Prepare dressing for slaw. Add and mix just before serving.
8. Prepare corn and refrigerate. Have oven ready.
9. Prepare potatoes, ready to place in oven and cook.
2 hours before serving:
10. Place meat in oven.
11. 40 minutes before, place potatoes and corn in oven (corn will not burn)
12. Make ice cream. Seal and pack to keep frozen.

JERKY STRIPS

1 ½ to 2 pounds flank steak
⅓ cup soy sauce
6 cloves garlic. crushed

6-8 dashes liquid smoke (optional)
⅛ teaspoon salt
¼ teaspoon pepper

Slice flank steak lengthwise, with the grain. into ¼ inch strips. Combine remaining ingredients; pour over steak strips, stirring to coat all sides of the meat. Marinate 30 minutes to 1 hour. Drain and arrange meat in a single layer on ungreased cookie sheet. Place meat on a rack if available. Bake in 150° oven for 12 hours. Do not open door. Let it cook overnight to save time. Cut into 1-inch strips. Store in tightly covered container. Not necessary to refrigerate. Note: Steak will cut easier if partially frozen.

SPINACH DIP

1 (10 oz) package frozen chopped spinach, cooked
   and drained thoroughly (squeeze with hands)
½ cup chopped green onions, use tops
½ cup chopped fresh parsley

1 cup mayonnaise
Garlic salt to taste
Hot sauce to taste

Chop through spinach (for better dipping). Combine all ingredients; mix well. Serve chilled or at room temperature. Yield: about 2 ½ cups. Place in salad puff bowl and serve with king size dip chips or crackers.

SALAD PUFF BOWL

⅔ cup water
¼ cup (½ stick) butter or margarine

1 cup biscuit mix
4 eggs

Heat water and butter to boiling. Add biscuit mix all at once. Stir over low heat and add one egg at a time, blending thoroughly after each egg. Beat until smooth. Spread on bottom (not sides) of a 9- or 10-inch pie pan. Bake at 400° for 35 or 40 minutes. Cool. Can be cooked day before if covered securely. 1 9-inch salad puff bowl.

OVEN BARBECUED RIBS

6-8 pounds pork ribs or loin cut into serving pieces
Salt to taste
¼ cup (½stick) butter or margarine
4 cloves garlic, crushed
4 onions, sliced
¼ cup prepared mustard
½ cup dark brown sugar

1 ½ cups chili sauce or catsup
2 tablespoons celery seed
¼ cup Worcestershire sauce
1 tablespoon salt
1 teaspoon black pepper
3 cups water
4 lemons, sliced thin

Lightly salt ribs. Place in baking pan, meat side down. Cover and bake at 450° for 30 minutes. Drain off excess fat. Melt butter, add garlic and onions and saute until brown. Add remaining ingredients. Bring to a boil. Cook one minute. Turn ribs to meat side up. Cover with sauce. Cover and bake at 350° for 1 ½ hours. Uncover, increase heat to 450° and bake 5-10 minutes or until brown. 6-8 servings. Note: Beef ribs may be used.

BAKED BEAN MEDLEY

1 (16 ounce) can Lima beans, drained
1 (16 ounce) can kidney beans, drained
2 (16 ounce) cans pork and beans, undrained
1 cup brown sugar, packed
1/2 teaspoon dry mustard

1/2 cup cider vinegar
7-8 slices bacon, cut into small pieces
2 medium onions, chopped
4 cloves garlic, crushed

Combine Lima beans, kidney beans and pork and beans in mixing bowl. Combine sugar, mustard and vinegar in small saucepan and heat until sugar is dissolved and mixture is hot. Add to bean mixture. In small skillet, saute bacon; add onions and garlic. Cook, stirring constantly, until onion is cooked, not browned. Add it to bean mixture. Pour into 9x13-inch or 3-quart baking dish and bake in 350° oven for one hour. 8-10 servings.

SLICED BAKED POTATO

8 large baking potatoes
1 cup (2 sticks) butter or margarine, melted

1/2 teaspoon salt
1/2 teaspoon pepper

Scrub potatoes, leaving skin intact. Arrange 6 pieces of heavy duty aluminum foil. Add salt and pepper to melted butter. Slice each potato into 3/4-inch slices. Dip each slice of potato in the melted butter mixture and reassemble the potato. Carefully wrap each potato in foil. Place potatoes in oven with ribs, or bake in 400° oven, or on hot coals. Bake for 40 minutes. 6-8 servings.

CORN ON THE COB WITH GARLIC DRESSING

8 ears fresh corn
1 teaspoon salt
2 cups mayonnaise
1/4 cup lemon juice

1/4 cup olive oil
4 cloves garlic, crushed
1 teaspoon hickory salt

Husk corn and remove silk. Combine remaining ingredients; spread generously on each ear of corn. Place each ear in the center of a square piece of aluminum foil. Wrap individually. Bake in 350° oven for 30 minutes or bake on the hot coals in grill. Serve corn wrapped. 8 servings. Will not burn. Keep in oven until serving time to keep hot.

APPLE SOUR CREAM SLAW

1 cup sour cream
2 tablespoons lemon juice
2 tablespoons cider vinegar
2 tablespoons sugar
1 teaspoon salt
1/4 teaspoon coarsely-ground black pepper
1 teaspoon dry mustard

1/2 cup sliced celery
2 cups shredded cabbage
1/2 cup shredded carrots
1 large red apple, cored, unpeeled,
    cut into small cubes
1/3 cup raisins
1/4 cup chopped salted peanuts (optional)

Combine first seven ingredients. Beat until smooth. Combine remaining ingredients; add to first mixture; toss to mix. 6-8 servings.

HOBO BREAD

1 pound package seedless raisins
1 tablespoon plus 1 teaspoon baking soda
2 ½ cups boiling water
1 ½ cup white sugar

3 ½ cups white all-purpose flour
2 eggs
3 tablespoons oil
1 teaspoon salt

Combine raisins, soda and boiling water. Allow it to set 8 hours or overnight. To the raisin mixture, add sugar, flour, eggs, oil and salt. Mix well and pour into 2 greased 9x5x2-inch loaf pans. Bake in 325° oven for 1 hour.

CRISPY CHOCOLATE CHIP COOKIES

½ cup butter or margarine
1 cup dark brown sugar, well-packed
1 egg beaten
1 teaspoon vanilla

1 ½ cups flour
½ teaspoon baking soda
2 cups crispy rice cereal
1 (12 ounce) package chocolate chips

Cream butter, add sugar gradually, add egg and vanilla, beat until smooth. Combine flour and soda. Add flour mixture to butter mixture. Stir in rice cereal and chocolate chips. Drop mixture from a teaspoon onto ungreased cookie sheet. Bake at 350° for 10 minutes. Yield: 4 dozen 2 inch cookies.

SATURDAY
Kiddies Party
Love sandwiches (grilled peanut butter and jelly) *
Large tray of items to pick and choose from to include:
1. Stuffed egg halves *
2. Cheese sticks; Cheddar, Gouda, Monterey Jack
3. Cold cut sticks; bologna, baked ham, smoked sausage, cold meat loaf
Bowl of dried fruit combination to eat by the handful to include:
1. Raisins
2. Dried apricot halves
3. Pitted prunes
4. Dried banana chips
5. Peanuts
Caramel dip (commercial) with fresh apple slices
Country style vanilla ice cream *
Graham cracker treats *

LOVE SANDWICHES
(Grilled peanut butter and jelly)

For each sandwich, spread 1 slice of bread with peanut butter, and another with the favorite jam or jelly. Close sandwich. Spread softened butter on the outside of top and bottom of sandwich. Grill until brown, Turn and grill the other side.

Variations: 1. Omit jelly and add a thin slice of boiled ham. 2. Add crumbled bacon to peanut butter and jelly sandwich or add crumbled bacon to peanut butter and omit the jelly.

STUFFED EGGS

8 hard-cooked eggs
1 teaspoon lemon juice
1 teaspoon prepared mustard
¹/₄ to ¹/₂ cup mayonnaise

¹/₄ teaspoon thyme
¹/₄ teaspoon salt
2 tablespoons butter or margarine, melted
Chopped parsley

Slice hard-cooked eggs in half lengthwise. Remove yolks, place in small bowl; add remaining ingredients, except parsley, and beat with beaters until smooth. Correct seasoning. Fill egg whites with yolk mixture. Place in refrigerator until ready to serve. Cut each half in half before serving. Sprinkle a little parsley on top of each egg piece. 8 servings.

COUNTRY STYLE VANILLA ICE CREAM

3 eggs
1 ³/₄ cups sugar
3 cups milk

3 cups whipping cream
2 tablespoons vanilla extract
¹/₄ teaspoon salt

In a large mixing bowl, beat eggs until foamy; gradually add sugar, beat until thickened. Add milk, cream, vanilla and salt. Mix thoroughly. Chill. Churn freeze. Yield: 3 quarts.

GRAHAM CRACKER TREATS

8 graham crackers
4 almond chocolate bars

8 large marshmallows

Place graham crackers on a sheet of aluminum foil. Top each with ½ of a chocolate bar, then a marshmallow. Put under broiler for a few minutes to toast marshmallow. Serve at once. Double recipe for seconds. 8 servings.

September

September - First Week

Poultry is so versatile and so popular that it frequents menus at all levels, from the most economical to the most elegant. Poultry includes domesticated chicken, turkey, goose, duck, squab and Cornish hen. The most important of these on the American table is chicken.

Chicken has exactly the same high-quality complete protein as red meat. In fact, few popular meats equal and none surpass the protein in chicken. The main difference is that chicken is "white" meat rather than "red" meat. The human body needs the high-quality protein for its essential amino acids that are essential for building, maintaining and replacing the body's tissue, muscle and cells. The amino acid content of chicken is equal to beef. For example, a 4-ounce portion of chicken contains 23.4 grams of protein and a 4-ounce serving of beef contains 20.6 grams.

Chicken is an excellent source of complete protein. It contains no carbohydrates, no vitamin C, is low in iron, riboflavin and thiamin. Chicken is the lowest in calories of popular meats. It is low in cholesterol, low in sodium, low in fat, and very easily digested. Chicken liver, however, is a rich source of vitamin A and the B vitamins and iron. Chicken skin has higher nutrient content than some meats, and has fewer calories and less fat than sirloin of beef. It nearly equals beef in protein. However, if one is cooking for low fat or low calorie dieters, chicken skin should be removed.

SUNDAY
Quick crab quiche *
Buttered Lima beans
Fresh fruit salad / Flour tortillas
Instant pot de creme *

QUICK CRAB QUICHE

1 (9 inch) unbaked pie shell (your own or deep-dish frozen)
1 package (6 ounce) frozen crabmeat, thawed, well drained and flaked, or 1 can (6 ounce) crabmeat, well drained and flaked
1/2 cup (2 ounces) shredded Swiss or Cheddar cheese
6 eggs

1 1/2 cups half & half, light cream or milk (or part crabmeat liquid, if you like)
1 tablespoon instant minced onion
1 tablespoon dry white wine (optional)
1/2 teaspoon salt
1/2 teaspoon dry mustard
1/2 teaspoon dried, crushed tarragon leaves

Sprinkle crabmeat and cheese into pie shell. Beat together remaining ingredients until combined. Pour over crabmeat and cheese. Bake in pre-heated 375° oven 30 to 35 minutes or until knife inserted near center comes out clean. Let stand 5 minutes before serving. (6 servings)

INSTANT POT DE CREME

1 pint chocolate ice cream or ice milk or frozen chocolate yogurt
1/3 cup half & half

1 (4 ounce) package instant chocolate pudding and pie filling

Beat one pint chocolate ice cream until creamy and then stir in one-third cup light cream or half & half. Gradually add one (4 ounce) package instant chocolate pudding and pie filling, beating until well blended, about 10 minutes. Turn into six individual pot de creme cups or small dessert dishes. Cover and chill until ready to serve. Garnish with a dollop of vanilla ice cream or whipped cream or whipped topping. (6 servings)

MONDAY
Low-fat chicken baked in mild barbecue sauce *
Mixed vegetable casserole *
Creamy cole slaw
Biscuits
Ice milk with fruit topping

LOW-FAT CHICKEN BAKED IN MILD BARBECUE SAUCE

2 whole chicken breasts, halved and skinned	*1/4 teaspoon oregano leaves*
1 medium tomato, coarsely-chopped	*1/4 teaspoon paprika*
1 large onion, cut in wedges	*1/8 teaspoon garlic powder*
1 tablespoon brown sugar, packed	*1/8 teaspoon dry mustard*
1 tablespoon cider vinegar	*1/2 teaspoon salt*
1/2 teaspoon ground cumin	*Parsley sprigs for garnish*

In 10x6-inch baking dish, arrange chicken flesh side up. In blender at medium speed, blend tomato, onion, sugar, vinegar, cumin, oregano leaves, paprika, garlic powder and mustard, until smooth. Pour tomato mixture over chicken. Bake 45 minutes in 375° oven, or until chicken is fork-tender. Garnish with parsley. (4 servings)

MIXED VEGETABLE CASSEROLE

2 (16 ounce) cans mixed vegetables, drained	*1 cup shredded sharp Cheddar cheese*
1 cup mayonnaise	*1/4 cup Parmesan cheese*
1 cup chopped onion	*2 tablespoons butter or margarine, melted*
1 cup chopped celery	*1 cup cracker crumbs*

Combine vegetables, mayonnaise, onion, celery, Cheddar cheese and Parmesan cheese. Pour into 2-quart baking dish. Combine butter with crumbs. Sprinkle on vegetable mixture. Bake in 350° oven for 30 minutes. (6-8 servings)

TUESDAY
Stove-top meat loaf *
Baked potato
Minted peas
Broccoli salad *
Coffee ice milk with Quick and Easy caramel pecan sauce

STOVE-TOP MEAT LOAF

1 pound lean ground beef	*2 tablespoons steak sauce*
1/2 cup oatmeal	*1/4 teaspoon Tabasco sauce (optional)*
1 egg	*1 (8 ounce) can tomato sauce*
2 tablespoons Worcestershire sauce	

Combine ground beef, oats, egg, Worcestershire sauce, steak sauce, and Tabasco sauce and make a round, rather flat, meat loaf. Place in greased electric skillet. Pour tomato sauce over meat loaf. Cover and cook at 300° until done — about 1 hour. (4 servings)

BROCCOLI SALAD

2 bunches broccoli
³/4 cup raisins
½ medium onion, chopped
10 slices bacon, cooked and crumbled

1 (8 oz) can sliced water chestnuts, drained
1 cup mayonnaise
⅓ cup sugar
1 tablespoon vinegar

Cut flowerets from broccoli. Use remaining parts later. Layer broccoli, raisins, onion, bacon and water chestnuts in bowl. Combine remaining ingredients and pour over salad. Refrigerate overnight. Stir together before serving. (6-8 servings)

QUICK AND EASY CARAMEL PECAN SAUCE

½ cup brown sugar, packed
½ cup light corn syrup
2 tablespoons butter or margarine
⅛ teaspoon salt

³/4 cup pecans, toasted and chopped
¼ cup evaporated milk
1 teaspoon vanilla extract

In medium saucepan, combine sugar, corn syrup, butter and salt. Stir over medium heat until mixture comes to a boil and sugar is dissolved. Remove from heat. Stir in nuts, milk and vanilla. Serve hot. (Yield: 1 ½ cups) To reheat: Place in small, heavy-bottomed saucepan over medium-low heat for 3 to 4 minutes.

WEDNESDAY
Potato and carrot chowder
Corned beef sandwich on rye
Fresh green salad
Cream cheese pound cake

POTATO AND CARROT CHOWDER

3 cups diced potatoes
2 cups diced carrots
1 ½ cups sliced onions
2 cups boiling water
1 ½ teaspoons salt

⅛ teaspoon pepper
Dash of paprika
3 cups milk
2 tablespoons butter
Parsley

Cook the vegetables in boiling water plus 1 teaspoon salt until tender. Mash vegetables in water. Heat milk, add to vegetables with remaining salt, pepper and paprika. Heat thoroughly. Correct seasonings, add butter and serve topped with a sprinkling of chopped parsley. (6 servings)

THURSDAY
Baked fish fillets
Rice pilaf
Brussels sprouts with creamy egg sauce
Orange and onion slices with French dressing
Raspberry muffins *

RASPBERRY MUFFINS

2 cups all-purpose flour
1 cup sugar
1 tablespoon baking powder
½ teaspoon salt
1 cup half & half

½ cup cooking oil
1 teaspoon lemon extract
2 eggs, slightly beaten
1 cup fresh or frozen raspberries without
  syrup (do not thaw frozen berries)

Line 12 large or 16 medium muffin cups with paper baking cups. Lightly spoon flour into measuring cup; level off. In large bowl, combine flour, sugar, baking powder and salt; mix well. In small bowl, combine half-and-half, oil, lemon extract and eggs; blend well. Add to dry ingredients; stir until dry ingredients are just moistened. Carefully fold in raspberries. Fill paper-lined muffin cups ¾ full. Bake in preheated 425° oven 18 to 23 minutes or until golden brown. Cool 5 minutes. Remove from pan. (Yield: 12-16 muffins)

FRIDAY
Friday Night Get Together
Seafood gumbo *
Cole slaw
French peasant bread
Lemon chiffon pie

SEAFOOD GUMBO

1 cup salad oil or bacon drippings
1 cup all-purpose flour
2 large onions, chopped (2 cups)
2 ribs celery, chopped
1 large green pepper, chopped (1 ½ cups)
6 cloves garlic, crushed
2 ½ quarts warm water
4 cups sliced okra
1 ½ quarts stewed tomatoes
6 bay leaves
¼ cup Worcestershire sauce

2 tablespoons salt
Red and black pepper to taste
1 pint oysters, undrained
1 pound fresh or frozen crabmeat or 1 (6 ½-oz) can
1 ½ to 2 pounds fresh or frozen medium shrimp,
  peeled and de-veined
½ cup chopped parsley
½ cup chopped green onion tops
Hot cooked rice
Gumbo file (optional)

Combine oil and flour in heavy pot over medium heat. Cook, stirring constantly, until mixture (called *roux*) is the color of a copper penny (about 10 to 15 minutes). Add onion, celery, green pepper, and garlic to roux; cook, stirring constantly, until vegetables are tender.
Do not burn roux. It will ruin gumbo.
Reduce heat, if necessary. Gradually add warm water to roux, in small amounts at first, blending well after each addition; add okra, tomatoes, bay leaf and Worcestershire sauce. Bring mixture to a boil. Reduce heat; simmer, stirring occasionally, at least 20 minutes (1 hour is better, as the roux develops more flavor at this point). Stir in salt, pepper and seafood. Bring gumbo to a boil and simmer 10 minutes. Add parsley and green onion; simmer 5 minutes longer. Remove from heat and serve gumbo over hot rice. Gumbo can be further thickened, if desired, by adding a small amount of file to each serving. (12-14 servings)

FRENCH PEASANT BREAD

2 cups lukewarm water
1 package dry yeast
1 tablespoon sugar
2 teaspoons salt

4 cups all-purpose flour
1 tablespoon corn meal
Melted butter

In a large bowl, combine water, yeast, sugar and salt. Stir until dissolved. Stir in flour. Place dough in another large bowl that is greased with butter. Turn dough to grease the sides. Cover with a damp cloth. Let rise in a warm place for 45 minutes or until double in size. Grease a baking sheet and sprinkle with 1 tablespoon corn meal. Flour hands and divide the dough evenly into two parts, shaping each into an oblong loaf. Do not knead. Place both loaves on the prepared baking sheet. Let loaves rise another 45 minutes or until almost doubled in size. Brush tops with melted butter. Bake in a preheated 425° oven for 10 minutes. Reduce the temperature to 375° and bake 20 minutes. Remove bread from oven and brush again with melted butter. Serve hot.

SATURDAY
Brunch - Weekend Company
Mimosas * or orange juice
Cheese crispies *
Baked ham slices / Eggs Florentine *
Joyce's garlic grits *
Peaches and cream *
Scalloped pineapple *
Morning bread * / Bagels and cheese

Plan Of Work
Day before:
1. Prepare cheese crispies
2. Prepare morning bread
3. Prepare garlic grits
4. Prepare sauce for eggs Florentine
Two hours before serving:
5. Prepare scalloped pineapple (bake one hour before)
6. Prepare peaches and place in oven 15 minutes before serving.
Thirty minutes before serving:
7. Place ham slices in the oven and bake only until heated through.
8. Prepare eggs Florentine and bake.
9. Heat grits along with other items in oven.
10. Bread can be served at room temperature or warmed slightly.
11. Prepare mimosas as they are ordered.

MIMOSAS BY THE GLASS

1 part champagne
1 part orange juice

Triple sec
Orange wheels

Mix chilled champagne and orange juice in a large champagne glass, add dash of triple sec and garnish with orange slices.

CHEESE CRISPIES

2 cups shredded sharp Cheddar cheese
1 cup (2 sticks) margarine, softened
2 cups sifted flour
2 cups crisp rice cereal

¹/₂ teaspoon red pepper
1 teaspoon seasoned salt
1 teaspoon Worcestershire sauce

Mix cheese and margarine. Work in flour. This can best be done by mixing with hands. Put in pepper, salt and sauce, mixing well. Pour in cereal and, using hands, mix without crushing cereal unnecessarily. Shape into small balls (not quite as big as walnuts) and place on ungreased cookie sheets. Flatten each ball with fork. Bake at 375° until balls are light brown, about 10 minutes. (Yield: 3-4 dozen)

EGGS FLORENTINE

1 pound fresh spinach
1 teaspoon seasoned salt
4 eggs
2 tablespoons butter or margarine

2 tablespoons flour
1 cup milk
1 cup (4 ounces) shredded Cheddar cheese

Cook spinach in very little salted water for five minutes. Drain and spread in bottom of buttered baking dish. Make 4 depressions, equally separated in the spinach. Break an egg into a small dish and slide each into a depression. Melt butter. Stir in flour. Add milk and stir until thick. Spoon sauce onto the eggs and top with shredded cheese. Bake at 350° for 30 minutes. (4 servings)

JOYCE'S GARLIC GRITS

4 cups water
1 cup quick cooking grits
1 teaspoon salt
¹/₂ teaspoon white pepper (black can be used)
2 cups (8 ounces) shredded sharp Cheddar cheese,
   or 1 (6 ounce) package garlic cheese spread

¹/₄ teaspoon garlic powder
¹/₂ cup margarine
2 eggs
¹/₂ cup half & half (light cream)
Garlic salt to taste

Pre-heat oven to 350°. Bring water to a boil, add salt and grits, stir until smooth and thick. Add pepper. Stir cheese into hot grits; add garlic powder and margarine. Cool. Beat eggs with cream. Stir slowly into grits. Add garlic salt to taste. Pour into a 1 ¹/₂-quart greased casserole. Bake for 1 to 1 ¹/₂ hours.

PEACHES IN CREAM

1 (16 ounce) can peach halves
¹/₃ cup sugar
¹/₃ cup water

¹/₂ teaspoon ground cinnamon
¹/₄ cup heavy or whipping cream

Place peach halves in casserole. In small bowl, combine sugar, water and cinnamon; pour over peaches. Bake at 375° for 15 minutes, or until peaches are tender. Pour cream over peaches and bake 5 minutes longer. Fresh peaches or apricots may be substituted for the canned peaches. (Yield 4-6 servings)

SCALLOPED PINEAPPLE

3 eggs, well-beaten
2 cups sugar
1 (20 ounce) can crushed pineapple, undrained

4 cups (1 inch cubes) fresh bread
1 cup margarine, cut into 1-inch squares

Combine all ingredients in a medium mixing bowl, and mix well. Pour into a greased 13x9x2-inch baking pan. Bake at 350° for 1 hour. Freeze leftovers. (Yield: 10-12 servings).

MORNING BREAD

6 slices bacon, diced
6 eggs
³/₄ cup milk
1 ½ cups flour
2 ½ teaspoons baking powder

½ teaspoon salt
1 cup chopped cooked ham
2 cups (8 ounces) shredded sharp or extra sharp Cheddar cheese

Brown bacon until light golden; drain. Beat eggs until foamy. Add milk, flour, baking powder and salt. Beat by hand until smooth. Stir in bacon, ham and cheese. Blend well. Pour into greased 9x5-inch loaf pan. Bake at 350° for 50 to 60 minutes. Cool on rack before removing from pan. Serve warm or store in refrigerator, slice and toast to serve. 1 loaf.

September - Second Week

In order to select chicken for the use intended, it is necessary to know the market classes that are available. Chickens are classified by age and weight. The classes available are:

Broilers, or very young birds of either sex weighing from 1 to 2 ½ pounds. They have smooth, thin skins, tender muscles with very thin connective tissue, and are therefore very tender. They are usually pan fried, grilled or broiled.

Fryers, or very slightly older, usually weighing 2 ½ to 3 ½ pounds. These are a tender class.

Roasting chickens are fully developed birds of either sex and are still young and tender, weighing 3 ½ to 5 or 6 pounds.

Capons are unsexed male birds weighing from 4 to 8 pounds. They are tender and flavorful.

Stewing chickens are older birds generally weighing from 4 to 6 pounds. They have well-developed muscles with thick connective tissue, and a high proportion of fat under the skin. They are usually cooked a long time in water in order to tenderize the meat.

Today it is possible to purchase chicken by the parts and the exact number needed. This prevents overbuying. The most popular chicken cuts available and the method of cooking are as follows:

Split broiler - chicken cut in half and usually broiled
Chicken quarters - usually baked or broiled
Breasts, whole or split - usually broiled or baked
Thigh, the meaty portion of dark meat - can be broiled, baked or pan fried
Drumstick - pan fried, or broiled or baked
Wings - can be stewed, baked or fried
Backs and necks - can be simmered for the broth
Gizzard and heart - can be pan fried or simmered
Chicken livers - can be fried, simmered or baked. (This dish is very popular.)
The rule for amounts per serving can be varied to fit the eating habits of the family or as follows:
Frying - ³/₄ to 1 pound per serving
Roasting - ½ to ³/₄ pound per serving
Broiling - ½ chicken or 1 pound
Stewing - ½ to ³/₄ pound per serving

In selecting chicken:
- Choose kind and weight best suited for your purpose.
- Read label to learn kind, weight, price, wholesomeness and quality.
- Examine the bird for the U.S.D.A. inspection stamp to prove wholesomeness.
- Look for grade labeling such as U.S. Grade A, B, or C.
- Check for freshness, fleshy soft flexible breast, meaty legs and firm flesh.

SUNDAY
Baked crab sandwich *
Herbed couscous with vegetables*
Buttered asparagus
Lettuce and tomato with Ranch-style dressing
Lemon meringue pie

BAKED CRAB SANDWICH

12 slices bread	*¼ teaspoon Tabasco sauce*
1 lb crabmeat, or 2 (6 oz) cans crabmeat, drained	*1 tablespoon lemon juice*
1 small onion, chopped	*3 cups milk*
½ cup sliced celery	*4 eggs, beaten*
1 small green pepper, chopped	*1 (10 ½ ounce) can cream of mushroom soup*
1 cup mayonnaise	*½ teaspoon salt*
½ teaspoon salt	*¼ teaspoon pepper*
½ teaspoon white pepper	*1 ½ cups (6 oz) shredded sharp Cheddar cheese*
1 tablespoon Worcestershire sauce	

Butter a 9x13-inch baking dish; line with 6 slices of bread. Combine crab, onion, celery, green pepper, mayonnaise, salt, white pepper, Worcestershire sauce, Tabasco sauce and lemon juice. Spread on bread; top with remaining 6 slices of bread. Combine milk, eggs, mushroom soup, salt and pepper, and pour over top of bread. Top with cheese. Allow to remain in refrigerator 6 hours or overnight. Bake at 350° for 1 hour. (6 large servings)

HERBED COUSCOUS WITH VEGETABLES

1 cup sliced fresh mushrooms	*½ teaspoon garlic salt*
1 small onion, chopped	*¼ teaspoon dried oregano leaves, crushed*
1 cup fat-free chicken broth	*¼ teaspoon black pepper*
2 tablespoons butter or margarine	*²/₃ cup couscous*
1 tablespoon chopped parsley	*1 medium tomato, peeled, chopped (optional)*
½ teaspoon dried basil, crushed	

In a medium sauce pan, saute mushrooms and onion in butter until tender. Add chicken broth, stir in parsley, basil, salt, oregano and pepper. Bring to a boil. Add couscous. Remove from heat, cover and let stand 5 minutes. Stir in tomato. (4 servings)

MONDAY
Linguine with fresh tomato sauce *
Green salad with sour cream dressing *
Italian bread
Cocklebur cake *

LINGUINE WITH FRESH TOMATO SAUCE

2 tablespoons oil
1 small onion, chopped
2 cloves garlic, crushed
3 lbs fresh tomatoes or 2 (14 oz)
  cans diced tomatoes
½ cup coarsely-chopped basil

3 tablespoons red wine vinegar
Salt
Pepper
1 pound linguine
1 tablespoon olive oil
Grated Parmesan cheese

Heat 2 tablespoons oil in a skillet, add onion and garlic. Cook until onions are tender, not brown, about 3-5 minutes. Add tomatoes and cook 10 minutes; add fresh basil, vinegar, and salt and pepper to taste. Just before serving, cook linguine in barely-salted water until firm but tender (al dente). Drain. Transfer to serving bowl. Add 1 tablespoon olive oil, toss well. Add sauce. Toss again. Pass Parmesan cheese. 6 servings.

SOUR CREAM DRESSING

1 cup sour cream
2 tablespoons red wine vinegar
1 teaspoon sugar
½ teaspoon salt

½ teaspoon celery seed
¼ teaspoon pepper
¼ teaspoon thyme

Combine all of the above ingredients. Chill. Serve on mixed green salad.

COCKLEBUR CAKE

½ cup (1 stick) butter or margarine
1 cup light brown sugar, firmly-packed
1 cup flaked coconut
1 cup light corn syrup

1 cup seedless raisins
½ cup chopped nuts (optional)
1 cup Maraschino cherries
1 (18.5 ounce) package yellow cake mix

Melt butter in 9x13-inch baking pan. Pat brown sugar and coconut over butter. Pour on corn syrup and sprinkle with raisins and nuts. Place cherries randomly. Prepare cake mix according to package directions. Pour over mixture in pan. Bake at 350° for 45 minutes. Turn out of pan while hot.

TUESDAY
Beef Stroganoff on steamed rice
Buttered fresh green beans
Mixed vegetable salad, Italian dressing
Finger rolls
Baked apples with fresh orange sauce *

BAKED APPLES WITH FRESH ORANGE SAUCE

6 or 8 red baking apples, washed and cored
Nutmeg
⅓ cup sugar

½ cup water
Orange Sauce

Starting at stem end, peel cored apples ¼ of the way down. Arrange apples in shallow baking dish. Sprinkle centers of apples with nutmeg and sugar. Pour water into bottom of baking dish. Bake uncovered in a 350° (moderate) oven, 40 to 60 minutes (depending on size of apples). Serve warm or cold with Orange Sauce. (6-8 servings)

Orange Sauce

½ cup sugar
3 tablespoons cornstarch
1 cup water

1 cup fresh orange juice
2 tablespoons grated orange peel
2 oranges, peeled, cut into bite-size pieces

Combine sugar and cornstarch in sauce pan; gradually add water and orange juice. Bring mixture to boil and cook over low heat for 5 minutes, stirring constantly. Stir in grated orange peel and orange pieces. Serve hot or cold over apples. (2 ½ cups sauce)

WEDNESDAY
Roast herb turkey breast *
Mashed potatoes
Buttered corn on the cob
Marinated tomato and artichoke salad
Cornbread
Blueberry delight *

ROAST HERB TURKEY BREAST

½ turkey breast (about 4 to 4 ½ pounds)
1 tablespoon lemon juice
1 ½ teaspoons salt
2 tablespoons butter
¼ teaspoon paprika
⅛ teaspoon powdered thyme
⅛ teaspoon powdered basil

⅛ teaspoon white pepper
½ cup rose´ wine
1 chicken bouillon cube, crushed
2 cups small fresh mushrooms
*1 (8 ounce) can small whole onions, drained *
Corn starch

Sprinkle turkey breast with lemon juice and season under side with ½ teaspoon salt. Mix remaining teaspoon salt with butter, paprika, herbs, and pepper, and rub over skin. Place turkey skin-side up in shallow pan. Roast in hot oven (400°) for 20 minutes, until skin begins to brown. Re-set thermostat to moderately slow (325°) and roast 1 to 1 ½ hours, until meat is tender, basting frequently with wine mixed with bouillon cube. Add mushrooms (halved or whole) and onions last 20 minutes turkey roasts. If desired, pan juices may be thickened slightly with cornstarch. (Makes 6 servings) Note: If canned onions are not available, steam 1 cup fresh onion slices and proceed according to directions.

BLUEBERRY DELIGHT

2 cups plain flour
1 cup finely-chopped nuts (walnuts or pecans)
1 cup (2 sticks) butter or margarine, melted
⅓ teaspoon salt

1 box powdered sugar
1 (8 ounce) package cream cheese
1 (9 ounce) package whipped topping
1 can blueberry pie filling

Combine flour, nuts, butter and salt, blend, and press into a greased 9x13-inch baking dish. Bake at 350° for 30 minutes or until lightly browned. Combine sugar and cheese. Blend in whipped topping. Pour over baked crust. Top with pie filling. Refrigerate overnight. (12-15 servings)

THURSDAY

Meat balls in tomato sauce
Garlic noodles *
Buttered fresh spinach
Lettuce and tomato salad
Heated focaccia (commercial bread)
Chocolate covered nuts

GARLIC NOODLES

1/4 cup (1/2 stick) butter or margarine
1/4 cup olive oil
1/4 cup minced fresh parsley
5 cloves garlic, crushed
3 tablespoons dried basil or 1/4 cup fresh, minced

1/4 teaspoon salt
1/2 teaspoon freshly-ground black pepper
1/8 teaspoon cayenne pepper
8 ounces noodles or spaghetti
1 cup grated Parmesan cheese

Combine butter, oil, parsley, garlic, basil, salt, black pepper and cayenne. Heat until butter is melted and garlic slightly brown. Cook noodles according to package directions; drain. While hot, add butter mixture and stir to mix well. Add cheese to coat cooked noodles or spaghetti. Serve hot. (4 servings)

FRIDAY

Left over turkey slices
Onion pie supreme *
Fresh fruit salad / Bread sticks
Cookies

ONION PIE SUPREME

3 cups thinly-sliced onions, preferably Vidalia
1/4 cup (1/2 stick) butter or margarine, melted
1 (9 inch) deep-dish pie shell, baked
1/2 cup milk
1 1/2 cups sour cream

3 tablespoons flour
1 teaspoon salt
1/4 teaspoon pepper
2 eggs, well-beaten
1 teaspoon dried parsley flakes

Cook the onions in butter until lightly browned; spoon into pastry shell. Blend milk with sour cream. Blend flour, salt and pepper with remaining 1/4 cup sour cream. Combine both mixtures; add beaten eggs and mix thoroughly. Pour over onions. Sprinkle on parsley flakes. Bake in 325° oven for 40 minutes or until firm in center. (6-8 servings)

SATURDAY
Tailgate time again!
Chicken fillet strips *
Nippy pineapple dipping sauce *
Ham slices - mustard sauce *
Marinated picnic vegetables *
Cream cheese and olive sandwiches on whole wheat bread *
Mini-Swiss cheese tarts *
Peanut bars *
French applesauce cake *

Plan Of Work

Most of the food in this meal can be done ahead of time. This will give hostess time to be with out-of-town company.

Early in the week (or two weeks before):

1. Marinate the vegetables.
2. Order chicken to be cooked, and make arrangements to pick up the order the morning of the party. (Chicken fingers have no waste. It makes clean-up simpler.)
3. Make peanut bars.

Day before:

4. Bake ham, cool and slice.
5. Prepare dipping sauce for chicken.
6. Prepare hot mustard sauce.
7. Prepare sandwich filling.
8. Prepare pastry and filling for cups.
9. Prepare applesauce cake.

Day of party:

10. Prepare sandwiches.
11. Prepare mini-cheese tarts
12. Pick up chicken at deli.

CHICKEN FILLET STRIPS

(If it is more desirable, cook at home or have it done at the local delicatessen.)

4 pounds chicken fillet strips (buy at the meat market all ready to fry)
2 cups corn oil
1 cup flour
1 1/2 teaspoon salt
1/2 teaspoon pepper

Keep chicken refrigerated until ready to cook. Heat oil. Place flour, salt and pepper in plastic bag. Shake chicken pieces in the bag of flour; shake off excess. Drop into hot fat, a few pieces at a time. Fry about 4 minutes or until golden brown. Drain on paper towels.

Nippy Pineapple Dipping Sauce

1 (12 ounce) jar pineapple preserves
1 cup prepared mustard
1/2 cup horseradish sauce

In a medium saucepan, combine pineapple preserves, mustard and horseradish sauce. Heat, stirring constantly until all is dissolved.

BAKED HAM, BONELESS

Even though the ham is fully cooked, many hostesses cook it for 15 minutes per pound. Allow the ham to cool and slice later.

Orr's Mustard Sauce

1/2 cup sugar
1/4 cup plus 1 tablespoon dry mustard
1/2 teaspoon salt
2 tablespoons flour
1 cup milk
1 egg yolk, beaten
1/2 cup vinegar

In medium-size bowl, sift together sugar, mustard, salt and flour. Set aside. Combine milk, egg yolk and vinegar. Gradually stir milk mixture into the dry mixture. Cook over low heat, stirring constantly until thick, approximately 10 minutes. Serve with baked ham. (Yield: about 1 ½ cups)

MARINATED PICNIC VEGETABLES

1 quart white vinegar
1 ½ cups sugar
Dash salt
4 carrots, scraped and cut in strips
3 green peppers, cut in strips
3 celery ribs, cut into 3-inch strips

1 small onion, sliced thinly into rings
6 cups cauliflowerets
2 cloves garlic
2 teaspoons dried oregano leaves
3 dill pickles

In a large kettle, combine vinegar, sugar, salt and 2 cups water. Bring to boiling, stirring; remove from heat. Let cool completely. Add remaining ingredients. Put in quart jars with tight-fitting lids. Refrigerate, covered. Should hold for two weeks before serving. (Not absolutely necessary.) (Yield: 3 quarts)

CHEESE AND OLIVE SANDWICHES

1 (8 ounce) package cream cheese, softened
½ cup mayonnaise
1 cup stuffed olives, chopped finely

2 tablespoons olive juice
½ cup finely-chopped pecans
Tabasco sauce to taste

Combine all of the above ingredients. Mix well. Mixture will be soft. Place in refrigerator overnight; it will become firm enough to spread. Spread on very thin sliced bread. (Makes 3-4 dozen finger sandwiches)

MINI SWISS CHEESE TARTS
Shells

6 tblsp (³/₄ stick) butter or margarine, softened
3 ounces cream cheese, softened
1 cup flour

½ cup corn meal
Pinch of salt

Cream butter and cheese. Combine flour, corn meal and salt. Add to butter mixture slowly. Stir constantly until well blended. Knead very lightly with hands. Divide dough into one-inch balls. Press into small tins using fingers. (Yield: 48 small tart shells)

Swiss Cheese Filling

1 tablespoon finely-chopped onions
1 tablespoon butter or margarine
½ cup shredded Swiss cheese
1 egg, well beaten
½ cup whipping cream (can use milk)

¼ teaspoon salt
¼ teaspoon dry mustard
Cayenne pepper to taste
Black pepper to taste

Saute onions in butter; add remaining ingredients and mix well. Fill unbaked tart shells. Bake in 350° oven for 20-25 minutes until filling is brown.

PEANUT BARS

1½ cups flour
⅔ cup brown sugar, firmly-packed
½ teaspoon baking powder
½ teaspoon salt
¼ teaspoon soda
½ cup butter or margarine, softened
1 teaspoon vanilla
2 egg yolks, beaten

3 cups miniature marshmallows
⅔ cup corn syrup
¼ cup butter or margarine
2 teaspoons vanilla
1 (12 ounce) package peanut butter chips
2 cups rice cereal
2 cups salted peanuts (unsalted may be used)

Combine flour, sugar, baking powder, salt, soda, ½ cup butter, 1 teaspoon vanilla and egg yolks. Blend to a crumb mixture. Press into an ungreased 9x13x2-inch baking dish. Bake 12 to 15 minutes at 350°. Remove from oven and immediately sprinkle on marshmallows. Return to oven for 1 to 2 minutes or until marshmallows begin to appear puffed. In saucepan combine syrup, ¼ cup butter, 2 teaspoons vanilla and peanut butter chips. Heat and stir until chips are melted. Remove from heat and add cereal and nuts. Immediately spoon over marshmallow layer and spread to cover. Chill and cut into bars. (Approximately 36 bars)

FRESH APPLESAUCE CAKE

1 (1 pound 2¼ ounce) package yellow cake mix
1 (3 ½ ounce) package French vanilla or
  vanilla-flavored instant pudding and pie filling
4 eggs
⅓ cup vegetable oil

⅓ cup sour cream
1 cup commercial applesauce
1 cup finely-chopped raisins
½ teaspoon cinnamon
¼ teaspoon nutmeg

Blend all ingredients in large mixer bowl. Beat 4 minutes at medium speed of electric mixer. Pour into greased and floured Bundt pan. Bake at 350° for 50 to 55 minutes, or until cake springs back when lightly pressed and pulls away from sides of pan. Do not underbake. Cool in pan 15 minutes; remove and cool on rack. Top with Confectioners Sugar Glaze.

Confectioners Sugar Glaze

Stir about 1 tablespoon hot milk or water into 1 cup sifted confectioners sugar.

September - Third Week

Peanuts and peanut butter are no longer considered just a ball game snack or part of a kid's sandwich, says the Peanut Advisory Board. Nutrition-minded consumers also recognize the importance of the peanut as an alternative to traditional protein foods such as meat, fish and poultry. By using peanuts and other plant protein sources in everyday menus, one can add variety, reduce cost and provide a balanced intake of nutrients. With nutritionists recommending a reduction in the intake of saturated fat, peanuts are a good choice since they're low in saturated fat and contain no cholesterol.

When using vegetable proteins such as peanuts in place of animal protein, keep in mind that the value of the protein is classified in terms of its amino acid composition. Of the 20 or more amino acids that are known, our bodies cannot manufacture eight, which are called essential amino acids. Therefore, our everyday diet must provide them. Animal protein provides all of the essential amino acids, while vegetable proteins must be "paired up" with each other to assure that all eight essential amino acids are present in a meal. For example, peanut butter becomes a complete protein source when served with bread. Peanuts and rice constitute another pair of vegetable proteins that, when served together, are "complete" and provide all eight of the essential amino acids.

Here are more interesting facts concerning peanuts and peanut butter:

1. Defatted peanuts with the oil squeezed out are now being sold nationwide. One-fourth of a cup of these low-calorie peanuts contain about 100 calories, or about half the calories of regular peanuts.

2. Peanuts contain fiber or "roughage" valuable in assisting the digestive system.

3. An ounce of cocktail-type peanuts contains less salt than leading brands of cornflakes.

4. The digestibility of peanuts is very high, with little difference between raw and processed nuts. Peanut butter is one of the most nutritious foods available to Americans. It is 26 percent protein, which exceeds the protein content in most other foods. Peanut butter is also a good source of niacin, thiamin, and other B vitamins, as well as eleven of the thirteen essential minerals. A child can get 40 percent of his daily protein needs from only four tablespoons of peanut butter (the amount usually used for two sandwiches). Two peanut butter sandwiches, a glass of milk and a serving of fruit can supply about one-third of the daily nutritional needs of a growing child. When served as a main dish item, one-fourth cup of peanut butter may be used in place of one serving of meat.

Peanut butter was first used as a food for invalids because of its high nutritive value, easy digestibility, and palatability. By federal regulations, 90 percent of peanut butter must be peanuts. No artificial flavors or sweeteners, chemical preservatives, natural or artificial color, purified vitamins or minerals are allowed. Additives are limited to salt, sweeteners, and stabilizers.

SUNDAY
Broiled lamb chops
Creamed potatoes
Minted carrots and peas *
Tomato aspic / Bran muffins
Quick Black Forest pie *

MINTED CARROTS AND PEAS

½ pound carrots, scraped and sliced
½ teaspoon sugar
1 teaspoon salt
Boiling water

1 (10 ounce) package frozen green peas
2 tablespoons butter or margarine
1 tablespoon fresh mint leaves or ½
tablespoon of dried mint

Combine carrot slices, sugar and salt in sauce pan. Cover with water, bring to a boil and cook about 15 minutes. Add peas and cook 10 minutes longer, or until carrots and peas are tender. Melt butter and stir in mint leaves. Drain vegetables and toss with minted butter. (4 servings)

QUICK BLACK FOREST PIE

1 (3 ounce) package instant chocolate pudding
and pie filling
1 cup milk

1 (8 oz) package frozen whipped topping, thawed
1 prepared graham cracker crust
1 (21 ounce) can cherry pie filling

Combine in a bowl, pudding and milk; mix for one minute. Fold in 1 ½ cups whipped topping. Frost pie with remaining topping. Cover topping with 1 can of cherry pie filling. Refrigerate for at least 2 hours before serving.

MONDAY
Cucumber soup *
Chicken salad pocket sandwiches *
Relish tray - carrots, celery, green pepper
Ginger snaps

CUCUMBER SOUP

3 cucumbers, peeled and sliced
3 cups chicken broth, plus 4 chicken bouillon cubes
1/4 cup chopped onion
1/4 cup flour
1 bay leaf
1 teaspoon salt

3 cucumbers, peeled, seeded and sliced
1 cup heavy cream or half & half
1 cup sour cream
2 tablespoons fresh lemon juice
Fresh chopped parsley or fresh dill

In a large saucepan, add 3 cucumbers, sliced, chicken broth and bouillon cubes, onion, flour, bay leaf and salt. Bring to a boil; turn heat down and simmer for 15 minutes. Place in a blender jar and blend until smooth. Chill. Place remaining cucumbers in blender jar and blend until smooth. Add to hot mixture. Combine cream, sour cream and lemon juice; add to cucumber mixture; blend thoroughly. Correct seasoning. Serve cold, in punch cups, topped with chopped parsley or dill. 6 servings.

CHICKEN SALAD POCKET SANDWICH

2 cups cooked chicken, chopped
1/2 cup finely-chopped celery
1/4 cup green onion, use tops also
2 hard-cooked eggs, chopped
1 tablespoon lemon juice

1/2 teaspoon salt
1/4 teaspoon pepper
Dash cayenne pepper
3/4 cup mayonnaise

Combine all ingredients, mixing well. Can be covered and refrigerated for several hours to allow flavors to blend. Use as a sandwich filling for pita bread or your favorite sandwich bread. (4 sandwiches)

Pita bread (Pocket bread)

1 teaspoon sugar
1/2 teaspoon salt
3/4 cup hot water

1 envelope (1 tablespoon) dry yeast
2 cups flour

In mixing bowl, combine sugar, salt and hot water; stir to dissolve sugar and salt. Allow to cool to lukewarm. Sprinkle yeast over mixture and allow to dissolve. Add flour, 1/2 cup at a time. Turn dough onto floured surface and knead thoroughly. Divide dough into 12 small pieces. Roll dough pieces into balls. With rolling pin, roll each ball into a 5-inch circle and place on baking sheet. Bake at 500° for 5-7 minutes, or until puffed and golden. (Makes 12 rounds)

TUESDAY
Lentil soup *
Minute steaks in garlic butter
Buttered beets
Tossed salad / Orange muffins *
Chocolate custard *

LENTIL SOUP

¹/₂ cup chopped onions
¹/₂ cup chopped celery
1 pound bulk hot pork sausage
1 pound hamburger
2 cups lentils
8 cups water
2 cans tomato paste

2 bay leaves
¹/₂ teaspoon oregano
1 teaspoon basil
1 teaspoon garlic salt
¹/₄ cup brown sugar
Salt and pepper to taste

Saute onions and celery together in oil. Brown sausage and hamburger and drain off grease. Combine sauteed onion and celery with meat, lentils and water. Add tomato paste, basil, garlic salt, brown sugar, salt and pepper. Simmer until lentils are cooked, about 30 minutes. 6-8 servings.

ORANGE MUFFINS

2 eggs
¹/₂ cup oil
1 can (6 ounce) frozen orange juice
Grated rind of 2 oranges
1 cup applesauce
4 cups flour

1 ¹/₂ cups sugar
1 tablespoon baking powder
2 teaspoons baking soda
¹/₂ teaspoon mace
¹/₂ cup sugar
¹/₂ cup chopped nuts

Place eggs and oil in mixer bowl. Mix thoroughly. Add orange juice and rind of one orange and applesauce; continue beating. Sift flour, sugar, baking powder, soda and mace. Stir into the egg mixture until well-blended. Spoon into greased muffin tins. (May be lined with paper) Blend ¹/₂ cup sugar, nuts and rind of one orange; sprinkle on top of each muffin. Bake in a 375° oven for 20 to 25 minutes. (Yield: 24 muffins)

CHOCOLATE CUSTARD

1 egg
1 cup chocolate chips
1 teaspoon vanilla

1 teaspoon instant coffee
²/₃ cup milk

Place egg, chocolate chips, vanilla, coffee in blender jar; blend. Bring milk to a boil. Add boiling milk to the blender. Blend for one minute. Place in individual cups or in a pint-size mold. Chill for 2-3 hours before serving. Note: Two tablespoons of Amaretto may be added to the custard before the milk is added. If too stiff, add 2 tablespoons of milk.

WEDNESDAY
Seafood dinner casserole deluxe
Chicken wild rice salad *
Buttered broccoli spears
Pickled peaches
French lemon puffs *

SEAFOOD DINNER CASSEROLE DELUXE

2 cups cooked and peeled shrimp	*1 medium onion, chopped*
1 (6 ounce) can crab meat	*1 large green pepper, chopped*
1 (6 ½ ounce) can tuna fish in water or 1 cup raw oysters	*¼ cup Worcestershire sauce*
1 cup frozen peas, thawed but uncooked	*1 teaspoon salt*
1½ cups cooked rice	*½ teaspoon pepper*
1 cup mayonnaise	*2 tablespoons butter or margarine, melted*
1 cup chopped celery	*1 cup cracker or bread crumbs*

Combine all ingredients except butter and crumbs. Pour into 1½ quart casserole. Combine butter and crumbs; sprinkle over casserole. Bake in 350° oven for 35-45 minutes.

FRENCH LEMON PUFFS

1 egg	*2 cups biscuit mix*
2 tablespoons sugar	*⅓ cup butter or margarine, melted*
Thin rind of 1 lemon	*½ cup sugar*
1 cup milk	

Put egg, sugar, rind and milk into blender container. Combine, cover and process at MIX until rind is chopped fine. Remove cover and add biscuit mix; continue processing only until mixture is smooth. Fill greased muffin tins one-half full. Bake in 400° oven for 12 to 15 minutes, until lightly browned. While muffins are hot, dip tops into melted butter, then into sugar. Work fast so muffins will not cool. (Makes 18-21 puffs, depending on size of muffin cups.)

THURSDAY
Baked ham with sour cream mustard sauce *
Baked sweet potato (in skin)
Green beans with almonds
Lettuce with thick Roquefort dressing
Homemade pumpernickel bread *
Orange sherbet with mandarin topping

SOUR CREAM MUSTARD SAUCE

1 cup sour cream	*½ teaspoon salt*
1 tablespoon lemon juice	*1 tablespoon prepared mustard*
2 tablespoons sugar	*1 egg yolk, beaten*

Whip sour cream. Continue beating and slowly blend in remaining ingredients.

PUMPERNICKEL BREAD

1 ½ cups cold water	*1 tablespoon caraway seeds*
¾ cup yellow corn meal	*2 packages active dry yeast*
1 ½ cups boiling water	*¼ cup very warm water*
1 ½ teaspoons salt	*2 cups mashed potatoes*
2 tablespoons sugar	*4 cups rye flour*
2 tablespoons butter or margarine	*4 cups whole wheat flour*

Add cold water to cornmeal in a saucepan, stir until smooth. Stir in boiling water and cook, stirring constantly, until thick. Add salt, sugar, butter and caraway seeds. Cool to lukewarm. Dissolve yeast in warm water. Add yeast and mashed potatoes to cornmeal mixture. Mix well. Combine rye and whole wheat flour and stir into mixture. Knead until smooth and satiny. Put into greased bowl, turn once, cover and let rise until doubled, about 1 hour. Punch down, divide dough into 3 portions and form into round loaves. Place on greased pans and let rise until doubled, about 45 minutes. Bake in a moderately hot oven (375°) for about 1 hour. (Makes 3 loaves; freeze two if desired.)

FRIDAY
Teens' Supper After the Football Game
Pigs in a blanket *
Baked beans
Potato casserole
Carrot and raisin salad
Chocolate fondue with fruit *

PIGS IN A BLANKET

1 package refrigerated crescent rolls   *Chopped onions*
Catsup   *8 frankfurters*
Mustard

Unroll dough from 1 package refrigerated crescent rolls. Separate dough along perforation. For each sandwich, place frankfurters at shortest side of triangle. Top with mustard and sprinkle with chopped onions. Brush with catsup if desired. Roll up to opposite point. The ends of the hot dog will peek out from biscuit "blanket." Put sandwiches on an ungreased baking sheet, point side of roll down. Bake at 450° for 10-12 minutes. Biscuits should be lightly browned. Serve hot. (Makes 4-8 servings)

CHOCOLATE FONDUE WITH FRUIT

1 cup (6 oz package) semi-sweet chocolate pieces   *²/3 cup undiluted evaporated milk*
½ cup creamed white honey

Melt chocolate pieces and honey in medium sauce pan over low heat. Add milk. Beat to blend well. Pour into a fondue pot or small chafing dish and keep warm while serving. For dunking, use pieces of fruit, cake or large marshmallows speared on wooden picks or fondue forks. For example, use drained canned pineapple cubes, drained mandarin oranges, banana chunks, fresh apple slices, seedless grapes or angel food cake torn into bite-size pieces. (6 servings) For a great chocolate sundae, pour warm fondue sauce over vanilla ice cream.

SATURDAY
Kiddies' Lunch Party
Have fun cooking and eating together!
Outer space tuna sandwiches *
Relish tray - carrot sticks, celery sticks, apple slices, quartered hard-cooked eggs,
Cheddar cheese sticks, strawberries, raisins, peanuts
Commercial ice cream bars
Rocky road toads *
Pineapple bubble-up * and chocolate milk

Plan Of Work

Day before:

1. Let the children hosting the party help make the cookies.
2. Purchase commercial ice cream bars and freeze.

Early in the day:

3. Children and parents make the sandwiches.

About 1 hour before the party:

4. An adult should prepare the relish tray since it involves the use of sharp objects in preparation.
5. Mix beverage (pineapple bubble-up) ahead, except the lemon-lime carbonated beverage is added at the time of serving. *Guests take home leftover cookies.*

OUTER SPACE TUNA SANDWICH

2 (6 ½ or 7 ounce) cans tuna, drained and flaked	2 tablespoons chopped onions
2 hard-cooked eggs, chopped	½ cup mayonnaise
³/₄ cup chopped celery	16 slices whole wheat bread
½ cup chopped sweet pickle chips	

Combine all ingredients and mix well. Spread generously over 8 slices of bread. Top with the remaining slices. 8 thick sandwiches, cut in thirds.

ROCKY ROAD TOADS

2 (6 ½-ounce) bars milk chocolate	1 cup miniature marshmallows
1 cup seedless raisins	½ cup chopped walnuts or pecans

Break chocolate up into top of double boiler. Set over warm water. (Warning: the water must never get really hot or the chocolate will have white streaks when it sets. Set the double boiler over very low heat, or simply keep changing water in the lower pan and don't put it on the stove at all.) Stir the chocolate frequently, and when it is completely melted, stir in the raisins, marshmallows and nuts. Cover a baking sheet with waxed paper. Dip a teaspoonful of candy, and push it off onto the waxed paper with another spoon. Makes about 2 dozen large pieces.

PINEAPPLE BUBBLE-UP

1 (46 oz) can unsweetened pineapple juice, chilled	1 (1 liter) bottle lemon-lime carbonated beverage
1 (6 ounce) can frozen lemonade concentrate	Ice

Stir pineapple juice and lemonade concentrate together. Mix well. Just before serving, add the carbonated beverage. Serve over ice cubes in a punch bowl or in individual glasses. 9 servings.

September - Fourth Week

Ham has really come a long way. It is a popular meat because it is economical, nutritious and convenient. It also has lots of fine flavor and appetite appeal. But there are certain facts the consumer should know about ham to receive maximum value and satisfaction.

Like all red meat, ham and other processed pork are outstanding sources of high-quality protein which the body needs to build, maintain and repair tissue, and help fight infection and disease. The body constantly tears down and builds up tissue, but stores little protein; therefore, high protein foods such as ham and other meats should be eaten daily.

Ham contains the B vitamins needed for normal metabolism of other nutrients and for good vision, clear eyes, normal appetite, healthy skin and includes riboflavin (B2), niacin, thiamin (B1), B-6 and B-12. Thiamine deserves special mention because pork is the leading meat source of thiamine, containing three times as much as any other food. Two important minerals found in smoked ham are iron and zinc. Food iron is essential in forming and maintaining red blood cells and in prevention of anemia. Scientists claim that when meat is included in a meal, the absorption of iron from other foods in the diet is enhanced. Zinc is necessary for children's growth and normal development, to hasten wound healing and for normal senses of taste and smell.

Also, ham is not high in calories. According to the USDA listing of the Nutritive Value of American Foods, a 3-ounce portion of ham, lean without visible fat and boneless, contains 184 calories compared to 222 calories in a 3-ounce portion of round steak. Ham trimmed of excess visible fat is a nutritional bargain.

Since ham is one of the old-fashioned American favorite foods, correct decisions about ham and other smoked pork products must be made at home and at the market concerning selection, cooking and storage information. Food ads can help meal planners achieve variety and economy. There are so many styles and types of ham and one kind is usually the buy of the week.

Meat costing the least per pound may not always be the best buy. Cuts should be compared by cost per serving, not cost per pound. To figure the cost per serving, divide the price per pound by the number of servings per pound.

Here are general guidelines to number of servings:
• Boneless or canned hams - 5 servings per pound.
• Cuts with some bone - 2 to 3 servings per pound.
• Cuts with a large amount of bone - 1 to 1 ½ servings per pound.

Buying large cuts and cutting into smaller portions at home can mean big savings because less labor is required for cutting and packaging at the market. In selecting ham cuts, the lean should be firm, fine-grained, free from excess moisture and pink in color. The fat covering should be firm and white. Sometimes an iridescence or rainbow-like appearance will show on the cut surface. This is caused by the refraction of light on the cut ends of the muscle fiber and is in no way harmful.

Read the label to identify the ham. It can serve as a cooking guide; for example, "fully cooked" means the ham has been completely cooked and needs to be heated only if it is to be served warm. "Cook before eating" means it was not fully cooked during processing and should be cooked to the internal temperature of 160°. If no label is present, assume the ham has not been cooked at all.

The term "water added" may also appear on the label. Most processed hams are pumped with a curing solution and then smoked. If enough moisture does not evaporate during smoking to return the ham to its original fresh weight, it is labeled "water added." These hams may contain up to 10 percent added moisture; hams over 10 percent must be labeled "imitation."

Proper handling is essential to protect the flavor and quality of ham and other smoked pork cuts. These products should be placed in the coldest part of the refrigerator promptly and can usually be stored in their original wrapping for at least a week. Some packages have a freshness date that will aid in determining how long these can be stored. Use ham slices within 3 to 4 days.

Leftover cooked ham should be tightly wrapped or covered and refrigerated within 1 to 2 hours after cooking. It may be stored in the refrigerator for 4 to 5 days.

Ham and other smoked pork products do not keep their high quality long in the freezer because changes in flavor and texture can occur. If freezing, tightly seal in moisture-proof and vapor-proof wrap and store at 0° or lower for no longer than 2 months.

SUNDAY
Turkey and rice pie *
Buttered peas
Relishes - green onions, radishes, celery, pickles
Hot buttered rolls
Pineapple baked apples *

TURKEY AND RICE PIE
Turkey Crust

1 pound ground turkey	*¼ cup catsup*
½ cup bread crumbs	*½ teaspoon salt*
¼ cup onion	*¼ teaspoon pepper*
¼ cup chopped green pepper	*⅛ teaspoon oregano*

Combine all ingredients and mix thoroughly. Pat into bottom and sides of a 9-inch pie plate and pinch fluting around edges. Set aside. (Ground turkey may be purchased. If not available, use 2 cups raw turkey ground at home.)

Filling

1 ⅓ cups packaged precooked rice	*1 ¼ cup shredded Cheddar cheese (divided)*
1 (8 ounce) can tomato sauce	*1 cup sour cream*
1 cup water	*2 tablespoons chili sauce*
½ teaspoon salt	

Combine rice, tomato sauce, water, ½ cup cheese and salt. Spoon into meat shell and cover with foil. Bake at 350° for 30 minutes. Remove from oven; remove foil. Sprinkle with ½ cup shredded cheese. Bake 10 minutes. Combine sour cream and chili sauce. Just before serving, "frost" with sour cream/ chili sauce mixture and sprinkle with remaining ¼ cup of cheese. Cut into pie-shaped pieces (6 servings).

PINEAPPLE BAKED APPLE

6 large apples	*¾ cup of juice-packed, crushed pineapple*
2 cups water	

Core apples without cutting through bottom. Place apples in a small baking dish. Fill center with drained, crushed pineapple. Pour a small amount of water around the apples (do not pour water over the apples). Bake covered at 375° for about 60 minutes or until apples are tender. (6 servings) Variations: raisins, cinnamon or nutmeg may be added to the pineapple.

MONDAY
Ham 'n egg pudding *
Steamed cauliflower and peas
Fried apple slices
English muffins with jam

HAM 'N EGG PUDDING

2 cups milk	*1 teaspoon salt*
2 cups soft bread crumbs	*⅛ teaspoon pepper*
1 cup diced cooked ham	*6 eggs, separated*
2 tablespoons butter, melted	*¼ teaspoon cream of tartar*
1 tablespoon dried minced onion	*¼ cup grated Parmesan cheese*

Combine milk, bread crumbs, ham, butter, minced onion, salt and pepper. Beat egg yolks until thick and lemon-colored, about 5 minutes. Stir egg yolks into bread mixture. Beat egg whites and cream of tartar until stiff but not dry, or just until whites no longer slip when bowl is tilted. Gently fold whites into yolk mixture. Pour into greased 12x7x2-inch baking dish. Top with Parmesan cheese. Bake in preheated 325° oven for 30 minutes or until knife inserted near center comes out clean. Serve immediately. (6 servings)

TUESDAY
Knoxville chicken *
Celery and potato bake *
Citrus fruit with honey mustard dressing
Bread sticks
Pound cake with raspberries and whipped topping

KNOXVILLE CHICKEN

3 whole broiler-fryer chicken breasts, cut in half	*¼ cup chopped chutney*
2 tablespoons butter or margarine	*1 ½ cups orange juice*
1 teaspoon salt	*½ teaspoon cinnamon*
¼ teaspoon pepper	*½ teaspoon curry powder*
½ cup blanched, slivered almonds	*⅟₁₆ teaspoon or a pinch of thyme*
½ cup raisins	

In greased, large, shallow baking pan, place chicken in a single layer, skin side up. Dot with butter. Sprinkle salt and pepper on chicken. Bake in 425° oven for 15 minutes. In sauce pan combine almonds, raisins, chutney, orange juice, cinnamon, curry and thyme; simmer about 10 minutes or until flavors blend. Pour sauce over chicken. Reduce heat to 350° and bake about an hour longer or until fork can be inserted in chicken with ease. (6 servings)

CELERY AND POTATO BAKE

3 cups thinly-sliced celery	*⅛ teaspoon black pepper*
3 cups thinly-sliced unpeeled new potatoes	*¼ cup (½ stick) melted butter or margarine*
1 ½ cups thinly-sliced onions	*½ cup dry bread crumbs*
3 tablespoons all-purpose flour	*¼ cup grated Parmesan cheese*
½ cup milk	*¼ teaspoon garlic powder*
¼ cup (½ stick) butter or margarine	*1 tablespoon paprika*
1 ³/₄ teaspoons salt	

Fill a 2-quart casserole with alternating layers of celery, potatoes and onions, sprinkling 1 tablespoon flour evenly over each layer. Combine milk, ¼ cup butter, salt and pepper. Heat and pour over the casserole. Cover and bake at 350° for 30 minutes. Uncover casserole. Combine the melted butter, bread crumbs, cheese, garlic powder and paprika. Sprinkle over the top. Continue baking, uncovered, for 20 minutes. (6 servings)

WEDNESDAY
Baked cabbage and beef casserole *
Apple and nut salad
Corn muffins / Cherry brownie pie *

BAKED CABBAGE AND BEEF CASSEROLE

4 strips bacon, finely-chopped	*1 egg, slightly beaten*
½ cup finely-chopped onion	*¼ cup soft bread crumbs*
1 teaspoon salt	*1 pound ground beef*
Pepper to taste	*1 small head cabbage, shredded*
½ teaspoon poultry seasoning	*1 cube beef bouillon, dissolved in 1 cup boiling water*

Fry bacon until crisp; crumble and set aside. Add onion and saute until it is transparent. Combine beef, salt, pepper, poultry seasoning, egg and bread crumbs. Add onion and half of the bacon. Place a layer of shredded cabbage in a 1 ½-quart baking dish; top with layer of meat mixture. Continue alternating layers, ending with cabbage. Pour bouillon over all. Sprinkle remaining half of crumbled bacon over top. Cover and bake at 350° for 1 hour. Remove cover during last 15 minutes, to brown. (6 servings)

CHERRY BROWNIE PIE

⅓ cup butter or margarine	*2 ounces unsweetened chocolate, melted*
¾ cup sugar	*⅔ cup sifted flour*
1 teaspoon vanilla	*½ teaspoon salt*
2 eggs, beaten	*1 cup cherry pie filling*
⅓ cup light corn syrup	

Combine butter, sugar and vanilla in mixing bowl until well-blended. Add eggs and corn syrup; beat until smooth. Blend in melted chocolate. Combine flour and salt; stir into chocolate mixture. Spread cherry filling in bottom of greased 9-inch pie plate to about 1 inch from edge. Spoon brownie mixture over cherries; spread to edges of plate. Bake in 350° oven for 40 to 45 minutes or until cake tester comes out clean. If desired, serve with ice milk. Note: If metal pie pan is used, bake 30 to 35 minutes.

THURSDAY
Supper sandwiches *
Fresh fruit salad / Carrot 'n pudding cake *

SUPPER SANDWICHES

1 (10 ounce) package frozen broccoli spears	*1 tablespoon prepared mustard*
6 servings thinly-sliced cooked ham (commercial)	*1 tablespoon lemon juice*
2 tablespoons butter	*1 (2 ½ oz) can mushrooms, drained and diced*
2 tablespoons flour	*6 slices toasted rye bread*
½ teaspoon salt	*⅓ cup shredded Cheddar cheese*
2 cups undiluted evaporated milk	

Cook broccoli according to package directions. Wrap ham in foil and heat in slow oven (325°) until warm. Melt butter in sauce pan over medium heat. Blend in flour and salt. Gradually add milk; stir until blended. Cook over medium heat until smooth and thickened, stirring constantly. Stir in mustard, lemon juice and mushrooms. Place toast slice in bottom of each of 6 individual casseroles or all six slices on cookie sheet. Top toast slice with one serving hot ham and 2 to 3 spears hot cooked broccoli. Spoon about ⅓ cup sauce over each sandwich; sprinkle with cheese. Broil 30 seconds or until cheese melts. (6 servings)

CARROT 'N PUDDING CAKE

1 (1 pound 2 ¼-ounce) package yellow cake mix
1 (3 ½-ounce) package instant vanilla pudding and pie filling
4 eggs
⅓ cup water
¼ cup oil

3 cups grated carrots
½ cup raisins, finely-cut
½ cup walnuts or pecans
½ teaspoon salt
2 teaspoons cinnamon

Place all above ingredients into a processor bowl. Beat until well mixed. Pour batter into 2 greased and floured 8x4-inch loaf pans. Bake in 350° oven for 45-50 minutes or until cake springs back when touched. Do not overbake. Cool in pan 15 minutes. Remove and cool on racks. Frost with Orange Cream Cheese Frosting.

Orange Cream Cheese Frosting

1 tablespoon butter or margarine
1 (3 ounce) package cream cheese
1 teaspoon grated orange rind

2 ½ cups sifted confectioners' sugar
1 tablespoon orange juice

Blend butter and cheese. Add orange rind and beat until smooth. Alternately add sugar with orange juice. Beat until smooth. Frost tops of the cakes.

FRIDAY
Tuna croquettes *
Fresh tomato casserole *
Western carrots *
Jellied pineapple salad *
Whole wheat bread slices
Ice cream with caramel sauce

TUNA CROQUETTES

3 tablespoons butter or margarine, divided
⅓ cup flour
½ cup milk
2 tablespoons finely-chopped onion
1 tablespoon snipped parsley
2 teaspoons lemon juice
¼ teaspoon salt

Dash pepper
Dash paprika
2 (6 ½ or 7 oz) cans tuna, drained & flaked
¾ cup fine dry bread crumbs
1 egg, beaten
2 tablespoons water

Melt 2 tablespoons of butter, then blend in flour. Add milk. Cook and stir over medium heat until very thick and smooth; remove from heat. Add onion, parsley, lemon juice, salt, pepper and paprika; stir in tuna. Chill. Shape tuna mixture into 8 cones, about ¼ cup for each. Roll in crumbs. Combine egg with water. Dip cones in egg mixture; roll in crumbs again. In electric skillet, add 1 tablespoon of butter, fry a few croquettes at a time at 350°, until brown and hot, about 3 minutes. Turn if necessary for even cooking. Drain on paper towel. Keep croquettes hot. (4 servings)

FRESH TOMATO CASSEROLE

1 ¼ cups packaged onion and garlic croutons
3 medium-sized ripe tomatoes (1 pound) cut
   in ¼-inch slices
6 ounces Mozzarella cheese, cut in thin slices

2 tablespoons chopped fresh basil
1 tablespoon snipped fresh chives
Freshly ground black pepper, to taste
2 tblsps bottled red wine vinegar and oil dressing

Scatter croutons over bottom of 9-inch glass pie plate. Overlap alternate slices of tomato and Mozzarella cheese on top in a circular pattern to cover the layer of croutons. Sprinkle with basil, chives and pepper. Microwave uncovered on HIGH 3 ½-4 ½ minutes until cheese is melted. Remove from oven, spoon dressing on top. Let stand 5 minutes for flavors to develop. (6 servings)

JELLIED PINEAPPLE SALAD

2 tablespoons (2 envelopes) plain gelatin
¼ cup cold water
1 cup pineapple juice
2 tablespoons lemon juice
2 tablespoons sugar

Pinch of salt
¾ cup drained crushed pineapple
½ cup finely-chopped celery
1 cup cottage cheese

Soak gelatin in the cold water for 5 minutes. Combine pineapple juice, lemon juice, sugar, salt and gelatin. Heat and stir until gelatin is dissolved. Chill until partially set. Stir in the pineapple, celery and cottage cheese. Pour into a 1-quart mold and chill until firm. (6-8 servings)

WESTERN CARROTS

¾ cup water
6 medium carrots, sliced
3 tablespoons butter or margarine
¼ cup bacon, cooked and crumbled

2 green onions, sliced; use tops
1 tablespoon firmly-packed brown sugar
¼ teaspoon salt
⅛ teaspoon pepper

In 2-quart sauce pan, bring water to a boil. Add carrots. Cover; cook over medium heat until carrots are crisply tender, 10 to 12 minutes. Drain. In same sauce pan, add butter, carrots, bacon, green onions, brown sugar, salt and pepper. Cover; cook over medium heat, stirring occasionally, until heated through, 5 to 7 minutes. (4 servings)

SATURDAY
Neighborhood Saturday Night Supper
Braised beef tips on buttered rice *
Golden corn and tomato casserole *
Quick wilted lettuce salad *
Sour cream biscuits (commercial)
Praline sundae *
Oatmeal squares *

Plan Of Work

Day before:

1. Prepare praline topping and glazed oatmeal squares.

Two hours before serving time:

2. Start preparing the beef strips.

One hour before serving:

3. Assemble vegetable casserole.

4. Wash lettuce and have ingredients ready for preparing salad dressing.

5. Place vegetable casserole in oven.

6. Prepare rice on range top.

Fifteen minutes before serving:

7. Cook salad dressing.

8. Complete salad.

9. Heat biscuits.

10. Have praline topping at room temperature.

BRAISED BEEF STRIPS

1 ½ pounds beef bottom round steak, cut ³/₄ to 1-inch thick	½ cup hot water
1 teaspoon salt	2 (10 oz) packages, cut frozen green beans, defrosted
½ teaspoon thyme	8 ounces mushrooms, sliced
⅛ teaspoon pepper	³/₄ cup buttermilk
1 beef bouillon cube	1 tablespoon cornstarch

Trim separable fat from steak; slowly heat fat in large frying pan or Dutch oven to obtain 1 tablespoon drippings. Discard fat. Cut steak into ³/₄ to 1-inch cubes; brown in drippings. Combine salt, thyme and pepper and sprinkle over meat. Crush bouillon cube and dissolve in hot water; add to meat. Cover tightly and cook slowly 1 ½ hours. Stir in green beans and mushrooms; continue cooking, covered, 13 minutes. Add buttermilk to cornstarch, stirring to blend; gradually add to meat mixture and cook until thickened, stirring occasionally. Continue cooking 2 minutes. (4-6 servings)

GOLDEN CORN AND TOMATO CASSEROLE

8 slices of bacon, cut into halves	Salt to taste
2 cups fine bread crumbs	Pepper to taste
2 cups tomatoes, peeled and chopped	¼ cup (½ stick) butter or margarine, melted
1 green pepper, chopped	
3 cups corn kernels, uncooked, or 2 (10 ounce) packages of frozen whole kernel corn	

Put four slices of the bacon in the bottom of a shallow 2-quart casserole. Top with half of the bread crumbs. Add in layers the tomatoes, green peppers and corn, which have been seasoned with salt and pepper. Combine remaining cup of bread crumbs with the melted butter. Sprinkle on top. Cover with the remaining bacon and bake in 375° oven for 40 minutes or until lightly browned. (6 servings)

QUICK WILTED LETTUCE SALAD

1 head lettuce
6 slices bacon
3 tablespoons warm bacon drippings

1 ½ teaspoons sugar
³/₄teaspoon salt
⅓ cup vinegar

Wash, core and drain lettuce. Cut or tear lettuce in bowl. Cook bacon until crisp. Crumble and set aside. In 3 tablespoons of warm drippings, add sugar and salt; stir and dissolve. Add vinegar to bacon dripping mixture. Sprinkle bacon on lettuce and pour hot mixture over lettuce. Toss lightly. (6 servings)

PRALINE SUNDAES

⅓ cup water
⅓ cup brown sugar, packed
1 cup white corn syrup
1 cup chopped pecans

⅛ teaspoon rum extract
⅛ teaspoon maple extract
Vanilla ice cream

Combine water, sugar and corn syrup in saucepan. Cook on low heat until mixture comes to a boil. Add nuts and flavoring. Cool. Cover and refrigerate. Warm to room temperature and serve over vanilla ice cream. 1 pint sauce.

GLAZED OATMEAL SQUARES

1 ¼ cups boiling water
1 cup quick oats
½ cup (1 stick) butter or margarine
1 cup sugar
2 eggs, slightly beaten

1 ⅓ cups flour
1 cup brown sugar, firmly-packed
1 teaspoon baking soda
½ teaspoon cinnamon

In a large mixing bowl, combine the boiling water, oatmeal and butter. Allow to set 20 minutes. Add the remaining ingredients and stir until smooth. Pour into a greased 9x13-inch pan. Bake at 350° for 35 minutes.

Topping

½ cup (1 stick) butter or margarine
¼ cup evaporated milk
½ cup sugar

1 teaspoon vanilla
1 cup flaked coconut
1 cup chopped pecans

Combine all the ingredients; mix and spoon over cake while still warm. Put under broiler for 2 minutes. Yield: 24 squares.

October

October - First Week

Beef, by demand, is one of America's favorite foods. When excess fat is removed, beef is an excellent source of good quality protein, iron, the essential B vitamins and other nutrients. According to the National Meat Board, there are 19 cuts of beef under 300 calories per 3 ½ ounces cooked, boneless serving. This includes the meat and the marbling, which is the long network of fat embedded within the muscle tissue. Even weight watchers can include beef in their diets.

To retain its quality, fresh beef should be stored uncovered or loosely wrapped in the coldest part of the refrigerator or in the compartment designed for meat storage. Beef prepackaged for self-service should have the wrapper loosened before placing in the refrigerator or in the meat compartment. Cooked beef will keep better if left in large pieces and not cut until ready to use. This helps prevent contamination.

The method selected for cooking fresh beef depends upon the tenderness, size and thickness of the cut and the available cooking facilities. Tender cuts of beef from the loin area can be cooked by dry heat methods, which are: roasting, broiling, outside grilling and pan frying. Large cuts, including rib, rump and sirloin tip, should be roasted at 300° to 325° until the inserted meat thermometer registers rare, medium or well-done. It is best to allow large cuts to set 15 to 30 minutes before carving.

Tender steaks, such as T-bone, porterhouse, sirloin and filet mignon, cut one inch or more thick, should be broiled or grilled to desired degree of doneness. Tender steaks cut less than one inch thick may be pan broiled or pan fried.

Less tender cuts such as the shoulder cuts, referred to as chuck, the hind quarter which includes the rump, round, leg and flank steak, can be made tender by cooking in moist heat (such as stewing or braising), which consists of browning the meat, then adding water, broth or tomato juice to complete cooking.

The grade of the meat and the cut of the meat, which indicates the location of the cut on the animal body, will determine the tenderness. The parts of the animal body which get the most exercise, which develops connective tissue, are the least tender.

However, the less tender cuts of meat can be equally as tender and juicy if cooked correctly. So, whether it is a steak, pot roast or left over beef hash, the meat will be high in the same nutritive value to the health and welfare of the entire family.

SUNDAY
Company for a Chilly Sunday Lunch
Creamy green soup
Stuffed fillet of sole with shrimp sauce
Brussels sprouts with pecan butter
Honey fruit salad
Buttered biscuits (commercial)
Cranberries jubilee

Plan Of Work

Day before:

1. Prepare soup and reheat before serving.
2. Prepare cranberry jubilee, reheat and ignite just before serving.
3. Cook rice for fish dish.
4. Prepare shrimp sauce for fish dish and reheat before serving.

About an hour before serving:

5. Prepare salad and refrigerate.
6. Prepare fillet of sole.
7. While fish is cooking, prepare Brussels sprouts and reheat soup, and shrimp sauce.
8. Turn heat to low to heat jubilee slowly. It will be hot at the time of serving.

CREAMY GREEN SOUP

1 quart chicken broth (canned or home made)	1 large clove garlic, crushed
1 pound kale, washed and finely chopped	5 scallions, chopped, use tops
1/2 pound bok choy, washed and finely chopped	2 tablespoons flour
3 sprigs fresh tarragon or 1 teaspoon dried	1 cup evaporated milk
2 tablespoons olive oil	Freshly ground black pepper
1 large onion, chopped	Yogurt

In a large saucepan, bring chicken broth to a boil. Add kale, bok choy and tarragon; turn down heat and simmer 20-30 minutes. In a small skillet, heat oil, add onions, garlic and scallions, saute 2-3 minutes or until the onion is tender, do not brown. Sprinkle flour over the onion mixture and cook about 3 minutes over low heat, stirring constantly. Gradually add the onion and flower mixture to the liquid, stirring constantly, until it is slightly thickened. Transfer the soup mixture to a blender or food processor. Puree. Transfer soup back to a saucepan, and add evaporated milk. Heat and serve warm, with a dollop of yogurt. 6 servings.

FILLET OF SOLE WITH SHRIMP SAUCE

1 cup diced celery	1 teaspoon salt
1 cup sliced onion	1/4 teaspoon pepper
1 tablespoon butter or margarine	2 pounds sole fillets (or any fish)
3 cups cooked rice	Shrimp sauce
2 tablespoons diced pimiento	

Saute celery and onions in butter until tender. Add rice, pimiento and seasonings. Turn into a buttered 2-quart shallow baking dish. Arrange filets on top of rice. Season with additional salt and pepper. Bake at 375° for 15 minutes. Serve, topped with shrimp sauce. 6 servings.

Shrimp Sauce

3 tablespoons cornstarch	1/2 teaspoon basil
2 cups chicken broth	1/2 teaspoon garlic powder
2 (4 ounce) cans sliced mushrooms with liquid	18 shrimp, peeled and sliced in half lengthwise

Combine all ingredients and cook over low heat, stirring constantly, until thickened.

BRUSSELS SPROUTS WITH PECAN BUTTER

1 ½ pounds Brussels sprouts	½ cup coarsely-chopped pecans
1 inch boiling chicken stock	¼ cup (½ stick) butter or margarine
2 tablespoons chopped onion	Pimiento strips
½ teaspoon salt	Fresh parsley

Wash and trim Brussels sprouts. Soak in salted water to cover 20 minutes, using 1 teaspoon salt to 1 quart water. Drain and rinse with cold water. Place them in a saucepan with 1 inch boiling chicken stock, onion and salt. Bring to boiling point and cook, uncovered, 5 minutes. Cover and cook 10 minutes or until barely crisp-tender. Drain if necessary and keep hot. Saute pecans in butter 2-3 minutes or until butter is golden. Pour over Brussels sprouts. Toss lightly. Garnish with pimiento strips and a sprig of fresh parsley. 6 servings.

HONEY FRUIT SALAD

1 (20 ounce) can pineapple chunks, undrained	½ cup nuts (pecans or walnuts) coarsly chopped
2 medium oranges, peeled and sectioned	½ cup orange juice
1 large apple, unpeeled, sliced	¼ cup honey
1 banana, peeled, sliced	1 tablespoon lemon juice

Combine pineapple, oranges, apple, banana and nuts. Set aside. In small bowl, combine orange juice, honey and lemon juice. Pour over fruit, mix gently. Chill. 6 servings.

CRANBERRIES JUBILEE

1 cup sugar	¼ cup brandy
1 ½ cups water	Vanilla ice cream
2 cups (½ pound) fresh cranberries	

Combine sugar and water in saucepan; stir to dissolve sugar. Bring to a boil; boil 5 minutes. Add cranberries and bring to a boil again; cook 5 minutes. Turn into heat-proof bowl or blazer pan of chafing dish. Heat brandy. Ignite brandy and pour over cranberry mixture. Blend into sauce and serve immediately over ice cream. 6-8 servings.

MONDAY
Poultry and onion stew *
Scalloped potatoes
Savory green beans
Sliced tomatoes and cucumbers and green onions
Autumn apple bread and jam *

POULTRY AND ONION STEW

4 turkey thighs or fryer cut up	½ cup cider vinegar
12 small onions	Salt and pepper to taste
3 cloves garlic, whole	1 (16 ounce) can tomatoes
2 teaspoons pickling spices	1 (6 ounce) can tomato paste
2 tablespoons olive oil	1 teaspoon sugar

Wash meat and pat dry with paper towel. Brown slightly in 2 tablespoons oil. Peel onions and leave whole. Place half of the meat in the bottom of a Dutch oven. Add 6 onions on top. Place remaining meat on the onions, finishing with the remaining onions. Add garlic, cloves and pickling spices tied in cheesecloth bag. Then add vinegar, tomatoes, tomato paste and sugar. Cover tigthtly and heat to boiling. Turn heat low, cover and simmer 2 to 2 ¼ hours, until meat is tender and the liquid is reduced to a delicious sauce. Remove spices at once. 6-8 servings.

AUTUMN APPLE BREAD

¼ cup shortening
⅔ cup sugar
2 eggs, well-beaten
2 cups sifted flour
1 teaspoon baking powder

1 teaspoon baking soda
1 teaspoon salt
2 cups coarsely-grated apples
1 tablespoons grated lemon peel
⅔ cup chopped walnuts

Cream shortening and sugar until light and fluffy; beat in eggs. Mix and sift flour, baking powder, baking soda and salt; add alternately with grated apple to egg mixture. Stir in lemon peel and walnuts (batter will be stiff). Bake in greased and floured loaf pan, 8x5x2 inches, at 350° 50-60 minutes. Do not slice until cold.

TUESDAY
Ziti with fresh tomato sauce *
Mixed vegetable salad
Italian bread
Spumoni ice cream

ZITI WITH FRESH TOMATO SAUCE

¼ cup olive oil
3 large cloves garlic, crushed (may use more)
1 medium onion, chopped
1 small green pepper, chopped
6 or 7 fresh large tomatoes (about 3 pounds, chopped)
½ cup chopped fresh basil

3 tablespoons red wine vinegar
Salt to taste
Pepper to taste
1 (8 ounce) can mushroom stems and pieces, drained
1 (8 ounce) package ziti
Parmesan cheese (optional)

Heat oil in large skillet, add garlic, onions and pepper. Cook over low heat 3-5 minutes until vegetables are tender. Do not burn. Add tomatoes, basil, vinegar, salt, pepper and mushrooms. Cook about 3 minutes. Store until ready to use. May be done the day before. Cook ziti until cooked firm but tender (al dente). Do not overcook. Drain. Add most of the sauce, stir to mix well. Pour ziti into serving bowl, top with remaining sauce. Pass the Parmesan cheese. 4 servings.

WEDNESDAY
Savory pot roast with sour cream gravy *
Buttered noodles
Steamed carrots and peas
Broccoli-cheese salad *
Zucchini bread and cream cheese *

SAVORY POT ROAST WITH SOUR CREAM GRAVY

3-4 pound beef blade roast or arm pot roast
2 tablespoons cooking oil
1 beef bouillon cube
1 cup boiling water
¼ cup catsup
1 tablespoon Worcestershire sauce
1 tablespoon instant minced onion

2 teaspoons salt
1 teaspoon caraway seed
½ teaspoon pepper
1 (4 ½ ounce) can mushrooms
¼ cup flour
1 cup sour cream
Cooked noodles

Brown meat in cooking oil in large frying pan or Dutch oven. Pour off drippings. Crush bouillon cube and dissolve in boiling water. Add catsup, Worcestershire sauce, instant minced onion, salt, caraway seed and pepper; add to meat, cover and cook slowly, 2 to 2 ½ hours or until meat is tender. Drain mushrooms, reserving liquid. Add water to mushroom liquid to make ½ cup. Remove pot roast from pan. Blend flour and mushroom liquid and use to thicken gravy. Serve pot roast with noodles and gravy. 8 servings.

BROCCOLI-CHEESE SALAD

³/₄ pound broccoli (about 2 cups)
Boiling water
4 oz Cheddar cheese, cut in matchstick-sized pieces

¼ pound medium mushrooms, thinly slices
Creamy onion dressing (commercial)
Radishes (optional)

Trim broccoli stem ends and peel outer layer of stalks. Cut flowerets from stalks and cut stalks crosswise in thin slices. Place broccoli in steamer basket; set in kettle over 1 inch boiling water. Cook, covered, until barely tender when pierced (about 5 minutes). Drain, rinse under cold water, and drain again. To serve, gently combine in a salad bowl, broccoli, cheese, mushrooms and dressing, coating vegetables well. Garnish with radishes. 4 servings.

ZUCCHINI BREAD

2 cups flour
½ teaspoon baking powder
2 teaspoons baking soda
1 teaspoon salt
3 teaspoons ground cinnamon
½ teaspoon ground cloves
½ teaspoon nutmeg
3 eggs

½ cup brown sugar
1 cup white sugar
3 medium sized zucchini (2 cups), processed in
* blender (cut zucchini into chunks, add to*
* blender, process a few seconds at CHOP, drain)*
2 teaspoons vanilla
1 cup chopped walnuts
1 cup raisins

Combine flour, baking powder, baking soda, salt, cinnamon, cloves and nutmeg; sift. Beat eggs in large mixing bowl on high for 15 seconds. On medium speed, gradually add oil, sugars, zucchini and vanilla, mixing about 2 minutes until thoroughly combined. Add sifted dry ingredients, nuts and raisins. Mix thoroughly at medium speed, about 2 minutes. Divide batter into 2 well-greased 4x5x3-inch loaf pans (3 cups batter per pan). Bake on a rack in preheated (420°) frypan for 1 hour 15 minutes. Remove, cool 10 minutes, remove from pans and cool completely. Makes 2 loaves. Note: For a fluted or tube pan, spoon batter into a well- greased fluted or tube pan. Bake on a rack in the frypan (preheated at 420°) for 1 hour, 20-30 minutes. Remove, cool 10 minutes, remove from pan and cool completely. If no rack is available, put pans on pennies. Bread can also be baked in the oven at 350° for 65-70 minutes.

THURSDAY
Baked chicken breasts
Creamed potatoes
Colorful fresh pepper medley *
Onion spoon bread *
Honey crinkles *

COLORFUL FRESH PEPPER MEDLEY

5 bell peppers, 2 green, 2 red, 1 yellow	*1 teaspoon dried basil*
2 tablespoons olive oil	*1/2 teaspoon salt*
1 (4 ounce) can mushroom stems and pices, drained	*1/4 teaspoon black pepper*
2 teaspoons Worcestershire sauce	

Slice peppers, remove stems and seeds. Sauté in olive oil for 2-3 minutes or until tender. Add mushrooms, Worcestershire sauce and basil. Turn heat to low; cover tightly and steam until peppers ar tender, about 5-10 minutes. Remove cover and cook, stirring constantly, until slightly brown. Add salt and pepper; correct seasonsing. 6 servings.

ONION SPOON BREAD

1 quart milk	*2 tablespoons finely chopped onion*
2 cups corn meal	*3 eggs, separated*
1 teaspoon salt	*3 tablespoons butter or margarine*

Scald milk, add corn meal, salt and onions. Cook until thick. Cool, add egg yolks and butter; mix well. Beat egg whites until stiff, fold into onion mixture. Pour into a well-greased 2-quart casserole dish. Bake in a 350° oven for 40 minutes.

HONEY CRINKLES

1/2 cup shortening	*2 cups graham cracker crumbs*
1/2 cup peanut butter (creamy or chunky style)	*1/2 cup sifted flour*
1/2 cup mashed ripe banana (about 1 large)	*1 teaspoon salt*
1 teaspoon vanilla	*1 1/2 teaspoons baking powder*
1 cup honey	*1 cup raisins or diced dates or prunes*

Cream together shortening, peanut butter, banana and vanilla. Continue creaming while slowly adding honey in a fine stream. Combine graham cracker crumbs, flour, salt, baking powder and raisins. Add to creamed mixture and stir until well blended. Dough will be very soft. Chill at least one hour before baking. Drop from teaspoon, 1 inch apart, on greased baking sheet. Bake at 325° for 15-18 minutes. Do not overbake. 4 1/2 dozen cookies.

FRIDAY
Shrimp Jambalaya *
Caesar salad
Hot garlic French Bread
Piña Colada Cake *

SHRIMP JAMBALAYA

3 (5 ounce) cans shrimp	1 ½ cups water
1 cup chopped green peppers	1 cup uncooked rice
1 medium onion onion, chopped	½ teaspoon crushed whole thyme
3 cloves garlic, crushed	½ teaspoon salt
¼ cup melted fat or oil	1 bay leaf
1 (16 ounce) can tomatoes or 1 (14 ½ ounce)	Dash pepper
can diced tomatoes	¼ cup chopped parsley

Drain shrimp. Cover shrimp with ice water and let stand for 5 minutes, drain. Cook green pepper, onion and garlic in fat until tender. Add remaining ingredients except parsley and shrimp. Cover and cook for 25-30 minutes or until rice is tender; stir occasionally. Add parsley and shrimp; heat. Remove bay leaf. If mixture gets too dry, add some water. 6 servings.

PIÑA COLADA CAKE

⅓ cup dark rum	4 eggs
1 (3 ½ ounce) package vanilla flavored or	½ cup water
coconut cream instant pudding or pie filling	¼ cup oil
1 (18¼ ounce) package white cake mix	1 cup flaked coconut

Add rum, pudding, cake mix, eggs, water and oil to processor container. Process until well-mixed. Pour into 2 greased and floured 9-inch layer pans or 13x9x2-inch baking dish. Bake in 350° oven for 25-30 minutes or when cake springs back when lightly touched. Do not overbake. Cool in pan 15 minutes. If using baking dish, leave cake in container and frost in the container. If using layer pans, remove from pans, fill and frost. Sprinkle with coconut. Refrigerate.

Piña Colada Frosting

1 (8 ounce) can crushed pineapple in juice	⅓ cup rum
1 (3½ ounce box) vanilla or coconut cream	1 (8 ounce) container whipped topping, thawed
pudding and pie mix	

Combine pineapple, pudding mix and rum; beat until well-mixed. Fold in whipped topping. Refrigerate cake.

SATURDAY
Broiled beef steaks
Cottage fried potatoes
Cauliflower topped with cheese sauce
Hot rolls (commercial)
Evergreen salad *
Tipsy cake *

EVERGREEN SALAD

1 small head lettuce	3 medium oranges, peeled and thinly sliced
1 bunch spinach, washed and trimmed	1 medium cucumber, peeled and thinly sliced
1 small onion, sliced & separated into rings (red is preferred)	Yogurt-Cumin dressing

Core, rinse and thoroughly drain lettuce. Chill in plastic bag or plastic crisper. Tear lettuce; toss with spinach leaves and arrange on 8 individual salad plates. Arrange onion rings, orange and cucumber slices over the greens. Serve with dressing. 8 servings.

Yogurt-Cumin Dressing

1 cup plain yogurt
2 tablespoons mayonnaise
2 tablespoons orange juice

1 teaspoon grated orange rind
¼ teaspoon ground cumin
¼ teaspoon salt

Combine yogurt, mayonnaise, orange juice, orange rind cumin and salt. Mix well. Double if needed.

TIPSY CAKE

1 (18¼ ounce) box yellow cake mix
1 (3½ oz) box instant vanilla pudding and pie mix
¹/₄ cup Bourbon
4 eggs, slightly beaten
1 cup oil

1 cup milk
¼ cup chopped nuts
½ cup (1 stick) butter or margarine
1 cup sugar
³/₄ cup Bourbon

In large mixing bowl, combine cake mix, pudding mix, ¼ cup Bourbon, eggs, oil and milk. Beat for 5 minutes. Fold in nuts. Pour into greased and floured bundt pan or 10-inch tube pan. Bake in 350° oven for 50 minutes. Cool 20 minutes in pan then turn onto a dish with sloping sides. In a small saucepan, combine butter, sugar and ³/₄ cup Bourbon. Cook until butter is melted and sugar is dissolved. Pierce cake with paring knife or fork many times over all the surface. Pour on half the glaze, using a brush to get the sides. Allow the cake to stand for 1 hour and re-glaze with the remainder of the sauce. Store in air-tight container for several days before serving, if possible. This cake improves with age.

October - Second Week

Hamburger is one of the most popular meats in the American household. Some questions and comments about hamburger include the following:

1. Ground beef often is labeled differently. Sometimes the words "regular," "lean," and "extra lean" are used, and other times it is ground chuck, ground round or ground sirloin. Why? Regular, lean and extra lean refer to the fat content in ground beef. Ground chuck, ground round and ground sirloin refer to the cut of meat being ground. The U.S. D.A. has standards for these names which are applied only when the meat is ground in a federally-inspected or state-inspected plant. However, supermarkets which grind and package beef themselves sometimes label their ground beef packages according to their own preferences. Some consumers prefer to select a piece of beef and have the supermarket grind it for them.

2. Are there federal grades for ground beef or hamburger? No. Ground beef or hamburger may be made from graded (U.S. prime, choice, good, etc.) or ungraded meat. There is no way of telling what quality of meat you may be purchasing because the trimmings used to make ground beef lose their identity during grinding. The U.S.D.A. recommends that you buy ground beef or hamburger by price.

3. How much fat is in regular, lean and extra lean ground beef? Many stores follow this rule: Regular - no more than 30% fat; lean - approximately 23% fat; extra lean - approximately 15% fat.

4. Does the U.S.D.A. set a limit for fat in ground beef? Yes, but only for products ground in federally-

or state-inspected packing plants. The limit for fat in these products is 30% by weight, equivalent to regular ground beef. Most ground beef, though, is ground in local supermarkets to maintain freshness. The grinding is not subject to federal inspection regulations on fat content. Most states and cities, however, do set standards for store-packed ground beef.

5. Many people call ground beef "hamburger," yet it's not often labeled that way in the store. Is there a difference? The U.S.D.A. distinguishes between ground beef and hamburger only if they are ground in and packaged in a federally- or state-inspected plant. The U.S.D.A. applies no distinction to beef that is ground in a local supermarket. According to U.S.D.A. standards, hamburger is ground beef to which seasonings and beef fat may be added while the meat is being ground. No water, extenders or binders are permitted. Ground beef is just what the name implies. No extra fat, water, extenders or binders are permitted. Seasonings, however, may be added as long as they are identified on the label. Both ground beef and hamburger are limited to 30% fat by weight.

6. From what kind of beef is ground beef made? Generally, ground beef is made from the less tender and less popular cuts of beef. Trimmings from higher priced cuts may also be used. These cuts contain varying amounts of fat and lean. Because ground beef is so popular, many supermarkets and butchers cannot get enough meat from a carcass of beef after they have removed the steaks, roasts and other cuts to fill the demand. Consequently, they may buy less tender meats or less popular wholesale cuts specifically for grinding into ground beef. Some stores may buy imported frozen boneless beef and grind it after adding trimmings from their own meat cutting operations. While most steaks and roasts may come from younger steers or heifers, much ground beef is prepared from the meat of older animals, which is tougher. Grinding tenderizes it, and the addition of fat reduces its dryness and improves flavor.

7. Why is prepackaged ground beef often red on the outside and dull, grayish brown on the inside? The pigment is responsible for the red color of meat. When exposed to air, the pigment combines with oxygen to produce the red color, which is referred to as bloom. The interior of the meat does not have the red color due to lack of oxygen to cause the bloom to appear.

SUNDAY
Chuck roast in foil (gravy included)
Steamed potatoes, onions and carrots
Three green salad with honey lime dressing *
Hard rolls / Fruit surprise pie *

THREE GREEN SALAD WITH HONEY LIME DRESSING
Three Green Salad

2 avocados, diced
1/2 medium head lettuce, torn, chilled

1 (10 ounce) package fresh spinach, torn, chilled
1 tablespoon sesame seeds, toasted (optional)

Put avocado, lettuce and spinach is a quart-sized salad bowl. Before serving, toss with honey lime dressing. Top with sesame seeds. 4 servings.

Honey Lime Dressing

1/2 cup salad oil
1/4 cup honey
1/4 cup lemon juice

1/4 cup lime juice
1/2 teaspoon salt
1/4 teaspoon dry mustard

Combine all ingredients in a small bowl. Stir until well mixed. Chill. 1 cup dressing.

FRUIT SURPRISE PIE

³/₄ cup (1 ¹/₂ sticks) butter or margarine, melted
³/₄ cup sugar
³/₄ cup milk

1 can cherries for pie
³/₄ cup self rising flour

Place butter in a deep-dish pie pan. Combine sugar, milk and flour; mix well. Pour over butter in pan. Drain cherries, reserve juice. Combine ⅓ cup cherry juice with cherries and pour on top of flour mixture. Bake in 350° oven for 45 minutes. Note: If desired, a can of cherry pie filling can be used instead of cherries.

MONDAY
Noodles Romanoff *
Steamed carrots with bacon
Cran-raspberry molded salad *
Hot buttered Italian bread
Coffee mousse *

NOODLES ROMANOFF

1 (8 ounce) package egg noodles
1 ¹/₂ cups cottage cheese
2 cloves garlic, crushed
1 tablespoon Worcestershire sauce
1 cup sour cream

4 green onions, finely-chopped
1 ¹/₂ teaspoons garlic salt
¹/₈ teaspoon cayenne pepper
³/₄ cup Parmesan cheese

Cook noodles in boiling water al dente, about 10 minutes; drain well. Combine noodles, cottage cheese, garlic, Worcestershire sauce, sour cream, onion, garlic salt, cayenne and ½ cup Parmesan cheese. Pour into a 2-quart buttered baking dish. Sprinkle top of mixture with ¼ cup Parmesan cheese. Bake in 350° oven for 20 minutes. 4 servings.

CRAN-RASPBERRY MOLDED SALAD

1 envelope plain gelatin
2 tablespoons water
2 (3 ounce) packages raspberry flavored gelatin
2 cups boiling water

1 pound fresh cranberries, ground
1 cup coarsely chopped pecans
Crisp salad greens
Mayonnaise

Cover plain gelatin with cold water. Let stand 2-3 minutes. Add plain gelatin and raspberry flavored gelatin to the boiling water, stir until dissolved. Chill until partially set. Fold in the cranberries and pecans. Pour into a 6 cup mold. Chill. Unmold on crisp salad greens. Top with calorie-reduced mayonnaise, if desired. 6 servings.

COFFEE MOUSSE

*1 cup strong, hot coffee **
1 (6 ¹/₄-ounce) bag miniature marshmallows
3 tablespoons coffee liqueur

1 cup heavy cream, whipped
¹/₂ cup heavy cream, whipped (optional)
Shaved chocolate (optional)

Combine coffee and marshmallows in a 1 ½-quart saucepan. Heat until marshmallows are melted. Cool to room temperature or place in a pan of ice water to hasten cooling. Stir in liqueur. Fold in 1 cup of whipped cream. Pour into 6 dessert compotes or one large compote. Refrigerate. At serving time, top with additional whipped cream and shaved chocolate, if desired. 6 servings. Note: If coffee is not strong enough, add 2 teaspoons of instant and stir until dissolved.

TUESDAY
Fettucine Ferrara *
Spinach souffle *
Tossed salad with low-calorie blue cheese dressing *
Sourdough hard rolls
Apricot mousse

FETTUCINE FERRARA

9 ounce package fettucine, or other pasta	*6 ounces ham, cut in ¼ inch cubes*
⅓ cup olive oil	*2 egg yolks*
2 bunches green onions, chopped	*½ cup heavy cream*
2 cloves garlic, crushed	*¾ cup grated Parmesan cheese*
1 (16 ounce) can diced tomatoes	*Salt and freshly-ground pepper to taste*

In a large kettle, cook the fettucine in boiling, salted water to "al dente" texture. Drain thoroughly. Melt the butter in a medium skillet; add the onions and garlic, cooking gently until the onions are tender. Add the tomatoes and sauté for 1-2 minutes. Add ham to heat through. Beat the egg yolks, then beat the cream into the egg yolks only until well mixed. Stir slowly into the tomato and ham mixture with a flat whisk and cook until just thickened and well blended. Add remaining ingredients and mix. Remove from heat and add to the hot fettucine, toss and serve immediately. 6 servings.

SPINACH SOUFFLE

3 tablespoons butter or margarine	*1 cup milk*
¼ cup flour	*¼ pound Swiss cheese, shredded (1 cup)*
1 teaspoon salt	*1 (10 ounce) package frozen chopped spinach*
¼ teaspoon pepper	*3 eggs, separated*
Pinch of nutmeg	

Melt butter and blend in flour, salt, pepper and nutmeg. Gradually add milk, stirring until well-blended. Cook over low heat, stirring constantly, until the mixture is thick and smooth. Add cheese and spinach and cook until the cheese is melted. Cool. Beat egg whites until stiff and dry, then beat egg yolks until thick and lemon colored. Add yolks to spinach mixture. Fold in egg whites. Pour into a buttered 1 ½-quart straight-sided baking dish. Bake in preheated slow oven (325°) for 40-45 minutes or until firm in the center. Serve immediately. 4 servings.

LOW-CALORIE BLUE CHEESE SALAD DRESSING

4 ounces (1 cup) blue cheese, crumbled	*¼ teaspoon garlic powder*
1 (8 ounce) carton sour cream	*1 teaspoon garlic salt*
2 tablespoons lemon juice	*¼ teaspoon black pepper*

Combine blue cheese, sour cream, lemon juice, garlic powder, garlic salt and black pepper. Blend well by hand; do not use blender. Yield: 2 cups.

WEDNESDAY
Sausage casserole *
Grits
Buttered broccoli
Cranberry muffins *
Carrot and celery sticks
Apple sauce

SAUSAGE CASSEROLE

1 ½ cups dried chicken noodle soup	½ teaspoon butter or margarine
2 ½ cups boiling water	2 cloves garlic, crushed
½ cup rice	½ pound (1 cup) bulk sausage
1 cup chopped celery	½ cup slivered almonds
½ cup chopped onion	½ can mushroom soup
½ cup chopped green peppers	

Place dried chicken soup in large saucepan. Pour boiling water over dried soup. Add rice and cook 15 minutes or until thick. In a skillet, melt butter, add celery, onion and green peppers, saute 5 minutes. Add to rice mixture. In a skillet, add butter, garlic and sausage, fry until all pink has left the meat. Drain and add to the rice mixture. Stir in almonds and mushroom soup. Pour into a 2-quart baking dish. Bake in a 350° oven for 45 minutes. 4 servings.

CRANBERRY MUFFINS

1 can whole cranberry sauce	1 egg, beaten
2 cups biscuit mix	¾ cup milk
⅓ cup sugar	2 tablespoons oil or melted butter or margarine

Break up cranberry sauce, set aside. Combine remaining ingredients. Mix only until flour mixture is moistened. Fold cranberry sauce into mixture very carefully. Fill greased muffin tins ⅔ full. Bake in 425° oven for 20-25 minutes. 18 muffins.

THURSDAY
Baked chicken slices
Oven roasted potato quarters
Herbed baked tomatoes *
Lettuce wedges with Roquefort cheese dressing
Biscuits / Fudgy Kahlua brownies *

HERBED BAKED TOMATOES

4 medium tomatoes	⅛ teaspoon oregano
½ teaspoon garlic salt	¼ teaspoon pepper
½ teaspoon sugar	½ cup cracker crumbs
¼ teaspoon onion powder	Butter or margarine
⅛ teaspoon basil	Chopped parsley

Preheat oven to 350°. Cut tops off the tomatoes, and scoop out a small portion of the pulp. Mix pulp together with salt, sugar, onion powder, basil, oregano and pepper. Stuff tomatoes with this mixture. Top with cracker crumbs, dot with butter and sprinkle with chopped parsley. Bake for 20 or 30 minutes, until the tomatoes are tender. 4 servings.

FUDGY KAHLUA BROWNIES

2 1/4 cups flour, divided
1 cup sugar, divided
1 cup (2 sticks) butter or margarine
1/2 cup unsweetened cocoa
1/2 teaspoon baking powder
1 (14 ounce) can sweetened condensed milk

1 egg, slightly beaten
2 tablespoons Kahlua (can use very strong coffee
 plus 1 teaspoon sugar)
1 teaspoon vanilla
1 cup finely-chopped nuts (walnuts or pecans)

Combine 2 cups flour, 1/2 cup sugar and butter. Blend until it resembles coarse corn meal. Press firmly on the bottom of a 13x9x2-inch baking pan. Bake in 350° oven for 15 minutes. Combine 1/4 cup flour, 1/2 cup sugar, cocoa, and baking powder. Add milk, egg, Kahlua and vanilla. Mix well. Stir in nuts. Spread over crust, Bake in 350° oven 20 minutes or until center is set. Cool. Yield: about 3 dozen brownies. (Nice to use at holiday parties)

FRIDAY
Early Autumn Dinner
Fish fillet in champagne sauce *
Pat's squash casserole *
Peas and bacon, Italian style
Fresh fruit salad with grenadine dressing *
Commercial hot rolls
Oatmeal cake *

Plan Of Work
Day before:
1. Prepare oatmeal cake.
2. Prepare salad dressing.
About 1 hour before serving:
3. Prepare marinade and marinate fish.
4. Prepare fruit for salad.
5. Prepare squash casserole. Place in oven 30 minutes before serving.
6. While squash is baking, prepare the peas and bacon.
7. Finally, finish preparation of the fish.

FISH FILLET IN CHAMPAGNE SAUCE

1 cup champagne or sparkling white wine
2 teaspoons curry powder (Madras if possible)
Juice of one lemon or 3 tablespoons lemon juice
Salt to taste
Pepper to taste

4 firm catfish fillets or any white fish
2 tablespoons (1/4 stick) butter or margarine
3 medium onions, chopped-finely
Finely-chopped fresh dill
Cooked wild rice

Combine champagne, curry powder, lemon juice, salt and pepper. Mix thoroughly. Marinate fish in this sauce for 45 minutes. In a large skillet, melt butter, add and saute onions until soft and transparent, about 5 minutes, do not burn. Add fish and marinade and simmer until the fish is just cooked, about 10-15 minutes. Add more champagne during cooking if it is necessary. Garnish with dill; serve on a bed of wild rice. (If wild rice is not available, use the combination of regular plus wild.) 4 servings.

PAT'S SQUASH CASSEROLE

2 pounds (6 cups) diced summer squash
1/2 cup water
1/4 cup chopped onions
1 (10 1/2-ounce) can cream of chicken soup

1 cup sour cream
1 cup shredded carrots
1/2 cup melted butter
1 (8 ounce) package herb flavored stuffing mix

In large saucepan, add squash, water and onion. Cook for 5 minutes. Drain. Add soup, sour cream and carrots. Combine butter and stuffing mix; spread half the stuffing over the bottom of a 2-quart baking dish. Add the squash mixture. Top with remaining stuffing mix. Bake in a 350° oven for 25-30 minutes. 6-8 servings.

PEAS AND BACON, ITALIAN STYLE

2 (10 ounce) packages frozen peas
6 slices bacon
Salt to taste

Pepper to taste
1 cup chopped pimiento

Cook peas according to package directions, drain. Dice bacon and cook in a skillet until cooked but not crisp. Add peas to bacon in skillet. Correct seasoning. Add pimiento just before serving. 6 servings.

FRESH FRUIT SALAD WITH GRENADINE DRESSING

1/2 cup plus 2 tablespoons sugar
1/2 cup plus 2 tablespoons grenadine syrup
1 teaspoon dry mustard
1 teaspoon salt
1/4 cup vinegar
1 cup oil

1 teaspoon celery seed
1/4 teaspoon dried onion bits
1 teaspoon poppy seed
1/2 tablespoon lemon juice (optional)
6-8 cups fresh fruit of your choice

In small bowl of electric mixer, combine sugar, syrup, mustard, salt, vinegar and oil. Beat until well mixed. Add celery seed, onion, poppy seed and lemon juice; continue beating until well mixed. Add to the fruit just before serving. 6-8 servings, 1 1/2 cups.

OATMEAL CAKE

1 1/4 cup boiling water
1 cup oatmeal, quick or old fashioned
1/2 cup butter or margarine, softened
1 cup granulated sugar
1 cup firmly-packed brown sugar
1 teaspoon vanilla

2 eggs
1 1/2 cup sifted all-purpose flour
1 teaspoon baking soda
1/2 teaspoon salt
3/4 teaspoon cinnamon
1/4 teaspoon nutmeg

Pour boiling water over oats; cover, and let stand for 20 minutes. Beat butter until creamy; gradually add sugars and beat until fluffy. Blend in vanilla and eggs. Add oats mixture, mix well. Sift together flour, soda, salt, cinnamon and nutmeg. Add to creamed mixture, mix well. Pour batter into well-greased 9-inch cake pan. Bake at 350° for 50 minutes. Do not remove from pan. While cake is baking, prepare frosting.

Frosting

½ cup butter or margarine, melted
½ cup firmly-packed brown sugar
3 tablespoons sweetened condensed milk

⅓ cup chopped nuts
³/₄ cup flaked coconut

Combine all ingredients, mix well. Spread evenly over cake. Broil until frosting becomes bubbly. Serve warm or cold.

SATURDAY
Meat loaf
Hash brown casserole *
Buttered fresh green beans
Apple salad
Sliced whole wheat bread
Angel crisp tea cookies *

HASH BROWN CASSEROLE

2 pounds frozen hash brown potatoes, thawed
½ cup butter or margarine, melted
1 tablespoon salt
1 tablespoon pepper
1 (10 ½-ounce) can cream of chicken soup

½ cup chopped onion
1 (16 ounce) carton sour cream
3 cups (12 ounces) shredded sharp Cheddar cheese
2 cups crushed corn flakes
¼ cup butter or margarine, melted

Combine potatoes, ½ cup butter, salt, pepper, soup, onion, sour cream and cheese. Pour into 2 greased 1 ½-quart casseroles or one 3-quart. Combine corn flake crumbs with ¼ cup melted butter. Sprinkle on casserole. Bake in 350° oven for 1 hour. 12 servings for large casserole. For 6 servings use 2 casseroles and freeze one for future use.

ANGEL CRISP TEA COOKIES

1 cup sugar
½ cup (1 stick) butter or margarine
½ cup shortening
1 egg, beaten slightly
2 ½ cups flour

½ teaspoon salt
1 teaspoon baking soda
1 teaspoon cream of tartar
1 teaspoon vanilla

Cream sugar, butter and shortening until smooth and well-mixed. Add eggs, mix well. Combine flour, salt, soda, cream of tartar and vanilla; stir into the creamed mixture, mix well. Pinch off a piece of batter the size of a walnut and roll into a ball. Place on ungreased cookie sheet. Continue until all batter is used. Dip a fork in water and flatten the cookie balls. Make as thin as you can. Bake in 300° oven for 10-15 minutes. Watch carefully, cookies will burn easily. Yield: about 3 dozen.

October - Third Week

More about the purchase, use and storage of ground beef:

1. Make sure the package has not been torn. Select a package that feels cold. Most important of all, make ground beef one of your last purchases before leaving the store and refrigerate it or freeze it immediately.

2. Ground beef, like other fresh meats, should be refrigerated or frozen as soon as possible after purchase. If you plan to use the ground beef within a day or two, it can be stored in the coldest part of the refrigerator. Ground beef wrapped in transparent film can be refrigerated without rewrapping. But ground beef wrapped in butcher paper should be unwrapped and repackaged in transparent film or wax paper. If ground beef is to be stored in a freezer for 2 weeks or less, it may be kept in transparent film without moisture loss. For longer storage, it should be wrapped tightly in moisture-resistant material like aluminum foil, freezer paper or plastic bags. Ground beef kept frozen at 0° can be stored for up to 3 months with little loss of quality. Mark your packages with the date they were placed in the freezer so you can keep track of storage time.

3. Ground beef should be thawed in the refrigerator. Keeping the meat cold while it is thawing is essential to prevent growth of bacteria. If you must thaw ground beef rapidly, put the meat in a watertight wrapper in cold water or in a closed double paper bag at room temperature; then cook it as soon as it is thawed.

4. High bacterial counts are not necessarily a hazard to health as long as the meat is thoroughly cooked before eating and proper handling procedures are followed. Ground beef, made as it often is from trimmings, has been handled more than other cuts of beef. Grinding exposes more of the meat surface to bacteria normally occurring in the air, on the butcher's hands and on the equipment. These bacteria are not usually harmful, but they will cause loss of quality and spoilage if the meat is mishandled. To keep bacterial levels low, keep ground beef cold (40° or lower) during storage and cook it thoroughly. Also wash your hands thoroughly with soap and water immediately before and after handling ground beef to make sure you don't spread bacteria. To avoid cross-contamination, don't reuse any packaging materials or utensils which have come in contact with the raw meat unless they are washed thoroughly with soap and hot water.

5. In making ground beef, some retail stores grind the meat while it is still frozen. Ice crystals, which are incorporated into the meat, melt when the meat is cooked, which accounts for the large amount of moisture often associated with ground beef. The same thing can occur from home freezing. If large packages of ground beef are frozen, freezing will be slow, causing large ice crystals to form in the cell walls. As a result, cellular fluids or meat juices are released during cooking.

6. All meat will shrink in size and weight during cooking. The amount of shrinkage will depend on its fat content, the temperature at which the meat is cooked, and how long it is cooked. Basically, the higher the cooking temperatures, the greater the shrinkage. Cooking ground beef at moderate temperature (325° - 350°) will reduce shrinkage and help retain juices and flavor. Over-cooking draws out more juices from ground beef and results in more shrinkage and a dry unpalatable product. Season with salt after cooking to reduce the drawing out of juices from the meat and reduce shrinkage. However, if you want to enhance the flavor of the ground beef, you should salt the beef before cooking

7. The U.S.D.A. advises against eating raw ground beef since harmful food-poisoning bacteria could be present. Beef Tartar, a popular raw ground beef spread, can be dangerous since it is hard to know how long it has been at room temperature, how it was handled during preparation or when it was prepared.

8. The U.S.D.A. recommends thorough cooking for safety's sake. If you enjoy your hamburgers rare, make sure the meat is at least brownish-pink in color. That would be the equivalent of cooking the meat to an internal temperature of 145°. And be sure to handle the meat carefully; keep it refrigerated until cooked and eat it soon after it is cooked to minimize the risk from harmful bacteria.

SUNDAY

Dip and bake pork chops *
Baked sweet potato in skin
Layered artichoke bake *
Citrus salad with citrus dressing
New Orleans bread pudding with tipsy sauce

DIP AND BAKE PORK CHOPS

1 cup flour	*$1/4$ teaspoon pepper*
1 cup grated Parmesan cheese	*$1/3$ cup milk*
$1/2$ teaspoon marjoram	*1 egg, beaten*
$1/2$ teaspoon thyme leaves, crushed	*6 pork chops, cut $1/2$ to $3/4$ inch thick*
$1/2$ teaspoon salt	*$1/4$ cup butter or margarine, melted*

Combine flour, cheese, marjoram, thyme, salt and pepper; set aside. In flat pan, combine milk and egg. Coat chops with combined dry ingredients. Dip chops into combined milk and egg. Coat again with combined dry ingredients. Place in foil-lined large shallow baking pan. Drizzle butter over meat. Bake in 400° oven for about 45 minutes or until tender and golden brown. 6 servings.

LAYERED ARTICHOKE BAKE

1 tablespoon butter or margarine	*$1/2$ cup crushed herb seasoned stuffing mix .*
1 (9 ounce) package frozen artichoke hearts,	*$1/4$ cup grated Parmesan cheese*
thawed, drained or 1 (14 ounce) can hearts,	*2 tablespoons butter or margarine, melted*
drained and quartered	*$1/4$ teaspoon salt (optional)*
2 small tomatoes, cut into $1/4$-inch slices	*2 green onions, sliced*

In ungreased 8-inch square baking dish, melt 1 tablespoon butter in 350° oven. In melted butter, layer artichokes and tomato slices. Set aside. In small bowl, combine stuffing mix, cheese, 2 tablespoons butter and salt. Sprinkle stuffing mixture over vegetables. Bake, uncovered, for 25 to 30 minutes, or until heated through. Sprinkle with green onions. 4 servings.

MONDAY

Barbecued beef patties *
Baked beans
Buffet macaroni salad *
Relish tray and carrot sticks
Ice cream

BARBECUED BEEF PATTIES

2 pounds ground beef
2 cups milk
1 1/3 cups quick cooking oatmeal
3 tablespoons grated onion

2 teaspoon salt
1/2 teaspoon chili powder
1/8 - 1/4 teaspoon pepper

Combine all ingredients; shape into 8-10 patties. Place in a 13x9 1/2x2-inch baking pan. Pour barbecue sauce (see next recipe) over patties. Bake in 350° oven for 1 hour.

Barbecue Sauce

3-4 medium onions, finely-chopped
1 cup catsup
1 cup water
3 tablespoons vinegar

1 1/2 tablespoons Worcestershire sauce
3/4 tablespoon paprika
3/4 tablespoon chili powder

Combine all ingredients for sauce, simmer 30 minutes. Pour over patties. Bake in 350° oven for 1 hour. Serve in flat bowl surrounded by sesame buns. Garnish with parsley. 8 servings. Note: If this recipe is used for sandwiches, double the sauce recipe for spreading consistency.

BUFFET MACARONI SALAD

3/4 cup mayonnaise
1/2 teaspoon dry mustard
1/2 teaspoon salt
1/4 teaspoon garlic salt
1/4 teaspoon pepper
2/3 cup undiluted skim evaporated milk
2 tablespoons vinegar

4 cups hot, cooked elbow macaroni
1/2 cup thinly-sliced celery
1/3 cup thinly-sliced carrot
1/3 cup thinly-sliced radish
1/4 cup chopped green pepper
2 tablespoons finely-chopped onion
1 tablespoon chopped pimiento

Combine mayonnaise, mustard, salt, garlic salt, pepper and evaporated milk in a large bowl. Stir in vinegar until well blended and slightly thickened. Add macaroni, celery, carrot, radish, green pepper, onion and pimiento. Toss well. Chill. 6-8 servings.

TUESDAY
Vegetable sausage soup *
Cheese and olive sandwich
Green salad medley with Italian dressing *
Apple cobbler

VEGETABLE SAUSAGE SOUP

1 1/4 pounds Italian sweet sausage
1/4 cup water
3 1/2 cups chicken broth
1 (16 ounce) can tomatoes
1 (8 ounce) can tomato sauce

1/2 teaspoon basil leaves, crushed
1/2 teaspoon dried parsley flakes
1/4 teaspoon sugar
2 cups cooked small shell macaroni
2 (10 ounce) packages frozen mixed vegetables

In a large heavy pan, combine sausage and water. Cover; cook over low heat 10 minutes. Drain. Cut sausage into thin slices. Return sausage to pan; brown. Add remaining ingredients except macaroni and vegetables. Cover; cook over low heat 30 minutes. Add macaroni; cook 5 minutes. Add frozen vegetables; cook 5 minutes more or until done. stir occasionally. Freeze leftover soup. 6-8 servings.

GREEN SALAD MEDLEY WITH ITALIAN DRESSING

¹/₂ head lettuce	2 tablespoons granulated sugar
¹/₂ head endive	2 tablespoons snipped fresh parsley
1 cucumber, thinly sliced	1 teaspoon monosodium glutamate (optional)
1 large green pepper, cut into long strips	1 teaspoon garlic salt
5 green onions, use tops, sliced	¹/₂ teaspoon oregano
¹/₂ cup cooked green peas or frozen peas, thawed only	1 teaspoon coarsely-ground black pepper
	1 cup salad oil or olive oil
1 rib celery, sliced diagonally	¹/₃ cup wine vinegar

Place greens, cucumber, green pepper, onions, green peas and celery in salad bowl; refrigerate until ready to use. Combine remaining ingredients in a jar. Shake vigorously. Pour on vegetables. Toss gently until all vegetables are well coated. Serve immediately. Refrigerate extra dressing. 6 servings.

WEDNESDAY
Quick & easy Sauerbraten and gravy *
Mashed potatoes
Cabbage and apple medley *
Marinated tomatoes and onions
French bread slices / Spiced tomato cake *

QUICK & EASY SAUERBRATEN AND GRAVY

1 (5 pound) beef rump roast	1 bay leaf
¹/₂ cup vegetable oil	12 whole cloves
1 cup vinegar	¹/₂ cup raisins
¹/₂ cup brown sugar, packed	6 small onions
1 tablespoon salt	¹/₄ cup corn starch
	¹/₄ cup water

Brown roast in vegetable oil in heavy pan or kettle, just large enough to hold roast flat. After browning roast, pour off oil and add vinegar, brown sugar, salt, bay leaf, cloves, raisins and onions. Add about 1 cup water or just enough to come up sides of roast. Cover pan tightly and simmer for about 2 hours or until meat is tender. Add water, if necessary, while meat is cooking, Keep level of liquid about half-way on side of roast, and turn roast occasionally while meat is cooking. After meat is tender, remove to platter and thicken sweet-sour gravy with ¹/₄ cup cornstarch in ¹/₄ cup of lukewarm water. Cook gravy until thick and serve over roast. 8-10 servings. Increase corn starch & water if sauce is too thin.

CABBAGE AND APPLE MEDLEY

1 cup water	¹/₂ teaspoon salt (optional)
4 cups (¹/₂ small head) cabbage, cubed into 1-inch cubes	¹/₄ teaspoon nutmeg
	2 medium tart red apples, unpeeled, cubed
2 tablespoons butter or margarine	2 tablespoons chopped fresh parsley

In a 2-quart saucepan, bring water to a boil. Add cabbage. Cover; cook over medium heat, stirring occasionally, until cabbage is crisply tender (5-6 minutes). Drain. To same saucepan add butter, salt, nutmeg and apples. Cover; cook over medium heat, stirring occasionally, until apples are crisply tender (3-4 minutes). Sprinkle with parsley before serving. 6 servings.

TOMATO SPICE CAKE

2 ⅓ cups cake flour or 2 cups all-purpose flour	½ teaspoon ground cloves
1 ⅓ cups sugar	1 (10 ¾-ounce) can condensed tomato soup
2 teaspoons baking powder	½ cup shortening
1 teaspoon baking soda	2 eggs
1 ½ teaspoon allspice	¼ cup water
1 teaspoon cinnamon	

Measure dry ingredients into large bowl. Add soup and shortening. Beat at low to medium speed for 2 minutes, scraping sides and bottom of bowl constantly. Add eggs and water. Beat 2 minutes more, scraping bowl frequently. Pour into 13x9x2-inch pan. Bake in 350° oven for 35-40 minutes. Let stand in pan 10 minutes; remove from pan. Cool. Frost with cream cheese frosting (optional) **(see index)**. To prepare in bundt pan: Proceed as above. Bake in well-greased and lightly-floured 2 1/2-quart bundt pan at 350° for 50 to 60 minutes or until done. Cool right side up in pan 15 minutes; remove from pan. Cool. If desired, sprinkle with powdered sugar.

THURSDAY
Brunswick stew *
Pork barbecue
Cole slaw
Peanut butter and jelly cake *

BRUNSWICK STEW

2 pounds chicken	2 cups fresh corn or 1 (16 ounce) can whole
3 cups water	kernel corn, undrained
1 ½ teaspoons salt	1 teaspoon sugar
1 cup diced potatoes	Salt to taste
1 ¾ cups canned or frozen, thawed Lima beans,	½ teaspoon pepper
drained	½ teaspoon oregano
1 ¾ cups tomato sauce	½ teaspoon poultry seasoning
1 cup chopped onions	Few grains of cayenne pepper

Simmer chicken in salted water until tender, about 2 to 2 ½ hours. Drain off the broth and set aside. Separate the meat from the bone and skin and cut into small pieces. Skim fat from the broth. Boil broth to concentrate it to about 2 cups. Add potatoes to broth and simmer 10 minutes. Add Lima beans, tomato sauce and onion. Cook 20 minutes longer. Add chicken, corn, sugar, salt, pepper, oregano, poultry seasoning and cayenne. Cook 15-20 minutes longer or until vegetables are tender. 6 servings.

PEANUT BUTTER AND JELLY CAKE

¹/₂ cup crunchy peanut butter
¹/₂ cup butter or margarine
1 cup brown sugar, firmly packed
¹/₂ cup granulated sugar
2 eggs
2 cups flour
1 tablespoon baking powder

¹/₂ teaspoon salt
³/₄ cup undiluted evaporated milk
¹/₂ cup water
1 teaspoon vanilla
1 (10 ounce) jar currant jelly
1 recipe vanilla icing
¹/₄ cup chopped peanuts

Cream peanut butter and butter together in mixing bowl. Add sugars; beat until light and fluffy. Add eggs, one at a time, beating well after each addition. Sift flour, baking powder and salt together. Combine milk, water and vanilla. Add sifted dry ingredients alternately with milk mixture to creamed mixture, beginning and ending with dry ingredients. Beat after each addition, scraping sides of bowl constantly. Continue beating until mixture is smooth. Pour batter into buttered 13x9x2-inch baking pan. Bake in moderate oven (350°) 35-40 minutes. Cool. Break up jelly with spoon; spread evenly over cake. Prepare vanilla icing. Carefully spread icing over jelly on cake; sprinkle with peanuts.

Vanilla Icing

Combine ¹/₃ cup undiluted evaporated milk, 4 cups sifted confectioners sugar and 1 teaspoon vanilla; blend until smooth. Add ¹/₄ cup softened butter or margarine; beat until creamy.

FRIDAY
Shrimp in sherry *
Buttered asparagus
Corn on the cob
Molded fruit salad
Scones
Lemon sherbet

SHRIMP IN SHERRY

1 pound cooked shrimp, peeled, deveined
¹/₂ cup melted butter or margarine
¹/₄ cup chopped parsley
¹/₄ teaspoon paprika

1 teaspoon garlic salt
2 tablespoons garlic juice
¹/₄ cup cooking sherry (regular sherry can be used)
1 cup fine bread crumbs

Cut large shrimp in half. Add seasonings to melted butter. Stir in sherry. Lightly mix in bread crumbs. Place shrimp in small individual baking dishes. Form a crust over each with buttered crumbs. Bake 25 minutes at 325°F. 4 servings.

SATURDAY
Chinese Sundae Supper
Sherry
Cheese mold with chutney topping with crackers *
Chinese sundae *
Vegetable salad with Italian dressing *
Bread sticks / Raspberry yogurt with raspberry topping

Plan Of Work

Day before:

1. Prepare cheese mold. Refrigerate.
2. Cook chicken and get ready for "Chinese sundae."
3. Prepare dressing for salad.

Early in the day:

4. Prepare all condiments; place in serving dishes, covered.
5. Creamed chicken can be made early and reheat before serving. Set up carefully for serving; need plenty of room.

Thirty minutes before serving:

6. Prepare salad, keep chilled.
7. Unmold cheese onto a lettuce lined dish. Cover top of mold with chutney. Serve as an hors d'oeuvre.
8. Reheat chicken before serving.
9. Dessert will be assembled just before serving.

CHEESE MOLD WITH CHUTNEY TOPPING

2 cups (8 ounces) shredded sharp Cheddar cheese	*¼ cup mayonnaise*
1 (8 ounce) package cream cheese, softened	*½ teaspoon garlic salt*
1 tablespoon Worcestershire sauce	*¼ teaspoon Tabasco sauce*
¼ cup finely-chopped onion	*1 (8 ounce) bottle chutney (large pieces chopped)*

Combine all ingredients except chutney. Pack into a mold lined with plastic wrap. Refrigerate. At serving time, unmold cheese mixture onto a serving dish. Cover mold with chutney, allow it to drip around the sides of the mold. Garnish with parsley. Serve with crackers.

CHINESE SUNDAE
"Creamed chicken and a whole lot more!"

¼ cup chicken fat, butter or margarine	*¼ cup (½ stick) butter or margarine*
¼ cup flour	*½ cup chopped onions*
1 teaspoon salt	*¼ cup diced green peppers*
¼ teaspoon white or black pepper	*1 (8 ounce) can mushroom stems and pieces, drained*
1 cup chicken stock or canned chicken consomme	*⅓ cup diced pimientos*
1 cup half & half (milk can be used)	*3 or 4 cups diced cooked chicken*

Melt fat in a large saucepan; blend in flour, salt and pepper. Add chicken stock gradually, stirring constantly; add half & half and cook, stirring, until sauce thickens. Saute onions and green peppers in $^1/_4$ cup butter until onions are translucent and tender; add to sauce. Add mushrooms, pimiento and chicken. Cook until warmed through. 6 servings.

Condiments

4 cups cooked rice (can prepare instant rice)	*2 cups drained crushed pineapple*
2 cans Chinese noodles	*1 ½ cups coconut*
1 pound (4 cups) shredded sharp Cheddar cheese	*2 cups finely-chopped nuts (pecans or walnuts)*
1 ½ cups chopped green onions, use tops	*Creamed chicken*
1½ cups chopped celery	

All of the above condiments should be put into individual bowls, all looking alike if possible. Each individual serves himself. Start by placing a serving of rice in the center of the plate. Top with a portion of each condiment, in layers in the order given and end with a serving of creamed chicken poured over the top of it all. *Great flavor!*

VEGETABLE SALAD WITH ITALIAN DRESSING

½ head lettuce
½ bunch endive
1 cucumber, thinly sliced
1 large green pepper, cut into long strips
5 green onions (use tops), sliced
½ cup cooked green peas, or frozen peas,
*   thawed only*
1 stalk celery, sliced diagonally

2 tablespoons granulated sugar
2 tablespoons snipped fresh parsley
1 teaspoon monosodium glutamate
1 teaspoon garlic salt
½ teaspoon oregano
1 teaspoon coarsely-ground black pepper
1 cup salad oil or olive oil
⅓ cup wine vinegar

Place greens, cucumber, green pepper, onions, peas, and celery in a salad bowl; refrigerate until ready to use. Combine remaining ingredients in jar. Shake vigorously. Pour over vegetables. Toss gently before serving until all vegetables are well-coated. Serve immediately. 6 servings.

October - Fourth Week

One way to tell high quality pork is by its color. The lean high quality pork is grayish pink, has a fine texture and is firm. The fat is very white and is medium soft. In pork of poor quality, the lean is a deep red and both lean and fat is coarse and flabby. Pork should have the round "U. S. Inspected and Passed" stamp on it to assure you the meat is clean and wholesome.

Most cuts of fresh pork are tender, but it must be thoroughly cooked to avoid the risk of trichinosis. This is a disease contracted from eating raw or under-cooked infected pork (less than 10 percent of the pork in the U.S. is infected).

When pork is in great abundance, it is one of the best buys on the market. In general, the most economical buys are liver, ground pork, ham shanks and shoulder roasts which are usually roasted or broiled. Pork loin is the most expensive cut, but is also the most desirable.

All fresh meat is perishable and must be stored in the refrigerator immediately upon return from the market. Pre-packaged, cured or smoked meats, bacon, sausage and frankfurters are best stored in the refrigerator in their original wrapping. Packaged frozen meat should be left frozen at 0° or below.

In addition to the nutritional properties of other meats, pork is the highest in thiamine content of all the meats. Thiamine is an essential nutrient of the B vitamin group.

SUNDAY
A Great Sunday Night Supper
Baked Italian fish fillets *
Buttered spaghetti
Buttered Lima beans
Broccoli salad with pepper dressing *
Hot garlic sticks
Creamy chocolate mousse *

BAKED ITALIAN FISH FILLETS

1 pound frozen fish fillets, thawed
1 medium onion, chopped
2 tablespoons butter or margarine
1 (15 ounce) can tomato sauce
1 teaspoon oregano

1 teaspoon basil
1/2 teaspoon garlic salt
1/4 teaspoon pepper
1/4 cup grated Parmesan cheese

Place fish, skin side down, in a shallow 2-quart baking dish. Saute onion in butter until tender. Add tomato sauce, oregano, basil, garlic salt and pepper. Stir to blend. Pour over fish. Top with cheese. Bake at 350° (moderate oven) until fish flakes easily when tested with a fork, about 45 minutes. 4 servings.

BROCCOLI SALAD WITH PEPPER DRESSING

1 bunch fresh broccoli
2 tablespoons salad oil (olive oil is best)
1 teaspoon coarse-ground black pepper
1/4 teaspoon Tabasco sauce

2 tablespoons cider vinegar
1 tablespoon brown sugar
1 tablespoon soy sauce
1/4 teaspoon garlic salt (optional)

Peel the broccoli stems. Cut the stems and flowerets into 1- inch sections. Set them in a vegetable steamer and steam until broccoli has barely lost its crunch, about 5 minutes. Cool. Combine oil, pepper, Tabasco sauce, vinegar, brown sugar, soy sauce and salt. Stir vigorously until well-mixed. Arrange cooled broccoli on a serving dish. Pour on dressing and toss gently. Refrigerate, uncovered, until serving time. 4 servings.

CREAMY CHOCOLATE MOUSSE

1 (8 ounce) package cream cheese, softened
1 3/4 cups milk
1 (4 1/8 oz) package instant pudding and pie filling

1 1/2 teaspoon brandy extract
Whipped cream or whipped topping
Orange sections

Whip cheese until soft and smooth; gradually add milk. Add pudding, beat slowly until well-blended, about 2 minutes. Pour at once into dessert dishes. Just before serving, garnish with whipped cream or whipped topping and sections of mandarin or fresh orange. 4-6 servings.

MONDAY
Ricotta-stuffed jumbo macaroni shells *
Buttered asparagus
Lettuce and tomato salad
Garlic bread sticks
Baked fudge pudding

RICOTTA-STUFFED JUMBO MACARONI SHELLS

16 jumbo macaroni shells
1 (10 oz) package frozen chopped spinach, thawed
2 tablespoons Parmesan cheese
1 cup (8 ounces) ricotta or cottage cheese
1 cup (4 oz) shredded Swiss or Mozzarella cheese
1 tblsp chopped fresh parsley or 1 teaspoon dried
1/4 teaspoon nutmeg
1 teaspoon garlic salt
1/4 teaspoon pepper
1 egg, slightly beaten

1 teaspoon oil
3 cloves garlic, crushed
1 medium onion, chopped
2 cups tomato sauce
1/2 teaspoon basil
1/2 teaspoon oregano
1/2 teaspoon fennel seeds
1 teaspoon salt
1/4 teaspoon pepper

Cook shells according to package directions. Do not over cook. Drain and place on paper towels to dry slightly. Drain spinach and squeeze out any excess water. Combine spinach, Parmesan cheese, ricotta, Swiss cheese, parsley, nutmeg, garlic salt, pepper and egg. Mix thoroughly and stuff into macaroni shells. In small saucepan, saute garlic and onion in oil until tender. Add tomato sauce, basil, oregano, fennel seed, salt and pepper. Simmer about 10 minutes. Spread a little sauce over bottom of 10-inch baking dish. Top with stuffed macaroni shells. Pour remaining sauce on top. Sprinkle with additional Parmesan cheese. Bake in 350° oven for 30 minutes. If more sauce is desired, double the sauce recipe. 4 servings.

TUESDAY
Creamed fresh mushrooms and chicken in popovers *
Baked tomato halves
Carrot and cabbage slaw
Squash pie *

CREAMED FRESH MUSHROOMS AND CHICKEN IN POPOVERS
Popovers

1 cup flour
1/2 teaspoon salt
2 eggs

1 cup milk
1 tablespoon butter or margarine, melted

Sift flour and salt into mixing bowl. Add unbeaten eggs and cup of milk. Beat until smooth, using rotary beater, whisk or spoon. Add melted butter and continue to beat for 1 minute. Pour into buttered deep muffin pans or glass custard cups, filling each one 1/2 full. Place in preheated hot oven (450°). Bake 30 minutes. Reduce heat to 350° and bake 10 minutes longer. Cut off tops of popovers and fill with creamed chicken mixture or cut popovers in half and fill each half and leave open. 8 popovers.

Creamed fresh mushroom and chicken filling

1 cup sliced fresh mushrooms
1/4 cup butter or margarine, melted
1/4 cup all-purpose flour
1 cup chicken broth
1 cup milk

1 teaspoon salt
1/4 teaspoon pepper
2 cups diced cooked chicken
1/4 cup Sherry
3 eggs, hard-cooked, chopped

Lightly brown mushrooms in butter. Add flour; blend and add chicken broth, milk and seasonings. Cook until thick, stirring constantly. Add chicken, sherry and eggs; stir until hot. Serve in popovers. Makes 6 servings.

SQUASH PIE

1 (2 pound) butternut squash	1 teaspoon cinnamon
1 cup evaporated milk	1/2 teaspoon nutmeg
2 eggs, beaten	1/2 teaspoon ginger
3/4 cup firmly-packed brown sugar	1 (9 inch) unbaked pie shell
3/4 teaspoon salt	Whipped cream (optional)

Peel squash; slice in half, lengthwise and remove seeds. Cut into slices; place in saucepan and cover with water. Cover and cook for 15 minutes or until tender. Drain. Mash pulp thoroughly; set aside 1 3/4 cups mashed squash. Store remainder in refrigerator for other uses. Combine 1 3/4 cups squash, milk, eggs, brown sugar, salt, cinnamon, nutmeg and ginger in a medium bowl. Mix well. Pour squash mixture into pie shell. Bake at 450° for 15 minutes. Reduce heat to 300° and continue baking for an additional 45 minutes. Cool. Garnish with whipped cream. Makes one 9-inch pie. Note: To cook squash in microwave oven, pierce squash 10-15 times with a fork. Place squash on paper towel in microwave oven. Microwave on high for 16-18 minutes, turning squash after 8 minutes. Let stand 5 minutes. Cut in half, discard seeds, scoop out pulp and discard shell.

WEDNESDAY
Marinated pork chops *
Chunky cheese potatoes *
Buttered carrots with green onions
Fresh fruit with tomato French dressing
Flour tortillas / Baked fudge pudding*

MARINATED PORK CHOPS

4 pork chops 1 to 1 1/2 inches thick	1/2 teaspoon garlic powder
1/3 cup lemon juice	1 teaspoon ground ginger
1/3 cup soy sauce	

Place pork chops in a shallow baking dish. Combine remaining ingredients; mix well. Pour over pork chops. Refrigerate, covered, for 6 hours or overnight, turning occasionally. Bake at 350° for 45 minutes with half the marinade; then broil inside or on outside grill basting with remaining marinade until golden brown. 4 servings.

CHUNKY CHEESE POTATOES
(use leftover baked potatoes)

4 medium-sized prebaked potatoes, cut into large chunks	1 cup (4 ounces) shredded sharp Cheddar cheese
1/4 cup (1/2 stick) butter or margarine, melted	2 slices dry bread, crumbled
	1/4 teaspoon paprika

Arrange chunks of potato in 1 1/2-quart greased baking dish. Brush potato pieces with melted butter. Combine shredded cheese, bread crumbs and paprika; sprinkle over potatoes. Bake in 375° oven for 15 minutes, or until cheese melts and potatoes are hot. 4 servings.

BAKED FUDGE PUDDING

2 ½ cups flour
1 tablespoon plus 2 teaspoons baking powder
1 ¼ teaspoons salt
2 cups sugar
¼ cup plus 1 tablespoon cocoa
¼ teaspoon ground cloves
2 ½ teaspoons vanilla

1 ¼ cup milk
¼ cup plus 1 tblsp butter or margarine, melted
1 ½ cups chopped nuts, divided
1 teaspoon cocoa
3 tablespoons brown sugar
1 ½ cups hot water
Whipped cream or whipped topping

Sift together flour, baking powder, salt, sugar, ¼ cup plus 1 tablespoon cocoa and cloves in a mixing bowl. Combine vanilla and milk; add to dry ingredients. Add melted butter and ½ cup nuts, mix until well blended. Pour into well greased 9x9x2-inch square pan. In a separate small bowl, combine 1 cup nuts, 1 teaspoon cocoa and brown sugar. Sprinkle over the batter. Pour 1 ½ cups water over the entire surface. Bake in a 350° oven for 40-45 minutes. Serve topped with whipped cream or whipped topping. 6 - 8 servings. (Not a pretty dish, but great tasting. Serve from the kitchen. Place in dessert dishes topped with whipped cream, whipped topping or ice cream.)

THURSDAY
Deviled Swiss steak *
Buttered couscous
Spinach with shredded egg yolk
Raw vegetable salad with ranch dressing
Soft molasses cookies *

DEVILED SWISS STEAK

3 pounds bottom round of beef (½ inch thick)
¼ cup flour
¼ teaspoon pepper
2 tablespoons vegetable oil
1 large onion, sliced

1 cup water
4 beef bouillon cubes
⅓ cup steak sauce
3 tablespoons Dijon-style mustard
2 tablespoons brown sugar

Flatten beef with mallet or dish. Combine flour and pepper. Dredge meat in flour mixture. Brown on both sides in vegetable oil. Remove from pan and add onion, water, bouillon cubes, steak sauce, mustard and brown sugar. Bring to a boil; simmer until bouillon cubes and sugar dissolve. Add meat, cover and cook 1 ½ to 2 hours at low temperature. Transfer meat and onions to serving platter. Skim fat from sauce. Serve in gravy boat. 6 servings.

SOFT MOLASSES COOKIES

2 ½ cups sifted flour
1 tablespoon plus 1 teaspoon baking powder
½ teaspoon salt
¼ teaspoon baking soda
1 egg
1 cup soft shortening
½ cup light molasses

½ cup milk
½ teaspoon lemon extract
1 cup brown sugar, firmly packed
1 teaspoon cinnamon
1 teaspoon ground ginger
½ teaspoon ground cloves
Raisins for topping

Sift flour, baking powder, salt and soda into large mixing bowl. Put egg, shortening, molasses, milk, extract, sugar, cinnamon, ginger and cloves into blender container; cover and process on BLEND until smooth. Pour onto dry ingredients and mix well. Chill for 1 hour. Drop by teaspoonfuls onto greased cookie sheets; top each with a raisin. Bake 12 -15 minutes at 375°. 6-7 dozen cookies.

FRIDAY
Costumed Halloween Supper
Hot pepper cheese and crackers
Southern barbecue sauce on country style spare ribs *
Parmesan baked potato slices *
Marie's corn bread casserole *
Fruited spinach salad *
Orange sherbert with raisin garnish

Plan Of Work
Day before:
1. Prepare lemon bars and store properly in air tight container.
2. Prepare barbecue sauce, refrigerate until needed.
About 4:00 pm:
3. Put spare ribs on the grill or bake in the oven for 1 ¹/₂ hours. When finished, keep warm until served.
4. Prepare salad dressing, cook bacon and wash spinach. Prepare other salad ingredients, ready to assemble just before serving.
About 1 hour before serving:
5. Assemble ingredients for corn bread casserole. Place in oven 30 minutes before serving.
6. Prepare potatoes and place in same oven 30 minutes before serving.

SOUTHERN BARBECUE SAUCE ON COUNTRY STYLE SPARE RIBS

2 cups catsup	1 large lemon
¹/₄ pound (¹/₂ stick) butter or margarine	1 tablespoon grated fresh ginger (optional)
¹/₄ cup Worcestershire sauce	Salt to taste
5 cloves garlic, crushed	Tabasco sauce to taste
¹/₂ cup packed dark brown sugar	3 pounds country style spare ribs

Combine catsup, butter, Worcestershire sauce, garlic and brown sugar in medium-sized saucepan. Cut lemon in half, remove seeds, squeeze juice into sauce. add the squeezed lemon, also. Over medium heat, bring sauce to a boil, add ginger, salt and Tabasco sauce, stirring constantly, until sugar is dissolved. Grill spare ribs about 1 ½ hours or until almost done, then baste with sauce the last 30 minutes of grilling. Refrigerate any extra sauce. (Ribs may be cooked in the oven if weather does not permit grilling.) 4 servings, 3 cups sauce.

PARMESAN BAKED POTATO SLICES

¹/₄ cup (¹/₂ stick) butter or margarine	2 tablespoons grated Parmesan cheese
¹/₂ teaspoon salt	2 tablespoons chopped fresh red or green pepper
¹/₄ teaspoon pepper	2 tablespoons chopped fresh parsley
3 medium baking potatoes, washed, unpeeled, cut into ¹/₈-inch slices	

In ungreased 12x8-inch baking dish, melt butter in oven (5 to 7 minutes). Stir in salt and pepper. Stir in potatoes until coated with butter. Cover with foil; bake at 350° for 30 minutes. Remove foil; sprinkle Parmesan cheese over potatoes. Continue baking, uncovered, for 20-30 minutes, or until potatoes are crisply tender. Sprinkle with red pepper and parsley before serving. 4 servings.

MARIE'S CORN BREAD CASSEROLE

1 large onion, cut in thin slices
1/4 cup butter or margarine
1 (7 ounce) box corn bread mix
1 (8 ounce) can cream style corn
1 egg, beaten

1/3 cup milk
1 cup sour cream
1/2 teaspoon salt
1/2 teaspoon dill weed
3/4 cup shredded sharp Cheddar cheese

Saute onions in butter until tender. Add mix, corn, egg and milk. Mix well; pour in a greased 8x8-inch baking dish. Combine sour cream, salt and dill weed; spoon over batter in pan. Sprinkle cheese on top of all. Bake in 435° oven for 30 minutes.

FRUITED SPINACH SALAD

1 (15 1/2-ounce) can pineapple tidbits
5 cups spinach leaves
4 strips bacon, cooked and crumbled
1 cup sliced mushrooms
1 orange, peeled and sliced crosswise
3 tablespoons sliced almonds, toasted
3/4 cup cooking oil
3 tablespoons orange juice

2 tablespoons vinegar
1 tablespoon Dijon mustard
1 teaspoon dill weed
1/2 teaspoon grated orange rind
1/4 teaspoon garlic powder
1/4 teaspoon salt
Dash pepper

Drain pineapple, reserving 1/4 cup juice. Set aside. Thoroughly clean spinach; drain and tear into bite-sized pieces. In salad bowl, combine spinach, bacon, mushrooms, orange, pineapple and almonds. Thoroughly blend reserved juice, oil, orange juice, vinegar, mustard, dill, orange rind, garlic powder, salt and pepper. Toss 1/2 cup dressing with salad. Serve remaining dressing with salads. 4 servings.

SATURDAY
Standing rib roast and gravy *
Mashed potato casserole
Brussels sprouts
Green salad
Hot rolls
Praline cheese cake *

STANDING RIB ROAST AND GRAVY

3-4 pound rib roast, cut from the loin end or center of the rib of beef

1 tablespoon salt (optional)

Wipe the meat with a clean damp cloth. If a meat thermometer is used, insert so that the center of the bulb extends to the center of the thickest muscle of meat, but does not touch any bone. Rub the roast lightly with salt if desired. Place the roast, fat side up, on rack in the open roasting pan. Do not cover the pan and do not add water. Bake in a 300° oven to the desired degree of doneness. Use a constant temperature throughout the roasting period. (Rare, 18 to 20 minutes per pound. Medium, 22 to 25 minutes per pound. Well done, 30 to 35 minutes per pound.) Place on hot platter and serve with gravy. 6-8 servings.

Roast-Beef Gravy

3-4 tablespoons fat and drippings from roast
3-4 tablespoons flour
2 cups cold water, beef bouillon or milk

1 teaspoons salt
$1/8$ teaspoon pepper

When the roast is done, remove it to a platter. Pour the fat and juices from the roasting pan carefully into a cup or container. Measure 3 tablespoons of juice and 3 tablespoons flour into a bowl. Mix to a smooth paste and pour back into the unwashed roasting pan. Cook, stirring constantly, until a smooth, brown mixture is obtained. Add cold water, bouillon or milk. Season with salt and pepper. Serve hot with roast. 2 cups.

PRALINE CHEESE CAKE
Crust

$1/2$ cup (1 stick) lightly-salted butter or margarine
1 cup very-finely ground vanilla wafer crumbs
1 cup finely-chopped pecans

2 tablespoons white sugar
2 tablespoons brown sugar

Melt butter over very low heat. Combine butter with crumbs, nuts and sugars until well-blended. Press mixture over bottom and up sides of an ungreased 10-inch springform pan. There should be enough to coat the entire pan.

Filling

2 pounds (four 8-ounce packages) cream cheese
$3/4$ cup white sugar
$3/4$ cup brown sugar
3 tablespoons praline liqueur or rum

$1/2$ cups chopped nuts
Pinch of salt
4 large eggs

In a mixer, combine cream cheese and sugar and beat for 2 minutes, or until soft. Add praline liqueur, nuts and salt and blend thoroughly. Add eggs, one at a time, keeping mixer on lowest speed, just until each egg is incorporated into batter. Pour filling into crust and bake in 350° oven for 45-50 minutes. Remove from oven and let stand 10 minutes while topping is prepared.

Topping

2 cups sour cream
$1/4$ cup brown sugar, firmly-packed

1 teaspoon praline liqueur or rum
$1/2$ teaspoon maple syrup

Combine all ingredients. Spread evenly over top of baked filling and return to oven for 10 minutes. Remove and place immediately in refrigerator.

November

November - First Week

This is the season to entertain and be entertained, when most people think the house must be full of wonderful cookies, candies and sweet beverages. Hospitality prevails as families and friends join together and this means a lot of eating. So, to keep the spirit of hospitality and still hold everyone's weight down, try planning snacks that are colorful, tasty and low calorie, along with some of the traditional high-calorie snacks so that people do have a choice. Here are some suggestions:

1. There is nothing more beautiful than a colorful bowl of fresh fruits, and there is such a variety on the market now.

2. Have an attractive bowl of nuts on the shelf, with a nutcracker nearby. If people have to crack their own, chances are they will eat less. Skip the salted nuts that are shelled and ready to eat.

3. If homemade cookies and candy must be around, exercise a little portion control and make them very small so that two or three would equal one normal size. Most people won't take more than two or three.

4. Serve un-iced cakes and cookies; this adds fewer calories. In slicing cakes or pie, make them about 1/3 of the normal size serving. Often a small taste is as satisfying as a huge one. The size of the portion is as important as what it contains or how it is prepared. Cookies and cakes containing fruits, nuts and peanut butter certainly supply a lot of good nutrition. Serve them small also.

5. Many great low-calorie snacks can come out of the refrigerator:

a. Keep a bowl of marinated fresh vegetables, such as strips of carrots, celery, green peppers and mushrooms. Children like them plain; perhaps we should imitate the children.

b. Have slivers of cheese already cut to pick up with fingers. Cut the pieces small and skip the crackers.

c. Pickled eggs keep a long time and serve as a satisfying snack. The tiny pickled eggs are great left whole; if large, cut them in half or quarters. A whole large egg is usually too much.

d. Avoid tiny pastry tarts filled with a sweetened condensed milk mixture. The caloric content of this product is very high. Fill them with a cooked fruit mixture or old-fashioned lemon filling.

e. For beverages, have low calorie drinks and unsweetened fruit juices. Also, serve low-fat milk.

f. Encourage people to get their own snacks between meals. When they have to fix their own, they often lose interest or simply do not want to take the time to fix it and clean up afterward. The secret is for the homemaker to exercise these calorie cuts, but not to talk about them.

SUNDAY
Grilled steak with garlic sauce *
Oven baked potatoes
Sauteed green peppers and mushrooms
Harvest fruit ring with poppy seed dressing *
Banana nut bread
Chocolate pudding with whipped topping

GARLIC SAUCE FOR STEAKS AND HAMBURGERS

1 clove garlic	*1 tablespoon Worcestershire sauce*
2 tablespoons butter or margarine	*1 teaspoon paprika*
1/4 cup catsup	*1/2 teaspoon dry mustard*
1/4 cup vinegar	*Tabasco sauce to taste*

Place all in blender. Blend about 20 seconds, and serve with meat.

HARVEST FRUIT RING WITH POPPY SEED DRESSING

1 ½ envelopes (1 ½ tblsp) unflavored gelatin
⅓ cup cold water
1 ½ tablespoons finely-shredded preserved ginger
⅓ cup lemon juice
⅓ cup canned pineapple juice
⅓ cup sugar
¼ teaspoon salt

2 cups ginger ale
1 cup green grapes (or Tokay grapes, halved and seeded)
1 (11 ounce) can mandarin oranges, drained
⅔ cup pineapple tidbits, drained
Curly endive

Soften gelatin in cold water. Dissolve over hot water. Stir in shredded ginger. Add lemon juice, pineapple juice, sugar and salt; stir until sugar is dissolved. Add ginger ale. Arrange grapes (cut side up if using Tokay grapes) evenly around bottom of ring mold and pour just enough gelatin mixture barely to cover the grapes. Chill until set. Chill remaining ginger ale mixture until slightly thick. Stir in fruit. Spoon into ring mold. Allow to set several hours. Unmold on serving plate; garnish with curly endive. Serve with Poppy Seed Dressing (see index). (8 servings)

MONDAY
Tuna quiche *
Buttered Lima beans
Marinated tomatoes *
Cookies

TUNA QUICHE

1 frozen deep-dish pie crust shell
1 (6½ ounce) can tuna fish, drained
1 ½ cups shredded Swiss cheese or
　Monterey Jack cheese
1 medium onion, finely-chopped

2 eggs, beaten
1 cup evaporated milk
1 tablespoon lemon juice
1 teaspoon garlic salt
¼ teaspoon pepper

Thaw pie crust as package directs. Prick bottom and sides with fork. Bake on cookie sheet at 450° for five minutes. Remove from oven. Distribute tuna over bottom of pastry shell. Sprinkle cheese and onion over tuna. Beat together eggs, milk, lemon juice and seasonings. Pour over tuna mixture. Bake on cookie sheet at 450° for 15 minutes. Reduce oven to 350° and bake an additional 12 to 15 minutes or until top is golden. (4-6 servings)

MARINATED TOMATOES

½ cup oil
3 tablespoons cider vinegar
2 teaspoons Worcestershire sauce
¾ teaspoon salt (garlic salt may be used)
¼ teaspoon pepper
1 tablespoon sugar

1 clove garlic, crushed
1 teaspoon sweet basil
¼ teaspoon thyme
4 green onions, chopped (use tops)
2 or 3 ripe tomatoes, sliced
Lettuce

Combine oil, vinegar, Worcestershire sauce, salt, pepper, sugar, garlic, basil, thyme and onions. Mix well. Slice tomatoes (not necessary to remove skins). Add to marinade. Marinate overnight. Line individual dishes or large serving dish with lettuce. Top with tomato slices, drained. From marinade, spoon green onions on top of tomato slices before serving. (4-6 servings)

TUESDAY
Broiled whitefish fillet
Buttered rice
Stir-fry yellow squash
Golden congealed salad *
Corn sticks
Ice cream with praline topping *

GOLDEN CONGEALED SALAD

3 tablespoons (3 envelopes) unflavored gelatin
1 ½ cups cold orange juice
½ cup pineapple juice (drained from canned pineapples; add orange juice if necessary to make ½ cup)

1 cup mayonnaise
1 ½ cups finely-grated carrots
1 (20 ounce) can crushed pineapple, drained
½ cup chopped nuts (optional)

Sprinkle gelatin over ½ cup cold orange juice. Allow to stand until all gelatin is moist. Heat pineapple juice to boiling. Add gelatin and stir until dissolved. Add remaining cold orange juice. Chill until consistency of egg whites. Add mayonnaise and stir until evenly distributed. Add carrots, pineapple and nuts; mix well. Pour into 2-quart mold that has been rinsed in cold water. Cover and chill until firm. (8 servings)

CORN STICKS

1 egg
1 cup milk
2 tablespoons melted butter
2 cups white or yellow cornmeal

¼ cup flour
1 tablespoon sugar
2 teaspoons baking powder
½ teaspoon salt

Beat egg, add milk and melted butter. Sift together cornmeal, flour, sugar, baking powder and salt. Add egg mixture and mix well. Preheat corn stick pans in oven and grease thoroughly. Pour batter in hot corn stick pans. Bake in 450° oven for 12-15 minutes.

CRUNCHY PRALINE TOPPING

½ cup (1 stick) butter or margarine
1 cup brown sugar

½ cup chopped pecans
2 ½ cups corn flakes or other cereal flakes

Melt butter and sugar in pan. Bring to a boil and immediately remove from heat. Add pecans and corn flakes; toss together to coat cereal and nuts. Cool. Store in air tight container. Serve over ice cream. (Yield: 3 cups)

WEDNESDAY
Onion pot roast *
Mashed potatoes
Steamed okra and tomatoes
Cole slaw
Biscuits
Lovey's creamy peanut butter pie *

ONION POT ROAST

2-3 tablespoons fat drippings or a piece of fat
    cut from the meat
4-pound rump roast or beef round
1 teaspoon salt

¼ teaspoon pepper
½ - 1 cup water
3 or 4 onions, quartered

Place fat or drippings in heavy skillet and heat. Add meat and brown on all sides. Season meat as it is browned. Place a rack under the meat after it is completely browned. Add a small amount of water if desired. Pot roasts look better and have better flavor when the amount of water added is kept at a minimum. Add onions. Simmer slowly over low heat for 3 to 4 hours until tender. Serve hot. Drain liquid and fat in kettle and make gravy if desired. (6-8 servings)

CREAMY PEANUT BUTTER PIE

1 (8 ounce) package cream cheese, softened
³/₄ cup sifted powdered sugar
³/₄ cup crunchy peanut butter
1 (9 oz) package of frozen whipped topping, thawed

1 (8 inch) graham cracker pie shell
Coarsely-chopped peanuts, optional
Whipped topping, optional
Chocolate syrup, optional

In small mixer bowl, beat together cream cheese and sugar until light and fluffy. Add peanut butter, beating until smooth and creamy. Fold 9-ounce container of whipped topping into peanut butter mixture. Turn into prepared crust. Chill 5 to 6 hours or overnight or freeze. Top with more whipped topping. Garnish with coarsely chopped peanuts or lace chocolate syrup on the top of the pie.

THURSDAY
Skillet Pasta *
Peas and bacon
Sicilian tomato salad *
Hot Italian bread with garlic butter
Fresh fruit

SKILLET PASTA

1 pound ground beef, or bulk sausage
1 cup chopped onion
Dash of pepper
1 teaspoon oregano
1 teaspoon basil
2 teaspoons fennel seed (optional)
¼ cup chopped green pepper
2 (14 ounce) cans of diced tomatoes

½ cup tomato juice
1 ½ teaspoons garlic salt
1 teaspoon chili powder
1 (8 oz) package spaghetti, broken into small pieces,
    or 2 ½ cups elbow macaroni, egg noodles
    or any desired pasta
Parmesan cheese

In a large frying pan, add meat, onions, pepper, oregano, basil, fennel seed and green pepper; cook over medium heat until meat is brown and onions and green pepper are tender. Pour tomatoes and tomato juice over meat mixture and add garlic salt and chili powder. Bring to a boil. Add spaghetti or noodles and stir to moisten. Cover, reduce heat to as low as possible, and cook 40 minutes or until pasta is tender. Correct seasoning. Serve from the skillet and pass the Parmesan cheese at the table. (6 servings)

SICILIAN TOMATO SALAD

4 medium-size tomatoes	*1 tablespoon red wine vinegar*
Lettuce leaves	*1 ¼ teaspoons basil leaves*
1 medium-size red onion, sliced	*1 garlic clove, crushed*
½ cup (2 ounces) shredded Mozzarella cheese	*2 anchovy fillets, minced (optional)*
3 tablespoons olive oil	*¼ teaspoon salt*

Hold tomatoes at room temperature until fully ripe. Remove stem ends; slice tomatoes. Line the serving platter with lettuce. Arrange tomatoes and onions on top; sprinkle with cheese. Set aside. Combine oil, wine vinegar, basil, garlic and one anchovy. Pour over tomatoes. Garnish with one anchovy, if desired. Let stand at least 15 minutes before serving. (4-6 servings)

FRIDAY

Oven barbecued chicken *
Baked potatoes
Turnip greens with ham chips
Corn muffins
Pound cake with ice cream (optional) and sinful sauce *

OVEN BARBECUED CHICKEN

1 (2 ½ pound) broiler or frying chicken,	*1 ½ tablespoons Worcestershire sauce*
* cut into serving pieces*	*1 teaspoon salt*
¼ cup butter or margarine, melted	*¼ teaspoon pepper*
1 cup water	*1 teaspoon celery salt*
½ cup catsup	*½ teaspoon chili powder*
1 tablespoon vinegar	*½ tablespoon prepared mustard*
1 tablespoon brown sugar	*2 dashes Tabasco sauce or to taste*

Brush chicken with butter, place skin side down in broiler pan. Put all remaining ingredients in a pint jar and shake well. On each chicken half, pour 2 or more tablespoons sauce; cover with aluminum foil. Bake in 300° oven for 1 hour. Remove foil, turn chicken and add remaining sauce and cook until tender. (Foil may be used during last part of cooking time to prevent excessive browning.) Serve with or without sauce. (4-6 servings) Note: Sauce may be doubled and used another time.

SINFUL SAUCE

½ cup milk	*½ teaspoon vanilla*
⅔ cup honey	*1 cup creamy peanut butter*
¼ cup brown sugar, packed	*4 tblsp chopped salted cocktail peanuts (optional)*
1 teaspoon grated lemon peel	

In a medium sauce pan, combine milk, honey, sugar, lemon peel and vanilla. Stir in peanut butter until smooth. Place over medium heat, stirring occasionally until heated through. Serve over ice cream, waffles or pound cake. Can top sauce with salted cocktail peanuts. (8-10 servings) Note: Recipe may be prepared ahead and refrigerated. Simply heat and serve. (Yield: 2 cups)

SATURDAY
Saturday Night Get Together
Cold artichokes with quick Hollandaise sauce
Grilled butterfly leg of lamb vermouth
Western succotash
Buttered broccoli spears with Parmesan cheese
Beet relish with sour cream dressing *
Commercial whole wheat rolls
Sherry chiffon pie *

Plan Of Work
Day before:
1. Cook artichokes and make Hollandaise sauce
2. Prepare sherry chiffon pie
3. Prepare salad and dressing
One hour before:
4. Prepare lamb for grilling. Assign a family member to man the grill while lamb is cooking.
5. While grilling lamb, prepare the succotash and broccoli spears and heat the bread.

ARTICHOKES WITH QUICK HOLLANDAISE SAUCE
Wash artichokes thoroughly. Cut off stem. Pull off coarse outer leaves. Trim off about one inch from the top by cutting across the top with a sharp knife, letting the artichoke rest on a cutting board. Snip off any thorny tips from the leaves with kitchen shears. Drop the artichokes into a large kettle of boiling salted water. Cover and boil until tender, from 15 to 45 minutes. The artichoke is tender when the leaves may be pulled off easily or the stem can be easily pierced with a fork. Remove from water and turn upside down to drain thoroughly. Chill. Place in center of a dish, with Hollandaise on the side for dipping.

Quick Hollandaise Sauce

½ cup (1 stick) butter or margarine	*½ teaspoon salt*
3 egg yolks	*¼ teaspoon Tabasco sauce*
2 tablespoons lemon juice	*1 teaspoon dry mustard*

Melt butter but do not brown. Set aside. Place egg yolks, lemon juice, salt, Tabasco and mustard in the blender. Cover. Turn blender on and off once. Turn to high speed and quickly pour in the hot melted butter. Sauce will be emulsified. Keep warm to serve or refrigerate and heat as needed. If sauce thickens too much, re-blend with one or two tablespoons of water or lemon juice.

GRILLED BUTTERFLY LEG OF LAMB VERMOUTH

1 (6 to 7 pound) leg of lamb	*1 cup dry vermouth*
2 cloves garlic	*2 cloves garlic, crushed*
2 teaspoons salt	*2 tablespoons olive or salad oil*
½ teaspoon of black pepper	*Butter or margarine*
1 teaspoon fresh or ½ teaspoon dried rosemary	*Chopped parsley*

Have lamb boned at the market or do it yourself. Remove excess fat and sinews. Cut garlic cloves in half and rub meat on both sides. Sprinkle meat with salt, pepper, and rosemary, particularly on the cut side. Place meat in hinged wire broiler, spreading it out as you would a steak. Grill lamb over a rather low fire, turning it several times. Heat vermouth, crushed garlic and oil in small sauce pan and brush over the meat several times during the browning. It should take about 30 minutes to grill the lamb to a beautiful brown color and have the inside still juicy and pink. Place meat on a warm carving board and spread with a little softened butter or margarine and chopped parsley. Slice into thin slices. Simmer remaining vermouth mixture for a few minutes, then pour over each serving. (8-10 servings)

BEET RELISH WITH SOUR CREAM DRESSING

1 (16 ounce) can beets, drained (save juice)
 and chopped finely
1 (3 ounce) package lemon-flavored gelatin
Beet juice
$1/_2$ cup cold water

2 tablespoons vinegar
2 tablespoons grated onion1 teaspoon salt
$1/4$ teaspoon Tabasco sauce
2 cups lettuce
Sour cream dressing

Bring beet juice to a boil. Add gelatin and stir until dissolved. Add cold water, vinegar, onion, salt and Tabasco. Chill until thick. Fold in chopped beets. Pour into one-quart mold. Chill until firm. Garnish with chopped lettuce and topped with sour cream dressing.

Sour Cream Dressing

1 cup dairy sour cream
1 tablespoon vinegar
2 tablespoons grated onion
1 teaspoon salt or dill salt

$1/4$ teaspoon pepper
$1/2$ teaspoon sugar
Pinch dried dill (optional)

Combine all ingredients in bowl and mix until smooth and well blended. (6-8 servings)

WESTERN SUCCOTASH

$1/4$ pound fresh okra or 1 (10 ounce) package
 frozen okra, thawed
1 cup zucchini slices
$1/2$ cup onion rings
1 tablespoon butter or margarine

1 (10 ounce) can whole kernel corn, drained
1 cup chopped tomato
2 cups ($1/2$ pound) Jalapeno Pepper Pasteurized
 Process Cheese Spread, cubed

Saute okra, zucchini and onion in butter. Stir in corn and tomato; bring to a boil. Cover; simmer 10 minutes. Add process cheese spread. Heat until process cheese spread is melted, stirring occasionally. (6-8 servings)

SHERRY CHIFFON PIE

1 envelope unflavored gelatin
$1/4$ cup cold water
2 eggs, separated
6 tablespoons sugar
1 $1/2$ cups hot milk
$1/4$ cup sherry

$1/2$ teaspoon almond extract
$1/4$ teaspoon salt
$1/2$ to 1 cup whipping cream
Baked pie shell
Grated chocolate (optional)

Add gelatin to cold water. Beat egg yolks and add 2 tablespoons sugar at a time until all 6 tablespoons are used. Slowly stir hot milk into egg yolks. Cook over hot water until mixture coats a spoon. Remove from heat and add gelatin, stirring until thoroughly dissolved. Add sherry and almond extract. Mix well. Chill until only slightly thickened. Beat salt and egg whites until stiff. Fold into above mixture. Whip cream and fold into mixture. Pour into baked pie shell. Chill 4 hours before serving. Grated chocolate may be sprinkled over top before serving.

November - Second Week

When the fall holiday season comes around, our thoughts immediately turn to good food. The foods that take top billing are turkey, dressing, starchy vegetables such as sweet potatoes, the sweet congealed salads, and the luscious sweet desserts. All this adds up to good taste and a lot of calories. Two important items that are almost totally ignored are vegetables and fresh vegetable salads. These two items have so much to offer a holiday meal. For example:
1. They offer vitamins and minerals that are essential to a normal diet; good health does not take a holiday. We must work at obtaining it everyday. Fruits and vegetables add very few calories, but a lot of other good things.
2. Vegetables add vivid colors, if not overcooked. Overcooking destroys the natural color. So, choose the color you need to enhance your meal; it could be red, yellow, orange, green or white. Select the vegetable, then cook it properly with the minimum amount of time, heat and water. Too much of any of these will destroy nutrients as well as color.

Many meals need a variety of texture to make them appealing. If you need something crunchy, add a crisp raw vegetable salad or add water chestnuts or nuts to a vegetable or casserole as you cook. Stir-fry vegetables to maintain crispness. Your favorite vegetables blanched for 30 seconds to a minute in boiling water, then marinated in a favorite dressing, can be prepared ahead of time. This adds color, texture and flavor.

Steamed vegetables retain their crisp, tender state very well and can be served without fat. The calorie content is reduced, but the good vegetable flavor is still there. Try carrots and whole onions and cauliflower. Place the vegetables in a shallow pan, add about 2 tablespoons of water, and sprinkle seasoning on the vegetables. Cover tightly with foil and bake in the oven. All good natural flavor is retained. You can make any combination of vegetables and steam them. The secret to cooking the easy way is to have vegetables cleaned and prepared for cooking so that, at the last minute, you can cook with ease.

Before the meal, if serving hors d'oeuvres such as dip, instead of the usual crackers or chips, use only raw carrots, celery or green pepper sticks. Here again, you have color, texture, flavor, and above all good nutrition; to top it all, it is less expensive. Plan a holiday meal that is complete by including fresh vegetables.

If you are tired of the natural flavor, season vegetables with a suitable herb or spice. Try a little nutmeg on carrots or pep up acorn squash by adding a bay leaf, a little marjoram, sage or thyme. Use mint with English peas. Start by adding a small amount. Increase the amount until you get the flavor you like.

Flavored butter is a nice seasoning for vegetables. Melt the butter or margarine and then add the herb or spice. Butter with minced chives and parsley will improve potatoes, cauliflower, zucchini, green beans, asparagus or corn. Oregano mixed with butter is good with peas, corn or eggplant.

Whatever your choice, make vegetables special for your holiday meal.

SUNDAY
Sunday Night Supper
Healthy and hearty kale soup *
Canadian meat pie *
Tossed salad
Biscuits
Crunchy oatmeal cookies *

HEALTHY AND HEARTY KALE SOUP

1 lb. of fresh kale or 2 cups of canned kale, drained
2 tablespoons olive oil
1 medium-size yellow skinned onion
2-3 large cloves garlic, crushed
2 large potatoes, peeled and cut into ¹/₂-inch slices

1 cup cooked chopped smoked ham or ¹/₂ pound of
chorizo or Andouille sausage, sliced and cooked in
microwave for 4-5 minutes to remove fat
4-6 cups canned chicken broth
Salt and pepper to taste

If using fresh kale, remove tough stems. Wash and dry leaves in paper towels. Cut crosswise in ¹/₄- to ¹/₂-inch ribbons. Heat two tablespoons olive oil in a large sauce pan or deep skillet. Add onions and garlic and saute over medium heat until tender, about 5-7 minutes. Do not brown. Add kale, potatoes and chicken broth. Bring to a boil, turn heat down to medium and simmer until kale is tender and potatoes are cooked, 30 to 45 minutes (if canned kale is used, reduce cooking time to 15 to 20 minutes). Add meat and cook about 15 minutes longer to allow the flavors to blend. Season with salt and pepper. Serve hot. (4 servings). Note: Kale is a tough green vegetable and usually needs longer time cooking. If in a hurry, use canned kale. (6-8 servings)

CANADIAN MEAT PIE

Pastry for a double crust pie
¹/₂ pound ground beef
¹/₂ pound ground pork
¹/₂ cup chopped onions
¹/₄ cup water
1 ¹/₂ teaspoons garlic salt

¹/₄ teaspoon pepper
¹/₂ teaspoon dry mustard
¹/₂ teaspoon leaf thyme, crusted
¹/₂ teaspoon leaf sage, crushed
¹/₈ teaspoon ground cloves

Line a 9-inch pie pan with one-half of the pastry. Roll remaining pastry for top; cut a few slits for steam to escape, reserve. Combine remaining ingredients in a large skillet. Cook, stirring constantly, until meat has lost the pink color, but is still moist. Cool. Fill pastry-lined pan with cooled meat mixture. Cover with remaining pastry. Press edges together to seal. Crimp with flour-dipped tines of fork. Bake at 400° for 25 to 30 minutes. (4-6 servings)

CRUNCHY OATMEAL COOKIES

¹/₂ cup softened butter or margarine
¹/₂ cup granulated sugar
¹/₂ cup firmly-packed light brown sugar
1 egg
¹/₂ cup vegetable oil
¹/₂ teaspoon vanilla
1 ³/₄ cups all-purpose flour

¹/₂ teaspoon baking soda
¹/₄ teaspoon salt
¹/₂ cup regular oats (uncooked)
¹/₂ cup crushed corn flakes
¹/₄ cup flaked coconut
¹/₄ cup chopped pecans or walnuts

Cream butter. Gradually add sugars, beating well at medium speed. Add egg and beat well. Add oil and vanilla and mix well. Combine flour, soda and salt and add slowly to creamed mixture. Stir in oats and remaining ingredients. Shape dough into 1-inch balls. Place on ungreased cookie sheets and flatten each ball with the tines of a fork. Bake in a 325° oven for 15 minutes. Cool slightly. Remove from cookie sheet and cool. (Yield: 5 dozen)

MONDAY
Pronto beef Stroganoff *
Angel hair pasta
Quick glazed carrots *
Fruit and cottage cheese salad
Rye bread slices
Apple pie with crumb top

PRONTO BEEF STROGANOFF

1/4 cup (1/2 stick) butter or margarine (or oil)	1/4 teaspoon pepper
1 medium onion, chopped	1/4 teaspoon paprika
1 pound ground round steak	1 (8 oz) can mushroom stems and pieces, undrained
3 cloves garlic, crushed	1 (10 1/2-ounce) can cream of chicken soup
1 tablespoon cornstarch	1 cup sour cream
2 teaspoons salt	1/4 cup chopped chives

Place butter in large skillet. Add onion and round steak and brown. Add garlic, cornstarch, salt, pepper, paprika, mushrooms and simmer about five minutes. Add soup, simmer for 10 more minutes. Stir in sour cream and garnish with chopped chives. (4 servings)

QUICK GLAZED CARROTS

12 medium-size carrots, scraped, cut in half	1/2 cup syrup
Boiling water to cover	1/4 cup (1/2 stick) butter or margarine, melted
1/2 cup water	1/2 teaspoon salt

Parboil scraped carrots in boiling water until almost tender. Drain well. Arrange in buttered baking dish. Combine water, syrup, melted butter and salt together. Pour over carrots. Bake uncovered in a moderate oven at 350° for 20 to 30 minutes, basting occasionally. (6 servings)

TUESDAY
Tortilla soup *
Sausage and creamed cabbage *
Green salad
Sour dough raisin bread *
Ice cream with peach sauce *

TORTILLA SOUP

1 small onion, chopped
2 cloves garlic, crushed
1 tablespoon olive or vegetable oil
1 (4 ounce) can chopped green chilies
1 lemon, peeled and chopped
1 (10½ ounce) can beef bouillon
1 (10½ ounce) can chicken broth
1½ cups water

1 teaspoon ground cumin
1 teaspoon chili powder
⅛ teaspoon black pepper
1 tablespoon Worcestershire sauce
1 tablespoon bottled steak sauce
3 flour tortillas, cut into ½ inch strips
¼ cup shredded Cheddar cheese

Saute onion and garlic in oil until soft, not brown. Add remaining ingredients except flour tortillas. Bring to a boil, turn down heat and simmer for 45 - 60 minutes. Add flour tortillas and simmer for 10 minutes. Serve in bowl and sprinkle with cheese. 4-6 servings.

SAUSAGE AND CREAMED CABBAGE

8 ounces Sausage Links (or use brown and serve
* sausage links)*
1 (10½ ounce) can condensed cream of celery soup

2 teaspoons prepared mustard
4 cups shredded cabbage

Brown sausage in skillet until cooked through. Add soup, mustard and cabbage. Stir to combine. Cover and cook 10 minutes or until cabbage is tender. (4 servings)

SOUR DOUGH BREAD WITH WHITE RAISINS

1 cup starter (left at room temperature 8-12 hours)
1½ cups warm water
½ cup vegetable oil (not olive oil)
¼ cup sugar (or 3 tablespoons honey)

½ tablespoon salt
6 cups bread flour
1 cup white raisins (dark raisins can be used)

Combine starter, water and oil. Add sugar or honey, salt, flour and raisins. Mix well. Cover lightly. Let stand overnight. Punch dough down. Divide into 3 portions. Shape and place each portion in a 9x5-inch greased loaf pan. Let dough rise until just above edge of pans (3-8 hours, depending on room temperature). Bake in a 350° oven for 30 to 40 minutes. Cool in pan for about 5 minutes; remove.

Starter

2 cups flour
2 cups warm water

1 package dry yeast

Combine flour, water and yeast. Let stand in a warm place overnight up to 48 hours. The longer the mixture stands, the stronger the fermentation will be. After fermenting, the starter is ready to use or to store in refrigerator. "Feed" once or twice a week with 1 cup milk, 1 cup flour, 1/4 cup sugar.

RUTH'S PEACH SAUCE

3 cups mashed peaches
3 cups finely-chopped peaches
2 cups sugar

¼ teaspoon ascorbic acid
1 package Sure Jell

Combine and chill. Serve over ice cream. Refrigerate left overs.

WEDNESDAY
Pork chops on fruit pilaf *
Basic eggplant casserole *
Buttered spinach
Chocolate layered dessert *

PORK CHOPS ON FRUITED PILAF

4 lean pork chops, about ½-inch thick
Seasoned salt
³/4 cup uncooked regular rice
4 sliced green onions, including tops, but separated
1 cup chicken broth

1 can (17 ounces) chunky mixed fruit
(drain, reserve syrup)
2 teaspoons lemon juice
¼ teaspoon grated lemon peel

Sprinkle chops with salt and brown on each side in a lightly greased ovenproof skillet. Remove chops. Add rice and white part of onions. Cook until golden brown. Stir in broth, ³/4 cup of reserved syrup, lemon juice and lemon peel. Bring to a boil. Place chops over rice mixture. Cover and bake at 350° for 20 minutes. Stir in fruit and onion tops. Adjust seasonings, if necessary. Replace cover and continue baking 15 minutes longer, or until liquid is absorbed and rice is tender. Fluff lightly with a fork. Recipe may be doubled. (4 servings)

BASIC EGGPLANT CASSEROLE

1 pound eggplant, peeled and cubed
1 large onion, finely-chopped
1 tablespoon water
⅓ cup cracker crumbs
⅓ cup soft bread crumbs (packed)

1 ½ teaspoons Worcestershire sauce
1 egg, beaten
1 teaspoon baking powder
⅓ cup Parmesan cheese
1 cup (4 oz) shredded sharp Cheddar cheese, divided

Combine eggplant and onion and water in sauce pan. Cover and steam until vegetables are tender. Drain and mash with a fork. Add cracker and bread crumbs. Mix well and cool. Stir in Worcestershire sauce, egg, baking powder, Parmesan cheese and ¼ cup of the Cheddar cheese. Combine well. Place in a greased 1-quart casserole dish. Bake in a 350° oven for 1 hour. Remove from oven. Sprinkle with remaining Cheddar cheese and bake for another 5 minutes or until cheese melts. (6 servings)

CHOCOLATE LAYERED DESSERT (4 layers)

1 ½ cups flour
³/4 cup (1 ½ sticks) butter or margarine
1 cup chopped nuts, divided
1 (8 ounce) package cream cheese, softened
1 cup confectioners sugar

1 (9 ounce) package frozen whipped topping,
thawed, divided
1 (6 ounce) package instant chocolate pudding
and pie filling
3 cups milk

First layer: Combine flour, butter and ½ cup nuts; mix well. Spread on bottom of an ungreased 9x13x2-inch baking dish. Bake in a 375° oven for 20-25 minutes. Cool.
Second layer: Combine cream cheese, sugar and 1 cup whipped topping; mix well. Spread on top of the first layer. (Do not disturb first layer.) Third layer: Place chocolate pudding and milk in a blender jar. Blend at low speed for 2 minutes. Spread on top of second layer. Fourth layer: Spread remaining whipped topping on third layer. Sprinkle with remaining nuts. Refrigerate for 1 or 2 days. Refrigerate left overs. 15 servings.

THURSDAY
Baked chicken slices
Pasta pilaf *
Green beans in citrus sauce *
Slaw
Rolls
Apple pudding cake *

PASTA PILAF

2 tablespoons butter, margarine, or olive oil
1 medium onion, chopped
1 clove garlic, crushed
1 ½ cups chicken broth

1 cup very tiny pasta (orzo, a rice-shaped pasta,
  is preferred)
½ cup shredded Swiss or Gruyere cheese

Melt butter in medium skillet over low heat. Add onion and garlic. Cook until onion is translucent, stirring occasionally. Add broth, bring to a boil. Add pasta, bring to a boil. Cover, turn off heat. Let stand for about 25 minutes, or until all liquid is absorbed. If too dry, add a little more broth. Stir in cheese until melted. Serve from stove or place in casserole to serve buffet. (4 servings)

GREEN BEANS IN CITRUS SAUCE

1 pound green beans (two 10 oz packages) frozen,
  or 1 (16 ounce) can of green beans
1 inch boiling water
1 teaspoon salt
½ cup orange juice
¼ cup lemon juice

1 teaspoon cider vinegar
2 teaspoons cornstarch
2 ½ tablespoons brown sugar
1 teaspoon salt
¼ cup butter or margarine
½ teaspoon grated lemon peel

Remove stem ends from beans. Cut into 1-inch pieces. Add 1 teaspoon salt to boiling water; add beans and cook 15 minutes or until crisp tender. Drain. Combine orange juice, lemon juice, vinegar and cornstarch. Cook, stirring constantly, over low heat until thickened and smooth. Add sugar, 1 teaspoon salt, butter, lemon peel and beans. Cook gently until heated throughout. Serve immediately. (4-6 servings)

APPLE PUDDING CAKE

¼ cup butter or margarine
½ cup sugar
¾ cup apples, grated and peeled
1 cup all-purpose flour
½ teaspoon baking soda

½ teaspoon cinnamon
½ teaspoon allspice
½ teaspoon salt
½ cup walnuts, chopped
1 cup drained, soaked raisins

Cream butter or margarine and sugar together until light and fluffy. Blend in grated and peeled apples. Sift together flour, baking soda, cinnamon, allspice and salt. Stir this flour mixture into apple mixture. Stir in walnuts and raisins. Spread this batter in greased and floured 9-inch square baking pan. Bake in moderate oven (350°) for 30 to 40 minutes. While cake bakes, mix the topping.

Topping

½ cup sugar
1 tablespoon butter

Grated peel of 1 orange
Juice of 1 orange

Combine butter, sugar and grated peel and juice of orange. Cook in sauce pan until boiling, then reduce the heat and simmer until sugar is dissolved. Pour hot topping over the cake when it comes from the oven. Serve slightly warm, with whipped cream on top.

FRIDAY
Casual Dinner on a Chilly November Evening
Seafood Newburg on toast *
Lemon broccoli almondine *
Avocado salad with mushroom dressing *
Cran-apple cobbler *

Plan Of Work
Day before:
1. Prepare mushroom dressing, store in refrigerator.
Early in the day:
2. Prepare seafood for Newburg.
3. Clean broccoli
One hour before serving:
4. Prepare cran-apple cobbler and place in oven.
5. While dessert is cooking, prepare material for salad. Store in refrigerator.
6. Cook broccoli.
7. Prepare Newburg last.
All should be ready to serve at once. Cobbler can be served warm if taken from oven a few minutes before serving. It is a nice holiday dessert.

SEAFOOD NEWBURG

¹/₄ cup butter or margarine
2 tablespoons cornstarch
1 teaspoon salt
1 teaspoon paprika
Dash cayenne pepper
2 cups light cream or half & half

¹/₂ cup dry sherry
2 egg yolks, slightly beaten
2 cups cut up cooked lobster meat or crabmeat or
* cleaned cooked shrimp*
6 slices toast (or 6 pastry shells)

Melt butter in sauce pan. Blend in cornstarch, salt, paprika and cayenne. Remove from heat. Gradually blend in cream. Cook over medium heat, stirring constantly, until mixture comes to a boil and boils 1 minute. Reduce heat. Gradually stir in sherry. Blend a little hot mixture into beaten egg yolks, then stir all into remaining hot mixture in sauce pan. Add selected seafood. Heat, but do not boil. Serve over toast or in patty shells. (6 servings)

LEMON BROCCOLI ALMONDINE

¹/₂ cup water
³/₄ pound broccoli, trimmed, cut into spears
¹/₄ cup (¹/₂ stick) butter or margarine
¹/₄ cup sliced almonds, toasted

¹/₄ teaspoon salt
1 teaspoon lemon juice (more, if desired)
¹/₄ teaspoon grated lemon peel

In 2-quart sauce pan, bring water to a boil. Add broccoli. Cover; cook over medium heat until broccoli is crisply tender (8 to 10 minutes). Drain. In 1-quart sauce pan, melt butter. Stir in almonds, salt, lemon juice and lemon peel. Cook, uncovered, over medium heat, stirring occasionally, until heated through (2 to 3 minutes). To serve, spoon lemon-butter sauce over warm broccoli spears. (4 servings)

AVOCADO SALAD WITH MUSHROOM DRESSING

1 (4 ounce) can mushroom buttons, drained	*2 or 3 tablespoons olive oil*
1/3 cup finely-chopped celery	*1 teaspoon chopped parsley*
2 tablespoons thinly-sliced green onions	*3/4 teaspoon seasoned salt*
1 tablespoon chopped pimiento	*3 cups shredded lettuce*
1 tablespoon lemon juice	*2 medium-sized avocados*

Combine mushrooms, celery, onions, pimiento, lemon juice, oil, parsley and salt. Mix well. Arrange ³/₄ cup shredded lettuce on each individual salad plate. Cut each avocado in half and remove seed and skin. Slice ½ of each avocado over each serving of lettuce. Just before serving, top each salad with ¼ cup dressing. (4 servings)

CRAN-APPLE COBBLER

3 cups peeled, cored, sliced apples	*3/4 cup sugar*
2 cups chopped cranberries	*1/2 teaspoon ground cinnamon*
3/4 cup light or dark corn syrup	*1/2 cup mayonnaise*
1 cup unsifted flour	*1/2 cup chopped nuts*

Combine apples, cranberries and corn syrup; toss to mix well. Pour into greased 8x8x2-inch baking dish. In bowl, combine flour, sugar and cinnamon. With pastry blender or two knives, cut in mayonnaise until mixture resembles coarse crumbs. Stir in nuts; sprinkle over fruit. Bake in 400° oven for 30 to 35 minutes or until lightly browned. Serve warm. Save leftovers for lunch. (8 servings)

SATURDAY
Saturday Noon Meal
Congealed shrimp salad *
Broccoli in sour cream sauce *
Fruit salad with celery seed dressing *
Croissants
Raspberry yogurt

CONGEALED SHRIMP SALAD

2 cans condensed cream of tomato soup, undiluted	*2 cups mayonnaise*
1 (6 ounce) package of lemon-flavored gelatin	*2 cups (16 ounces) cottage cheese (small curd)*
1 cup finely-chopped celery	*1 (8 ounce) package frozen cooked shrimp, thawed*
1 small onion, chopped	*(Double amount of shrimp, if desired.)*
2/3 cup chopped green pepper	

Heat tomato soup, add the lemon-flavored gelatin. Chill. When slightly thickened, add celery, onion, green pepper, mayonnaise, cottage cheese and shrimp. Pour into a 13x9x2-inch baking dish or a 3-quart baking dish. Chill until firm. (15 servings) (This recipe can be divided in half. Use one 3-ounce package of lemon gelatin.)

BROCCOLI OR CAULIFLOWER IN SOUR CREAM SAUCE

1 bunch fresh broccoli (about 1 ½ pounds) or
2 packages (10 ounces each) frozen broccoli
spears (Use same amount for cauliflower)
2 tablespoons butter
2 tablespoons finely-chopped onion

2 teaspoons sugar
1 teaspoon vinegar
⅛ teaspoon pepper
1 cup sour cream
¼ cup chopped nuts (optional)

Cook broccoli or cauliflower. In top of double boiler, melt butter; saute onion until tender. Stir in sugar, vinegar and pepper. Gently blend in sour cream. Place top of double boiler over warm, not boiling, water. Heat until sauce is warm. Serve over broccoli. Top with nuts, if desired. (6 servings)

CELERY SEED DRESSING (For Fruit Salad)

1 cup plus 2 tablespoons sugar
1 teaspoon dry mustard
1 teaspoon salt
1 onion, grated
½ cup vinegar

1 cup salad oil
2 teaspoons celery seed
6 cups mixed fruit
Salad greens

Blend sugar, mustard, salt, onion and vinegar for about 15 minutes in blender at low speed. Remove cap and add oil slowly. Pour into bowl and stir in celery seed. Excellent on avocado and pineapple, but any fruit may be used. Will keep at least a month. Stir or shake just before serving, and pour on salad at last minute. (Yield: approximately 1 ½ cups)

November - Third Week

Advance food planning can save time, energy, money, nerves, disposition, and general good health, not to mention happy family relationships. It is always a comfortable feeling to have an adequate supply of prepared food on hand and in the freezer, to supplement every hasty meal served during this glorious festive season. Breads freeze well, so always prepare more than is needed, wrap and be sure to label with the name of the product and the date it is put in the freezer.

Always be aware of budget meat prices and plan holiday meals around the best you can get; freeze the meat and never tell your guests you "bought it on sale" — for some reason, it takes the festive feeling out of eating.

If you like banana breads or cakes during the holiday, buy overripe bananas at bargain prices. Mash them and freeze in the amounts called for in your recipe, and use as soon as you can.

Many times cheese is reduced, so shred it and freeze in cup-sized packages ready to add to any food combination. If bacon is reduced in price, buy it, cook it, and freeze in strips ready to be thawed, heated and bragged about at serving time.

On a dull chilly evening, make up various batches of salad dressings and have them ready to serve right out of the refrigerator.

For a quick, easy and charming dessert, don't forget the fruit you preserved last summer. A crystal compote, a dash of wine, a dab of topping, topped with a nut half, makes a dessert with glamour and flavor.

So, when cooking foods that freeze well for the next month, be sure to prepare enough for another meal, including spaghetti sauces, pie crusts, cakes, breads of all kinds, casseroles, and a whole lot more. Planning ahead at this time means more time for family fun.

Good Oven Sense

With so much holiday cooking going on this month, save time, money and energy by using a tried-and-true technique. If you use your oven for one dish, why not use it for the entire meal or for food to be used later. It takes very little more electricity to cook several items in the oven than if only one is cooked. It also relieves the cook from standing, stirring and watching; both time and money are saved. Here are a few rules to follow: Cook the protein dish (meat, usually) at the recommended temperature. Vegetables and most oven desserts, pies and quick breads, can be cooked successfully at temperatures 25 degrees lower than recommended for a longer time, or 25 degrees higher for a shorter time. All foods do best on the middle rack of the oven when there is room. However, if both racks are required, place meat and vegetables on the lower rack and breads and desserts on the higher one. Do not cook meats or poultry at a temperature higher than the one recommended because excessive high temperatures will cause meat and poultry to shrink and lose volume, fats to break down and raise the possibility of smoke; eggs and cheese-covered dishes become rubbery and custard will curdle. High temperatures can destroy most of the vitamin B1 (thiamine) and vitamin C.

SUNDAY
Broiled loin lamb chops with pineapple *
Italian tomato saute *
Zucchini wheels with basil and olive oil
Melon wedge topped with blueberries
Refrigerator rolls
Custard pie

BROILED LOIN LAMB CHOPS WITH PINEAPPLE SLICES

4 lamb chops, 1 ½ inches thick, cut from	*Few grains pepper*
the loin of lamb	*4 slices pineapple*
1 teaspoon salt	

Place chops on the rack of the broiler pan, two inches from the source of heat. Place slices of fresh or canned pineapple underneath the rack of the broiler pan. When half the cooking time is over and the surface is well-browned, turn the chops. Allow about 8 minutes for broiling each side of chop. When second side is well-browned, remove chops and pineapple from the rack and pan and place on hot platter to serve. (4 servings)

ITALIAN TOMATO SAUTE

4 medium-sized tomatoes	*1 clove garlic, crushed*
2 tablespoons butter or margarine	*³/₄ teaspoon salt*
1 cup diced celery	*1 teaspoon oregano leaves*
½ cup sliced onion	*⅛ teaspoon black pepper*

Hold tomatoes at room temperature until fully ripe. Cut each tomato into 6 to 8 wedges; set aside. In a large skillet, melt butter. Add celery, onion and garlic; saute for 5 minutes. Stir in salt, oregano and black pepper; cook and stir for one minute. Add reserved tomatoes; stir gently over moderate heat just until tomatoes are hot, about 3 minutes. (6 to 8 servings)

MONDAY
Fireside Supper for Family and Friends
Family-style vegetable beef soup *
Grilled ham and cheese on croissants *
Cabbage and pineapple slaw with sweet-sour dressing *
Ultimate Cappuccino and hot chocolate * / Raisin oatmeal cookies *

Plan Of Work
Day before:
1. Prepare raisin oatmeal cookies
Early in the day:
2. Prepare the vegetable soup and reheat before serving.
3. Prepare the salad to chill before serving.
Ten minutes before the dinner is served:
4. Prepare the sandwiches and serve hot.
Note: Prepare cappuccino just before serving; prepare hot chocolate for children.

FAMILY-STYLE VEGETABLE BEEF SOUP

1 ½ pounds beef chuck, cut into cubes	*1 cup chopped cabbage*
1 teaspoon salt	*1 (16 ounce) can tomatoes, undrained ****
½ teaspoon pepper	*1 tablespoon Worcestershire sauce*
2 bay leaves	*½ teaspoon oregano*
4 large carrots, scraped and sliced	*1 beef bouillon cube*
1 medium onion, chopped	*1 (16 ounce) can whole kernel corn,*
1 cup chopped celery	*undrained (optional)*

In 3-quart pan, add meat; cover with water. Add salt, pepper and bay leaves. Bring to a boil. Reduce heat and simmer for ½ hour. Add carrots, onion, celery and cabbage; simmer for another hour. Add tomatoes, Worcestershire sauce, oregano, bouillon and corn. Simmer for another 30 minutes. (6 servings). **Note:** You can substitute 2 (14 oz) cans stewed tomatoes or diced tomatoes for a richer flavor and a soupier texture. One or two cubed potatoes may be added.

BROILED HAM AND CHEESE SANDWICHES

12 slices whole wheat bread, buttered	*2 tablespoons catsup*
6 slices boiled ham	*2 tablespoons prepared mustard*
6 slices American cheese	*Melted butter*

Lay 6 slices of bread on cookie sheet, buttered side up. Place one slice ham and one of cheese on each slice of bread. Combine and mix catsup and mustard. Spread on buttered side of the other 6 slices bread. Place on top of ham and cheese. Brush outside of each sandwich with melted butter. Toast under a broiler or in a sandwich grill or in a skillet. Serve immediately. (6 servings)

CABBAGE-PINEAPPLE SLAW AND SWEET-SOUR DRESSING

⅓ head cabbage, shredded
1 (20 ounce) can crushed pineapple, drained
½ cup raisins
½ cup chopped pecans or walnuts

½ cup chopped celery
1 tablespoon poppy seeds
½ cup sour cream
½ cup honey

In a large mixing bowl, combine the cabbage, pineapple, raisins, nuts and celery. In a small bowl, combine the poppy seeds, sour cream and honey. Pour the dressing over the salad and mix thoroughly. Chill before serving. (4 servings)

RAISIN OATMEAL COOKIES

1 cup granulated sugar
1 cup firmly-packed brown sugar
1 cup shortening
2 eggs
⅓ cup molasses
3 cups flour
1 teaspoon salt
1 teaspoon cinnamon

⅓ teaspoon nutmeg
½ teaspoon cloves
1 teaspoon soda
1 teaspoon baking powder
1 cup undiluted evaporated milk
3 cups quick oats
2 cups seedless raisins
1 cup chopped nuts, if desired

Blend sugars, shortening, eggs and molasses until light and fluffy. Sift flour, salt, spices, soda and baking powder together. Add dry ingredients alternately with milk until well mixed. Stir in oats, raisins and nuts. Drop by heaping teaspoonful on greased baking sheet. Bake in moderate oven (350°) for 15-18 minutes or until light brown. Cool on wire racks. (Yield: 7 dozen cookies)

ULTIMATE CAPPUCCINO

3 cups coffee
3 cups half & half
½ cup (4 ounces) dark creme de cacao

¼ cup (2 ounces) rum
¼ cup (2 ounces) brandy

Combine all ingredients and heat. Serve immediately. (6-8 servings)

TUESDAY
Baked ham slices
Sweet potato bake
Onion pie *
Autumn fruit salad *
French silk pie *

ONION PIE

8 slices bacon, cut into small pieces
2 large onions, chopped (preferably Vidalia, but
  white or Spanish may be used)
1 cup milk
½ cup sour cream
3 eggs

1 teaspoon salt
½ teaspoon pepper
1 ½ teaspoons dried chives
¾ cup biscuit mix
Caraway seeds

Cook bacon and onions until onions are tender. Put into deep 9-inch pie pan. In blender jar, combine milk, sour cream, eggs, salt, pepper chives and biscuit mix. Blend until thoroughly mixed. Pour over onion in pie pan. Sprinkle with caraway seeds. Bake in 350° oven for 30-35 minutes. (6 servings)

AUTUMN FRUIT SALAD BOWL

1 head romaine lettuce
½ pineapple, pared and sliced
1 grapefruit, peeled and sectioned

½ red apple, sliced, unpeeled
¼ pound seedless red or green grapes
1 orange, peeled and sectioned

Line large salad bowl with romaine. Arrange fruit in sections around the serving plate. Dressing is not necessary. Fill center opening with fruit, nuts or cottage cheese. (4-6 servings)

FRENCH SILK PIE

1 ¼ cups (2 ½ sticks) butter or margarine, softened
³/4 cup sugar
2 eggs, beaten

1 teaspoon vanilla
1 ½ ounces melted semi-sweet chocolate
1 graham cracker crust

Cream butter and sugar with electric beater until smooth. Continue beating until mixture is very fluffy. Add eggs, vanilla and chocolate. Blend well. Pour into pie shell. Chill until ready to use. May be served cold or at room temperature. (6-8 servings)

WEDNESDAY
Luncheon
Clams au gratin *
Stir-fried spinach *
Grapefruit and almond salad in lemon French dressing*
Frozen coffee yogurt
Peanut butter cookies *

CLAMS AU GRATIN

1 pound (4 cups) Monterey Jack cheese, shredded
3 (6 ½-ounce) cans chopped clams, drained
2 tablespoons finely-chopped parsley
2 tablespoons chopped chives

2 cloves garlic, crushed
Dash red pepper
Dash black pepper
8 slices rye or pumpernickel bread

Combine cheese, clams, parsley, chives, garlic and pepper. Mix until well-blended. For each serving, place a bread slice in the bottom of an au gratin dish. Divide clam mixture among the dishes. Broil until golden brown and bubbly. Serve immediately. (6-8 servings)

STIR-FRIED SPINACH

1 pound fresh spinach
2 tablespoons oil
2 cloves garlic, crushed

½ teaspoon salt
¼ teaspoon sugar
⅛ teaspoon pepper

Remove tough stems from spinach. Wash spinach leaves and dry thoroughly. Heat wok or skillet. Add oil, salt and garlic and stir-fry 5 seconds. Add spinach; stir-fry 10 seconds. Cover pan and continue to cook 45 seconds. Uncover pan, add sugar and pepper and stir-fry 5 seconds. Serve hot. (4 servings)

GRAPEFRUIT AND ALMOND SALAD

2 ½ cups grapefruit segments   *1 green pepper, cut into rings*
1 cup slivered blanched almonds   *Lettuce cups*
½ cup dates   *Lemon French dressing (optional)*

Combine grapefruit, almonds, dates and green pepper rings. Mix well. Serve in lettuce cups. Top with dressing. (6-8 servings)

Lemon French Dressing

½ cup lemon juice   *2 tablespoons sugar or honey*
½ teaspoon salt   *½ cup olive or salad oil*
Few grains cayenne

Place lemon juice, salt, cayenne and sugar in blender jar. Pulse 2 or 3 times. With blender running, add oil. A temporary emulsion will form. About 1 cup.

PEANUT BUTTER COOKIES

1 cup sugar   *1 egg*
1 cup peanut butter

Combine above ingredients. Mix well. Roll into balls size of walnut; place on greased cookie sheet. Press with bottom of glass, then with a fork in criss-cross fashion. Bake in 350° oven for 8 minutes.

THURSDAY
Fresh Italian tomato sauce with meatballs on pasta *
Green salad
Hot garlic bread
Fresh fruit compote
Shortbread cookies

FRESH ITALIAN TOMATO SAUCE WITH MEATBALLS ON PASTA

8 ounces linguine or any pasta   *6 quarts boiling water*
2 teaspoons salt (optional)

Add pasta and salt to boiling water; cook until tender (al dente). Drain; top with fresh tomato sauce, meatballs and Parmesan cheese. (6-8 servings)

Tomato Sauce

1 to 2 tablespoons olive oil   *1 teaspoon fennel seed*
1 large onion, chopped   *5 cloves garlic, crushed*
4 green peppers, coarsely chopped   *Salt to taste*
1 banana pepper, finely-chopped   *Pepper to taste*
4 to 5 large fresh tomatoes   *Meatballs (optional; recipe follows)*
¼ cup chopped fresh basil or 1 tablespoon *Parmesan cheese*
*   dried basil*

Heat oil; saute onion, green peppers and banana pepper until slightly tender. Add tomatoes, basil, fennel and garlic. Simmer for 30-35 minutes. Add meatballs, if desired and simmer for 20 minutes longer. Serve over hot pasta and top with Parmesan cheese.

Meat Balls

1 pound lean ground beef
½ pound sausage
1 cup bread crumbs
1 small onion, finely-chopped
2 cloves garlic, crushed

1 teaspoon ground sage
2 teaspoons salt
½ teaspoon black pepper
2 eggs, beaten

Mix all ingredients and shape into balls of desired size. Place on a cookie sheet. Bake at 375° for 20 minutes. Drain all fat. Put in sauce and simmer as directed above.

FRIDAY
Liver fricassee over noodles *
Baked squash salad *
Relish tray - carrots, celery, radishes, apple slices, green onions, green and red pepper rings
Iced orange spice cake *

LIVER FRICASSEE OVER NOODLES

1 ½ pounds beef liver, cut into long
   strips (1x2-inch strips)
2 tablespoons vegetable oil
⅓ cup sherry
2 (14 ounce) cans stewed tomatoes
1 teaspoon sweet basil

1 teaspoon salt
¼ teaspoon pepper
2 cloves garlic, crushed
3 cups hot cooked noodles, buttered
   (2 tablespoons butter or margarine)

Brown liver on each side in oil. Drain off excess fat. Add wine and simmer gently for 5 minutes. Add tomtoes, basil, salt, pepper and garlic. Cover and continue to simmer for 45 minutes or until liver is tender. Remove cover and allow sauce to thicken if necessary. Serve over hot cooked and buttered noodles. (6 servings)

BAKED SQUASH SALAD

1 ½ pounds yellow squash, cooked and drained
½ tablespoon sugar
¾ cup mayonnaise
2 medium onions, finely-chopped
1 green pepper, chopped
¾ cup chopped nuts (pecans or walnuts)
*2 eggs **

1 cup (4 ounces) shredded Cheddar cheese
1 (4 ounce) jar chopped pimiento
1 ½ teaspoons garlic salt
½ teaspoon black pepper
¼ cup (½ stick) butter or margarine, melted
2 cups bread crumbs

Mash squash, add sugar, mayonnaise, onion, green pepper, nuts, eggs, cheese, pimiento, salt and pepper. Place in a 1 ½-quart baking dish. Combine butter and crumbs. Sprinkle on top of casserole. Bake in a 350° oven for 50 minutes. Note: If recipe is doubled, use 3 large eggs. (6 servings)

ICED ORANGE SPICE CAKE BARS

1 (6 oz) can frozen orange juice concentrate, thawed	2 cups sifted all-purpose flour
1/2 cup rolled oats	1/4 teaspoon salt
1 cup chopped nuts	1 teaspoon baking soda
1/2 cup shortening	1 teaspoon ginger
1/2 cup sugar	1 teaspoon cinnamon
1/2 cup unsulphured molasses	Orange Icing
1 egg	Candied cherries (optional)

Combine undiluted orange juice concentrate, rolled oats and nuts; reserve. Combine and cream shortening and sugar; beat until fluffy. Add molasses and egg; mix well. Combine and sift flour, salt, soda, ginger and cinnamon. Stir into molasses mixture. Add nuts; blend well. Turn into greased 13x9-inch baking pan; spread evenly. Bake in slow oven (325°) for 40 minutes. Cool. Frost with Orange Icing. Cut into 3x1-inch bars. Decorate with candied cherries, if desired. (Makes about 36 bars). Note: 1/2 cup candied fruit may be substituted for 1/2 cup nuts.

Orange Icing

1 1/2 cups sifted powdered sugar	2 1/2 tablespoons orange juice

Combine sugar and orange juice. Blend to spreading consistency.

SATURDAY
Baked eye of the round *
Herbed new potatoes via microwave *
Festive fresh onions *
Frozen cranberry salad *
Hard French rolls
Caramel cake

BAKED EYE OF THE ROUND

1 (4 pound, approximately) eye of the round roast	Seasoned salt (optional)

Rub surface of the roast with seasoned salt, if desired. Place in a 325° oven. Do not cover, and do not add water. Bake for 45 minutes; turn off heat. Do not open oven door. Leave roast in closed oven for 45 minutes more. Use left overs for sandwiches. (8 servings, while hot)

HERBED NEW POTATOES - Via microwave

1 1/2 pounds uniformly small red-skinned potatoes	2 tablespoons chopped fresh dill or parsley
1 tablespoon butter or margarine, cut up	Salt and freshly-ground black pepper to taste

Scrub potatoes and peel half-inch-wide strip from around middle of each. (For artistic effect, remove peel in spiral pattern.) Place potatoes and butter or margarine in microwave-safe 2-quart shallow casserole dish and cover tightly with plastic wrap, venting edge. Microwave on HIGH for 8-10 minutes or until potatoes are tender, stirring once, halfway through cooking time. Let stand, covered, 3 minutes. Sprinkle with parsley or dill, salt and pepper, and stir to coat well. Let cool slightly before serving. (4 servings)

FESTIVE FRESH ONIONS

18 small white onions
1 inch boiling water
1 teaspoon salt
1/4 cup butter or margarine

1/2 teaspoon sugar
1/4 teaspoon white pepper
1/4 cup sherry
Chopped fresh parsley

Peel onions and place, whole, in a sauce pan with boiling water and salt. Bring to a boil and cook, uncovered, 5 minutes. Cover and cook 12 to 15 minutes or until onions are tender. Drain if necessary. Add butter, sugar, pepper and sherry. Cook, uncovered, 5 minutes. Correct seasonings. Turn into serving dish. Sprinkle with chopped parsley. (6 servings)

FROZEN CRANBERRY SALAD

1 (15 ounce) can whole cranberry sauce, broken up
1 (8 ounce) carton of sour cream
1 cup chopped pecans

1 (20 ounce) can crushed pineapple, drained
6 lettuce cups

Combine all ingredients, place in freezer tray; freeze at least 2 hours. Cut into squares and serve on lettuce cups. (6 servings)

November - Fourth Week

"How do we keep our balance? Through tradition," says Tevye in *Fiddler on the Roof.* The great tradition of Thanksgiving in America is serving the festive bird — the turkey.

The real American tradition is to spend Thanksgiving on the farm. For most people that's now impossible, but the feeling is there when you serve a big broad-breasted turkey in an old-fashioned, deliciously roasted way — with cornbread stuffing and giblet gravy. That's a Southern tradition. Team it with all the delicious foods traditionally served at Thanksgiving, and you've given your family a touch of the past, a taste of the old-fashioned homey Thanksgivings of years gone by.

Actually, today's turkey is much better than the one Grandmother served; it is broader-breasted, more tender, cleaned and fresh-frozen so that it's at its best when you get it. Even the method of preparation has been improved to give the most succulent finished product.

Not only is the turkey a geat tradition and a favorite dish, but it is the highest in protein of any meat, high in the important vitamins riboflavin and niacin and even iron, yet low in fat and cholesterol. And, per haps best of all, its price has increased the least of all of the meats since Grandmother's day.

Thanksgiving or not, turkey is a great buy. No wonder it was the Pilgrim's Pride.

Following is the modern way to Oven-roasted Turkey:

To thaw — leave turkey in original bag and use one of the following three methods:

1. No hurry: place on tray in refrigerator 3 to 4 days.
2. Faster: place on tray at room temperature, 1 hour per pound of turkey.
3. Fastest: cover with cold water, changing water frequently. One-half hour per pound of turkey.

Refrigerate or cook turkey as soon as thawed. If you plan to stuff the turkey, do so just before roasting. Follow instructions on bag for commercially-stuffed turkeys. Refreezing uncooked turkey is not recommended.

Remove plastic bag. Remove neck and giblets from cavities. Rinse turkey and wipe dry. Cook neck and giblets for broth for flavoring dressing and for giblet gravy.

The big question is whether or not to stuff a turkey. The U.S.D.A. recommends against stuffing, but if you must, stuff just before roasting — not the day before. Follow your favorite dressing recipe if you wish to stuff the turkey, or bake stuffing on the side. To stuff turkey loosely requires 3/4 cup stuffing per pound oven-ready weight. Unstuffed turkeys require about 1/2 hour less roasting time. If not stuffed, rub salt generously in cavities, and, if desired, insert pieces of celery, carrots, onion and parsley for added flavor.

Fasten down legs either by tying or tucking under skin band. Neck skin should be skewered to back and wings twisted akimbo.

To roast: Place turkey breast up on rack in shallow roasting pan. Brush with butter, margarine, or cooking oil if desired. If a roast-meat thermometer is used, insert into the thick part of the thigh. Bulb must not touch bone or be embedded in fat. Roast in 325° oven. Time chart below is your guide to length of roasting time. When the thermometer registers 180-185°, the turkey is done. A "tent" of foil placed loosely over turkey will eliminate need of basting, although turkey may be basted if desired. Remove foil last half hour for final browning. If turkey is not too heavy for convenient handling, it can be roasted breast down (using V rack) for the first half of roasting time. Insert thermometer after turkey is turned breast side up. The breast-down method results in juicier white meat. Turkey is done when:

1. Roast-meat thermometer registers 180-185°.
2. Thick part of drumstick feels soft when pressed with thumb and forefinger.
3. Drumstick and thigh move easily.

APPROXIMATE COOKING TIME FOR TURKEY AT 325°:

Weight	Cooking Times for Unstuffed Bird	Cooking Times for Stuffed Bird
6-8 pounds	2 ¼ to 3 hours	2 ¾ to 3 ½ hours
8-12 pounds	3 to 4 ½ hours	3 ½ to 5 ¼ hours
12- 16 pounds	4 ½ to 5 hours	5 ¼ to 6 hours
16-20 pounds	5 to 6 ¼ hours	6 to 7 ¼ hours

We are at our most traditional when planning a Thanksgiving dinner. Here is a Thanksgiving dinner served to soldiers at Fort Morgan, Alabama, in November, 1912. Compare to ours.

Olives and Pickles
Oyster Soup
Roast Turkey
Oyster Dressing
Giblet Gravy
Cranberry Sauce
Celery
Candied Sweet Potatoes
Mashed Potatoes
Creamed Peas
English Plum Pudding with Brandy Sauce
Coconut Cream Pie
Mixed Candies and Assorted Nuts
Claret, Punch, Cocoa
Have a grateful day!

SUNDAY
Noon Day Meal
Creamy carrot soup *
Sweet and sour mushrooms *
Buttered rice / French peas and onions *
Confetti corn bread *
Danish raspberry bars*

CREAMY CARROT SOUP

1 pound carrots, peeled, thinly-sliced
4 ½ cups chicken broth
⅓ teaspoon salt
Pepper, white, if available

1 medium onion, sliced
1 ½ tablespoon butter
1 ⅓ cup yogurt
Unpeeled and thinly-sliced cucumbers for garnish

In sauce pan, combine carrots, broth, salt and pepper. Bring to a boil. Reduce heat and simmer until carrots are tender. Saute onions in skillet until tender (5 minutes). Do not let onions brown. Add onion to carrot mixture. (1 teaspoon curry powder (optional) may be added at this step). Puree half of the mixture at a time in blender until smooth, adding ½ of the yogurt to each batch. Chill overnight. Garnish. Soup should be very thick.

SWEET 'N SOUR MUSHROOMS

1 egg, beaten
2 tablespoons all-purpose flour
½ teaspoon salt
1 pound fresh mushrooms
Deep fat for frying
1 (8 ounce) can chunk pineapple in unsweetened pineapple juice
3 tablespoons cornstarch
3 ³/₄ cup sugar

⅓ cup cider vinegar
¼ cup soy sauce
1 tablespoon vegetable oil
2 small cloves garlic, minced
2 small onions, quartered and separated
2 carrots, peeled and thinly-sliced
1 medium-sized green pepper, cut in ½-inch pieces
Hot cooked rice

In small bowl, combine egg, flour and salt. Coat mushrooms very lightly. Fry in deep hot fat (360°) for 2 to 3 minutes or until lightly browned. Drain on absorbent paper. Keep warm. Drain pineapple. Add enough water to juice to make ⅔ cup. Remove ¼ cup and combine with corn starch. Set aside. To remaining juice, add sugar, vinegar, soy sauce and catsup. Set aside. Heat 2 tablespoons oil in large heavy skillet or wok. Stir-fry garlic, onion and carrots for 2 minutes. Add sugar mixture. Bring to boiling. Gradually stir in cornstarch mixture. Continue to cook, stirring constantly, until thickened and bubbly. Stir in mushrooms, pineapple chunks and green pepper. Heat through (about 5 minutes), stirring occasionally. Serve over rice. (4 servings)

FRENCH PEAS AND ONIONS

2 (10 ½-ounce) packages frozen peas, thawed
1 (16 ounce) can small onions, drained
1 (8 oz) can mushrooms stems and pieces, drained

3 tablespoons half & half
½ teaspoon sugar

Combine vegetables, add half & half and sugar and heat thoroughly. Stir until vegetables are well coated with half & half. (6-8 servings)

CONFETTI CORN BREAD

2 eggs, lightly-beaten
³/₄ cup milk
¹/₃ cup corn oil
1 (16 ounce) can cream-style corn
1 medium onion, finely-chopped
1 (2 ounce) jar chopped pimiento, drained

1 cup yellow corn meal
1 teaspoon salt
¹/₂ teaspoon baking powder
1 tablespoon plus 2 teaspoons sugar
1 (4 ounce) can chopped green chilies, drained
³/₄ cup shredded sharp Cheddar cheese

Combine all above ingredients except the sharp cheese. Pour into a greased 9x13x2-inch baking dish. Bake in 350° oven for 45 minutes. Remove from oven, sprinkle with cheese. Bake another 5 minutes or until cheese melts. Cut into squares. (12 servings)

DANISH RASPBERRY BARS

1 ¹/₂ cups sifted flour
¹/₂ teaspoon baking powder
1 ¹/₂ cups quick-cooking oats
¹/₂ cup sugar
¹/₂ cup brown sugar, firmly packed

³/₄ cup butter or margarine, melted
³/₄ cup red raspberry preserves
³/₄ up chopped almonds
Powdered sugar

In mixing bowl, combine flour, baking powder, oats and sugars. Add melted butter and stir to blend. Press about two-thirds of oat mixture in the bottom of an ungreased 9-inch square cake pan. Spread evenly with preserves. Add almonds to remaining oat mixture and sprinkle over preserves; pat down slightly. Bake 30 to 35 minutes or until golden brown in a 375° oven. Sift powdered sugar over top. Cool and cut into bars. (24 bars)

MONDAY
Creamy kale soup *
Toasted salmon sandwiches *
Do ahead salad *
Ice milk bars, commercial

CREAMY KALE SOUP

1 quart chicken stock or canned broth
1 pound fresh kale, washed and chopped
8 oz fresh bok choy, washed and chopped (optional)
3 sprigs tarragon (or 1 teaspoon, dried)
2 tablespoons olive oil
1 medium-sized onion, chopped

2-3 cloves garlic, chopped
5 scallions (green onions), sliced thinly
2 tablespoons flour (whole wheat is good)
1 ¹/₂ cups evaporated milk (may use skim)
Black pepper
Plain low-fat yogurt

In a large sauce pan, heat broth to boiling. Add kale, bok choy and tarragon. Reduce heat to a simmer. In a small skillet, heat olive oil. Saute onions, garlic and scallions for about 3 minutes, or until the onion is tender and translucent. Stir flour into the onion mixture and cook over medium heat for 4 minutes. Do not let the flour brown. Gradually add the onion and flour mixture to the liquid, stirring constantly until the mixture thickens. Simmer uncovered for 30 minutes. Cool slightly. If so desired, put soup in blender jar and puree the whole soup. Transfer soup back to sauce pan and reheat. Serve warm with a dollop of sour cream. (4-6 servings)

TOASTED SALMON SANDWICHES

1 (16 ounce) can salmon
12 slices white or whole wheat bread
1/4 cup (1/2 stick) butter or margarine, softened
1 (10 ounce) package frozen green peas, thawed
1/2 cup finely-chopped onions or 1/4 cup instant minced onion

1 (10 1/4-ounce) can cream of mushroom soup
4 large eggs
2 cups milk

Butter 6 slices of bread, place in a buttered 9x13x2-inch casserole dish, butter side up. Combine peas, onions and salmon. Spread on bread. Top with 6 slices bread, buttered side up. Combine soup, eggs and milk, and pour over bread. Bake 1 hour at 350°. Serve at once. (6 servings)

DO-AHEAD SLAW

1/2 medium-sized head green cabbage, shredded
1 green pepper, chopped
1 medium onion, sliced into rings
2 tablespoons sugar
1/3 cup white vinegar

2 tablespoons vegetable oil
1 teaspoon sugar
1 teaspoon salt
1/2 teaspoon celery salt
1/2 teaspoon dry mustard

In large bowl place shredded cabbage; top with layer of chopped green pepper and a layer of onion slices. Sprinkle 2 tablespoons sugar over top of onions. In sauce pan, combine vinegar, oil, 1 teaspoon sugar, salt, celery salt and dry mustard. Bring to a boil, stirring constantly. Pour over slaw in bowl. Cover, refrigerate at least 4 hours. To serve, toss salad to mix well. (4 servings)

TUESDAY

Italian meat loaf with tomato sauce *
Celery casserole *
Tossed salad
Hot garlic bread / Apple crisp *

ITALIAN MEAT LOAF WITH TOMATO SAUCE

2 pounds ground beef
3 cloves garlic, minced
1 cup bread pulled into small pieces, or oatmeal
1 large onion, chopped
2 teaspoons salt
1/2 teaspoon crushed red pepper

3/4 teaspoon oregano
1/4 teaspoon fennel seed, optional
1 teaspoon sage
1/2 cup parsley, chopped, or 4 tablespoons
   dried parsley leaves
1/2 cup grated Parmesan cheese

Put all ingredients into a large bowl and mix thoroughly. Shape into a loaf and bake in a loaf pan at 350° for 1 hour. (6-8 servings)

Tomato Sauce

3 tablespoons oil, preferably olive oil
4 cloves garlic, crushed
1 medium onion, chopped
1 (28 ounce) can tomatoes
1 (12 ounce) can tomato paste

1 teaspoon salt
1 teaspoon freshly-ground black pepper
1 tablespoon basil
1 tablespoon oregano

Saute onion and garlic in oil until soft. Put remaining ingredients into heavy pot. Add onions and garlic and simmer, uncovered, for at least two hours, longer if the sauce has not been reduced enough to be thick. Correct seasoning to taste. Pour sauce over the hot meat loaf and serve immediately. Note: This sauce is excellent over spaghetti, too; add chopped mushrooms for an extra touch.

CELERY CASSEROLE

2-3 cups celery, sliced	1 cup chicken broth
1/4 cup slivered almonds	3/4 cup half & half
1 (5 ounce) can water chestnuts, sliced	1 (4 ounce) can mushroom stems and pieces
3 tablespoons butter or margarine	1/2 cup Parmesan cheese
3 tablespoons flour	1/4 cup bread crumbs
1 teaspoon salt	2 tablespoons butter or margarine
1/4 teaspoon pepper	

Parboil celery for 5 minutes in salted water (1 teaspoon salt in water to cover). Drain, place in quart-size casserole. Add almonds and water chestnuts. Heat 3 tablespoons butter, stir in flour to make a smooth paste. Slowly stir in broth and half & half. Cook, stirring until thick and smooth. Add mushrooms. Pour sauce over celery. Top with cheese and crumbs mixed with 2 tablespoons of butter. Bake at 350° for 30 minutes. (4-6 servings)

APPLE CRISP

4 cups sliced cooking apples (peeled or unpeeled)	1/2 cup brown sugar
1 tablespoon lemon juice	1/2 teaspoon salt
1/3 cup sifted flour	1 teaspoon cinnamon
1 cup corn flakes, crushed	1/3 cup butter or margarine

Place apples in a greased shallow baking dish. Sprinkle with lemon juice. Combine flour, corn flakes, sugar, salt and cinnamon. Melt butter or margarine and mix with dry ingredients until crumbly. Sprinkle crumb mixture on top of apples and bake at 350° for 30 minutes. (6 servings)

WEDNESDAY
Sauteed ham slices
Broccoli and cauliflower supreme *
Couscous with mushrooms *
Fresh fruit with sour cream ginger dressing *
Toasted English muffins and jam

BROCCOLI AND CAULIFLOWER SUPREME

1 (10 ounce) package chopped frozen broccoli	1 (8 oz) package calorie-reduced cream cheese, cubed
1 (10 ounce) package frozen cauliflower	1/4 cup milk
1 medium onion, chopped	1/2 teaspoon basil
1 clove garlic, crushed	1/2 teaspoon marjoram
8 ounces fresh mushrooms, sliced	Salt and pepper to taste
2 tablespoons butter or margarine	2 cups Cheddar cheese, shredded

Cook broccoli and cauliflower according to package directions (slightly undercook). Drain. Place broccoli in greased 1 ½ quart casserole; add cauliflower. Saute onion, garlic and mushrooms in butter; put over vegetables. Combine cream cheese and milk in sauce pan, heat until cheese is melted. Add basil, marjoram, salt and pepper. Pour over vegetables. Top with Cheddar cheese. Heat until cheese is melted, if desired. (4-6 servings)

COUSCOUS WITH MUSHROOMS

1 cup fresh mushrooms, sliced
1 small onion, chopped
1 tablespoon butter or margarine
1 cup defatted* chicken broth
1 tablespoon snipped parsley
½ teaspoon garlic salt

½ teaspoon dried basil
¼ teaspoon dried oregano, crushed
¼ teaspoon pepper
²/₃ cup couscous
1 medium tomato, peeled and chopped

In a medium sauce pan, saute onions and mushrooms in hot margarine. Stir in broth, parsley, basil, salt, oregano and pepper. Bring to a boil; remove from heat. Stir in couscous, cover, let stand for 5 minutes. Stir in tomato. (4 servings)
* Chill broth, grease will float on the top and solidify. Remove fat and discard.

SOUR CREAM GINGER DRESSING (For Fresh Fruit)

2 tablespoons chopped crystallized ginger   *1 cup dairy sour cream*

Gently fold ginger into sour cream; chill. Let stand few hours or overnight before serving. (Yield: 1 cup)

THURSDAY
A Thankful Thanksgiving Dinner
Cranberry sangria, * champagne or cranberry juice
Roast turkey with corn bread or oyster dressing *
or Bread and chestnut dressing *
Holiday cranberry sauce *
Whipped potatoes * with giblet gravy *
Sweet potato souffle * or Creamy broccoli casserole *
or Double corn casserole *
Marinated tomatoes and onion salad **(see index)**
Overnight rolls **(see index)**
Old fashioned pumpkin pie *
Fresh apple cake with butterscotch sauce*
Currant tarts *
Ambrosia *

Plan Of Work

Day before:

1. Prepare corn bread for crumbs for dressing.
2. Prepare cranberry sauce.
3. Be certain turkey is thawed and ready to bake. Do not stuff.
4. Cook giblets for broth and gravy.
5. Prepare the overnight rolls (or buy commercial).
6. Prepare pumpkin pie.
7. Section oranges for ambrosia, combine with pineapple. Refrigerate and complete next day.
8. Prepare fresh apple cake and butterscotch sauce.

Early in the day:

9. Follow directions for the turkey and check timing according to the size of the bird.
10. Prepare dressing and refrigerate until ready to use.
11. Prepare giblet gravy. Refrigerate and heat before serving.
12. Check timing for rolls to be sure they will rise and be ready for oven as vegetables come out of the oven.

About two hours before:

13. Prepare broccoli and corn casserole.
14. Prepare sweet potato souffle.
15. Prepare whipped potatoes.
16. Assemble ambrosia.
17. When turkey comes out of the oven, immediately put in the broccoli and corn casserole, souffle and dressing. As soon as vegetables come out of the oven, put in bread.
18. Warm sauce for apple cake.

Have a great and comfortable dinner!

CRANBERRY SANGRIA

6 cups (48 ounces) cranberry juice cocktail	*1 lemon, sliced*
3 cups sweet red wine	*Sugar to taste*
1 orange, sliced	

In a tall pitcher, combine cranberry juice cocktail, wine and orange and lemon slices. Sweeten to taste. Chill several hours to blend flavors. Serve in large wine glasses with fruit. (12 servings)

ROAST TURKEY

Follow directions in the introduction to this section.

CORN BREAD AND OYSTER DRESSING

1 pint oysters*	*2 2/3 teaspoons seasoning salt*
1 cup finely-chopped onion	*1/2 teaspoon pepper*
2 cups chopped celery (stalk and leaves)	*2 teaspoons crushed sage leaves*
1 1/3 cups butter or margarine	*1 1/3 teaspoons thyme leaves*
12 cups coarse corn bread crumbs**	*1-2 cups chicken broth*

In large skillet, melt butter; add onion, oysters and celery. Cook and stir until onion is tender. Stir in about one-third of corn bread crumbs. Turn into deep bowl. Add corn bread, salt, pepper, sage, thyme and oyster liquor. Add as much broth as necessary to reach desired consistency. Stuff turkey just before roasting. Makes 12 cups, enough for a 16-pound turkey. Or, pack into a baking dish and bake one hour.

* 2 cups of bread or biscuit crumbs may be substituted for oysters.

** Corn bread may be made either from a mix or by your favorite recipe a week or two early, if desired. Then crumble and freeze until time to make dressing.

BREAD AND CHESTNUT STUFFING

³/4 (1 ½ sticks) butter or margarine
1 large onion, chopped
3 ribs celery, chopped
12 cups dry bread cubes or bread crumbs
3 tablespoons fresh parsley, chopped

1 ½ teaspoons salt
1 tablespoon poultry seasoning or 1 tablespoon sage
¼ to ½ teaspoon ground pepper
1 cup sliced water chestnuts, optional
About ³/4 cup broth or water

In skillet, cook butter, onion and celery until tender, stirring occasionally. In large bowl, combine bread cubes, parsley, salt, poultry seasoning and pepper. Mix to combine. Add butter-onion mixture and water chestnuts. Toss, adding as much liquid as desired. Pour in a 3-quart casserole for 45 minutes or until hot. (12 servings)

HOLIDAY CRANBERRY SAUCE

1 cup sugar
1 cup water
1 package (12 ounces) fresh or frozen cranberries

1 apple, washed, diced, unpeeled
1-2 ribs celery, chopped fine
1-2 cups nuts, coarsely chopped

Dissolve sugar in water in sauce pan. Cook cranberries in water with sugar until the cranberries pop and split. Cool. Add apple, celery and nuts. Refrigerate until used. (Yield: 4-5 cups)

WHIPPED POTATOES

6 potatoes, scrubbed, do not peel
3 tablespoons butter or margarine
⅓ cup hot milk or half & half

1 teaspoon salt
Pepper to taste

Place potatoes in pan and cover with water. Bring water to a boil and cook until potatoes are tender. Peel, cut into small pieces and place in mixer bowl. Start mixing immediately. (Do not let potatoes cool, or they will get gummy.) While mashing and beating, add the butter, half the milk and the salt and pepper. Add milk as necessary to reach desired consistency. Beat until creamy and light. Serve hot. (6 servings; may be doubled)

GIBLET GRAVY

¼ cup plus 2 tablespoons fat
¼ cup plus 2 tablespoons flour

4 cups broth, milk or water (use broth from cooking giblets)

When turkey is done, remove to warm platter and keep hot. Allow about ¼ cup gravy for each serving. Pour drippings (fat and meat juice in the roasting pan) into a bowl, leaving all the brown particles in pan. Let fat rise to top of drippings. Skim off all the fat. Measure the amount of fat needed for gravy and return it to roasting pan. The meat juice under the pan should be used as part of the liquid for the gravy. Set roasting pan with fat over low surface heat. Blend in flour and cook until bubbly, stirring constantly. If desired, brown fat and flour slightly to give more color and flavor. Add liquid which is cool or lukewarm, not hot, all at once. Cook, stirring constantly, until uniformly thickened. While stirring, scrape the brown particles from the bottom and sides of pan and blend into gravy. Simmer gently about 5 minutes. Trim any gristle from cooked giblets. Dice meat and add to gravy. Season to taste with salt and pepper. Serve hot.

Giblets

Turkey gizzard, heart and neck	*1 small bay leaf*
Water	*1 small onion, chopped*
1 teaspoon salt	*½ cup chopped celery*
3 peppercorns	*1 small carrot, sliced*
3 cloves	

The gizzard, heart and neck should be cooked promptly after being cleaned and washed. They must be cooked tender before they are added to gravy or stuffing. Use giblet broth as liquid in gravy or stuffing. Cover gizzard, heart and neck with water. Add salt, peppercorns, cloves, bay leaf, onion, celery and carrot. Simmer 2 to 3 hours, or until gizzard is fork-tender. Refrigerate unless used immediately.

SWEET POTATO SOUFFLE

5-6 large sweet potatoes, cooked in skin until tender	*1 ½ cups milk*
3 eggs	*3 cups miniature marshmallows*
1 ½ cups sugar	*½ cup (1 stick) butter or margarine*

Topping

½ cup (1 stick) butter or margarine, melted	*1 ½ cups crushed corn flake crumbs or wheat*
1 cup chopped nuts	*germ (optional)*
¾ cup brown sugar	

For topping: Combine butter, nuts and brown sugar in double boiler or over very low heat until butter is melted. Pour over potatoes before baking. Top with corn flake crumbs, if desired.

For potatoes: Remove skin from hot potatoes. Cut into small pieces or put through a ricer. Put potatoes in large bowl of electric mixer. While mixing, add eggs, sugar and half the milk. Add more milk as needed. Beat until smooth and creamy. In top of double boiler or over very low heat, combine butter and marshmallows. Cook until all is melted and smooth. Add to potato mixture. Mix well. Pour into a greased 3-quart baking dish. Add topping. Bake in a 400° oven for 40 minutes. (12 servings)

CREAMY BROCCOLI CASSEROLE

3 cups broccoli, chopped, cooked and drained, or 3	*½ cup chopped onion*
(10 ounce) boxes broccoli, frozen and thawed	*1 cup shredded Cheddar cheese*
1 cup mayonnaise	*1 (10 ¾ ounce) can cream of chicken soup*
1 egg, beaten	*½ cup seasoned bread crumbs*

Place broccoli in casserole. Combine mayonnaise, egg, onion, beat well. Stir in cheese and soup. Pour over broccoli. Sprinkle with bread crumbs. Bake in 350° oven for 30 minutes.

DOUBLE CORN CASSEROLE

1 (15 ounce) can cream-style corn
1 (16 ounce) can whole kernel corn, undrained
1 (8 ounce) carton sour cream

1 1/2 boxes corn bread or corn muffin mix
(about 12 ounces)
1/2 cup butter or margarine, melted

Combine all ingredients in large bowl. Pour into lightly greased 9x13-inch baking dish and bake at 350° for 45 minutes or until center is firm. (10-12 servings)

OLD-FASHIONED PUMPKIN PIE

2 eggs, lightly beaten
3/4 cup granulated sugar
1 (16 ounce) can solid packed pumpkin
1/2 teaspoon salt
1 1/2 teaspoon cinnamon

3/4 teaspoon ginger
1/4 teaspoon ground cloves
1 (12 ounce) can evaporated milk
1 (9-inch) pie crust
Whipped cream, optional

Place all above ingredients except pie crust in blender jar. Blend until smooth. Pour into pie crust. Bake in 425° oven for 15 minutes. Reduce heat to 350°. Bake additional 45 to 50 minutes or until knife inserted into center comes out clean. Cool. Garnish with whipped cream. (6-8 servings)

FRESH APPLE CAKE WITH BUTTERSCOTCH SAUCE

1 cup flour
1 cup sugar
1 teaspoon soda
1/4 teaspoon nutmeg
1/4 teaspoon cinnamon
1/4 teaspoon salt

1 egg
2 tablespoons evaporated milk
1 teaspoon vanilla
1/2 cup chopped nuts
4 medium apples, peeled and thinly sliced

Combine flour, sugar, soda, nutmeg, cinnamon and salt. Beat egg; add milk and vanilla. Add egg mixture to dry ingredients. Fold in nuts and apples. Beat well for at least a minute. Pour into a 9x9x2-inch baking pan.

Butterscotch Sauce

1/2 cup firmly-packed brown sugar
1/2 cup white sugar

1/2 cup (1 stick) butter or margarine
1/2 cup evaporated milk

Combine sugars, butter and milk in sauce pan. Cook over medium heat until sugars are dissolved. Serve warm over apple cake. (Yield: 2 cups)

CURRANT TARTS

1 cup currants or raisins, chopped fine
1 cup brown sugar
2 tablespoons butter
1 egg

1/2 teaspoon vanilla
1/2 teaspoon nutmeg
1/2 cup coconut
16 tart shells, unbaked

Cover currants or chopped raisins with boiling water. Drain and while hot, add butter, then sugar and beaten eggs. Add remaining ingredients and put in unbaked tart shells. Put pastry dough in muffin tins for tart shells. Bake at 400° for 15 minutes. (Yield: 16 tarts)

Pastry Mix

6 cups flour
1 tablespoon salt

1 pound shortening

Sift together fat and salt. Blend in fat until about the size of small peas or smaller. Store in covered containers. This will keep at least 6 weeks or more.

Tart Shells

Pinch off amount the size of a walnut and press with fingers into greased muffin tins.

AMBROSIA

6 apples, peeled and cut in thin slices
6-8 navel oranges, peeled, seeded and sectioned
2 (20 ounce) cans pineapple chunks, drained, juice reserved

4-6 cups canned moist and flaky coconut or grate 4 coconuts
3/4 cup sugar

In a large crystal bowl, layer apples, oranges and pineapple. Sprinkle each layer with generous amount of coconut and sugar. Repeat layers, end with coconut. Pour two or more cups of orange juice on all, then 1/2 cup of the reserved pineapple juice. Cover and refrigerate. (About 12 servings)

FRIDAY
Fettucine Alfredo *
Buttered spinach
Dilled green pea salad *
Hot Italian bread
Leftover Thanksgiving desserts

FETTUCINE ALFREDO

1 pound slim egg noodles
Salt
1/4 pound (1 stick) butter, softened

1 cup heavy cream
1 cup grated Parmesan cheese
Finely-ground black pepper

Cook noodles according to package directions in large pot of salted boiling water about 8 minutes. Drain well. Combine butter, heavy cream and half-cup of the cheese. Add to hot, dry noodles and toss thoroughly. Serve on plate topped with pepper and additional Parmesan cheese. (6-8 servings)

DILLED GREEN PEA SALAD

2 (10 ounce) packages frozen peas
3 tablespoons salad oil
1 1/2 tablespoons lemon juice
1/4 teaspoon dried dill weed
1/4 teaspoon basil

1 clove garlic (peeled and left whole)
Salt and pepper to taste
1 cup thinly-sliced celery
Lettuce
Hard-cooked eggs

Cook peas as directed on package, reserving ⅓ cup of the cooking water. Combine peas, the reserved cooking water, salad oil, lemon juice, dill weed, basil, garlic, salt and pepper. Chill thoroughly, at least 2 hours; discard garlic. Toss chilled ingredients with celery. Serve from lettuce-lined bowl; decorate with hard-cooked eggs. (6 servings)

SATURDAY
Beef cubes in beer *
Okra and tomatoes *
Spinach salad with bacon dressing *
Skillet muffins *
Ice cream with a choice of sauce:
Creamy caramel sauce *
Hot fudge sauce*

BEEF CUBES IN BEER

¼ cup (½ stick) butter or margarine	¼ cup flour
2 large onions, thinly sliced	2 cloves garlic, crushed
2 tablespoons oil or butter	1 cup beer
2 pounds chuck steak, cut in 2-inch cubes	Salt to taste
1 ½ teaspoons salt	Pepper to taste
¼ teaspoon pepper	

Melt butter in 10-inch skillet and saute the onions until soft and lightly browned. Dry the beef cubes and sprinkle lightly with salt, pepper and flour. Add oil to Dutch oven and brown meat, a few pieces at a time, over medium-high heat. Don't crowd the meat or it won't brown. When all the pieces of steak are nicely browned, add the sauteed onions, garlic and beer. Cover and simmer for approximately 1 ¼ hours or until tender. Taste for seasoning and serve at once. If sauce is thin, make a paste of 1 tablespoon flour and 1 tablespoon butter. Stir in and cook until slightly thickened. (6 servings)

OKRA AND TOMATOES

3 tablespoons bacon drippings or olive oil	1 small onion, chopped
2 ribs celery, chopped	2 medium tomatoes, peeled and cut into pieces
½ green pepper, chopped	1 tablespoon salt
1 pound fresh okra, sliced thin, or 2 (10-ounce) packages frozen okra in pieces	Salt and pepper, to taste

Saute celery, pepper and onion in bacon drippings until tender. Add remaining ingredients; cover with enough water to simmer. Cook slowly until done. May be served on rice. (4-6 servings)

BACON DRESSING

4 slices bacon, diced fine	1 tablespoon sugar
½ small onion, chopped	¼ cup vinegar (diluted if desired)
1 teaspoon salt	

Fry bacon until crisp; add onion and cook until tender but not brown. Add remaining ingredients. Heat and pour over salad ingredients, lettuce or spinach. (4 servings)

SKILLET ENGLISH MUFFINS

Canned buttermilk biscuits   *Cornmeal*

Separate each biscuit and flatten out to appear as size and shape of an English muffin. Dip each into cornmeal. Grease skillet. Preheat to 300°. Brown 7 minutes on each side. Serve with butter, jellies.

CREAMY CARAMEL SAUCE

3/4 cup light brown sugar   *1/2 teaspoon salt*
1/2 cup heavy cream (whipping cream)   *2 tablespoons butter*
1/3 cup light corn syrup

Combine in a pan. Bring to a simmer. Turn heat to low, cook until it coats the spoon, about 10 minutes. Add butter and blend until smooth. Will keep 10 days in the refrigerator. Pack in canning jar to store and refrigerate.

HOT FUDGE SAUCE

4 ounces semi-sweet chocolate   *1/2 cup brown sugar*
1/2 cup cream   *1/8 teaspoon salt*
2 tablespoons butter or margarine

Pour all of the ingredients into the top of a double boiler or on low heat and cook, stirring constantly, until well blended.

December

December - First Week

This festive holiday month is a great time to bring old friends together, especially students who are home for the holidays. Along with these festivities come many parties, and eating at fast food restaurants. As a result, American youths are eating more meat, fat and sugar. This does not mean that these foods do not have any nutrients. Most of them do: for example, hamburger, fish and chicken contribute good quality protein, iron and a good supply of the B vitamins. The enriched buns contain the B vitamins, as well as fiber and carbohydrates. Many fast food places now offer salad bars, whole grain bread and milk. However, you can still get too much fat. So, why not use your own kitchen for fast foods. Forget so much frying, especially the extra crispy chicken (it means the chicken remains in the fat longer), and the gob of mayonnaise on all sandwiches. At home, for a salad, you can also control the amount of salt added, and you will probably skip the bacon bits, croutons, excessive amount of cheese, and salty or pickled vegetables. Your pizza at home will probably not have the double-thick crust and unnecessary double supply of cheese. You can bake a potato at home and skip the high-calorie toppings. Most people eat the high-calorie additions because they are paying for them whether they want them or not. So, set up a fast food system at home. Go for the low-calorie drinks or milk when away from home.

Another idea: make your dips and topping with yogurt, not sour cream, and save over 250 calories per cup.

Remember the popular deep-fried vegetables in restaurants are great, but carry many more calories than the raw ones.

Being home for the holidays can be fun, healthy and non- fattening. All it requires is a little quiet thinking. And don't ruin eating for others by talking about cutting calories. Happy holiday fun!

This year, play it smart and prepare the Christmas goodies a day, a week, or maybe even a month early, and freeze them. You will be a giant step in front, ready for really unruffled entertaining. Then spend that bonus time with your family, making memories and following wonderful family traditions. Follow this guide to freezing cooked foods:

General Freezing Information: Garlic, pepper and celery intensify in flavor when frozen; onion, salt and chili powder lose flavor. Cool hot meats quickly by placing pan of cooked food in sink of ice water; cool food to room temperature before packaging. Freeze in family-size portions. Allow for head- space; some foods expand when frozen. Wrap with moisture- vaporproof materials; seal well. Label with contents and date.

For Yeast Breads: Bake as usual; cool quickly. Wrap and seal. Freeze up to 2 months. Thaw in package at room temperature about 3 hours.

For Quick Breads: Bake as usual; cool. Wrap and seal. Freeze up to 2 months. Thaw in package at room temperature about 2 hours. Or thaw, wrapped, in 250° to 350° oven.

For Cakes: Remove baked cake from pan; cool. Wrap and seal. Freeze up to 6 months. Thaw in package at room temperature 2 to 3 hours for large cake, 1 hour for layers. (Unfrosted cakes freeze better than frosted; store frosted cakes up to 2 months.)

For Rolled or Drop Cookies: Pack unbaked dough in freezer container; seal. Freeze 6 to 12 months. Thaw in package at room temperature till soft enough to be shaped. Bake as usual.

For Bar cookies: Spread dough in baking pan; wrap and seal. Freeze 6 to 12 months. Bake cookies, without thawing, according to recipe directions, increasing baking time if necessary.

For Baked Cookies: Bake as usual; cool thoroughly. Place in containers with waxed paper between layers and in air spaces; seal. Freeze 6 to 12 months. Thaw in package at room temperature.

For Unbaked Fruit Pies: Treat light-colored fruits with ascorbic acid, which is a color keeper to prevent darkening. Prepare pie as usual but don't slit top crust. Use metal or glass pie plate; cover with inverted paper plate. Wrap and seal. Freeze up to 2 months. To use, unwrap frozen pie; cut vent holes in top crust. Bake in 450° to 475° oven for 15 to 20 minutes, then in 375° oven till done. Bake frozen cherry or berry pies in 400° oven.

For Casseroles: Poultry fish or meat with vegetable or cereal product. If unbaked mixture is hot, cool thoroughly. Turn into oven-proof freezer container or foil-lined casserole. Cover and seal. Freeze 2 to 4 months. Uncover; bake in 400° oven for 1 hour for pints, 1 3/4 hours for quarts, or till food is hot.

For Meats (Roast Meat or Poultry): Cook as usual; remove excess fat and bone. Cool quickly. Wrap and seal. To freeze small pieces or slices, cover with broth, gravy or sauce. Wrap tightly; seal. Freeze 2 to 4 months. Thaw large pieces in refrigerator before heating. Heat meats in sauces in top of double boiler. Deep-fried meats or poultry do not freeze well.

For Fruit: If overripe bananas are on sale, buy them, mash them, add a little lemon juice to keep from darkening and freeze for holiday baking.

SUNDAY
December Breakfast Buffet
Assorted chilled fresh fruit in compote *
Individual ham loaves on pineapple rings *
Eggs and mushroom scramble *
Cheesy grits casserole *
Orange rolls *
Angel biscuits *
Filled coffee cake *

Plan Of Work

Day before:
1. Prepare fruit compote and chill to be ready to put in individual compotes.
2. Prepare the ham loaves. Cook, cool and refrigerate.
3. Prepare cheesy grits casserole. Cook, cool and refrigerate.
4. Prepare the orange rolls and the filled coffee cake, wrap in foil.

Two hours before serving:
5. Prepare angel biscuits

Thirty minutes before:
6. Put grits in oven to re-heat.
7. Put the ham loaves in oven to re-heat.
8. Egg and mushroom scramble should be prepared last.

This is a great party buffet without last minute preparations!

ASSORTED CHILLED FRESH FRUIT COMPOTE

1 cantaloupe	*1 pint fresh strawberries*
1 honeydew melon	*3 kiwi*
2 bananas	*Orange juice (optional)*

Remove rind and seeds from melons and cut into one-inch cubes. Wash and remove stems of strawberries. Store melon cubes and strawberries in refrigerator until ready to combine with other fruit. Just before serving, peel bananas and slice crosswise. Remove peel from kiwi and slice crosswise. Combine all fruit, cover with orange juice, and chill until ready to serve. (6-8 servings)

INDIVIDUAL HAM LOAVES

2 pounds ground smoked ham
6 slices canned pineapple
6 ½-inch squares pimiento
1 (5 ⅓-ounce) can of evaporated milk
½ teaspoon curry powder

1 tablespoon instant minced onion
1 egg, beaten
½ cup crushed unsalted crackers
2 tablespoons catsup
1 tablespoon chopped parsley

Place a pineapple slice in the bottom of each of 6 aluminum tart pans. Fill center of each pineapple slice with a square of pimiento. Mix 2 tablespoons evaporated milk with curry powder and sprinkle 1 teaspoon of the liquid over each pineapple slice. Add remaining evaporated milk to instant onion. Lightly but thoroughly combine ground ham, egg, cracker crumbs, catsup and parsley; mix in evaporated milk with onion. Divide meat mixture into sixths and place 1 portion on pineapple ring in each pan, pressing lightly to mound. Cover each pan tightly with aluminum, securing around rim of pan. Cook in 350° oven for 45 to 55 minutes or until done. Invert pans to remove loaves and serve pineapple side up. 6 servings)

EGG AND MUSHROOM SCRAMBLE

½ cup (1 stick) butter or margarine, divided
1 pound fresh mushrooms, sliced
10 eggs, beaten
4 green onions, finely chopped (use tops)

¼ cup half & half
³/₄ teaspoon salt
³/₄ teaspoon coarsely-cracked black pepper

In a large skillet, melt ¼ cup (½ stick) butter. Add mushrooms and saute until tender. Remove to a container and keep hot. Combine eggs, green onion, half-and-half, salt and pepper. Beat until frothy. Add remaining butter to skillet and heat. Pour egg mixture into the hot skillet and move about gently to cook until just set and still slightly moist. Put into serving dish and top with mushrooms. (6 servings)

CHEESY GRITS CASSEROLE

2 cups instant grits
½ teaspoon garlic powder
1 teaspoon garlic salt
1 teaspoon coarsely-cracked black pepper
2 cups boiling water

2 cups (½ pound) sharp Cheddar cheese,
*   cut into ½-inch cubes*
1 cup (4 ounces) shredded sharp Cheddar cheese
1 tablespoon Worcestershire sauce
2 eggs, beaten

In a large mixing bowl, combine grits, garlic powder, salt and pepper. Add boiling water and stir until absorbed. Add cheese cubes, shredded cheese, Worcestershire sauce and eggs. Stir to mix. Pour into a greased 1 ½-quart casserole and bake for 30 to 40 minutes or until firm. (6-8 servings)

ORANGE ROLLS

½ cup orange juice
1 cup sugar, divided
1 tablespoon grated orange rind, divided
³/₄ cup (1 ½ sticks) butter or margarine, divided
2 packages active dried yeast

1 ¼ cups warm water
1 teaspoon salt
2 eggs, beaten
3 ¼ cups all-purpose flour

In small sauce pan, combine orange juice, ³/₄ cups sugar, 2 teaspoons rind, ¼ cup (½ stick) butter; cook over medium heat for 2 minutes. Spoon 2 to 3 teaspoons in muffin cups. In large mixer bowl, add yeast and warm water, stir until dissolved. Add ¼ cup sugar, salt, ½ cup (1 stick) butter, eggs, 1 teaspoon rind, 2 cups flour. Blend at low speed. Beat 2 minutes at medium speed. Blend in 1 ¼ cups flour. Beat one minute. Spoon in cups. Let rise for 30 minutes. Bake in 375° oven for 20 minutes. Remove from pan immediately. (Yield: approximately 12 rolls)

ANGEL BISCUITS

2 packages (¼ ounce each) active dry yeast
¼ cup warm water
2 cups warm buttermilk
5 cups all-purpose flour
⅓ cup sugar

1 tablespoon baking powder
1 teaspoon baking soda
2 teaspoons salt
1 cup shortening
Melted butter or margarine

Dissolve yeast in warm water. Let stand 5 minutes. Stir in buttermilk; set aside. In a large mixing bowl, combine flour, sugar, baking powder, soda and salt. Cut in shortening with a pastry blender until mixture resembles coarse meal. Stir in yeast-buttermilk mixture; mix well. Turn out onto lightly floured surface; knead lightly 3-4 times. Roll to ½-inch thickness. Cut with a 2 ½-inch biscuit cutter. Place on a lightly-greased baking sheet. Cover and let rise in a warm place about 1 ½ hours. Bake in a 450° oven for 8-10 minutes. Lightly brush tops with melted butter. Yield: about 2 ½ dozen.

FILLED COFFEE CAKE

1 cup (2 sticks) butter or margarine, softened
2 cups sugar
3 eggs
1 (8 ounce) carton commercial sour cream
1 teaspoon vanilla extract
2 cups all-purpose flour

2 teaspoons baking powder
¼ teaspoon salt
³/₄ cup chopped nuts (pecans or walnuts)
2 tablespoons sugar
1 teaspoon ground cinnamon

Cream butter and sugar until light in a large mixing bowl; add eggs, one at a time, beating well after each addition. Add sour cream and vanilla; mix well. Combine flour, baking powder and salt, stir into batter; set aside. Combine nuts, 2 tablespoons sugar and cinnamon; set aside. Pour ½ of the batter into a greased and floured 10-inch Bundt or tube pan; sprinkle with ½ of the nut mixture. Repeat process with remaining batter and nut mixture. Bake at 350° for 55 to 60 minutes or until done. Let cool slightly in pan; remove from pan and cool completely. (Yield: 12-16 servings)

MONDAY
Borscht *
Chicken Marengo*
Buttered peas
Grapefruit salad
Custard cup

BORSCHT

1 small onion, chopped	*1-2 tablespoons red wine vinegar*
1 clove garlic, minced	*3 cups beef bouillon*
1 tablespoon cooking oil	*¼ small head of cabbage, shredded*
1 carrot, sliced	*1 large potato, pared and diced*
1 tomato, chopped	*½ pound Polish or hickory-smoked sausage, sliced*
1 teaspoon salt	*1 (16 ounce) can julienne beets, optional*
⅛ teaspoon pepper	*Sour cream or yogurt, optional*

In a 2-quart kettle, saute onion and garlic in oil until soft. Add carrots and cook two more minutes. Add tomato, salt, pepper, vinegar and bouillon. Heat to boiling. Reduce heat, cover, simmer 30 minutes. Add cabbage, potato and sausage; simmer 15 minutes longer or until potato is tender. Serve in bowl, top with beets and sour cream. (4-5 servings)

CHICKEN MARENGO

1 frying chicken, cut into serving pieces	*½ cup chicken stock or bouillon*
½ cup flour	*1 clove garlic, crushed*
½ teaspoon salt	*½ cup dry white wine, optional*
¼ teaspoon pepper	*12 mushroom caps*
3 tablespoons oil	*1 tablespoon butter*
1 small onion, chopped	*½ cup croutons, optional*
3 tomatoes	*Parsley*
3 tablespoons tomato sauce	

Combine flour, salt and pepper in plastic bag. Add chicken pieces and shake to cover. Cook chicken in hot oil to golden brown on all sides. Add onion and saute. Add tomatoes, sauce, stock and garlic. Season with salt and pepper. Cover, simmer 1 hour. Add wine, cook 15 minutes. Saute mushroom tops in butter. Serve chicken on hot platter. Put croutons on chicken. Pour sauce over all. Garnish with mushroom caps and parsley. (4-6 servings)

TUESDAY
Pot roast with potatoes and carrots *
Cheese rice mold *
Green pepper and celery sticks
Old fashioned custard pie *

POT ROAST WITH POTATOES/CARROTS

2 tablespoons oil	1 bay leaf
3-4 pounds of beef pot roast (chuck or rump)	1 cup boiling water
½ cup chopped onion	4-6 potatoes
2 ½ teaspoons seasoned salt	4-6 carrots
¼ teaspoon black pepper	

Heat the oil for about three minutes in Dutch oven or heavy pan. Brown meat about 8 minutes on each side. Add onion, seasonings and boiling water. Cover and bring to boil quickly. Turn heat down and simmer for 3 hours. Add potatoes and carrots. Cover and bring to boil quickly. Turn heat down. Simmer for 45 minutes or until vegetables are tender. (4-6 servings)

CHEESE RICE MOLD

1 cup rice	1 cup (4 ounces) Swiss cheese, shredded

Cook rice according to package directions. Remove from heat. Add cheese and toss lightly. Pack into 3-4 cup buttered mold. Invert immediately onto serving plate. (4 servings)

OLD FASHIONED CUSTARD PIE

2 ½ cups whole milk	¼ teaspoon salt
3 eggs	1 teaspoon black walnut flavoring or vanilla
½ cup sugar	

Scald milk in double boiler. Beat eggs slightly and add sugar, salt and flavoring. Add scalded milk to egg mixture. Pour into unbaked 9-inch pie shell. Bake in 450° oven for 10 minutes; reduce heat to 350° and cook for 5 minutes or until done. 6 servings.

WEDNESDAY
Vegetable stuffed cabbage rolls *
Praline acorn squash *
Mixed fresh fruit
Soft raisin cookies *

VEGETABLE STUFFED CABBAGE ROLLS

8 medium-sized cabbage leaves	⅓ cup grated Parmesan cheese
2 cups finely-chopped cabbage	1 teaspoon salt
¼ cup minced onion	¼ teaspoon black pepper
3 tablespoons butter or margarine	1 cup tomato sauce
1 cup cooked rice	

Immerse cabbage leaves in boiling water for 3 minutes. Drain. Saute chopped cabbage and onion in butter. Add rice, cheese, salt and pepper. Divide the mixture among the cabbage leaves. Fold insides and roll to enclose filling; fasten with wooden picks. Place rolls in a single layer in a shallow sauce pan. Add tomato sauce. Simmer for 20 minutes. (4 servings)

PRALINE ACORN SQUASH

2 medium acorn squash, halved lengthwise;
   remove seeds
1/2 cup water
2 tablespoons butter or margarine, softened

1/3 cup pecans
1/4 cup firmly-packed brown sugar
1/4 teaspoon mace
2 teaspoons vanilla

In ungreased 12x8-inch baking pan, place squash cut side up. Pour water into pan; set aside. In small bowl, combine butter, pecans, sugar, mace and vanilla. Divide mixture evenly among squash halves. Cover; bake for 45 minutes in 400° oven, or until tender. (4 servings)

SOFT RAISIN COOKIES

1 cup water
2 cups raisins
1 3/4 cups sugar
2 eggs, slightly beaten
1 teaspoon vanilla
3 1/2 cups all-purpose flour

1 teaspoon baking powder
1 teaspoon baking soda
1 teaspoon salt
1/2 teaspoon ground cinnamon
1/2 teaspoon ground nutmeg
1/2 cup chopped walnuts

Combine raisins and water in a small saucepan; bring to a boil. Cook for 3 minutes; remove from heat and let cool (do not drain). In a mixing bowl, cream shortening; gradually add sugar. Add eggs and vanilla. Combine dry ingredients; gradually add to creamed mixture and blend thoroughly. Stir in nuts and raisins. Drop by teaspoonfuls 2 inches apart on greased baking sheets. Bake in 350° oven for 12-14 minutes. Yield: about 6 dozen.

THURSDAY
Meat balls with quick mushroom sauce *
Rice
Buttered peas
Tomato jelly ring *
Lemon custard pudding cake *

MEAT BALLS WITH QUICK MUSHROOM SAUCE

2 pounds ground beef
1 pound ground pork
1 1/2 cups quick cooking oats, uncooked
1 1/2 teaspoons salt
1/2 teaspoon pepper
1 teaspoon sage

1/2 teaspoon garlic powder
3 eggs
1 medium onion, finely chopped
1 teaspoon Worcestershire sauce
1 cup milk
Quick mushroom sauce

Combine all ingredients except Quick mushroom sauce in large mixing bowl in order listed; mix well. Roll into meat balls about the size of a walnut. Place in a baking pan and bake in a 350° oven for 20 minutes or until done (pour off grease). Pour mushroom sauce over meat balls; cover pan tightly and heat about 8 minutes. Serve in puffed pastry shells, on toast or over hot rice. Garnish with pimiento strips. 10-12 servings.

Quick Mushroom Sauce

2 (8 ounce) packages cream cheese
2 (10 ³/4-ounce) cans cream of mushroom soup,
  undiluted

1 (8 oz) can mushroom stems and pieces, drained
Garlic salt to taste
Pepper to taste

Melt cream cheese in top of double boiler or over low heat, stirring constantly. Add soup and mushrooms; stir until blended. Yield: 10-12 servings.

TOMATO JELLY RING

1 ½ tablespoons (1 ½ envelopes) plain gelatin
¼ cup water
2 cups vegetable cocktail juice
1 cup finely-chopped celery

¼ cup finely-chopped onions
1 teaspoon lemon juice
Tabasco sauce to taste
Curly endive

Dissolve gelatin in water. Heat 1 cup vegetable juice. Dissolve softened gelatin in vegetable juice, stir until it is all dissolved. Add the remaining ingredients. Pour into a 1 or 1 ½-quart ring mold. Chill. Unmold on a bed of curly endive.

LEMON CUSTARD PUDDING CAKE

¼ cup plus 2 tablespoons all-purpose flour
¼ cup plus 2 tablespoons (³/4 stick) butter or
  margarine, melted
2 cups sugar, divided
4 eggs, separated

1 ½ cups milk
Grated peel of one lemon
2 tablespoons fresh lemon juice
Confectioners' sugar

In a large mixing bowl, combine flour, butter and 1 ½ cups sugar. Beat egg yolks; add to mixing bowl along with milk and lemon peel. Mix well. Add lemon juice. In another bowl, beat egg whites until stiff, slowly adding remaining ½ cup sugar while beating. Fold into batter. Pour into a greased 2-quart baking dish or individual ramekins. Place in a shallow pan of hot water and bake in 350° oven for 55-60 minutes or until lightly browned. Serve warm or chilled with confectioners' sugar dusted on top. Yield: 6-8 servings.

FRIDAY
Macaroni and ham casserole *
Buttered cabbage
Mixed vegetable salad
Bagels with calorie-reduced cream cheese
Pumpkin cookies *

MACARONI AND HAM CASSEROLE

8 ounces elbow macaroni
2 cups (16 ounces) cubed ham
2 cups (8 ounces) shredded sharp Cheddar cheese
1 (10 ½-ounce) can cream of celery soup
¼ cup milk

1 teaspoon garlic salt
¼ teaspoon black pepper
1 medium onion, chopped
1 tablespoon butter, margarine or oil
¼ cup grated Parmesan cheese

Cook macaroni according to package directions. Drain, pour into a large mixing bowl. Add ham, cheese, soup, milk, salt and pepper, and mix. Saute onion in butter. Cook until tender, not brown. Add onion to macaroni mixture. Pour into a greased 2-quart baking dish. Sprinkle Parmesan cheese on top of macaroni mixture. Bake at 350° for 30 minutes. (4-6 servings)

PUMPKIN COOKIES

2 ³/4 tablespoons (¹/3 stick) butter or margarine | *2 cups whole wheat flour*
or 3 tablespoons oil | *1 teaspoon baking soda*
¹/4 cup sugar | *1 ¹/2 teaspoons nutmeg*
¹/3 cup brown sugar, packed | *Pinch salt*
1 egg, well beaten | *1 cup canned pumpkin*
1 tablespoon honey | *¹/2 cup raisins*
1 teaspoon vanilla | *¹/2 cup walnuts or almonds*

Cream butter with sugars. Beat in egg, honey and vanilla. Combine flour, soda, nutmeg and salt. Fold into butter mixture. Fold in pumpkin and mix well. Stir in raisins and nuts. Drop by teaspoon onto cookie sheet. Do not press to flatten. Bake in a preheated 300° oven for 15 to 20 minutes, until cookies are light brown. (Yield: 2 dozen)

SATURDAY
Veal Formia *
Buttered angel hair pasta
Tomato and cheese salad *
Quick onion bread *
Cranberry holiday bake with butter sauce *

VEAL FORMIA

2 pounds veal fillets, cut into two-ounce slices | *2 cloves garlic, crushed*
1 cup flour | *1 cup (2 sticks) butter or margarine*
1 teaspoon salt | *¹/2 cup dry white wine*
¹/4 teaspoon pepper | *1 tablespoon lemon juice*
2 tablespoons olive oil | *1 pound fresh mushrooms, cleaned and sliced*

Pound veal gently with a mallet or end of a dish. Sprinkle lightly with flour, salt and pepper. Heat olive oil, garlic and 2 tablespoons butter. When pan is hot, saute veal on both sides but do not brown. Remove, set aside, keep warm. Add wine to pan, heat a little, add remaining butter and lemon juice. Saute mushrooms just a few minutes. Place several veal slices on each plate and cover with mushrooms and sauce left in the pan. (6-8 servings)

TOMATO AND CHEESE SALAD

2 large ripe tomatoes, sliced 1/4-inch thick | *¹/4 cup olive oil*
1 large sweet onion, sliced thin | *1 teaspoon basil leaves*
8 ounces Mozzarella cheese slices | *¹/4 teaspoon pepper*
(cut in half crosswise) | *Garlic salt to taste*

Arrange tomato, onion and cheese slices in overlapping rows on a serving platter. Combine oil, basil, pepper and garlic salt. Before serving, drizzle dressing on tomato platter. (6 servings)

QUICK ONION BREAD

2 cups biscuit mix
½ cup cold water
1 tablespoon instant minced onion

1 tablespoon soft butter or margarine
Poppy seeds

Stir biscuit mix, water and onion to a soft dough. Roll dough on greased baking sheet into an oblong, 10x8 inches. Spread dough with butter and sprinkle with poppy seeds. Bake 10 minutes at 450°. Serve hot. (6 servings)

CRANBERRY HOLIDAY BAKE WITH BUTTER SAUCE

¼ cup butter or margarine
1 ¼ cups sugar
2 ½ cups flour
1 tablespoon plus 1 teaspoon baking powder

½ teaspoon salt
1 ¼ cups milk
4 cups fresh cranberries

Cream butter, gradually beat in sugar. Combine flour, baking powder and salt. Add dry mixture to butter/sugar mixture, alternately with milk. Begin and end with dry mixture. Wash cranberries and remove damaged ones. Fold into batter. Pour into 9x13-inch greased baking pan. Bake in 350° oven for 35-40 minutes. Serve warm and top each serving with butter sauce.

Butter Sauce

1 ½ cups sugar
1 ½ tablespoons flour
³⁄₄ cup (1 ½ sticks) butter or margarine

³⁄₄ cup cream or half & half or evaporated milk
1 ½ tablespoons vinegar
1 ½ teaspoons vanilla

Combine sugar and flour, add butter, cream and vinegar. Stir until smooth. Cook, stirring constantly, until thick and smooth. Add vanilla. Serve warm over warm holiday cake.

December - Second Week

Planning meals ahead at the holiday season is really a great time-saver, but planning to prepare extra food is called "planned-over food," not left over food. It is done on purpose. You probably have a few ideas of your own in this area.

However, planning ahead is really our thing in the festive fall season, and included this week is an **Orange Cranberry Relish**, which is becoming a holiday tradition. It is great as a relish, but it can also be used in so many other foods to add zest, color and interest to a meal, and flavor to other foods. So, when preparing the Orange Cranberry Relish, make a lot extra and prepare the following novel recipes with it.

ORANGE CRANBERRY RELISH

2 oranges, quartered and seeded
4 cups (1 pound) fresh cranberries, partially frozen

2 cups sugar

Put orange quarters with peel and cranberries through food chopper. Add sugar. Chill. Relish keeps well in refrigerator for several weeks, or freeze in smaller portions. (Yield: 1 quart.)

1. Surprise Muffins: Fill greased muffin cups half full with your favorite plain muffin batter. Top with 1 heaping teaspoonful Orange Cranberry Relish. Add more batter to fill each cup ²/₃ full, Bake in 400° oven 25 minutes.

2. Orange Cranberry Cream: Fold ½ cup Orange Cranberry Relish into 1 cup heavy cream, whipped. If desired, add sugar to taste. Use as topping for sponge cake or filling for tart shells. Garnish with orange sections.

3. Orange Cranberry Salad Molds: Prepare one (3 ounce) package lime-flavored gelatin according to package directions. Chill to consistency of unbeaten egg white. Fold in 1 cup Orange Cranberry Relish. Turn into a 3-cup mold or individual molds.

4. Orange Cranberry Upside-Down Cake: Combine 2 cups Orange Cranberry Relish, ⅓ cup sugar, and 1 tablespoon butter in 10-inch skillet. Bring to a boil, stirring occasionally. Prepare one 9-inch yellow cake layer (½ box cake) and place over mixture. Cover skillet. Reduce heat to low and cook 10 minutes. Invert on serving plate. Serve warm or cold with whipped cream or ice cream.

5. Orange Cranberry Apple Pie: Combine 2 cups Orange Cranberry Relish, 2 cups chopped apples and ½ cup sugar. Turn into an unbaked 9-inch pie shell. Adjust top crust. Bake in a hot oven (425°) for 45 minutes. Serve warm or cold with whipped cream or ice cream.

6. Cranberry Relish Squares: 2 (3 ounce) packages raspberry-flavored gelatin, 2 cups boiling water, 2 ½ cups Orange Cranberry Relish, 1 (7 ounce) bottle (about 1 cup) lemon-lime carbonated beverage. Dissolve gelatin in boiling water. Stir in the Orange Cranberry Relish. Carefully stir in the carbonated beverage. Pour into 8x8x2-inch pan. Chill until firm. Cut into squares. (8 servings)

7. Cranberry-Raspberry Ring: 1 (3 ounce) package raspberry-flavored gelatin, 1 (3 ounce) package lemon-flavored gelatin, 1 ½ cup boiling water, 1 (10 ounce) package frozen raspberries, thawed 1 cup Orange Cranberry Relish, 1 (7 ounce) bottle (about 1 cup) lemon-lime carbonated beverage. Dissolve raspberry and lemon-flavored gelatins in the boiling water. Stir in frozen raspberries, breaking up large pieces with fork. Add Orange Cranberry Relish. Chill until cold but not set. Resting bottle on rim of bowl, carefully pour in lemon-lime carbonated beverage; stir gently. Chill until partially set. Turn into 5 or 5 ½-cup ring mold. Chill until firm. Unmold on lettuce leaves. (8-10 servings)

8. Rosy Salad Dressing: 1 (8 ounce) package cream cheese, softened, 1 cup sour cream, ³/₄ cup Orange Cranberry Relish Combine cream cheese and sour cream. Beat until smooth. Stir in Orange Cranberry Relish. Chill at least 2 hours. Serve on fruit salad. (Yield: 3 cups)

9. Svengali Tomatoes: In sauce pan, combine one (16 ounce) can tomatoes, cut up, ¼ cup Orange Cranberry Relish, 2 tablespoons raisins, 1 tablespoon sugar, 1/2 teaspoon salt, ½ teaspoon ground ginger, and ¼ teaspoon cayenne. Simmer 8 to 10 minutes. Serve warm or chilled as an accompaniment to meat or poultry. (2 cups)

During the busy holiday season, use the free hours in the week before the holidays to prepare foods and freeze them. There are a few basic rules to know.

Combination casserole dishes such as lasagne, meat loaf, stews, chicken and seafood casseroles freeze well if excess fat from the cooked dish has been removed. Baked goods such as rolls, breads, cakes, pies and sandwiches freeze well.

Avoid freezing the following:

1. Most fried foods except French fried potatoes and onion rings, because they lose their crispness;
2. Milk sauces, custards, cream fillings, since they may curdle, become watery or lumpy;
3. Potatoes, which do not have a good texture after freezing;
4. Lettuce, fresh greens and tomatoes lose their crispness;
5. Cooked egg whites and meringues, since they toughen and get rubbery.

Wrap food properly and be ready for happy holiday eating. Finally, thaw foods in the refrigerator for safety reasons.

SUNDAY
Creamy chicken dinner *
Steamed rice
Rotatouille Provincale (egg plant casserole) *
Waldorf salad / Pineapple cheese torte *

CREAMY CHICKEN DINNER

1 (10 ³/4-ounce) can cream of celery soup
1 cup sour cream
2 tablespoons vermouth, white wine or sherry

1 (15 ¹/2-ounce) can onions
2 whole chicken breasts, skinned, boned and halved
¹/4 cup grated Parmesan cheese

Combine soup, sour cream and vermouth, wine or sherry in 1 ¹/2-quart baking dish with lid or in Dutch oven. Drain onions and stir gently into soup mixture. Wash and dry chicken breasts and arrange them in baking dish. Spoon soup mixture over them. Sprinkle cheese over chicken. Cover baking dish and bake in 350° oven for 45 minutes. (4 servings)

ROTATOUILLE PROVINCALE (Eggplant Casserole)

¹/3 cup olive oil
1 onion, thinly sliced
2 cloves garlic, crushed
4 green peppers, cut into tiny slivers
2 ¹/2 cups peeled, diced eggplant

3 cups zucchini wheels, cut in ¹/2-inch slices
2 cups peeled, quartered tomatoes
Salt to taste
Pepper to taste
Olive oil

In a deep skillet or casserole, place oil, add onions and garlic and saute until golden brown. Remove onion and garlic from skillet. Add vegetables in individual layers. Add to each layer onion and garlic mixture, salt and pepper. Simmer, covered, over very low heat for 35-45 minutes. Uncover and continue to heat 10 minutes longer to reduce the amount of liquid. Serve hot as a side dish or cold as an hors d'oeurve. 8 servings.

PINEAPPLE CHEESE TORTE

1 cup all-purpose flour
¹/4 cup confectioners' sugar
¹/4 cup finely chopped almonds
¹/3 cup butter or margarine, softened
Filling

2 (8 ounce) packages cream cheese, softened
¹/2 cup sugar
2 eggs
²/3 cup unsweetened pineapple juice

Pineapple Topping

¹/4 cup all-purpose flour
¹/4 cup sugar
1 (20 ounce) can crushed pineapple, juice drained and reserved

¹/2 cup whipping cream

Combine flour, sugar, almonds and butter; pat into the bottom of a 11x7x2-inch bakiing dish. Bake in a 350° oven for 25 minutes. Beat cream cheese in a mixing bowl until fluffy; beat in sugar and eggs. Stir in juice. Pour filling over hot crust. Bake in 350° oven for 25 minutes or until center is set. **For topping**, combine flour and sugar in a saucepan. Stir in 1 cup of reserved pineapple juice. Bring to a boil, strirring constantly. Boil and stir 1 minute. Remove from heat; fold in pineapple. Cool. Whip cream until stiff peaks form; fold into topping. Spread carefully over dessert. Refrigerate 5 hours or over-night. Garnish with almond slivers. 12-16 servings.

MONDAY
Malfatti (spinach dumplings in spicy tomato sauce) *
Skillet slaw *
Quick cheese-bacon bread *
Tiramisu *

MALFATTI IN SPICY TOMATO SAUCE

2 (10 ounce) packages frozen chopped spinach
1 tablespoon salt
3 eggs
2 ½ cups of bread crumbs (12 ounces bread, about
  16 slices, crust removed)
1 pound ricotta
½ cup grated Parmesan cheese
½ cup finely-chopped green onions

½ cup chopped parsley, fresh
3-4 cloves garlic, crushed
1 tablespoon chopped fresh basil (2 teaspoons dried)
¼ teaspoon ground nutmeg
¼ teaspoon black pepper
All-purpose flour
6-8 quarts water
1 teaspoon salt

Cook spinach until thawed; drain, squeeze. Beat eggs and add spinach, crumbs, ricotta, cheese, onions, parsley, garlic, basil, nutmeg and pepper. Mix, cover and refrigerate for 12 to 24 hours. Roll ⅓ cup into oval form (3x1 ½-inches). Roll in flour. Place on foil or waxed paper. Do not let patties touch while waiting to cook. Bring water to a boil and add 1 teaspoon salt. Drop dumplings into water, one layer. When they float to the top, cook four minutes longer. Lift with a slotted spoon and drain well (keep warm at 250°). May be frozen. After poaching, place in baking dish and brush with melted butter and Parmesan cheese or spicy tomato sauce. Cook at 350° for ½ hour. 6-8 servings. Serve hot.

Spicey Tomato Sauce

6 tablespoons olive oil
½ cup chopped onion
1 quart (two 16-ounce cans) canned tomatoes and juice
1 clove garlic, minced
¼ cup dry white wine
2 tablespoons chopped fresh parsley

1 teaspoon dried basil
1 teaspoon fennel seed
½ teaspoon sugar
1 teaspoon salt
¼ teaspoon pepper (cayenne)
¼ cup chopped ripe olives

Combine all ingredients and simmer for one hour and add olives last three minutes. To serve malfatti, top with ¼ cup melted butter and 1 cup Parmesan cheese, or simmer in spicey tomato sauce. Yields about one quart.

SKILLET SLAW

4 slices bacon
¼ cup vinegar
1 tablespoon brown sugar, packed
1 teaspoon salt

¼ cup finely-chopped onion
3 cups shredded cabbage
⅓ cup chopped fresh parsley (optional)

Cook bacon until crisp. Remove from skillet and crumble. Add vinegar, sugar, salt and onion to bacon drippings in skillet. Heat thoroughly to dissolve sugar. Combine cabbage, parsley and bacon. Pour hot dressing over vegetables and toss. (4-6 servings)

QUICK CHEESE BACON BREAD

4 cups flour	*2 cups milk*
½ cup sugar	*½ cup vegetable oil*
2 tablespoons baking powder	*2 cups (8 ounces) shredded Cheddar cheese*
2 teaspoons salt	*⅔ cup cooked, crumbled bacon*
2 eggs, slightly beaten	*2 teaspoons caraway seeds*

Line two 9x5x3-inch loaf pans with heavy-duty aluminum foil, leaving ½-inch collar around edges; grease bottom and sides of foil. Combine flour, sugar, baking powder, salt, eggs, milk and oil in large bowl of mixer. Beat on medium speed ½ minute, scraping sides and bottom constantly. Stir in cheese, bacon and caraway seeds. Divide batter between prepared pans. Bake in a 350° oven for 45-50 minutes or until wooden pick comes out clean. Cool in pans for 5-10 minutes; remove from pans and cool thoroughly. Freeze extra loaf. (2 loaves)

TIRAMISU

6 egg yolks	*1 ¼ cups whipping cream, whipped*
1 ¼ cups sugar	*3-6 ounces lady fingers*
1 ¼ cups mascarpone or (10 ounces) cream cheese, softened	*⅓ cup coffee liqueur (Kahlua)*

Combine egg yolks and sugar in top of double boiler. Stir over boiling water until smooth and thick (about 8 minutes). Cut cheese into cubes and add to egg mixture. Stir until smooth. Remove from heat and gradually stir in whipped cream. Line sides of a 2-quart crystal bowl with lady fingers. Brush lady fingers with coffee liqueur. Pour in ½ of the dessert mixture. Lay remaining lady fingers on top of the dessert mixture; brush with remaining liqueur. Pour remaining dessert mixture on lady fingers. Chill for at least 2 hours. (Individual dessert dishes may be used.)

TUESDAY
Miller's meat cakes with piquant topping *
Asparagus Parmesan *
Buttered potatoes
Vegetable salad with creamy tart dressing
Cranberry fruit bread and butter *
Chilled apple sauce

MILLER'S MEAT CAKES WITH PIQUANT TOPPING

2 pounds ground beef	*1 teaspoon savory*
1 pound ground pork	*2 eggs*
1 ½ cup quick-cooking oats, uncooked	*1 tablespoon Worcestershire sauce*
1 ½ teaspoon salt	*½ cup vegetable juice or tomato juice*
½ teaspoon pepper	*½ cup chopped green peppers*
1 teaspoon sage	*¼ cup chopped parsley*

Combine all above ingredients in large mixing bowl in the order listed. Pack into well-greased muffin tins or individual baking pans (shaped like small pie pans). Bake in 350° oven for 20 minutes or until done. Cool. Remove from tins. Allow all fat to drain off. Place on cookie pan. Cover each meat cake with Piquant Topping. Reheat in oven for 10-15 minutes. Serve hot.

Piquant Topping

3 tablespoons brown sugar
1/4 cup ketchup

1/4 teaspoon nutmeg
1 teaspoon dry mustard

Combine all topping ingredients. Stir until well mixed. Spoon on top of cooked meat cakes, bake about 10-15 minutes longer.

ASPARAGUS PARMESAN

2 pounds fresh asparagus or 2 (10 ounce)
  packages frozen asparagus
1/4 cup (1/2 stick) butter or margarine
1 cup mayonnaise
1/2 teaspoon salt

1/4 teaspoon pepper
1/4 teaspoon dry mustard
3 tablespoons lemon juice or juice of one lemon
1 cup buttered bread crumbs
1 cup grated Parmesan cheese

Cook asparagus until tender. Drain and arrange in a 2-quart baking dish. Melt butter in small skillet, heat until it turns golden-brown. Blend in mayonnaise, seasonings and lemon juice. Pour over asparagus. Sprinkle bread crumbs all over the top and the Parmesan cheese. Bake in a 375° oven for 15-18 minutes, or until brown.

CRANBERRY FRUIT BREAD

2 cups chopped fresh or fresh-frozen cranberries
1 1/2 cups sugar
3 cups all-purpose flour
3/4 cup whole-wheat cereal
3 teaspoons baking powder
1 teaspoon salt (optional)
1 teaspoon cinnamon

1/2 teaspoon baking soda
1/8 teaspoon ground cloves
2 eggs, beaten
3/4 cup milk
1/4 cup vegetable oil
1/2 cup chopped walnuts

Preheat oven to 350°. Grease 9x5x3-inch loaf pan. Combine cranberries and sugar. Set aside. Stir together flour, cereal, baking powder, salt, cinnamon, baking soda and cloves. Combine eggs, milk and oil. Pour egg mixture over dry ingredients. Add cranberries and nuts. Stir just until thoroughly moistened. Pour into pan. Bake 65-70 minutes or until tester inserted in center comes out clean. Let cool before removing from pan.

WEDNESDAY
Pork chops stuffed with apple bread dressing *
Superb green beans *
Tossed fruit, vegetable and blue cheese salad *
Buttermilk biscuits, commercial / Pecan pie *

PORK CHOPS STUFFED WITH APPLE BREAD DRESSING

6 double-thick pork chops
Salt
Pepper
1/4 cup (1/2 stick) butter or margarine
1 tablespoon chopped onion
3 cups soft bread cubes

2 cups finely chopped apple
1/2 cup chopped celery
2 teaspoons chopped parsley
1/4 teaspoon salt
2 tablespoons cooking oil

Trim excess fat from chops, then slit chops from outer edge to the bone to make a pocket (or ask the butcher to do it). Sprinkle chops with salt and pepper inside and outside. Melt butter in sauce pan. Add onion and saute until lightly browned. Add bread cubes, apple, celery, parsley and salt and mix well. Stuff pork chops loosely with dressing mixture. Brown chops in oil in skillet on each side for 8 to 10 minutes. Place chops in large shallow greased baking pan. Cover, bake at 350° for 45 minutes. Uncover and bake 15 minutes longer. (6 servings)

SUPERB GREEN BEANS

4 cups cooked or 2 (16 ounce) cans green beans
1 onion, chopped
3 tablespoons butter or margarine
2 tablespoons all-purpose flour
2 tablespoons sugar

2 tablespoons vinegar
1/4 cup chopped parsley
1 cup sour cream
3 slices bacon, cooked crisp

Drain beans, reserving 1 cup liquid. Cook onion in butter until soft. Stir in flour. Stir in bean liquid, sugar, vinegar and parsley. Cook, stirring constantly, until thickened. Add sour cream and pour over the beans; heat through, but do not boil. Crumble bacon over top. (6-8 servings)

TOSSED FRUIT, VEGETABLE AND BLUE CHEESE SALAD

1 head lettuce or salad greens, any kind
1/2 cup diced celery
2 apples, unpeeled, cored, cut in thin wedges
1 cucumber, pared and sliced thin
4 oranges, peeled and sliced in cartwheels
1 grapefruit, peeled and sectioned
1/2 cup salad oil
1/3 cup lemon juice
1 tablespoon honey

1 teaspoon dry mustard
1/2 teaspoon salt
Dash of pepper
1/2 teaspoon paprika
1 teaspoon Worcestershire sauce
1/4 cup frozen chopped chives or finely chopped
  green onions
1/2 cup croutons
1/3 cup crumbled blue cheese

Line a large salad bowl with greens; arrange celery, apples, cucumber, oranges and grapefruit in bowl. In small bowl, combine salad oil, lemon juice, honey, mustard, salt, pepper, paprika, Worcestershire sauce and chives or green onions. Just before serving, pour enough dressing over salad to moisten; add croutons and blue cheese and toss lightly. (6-8 servings)

PECAN PIE

3 eggs
1/2 cup granulated sugar
1/2 cup brown sugar, well packed
1 cup light corn syrup

1 cup pecan halves
1 teaspoon vanilla
1 (9-inch) pie crust

Beat eggs and sugars until thick. Add corn syrup, nuts and vanilla. Pour into 9-inch pie crust. Bake in 300° oven for one hour.

THURSDAY
Casual Office Buffet Party
Favorite Happy Hour beverages
Tuna nut spread with crackers *
Chicken Imperial *
Potato celery bake *
Baked onions filled with spinach *
Overnight slaw *
Hot garlic bread / Assorted fruit bowl
Dutch apple pound cake *
Home-made custard ice cream *

Plan Of Work

Day before:

1. Prepare tuna nut spread, place on serving dish ready to place on table. Chill until ready to serve.
2. Prepare potato celery bake, have ready to place in oven. (Bake 1 ½ hours before serving.)
3. Prepare slaw to give time to develop flavors.
4. Prepare Dutch apple pound cake.
5. The custard part of the ice cream recipe can be made this day.

Morning of the party:

6. Cut and butter bread and wrap in foil, ready to heat in oven about 15-20 minutes before dinner is served.
7. Prepare stuffed onions ready to place in oven.

Afternoon of the party:

8. Three and one-half hours before serving, marinate the chicken for two hours. Place in oven one hour before serving.
9. One and a half hours before serving, place potato bake in oven.
10. Forty minutes before serving, place onions in oven.
11. About 30 minutes to 1 hour before serving, recruit guest to help make the ice cream. Whip egg whites and finish ice cream.
12. Put bread in oven 20 minutes before serving.

Enjoy!

TUNA NUT SPREAD

2 (6 ½ ounce) cans tuna fish (packed in water), drained and flaked

1 cup coarsely-chopped pecans or walnuts (can use more)

2 packages (1 ¼-ounces each) Italian salad dressing mix or ranch dressing mix

1-2 cups sour cream (use only enough to make it spreadable)

2 tablespoons chopped pimiento, drained

Tabasco sauce to taste

Parsley sprigs

Coarse-ground black pepper to taste

Assorted crackers

Combine tuna, nuts, dressing mix and mix thoroughly. Add only desired amount of sour cream to make a spread, pimiento and Tabasco sauce. Mix thoroughly; put in a quart mold. Chill until ready to serve. Unmold on plate and smooth with spoon. Garnish with parsley sprigs; sprinkle coarse-ground black pepper on top. Spread with a spatula on assorted crackers. Best if prepared a day ahead.

CHICKEN IMPERIAL

1 broiler fryer, cut into serving pieces
¼ to ½ cup sherry
1 ½ cups dry bread crumbs
²/₃ cup Parmesan cheese
½ teaspoon garlic powder
⅛ teaspoon pepper

1 ½ teaspoons salt
½ teaspoon dried parsley flakes
⅓ cup finely chopped blanched almonds
³/₄ cup (1 ½ sticks) melted butter or margarine,
  divided
Fresh parsley for garnish

Rinse chicken and pat dry. Soak the chicken pieces in sherry for two hours. Combine bread crumbs, Parmesan cheese, garlic powder, pepper, salt, parsley flakes and almonds. Mix well; add ¼ cup of the melted butter and stir. Drain the chicken and dip each piece in the remaining butter; roll in the bread crumb mixture. Place the pieces in an uncovered metal pan. Put a small amount of butter on each piece. Bake at 350° for one hour. Garnish with parsley; serve warm. (4 servings)

POTATO CELERY BAKE

3 cups thinly-sliced celery
4 cups thinly-sliced unpeeled new potatoes
1 ½ cups thinly-sliced onions
3 tablespoons all-purpose flour
½ cup milk
¼ cup (½ stick) butter or margarine, melted
1 ³/₄ teaspoons salt

½ teaspoon black pepper
¼ cup (½ stick) butter or margarine, melted
³/₄ cup dry bread crumbs
⅓ cup grated Parmesan cheese
½ teaspoon garlic powder
½ teaspoon paprika

Fill a 2-quart casserole with alternating layers of celery, potatoes and onions. Sprinkle 1 tablespoon of the flour evenly over each layer. Combine milk, ¼ cup butter, salt and pepper and pour over the casserole. Cover and bake at 350° for 1 hour. Uncover casserole. Combine the melted butter, bread crumbs, cheese, garlic powder and paprika. Sprinkle over the top. Continue baking, uncovered, for 20 minutes. (6 servings)

BAKED ONIONS FILLED WITH SPINACH

6 medium Spanish or Bermuda onions
¼ cup finely chopped onion
2 tablespoons butter or margarine
3 (10 ounce) packages frozen chopped spinach,
  thawed, drained, finely chopped
1 pound ricotta or cottage cheese

2 eggs, lightly beaten
¼ teaspoon ground nutmeg
1 cup (4 ounces) shredded Gruyere or Swiss cheese
Salt and pepper
1 cup chicken stock

Slice 1 inch from the stem end of each onion and shave the root end. Do not peel outer skin. Place onions in 2 quarts boiling water and boil for 20 minutes. Drain and peel outer skin. Slice 1 inch from stem end. Holding each onion stem- side up, lift out inner core with a fork. The center should pop out quite easily. Leave at least 2 whole layers of onion intact. Chop onion that has been removed. In a skillet, saute chopped onion in butter until golden, about 2 to 3 minutes. Add spinach and cook over medium heat until all liquid has evaporated. Combine ricotta, eggs, nutmeg, cheese and salt and pepper to taste. Combine with spinach mixture. Place onion cups in a shallow baking pan. Fill with spinach mixture. Pour chicken stock into pan, cover with foil and bake in a 350° oven for 20 minutes. Remove foil and continue baking for an additional 15 minutes. (6 servings)

OVERNIGHT SLAW

1 ½ pounds cabbage, shredded	½ cup sugar
1 medium onion, chopped	½ cup salad oil
1 green pepper, chopped	1 tablespoon salt
2 tablespoons chopped pimiento	1 ½ tablespoons prepared mustard
½ cup vinegar	1 teaspoon celery seed

Combine cabbage, onion, green pepper and pimiento in a 2-quart bowl. In a sauce pan, combine vinegar, sugar, oil, salt, mustard and celery seed; bring to a boil. Pour over vegetables, mix thoroughly. Refrigerate overnight in a covered container. Keeps several days in the refrigerator. (Yield: approximately 2 quarts)

DUTCH APPLE POUND CAKE

5 tablespoons sugar	½ teaspoon salt
1 ½ to 2 tablespoons cinnamon	1 cup vegetable oil
4 large (approximately 2 pounds) cooking apples, peeled, cored and thinly sliced	4 eggs, slightly beaten
	¼ cup orange juice
3 cups all-purpose flour	1 tablespoon vanilla
1 tablespoon baking powder	Powdered sugar
2 ½ cups sugar	

Combine 5 tablespoons sugar and the cinnamon. Add to apples, mix until apples are well coated; set aside. In large bowl of processor or electric mixer, add flour, baking powder, 2 ½ cups sugar, salt, oil, eggs, orange juice and vanilla. Beat until thoroughly mixed (batter will be thick). Spoon half of batter in a greased 10-inch tube pan. Top with half of the apples. Add remaining batter and top with remaining apples. Bake at 350° for 1 ¾ hours (cake should be brown and firm to touch). Cool cake for 1 ½ hours in pan. Remove from pan, cover with sifted powdered sugar. Best if served warm. Keep at room temperature.

HOME MADE CUSTARD ICE CREAM

8 eggs, separated	1 tablespoon vanilla
2 tablespoons flour	1 (13 ounce) can evaporated milk
2 ½ cups sugar	½ pint whipping cream
½ gallon milk	

Beat egg yolks. Add sugar and flour and beat well. In sauce pan, scald ½-gallon milk, slowly add about ⅓ of the scalded milk to sugar and egg yolk mixture, stirring constantly. Add this mixture to remaining scalded milk, stirring constantly. Pour this mixture into sauce pan and cook over medium heat, stirring constantly until mixture coats spoon. Cool slightly. Beat egg whites until stiff. Add egg whites and vanilla to slightly cooled custard. Cool thoroughly in refrigerator. Place evaporated milk in freezer tray and freeze until crystals form around outside. Whip evaporated milk and add to completely cooled custard. Refrigerate until ready to freeze. Add cream just before freezing. Freeze according to manufacturer's directions. (Yield: 5 quarts)

FRIDAY
Italian pasta bake *
Tossed salad
Parmesan sticks *
Hawaiian fruit pie *

ITALIAN PASTA BAKE

1 pound ground beef
1 small onion, chopped
1 small green pepper, chopped
2 cloves garlic, crushed
1 (6 ounce) can tomato paste
1/2 cup water
1 teaspoon garlic salt
1 teaspoon oregano leaves

1/2 teaspoon fennel or anise seed
4 ounces (2 cups cooked) noodles, cooked, drained
1/4 cup chopped fresh parsley or 1 tablespoon
dried parsley
1/2 cup mayonnaise
1 cup (4 ounces) grated Parmesan cheese, divided
2 eggs, beaten

Brown meat; drain. Add onions, green pepper and garlic; cook until vegetables are tender. Stir in tomato paste, water, garlic, salt, oregano and fennel or anise seed. Cover and simmer for 15 minutes. Combine noodles and parsley. Combine mayonnaise, 3/4 cup cheese and eggs. Layer noodles in a 10x6-inch baking dish. Add mayonnaise mixture; top with meat sauce. Sprinkle with remaining cheese. Bake in a 350° oven for 25 minutes. (6 servings)

PARMESAN STICKS

6 slices bread
1/2 cup (1 stick) butter or margarine, melted
1/2 cup corn flake crumbs

1 1/2-ounce can grated Parmesan cheese
1/2 teaspoon garlic salt

Trim crust from bread, if desired. Cut each slice into 4 strips. Combine corn flake crumbs, cheese and salt. Dip bread strips into melted butter, then into dry mixture. Bake in 425° oven for 7 minutes. (6 servings or 24 sticks)

HAWAIIAN FRUIT PIE

1 cup granulated sugar
1/2 cup (1 stick) butter or margarine, melted
2 eggs, beaten
1 tablespoon cornstarch
1 tablespoon lemon juice
1/2 cup chopped pecans

1/2 cup chopped dates
1/2 cup coconut
1 (8.5 ounce) can crushed pineapple, drained
1 unbaked (9- or 10-inch) pie shell
Whipped cream or topping or vanilla ice cream

Combine sugar, butter, beaten eggs, cornstarch and lemon juice. Blend thoroughly. Add chopped pecans, dates, coconut and pineapple. Stir until well blended. Pour into pie shell. Bake for 40-50 minutes in a 325° oven. Serve with whipped cream or vanilla ice cream.

SATURDAY
Poached fish with grapes and cream sauce *
Wild rice casserole *
Stewed okra and tomatoes
Oriental vegetable salad *
Sour cream apple pie *

POACHED FISH WITH GRAPES AND CREAM SAUCE

4 fresh flounder or sole fillets (about 1 pound) or	*1 tablespoon butter or margarine*
any white fish fillet	*1 tablespoon all-purpose flour*
2 cups water	*½ cup milk*
2 tablespoons lemon juice	*⅛ teaspoon ground thyme*
8 peppercorns	*1 cup seedless green grapes*
3 parsley sprigs	*1 teaspoon lemon juice*
1 bay leaf	*¼ teaspoon white pepper*

In a 10-inch skillet over high heat, combine fish, water, lemon juice, peppercorns, parsley sprigs and bay leaf; heat to boiling. Reduce heat to low; cover and simmer 5 to 10 minutes until fish flakes easily when tested with fork. With slotted pancake turner, carefully remove fish to warm platter. Reserve one-half of the cooking liquid. In a 2-quart sauce pan over medium heat, melt butter. Stir flour into hot butter until blended; cook, stirring constantly, until flour is light golden. Gradually stir in milk, thyme leaves and reserved liquid. Cook, stirring constantly, until gravy is thickened. Add grapes, heat through. Correct seasonings. Pour gravy over fish. (4 servings)

WILD RICE CASSEROLE

1 cup wild rice	*½ cup sliced almonds or water chestnuts*
½ pound mushrooms, sliced	*3 cups chicken broth*
¼ cup minced onion	*¼ cup (½ stick) butter or margarine*

Rinse wild rice under running water using strainer or in a bowl of water; drain. Combine rice, mushrooms, onion and almonds in a 2-quart casserole. Add broth, dot with butter. Cover and bake in 325° oven till rice is tender and liquid is absorbed, about 1 ½ hours. (6-8 servings)

ORIENTAL VEGETABLE SALAD

3 medium-sized tomatoes	*¼ teaspoon salt*
1 tablespoon soy sauce	*1 (6 ounce) package frozen snow peas, cooked,*
1 tablespoon oil	*drained and cooled*
1 teaspoon cider vinegar	*¼ cup sliced water chestnuts*
1 clove garlic, crushed	*3 scallions (green onions), sliced*
¼ teaspoon ground ginger	

Hold tomatoes at room temperature until fully ripe. In a large bowl, combine soy sauce, oil, vinegar, garlic, ginger and salt; mix well. Cut tomatoes into wedges; add tomatoes, chestnuts, snow peas and scallions to soy mixture; toss lightly to coat. Serve on a bed of lettuce, if desired. (6 servings)

SOUR CREAM APPLE PIE

2 eggs
1 cup (8 ounces) sour cream
1 cup sugar
¼ cup plus 2 tablespoons all-purpose flour, divided
1 teaspoon vanilla

¼ teaspoon salt
3 cups chopped, peeled cooking apples
1 unbaked pie shell (9 inches)
3 tablespoons butter or margarine, melted
¼ cup packed brown sugar

In a large bowl, beat eggs. Add sour cream. Stir in sugar, 2 tablespoons flour, vanilla and salt; mix well. Stir in apples. Pour in pie shell. Bake in 375° oven for 15 minutes. Meanwhile, with blender, combine butter, brown sugar and remaining flour. Sprinkle over top of pie. Return to oven for 20-25 minutes or until filling is set. Cool completely on a wire rack. Serve or cover and refrigerate. 8 servings.

December - Third Week

Those grand holidays — Christmas and New Year's — are a time for delicious feasts, not upset stomachs. Food safety is especially important during this time of year because food is being served in large quantities, festive styles, and prepared in a busy kitchen. All these contribute to the possibility of food poisoning. Here are a few things to keep in mind:
• It is important, first, to decide how many guests you can safely serve. Take refrigerator space into consideration. Remember, when foods are left for a long time on the buffet table, the chance of food poisoning increases. Keep buffet servings small and replenish as needed directly from the refrigerator or stove. Never leave cooked food at room temperature for more than 2 hours.
• Unfortunately, it is not always possible to tell by taste, looks, or odor of food if food is safe to eat. (Most germs that cause food poisoning are killed when food is cooked, but germs can get into it again.) Meat, poultry, fish and dairy products, left at room temperature, allow germs to grow to dangerous numbers. Even in large numbers, these germs seldom change the taste, odor, or looks of food. If you know the food has been left out of the refrigerator for more than 2 hours or handled carelessly, throw it out. To be sure your food is safe, keep meat, fish and poultry dishes COLD (below 40°) or HOT (above 140°) until serving time.
• Each year, many cases of food poisoning are reported from holiday dishes such as cold meat cuts, turkey stuffing, potato salad (and other salads) made with home-made mayonnaise, cream pies and egg nog. All these dishes contain meat, poultry or eggs — just what germs love. Also, these foods are handled more than other foods during preparation — especially for a fancy buffet — and it's easy for germs to spread from hands to the food. Keep your hands and utensils clean when preparing these foods. Refrigerate foods immediately if you prepare them ahead of time for serving.
• For safety's sake, don't stuff your turkey. The best way to cook the stuffing is separate from the bird. Germs love the ingredients in stuffing; the warm, moist inside of a turkey is the perfect place for germs to grow. The thick meat on the turkey protects the germs from extreme heat or cold so they continue to grow to dangerous numbers. The stuffing also gets a lot of handling in its preparation, so it's easy for germs to get inside the turkey. If you DO choose to stuff your turkey, mix the stuffing in advance, store it in the refrigerator separate from the bird, and stuff the bird just before cooking and cook the interior of the stuffing to 165°. Use a meat thermometer to make sure the heat has penetrated the stuffing. Remove all leftover stuffing from the bird and refrigerate the stuffing in a separate container.
• Even though cooking food thoroughly kills most germs, they can spread to food again once it has cooled. Germs on raw food can spread to cooked foods if the two come into contact. Remember that

germs can spread to any food as the result of contact with dirty hands and kitchen utensils. Germs from meat and poultry can spread, during handling, to other foods that you don't normally cook.

• To prevent the spread of germs, wash your hands and kitchen utensils with soap and hot water after handling one food and before moving onto another. You should never use the same cutting board and utensils for cooked meat that you used when the meat was raw, or you'll get the germs right back on your cooked food. Wash the cutting board and utensils first with soap and hot water.

• When preparing a hot dish ahead, place it in the refrigerator within 30 minutes after cooking. Reheat thoroughly just before serving. Never leave cold dishes at room temperature. Refrigerate immediately after preparation.

• To avoid the holiday rush, you might want to buy your groceries a few days ahead of the occasion. Make sure to use fresh meat, poultry, eggs and liquid dairy products within 3 to 5 days of purchase and keep them well refrigerated. Freeze fresh meat and poultry immediately after purchase if you plan to keep them longer.

• Plan ahead in your busy schedule to allow time for thawing frozen foods in the refrigerator. When frozen meats or poultry are thawed outside the refrigerator, the outer surfaces of the meat are exposed too long at temperatures that allow germs to grow. If it is necessary to thaw a large turkey outside the refrigerator, it may be thawed in a water-tight package under cold running water. Another alternative would be to place the bird in doubled brown paper bags to insulate it against too warm temperatures and uneven thawing. Cook promptly after thawing.

Foodborne illness can cause unpleasant symptoms that can last for several hours or even days! Don't let food poisoning ruin your holiday season!

SUNDAY
Peppered rib eye steaks *
Baked potatoes with mushroom and blue cheese topping *
Harvest bounty vegetable casserole * or
Western Italian beans *
Lettuce wedges with dressing
Hot French bread
Cranberry mousse *

PEPPERED RIB EYE STEAKS

4 beef rib eye steaks, 1 ¹/₂ inches thick	*1 ¹/₂ teaspoons pepper*
1 tablespoon olive oil	*1 teaspoon garlic salt*
1 tablespoon garlic powder	*1 teaspoon lemon pepper*
1 tablespoon paprika	*1 teaspoon cayenne pepper*
2 teaspoons dried ground thyme	*Orange slices (optional)*
2 teaspoons dried ground oregano	*Parsley sprigs (optional)*

Brush steaks lightly with olive oil. In a small bowl, combine remaining ingredients except orange slices and parsley sprigs. Sprinkle seasonings over steaks and press into both sides. Cover and chill for 1 hour. Grill steaks, turning once, over medium heat coals 14-18 minutes for rare; 18-22 minutes for medium; 24-28 minutes for well-done. Place on a cutting board; cut across the grain into thick slices. Put on serving platter. Garnish with orange slices and parsley, if desired. 8 servings.

BAKED POTATOES WITH MUSHROOM AND BLUE CHEESE TOPPING

8 medium potatoes, washed (pierce each with a fork)
5 tablespoons butter or margarine
12 ounces fresh mushrooms, sliced, or 1
  (8 ounce) can, drained

²/₃ cup sliced green onions, use tops
¹/₄ teaspoon garlic powder
¹/₄ cup crumbled blue cheese

Place potatoes on oven rack; bake for 60 to 75 minutes at 300°, or until potatoes are fork tender. In a small skillet, melt butter. Stir in mushrooms, onions and garlic powder. Cook, uncovered, over medium heat, stirring occasionally until mushrooms are crisply tender (2 to 4 minutes). Stir in blue cheese. Spoon about ¼ cup mushroom sauce over each hot, split, baked potato. (8 servings)

HARVEST BOUNTY VEGETABLE CASSEROLE

3 (16 ounce) cans cut green beans, drained
2 medium-sized green peppers, chopped
6 medium-sized tomatoes, chopped
3 cups biscuit mix

2 teaspoons salt
¹/₂ teaspoon cayenne pepper
1 cup milk
6 eggs, beaten slightly

In a greased 9x13x2-inch baking dish, spread beans and peppers. Spread with chopped tomato, then the cheese. In a blender jar, add biscuit mix, salt, pepper, milk and eggs. Blend until smooth. Pour over vegetables and cheese. Bake uncovered in a 350° oven for 45-50 minutes or until golden brown. Let stand 10 minutes before serving. The entire recipe can be prepared and part of it frozen or used up as leftovers. (12 servings)

WESTERN ITALIAN BEANS

4 bacon strips, diced
1 large onion, chopped
¹/₃ cup dry lentils
1 ¹/₃ cups water
2 tablespoons catsup
1 teaspoon garlic powder
³/₄ teaspoon chili powder

¹/₂ teaspoon ground cumin
¹/₄ teaspoon dried red pepper flakes
1 bay leaf
1 (14.5-ounce) can diced tomatoes with liquid
1 (15 ounce) can pinto beans, drained
1 (16 ounce) can kidney beans, drained

Lightly fry bacon in a heavy 3-quart saucepan. Add onions; cook until transparent. Stir in remaining ingredients. Cook over medium heat for 45 minutes or until lentils are tender, stirring once or twice. Remove bay leaf before serving. 8- 10 servings.

CRANBERRY MOUSSE

1 cup cranberry juice cocktail
1 tablespoon (1 envelope) unflavored gelatin
1 (3 ounce) package raspberry-flavored gelatin

1 (16 ounce) can whole berry cranberry sauce
1 cup heavy cream, whipped, or 2 cups
  whipped topping

Soften gelatin in 2 tablespoons cranberry juice. In a sauce pan, heat cranberry juice cocktail to boiling; stir in softened gelatin and raspberry gelatin until dissolved; stir in cranberry sauce. Chill until mixture begins to thicken. Fold in whipped cream and pour into serving bowl. Chill until firm. (6-8 servings)

MONDAY
Wedding soup *
Tomato risotto *
Green beans with mushrooms and garlic *
Tossed salad
Three-egg chiffon cake with peach topping *

WEDDING SOUP

1¹/₂ pound chicken parts, drumsticks, wings, backs	¹/₂ teaspoon salt
4 quarts water	¹/₆ teaspoon pepper
1 small onion, finely chopped	3 tablespoons finely-chopped onion
1 cup chopped celery	1 head endive, chopped
¹/₂ pound ground beef	2 eggs, beaten
1 egg	1 tablespoon Parmesan cheese

Combine chicken parts, water, onion and celery. Bring to a boil, reduce heat but keep water boiling gently for 1½ hours. Remove chicken from broth. Chill broth; remove fat from surface of broth. Remove meat from bones. Combine ground beef, egg, salt, pepper and onion. Roll meat mixture into 20 small (marble size) meat balls. Add meat balls and chicken to broth. Simmer 10 minutes. Add endive; simmer 10 minutes. Combine beaten eggs with cheese; pour into soup and stir. Keep water level at about 4 quarts. If low add additional canned broth or water and bouillon cubes. 10-12 servings.

TOMATO RISOTTO

2 pounds ripe tomatoes or 2 cans (14.5 ounce)	2 cups hot chicken broth or 1 (14 ¹/₂ oz) can broth
diced tomatoes	Pinch of salt to taste
1 tablespoon olive oil	Pepper to taste
1 large onion, chopped	¹/₂ teaspoon balsamic vinegar, optional
2 large cloves garlic, crushed	2 tablespoons sour cream
1 cup Arboria (Italian) rice or any long-grained rice	¹/₂ cup (loosely packed) basil leaves shredded
³/₄ cup dry white wine	or 1 tablespoon dried basil
1 ¹/₂ tablespoons tomato paste	¹/₂ cup grated Parmesan cheese (about 1 ¹/₂ ounces)

In a heavy medium sauce pan or skillet, combine olive oil, onions and garlic. Cover and cook over moderately low heat until the onions are translucent, about 5 minutes. Uncover, increase the heat to moderate and add the rice. Cook, stirring to coat thoroughly with oil, about one minute. Add the tomatoes and cook, stirring, until thoroughly incorporated, about 1 minute longer. Stir in wine, increase the heat to high and bring to a boil. Add tomato paste and 1 ½ cups of the hot chicken broth. Bring to a boil. Stir in ¼-cup chicken stock, continue stirring. Add another ¼-cup chicken broth and stir for about 5 minutes. Stir in additional ¼ cup stock, stirring until risotto is creamy and rice is tender, but still firm to the bite. If rice is still firm in the middle of the grain, add ¼-cup water and cook 5 minutes longer. Add salt, pepper, balsamic vinegar. Stir in sour cream. Serve individually or on a platter and top with shavings of fresh Parmesan cheese. (4-6 servings)

GREEN BEANS WITH MUSHROOMS AND GARLIC

1 pound fresh or frozen green beans	2 teaspoons onion powder
¹/₂ cup sliced fresh mushrooms	2-3 cloves garlic, crushed
6 tblsp butter or margarine or ¹/₃ cup olive oil	Salt and pepper to taste

Cook green beans in water to cover until tender. Meanwhile, in a skillet, saute mushrooms in butter until tender. Add onion powder and garlic. Cook 2 minutes. Drain beans; add to skillet and toss. Season with salt and pepper. 6 servings.

THREE-EGG CHIFFON CAKE WITH PEACH TOPPING

1 cup plus 2 tablespoons sifted cake flour
³/4 cup sugar
1 ½ teaspoons baking powder
½ teaspoon salt
¼ cup oil
3 eggs, separated

⅓ cup water
³/4 teaspoon vanilla flavoring
¼ teaspoon almond flavoring
¼ teaspoon cream of tartar
Sliced peaches, frozen or canned

Sift flour, sugar, baking powder and salt into large mixing bowl. Make a well in center and add oil, egg yolks, water and flavorings. Beat until smooth. In large bowl, beat egg whites and cream of tartar until mixture forms very stiff peaks when beater is raised. Gently fold flour mixture into egg whites, blending well. Turn batter into ungreased 9-inch tube pan. Bake in 325° oven for about 1 hour or until cake springs back when touched. Immediately invert pan over funnel or bottle and cool completely. Remove from pan. Top each serving with sliced peaches. Note: Cake may also be baked in ungreased 9x5x3-inch loaf pan in 325° oven for about 55 minutes. Invert cake to cool.

TUESDAY
Tamale casserole *
Overnight vegetable salad *
Garlic bread
Mexican hot chocolate * or chocolate marshmallow bars *

TAMALE CASSEROLE

2 cups chopped onion
1 cup chopped green pepper
1 cup water
2 pounds ground beef
3 (8 ounce) cans seasoned tomato sauce
2 (16 ounce) cans whole kernel corn, drained
1 cup black olives, coarsely chopped

3 cloves garlic, crushed
1 ½ tablespoons sugar
2 teaspoons salt
1 tablespoon chili powder
½ teaspoon black pepper
2 ½ cups shredded sharp Cheddar cheese

Combine onion and pepper in large skillet. Add water, cover and cook until vegetables are tender. Add ground beef and brown. Add tomato sauce, corn, olives, garlic, sugar, salt, chili powder and black pepper. Simmer 20 minutes or until thick. Add cheese. Pour into a 1 ½-quart baking dish. Bake at 375° for 40 minutes. (6-8 servings)

OVERNIGHT VEGETABLE SALAD

6 cups chopped lettuce
Salt to taste
Pepper to taste
1 tablespoon sugar
1 cup (4 ounces) shredded Swiss cheese
4 hard-cooked eggs, sliced

10 slices bacon, crisp-cooked, drained and crumbled
1 (10 ounce) package frozen peas, thawed
³/4 cup mayonnaise (more if needed)
1 cup (4 ounces) shredded Cheddar cheese
2 green onions, sliced, with tops

Place half of lettuce in bottom of large bowl; sprinkle with salt, pepper and sugar. Top with Swiss cheese. Layer eggs on top of Swiss cheese, standing some slices on edge, if desired. Sprinkle generously with salt. Next, layer in order, half the bacon, the remaining lettuce, and peas. Spread mayonnaise over top, sealing to edge of bowl. Cover and chill 24 hours or overnight. Top with remaining cheese. Garnish with remaining bacon and green onion. May be tossed before serving or left undisturbed. (10-12 servings)

MEXICAN HOT CHOCOLATE

3 ounces semi-sweet chocolate
3 tablespoons sugar
³/4 teaspoon ground cinnamon

¹/2 teaspoon vanilla extract
4 ¹/2 cups milk

In a 2-quart saucepan, combine semi-sweet chocolate, sugar, cinnamon and milk. Bring to a boil. When chocolate has softened, remove pan from heat and beat mixture with rotary beater until blended. Return pan to heat. Bring hot chocolate to a boil, add vanilla extract and beat well over heat to produce as much foam as possible. Pour into cups and serve immediately. (6 servings, ³/4 cup each)

CHOCOLATE MARSHMALLOW BARS

³/4 cup butter or margarine
1 ¹/2 cups sugar
3 eggs
1 teaspoon vanilla
1 ¹/3 cups all-purpose flour

¹/2 teaspoon baking powder
¹/2 teaspoon salt
3 tablespoons cocoa
¹/2 cup chopped pecans or walnuts
4 cups miniature marshmallows

Topping

1 ¹/3 cups (8 ounces) chocolate chips
3 tablespoons butter or margarine

1 cup peanut butter
2 cups crisp rice cereal

In a mixing bowl, cream butter and sugar. Add eggs and vanilla; beat until fluffy. Combine flour, baking powder, salt and cocoa; add to creamed mixture. Stir in nuts. Spread in a greased 10x15-inch pan. Bake in a 350° oven for 15-18 minutes. Sprinkle marshmallows evenly over cake; return to oven for 2-3 minutes. Using a knife dipped in water, spread the melted marshmallows evenly over cake. Cool. For topping, combine chocolate chips, butter and peanut butter in a small saucepan. Cook over low heat, stirring constantly, until melted and well blended. Remove from heat; stir in cereal. Spread over bars. Chill. About 3 dozen bars.

WEDNESDAY
Corn crispy catfish fillets *
Western carrots (**see index**)
Broccoli with creamy lemon sauce *
Onion corn bread casserole *
Cranberry salad *
Peach Bavarian cream *

CORN CRISPY CATFISH FILLETS

½ cup mayonnaise
¼ cup grated Parmesan cheese
2 tablespoons water

1 tablespoon instant minced onion
5 cups corn chips, coarsely crushed
2 pounds catfish fillets, skin removed

Line 13x9x2-inch baking pan with heavy-duty foil; grease foil. In shallow dish or pie pan, combine mayonnaise, cheese, water and onion. Spread crushed corn chips onto sheet of plastic wrap. Heat foil-lined pan in oven for 5 minutes. While pan is heating, dip fillets in mayonnaise mixture to coat both sides lightly; coat with crushed corn chips. Place fillets 1 inch apart in hot pan. Bake in 450° oven for 15 minutes or until fish flakes easily with a fork. Serve immediately. (4-6 servings)

CREAMY LEMON SAUCE

1 cup mayonnaise

3 tablespoons lemon juice

Combine mayonnaise and lemon juice. Mix well. Serve over hot asparagus or broccoli. (6 servings)

ONION CORN BREAD CASSEROLE

¼ cup butter or margarine
1 ½ cups chopped onion
1 cup sour cream
¼ teaspoon salt
1 cup (4 ounces) shredded sharp Cheddar cheese
1 (7 ½-ounce) package corn muffin mix

2 eggs, beaten
½ cup milk
1 (16 ounce) can cream-style corn
¼ teaspoon cayenne pepper
1 tablespoon grated Parmesan cheese

Saute onion in butter. Cool. Add sour cream, salt and ½ cup Cheddar cheese. In another bowl, combine muffin mix, eggs, milk, corn and cayenne pepper. Pour muffin mixture into a greased 9-inch baking pan. Spread batter evenly. Spoon onion mixture on top. Top with remaining Cheddar cheese, then 1 tablespoon Parmesan cheese. Bake at 425° for 30 minutes.

CRANBERRY SALAD

2 cups fresh cranberries
1 cup water
1 cup sugar
15 large marshmallows

1 (3 ounce) box cherry-flavored gelatin
1 cup chopped pecans
1 cup chopped apples
1 cup chopped celery

In 1 ½-quart sauce pan, combine cranberries, water and sugar; cook until berries pop (about 5 minutes). Remove from heat; add marshmallows and gelatin. Stir until marshmallows are melted. Cool and add pecans, apples and celery. Pour into a 1 ½-quart mold. Chill until firm. (6-8 servings)

PEACH BAVARIAN CREAM

1 (16 ounce) can sliced peaches

1 (6 oz) package peach or apricot flavored gelatin

½ cup sugar

2 cups boiling water

1 teaspoon almond extract

1 (8 oz) carton frozen whipped topping, thawed

Additional sliced peaches (optional)

Drain peaches reserving ⅔ cup of juice. Chop peaches into small pieces or place in jar of blender and puree; set aside. In a bowl, dissolve gelatin and sugar in boiling water. Stir in reserved syrup. Chill until slightly thickened. Stir extract into whipped topping; gently fold into gelatin mixture. Fold in peaches. Pour into an oiled 6 cup mold. Chill overnight. Unmold; garnish with additional peaches if desired. 8-10 servings.

THURSDAY

Holiday oyster stew *

Beef roast slices on toast with juice

Buttered asparagus

Raw vegetable tray

Apricot or prune-filled squares *

HOLIDAY OYSTER STEW

2 (12 ounce) cans oysters, fresh or frozen

2 slices bacon, chopped

⅓ cup chopped onion

1 (10 ¼-ounce) can frozen condensed cream of potato soup*

4 cups oyster liquor and half & half

1 ¼ teaspoons salt

Dash white pepper

Chopped parsley

Thaw frozen oysters. Drain oysters, reserving liquor. Fry bacon until crisp. Remove bacon from grease. Cook onion in bacon grease until tender. Add soup, oyster liquor, half-and-half, salt and pepper. Heat, stirring occasionally. Add bacon and oysters; heat for 3 to 5 minutes longer or until edges of oysters begin to curl. Sprinkle with parsley. (6 servings). Note: Canned or home-made cream of potato soup may be used.

APRICOT OR PRUNE-FILLED SQUARES
Filling

1 (12 ounce) package prunes or apricots, cooked and chopped

2 tablespoons liquid from prunes or apricots

2 tablespoons lemon juice

1 teaspoon grated orange peel

3 tablespoons sugar

⅛ teaspoon cloves

¼ teaspoon ginger

⅛ teaspoon nutmeg

Dash salt

Combine all ingredients. Cook over low heat, stirring occasionally, 8-10 minutes, or until thick. Cool to room temperature. Prepare crumb layer.

Crumb Layer

1 ¹/₄ cups sifted all-purpose flour
¹/₂ teaspoon cinnamon
¹/₂ teaspoon salt
³/₄ cup firmly-packed brown sugar

1 cup quick-cooking rolled oats
1 tablespoon poppy seed
¹/₂ cup (1 stick) butter or margarine

Combine flour, cinnamon and salt. Sift into a large bowl. Stir in brown sugar, rolled oats and poppy seed. Using a pastry blender or two knives, cut in butter until mixture resembles coarse meal. Spread half this mixture evenly over the bottom of a well-greased 8-inch square pan. Press down firmly. Cover with prune or apricot filling, spreading it evenly to edges and into corners. Sprinkle remaining crumb mixture over filling. Carefully press down crumbs to make a smooth top. Bake in 400° oven for 30 minutes or until top is browned. Cool in pan on cake rack. Cut into squares. Store in tightly-covered container. Cookies keep well. (About 16 cookies)

FRIDAY
Hot and tart baked chicken and rice *
Ccreamed peas and carrots
Corn tomato and sweet onion salad *
Linzertorte *

HOT AND TART BAKED CHICKEN AND RICE

1 fryer, cut into 4 quarters
¹/₃ cup butter or margarine, melted
¹/₂ cup vinegar
¹/₂ cup lemon juice
¹/₂ teaspoon salt
¹/₄ teaspoon pepper

1 (4 ounce) can chopped chili peppers, drained
¹/₂ teaspoon garlic salt
¹/₂ teaspoon onion powder
1 tablespoon instant minced onion, optional
1 cup rice, uncooked
1 ¹/₂ cups water

Combine butter, vinegar, lemon juice, salt, pepper, chili pepper, garlic salt, onion powder and minced onion. Pour over chicken; marinate for about 30 minutes. Put rice in greased 2-quart casserole and pour water over rice. Put chicken on top of rice and pour marinade over the chicken. Cover tightly with lid or foil and bake at 350° for about 45 minutes. Remove cover or foil and continue to bake 30 minutes to brown. (4 servings)

CORN, TOMATO AND SWEET ONION SALAD

3 very ripe tomatoes, cored and diced (2 ¹/₂ cups)
1 medium sweet onion, peeled and chopped
  (Vidalia or Bermuda)
1 (15 ¹/₄-oz) can whole kernel corn, well drained
1 tablespoon plus 1 teaspoon balsamic vinegar

¹/₈ teaspoon salt
1 tablespoon olive oil (extra virgin is best)
15 fresh basil leaves
Freshly-ground pepper

In a salad bowl, place tomatoes, onions and corn. In a small bowl, combine vinegar and salt. Slowly whisk in the olive oil. Slice basil into fine shreds. Add basil and dressing to the vegetable mixture and toss well to combine. Correct seasoning. Cover the salad with plastic wrap and refrigerate at least one hour. (4 servings)

LINZERTORTE

1 cup (2 sticks) butter or margarine
1 cup sugar
1 tablespoon grated orange or lemon peel
2 egg yolks
1 ½ cups sifted all-purpose flour
1 teaspoon baking powder
2 teaspoons cinnamon

½ teaspoon cloves
¼ teaspoon salt
1 cup ground nuts (filberts, almonds,
  pecans or walnuts)
1 cup currant, plum or raspberry preserves
Whipped cream

Cream the butter and add the sugar slowly, while continuing to cream. Add the grated peel. Add the egg yolks, one at a time, beating well after each. Combine and sift flour, baking powder, cinnamon, cloves and salt. Add slowly to creamed mixture. Stir in the nuts. Mix until all the ingredients are thoroughly combined. Chill. Pat two-thirds of the dough into the bottom of a 9-inch layer cake pan, preferably one with a removable bottom (a spring form). Spread preserves over the dough in the pan. Roll out the remaining dough and cut into eight strips, each ¾-inch wide. Place lattice-fashion on top of the preserves. Bake in 350° oven until edges of strips recede from the sides of the pan, 50 to 60 minutes. Cool. Garnish with whipped cream and cut into small wedges to serve, or cut into squares and serve as cookies. (10-12 servings)

SATURDAY
Family Birthday Party for Dad
Beverage of his choice
Prima Vera Dip with king-size dipping crackers *
Brie en croute with crackers *
Marinated and broiled flank steak *
Sherried sweet potatoes *
Old-fashioned succotash *
Elegante cauliflower and peas *
Tossed green salad with cheese cubes *
Whole wheat buttermilk rolls *
Natural apple pie *

Plan Of Work
Day before:
1. Prepare prima vera dip. It is best made the day before and drained before serving. Prepare Brie and refrigerate. Heat before serving.
2. Bake sweet potatoes and prepare the casserole. Bake 40 minutes before dinner. Can use canned yams to save time.
3. Prepare apple pie.
Early in the day:
4. Marinate the flank steak to develop the great flavor.
5. Prepare the succotash and reheat before serving.
6. Prepare cauliflower early and cook 20 minutes before dinner is served.
7. Have all salad ingredients ready to mix with dressing. Do not add dressing until just before serving.
Two hours before serving:
8. Prepare the Brie en croute.

PRIMA VERA DIP

3 medium tomatoes, chopped
6-8 green onions, chopped (use tops)
1 (4 ounce) can chopped green chilies
1 (14 oz) can pitted black olives, drained, chopped

3 tablespoons wine vinegar
1 1/2 teaspoons garlic salt
1/4-1/2 teaspoon black pepper
Tabasco sauce to taste

Combine all ingredients in bowl, refrigerate overnight. Drain before serving. Serve with small spoon. Use king-size chips or crackers. Refrigerate leftovers. Will keep several days. (3-4 cups)

BRIE EN CROUTE

1 (4 1/2-ounce) package Brie cheese
1 frozen puff pastry patty shell, thawed

1 egg yolk
1/4 cup cream

Roll shell until large enough to cover the cheese completely. Carefully pull dough over the top of the cheese. Cover sides and tuck under the bottom. Place on pie pan. Combine egg yolk and cream. Brush the mixture on top of the pastry. Cover all. Bake in 450° oven for 15 minutes, cool slightly. Serve with crackers as an appetizer. (6 servings) If time is limited, spread raspberry preserves on top of Brie and serve cold, with crackers.

MARINATED AND BROILED FLANK STEAK

1 flank steak
1/2 cup chopped onion
2 cloves garlic, crushed
1 tablespoon salad oil
2 tablespoons red wine vinegar

1/2 teaspoon dried rosemary
1/2 teaspoon dried basil
1 teaspoon salt (optional)
1 teaspoon black pepper

Score flank steak on each side. In small bowl, combine onion, garlic, oil, vinegar, rosemary, basil, salt and pepper. Pour marinade over steak. Spread marinade to cover steak on both sides. Marinate 4-6 hours in refrigerator. Broil steak in the oven or on a grill to the desired degree of doneness. To serve, cut thin slices on the slant and across the grain. Note: To broil in the oven for medium steak, broil 3 inches from heat for 5 minutes, turn, brush with remaining marinade. Broil 5 minutes more. (4-6 servings)

SHERRIED SWEET POTATOES

6 medium-size sweet potatoes*
1/2 cup maple syrup
1/4 cup water

2 tablespoons sherry
2 tablespoons butter or margarine

Cook sweet potatoes with skins on in boiling water until tender. Cool, peel, cut in halves or quarters. Place in casserole. Combine syrup, water, sherry. Pour over sweet potatoes. Dot with butter. Bake at 350° for 30 to 40 minutes. (6 servings). May used canned yams, drained, in place of raw potatoes.

OLD-FASHIONED SUCCOTASH

2 cups fresh or frozen Lima beans
2 cups fresh, cut corn from the cob (or use frozen)
1/2 teaspoon salt

1 cup warm milk
Few grains pepper
1/4 cup (1/2 stick) butter or margarine

Shell and wash the Lima beans. Cut the corn from the cob. Place Lima beans in sauce pan and barely cover with boiling water. Add salt. Cover sauce pan and cook until beans are tender (about 30 minutes). Add the corn and cook for 5 minutes longer. Add milk, pepper and butter; cook 1 minute to heat through. (6 servings). If too much water is left, drain before adding milk. If a thicker mixture is desired, combine 1 tablespoon corn starch with a little milk to make a smooth paste. Stir into vegetable mixture; cook until slightly thickened.

ELEGANTE CAULIFLOWER AND PEAS

1 medium head cauliflower, broken into flowerets,
  or use 2 (10 oz) packages frozen cauliflower
1 (10 ounce) package frozen peas, thawed

1 ½ cups commercial sour cream
1 ½ cups (6 ounces) shredded sharp Cheddar cheese
½ teaspoon pepper

Cook cauliflower in small amount of boiling water; drain. Layer half of cauliflower, peas, sour cream, cheese and pepper in a greased 1 ½-quart casserole; repeat layers. Bake at 350°for 20 minutes or until cheese is melted. (Yield: 6-8 servings)

TOSSED GREEN SALAD WITH CHEESE CUBES

1 clove garlic
¼ cup olive oil
2 quarts crisp salad greens
½ cup cubed sharp Cheddar cheese

²/₃ cup Italian salad dressing
1 cup crisp toasted bread cubes (½-inch)*
4 strips bacon, fried crisp, drained and crumbled

Add garlic to oil. Let stand 2 to 3 hours. At meal time, tear salad greens into bite-sized pieces and put into salad bowl. Add cheese and salad dressing. Mix salad lightly with two forks to blend ingredients. Don't overmix. Remove garlic from oil. Pour oil over the crisp toasted cubes. Stir to coat cubes thoroughly. Add to salad at once. Use forks to mix toasted cubes into salad. Serve immediately topped with crumbled bacon. (6 servings)

* If commercial croutons are used, omit oil, garlic and bread cubes.

QUICK WHOLE WHEAT BUTTERMILK ROLLS

1 cup whole wheat flour
3 to 3 ½ cups all-purpose flour
2 packages dry yeast
3 tablespoons brown sugar
1 teaspoon salt

½ teaspoon soda
½ cup shortening
1 ³/₄ cups buttermilk*
¼ cup (½ stick) butter or margarine,
  melted (optional)

In large mixer bowl, combine 1 cup whole wheat flour, 1 cup all-purpose flour, yeast, sugar, salt, soda and shortening. Mix well. Add buttermilk to flour mixture. Blend at low speed until moistened; beat 3 minutes at medium speed. By hand, gradually stir in enough of remaining flour (2 to 2 ½ cups) to make a firm dough. Knead on floured surface until smooth and elastic (about 5 minutes). Punch down. Divide dough into two balls. Shape each ball into a 12-inch rope and cut into 12 pieces. Form into balls. (Makes about 24 rolls). Place about 1/2 inch apart on greased cookie sheet or 15 ½x10 1/2x1 ½-inch pan. Cover, let rise in warm place until almost doubled (about 20 minutes). Bake at 400° for 25 minutes until golden brown. Remove from pan; brush with butter, if desired. Cool on racks. (Yield: 24 rolls)

*If buttermilk powder is available, use 5 tablespoons buttermilk powder (mix with dry ingredients), and 1 ³/₄ cups very warm tap water (120°-130°).

NATURAL APPLE PIE

1 (12 ounce) can frozen apple juice concentrate
1 tablespoon butter or margarine, softened
2 tablespoons cornstarch
1 teaspoon cinnamon

½ teaspoon nutmeg
6 slices unpeeled, sliced Delicious apples
1 recipe deep-dish double crust pastry*

Place apple juice in sauce pan and bring to a boil. Combine butter, cornstarch, cinnamon and nutmeg. Stir small amount of juice into the butter/spice mixture to make a smooth paste; stir into apple juice. In large mixing bowl, combine apples and juice mixture; mix thoroughly to coat all slices. Place mixture in 9-inch unbaked pie shell. Adjust top crust. Make slits in top crust to release steam. Bake in 350° oven for 30 minutes. Reduce heat to 325° for additional 30 minutes. Serve plain or warm, topped with sliced cheese or ice cream.
*Use favorite recipe or purchase two frozen crusts and use one for top crust.

December - Fourth Week

Gatherings at this glorious holiday season are the greatest. All ages mix happily; old friends, close friends, new friends and family sort themselves out to celebrate the religous holy days, mark the end of the old year with happy anticipation of a new one, or simply to follow a family tradition. For these brief holiday seasons including Thanksgiving, Christmas and ending with the New Year, we adhere to the ageless traditions based on love, faith and hope.

All holiday gatherings have something visibly traditional in them such as the decorated house, traditional music and especially the sharing of good food. Let's plan an open house with accent on impromptu, light and satisfying food. To prevent the last minute rush for time to prepare good food and with the food budget lagging behind, here are a few suggestions that will erase any visible signs of the lack of time and money.

Even though the food represents casual entertaining, the planning is not casual. For an open house, pick-up foods are easier to handle and do not create a build-up of people around the table. Use small paper plates, so guests can move around. Remember the food must be substantial if the party starts at six o'clock and continues. The early-comers are ready for food and the late arrivals' appetites have begun to build up again.

• The only traditional food served in the South on New Year's Eve and Day is black-eyed peas cooked with ham hocks. Cook as you wish, but serve it dry and well-seasoned in a bowl surrounded by crackers. Serve with a spreader. Avoid dips at large gatherings for sanitation reasons. Make your own tradition a safe and sanitary one.

• No time to make sandwiches, so prepare small hors d'oeuvre puffs (cream puff shells: **see index**), cook them, cut them and freeze them until the day of the party and fill them with a salad filling made of leftover holiday ham, chicken, turkey, or even a cheese spread. Plan for at least two per person.

• No time for making meatballs. Cut cooked boneless ham or turkey breast into 3/4-inch cubes. Pile on tray around bowl of sweet and sour sauce (recipe included). Serve with wooden picks.

• Add a festive touch to leftover crispy Cheddar cheese wafers (recipe included). Place on a tray around a bowl of green or red pepper jelly (a good way to use jelly received at Christmas time). Serve with a spreader and watch them disappear.

• All time New Year's favorite is pickled shrimp. Clean, peel, and pickle, and have no sauce to worry about dripping on the tablecloth. Use favorite pickled shrimp recipe. Replace part of the shrimp with quartered, canned artichoke hearts, canned button mushrooms, onion slices and even tortalini rings.

Prepare several days ahead, and it is ready to serve any time and you've avoided using too much shrimp. This saves time as well as money.

• For a sweet touch, here's an idea for leftover fruit cake. Cut into 1x2-inch slices. Sift confectioners' sugar over the top. Hence, a new face for an old favorite.

• Instead of preparing a last minute relish tray with dip, prepare vegetables to be served raw and marinate for a couple of weeks if necessary — all ready to serve.

• For something simple and elegant, drain pineapple chunks and cover lightly with white creme de menthe. Cover and refrigerate for at least one day. Stir occasionally. Serve in a crystal bowl with wooden picks. Chunks of honeydew melon can also be added. If you still have mint in your garden, top it with a sprig.

• Steam a couple of artichokes, serve cold with a dressing such as home-made or commercial mayonnaise, Hollandaise sauce, or any tart, creamy dressing for dipping the leaves. This becomes a challenge to some guests who are not familiar with eating the whole artichoke.

Think of your own family favorites to celebrate a tradition and serve holiday foods in a safe, sanitary and convenient manner.

SUNDAY
A Christmas Eve Tradition

Families all over the world have traditions which they practice regularly. They bring family and friends together in the same fashion, do the same things, and often eat the same food. This creates a bond that remains forever. A tradition is a gathering of old and new friends. Since Christmas Eve is a busy one for families and friends, any entertainment should be casual, flexible, short and fun. So, our tradition is an annual Egg Nog Party. Since children are invited, have two punch bowls, one for children and one for adults. To avoid leftovers, the egg nog is constantly being prepared by one member of the family, usually the father. The food does not replace a dinner since people come after dinner, after church and even other parties; here the food should be uncomplicated but interesting.

Egg Nog (with or without)
Sausage Con Queso
Pickled Red Hots
Party Onions
Pineapple Cheese Mold
Liverwurst Pate' Cheese Tray - Gouda, Sherry Cheddar, Sego, Swiss
Assorted Crackers
Cookies - Forgotten Cookies, Creme de Menthe Brownies, Snickerdoodles, Potato Chip Cookies,
Pumpkin Bars

SUPER EGG NOG

6 eggs, separated	*¹⁄₄ cup (4 ounces) Bourbon (optional)*
³⁄₄ cup sugar	*1 ¹⁄₂ cups whipping cream*
1 ¹⁄₂ cups milk	*Freshly grated nutmeg*

Separate eggs. Combine yolks, sugar, milk and bourbon. Whip cream to very soft peak and fold in to the egg mixture. Whip egg whites to soft peak and fold into egg mixture. Serve in punch cups with freshly grated nutmeg. 10 to 12 (4 ounce) servings. Recipe may be doubled.

SAUSAGE CON QUESA

1-2 pounds bulk hot sausage
1 (10 ounce) can tomatoes and chili peppers
3 pounds Cheddar cheese spread
1 tablespoon fennel seed

2 teaspoons oregano
Garlic salt to taste
Hot sauce to taste

Brown sausage, break up as fine as possible. Drain. In a 3-quart saucepan, place the tomatoes and chili peppers. Cut cheese into chunks. Add to tomatoes in pan. Add all seasonings and sausage. Place saucepan on low heat, stir often to prevent sticking. When cheese is melted, cook about 10 minutes longer so flavors will mellow. If too thin add more cheese and sausage. If too thick, add tomato or vegetable juice. Freezes very well. Prepare as far ahead as you wish. Serve from chafing dish hot with large size corn chips. Serves 25-30 people as hors d'oeuvres.

PICKLED RED HOTS OR FRANKFURTERS

2 pounds Red Hots or frankfurters
1 medium onion, thinly sliced
3 cups water
2 tablespoons sugar
2 teaspoons salt

1 teaspoon whole allspice
2 cups cider vinegar
1 tablespoon pickling spices
1 to 1 1/2 teaspoons dried crushed red pepper
1 teaspoon whole peppercorns

Slice Red Hots or frankfurters ¼- to ⅓-inch thick. Slice onion and separate into rings. Mix the remaining ingredients in large sauce pan. Heat only until sugar is dissolved, not to boiling. Place meat slices and onion in alternate layers in ½-gallon jar. Pour marinade over meat and onions. Refrigerate for two or three days. If fat from meat separates and solidifies, remove or warm before serving, only enough to melt fat. Serve with wooden picks as an hors d'oeuvre. Keeps for weeks in refrigerator. Serves 25 people for hors d'oeuvres.

LIVERWURST PATE

1 (8 ounce) package liverwurst
¼ cup (½ stick) butter or margarine, softened
6 slices bacon, cooked and crumbled

2 tablespoons green onion, sliced thinly
1 tablespoon Sherry
Coarsely-ground black pepper or sour cream

Combine all ingredients in blender, processer or by hand. Blend to a smooth texture. Form into a flat mold on plate. Sprinkle top with cracked pepper or spread with a thin layer of sour cream and chill before serving. Serve with crackers. Serves about 10 people for hors d'oeuvres.

PARTY ONIONS

2 large onions, preferably white skin or Vidalia
½ cup sugar
1 cup vinegar
2 cups water
½ cup (or less) mayonnaise or mayonnaise-style
*   salad dressing*

1 tablespoon dill seed
Garlic salt to taste
Tabasco sauce to taste
½ to 1 teaspoon monosodium glutamate (optional)

Chop onions finely. Combine sugar, vinegar and water. Add onions. Marinate 6 hours or overnight. Drain thoroughly. Add mayonnaise, dill seed, garlic salt, Tabasco and monosodium glutamate. Mix well. Serve with assorted crackers. (Yield: about 2 cups)

PINEAPPLE CHEESE MOLD

2 (8 ounce) packages cream cheese, softened
1 (8 ½-ounce) can crushed pineapple, well drained
   (squeeze out juice with hands)
2 cups chopped pecans, divided

¼ cup finely-chopped green pepper
2 tablespoons finely-chopped onion
Parsley (optional)

Combine cheese, pineapple, 1 ½ cups pecans, green pepper and onion. Mix well. Place on plate to be served or cover with plastic wrap and mold to the shape desired, a flat mold or a ball-shape. Refrigerate overnight. Before serving, sprinkle remaining ½ cup nuts on top and decorate with parsley, if desired. Remove from refrigerator for a few minutes before serving. Serve with spreader on crackers. Serves 30 for hors d'oeuvres.

FORGOTTEN COOKIES

2 egg whites
Pinch salt
²/₃ cup sugar

1 teaspoon vanilla flavoring
1 cup chocolate chips
1 cup chopped pecans

Chill bowl and beaters. Beat egg whites until frothy, add salt; continue beating until stiff. Add sugar and beat 10 minutes. Add vanilla and mix well. Stir in chips and pecans. Drop by heaping teaspoon on a foil-lined cookie sheet about 2 inches apart. Preheat oven to 350°, about 10 minutes. Put cookies in oven, turn off heat. Leave for at least 3 hours or overnight. 3 dozen cookies.

GLAZED CREME DE MENTHE BROWNIES

½ cup (1 stick) butter or margarine
1 cup sugar
4 eggs, beaten
1 cup all-purpose flour
½ teaspoon salt
1 (16 ounce) can chocolate syrup
1 teaspoon vanilla

2 cups confectioners' sugar
½ cup (1 stick) butter or margarine, softened
2 tablespoons green Creme de Menthe
1 cup chocolate chips
¼ cup plus 2 tablespoons (6 tablespoons)
   butter or margarine

Cream butter; add sugar. Beat until smooth and creamy. Add eggs; combine well. Combine flour and salt. To butter mixture, add flour mixture, syrup and vanilla. Beat until thoroughly blended. Pour into a greased 9x13x2-inch baking dish. Bake in 350° oven for 20-25 minutes. Cool thoroughly. Combine confectioners' sugar, ½ cup butter and Creme de Menthe. Spread over the thoroughly-cooled first layer. Place pan in refrigerator to set. In small sauce pan or top of double boiler, add chocolate chips and the 6 tablespoons of butter. Heat until chips are melted and well combined with the butter. Chill thoroughly until cold and thick. Spread over Creme de Menthe layer. Allow top layer to cool thoroughly before cutting. (Yield: 36 or more pieces)

SNICKERDOODLES

1 cup butter or margarine, softened
1 ½ cups sugar
2 eggs
2 ¼ cups all-purpose flour
2 teaspoons cream of tartar

1 teaspoon baking soda
1 teaspoon salt
2 tablespoons sugar
2 teaspoons cinnamon

Cream butter; add sugar and eggs and beat until light and fluffy. Sift together flour, cream of tartar, baking soda and salt, and stir into the creamed mixture. Chill dough. Roll into balls the size of small walnuts. Combine sugar and cinnamon. Roll balls in sugar-cinnamon mixture. Place about 2 inches apart on ungreased baking sheet. Bake until lightly browned, but still soft, at 400° for 8 to 10 minutes. These cookies puff up at first, then flatten out with crinkled tops. (Yield: 5 dozen 2-inch cookies)

POTATO CHIP COOKIES

2 cups (4 sticks or 1 pound) butter or margarine
1 cup sugar
2 teaspoons vanilla

3 ½ cups flour
2 ½ cups (4 ½ oz) coarsely-crushed potato chips

Cream butter and sugar; add vanilla. Beat in flour until a smooth but stiff mixture forms. Fold in potato chips. Mix until chips are completely folded into batter. Drop by teaspoon on an ungreased cookie sheet, about 1 ½ to 2 inches apart. Bake in 350° oven for 15-20 minutes. Allow to cool on pan. When cool, sift confectioners' sugar over all. Keep several weeks in refrigerator. (Yield: 6-7 dozen)

PUMPKIN BARS

4 eggs
1 ²/₃ cups granulated sugar
1 cup cooking oil
1 (16 ounce) can pumpkin
2 cups all-purpose flour

2 teaspoons baking powder
2 teaspoons ground cinnamon
1 teaspoon salt
1 teaspoon baking soda

Frosting

1 (3 ounce) package cream cheese
½ cup (1 stick) butter or margarine, softened

1 teaspoon vanilla
2 cups sifted confectioners' sugar

In mixer bowl, beat together eggs, sugar, oil and pumpkin until light and fluffy. Stir together flour, baking powder, cinnamon, salt and soda. Add to pumpkin mixture and mix thoroughly. Spread batter in ungreased 15x10x1-inch baking pan. Bake in a 350° oven for 25-30 minutes. Cool. Frost with cream cheese frosting. Cut into bars. (Yield: 2 dozen or more depending on size of cut)

Cream Cheese Frosting
Cream the cheese and butter. Stir in vanilla. Add confectioners' sugar, a little at a time, beating well until mixture is smooth.

Christmas Morning
Christmas morning breakfast must go fast if presents are to be opened before the big noonday Christmas dinner. So, let the menu be good, quick, and fun.

Fruit or vegetable juice
Breakfast pie *
Breakfast ring * (unless a friend gave you a breakfast bread for Christmas)

BREAKFAST PIE

5 eggs, beaten
2 tablespoons butter or margarine, melted
¼ cup all-purpose flour
½ teaspoon baking powder

1 (8 ounce) carton cream-style cottage cheese
2 cups (8 ounces) shredded Monterey Jack cheese
1 (4 ounce) can chopped green chilies, drained

Combine first 4 ingredients in a mixing bowl; beat well at medium speed of an electric mixer. Stir in remaining ingredients and pour into a well-greased 9-inch pie plate. Bake at 400° for 10 minutes, reduce heat to 350°, and bake about 20 minutes or until set. Cut into wedges to serve. (Yield: 6 servings)

BREAKFAST RING

½ cup (1 stick) butter or margarine, melted
½ cup brown sugar, packed
1 tablespoon water

Chopped nuts (optional)
1 (12 ounce) package of refrigerated biscuits
Cinnamon

Combine butter, sugar, water and nuts. Cut individual biscuits in half, crosswise. Roll biscuit pieces in butter mixture and sprinkle with cinnamon. Place in round casserole with each biscuit overlapping slightly to make a ring. Fill in the center. Microwave for 3 to 4 minutes on HIGH, or in a 400° oven for 12-14 minutes. 8-10 servings.

Christmas Dinner
Wassail bowl * or apple juice
Oyster-stuffed mushrooms *
Cream cheese topped with pepper jelly and crackers
Oven-smoked turkey *
Old-fashioned bread dressing *
Caramel sweet potatoes *
Chantilly potatoes * or Festive baked potatoes with crab stuffing *
Broccoli with Hollandaise sauce *
Stuffed onions au gratin *
Butterhorn rolls *
Cranberry cherry pie *
Impossible pumpkin pie *
Ambrosia variation *
Angel food cake with fluffy white icing *

WASSAIL BOWL

A festivebeverage that was served during the Christmas season under old English traditions. It was a very old custom, dating back to the days of the Saxons, and pronounced "was-hael."

2 cinnamon sticks
1 teaspoon ginger sticks
1 teaspoon ground ginger
1 teaspoon whole allspice
10 whole cloves
2 cups water

2 cups sugar
1 quart cider
½ cup lemon juice
1 quart orange juice or 1 pint sweet Sherry
1 quart ginger ale or beer
Small red apples

Place first 5 spices in cloth bag and tie securely. Simmer water, sugar, and bag of spices about 10 minutes. Stir until sugar is dissolved, then cover. Cool and add the cider and fruit juices or sherry. Reheat, if it is to be served hot, then add ginger ale or beer. Small red apples may be floated on the bowl of punch.

OYSTER-STUFFED MUSHROOMS

1 lb. large fresh mushrooms, stemmed, wiped clean
6 tablespoons (³/4 stick) butter or margarine
2 cloves garlic, crushed
1 tablespoon Worcestershire sauce
1 can (3 ³/4-oz) smoked oysters, chopped (reserve oil)

2 slices white bread, cubed (crust removed)
1/2 cup walnuts or pecans
1/4 teaspoon salt
1/8 teaspoon pepper

Finely chop mushroom stems. Melt butter in medium-size skillet. Add stems, garlic and Worcestershire sauce. Saute about 3 minutes or until stems are tender. Stir in chopped oysters and oil, bread cubes, nuts, salt and pepper. Fill mushroom caps. Place, filled side up, on baking sheet. Bake in 350° oven about 25 minutes or until hot. Garnish with parsley if desired. Makes about 8 servings for entree. Also good as an hors d'oeuvre. About 30 mushrooms.

OVEN SMOKED TURKEY

1 (6-7 pound) turkey
Salt and pepper
6 cloves garlic
1/3 cup liquid smoke, divided
1 cup water

12 peppercorns
1/4 teaspoon cayenne pepper
1 tablespoon mustard seed
1 bay leaf

Rinse turkey in cold water; pat dry with paper towels. Rub cavity and skin heavily with salt and pepper. Cut one clove of garlic and rub cavity, leaving the two halves inside the bird. Rub outer skin with a second clove of garlic and discard. Cut four little slits in skin of breast near crop and further back on each side, and insert a clove of garlic in each slit. Brush bird inside and out with 1/4 cup of liquid smoke. Leave in refrigerator overnight. Next day, insert thermometer in the thickest portion of the thigh. Preheat oven to 350°. Put turkey in shallow roasting pan and bake 15-20 minutes. Reduce heat to 300°; combine water, remaining liquid smoke, peppercorns, cayenne, mustard seed and bay leaf. Bring to a boil. Baste bird frequently with sauce and continue roasting about 2 hours, or until bird is tender and the thermometer registers 185°. Last 30 minutes, baste with drippings to give a brown color. To keep larger birds moist, double seasonings, cover with foil, and baste every 20 minutes until done. (6-8 servings)

OLD-FASHIONED BREAD DRESSING

1 quart diced celery
1 cup finely-chopped onion
1 cup (2 sticks) butter or margarine
4 quarts bread cubes, firmly-packed
  (2- to 4-day old bread)

1 tablespoon salt
1 teaspoon ground sage (more may be added)
2 teaspoons poultry seasoning
1/2 teaspoon pepper
1 1/2 to 2 cups chicken broth

Cook celery and onion in butter over low heat, stirring occasionally, until onion is tender but not browned. Meanwhile, combine bread cubes, salt, sage, poultry seasoning and pepper. Add celery and onion mixture; toss lightly to blend. Pour broth gradually over surface of bread mixture, tossing lightly. Add more seasoning as desired. Makes enough stuffing for neck and body cavities of a 14- to 18-pound, ready-to-cook turkey. Stuffing may be baked in loaf pan or casserole the last hour that the turkey is cooking. 1½ to 2 quarts stuffing.

CARAMEL SWEET POTATOES

½ cup walnut halves and pieces
⅓ cup butter, melted
1 cup brown sugar, packed
½ teaspoon salt

½ cup orange juice
6 medium sweet potatoes, cooked
⅓ cup brandy (optional)

Saute walnuts in melted butter over moderate heat until lightly toasted; remove walnuts from skillet. Add brown sugar, salt and orange juice to butter remaining in pan. Bring to a boil; boil 3 or 4 minutes. Peel and halve sweet potatoes. Add to syrup along with walnuts. Heat gently, basting with syrup. Heat brandy over water; pour over potatoes and flame, if desired. (6 servings)

CHANTILLY POTATOES

6 medium-sized potatoes*
2 tablespoons butter or margarine
¼ cup milk
Salt to taste

Pepper to taste
1 cup whipping cream, whipped
¼ cup grated Parmesan cheese
Paprika

Wash, peel and quarter potatoes. Cook in boiling water until done. Drain and mash; add butter and milk and beat until light and fluffy. Season with salt and pepper. Pour into buttered 1 ½-quart casserole; cover with cream, and sprinkle with the cheese and paprika. Bake in 350° oven until brown on top, about 15 minutes. (6 servings). Note: Instant mashed potatoes may be used, if desired.

FESTIVE BAKED POTATOES WITH CRAB STUFFING

4 medium large potatoes
½ cup (1 stick) butter or margarine
½ cup cream
1 teaspoon salt
¼ teaspoon pepper

1-2 tablespoons grated onion, pulp and juice
1 cup shredded sharp Cheddar cheese
1 (6 ½-ounce) can crab meat, drained, picked
over and flaked
1 (3 oz) can chopped & drained broiled mushrooms

Bake potatoes. When cooked, and still hot, cut in half, lengthwise, and scoop out insides. Cream well with butter and cream that has been heated. Stir in onion, 2/3 cup cheese, crabmeat and mushrooms. Pile into potato shells and sprinkle with remaining cheese. Bake in 350° oven until thoroughly heated and cheese has melted. Prepare a day ahead and heat just before serving.

BROCCOLI WITH HOLLANDAISE SAUCE

3 pounds broccoli
¼ cup cold water
1 tablespoons cornstarch
½ cup hot water

1 tablespoon lemon juice
⅛ teaspoon salt
2 egg yolks, slightly beaten
2 tablespoons butter

Wash broccoli thoroughly. Trim, slicing off tough end of stem. Make lengthwise slashes through stem up to flowerets. Place broccoli in large kettle in 1 inch of boiling salted water; cover and cook quickly until just tender, 15 to 20 minutes. Drain and serve with warm Hollandaise poured over top. Sprinkle with paprika. 6-8 servings.

Hollandaise Sauce

In small sauce pan, thoroughly blend cold water and cornstarch. Stir in hot water. Cook and stir over medium heat until cornstarch mixture begins to "gather" on bottom of pan. Turn heat to low and continue to cook and stir until smooth and thick, and mixture becomes clear. Remove from heat and stir in lemon juice and salt. Pour over slightly beaten egg yolks. Return mixture to pan, add butter, and reheat over medium low heat. Will not curdle; may be made ahead of time and reheated slowly. (Makes 1 cup) If Magic Hollandaise Sauce in blender can be used, **see index**.

STUFFED ONIONS AU GRATIN

6 medium-sized onions	*Salt and pepper*
1/2 cup shredded Cheddar cheese	*Onion stock*
1/2 cup toasted bread crumbs	*2 tablespoons melted butter*

Boil the onions until slightly tender; drain, reserve water. Remove the centers of onions with an apple corer; chop any removed onion. Combine chopped onion, cheese, crumbs and salt and pepper. Fill cavities in onions with the cheese mixture. Place onions in a baking dish. Add 1/2 cup of stock in which onions were boiled, salt and pepper. Top with butter and bake in a 350° oven until brown, about 15 minutes. (6 servings)

BUTTERHORN ROLLS

1 package (1 tablespoon) active dry yeast	*3 eggs, beaten (or 1 whole egg and 4 yolks)*
1/4 cup warm water (110°)	*3/4 teaspoon salt*
1/2 cup (1 stick) butter	*4 to 5 cups flour*
3/4 cup milk	*1/2 cup (1 stick) butter or margarine, melted*
1/2 cup sugar	

Combine yeast and warm water; allow to stand 5 minutes until it foams, then stir down. Melt butter in heavy sauce pan; add milk immediately and remove from heat. Blend in sugar, eggs, salt and dissolve yeast. Stir in enough flour to make soft dough. Cover and allow to rise until double, 2 to 4 hours. Turn dough (which is very soft and should remain so) onto floured board. Knead slightly to handle. Divide in half. Roll each half into 14-inch circle. Spread each circle with ¼ cup melted butter. Cut pie-fashion into 16 pieces. Roll each piece loosely from large end to small. Place on greased cookie sheet. Allow to rise in cool place 5 to 6 hours. Bake at 375° for 12 to 15 minutes or until lightly browned. 32 rolls.

CRANBERRY CHERRY PIE

3/4 cup sugar	*1 (21 ounce) can cherry pie filling*
2 tablespoons cornstarch	*2 deep-dish pie crusts*
2 cups raw cranberries, washed	

Combine sugar, corn starch and raw cranberries. Mix well, add cherry pie mix. Pour into a deep-dish pie crust. Flatten the extra crust and place on pie mixture. Bake in a 425° oven for 10 minutes. Reduce heat to 350° and bake 25-35 minutes. Chill before cutting.

IMPOSSIBLE PUMPKIN PIE

³/₄ cup sugar
½ cup buttermilk baking mix or any biscuit mix
1 (13 ounce) can evaporated milk
2 eggs

1 (16 ounce) can pumpkin
1 tablespoon pumpkin pie spice
2 teaspoons vanilla

Heat oven to 350°. Lightly grease pie pan (10x1 ½ or 9x1 ¼ inches). Beat all ingredients until smooth, or for 1 minute in blender on high speed, or for 2 minutes with hand beater. Pour into pie pan. Bake until golden brown and knife inserted in center comes out clean, 50-55 minutes. Refrigerate any remaining pie. Yield: 1 pie.

AMBROSIA VARIATION

6 apples, peeled and cut in slices
6-8 navel oranges, peeled and sectioned
2 (20 ounce) cans pineapple chunks, drained
* (juice reserved)*

1 (7 ounce) can flaked coconut (or grate
* fresh coconut)*
Sugar to taste
1 cup orange juice

In a large crystal bowl, layer the apples, oranges and pineapple. Sprinkle with coconut, then sugar. Repeat layers. Pour orange juice over all, then add about ½ cup of reserved pineapple juice. Cover and refrigerate. 8-12 servings.

ANGEL FOOD CAKE WITH QUICK FLUFFY WHITE ICING

Prepare 1 angel food cake mix according to package directions.

Quick Fluffy White Icing

2 egg whites
1 cup white corn syrup
¼ cup sugar

½ teaspoon cream of tartar
Pinch salt
1 teaspoon vanilla

Place all above ingredients in top of double boiler. Place over medium heat. Begin beating immediately. Beat until mixture stands in peaks, about 5 minutes. Remove from heat; continue beating as the mixture cools and add vanilla. Makes enough icing for a large angel food cake. Decorate with green and red Maraschino cherries for a Christmas dessert.

MONDAY
Quick and easy steak stew *
German potato salad *
Sour cream muffins *
Apple salad
Peanut butter bars *

QUICK AND EASY STEAK STEW

3 tablespoons all-purpose flour
1 teaspoon salt
1/4 teaspoon pepper
2 pounds beef cubed steaks (Porterhouse),
   cut into 2x2-inch pieces
3 tablespoons butter or margarine
2 garlic cloves, crushed

2 (16 ounce) cans Italian-style stewed tomatoes
   (with basil, garlic and oregano)
1 (8 ounce) can tomato sauce
1 (10 ounce) package frozen peas
1 (10 ounce) package frozen baby Lima beans
1 (16 ounce) can whole onions, drained

Combine flour, salt and pepper. Coat meat with mixture. In 12-inch skillet over medium-high heat, in hot butter, cook meat a few pieces at a time, until well-browned on all sides. Remove pieces as they brown. Reduce heat to medium; add garlic to drippings in skillet, cook until light brown. Return meat to skillet and add tomatoes with their liquid, tomato sauce, frozen peas and baby Limas. Heat to boiling. Reduce heat to low, cover and simmer 5 minutes. Add onions and cook 5 minutes longer or until vegetables are tender. (6 servings)

GERMAN POTATO SALAD

5 strips bacon
3/4 cup chopped onion
2 tablespoons all-purpose flour
2/3 cup cider vinegar
1 1/3 cups water

1/4 cup sugar
1 teaspoon salt
1/8 teaspoon pepper
6 cups sliced cooked peeled (or unpeeled)
   potatoes (about 2 pounds)

In a large skillet, fry bacon until crisp; remove and set aside. Drain all but 2/3 tablespoon drippings; add onion, cook until tender. Stir in flour; blend well. Add vinegar and water; cook and stir until bubbly and slightly thick. Add sugar and stir until it dissolves. Crumble bacon; gently stir in bacon and potatoes. Heat thoroughly, stirring lightly to coat potato slices. Serve warm. 6-8 servings.

SOUR CREAM MUFFINS

1 cup sour cream
2 cups self-rising flour

1/2 cup butter, melted

Combine all ingredients. Fill muffin tins about 3/4 full because they do not rise much. Bake in a 375° oven till brown, about 25 minutes.

PEANUT BANANA BARS

1 cup all-purpose flour
3/4 cup brown sugar
1 teaspoon baking powder
1/4 teaspoon salt
1/2 cup sliced ripe banana

1/4 cup peanut butter
2 tablespoons milk
2 tablespoons peanut oil
1/2 teaspoon vanilla
1 egg, beaten

Topping

1/2 cup all-purpose flour
1/2 cup brown sugar

1/2 cup chopped peanuts
1/4 cup butter or margarine

Combine first 10 ingredients and beat at medium speed in a large bowl. Beat one minute. Pour in a greased 9x13-inch pan. Combine all topping ingredients except peanuts. Stir until crumbly, then add peanuts. Sprinkle this mixture over batter. Bake in 350° oven for 25-30 minutes. Cool, cut into bars. (Yield: 2 ½ to 3 dozen bars)

TUESDAY
Hawaiian ham steak *
Southern eggplant casserole * or Swiss broccoli casserole *
Glazed beets *
Green salad
Peanut butter fudge cake *

HAWAIIAN HAM STEAK

½ cup brown sugar, packed
¼ cup butter or margarine
¼ cup red wine vinegar

1 fully-cooked smoked ham, center slice, cut
about ½ to ³/₄-inch thick (about 1 ½ pounds)
4 medium firm bananas, cut into 1 ½-inch chunks

In 12-inch skillet over medium heat, heat brown sugar, butter and vinegar until brown sugar is melted, stirring frequently. Add ham slice; cook five minutes on each side or until ham is heated through. Arrange ham on heated platter; keep warm. To brown sugar mixture in skillet, add bananas. Baste with sauce and cook until bananas are heated through, about 5 minutes. With spoon, carefully spoon banana chunks around ham slice. Spoon remaining sauce over ham and bananas. (6 servings)

SOUTHERN EGGPLANT CASSEROLE

1 pound eggplant
1 cup soft bread crumbs
½ cup milk
½ cup (1 stick) butter or margarine
1 onion, finely chopped

3 eggs, slightly beaten
½ teaspoon salt
2 cups (8 ounces) shredded sharp
Cheddar cheese, divided
Pepper to taste

Peel eggplants, cut into cubes and cook in a small amount of water until tender. Drain. Add crumbs to milk. Melt butter and saute onions until tender and light brown. Combine eggplant, milk and crumb mixture, onion, eggs, 1 cup cheese, salt and pepper to taste. Place in greased 1 ½-quart casserole. Bake in 400° oven for 20 minutes. Remove from oven and top with remaining 1 cup cheese and bake for 15 minutes longer. (4-6 servings)

SWISS BROCCOLI CASSEROLE

2 packages (10 ounce) frozen broccoli spears,
cooked and drained
3 hard-cooked eggs, sliced
1 can (10 ³/₄-ounce) cream of celery soup

½ soup can or ²/₃ cup of milk
1 can (3 ounce) French fried onions
½ cup (2 ounces) shredded Swiss cheese

Thoroughly combine soup and milk, Arrange broccoli in a 2-quart baking dish. Layer eggs, ½ can French fried onions, soup mixture and cheese over broccoli. Bake at 350° for 25 minutes. Top with remaining onions. Bake 5 minutes longer. (6 servings)

GLAZED BEETS

2 (16 ounce) cans sliced beets
1/2 cup vinegar
1/4 cup sugar

2 tablespoons corn starch
1/2 teaspoon salt
1/4 cup (1/2 stick) butter or margarine

Pour off liquid from beets. Combine 1/3 cup of the beet juice with vinegar. In small sauce pan, combine sugar, corn starch and salt. Stir in beet/vinegar liquid. Cook over moderate heat, stirring constantly until thick and clear. Add butter and beets and heat slowly, stirring occasionally, until heated through. If allowed to remain over very low heat for 15-20 minutes, the flavor will mellow.(6-8 servings)

PEANUT BUTTER FUDGE CAKE

1 cup (2 sticks) butter or margarine
1/4 cup cocoa
1 cup water
1/2 cup buttermilk
2 eggs, beaten
1 teaspoon vanilla

2 cups sugar
2 cups flour
1 teaspoon soda
Peanut Butter Mixture
Fudge Frosting

Combine butter, cocoa, water, buttermilk, eggs and vanilla. Bring to a boil. Combine sugar, flour and soda. Add to boiled mixture. Mix well with spoon (no mixer is needed). Pour into well-greased and floured 9x13-inch baking pan. Bake in 350° oven for 25 minutes. Cool in pan. Spread Peanut Butter Mixture over cooled cake. Top with Fudge Frosting. Cut into squares.

Peanut Butter Mixture

1 1/2 cups creamy peanut butter

1 1/2 tablespoons peanut oil

Combine peanut butter and peanut oil. Spread over cooled cake.

Fudge Frosting

1/2 cup (1 stick) butter or margarine
1/4 cup cocoa
1/4 cup plus 2 tablespoons buttermilk

1 (16 ounce) box powdered sugar
1 teaspoon vanilla

Combine butter, cocoa and buttermilk; bring to a boil. Pour boiled mixture over powdered sugar. Add vanilla and mix well. Spread over Peanut Butter Mixture.

WEDNESDAY
Baked turkey casserole (leftover turkey and dressing) *
Buttered peas
Lettuce wedges with no-calorie dressing*
Spicy orange buns *
Iced brown sugar squares *

BAKED TURKEY CASSEROLE (using leftover turkey)

Turkey dressing
Turkey slices

1 can cream of celery soup
1/3 cup water

Place dressing in casserole dish. Place turkey slices over the dressing. Combine soup and water. Pour over turkey slices. Bake in 325° oven for 45 minutes or until it bubbles. This dish can be frozen and baked.

NO-CALORIE DRESSING

1 cup wine vinegar	¼ teaspoon oregano or tarragon
2 cloves garlic, crushed	½ teaspoon salt or to taste
2 tablespoons chopped parsley	Pepper to taste

Combine in jar. Shake vigorously and pour over vegetable salad.

SPICY ORANGE BUNS

2 cups sifted flour*	1 teaspoon cinnamon
3 teaspoons baking powder	¼ cup (½ stick) butter or margarine
½ teaspoon salt	½ cup sugar
4 tablespoons shortening	1 (6 ounce) can frozen orange juice
¾ cup milk	(thawed and undiluted)
2 tablespoons sugar	

Combine and sift together flour, baking powder and salt. Cut in shortening until mixture resembles cornmeal. Stir in milk to form a smooth dough. Knead on lightly-floured board for ½ minute. Roll out lightly to rectangle about 1/2-inch thick. Blend sugar and cinnamon and sprinkle over dough. Roll up like jelly roll from long end and cut in nine equal slices. Place butter in small pan with sugar and orange concentrate. Stir over moderate heat just until butter is melted. Pour into baking pan (8x8x2-inches). Place buns in pan, cut side down. Bake in hot oven (425°) for 20-25 minutes.
*If time does not permit preliminary preparation, your favorite prepared biscuit mix can be substituted by thoroughly kneading the dough into a smooth ball. Proceed as directed above. Be sure to seal the edges by moistening with additional milk. (Yield: 9 buns)

ICED BROWN SUGAR SQUARES

1 cup (2 sticks) butter or margarine	2 cups all-purpose flour
1 cup firmly packed brown sugar	1 (12 ounce) package semi-sweet chocolate pieces
1 egg, slightly beaten	1-2 cups finely-chopped nuts
1 teaspoon vanilla extract	

Preheat oven to 350°. Cream butter; gradually add sugar, beating until well blended. Beat in egg and vanilla. Gradually blend in flour. Spread evenly in well-buttered 15 ½x10 ½x1-inch jelly roll pan. Bake 15 to 18 minutes until lightly browned. Remove from oven; quickly sprinkle chocolate pieces over baked cookie base. Return to oven 2 to 3 minutes to soften chocolate. Remove from oven; immediately spread chocolate evenly over cookie base. Sprinkle on chopped nuts. Chill until frosting is set. Cut in squares. (Yield: 50-70 squares)

THURSDAY
Creamy shrimp curry *
Curry condiments * / Relish tray
Last minute rolls * or Sweet potato muffins *
Cranberry apple pie *

CREAMY SHRIMP CURRY

¹/₄ cup (¹/₂ stick) butter or margarine
1 large onion, chopped
3 cloves garlic, crushed
1 teaspoon curry powder (if desired,
   add ¹/₂ teaspoon)
1 (10 ³/₄-ounce) can cream of mushroom soup

1 cup sour cream
1 teaspoon lemon juice
Salt to taste
Cayenne to taste
1 pound cooked peeled shrimp
3-4 cups hot cooked rice

Saute onion and garlic in butter until soft. Stir in curry powder and soup; heat thoroughly. Remove from heat; add sour cream, lemon juice, salt and cayenne. Before serving, add shrimp and heat thoroughly. Serve over steamed rice, accompanied by the following condiments. (4-6 servings)

Condiments

1 cup raisins
1 ¹/₂ cups peanuts
1 ¹/₂ cups chopped apple
4 hard-cooked eggs, chopped
1 ¹/₂ cups chutney

1 ¹/₂ cups shredded coconut
1 ¹/₂ cups pineapple chunks
4 bananas, sliced (optional)
10 slices crisp bacon, crumbled
1 large green pepper, chopped

Place a serving of rice on plate. Top with creamy shrimp curry. Add a teaspoon or more of each condiment, one on top of the other, in the order listed. Undesireable condiments may be eliminated as chosen by the individual.

LAST MINUTE ROLLS

1 ¹/₄ cups scalded milk
2 ¹/₂ tablespoons sugar
1 ¹/₂ teaspoons salt
¹/₄ cup (¹/₂ stick) soft butter or margarine

2 (¹/₄-ounce) packages active dry yeast
¹/₄ cup warm water
¹/₂ teaspoon lemon extract
3 ¹/₄ cups sifted all-purpose flour

About 1 ½ hours before dinner, pour scalded milk into a large bowl; stir in sugar, salt and butter. Cool until lukewarm. Sprinkle yeast into measuring cup containing 1/4 cup warm water; stir until dissolved. Stir dissolved yeast into lukewarm milk mixture. Add lemon extract. Add flour; stir until well blended, about one minute. Cover batter with waxed paper and clean towel; let rise in warm place (80° to 85°) until double in bulk. Stir well; then beat vigorously about ½ minute. Fill greased muffin pan cups ²/₃full. Bake in 400° oven about 25 minutes. Remove rolls from pan while hot. (Yield: one dozen rolls)

SWEET POTATO MUFFINS

²/₃ cup canned or cooked fresh sweet potatoes,
   well drained
¹/₄ cup (¹/₂ stick) butter or margarine
¹/₂ cup sugar
1 egg
³/₄ cup all-purpose flour
2 tablespoons baking powder

¹/₂ teaspoon salt
¹/₂ teaspoon cinnamon
¹/₄ teaspoon nutmeg
¹/₂ cup milk
¹/₄ cup chopped pecans or walnuts
¹/₄ cup raisins, chopped

Grease muffin tins. Puree the sweet potatoes in a food processor blender. Cream butter and sugar. Beat in eggs and pureed sweet potatoes. Sift flour, baking powder, salt, cinnamon and nutmeg. Add the dry ingredients alternately by hand with the milk and chopped nuts and raisins, mixing just until blended. Do not overmix. Spoon into the greased muffin tins, filling each tin completely full. A little sugar and cinnamon may be sprinkled on top of each muffin, if desired. Bake in a 400° oven for 25 minutes. 12 muffins or more depending on size of the cups.

CRANBERRY APPLE PIE

2 cups fresh cranberries
1 ½ cups sugar, divided
2 teaspoons grated orange rind
2 tablespoons orange juice
2 cups chopped apple

2 tablespoons flour
⅛ teaspoon ground cloves
⅛ teaspoon ground cinnamon
Double crust pastry, commercial or home made

Combine cranberries, 1 cup sugar, orange rind and juice in 2-quart sauce pan. Bring to boil and cook over medium heat about 10 minutes or until all cranberry skins pop open. Add apple. Combine remaining 1/2 cup sugar, flour, cloves and cinnamon. Stir into cranberry mixture. Turn into a pastry-lined 8- or 9-inch pie pan. Cover pie with top crust; seal and flute edge. Make several slits in top crust to permit escape of steam. Bake in a 425° oven about 35 minutes or until crust is golden brown. (Yield: one 8- or 9-inch pie)

FRIDAY
Potato gnocchi in tomato meat sauce *
Applesauce glazed pork roast *
Buttered spinach
Green salad
Italian bread
Ice cream with royal chocolate sauce *

POTATO GNOCCHI IN TOMATO MEAT SAUCE

2 ¼ cup hot mashed potatoes
1 cup plus 2 tablespoons all-purpose flour
Salt and pepper to taste
1 tablespoon olive oil

2 eggs
1 ½ tablespoons butter, melted
4 cups Meat Sauce
¾ cup freshly grated Parmesan cheese

Combine hot mashed potatoes with flour, salt and pepper and oil. Blend with a fork. Add egg and blend thoroughly. Turn dough onto a well-floured board and knead gently. The dough will be more pliable than bread dough but should not be sticky. If it is, add a little more flour. Cut off a piece of dough about the size of a golf ball. Roll into a cord about the thickness of a pencil. With a knife, cut the cord into 1-inch long pieces. Drop about 3 dozen gnocchi into simmering water; cover and allow to cook about 5 or 6 minutes. Remove with a slotted spoon; drain well, and place in a shallow pan. Mix with melted butter. Repeat with the remaining gnocchi, adding cooked gnocchi to shallow pan and turning gently each time to coat with butter. Keep them warm in a 150° oven. To serve, top with Meat Sauce, then cheese. (4 servings)

Meat Sauce

1 tablespoon oil (preferably olive oil)	*1 (8 ounce) can tomato sauce*
2 medium onions, chopped	*1 teaspoon oregano*
1 rib celery, sliced	*1 teaspoon fennel seed*
2 cloves garlic, crushed	*1/2 teaspoon thyme*
1 medium-sized green pepper, chopped	*1/2 teaspoon rosemary*
1 pound ground beef	*1/2 teaspoon basil*
1 (6 ounce) can tomato paste	*1 teaspoon salt*
1 (16 ounce) can tomatoes or 1 (14 ounce)	*1/2 teaspoon pepper*
can diced tomatoes, undrained	*1/2 cup dry red wine (optional)*

Heat oil in large skillet; add onion, celery, garlic and green pepper. Cook about 3 minutes, until tender but not brown, stirring constantly. Add meat, break into small pieces and cook until brown. Drain off any excess fat. Add tomato paste, tomatoes, tomato sauce, seasoning and wine. Bring to a boil, turn heat down and simmer 45 minutes to 1 hour. (Yield: approximately 4 cups). Note: If you prefer a lot of sauce, double sauce recipe and freeze the leftovers.

APPLESAUCE GLAZED PORK ROAST

4- to 5-pound boneless pork loin roast	*3/4 cup red currant jelly*
(double loin, rolled and tied)	*4 beef-flavor bouillon cubes*
1 1/2 cups applesauce	*1/4 teaspoon ground allspice*

Insert meat thermometer so bulb is in the center of the thickest part of roast. Place roast on rack in shallow pan. Roast at 325° uncovered about 2 1/2 hours or until meat thermometer registers 170°. Meanwhile, in sauce pan, combine remaining ingredients. Cook and stir until bouillon dissolves, about 5 minutes. Reserve about one-third of the sauce and baste during last 30 minutes of roasting. Serve remaining sauce warm with meat. Do not put the basting brush into the sauce to be served with the meat; use separate brushes. 10-12 servings.

ROYAL CHOCOLATE SAUCE

1 tablespoon cornstarch	*/2 cup water*
3 tablespoons cocoa	*3/4 cup marshmallow creme*
1/2 cup butter or margarine	*1 teaspoon vanilla*
1/2 cup honey	

Combine cornstarch, cocoa, butter, honey and water in a heavy sauce pan; bring to a boil, stirring constantly. Remove from heat. Add marshmallow creme and vanilla. Stir until blended. Serve warm over ice cream. (Yield: 2 cups) Refrigerate left over sauce. Reheat, if desired, before using again.

SATURDAY
New Year's Eve Cocktail Buffet and Open House

In setting up a cocktail buffet, the number of items or different dishes served is determined by the size of the house and the number of rooms opened up for guests. You will probably want at least one item in each of the rooms used. In the dining room, the table should look bountiful but not cluttered. Six items are usually enough on the dining table. Other items should be set up in various places as the hostess wishes. A separate area, such as a buffet, should be set up for sweets. Do not put sweets on the dining table with other foods. In the following menu some alternate items are suggested. If no alternate is given it is because the suggested item has been so well accepted that it should be used. Also included are several additional recipes that can be used at any cocktail buffet or open house. Select the ones that fit your needs.

Please note: Every item on the menu, and most of the recipes not on the menu, can be prepared several days ahead. The hot menu items should be reheated before serving. Sandwiches must be kept air-tight to avoid drying out. Frozen items such as asparagus rolls and rye pizza can be thawed at the last minute or cooked from the frozen state. I suggest starting preparation for a New Year's open house the day after Christmas, then, come New Year's Eve, no food preparation; just concentrate on decorations and serving.

NEW YEAR'S EVE COCKTAIL BUFFET
Main Table
Marinated and smoked catfish with crackers *
Steak bits* or tenderloin on the grill with finger rolls
Sausage, mushroom stroganoff in corn shells * or
Serendipity *
Hot ham and cheese on finger rolls * or
Petite mahogany drum sticks (the meaty section of chicken wings) *
Asparagus rolls *
V.P. spread (Vincent Price asked me to share this recipe) *
Crab pizza * or
Cheese mold with strawberry topping *
Sausage con quesa * or
Crab dip (if crab pizza is not used) *
Zucchini squares * or
Chili cheese squares *
Party rye pizza (to pass hot) *
Canned pineapple chunks and fresh fruit (melons, cantalope and strawberries) in white creme de menthe

Dessert Table
Peanut butter dipped cocoa bon bons *
Chocolate peanut butter balls *
Fruit cake or cookies left over from Christmas
Orange pecans *
White chocolate cereal mix *
5 minute chocolate fudge *
Peanut butter fudge *

HORS D'OEUVRE PUFFS

1 cup water
¹/₂ teaspoon salt
¹/₂ cup butter or margarine

1 cup sifted flour
4 eggs

Preheat the oven to 375°. Bring the water, salt and butter to a boil. When the butter is melted, pour in the flour all at once. Stir vigorously with a wooden spoon over low heat until the mixture forms a ball in the pan. Continue stirring and cooking for about 2 minutes. Remove from the heat and beat in the eggs, one at a time, continuing to stir until the mixture is smooth. Use two teaspoons to drop the batter onto a greased cookie sheet in amounts about the size of a hazelnut. Leave at least a 2-inch space between the mounds as the pastry swells and puffs in cooking. Bake until golden and no moisture shows, about 20-25 minutes. Do not underbake or the puffs will collapse. Remove from oven, cool, slit sides to release heated air. Store the puffs in an air-tight container or freeze until ready to fill and serve. Yield: about 36 puffs. Fill with turkey salad.

TURKEY SALAD FILLING

3 cups finely-chopped cooked turkey
1 cup finely-chopped celery
1 teaspoon salt

¹/₄ teaspoon pepper (white pepper, if available)
Mayonnaise to moisten and hold together

Combine all ingredients and stir until well mixed.

PINEAPPLE, MUSTARD AND HORSERADISH SAUCE
(Sweet and sour sauce for cooked ham, turkey cubes and chicken fingers)

1 (12 ounce) jar pineapple preserves
¹/₄ cup prepared horseradish

¹/₄ cup prepared mustard

Combine preserves, horseradish and mustard in a small saucepan. Heat until well blended, stirring constantly. Refrigerate until ready to use. Keeps for weeks in the refrigerator. (More horseradish or mustard can be added if desired.) Yield: 2 cups.

CRISPY CHEESE WAFERS

2 cups (8 ounces) shredded sharp Cheddar cheese
1 cup (2 sticks) butter or margarine
2 cups sifted flour
¹/₂ teaspoon cayenne pepper

1 teaspoon seasoned salt
2 teaspoons Worcestershire sauce
2 cups crispy rice cereal

Blend cheese and butter. Work in flour. Add pepper, salt and sauce; mix well, Pour in cereal and mix without crushing cereal unnecessarily. Shape into small balls and place on ungreased cookie sheets. Flatten each ball with a fork. Bake at 375° until light brown, about 10 minutes. Yield: about 3 to 4 dozen.

PICKLED SHRIMP, ARTICHOKES, MUSHROOMS AND ONIONS

2 to 2½ lbs. shrimp, cooked, peeled and deveined
4 medium onions, sliced thin
2 (14 ounce cans) artichoke hearts,
  drained and quartered
2 (8 ounce) cans button mushrooms, drained
¼ pound tortolini, cooked al dente
2 large bay leaves, diced
1 ¼ cups salad oil

¾ cup warmed white vinegar
1 ½ teaspoons salt
2 ½ teaspoons celery seed
1 tablespoon prepared mustard
2 ½ tablespoons capers and juice
Dash of hot sauce
¼ cup Worcestershire sauce

In a large pan arrange the shrimp in layers with the onions, artichoke hearts, mushrooms, tortolinis and bay leaves. Combine the remaining ingredients and mix well. Pour the sauce over each layer of shrimp mixture as it is placed in the pan. After the layers are covered with sauce, cover the pan and store in the refrigerator for at least 24 hours. It will keep a week or more. When serving, arrange the entire mixture on a large platter. Have cocktail picks handy. Nice with crackers. This is worth the time it takes.

MARINATED AND SMOKED CATFISH FILLETS

10 catfish fillets
1 cup soy sauce
½ cup lemon juice

¼ cup vegetable oil
8 cloves garlic, chopped finely or crushed

Wash and dry fillets. Set aside. Combine all remaining ingredients in a large pan. Mix well. Dip each fillet in the marinade and place in pan. Cover each layer of fish with a little more marinade. When all fish are dipped and in the pan, pour the remaining marinade over the fillets. Be sure all are covered. Marinate overnight at least, even longer if time permits. Cook in a smoker 2 to 2 ½ hours or until done. This is a great hors d'oeuvre; serve with crackers. Freezes well. Should serve about 35 people depending on the amount of other foods served. (I double the marinade recipe to have plenty. It will store in the refrigerator for a month or two, or use on other meat roasts.)

TENDERLOIN ON THE GRILL

1 (8 ounce) bottle Italian dressing
1 (5 ounce) bottle soy sauce
Juice of 2-3 lemons or ¼ cup lemon juice

½ teaspoon ground black pepper
1 teaspoon garlic powder
1 (8 pound) beef tenderloin, well trimmed

Combine all ingredients except the tenderloin; mix well. Place the tenderloin in marinade for about 2 hours, more if desired. Cook tenderloin on grill at medium heat, turning often, for 20 to 30 minutes or until it reaches the desired doneness. Slice thin and serve with small buns and Durkies dressing or horseradish sauce. Will serve 15 to 20 people as an hors d'oeuvre.

STEAK BITES

3-4 pounds sirloin steak
1 cup sherry
4 cloves garlic, crushed
1 (8 ounce) can mushrooms, undrained
½ cup (1 stick) butter or margarine
1 tablespoon dry mustard

1 teaspoon garlic salt
1 tablespoon Worcestershire sauce
¼-½ teaspoon liquid smoke
3 tablespoons cornstarch
Small finger rolls

Combine garlic and sherry; pour over steak and turn every 2 hours. Marinate all day or overnight. Reserve ⅓ cup marinade. Broil or grill steak to rare and cut into small slices to fit the buns. Set aside. Prepare sauce by combining undrained mushrooms, butter, mustard, salt, Worcestershire sauce, liquid smoke and ⅓ cup marinade. Combine cornstarch with enough sauce liquid to make a paste. Add cornstarch mixture to the sauce and heat, stirring, until it is slightly thick. Place cut meat in a chafing dish and cover with sauce. Serve hot with finger rolls. 50 servings.

DILL BITS

1 (11 ounce) package oyster crackers
½ cup oil
1 or 2 packages ranch dry dressing mix
 (not buttermilk)

½ teaspoon garlic salt
1 tablespoon dill weed
2-¾ teaspoon lemon pepper

Place crackers in a large bowl. Mix remaining ingredients. Pour over crackers; mix well and allow to stand overnight. They are dry and crisp after they stand. Keep well when stored in a tight container.

CORN SHELLS
(for Sausage, mushroom stroganoff)

¼ cup plus 2 tablespoons (¾ stick)
 butter or margarine
3 ounces cream cheese at room temperature

1 cup all-purpose flour
2 cup cornmeal
Pinch of salt

Cream butter and cheese; mix well. Combine flour, cornmeal and salt. Add flour mixture to creamed mixture a little at a time until all dry ingredients have been well blended. Knead lightly with hands. Wrap in plastic and place in refrigerator until ready to use. Pinch off dough the size of a walnut. Press into small (1 3/4 inches diameter) greased muffin cups. Adjust the size of the dough to the size of the muffin cups. Bake in a 350° oven for 20 minutes. 2-3 dozen shells. Fill with sausage, mushroom stroganoff.

SAUSAGE, MUSHROOM STROGANOFF

1 pound hot bulk sausage, browned and
 crumbled, set aside (optional)
¾ cup (1 ½ sticks) butter or margarine
4 cloves garlic, crushed
4 (8 oz) cans mushroom stems and pieces, drained
2 bunches (about 10) green onions, sliced, use tops

2 tablespoons flour
3 tablespoons finely-chopped parsley
1 ½ tablespoons lemon juice
1 tablespoon salt
2 teaspoons black pepper
2 cups sour cream

In a large skillet, melt butter. Add garlic, mushrooms and green onions; saute until onions are tender. Add cooked sausage. Stir in flour, mix well, cook about 1-2 minutes. Add parsley, lemon juice, salt, pepper and sour cream. Mix and correct seasoning. Place in chafing dish; surrounded by corn shells. Recipe may be doubled as many times as needed. Freezes well. Serves 50 for hors d'oeuvres. Serve with corn shells.

HAM AND CHEESE DINNER ROLLS

1 tablespoon Worcestershire sauce
2 tablespoons poppy seeds
¾ cup (1 ½ sticks) butter or margarine, softened
2 tablespoons prepared mustard

2 packages finger dinner rolls, split
Ham, tiny slices to fit roll
Cheese slices cut same size as the ham

Combine Worcestershire sauce, poppy seeds, butter and mustard; mix until smooth. Spread butter mixture on roll bottom. Top with slice of ham and cheese. Spread butter mixture on top half; close roll and bake in 400° oven for 10 minutes or 350° oven for 15 minutes until hot and cheese is melted. 48 rolls. (Can be prepared a day ahead if covered tightly with foil or plastic to prevent drying out.)

ASPARAGUS ROLLS

20 slices soft white bread
1 (3- or 4-ounce) package blue cheese
1 (8 ounce) package cream cheese
½ teaspoon Worcestershire sauce

2 (15 ounce) cans asparagus spears, drained and
  dried on paper towel
¾ cup (1 ½ sticks) butter or margarine

Remove crusts from bread slices. Roll each slice flat with a rolling pin. Set aside. Combine blue cheese, cream cheese and Worcestershire sauce; mix well. Spread thick layer of cheese mixture on each slice of bread. Place one asparagus spear down the side and roll into bread carefully. Place on cookie sheet seam side down. When all slices are rolled, wrap in plastic and place in freezer until ready to use. When ready to serve, remove from freezer, cut each roll in half or thirds*, brush with melted butter and bake in a 350° oven for 15 minutes. Serve warm or at room temperature
* For a luncheon, do not cut. Cut only when used for hors d'oeuvres.

My VP Spread
(Vincent Price asked me for this recipe)

1 (14 ounce) can artichoke hearts, drained,
  finely chopped
1 cup mayonnaise
1 cup sour cream

½ cup Parmesan cheese, divided
1 cup shredded sharp Cheddar cheese
Garlic salt to taste
½ teaspoon Tabasco sauce

Combine artichoke, mayonnaise, sour cream, ¼ cup Parmesan cheese, Cheddar cheese, garlic salt and Tabasco sauce; mix well. Spread in a 11 ½x8 ½x2-inch greased baking dish (2 quart). Sprinkle top with ¼ cup Parmesan cheese and dust lightly with curry powder (optional). Bake in a 325° oven for 20 minutes. Serve warm with king sized corn chips or crackers.

CRAB PIZZA

2 (8 ounce) packages cream cheese
2-3 tablespoons mayonnaise
2 teaspoons Worcestershire sauce
Garlic salt to taste
¼ teaspoon Tabasco sauce

6 ounces chili sauce
1 (6 ounce) can fancy white crab meat
Dried parsley
Curry powder

Combine cheese, mayonnaise, Worcestershire sauce, garlic salt and Tabasco sauce. Beat until light and fluffy. Spread on a flat plate. Form like a pizza base. Chill until firm. Remove from refrigerator, spread with chili sauce. Squeeze by hand as much water as possible from the crab and sprinkle crab on the chili sauce. Do not disturb the chili sauce. Sprinkle heavily with dried parsley and still be able to see the chili sauce and crab. Serves 25 or 30 people as an hors d'oeuvre.

ZUCCHINI SQUARES

3 cups thinly-sliced zucchini squash (4 small)	*1/2 teaspoon dried marjoram*
1 cup biscuit baking mix	*1/2 teaspoon oregano leaves*
2 small onions, finely chopped	*1/4 teaspoon pepper*
1/2 cup grated Parmesan cheese	*2 cloves garlic, crushed*
2 tablespoons finely-chopped parsley	*1/2 cup vegetable oil*
1/2 teaspoon salt	*4 eggs, slightly beaten*
1/2 teaspoon seasoned salt	*1 1/2 cups shredded Cheddar cheese*

Combine all ingredients. Spread in a greased 13x9x2-inch baking pan. Bake in a 350° oven for 1 hour. Cool. Cut into 2x2-inch squares. May be served warm or at room temperature. Yield: 2-3 dozen.

PARTY RYE PIZZA

1 pound ground beef	*4 cups shredded sharp Cheddar cheese*
1 pound hot bulk sausage	*1 teaspoon oregano*
1 small onion, chopped	*1/2 teaspoon garlic salt*
1 small green pepper, chopped	*1/2 teaspoon chili powder*
1 teaspoon fennel seed (optional)	*Party rye bread slices*

Brown the meat with onion, green pepper and fennel seed. Drain. Add cheese and mix well. Add oregano, garlic salt and chili powder; mix well. Spread on party rye slices. Place on a cookie sheet and bake at 300° for 5-10 minutes or until heated throughout, or broil for 5 minutes. Spread slices can be wrapped and frozen before baking. Remove from freezer and broil for 5 minutes or until heated through.

WHITE CHOCOLATE CEREAL/PARTY MIX

2 cups pecan halves	*1 pound white almond bark (imitation*
2 cups pretzel sticks	*white chocolate)*
2 cups Corn Chex	*2 tablespoons vegetable oil*
2 cups Rice Chex	

In very large mixing bowl, combine pecans, pretzels, Corn Chex and Rice Chex. Place almond bark in 1-quart glass measuring cup. Add vegetable oil. Microwave for 3 to 4 minutes or until almond bark is softened. Remove from oven and stir. Pour over cereal. Immediately stir the cereal so all pieces will be coated. Line counter with waxed paper or aluminum foil. Pour cereal on paper to cool and dry. Wonderful to give as Christmas gift in a pretty Christmas container.

ORANGE PECANS

1 pound pecan halves	*1 tablespoon vinegar*
1 pound brown sugar (use either dark or light)	*1/4 cup orange juice*
1 cup minus 2 tablespoons milk	

In medium-sized sauce pan, combine sugar, milk, vinegar and orange juice. Cook over medium heat to soft ball stage (about 230°), or when dropped in cold water, a soft ball will form. Remove from heat and add nuts. Stir until the nuts appear sugared. Pour out on counter lined with waxed paper. When completely cooled, separate nuts. Makes a good Christmas gift.

CRAB DIP

3 (8 ounce) packages cream cheese
3 (6 ¹/₂-ounce) cans crab meat, drained and flaked
1 (15 ounce) jar Cheese Whiz

¹/₄ cup plus 2 tablespoons whipping cream
1 ¹/₂ tablespoons Worcestershire sauce
¹/₂ teaspoon Tabasco sauce

Combine all the above ingredients. Heat until cheese melts and the mixture is hot. Correct seasoning. Serve in chafing dish. It can also be served at room temperature.

CHILI CHEESE SQUARES

2 cups (¹/₂ pound) shredded Monterey Jack cheese
2 cups (¹/₂ pound) shredded sharp Cheddar cheese
3 eggs, beaten slightly
1 (3 ounce) can chopped chili peppers, drained

1 teaspoon garlic salt
¹/₂ teaspoon monosodium glutamate, optional
Tabasco sauce to taste

Combine Monterey Jack and Cheddar cheeses. Place in bottom of a greased 7-inch pan. Combine eggs, chili peppers, salt and monosodium glutamate. Pour over cheese. Bake in a 350° oven for 30 minutes. Let it cool and set for 50 to 60 minutes before cutting into squares.

SERENDIPITY
To Be Served in Chafing Dish

1 tablespoon vegetable oil
1 pound ground beef
1 tablespoon sugar
1 large onion, finely chopped
1 large green pepper, finely chopped
1 ¹/₂ cups raisins

3 teaspoons chili powder
2 teaspoons oregano
1 (10 ¹/₂-ounce) can condensed tomato soup
1 (6 ounce) can tomato paste
³/₄ cup water (rinse out tomato paste can)
1 tablespoon soy sauce

Combine oil, meat, sugar, onion and pepper in large skillet. Cook until meat is brown and vegetables are tender, about 5 to 8 minutes. Add remaining ingredients; bring to a boil, reduce heat and simmer for 20-30 minutes. Do not burn, keep it dipping consistency. Serve in chafing dish with king-size corn chips. (Serves 25 people for appetizers)

CHEESE MOLD WITH STRAWBERRY TOPPING

1 pound (4 cups) shredded sharp Cheddar cheese
³/₄ cup mayonnaise
1 small onion, grated

1 cup chopped pecans
1 (8 ounce) jar strawberry preserves

Combine cheese, mayonnaise, onion and pecans; mix well with hands. Press into a flat mold, not a ring mold. Chill. When ready to serve, unmold on a flat plate and spoon preserves over the top, covering completely. Garnish with parsley. Serve with crackers. Serves 25 people as hors d'oeuvre.

SHRIMP CHEESE MOLD

1 (8 ounce) package cream cheese, softened
1 ¹/₂ teaspoons dry mustard
1 tablespoon grated onion
¹/₂ teaspoon lemon juice

¹/₄ teaspoon Tabasco sauce
Garlic salt to taste
1 (4 ounce) can tiny shrimp, washed and drained
²/₃ cup chopped pecans or walnuts

Combine cheese, mustard, onion, lemon juice, Tabasco sauce and salt in a bowl. Beat until light and fluffy. Fold in shrimp. Put into a flat dish or mold. Chill. Unmold and sprinkle top with nuts.

PETITE MAHOGANY DRUMSTICKS
(Meaty part of chicken wings)

2 teaspoons dry mustard
2 teaspoons monosodium glutamate (MSG)
1 cup soy sauce
²/₃ cup vegetable oil

1 teaspoon garlic powder
50 chicken wings or 100 with wing tips
  removed (petite drumsticks)

Combine mustard, MSG, soy sauce, vegetable oil and garlic powder. Add chicken wings; mix well. Marinate overnight. Line wings on cookie sheet; bake in 350° oven 25-30 minutes.

PEANUT BUTTER DIPPED COCOA BON BONS

2 (3 ounce) packages cream cheese
1 tablespoon milk
4 cups unsifted confectioners' sugar
¹/₃ cup cocoa

1 teaspoon vanilla
1 cup finely-chopped nuts
2 cups (12 ounces) peanut butter-flavored chips
2 tablespoons shortening

Beat cream cheese and milk until fluffy. Blend in sugar, cocoa and vanilla. Stir in nuts. Chill until firm to handle easily. Shape into ½-inch balls. Place on waxed paper. Chill 3 to 4 hours. In double boiler, stir peanut butter chips and shortening until melted. Dip balls in the peanut butter mixture. Place on waxed paper. Chill. Store in cool place. (Yield: 3 ½ dozen)

CHOCOLATE COATED PEANUT BUTTER BALL

2 cups butter or margarine, melted
1 ½ cups peanut butter
4 cups confectioners' sugar

1 ½ cups graham cracker crumbs
4 ounces wax
2 (4 ounce) packages German sweet chocolate

Combine butter, peanut butter, confectioners' sugar, graham cracker crumbs. Chill for ease of handling. Shape into small balls (½-inch). Chill. In top of double boiler, melt wax and chocolate. Dip balls in mixture. Let balls set until the chocolate covering is firm. (Yield: 2 ½ to 3 dozen)

FIVE MINUTE FUDGE

1 (5 ounce) can evaporated milk
1²/₃ cups sugar
½ teaspoon salt
1 (7 ounce) jar marshmallow creme

1½ cups semi-sweet chocolate chips
1 teaspoon vanilla
½ cup chopped nuts (optional)

Combine milk, sugar and salt in 3-quart saucepan. Bring to a boil. Boil to a soft ball stage (230°). Remove from heat. Stir in chocolate chips and marshmallow creme; stir until well blended. Pour into a well-greased 8-inch square pan. Cool. Cut into squares.

QUICK AND EASY PEANUT BUTTER FUDGE

²/₃ cup milk
2 cups sugar
1 cup crunchy peanut butter

1 (7 ounce) jar marshmallow creme
1 teaspoon vanilla

Combine milk and sugar in saucepan. Bring to a boil. Boil without stirring to a soft ball stage (230°). Remove from heat. Add peanut butter, marshmallow creme and vanilla. Stir until well blended. Pour into a 8-inch square pan. Place in refrigerator at least 20 minutes before cutting. Cut into squares. (Yield: 4-5 dozen)

Index

N-O

Appendices

❦ ❦ ❦

Substitutions for a Missing Ingredient

The following are substitute ingredients that cooks may use when they unexpectedly run out of a particular staple. These substitutions should be used only in unexpected situations, as results may vary.

Ingredient called for	Substitution
1 cup corn syrup	1 cup sugar and ¼-cup of liquid from recipe
1 cup whole milk	½-cup evaporated milk + ½-cup water OR ¼-cup non-fat dry milk + ⁷/₈-cup water + 2 tsp butter
1 cup buttermilk	1 cup milk + 1 tblsp vinegar or lemon juice (let stand)
1 cup honey	1 ¼-cups sugar + ¼-cup liquid
1 cup butter	1 cup margarine OR 1 cup shortening
1 teaspoon baking powder	¼ teaspoon baking soda + ½ teaspoon cream of tartar
1 cup sifted cake flour	1 cup sifted all-purpose flour minus 2 tablespoons
1 cup melted shortening	1 cup cooking oil (recipe *must* require *melted* shortening)
1 cup sour cream	⁷/₈-cup buttermilk + 3 tablespoons of butter
1 tablespoon corn starch	2 tablespoons of flour
1 cup cream or half & half	⁷/₈-cup milk + ½-tablespoon of butter
1 square (1 oz.) unsweetened chocolate	3 tablespoons cocoa + 1 tablespoon shortening
6 oz package melted semi-sweet chocolate	2 squares unsweetened chocolate + 2 tblsp shortening plus ½-cup sugar
3 oz. package flavored gelatin	1 tblsp plain gelatin + 2 cups fruit juice

Equivalent Chart

3 tsp...1 tblsp.

2 tblsp....................................⅛ cup

4 tblsp.................................$^1/_4$ cup

8 tblsp. ....$^1/_2$ cup

16 tblsp................................1 cup

5 tblsp. + 1 tsp. ....⅓ cup

12 tblsp.................................$^3/_4$ cup

4 oz.......................................½ cup

8 oz.......................................1 cup

16 oz.....................................1 lb.

1 oz.........................2 tblsp. fat or liquid

2 cups.................................1 pint

2 pints..................................1 qt.

1 qt.......................................4 cups

⅝ cups....................½ cup + 2 tblsp.

⅞ cups....................¾ cups + 2 tblsp.

8-10 egg whites.........................1 cup

12-14 egg yolks........................1 cup

1 cup unwhipped cream..2 cups whipped

1 lb. shredded American cheese.....4 cups

¼ lb. crumbled Bleu cheese..............1 cup

1 lemon..................3 tblsp. juice

1 orange.................⅓ cup juice

1 lb. unshelled walnuts..1½ cup shelled

2 cups fat.....................................1 lb.

1 lb. butter......................2 cups or 4 sticks

2 cups granulated sugar......................1 lb.

3 ½-4 cups unsifted powdered sugar.1 lb.

4 cups sifted flour..........................1 lb.

4 $^1/_4$ cups cake flour........................1 lb.

3$^1/_4$ cups whole wheat flour.........1 lb.

4 oz. (1 to 1¼ cups) uncooked macaroni..................2¼ cups cooked

7 oz. spaghetti...................4 cups cooked

4 oz. (1½ to 2 cups) uncooked noodles......................2 cups cooked

28 saltines...........................1 cup crumbs

4 slices bread.............1 cup crumbs

14 sq. graham crackers...1 cup crumbs

22 vanilla wafers..............1 cup crumbs

3 medium bananas.........1 cup mashed

10 miniature marshmallows.......1 large

1 tsp dried herbs..........1 tblsp fresh herbs

1 tblsp prepared mustard..........1 tsp dry

General Oven Chart

Very Slow Oven	**250° to 300° F.**
Slow Oven	**300° to 325° F.**
Moderate Oven	**325° to 375° F.**
Medium Hot Oven	**375° to 400° F.**
Hot Oven	**400° to 450° F.**
Very Hot Oven	**450° to 500° F.**

Alcohol Substitutes for Other Liquids in Cooking (& Vice-Versa)

In soups or other entrees	Substitution
Water Beef broth, bouillon or consommé Tomato or vegetable juice Apple cider	Dry red wine
Water Chicken broth, bouillon or consommé Carbonated beverages & white grape juice Liquid drained from mushrooms	Dry white wine

In cheese dishes	Substitution
Chicken broth White grape juice & carbonated beverages	Beer

In desserts	Substitution
Apple cider, canned fruit syrups	Brandy
Pineapple juice Syrups with almonds	Rum
Orange or pineapple juice Liquids drained from mushrooms, cider	Sherry
Syrup from berries, grapes or currants	Kirsch
Juice from peaches, apricots or pears	Cognac
Orange juice, both fresh and frozen	Cointreau
Spearmint extract, oil of spearmint Grapefruit juice	White creme de minth
Grape juice	Red Burgandy or claret
Ginger Ale	Champagne